By James R. Mellow

CHARMED CIRCLE:
GERTRUDE STEIN & COMPANY

NATHANIEL HAWTHORNE
IN HIS TIMES

INVENTED LIVES:
F. SCOTT AND ZELDA FITZGERALD

INVENTED

～ LIVES

HOUGHTON MIFFLIN COMPANY BOSTON

1984

F. Scott and Zelda Fitzgerald

James R. Mellow

Library of Congress Cataloging in Publication Data

Mellow, James R.
Invented lives.

Bibliography: p.
Includes index.
1. Fitzgerald, F. Scott (Francis Scott), 1896–1940—Biography.   2. Fitzgerald,
Zelda, 1900–1948—Biography.
3. Authors, American—20th century—Biography.   I. Title.
PS3511.I9Z686   1984   813'.52   [B]   84-9002
ISBN 0-395-34412-3

Printed in the United States of America

V 10 9 8 7 6 5 4 3 2 1

For permission to print or reprint previously unpublished or published materials,
the following are gratefully acknowledged:

Harold Ober Associates Incorporated: for previously unpublished material by F.
Scott and Zelda Fitzgerald, copyright © 1984 by Frances Scott Fitzgerald Smith,
all rights reserved; selections from previously published letters and materials by
Zelda Fitzgerald from *Zelda* by Nancy Milford, copyright © 1970 by Nancy
Winston Milford; selections from "Zelda: A Worksheet," which appeared in *The
Paris Review*, number 89, copyright © 1983 by Frances Scott Fitzgerald Smith;
selections from *As Ever, Scott Fitz*, copyright © 1972 by S. J. Lanahan, trustee,
Anne Reid Ober, and Matthew J. Bruccoli; selections from *Save Me the Waltz*,
copyright © 1932 by Charles Scribner's Sons, copyright renewed 1960 by Frances
Scott Fitzgerald Lanahan; selections from *F. Scott Fitzgerald in His Own Time: A
Miscellany*, copyright © 1971 by Matthew J. Bruccoli and Jackson R. Bryer;
selections from *F. Scott Fitzgerald's Ledger*, copyright © 1972 by Frances Scott
Fitzgerald Smith; selections from *The Romantic Egoists*, copyright © 1974 by
Frances Scott Fitzgerald Smith; selections from *The Notebooks of F. Scott Fitzgerald*,
edited by Matthew J. Bruccoli, copyright © 1972, 1978 by Frances Scott Fitz-
gerald Smith, reprinted by permission of Harcourt Brace Jovanovich, Inc., and
New Directions Publishing Corporation.

For Augie,
who gave up his vacations
in the service of this book:

*"Canaries in the morning, orchestras
In the afternoon, balloons at night."*

The whole earth is our hospital
Endowed by the ruined millionaire,
Wherein, if we do well, we shall
Die of the absolute paternal care
That will not leave us,
but prevents us everywhere.

T. S. ELIOT

Contents

Illustrations

xiii

"The New Generation in Literature" from *Vanity Fair*, February 1922 (courtesy *Vanity Fair*. Copyright © 1922, renewed 1950, by The Condé Nast Publications, Inc.)

Zelda in her traveling outfit, 1920 (courtesy Princeton University Library)

George Jean Nathan and H. L. Mencken, 1923 (courtesy Alfred A. Knopf)

At the honeymoon cottage at Westport, Connecticut, 1920 (courtesy Princeton University Library)

The *Hearst's International* photo of Scott and Zelda, 1923 (courtesy Princeton University Library)

FOLLOWING PAGE 364

Scott, Zelda, and Scottie in Paris, Christmas 1925 (courtesy Princeton University Library)

Maxwell Perkins (by John Hall Wheelock; photograph from *Editor to Author: The Letters of Maxwell E. Perkins*. Copyright 1950 Charles Scribner's Sons. Copyright renewed © 1978 John Hall Wheelock. Reprinted with permission of Charles Scribner's Sons)

Harold Ober (portrait by Willard H. Ortlip; photograph, Collection of Matthew J. Bruccoli)

Ernest Hemingway, 1931 (Collection of Matthew J. Bruccoli)

The Fitzgeralds aboard ship, ca. 1928–1931 (courtesy Princeton University Library)

The Hemingways en route to France, April 1929 (Patrick Hemingway Collection, courtesy Princeton University Library)

Laura Guthrie in her Gypsy fortuneteller's outfit, 1935 (courtesy Princeton University Library)

Fitzgerald at Chimney Rock, North Carolina, 1935 (courtesy Princeton University Library)

Sheilah Graham in Hollywood (The Bettmann Archive Inc.)

Scott and Zelda attending the theater in Baltimore, 1932 (The Bettmann Archive Inc.)

Ballerinas, painting by Zelda Fitzgerald, ca. 1938 (courtesy Montgomery Museum of Fine Arts, Montgomery, Alabama. Gift of the artist)

The illustrations on the endpapers, title page, and part-title pages are by Edward Shenton (courtesy Princeton University Library). Fitzgerald had "gotten very fond" of them when they first appeared in the magazine version of *Tender Is the Night* and recommended that they be used in the first edition of the book in 1934.

The dust-jacket photo of Scott and Zelda first appeared as an illustration for Fitzgerald's article "The Cruise of the Rolling Junk" in *Motor* magazine, 1924 (courtesy Princeton University Library).

Preface

W HEN I BEGAN *Invented Lives,* I intended to write a brief, brisk, semijournalistic account of the Fitzgeralds' marriage. It is common knowledge that the Fitzgeralds used their courtship— the romance of a Southern belle with a Northern lieutenant—and their stormy marriage as the basis for several novels and short stories. But as I read works by and about them, I began to feel that they had used these stories as a form of private communication, too. Fiction became a method of discourse about their marriage, allowing them to air their grievances and dissatisfactions, fix the blame, indulge in bouts of self-justification—even, it seemed, to play roles they had not managed to play in the reality of their marriage.

I did not expect chronology to be a problem. After all, the Fitzgeralds had always been public property, adepts at self-advertisement. In their lifetimes, they regularly made the gossip columns. After their deaths, their supposedly glamorous lives and antic dissipations, their unhappy fates, were detailed in memoirs written by contemporaries and in the subsequent biographies of others. Since I planned to write a book with a small focus, that public record would be a blessing.

I had not gotten far into the documentary material, both published and unpublished, when I realized, first, that the context of their lives was more important than I had allowed for. Their circle of friends provided them with alter egos, which they then used as characters in their stories, and with experiences, which they also

borrowed for their writings. Their connections with the hectic literary and theatrical worlds of the twenties and thirties had a more
important bearing on the work than I had supposed. Those connections gave a different meaning to the Fitzgeralds' ambitions and
accomplishments.

It was also readily apparent that there were gaps in the Fitzgerald chronology; the exact dates and sequences of events leading
up to some of the more important episodes in the Fitzgerald saga
were missing. When and where had Fitzgerald begun writing—and
rewriting—his first novel? What incidents from life had found their
way into his revisions? At what point had his premarital sexual affair
with Zelda begun? What were the real circumstances in the breaking-off of their engagement? How many abortions had Zelda had?
When did her affair with the French naval aviator, Edouard Jozan,
actually begin—if, indeed, it was a real affair and not a largely
fictionalized account of a summer flirtation? There were crucial aspects of their lives that had slipped through the cracks of the established chronology. I have to say that the answers to these questions
are, as they were in earlier biographies and recollections, a merger
of hazy factual detail and speculation drawn from the fictional use
the Fitzgeralds made of their experiences.

The Fitzgeralds' correspondence does not supply the conclusive
answers. Only some of Zelda's letters to her husband, many of them
written from clinics in Europe and America, were published, and
almost none was dated. In the Princeton University Library, they
are catalogued according to the opening sentences, rather like an
index of first lines for a volume of poetry; they make a strange
anthology of weather reports and bread-and-butter responses: "Thanks
again for the vacation," "Thanks for the money," "Thanks for the
perfume," or "The sky closed over the lake like a gray oyster shell."
Trying to determine some particular sequence of events in their lives,
or the sequence of the letters themselves, meant shuttling back and
forth through the undated letters in seven bulging file cases. There
was, fortunately, one useful clue for the biographer and researcher:
Zelda's preference for distinctive stationery—letter papers in a variety of plaids or with graph paper designs in assorted colors, or
stationery embossed with her name, in one case spelled out in elongated silver letters in a kind of Ziegfeld Follies graphic style. In an
age that relies on microfiche, microfilm, information storage, and
computerization, it was heartening to find that even a partial solution

to one research problem depended on a woman's taste in stationery—
the human touch.

Fitzgerald's correspondence—at least the most important letters—has already been published, but in scattered and sometimes
abridged versions. There are volumes of letters to his editor, Max
Perkins, and his agent, Harold Ober. (The letters and hasty telegrams to Ober were especially useful for filling gaps in the chronology. Fitzgerald was perpetually in need of money, so he was
careful to give Ober forwarding addresses and the dates of departures
and arrivals.) Edmund Wilson published a number of Fitzgerald's
letters to friends in *The Crack-Up,* though with the saltier passages
deleted. And there are, as well, the early 1963 volume of selected
Letters, edited by Andrew Turnbull, and the more expanded 1980
Correspondence of F. Scott Fitzgerald, with many important letters from
Zelda, edited by the Fitzgerald scholar Matthew J. Bruccoli.

But there is no definitive edition of Fitzgerald's correspondence
arranged in chronological order. Because the letters are scattered
through separate volumes, it was easy for biographers to overlook
certain of the less attractive elements of Fitzgerald's character. His
judgments of other writers, for instance, were remarkably volatile.
Within a week or two, or over a period of a month or more, his
opinion of Sinclair Lewis, given to various correspondents, could
swing 180 degrees, and closer to 360, depending on the critical
winds of the moment. In reading the correspondence, one might
easily forget his tendency to exaggerate the fees he was paid for his
work, or his gift for embellishing the truth in order to make a good
story better. Less forgivable was his habit of borrowing opinions
from others and passing them along as his own. In order to appear
up-to-date or look good in the eyes of his more intellectual friends,
Fitzgerald tried on new ideas like new suits. But the new clothes
did not make a new man.

The constant references to drinking and drinking sprees, and
the sly or abject apologies for his behavior that followed, became a
problem. A great deal of attention has been paid to this aspect of
Fitzgerald's personality. But the cumulative effect of the incidents,
when followed in chronological sequence, is devastating: a waste of
time and talent, repeated excuses for failures to meet deadline after
deadline, the ruin of relationships with old friends who no longer
cared to put up with his tiresome antics. I confess that, over the
years, I have become less and less sympathetic toward people with

major or minor talents in any field who waste their gifts on drugs and drink, egotism and temperamental behavior. When I began *Invented Lives,* I felt that the best approach would be not to let the glamorous Fitzgeralds get away with anything. That way, the sense of the real tragedy behind their lives would be all the more apparent in the end.

If, in the end, I was not more sympathetic to Fitzgerald's waste of his gifts, I did come away with a greater admiration for the way he stuck to his dreams of becoming one of the most important writers of his time and even for the considerable talent he brought to his supposedly commercial work. And I was struck, too, by the angry, complicated loyalty he maintained toward his marriage and his dearly purchased memories of his life with Zelda. He was a man who was committed to paying the bills for his mistakes in life.

But the ultimate fascination for me, as I picked through the scattered pieces of the Fitzgeralds' lives and letters, the history of their published writings, their relationships with contemporaries, was what masters of invention they became, creating new versions of themselves, putting themselves into their stories, acting out their stories in real life. Yet *Invented Lives* is also about the hazards of such invention: Zelda's life trailing through mental institutions, Fitzgerald's sliding downhill into alcoholism. Perhaps the most tragic element of Fitzgerald's saga was the desperate need of a first-rate writer to escape from his middle-class origins and pretend to be many of the things he was not—the war hero, the dazzling athlete, the passionate husband or lover, the intellectual author, and concerned social observer. Once, in one of his several moments of truth, Fitzgerald confessed to Max Perkins, "Five years have rolled away from me and I can't decide exactly who I am, if anyone."

Invented Lives is about the personal cost of American success and American failure.

A word about the peculiarities in the quoted material. Nineteenth-century authors tended to overpunctuate; twentieth-century writers have taken a somewhat laissez-faire attitude toward capitalization, spelling, the use of the comma and the period. The purist doctrine on a quotation is that it should in every case be printed exactly as found, with all errors indicated by the condemnatory *sic.*

Unless it indicates a particularly interesting Freudian slip of the pen, I prefer not to use the *sic* at all. Fitzgerald was notorious for misspelling and lax about punctuation. He almost never remembered that et cetera should be abbreviated etc., and not ect. If I were to use *sic* on a good many of his letters, the pages would be peppered with editorial knuckle-rappings. In a rash moment, I decided to supply the reader with several of his characteristic errors and then silently emend the rest for the remainder of the book.

My good intentions gave way when I began to wonder why, if I corrected Fitzgerald's misspellings and odd punctuation, I didn't do the same for Ernest Hemingway or Max Perkins, or tidy up the frantic capitalizations and unnecessary emphases of Sara Murphy's letters, or restore the quotation marks to the conversations recorded in the memoirs of Alice B. Toklas, who adopted the practice of her mentor, Gertrude Stein, and dispensed with commas and quotation marks as typographical impediments. Not wanting to pose as an authority on grammar and punctuation, I decided, with some relief, to restore the errors that I had corrected at random during the earlier drafts of *Invented Lives*. In only a few instances has the persistent misspelling of a proper name been corrected. And in very few instances a comma or a dash has been added to make a meaning plain. As a result, the book may look like a lexicon of typographical oddities. But that, I suppose, is a commentary, in itself, on the varieties of twentieth-century styles.

PART ONE

I

The Past Is Forever

THEY WERE relentless self-historians, keeping photograph albums, scrapbooks, diaries, notebooks, ledger accounts of their earnings. (They seldom bothered about their expenses.) They wrote about themselves on every offered occasion, creating the legend, inventing themselves afresh. Yet the truth is that they were like figures in a hall of mirrors: everything reflected back brilliant or attractive or distorted images of themselves, but it was difficult to know where the real substance was.

From this distance in time, details blur and fade — bleach out. Prompted by the legend or the easy recollection of some contemporary, one might take them for the foolish bride and bridegroom of a Sunday rotogravure section; not quite real, completely absorbed in themselves and in each other and in their special situation. At other times, when the legend is chastened by fact, their lives take on the hard, unforgiving accuracy of a snapshot.

But for now, she is nineteen and beautiful, barely out of adolescence, with the healthy look of a grown-up child, or not so very attractive, with a candy-box face and a little bow mouth. Her eyes are large and blue — or dark Confederate gray. Her hair is golden, tinged with auburn — "honey-gold." She is decidedly short — not more than five feet three or four — yet a poet will describe her as a "barbarian princess." She is frankly approving of the opposite sex. (Women are seldom her friends.) She is the kind of girl men instinctively stare at. In photographs she often seems to be pouting. Photographs sometimes lie.

He is twenty-three, with blond hair emphatically parted in the middle and with heavily lashed blue, or lavender, or gray, or ice-green eyes. He is five feet seven, or, as his passport will claim, five feet eight and a half. (Quite possibly he lied for the sake of the extra inch; he is sensitive about his stature.) He has a medium build that will go paunchy with age and too much drink. In time, he will use Sen-Sen to hide the alcohol on his breath; his medicine chest will be a forest of dandruff cures. But that time is not now. Now, his profile is said to rival that of the great Barrymore. A friend will meanly describe him as too pretty for a man.

It is the day of their wedding, April 3, 1920, a Saturday morning, not quite noon. A little band of friends and family is gathered in the rectory of St. Patrick's Cathedral. The bride is wearing a dark blue suit and hat, carrying a bouquet of orchids. (She loves flowers, is fond of exotics.) The groom is visibly impatient.

The wedding had originally been scheduled for the following Monday, April 5. But on March 30, from New York, he wired her in Montgomery, Alabama, WE WILL BE AWFULLY NERVOUS UNTIL IT IS OVER AND WOULD GET NO REST BY WAITING UNTIL MONDAY. He also informed her, FIRST EDITION OF THE BOOK IS SOLD OUT. So Zelda Sayre, after hastily putting together her trousseau, and accompanied by her sister Marjorie, took a train to New York to marry F. Scott Fitzgerald, whose first novel, *This Side of Paradise,* had become an overnight best seller.

Not only did Fitzgerald push forward the date of the wedding, but he is too impatient to wait for the arrival of Clothilde and John Palmer, Zelda's sister and brother-in-law. He insists that the officiating priest, the Reverend William B. Martin, start the ceremony a half-hour early. The other members of the wedding party are the matron of honor, Zelda's sister Rosalind, and her husband, Newman Smith, and Zelda's eldest sister, Marjorie Brinson. The best man is Ludlow Fowler, a Princeton classmate of Fitzgerald's. Neither the bride's nor the groom's parents attend.

The wedding ceremony at St. Patrick's is a formality. Zelda's family is Episcopalian, but she has little concern with religion at the moment. Fitzgerald has had a more or less Catholic education in Minnesota and upstate New York. There were early bouts of piety; Fitzgerald even entertained notions of the priesthood at various times. But much of that early religious fervor seems to have been the effect of energetic priests on an impressionable youth. At the time of his wedding, Fitzgerald had dissociated himself from the Church. "Last year as a Catholic" reads a 1917 entry in his ledger book; he was twenty-one when the lapse occurred.

The choice of a New York church wedding appears to have been that of Zelda's mother, Minnie Sayre, "because," so Zelda informed Fitzgerald, "she says you'd like to do it in St. Patrick's." That apparent act of tolerance is worth remembering; in a later, bitter time, Fitzgerald will twist it into an indictment against his mother-in-law and his bride. But now, the decision registers the characteristic ambivalence of Fitzgerald's life. It is a concession to priorities no longer felt—but it is performed in the most prestigious Catholic cathedral in the country. Father Martin pronounces his blessing on the mixed marriage. He advises the couple, "You be a good Episcopalian, Zelda, and, Scott, you be a good Catholic, and you'll get along fine." Fitzgerald will claim that this was the last piece of advice ever given him by a priest.

No sooner is the ceremony over than Fitzgerald whisks his bride off to their honeymoon suite at the Biltmore Hotel. There is no luncheon—no party of any kind for the members of the wedding. Rosalind Sayre Smith considers this an insult to the family, one that she does not forget.

There were understandable reasons for Fitzgerald's marrying in haste. His nearly two-year courtship of Zelda Sayre had been a torment of indecision, quarrels, and frustration. Fitzgerald was a cocky lieutenant with the 67th Infantry stationed at Camp Sheridan, Alabama, when he first met Zelda at a dance at the Montgomery Country Club in July 1918. One can easily paint the scene: the sultry summer evening, the dark sprawling silhouette of the club building, sheltered by tall oaks, flanked by pines and thick hedges of mock orange, the gleams of light and the strains of dance music, the sounds of laughter from the dark recesses of the wide verandah, the vivid girl with a sheen of blond hair who was the center of attraction among a stand of young officers from the camp and pilots from nearby Taylor Field. According to one report, Fitzgerald had promptly asked her for a late date after the dance; she had promptly answered, "I never make late dates with fast workers." Otherwise, the scenario and the setting were the same that Fitzgerald had used several times before in his collegiate stories written for the *Nassau Lit:* the bold and "unprincipled" girl, the handsome, somewhat stiffish, suitor, the dance attended by officers or gentlemen, the drifting refrain of some popular sentimental ballad like "Poor Butterfly."

Zelda, who had an instinct for reality, would remember the shabbier details of the scene: the sagging wire fence surrounding the tennis court, the trickling fire hydrant, the lawns scuffed thin by traffic like the front yard of some child's playhouse, the gravel driveway, the parked cars nosing into the round bed of cannas. But despite her sassiness, Zelda was young and impressionable, and Fitzgerald had definitely rushed her. Within a week or more of meeting her, he gave her a birthday party at the club. She would recall it, years later, as one of Fitzgerald's heroines might have recalled it—steeped in romance. "Remember," she wrote Fitzgerald, "there were 3 pines on one side and 4 on the other the night you gave me my birthday party and you were a young lieutenant and I was a fragrant phantom, wasn't I? And it was a radiant night, a night of soft conspiracy and the trees agreed that it was all going to be for the best. Remember the faded gray romance."

But Zelda in the flesh was much less tractable than a Fitzgerald heroine. Not quite eighteen, just graduated from Sidney Lanier High School, she was independent and artlessly selfish, with a keen sense of fun and a hatred of conformity. She smoked and drank, had acquired a local reputation as a "speed," was considered a highly prized date by the fraternity boys of Auburn and Georgia Tech. She was a late child; her sisters Marjorie, Rosalind, and Clothilde were all married by the time Fitzgerald met her; her brother, Anthony, was a practicing civil engineer in Mobile. Zelda was pampered and indulged by her mother. Fitzgerald always insisted that Mrs. Sayre had suckled the child for so many years that Zelda could probably have chewed sticks.

Minnie Sayre, forty when Zelda was born, was plump and matronly; she was fond of music and had literary aspirations. In her younger years, she had hoped to become an opera singer or an actress; now she wrote poetry for the local newspapers. She actively encouraged Zelda's interest in writing and dance, even produced some of the plays and skits for the local charity productions in which her daughter performed.

It was left to the elder Anthony Sayre, an associate justice of the Alabama Supreme Court, to stand guard over the family reputation and Zelda's worrisome behavior. Zelda admired her father's old-fashioned sense of propriety, but referred to him with randy innocence as "Old Dick" and evidently felt the need to ruffle his composure. According to one story, when Fitzgerald first went to dinner at number 6 Pleasant Avenue, Zelda managed to taunt her father to such a degree of rage that he chased her around the table with a carving knife. On a dull summer afternoon in Montgomery, she had been known to call the fire department, then climb to the roof of her house and push the ladder away so that she could be rescued. She had an instinct for provocative gestures; there were nights when she liked to drive past the local whorehouse — Madame Helen St. Clair's — and flick the spotlight on the boys she knew as they entered and left the establishment.

In her novel *Save Me the Waltz*, Zelda created a fictional vignette of Fitzgerald in his natty lieutenant's uniform, tailored for him by Brooks Brothers, on one of their early dates at the Montgomery Country Club. Her heroine, Alabama Beggs, is jealous of David Knight's "pale aloofness," his attractiveness to women. She is conscious of the odd, lilting gait of his walk: "There seemed to be some heavenly support beneath his shoulder blades. . . ." When the couple danced, her head on his shoulder, she found something memorable about the stiffness of his tunic collar and the scent of khaki and cambric. "He smelled like new goods," Zelda wrote. It was a clever simile. The amount of haberdashery in Fitzgerald's writings is impressive. Clothes are apt to have a symbolic importance. Like his hero Jay Gatsby, Fitzgerald, too, sensed an affinity between wealth and wardrobe. He was "overwhelmingly aware of the youth and mystery that wealth imprisons and preserves, of the freshness of many clothes. . . ."

Fitzgerald boasted that, although he did not have either of the two most important requirements, "great animal magnetism or money," he did have the two lesser qualities, "good looks and intelligence," so he always got "the top girl." But it is doubtful that he ever felt that secure about Zelda. He was painfully aware of her popularity, not only with fraternity boys and football heroes, but with the dashing young aviators of Taylor Field who routinely buzzed the Sayre house in their tributes to Zelda. A few weeks after Fitzgerald met her, one of her rejected suitors, Second Lieutenant Lincoln Weaver, had crashed on a speedway while attempting a tailspin. His stunt was featured in a local headline, in which he was described as "badly injured." The item was clipped for the Fitzgerald scrapbooks, and Weaver's name was enshrined in Fitzgerald's ledger book. The

man who died for the love of Zelda became a fixture in the legend
Fitzgerald contrived around his sweetheart. Out of admiration and
his envy of "animal magnetism," he created one of his enduring
symbols: the lover who dies in a plane crash, the cast-off man who
falls, like Icarus, from out the skies. The figure traces a curve
throughout Fitzgerald's fiction from beginning to end. But in this
case, the hero had not actually died. According to U.S. Army records,
Weaver survived and collected his separation pay the following year.
But Fitzgerald was a master of invention; for him, imagination would
always be more potent than fact.

Not only was Zelda popular and a femme fatale; she was an
accomplished tease even at the age of eighteen. Throughout their
courtship, she took a perverse pleasure in making Fitzgerald jealous
by sending him lively accounts of her dates with other men. When
Fitzgerald retaliated by mentioning that he had met some interesting
actresses in New York, she would suggest that he ought to have
dates, even affairs, with other women: "Anyway, if she's good-looking and you want to one bit — I know you could, and love me just
the same." She was also adept enough to go him one better by telling
him about her latest conquest at the country club dance: "One man
tried to elope to N.Y. with me — said I'd make a fortune Shaking-
It thusly up Broadway." Her nonchalance was the perfect weapon
to puncture Fitzgerald's old-fashioned and self-serving views on fidelity. And she also recognized that Fitzgerald courted his torment:
"I know you've worried — and enjoyed doing it thoroughly . . .
you're so morbidly exaggerative."

It had not been love at first sight, as the myth suggests. It was
not until September, according to his ledger, that Fitzgerald conceded
the affair had become serious: "Fell in love on the 7th." And his
anxieties about Zelda were not misplaced. At some point early in
the relationship, perhaps before Fitzgerald's unit was shipped north
on October 26, he and Zelda had sex together. It was not, apparently, an all-consuming, unavoidable, passionately physical involvement — only a brief sexual experiment, after which Zelda held back,
unwilling to commit herself further. The evidence for this does not
come from any detailed confession by either Fitzgerald or Zelda, but
from the scattered half-truths, near-truths, and evasions out of which
they constructed their fictional stories and the scraps of personal
history they related to friends. It comes, so to speak, from the loose
change of the documentary sources.

In a plot note for one of his later, absurd historical tales, dealing with the adventures of a ninth-century French nobleman, Philippe, designated the "Count of Darkness," Fitzgerald made a note about his heroine: "After yielding, she holds Philippe at bay like Zelda & me in summer 1917." The date is obviously wrong; Fitzgerald did not meet Zelda until the following summer. It is one of the oddities of the Fitzgeralds' history that, despite their interest in themselves, the crucial events of their lives are often blurred by uncertainties. Zelda's letters are almost never dated; only a random postmark fixes the time. The chronology of Fitzgerald's ledger entries is often haphazard and frequently doubtful. They spent their time as they spent their money, never concerned with keeping a strict record. The event was important and not the date.

Fitzgerald's biographer Matthew Bruccoli assigns 1918 as the time of their first sexual encounter. But it may also have occurred during the spring or summer of 1919, when Fitzgerald was working in New York and making regular visits to Montgomery. It was during this period that Zelda's usually breezy letters become especially warm and suggestive: "Sweetheart, I love you most of all the earth—and I want to be married soon—soon—Lover—Don't say I'm not enthusiastic—You ought to know." "Darling heart, I wish and wish we had eloped together—I'm all I'll ever be without you—and there's so much more room for growth—with you—All my mental faculties are paralyzed with loving you—and wanting you for mine."

But Fitzgerald's conquest, whenever it occurred, did not bring him any sense of security; he was never quite trusting of his dream girl afterward.

II

In his stories, Fitzgerald is always the sharp-eyed observer of his women characters; he notices their style, their clothes, their conversation, their techniques with men. He is intensely curious about what they think and feel, how they express themselves. That curiosity accounts for the vitality of his heroines as contrasted with the more pallid, circumspect, and conventionally minded heroes. Women are the focal points, the suns around which the plots and the male characters revolve.

It is astonishing, then, that Fitzgerald's mother played — or seems to have played — such a negligible role in his life and recollections. In the large commercial ledger book in which, some time between 1919 and the early 1920s, Fitzgerald began to chronicle the events of his life, month by month, year by year, as the "Outline Chart of My Life," Mary (Mollie) McQuillan Fitzgerald is treated in the most chilling and perfunctory terms. To be sure, Fitzgerald's record starts out as a third-person account of experiences and events from his birth, on September 24, 1896, and the earliest entries are mere comic accounts of such infantile moments as this tenth-month event: "He said his first word. It was the monosyllable 'up.'" But as the entries proceed from the crawling stage to his marriage at the age of twenty-three, through a welter of names and places, notes on trips to lakes and summer camps, through dances, courtships, and military service, it is easy to overlook that Fitzgerald gives only scant attention to his mother. Of some two thousand entries covering the period from his birth to his marriage, there are little more than a dozen mentions of Mollie Fitzgerald: bare recitals of such facts as her not letting him attend a party or her being away on a visit to relatives. Even the one entry that carries some hint of personal emotion, written when Fitzgerald was twenty, is a confession of his essential indifference:

> September 1916: I could now be sympathetic to Mother but she reacts too quickly.

The pertinent events involving his mother that Fitzgerald recalled when, at the age of twenty-three, he looked back over his life make up a very sparse inventory. After his marriage, there would be even fewer mentions of her. The peculiar truth is that throughout his life Fitzgerald spoke of his mother in disapproving terms, felt embarrassed about her, found it necessary to apologize for her on the rare occasions that he mentioned her to friends. Even in his dreams, he was unforgiving. Later in his life, he recorded an especially vivid dream, one that revealed his attitude toward his mother. It began with his being snubbed by a group of rich and handsome young men who refused to invite him to a party:

> I leave the house, but as I leave Mother calls something to me in a too audible voice from an upper story. I don't know whether I am angry with her for clinging to me, or because I am ashamed of

her for not being young and chic, or for disgracing my conventional sense by calling out, or because she might guess I'd been hurt and pity me, which would have been unendurable, or all those things. Anyhow I call back at her some terse and furious reproach.

Mollie McQuillan Fitzgerald was hardly a monster and certainly no venomous shrew. She was the somewhat plain, unexceptional eldest daughter of Philip McQuillan, an immigrant Irishman and self-made man who, in the course of a brisk career, turned his wholesale grocery business into a million-dollar concern. His wife, Louisa Allen, whom he married in 1860, was Irish as well, the daughter of an immigrant carpenter. Despite their lowly origins, the McQuillans became one of the prominent mercantile families in St. Paul, Minnesota, a mainstay of the Catholic Church there. Their three-story mansion, a Victorian hulk decked out with porticoes and porches, was one of the showplaces of St. Paul, until the area turned commercial and became less fashionably known as Lower Town. Fitzgerald seemed as ashamed of his origins — "straight 1850 potato-famine Irish" — as he was of his mother. He would tell a friend that the combination of being Irish and middle class "depresses me inordinately — I mean gives me a sort of hollow, cheerless pain. Half of my ancestors came from just such an Irish strata or perhaps a lower one."

Mollie McQuillan, educated at the Visitation Convent and then at Manhattanville College in New York, had traveled extensively; had toured Europe four times. Family photographs of her reveal a woman who seems, always, slightly past her prime, tightly corseted, not stylishly dressed (but not poorly dressed, either), a woman with a wan smile and a distracted, faraway look. She was an indiscriminate reader of innocuous novels and sentimental poetry. She had a liking for the maudlin verses of Alice and Phoebe Cary. Friends considered Mollie McQuillan eccentric and rather careless about dress. She was apt to arrive for a visit wearing one black shoe and one brown, because she preferred to break in a new pair one shoe at a time. An acquaintance described her as "dressed like the devil, always coming apart." She seemed doomed to spinsterhood — the fate of her two younger sisters, Annabel and Clara. But surprisingly, at the age of twenty-nine, she married thirty-seven-year-old Edward Fitzgerald, Maryland-born, but a St. Paul businessman. Local rumor had it that she had forced the issue by threatening to jump into the river if

Edward Fitzgerald did not propose. The story may well have been apocryphal and could be dismissed as a trivial piece of gossip, except that her son, when drunk and morose about a love affair, had a tendency to threaten to jump from the nearest window.

On February 12, 1890, Edward Fitzgerald and Mollie McQuillan were married in Washington, D.C., where both had family connections. They spent their honeymoon traveling in Europe. Mollie Fitzgerald was struck—as her son would be years later—by the atmosphere of the French Riviera. From Nice, she wrote her brother-in-law, John Fitzgerald, "The color of the water is so blue and the moon was shining so bright and altogether it was a perfect night for people in our situation." She went so far as to claim that, whatever might happen in the future, "this one time in our lives will be without a flaw to look back upon."

Edward Fitzgerald was a man of gentle and courteous manners, bound by the traditions of old-fashioned Southern gentility. He had been born on Glenmary Farm near Rockville, Maryland, and his family—the respectable half of the family, as far as his son was concerned—could trace its roots back to the Colonial legislators. He had attended Georgetown University, though he had not received a diploma. He lacked the aggressive spunk of the McQuillans. Photographs of him in his middle age (when Scott was a small boy) show him as a man with a taste for impeccable tailoring; a diffident and rather handsome man, with a neatly trimmed Vandyke beard and mustache and an expression of hurt around the eyes. He conveyed, to his son as well as to others, an air of good breeding and low vitality. In St. Paul, where the Fitzgeralds took up residence, Edward Fitzgerald operated a not too prospering wicker furniture business.

The marriage appears to have had none of the acrimony or violence that was to characterize the son's married life. Edward Fitzgerald, with fine distinction, would describe his wife as having "just missed being beautiful." Otherwise, the disappointments were less marital than financial. The couple had two daughters, both of whom died in an epidemic a few months before the birth of their first and only son, named Francis Scott Key Fitzgerald in honor of Edward's distant Maryland ancestor, the author of the anthem verse "The Star Spangled Banner." The double tragedy made Mollie Fitzgerald extremely nervous and fussy about her son's health. She pampered him and at the slightest sign of a cold kept him home from school.

Fitzgerald, who had a tendency to hypochondria in his later years, learned the tactical effectiveness of ill health at his mother's knee. And publicly, at least, he seems to have made something mythic out of the death of his sisters, as if that prenatal event had somehow conferred on him special powers: "I don't know how it worked exactly. I think I started then to be a writer."

Mollie Fitzgerald, who was addicted to sentimental keepsakes and souvenir books, recorded every important event in her son's infant life. His mother's habit must have encouraged Fitzgerald's tendency to historicize himself; he became a hoarder of valentines from childhood sweethearts and lists of his partners on dancing school programs.

Fitzgerald family life was peripatetic, partly because of financial difficulties and partly owing to Mollie Fitzgerald's incurable restlessness and dissatisfaction with any fixed abode. (Fitzgerald and Zelda also would never find a settled home for themselves.) In the fall of 1898, Edward Fitzgerald's company failed. He moved his family to Buffalo, New York, where he took a job as a salesman for the Procter & Gamble Company. The Fitzgeralds moved from one rented residence to another, first in Buffalo and then in Syracuse, where Scott's sister, Annabel, was born, in July 1901. Back in Buffalo again, in 1903, Fitzgerald attended school at the Holy Angels Convent, where he was allowed to go only half a day, making his own choice of which half he preferred. When the family moved again, this time to Highland Avenue, he was enrolled in Miss Ernestine Nardin's private academy for the children of Buffalo's well-to-do Catholic families.

If Mollie McQuillan Fitzgerald makes few appearances in the chronicles of Fitzgerald's early life, everything else of little or great importance is recorded on the long pages of his ledger, from his black cocker spaniel, Beautiful Joe, to his first bouts of religiosity: "He fell under the spell of a Catholic preacher, Father Fallon, of the Church of the Holy Angels." Fitzgerald noted his fights with rough boys, against whom he apparently held his own, his crushes on transient girl friends, dancing school frolics, trips to the Catskills, and family weddings in Maryland. Birthdays seem to have been more or less disappointing; the worst was his seventh, when, impeccably dressed in a sailor suit, he was prepared to play host — and no one came. At the precocious age of four, according to Fitzgerald's recollection, he had a "freudian shame" about exposing his bare feet and refused to swim or go barefoot around other boys. Whether this continuing fixation had something to do with a peculiar sequence of entries, set down for his seventh year, is not certain. Nonetheless, it reads like a clinical report on some minor psychic disturbance: "He took off John Wylie's shoes. He began to hear 'dirty' words. He had his curious dream of perversion."

He was approaching the combative phase in his relationships with other boys. At eight, he gave another boy a bloody nose "and ran home in consequence with a made up story." His close relationship with John Wylie went sour during this period, since the ledger records that he "hit John Wylie with a stick and ended their friendship." He wore his own battle wounds proudly. Having been hit accidentally on the head by a baseball bat wielded by Jack Butler, "son of an army officer" (social distinctions of this kind would be important to Fitzgerald throughout his life), he vowed that the scar would "always shine" in the middle of his forehead. It was during these impressionable years that he became infatuated with athletes who carried themselves with easy grace. At a basketball game, he "fell madly into admiration for a dark haired boy who played with a melancholy defiance." That beau ideal would trail after him through Princeton and into the fictional world of his stories and novels: "Perfection—black hair, olive skin, and tenor voice."

The years from 1905 until 1908 also marked the period of his regular attendance at Mr. Van Arnum's dancing school and the beginnings of an addiction to romance and falling in love. The first of his "serious" love affairs was a short-lived one with Nancy Gardiner, when he was nine. At eleven, he was smitten by Kitty Williams. (He preserved her crude hand-made valentine, along with a dance card on which her name appears several times.) Fitzgerald had tried to woo her with a large box of chocolates at Christmastime, but was "scared silly," and when she opened the door he thrust the gift at her and ran away in confusion.

In a private "Thoughtbook," which Fitzgerald, man of the world at thirteen, kept for a few months during the winter of 1910–1911, he looked back at his youthful affairs in Buffalo and gave a detailed account of the Kitty affair. He had asked her to be his partner in the Grand March. Kitty, who already had several suitors, passed down the word, through her girl friends, that Scott was not the first in her affections.

I dont remember who was first [he wrote] but I know that Earl was
second and as I was already quite over come by her charms I then
and there resolved that I would gain first place. . . . Finally she
asked me if I was going to Robin's party and it was there my
eventful day was. We played postoffice, pillow, clapp in and clapp
out and other foolish but interesting games. It was impossible to
count the number of times I kissed Kitty that afternoon. At any
rate when we went home I had secured the coveted 1st place. I held
this until dancing school stopped in the spring and then relin-
quished it to Johnny Gowns a rival. On valentines day that year
Kitty received no less than eighty four valentines.

A comic episode in the young life of a future author, perhaps. But,
noting the remarkable sangfroid of the thirteen-year-old writer, one
sees that the narrative is, in cameo, the model for many of Fitzgerald's later fictional situations: the top girl and the connoisseur of
kisses, the dance floor as the symbolic setting, the trivial ambitions
treated as matters of great magnitude. The strict accounting of the
number of valentines was important, as well. Fitzgerald had a healthy
respect for the evidence of success. Even the style, easy and conversational, with its mantle of sophistication, is prophetic.

It is significant that during this period of adolescence Edward
Fitzgerald assumed a more prominent and warmly human role in his
son's life than Mollie Fitzgerald could claim. A wary affection shows
through some of the ledger entries about Fitzgerald's father. Fitzgerald recalled, for instance, that when he was six, his father had
"egged" him into a boxing match with the grocer's son. He also
recalled a spanking his father had given him, on the Fourth of July
of that same year, because he had "wandered off" from home. With
Fitzgerald, as with writers like Ernest Hemingway, who were as
concerned with the image they projected as with the substance of
what they said, one has to take into consideration the occasion and
the audience for their personal revelations. In a later essay, "The
Death of My Father," in which Fitzgerald tried to come to terms
with his troubled relationship with his parent, he gave a more detailed account of the episode. And he heightened the poignancy of
the account by noting that he had run away from home:

I spent the day with a friend in a pear orchard and the police were
informed that I was missing and on my return my father thrashed
me according to the custom of the nineties — on the bottom — and

then let me come out and watch the night fireworks from the balcony with my pants still down and my behind smarting and knowing in my heart that he was absolutely right.

Compared with his mother's anarchic indulgence, which Fitzgerald perversely resented, his father's occasional strictness was evidently appreciated. He would remember, with affection, the summer Sunday mornings in Buffalo when he and his father walked downtown. He would wear his starched white duck trousers and carry his little cane — even at that age he was a dandy — while his father walked beside him, proud of "his handsome little boy." The pair would have their shoes shined — it was a Sunday ritual — then his father would light his cigar and the two would return home with the Sunday papers.

There were other occasions that Fitzgerald remembered with a sense of chagrin or shame, when his father, having had too much to drink, came out into the back yard and, tipsy, insisted on playing baseball with Scott and his friends. It is not known whether Edward Fitzgerald had a serious or growing problem as an alcoholic, or whether he drank under stress. Or even whether Fitzgerald was simply laying a groundwork of guilt and recrimination for his own later problems with alcohol. But two years after the baseball incidents, the Fitzgeralds' stay in Buffalo came to an end. It was one of those afternoons of an author which Fitzgerald would portray — this time for the benefit of an inquisitive reporter. He was at home when the phone rang; his mother answered it. He knew from the tone of her voice that it meant trouble. Earlier, she had given him a quarter to go swimming, and he was so convinced that something disastrous had happened that he returned it to her. He began to pray: "Dear God . . . please don't let us go to the poorhouse; please don't let us go to the poorhouse." Not long afterward, his father came home:

> I had been right. He had lost his job. That morning he had gone out a comparatively young man, a man full of strength, full of confidence. He had come home that evening an old man, a completely broken man. He had lost his essential drive, his immaculateness of purpose. He was a failure the rest of his days.

Fitzgerald's vignette ended with one of the few remembrances of his mother that showed any sense of warmth or compunction on his part. Mollie Fitzgerald had prodded her son: "Scott, say something to your father." Fitzgerald, unable to think of anything, went up to his father and asked, with inspired irrelevance, who his father thought would win the next presidential election. His father continued to stare out the window, then, without moving a muscle, answered, "I think Taft will."

Affecting as that scene may be, it is a mistake to take Fitzgerald's autobiographical stories altogether at face value. In this case, he was reciting his narrative for a reporter who regarded him as an alcoholic and a writer on the skids. Fitzgerald's little chronicle of his father's defeat must have included a certain amount of self-pity and self-justification. As a sensitive writer, Fitzgerald understood and mourned the loss of his father's "immaculateness of purpose." He no doubt regretted it as much as the loss of his own.

In the summer of 1908, when Fitzgerald was eleven, his family moved back to St. Paul and the sheltering security of the McQuillan money. At first, Scott and Annabel lived with Grandmother Louisa while their parents stayed with a friend. It was an uneasy time, and reinforced his sense of his father's failure. The McQuillans, "the black Irish half" of the family, clearly looked down their noses at the Maryland branch, which had the "breeding." Edward Fitzgerald attempted to rebuild a career, this time as a grocery salesman, renting desk space in his brother-in-law's office. It was not until 1913, when Louisa McQuillan died, leaving a considerable estate, that the Fitzgeralds were relatively well-off. In the meantime, the restless family moved from one rented apartment or house to another, usually on the fringes of the fashionable Summit Avenue area.

During the three years that Fitzgerald lived in St. Paul, he was enrolled in St. Paul Academy. Perhaps goaded by his father's failure, he made these adolescent years a bustle of activities, willing himself to succeed in all of them. He played basketball and football (and proudly noted that he had broken a rib in one of the St. Paul games), swam and boxed at the YMCA. He resumed regular attendance at a dancing school—this time Professor Baker's classes. It was around this time that he became an "inveterate author." (He was still an avid reader of boys' adventure stories, but he was now interested in Dickens and *Alice in Wonderland* and his father's favorite poets, Byron and Poe.) Within a year he was a published author. His first effort, "The Mystery of the Raymond Mortgage," a story with several loose ends and missing clues, appeared in the October 1909 issue of the school literary magazine, *Now and Then*. It caused a bout of author's fever; Fitzgerald hung around the printer's office until he became a nuisance. When the issues finally arrived in the classroom, he was so excited that he could not contain himself; he bounced up and down in his seat, mumbling, "They're here! They're here!" He followed up this success with stories of the heroism of a young football player ("Reade, Substitute Right Half") and of a Confederate soldier ("A Debt of Honor") who, having fallen asleep on sentry duty, redeems himself by dying in a charge at the Battle of Chancellorsville. The Civil War setting came from his father, whose stories Fitzgerald asked to hear again and again until he knew them by heart. At the age of nine, Edward Fitzgerald had rowed a Confederate spy across the Rockville River, and he could remember sitting on a fence one morning to watch as General Jubal Early's battalions marched toward Washington in an abortive attempt to take the capital.

Fitzgerald also began his career as a playwright and sometime actor-director. He wrote a series of plays — *The Girl from the Lazy J, The Captured Shadow, The Coward,* and *Assorted Spirits* — for the Elizabethan Drama Club, named after its sponsor and drama coach, Elizabeth Magoffin. The playbills and press clippings from the charity performances of *The Coward,* a Civil War drama, given at the YWCA and the White Bear Yacht Club, after Fitzgerald had gone east to a Catholic prep school, were pasted into his scrapbook with suitable captions: "The Great Event" and "Enter Success!" Before he was out of his adolescence, Fitzgerald had already basked in the glow of provincial fame.

It was in St. Paul, at the age of thirteen, that he began his "Thoughtbook," entering the names of two new crushes: "to wit — Margaret Armstrong and Marie Hersey — I have not quite decided yet which I like the best." And he added the saga of his summer romance with Violet Stockton, a dark-haired, brown-eyed Southern belle with a soft accent who was visiting St. Paul. Like most of Fitzgerald's desirable women, Violet had other admirers — in this case, Art Foley and Jack Mitchell. Violet had a book, a manual on flirting, that Fitzgerald and Mitchell managed to get away from her. Fitzgerald, who tended to be loose with confidences and secrets, showed it around to the other boys, with the result that "Violet got very mad and went into the house. *I* got very mad and therefor *I* went home . . . *I just hate Violet.*" There was a reconciliation of sorts; Violet gave him a box of candy on his birthday. But when she left town, she gave her ring to Art Foley and wrote to him, asking him for his photograph.

Despite his frenzied activities at St. Paul Academy, Fitzgerald was not popular; he was conceited, meddlesome, too high-handed for most of his classmates. It was not that he ignored them. He had, in fact, become something of an amateur psychologist and an observer of the mutability of his own affections and those of others. In his "Thoughtbook" he made mention of one of his early crushes: "One day Marie Hersey wrote me a note which began either 'Dear Scott, I love you very much or I like you very much' and ever since then she has been rather shy when she meets me." He also devoted a chapter to his waning infatuation for a classmate, Paul Ballion, "strong as an ox, cool in the face of danger, polite and at times very interesting," whom he had once regarded as his hero. "Now I don't dislike him. I have simply out grown him."

C. N. B. Wheeler, the athletic coach and the English teacher who encouraged Scott's literary ambitions, claimed that Fitzgerald's problem was that he saw through his classmates too readily and then "wrote about it." Wheeler thought Fitzgerald was destined to become an actor "of the variety type." Even Fitzgerald's membership in a series of secret societies, one of which, the Scandal Detectives, he had inaugurated, failed to improve his status. But however egotistical or imperious Fitzgerald may have been, he was forever curious about what others thought of him. In his "Thoughtbook," he noted Violet Stockton's measured opinion of his character: "that I was polite and had a nice disposition and that I thought I was the whole push and that I got mad too easily." Still, he enjoyed his reputation as the freshest boy in his circle. It evidently gave him a sly satisfaction to record in his ledger book a personal announcement that one of his academy classmates placed in the school paper: "Will someone poison Scotty or find some means to shut his mouth."

Later in life, Fitzgerald recognized that his self-centeredness had been a liability: "I didn't know till 15 that there was anyone in the world except me, and it cost me *plenty*." Hunting for the source of his character problems, Fitzgerald was inclined to blame his mother for having spoiled him. It was a curious indictment to bring against a relatively harmless, perhaps neurotic woman. Mollie Fitzgerald had a compulsive streak in her nature; Fitzgerald described her as being "pulled forward by an irresistible urge of boredom and vitality." Given the low-key, ineffectual character of his father, he may have found Mollie Fitzgerald's compulsiveness especially grating. But the only crime Fitzgerald adduces is that whenever his mother went on a trip or had an appointment, she insisted on being there an hour ahead of time, and that meant dull waits in waiting rooms. More troubling, perhaps, was her fussing over her son's health, though it was reasonable enough, following the death of her two daughters. There was a disposition to tuberculosis in the family, and Mollie Fitzgerald passed on her fears to her son. Later in life, Fitzgerald would have bouts of anxiety concerning the disease, fears that were sometimes convenient excuses for avoiding deadlines and at other times were valid. His later medical reports indicated old lesions on his lungs.

Like many an imaginative child with a literary bent, Fitzgerald fantasized that he was not his parents' offspring. He imagined, among other things, that he was a foundling, that he was descended from the royal Stuarts, that he was the son of a king—"a king who ruled the whole world." In a fictional portrait of himself—the hero at the age of ten—Fitzgerald made a startling confession of his desperate urge to see himself through the eyes of others, a need that seemed to convey a kind of immortality: "I had lived so much, not exactly within myself, but within mirrors of me that I found in other people, that I couldn't imagine myself a mortal. In the first place I was not to die. . . . I could think of the death of my whole family without a qualm—but myself—no!"

Such notions, harmless enough, crop up in his early stories and in the discarded version of his first novel. But Fitzgerald never altogether outgrew them. They found their perfect expression in his creation of Jay Gatsby, the man with no presumed ancestry, the man who "sprang from his Platonic conception of himself."

Fitzgerald's compelling urge to dissociate himself from his parents no doubt was a response to his judgment of them as mediocre. But that hardly explains or exonerates the bitterness he occasionally allowed to rise to the surface. Even in jest, his remarks could be cruel and insensitive. "My father is a moron and my mother is a neurotic, half insane with pathological nervous worry," he wrote. "Between them they haven't and never have had the brains of Calvin Coolidge." In his notebooks he remarked, "Advantages of children whose mother is dead." At times, he could be ruthless on the subject, and once boasted to a secretary: "If you want to be a top-notch writer, you have to break with everyone. You have to show your own father up. At first, they will throw you out for it, but in the end they will take you back on a different footing when the world acclaims you. You've got to go a lone, lone path." When Mollie Fitzgerald died, in 1936, Fitzgerald's mourning was tempered with dissatisfaction. Writing to Annabel, he was still critical: "Mother and I never had anything in common except a relentless stubborn quality, but when I saw all this it turned me inside out, realizing how unhappy her temperament made her and how she clung, to the end, to all things that would remind her of moments of snatched happiness."

Amazingly, for Fitzgerald had moments of startling obtuseness, he did not seem to recognize that his analysis of his mother read like a clinical diagnosis of his own problems in life. It is worth remembering, too, that Fitzgerald, who would admit to feminine traits in his nature, which he considered valuable for the delineation of his heroines, had a nagging urge to remake and re-educate the women he was involved with—his wife, his daughter, his mistress.

Fitzgerald, in fact, never resolved his ambivalent feelings toward the paired universe of his childhood, the unsatisfactory marriage of the problematic woman and the man who was a gentle failure. His dissatisfaction gave rise to the stringent demands he made on himself—his pursuit of the prized debutante, his compulsive hero worship. It was no accident that the two major themes of Fitzgerald's fiction were courtship and the conjugal life. In his major novels and most important stories, he explored the causes of marital failure; in his commercial stories, he tended to gloss over the difficulties with clever and conventional happy endings. "Fiction is a trick of the mind and the heart," Fitzgerald maintained in a provocative essay, "Author's House." Fiction, he said, was a method he had learned for dealing with "all the complicated dark mixture of my youth and infancy that made me a fiction writer instead of a fireman or a soldier." Having learned the craft, he suggested, he left those early feelings buried in the dark corners of the basement of his mind, where he couldn't look at them too closely.

But what had provided impetus for the work continued to goad him in life. In one of his more perceptive moments of self-analysis, Fitzgerald wrote:

When I like men I want to be like them—I want to lose the outer qualities that give me my individuality and be like them. I don't want the man, I want to absorb into myself all the qualities that make him attractive and leave him out. I cling to my own innards. When I like women I want to own them, to dominate them, to have them admire me.

It is significant that he mistakenly regarded women as the less complicated, more easily solved, problem of the two.

III

In the fall of 1911, Fitzgerald, just turning fifteen, went to Newman, a Catholic prep school situated on a fourteen-acre estate in Hackensack, New Jersey. The school's emphasis on athletics, in addition to its classical studies program, was more to Fitzgerald's liking. He tried out for the football team and was accepted. But during his two years at Newman, Fitzgerald excelled at neither studies nor athletics. He did achieve some fame, at first, for successfully running the ball and setting up a winning touchdown play for quarterback Charles (Sap) Donahoe in one of the early games. Donahoe, Irish and from Montana, had the dark good looks and literary inclinations (he was editor of the school paper) that suited Fitzgerald's need for a hero to worship. The two became good friends during their Newman and Princeton years. In a later Newman game, however, Fitzgerald flubbed a tackle and earned a reputation for being "yellow" on the field. He compensated by writing a poem, "Football," which, published in the *Newman News,* temporarily restored him to favor and brought him some welcome renown. Edward Fitzgerald was especially proud of his son's ringing and descriptive quatrains:

> Good, he's free; no, see that halfback
> Gaining up behind him slow.
> Crash! they're down; he threw him nicely, —
> Classy tackle, hard and low. . . .

As a result, Fitzgerald developed the idea that writing was a substitution for the real action on the playing fields, a way of experiencing it with the "same intensity." With a strange metaphor, he characterized writing as "a back door way out of facing reality."

In an early attempt at a novel, Fitzgerald made a striking catalogue of what he considered his own assets and liabilities on the verge of adolescence: "I marked myself handsome; of great athletic *possibilities,* and an extremely good dancer." Socially: "I was convinced that I had personality, charm, magnetism, poise, and the ability to dominate others. Also I was sure that I exercised a subtle fascination over women." On the debit side were his freshness and unpopularity, his "surly sensitiveness." But most damaging of all was this stunning admission: "At bottom, I lacked the essentials. At the last crisis, I knew I had no real courage, perseverance or self-respect." His self-esteem was so fragile, he realized, that it could be toppled "by an unpleasant remark or a missed tackle."

At Newman, he continued writing stories and poems for the school paper. When he was home on vacation, he busied himself with the affairs of the Elizabethan Drama Club. His ledger entries note his frequent trips to New York, where he usually haunted Broadway, sometimes with Newman chums like Martin Amorous. It is little wonder that his scholastic record was poor and that he was often kept "on bounds." Away from home, he worried that he had consumption. He had begun to drink and had his first taste of whiskey. There were assorted quarrels with other boys, including a spate of bickering with Sap Donohoe, and an admission that he was becoming unpopular.

As with most of Fitzgerald's education, lower and higher, the important influences were never scholastic, but personal. In this case, it was his meeting, in his second year at Newman, Father Cyril Sigourney Webster Fay, a thirty-seven-year-old convert from the Episcopalian faith, an accredited Easterner, descendant of old-line Boston and Philadelphia families. Father Fay, a trustee of Newman (he later became its headmaster), was a pudgy, tow-headed, bespectacled old aunty of a man with several chins to his credit and a beaming smile. He lived with his mother in Washington, but frequently visited Newman; he was addicted to good food, good wine, and good company. He recognized that asceticism was "a special call," one that he had not personally heard. "It seems to me," he would say, "that we praise God better by enjoying and thanking Him for the good things He sends our way."

Fay numbered among his friends the Anglo-Irish novelist Shane Leslie, a Catholic convert and first cousin to Winston Churchill, a gossipy and acerbic man, a romanticist in his views on the Irish question. Fay was also an old friend of Henry Adams, then living in Washington. Adams appreciated his wit and humor and considered the priest a "genial sinner." He was amused by Fay's efforts to proselytize him. Another of Fay's admirers was Mrs. Winthrop Chanler, a wealthy Catholic matron, an old friend of Edith Wharton, and mother of the future composer Theodore (Teddy) Chanler. Daisy Chanler was a woman of wry sentimentality, an accomplished horse-woman whose Genessee River estate was a haven for the fox-hunting and polo-playing set. At Sweet Briar Farm, near Geneseo, she had built her own chapel, where Father Fay, the childlike favorite of her own children, served mass during his usual summer visits. (With great ceremony, he also blessed the house, the stables, the horses, the gardens and flowers, and once exorcised a plague of army worms that was threatening the wheatfields.)

Father Fay immediately took the blond young Fitzgerald under his wing, introduced him to his upper-class friends like Mrs. Chanler and Leslie, invited him to his home in Washington, where, as Fitz-gerald later described it, the priest ruled "rather like an exiled Stuart king, waiting to be called to the rule of his land"—thus establishing an idealized link between the priest-king and the Stuart prince he imagined himself to be. The truth is that over the next several years Fay served as a substitute mother and father to the boy, who was impressed with his style and class, with the great world of wealth and high office to which he obviously had entrée. On his Washington visits, Fitzgerald was wined and dined at the priest's table, offered cigarettes like any other man of the world, and introduced to Fay's equally worldly assistant, Father William Hemmick, a Jesuit with a taste for Parisian-tailored cassocks and smart pumps with silver buckles. It was through Fay that Fitzgerald met Henry Adams, who figures in *This Side of Paradise* as Thornton Hancock, the weary agnostic and retired diplomat who has conversed with Parnell, Glad-stone, and Bismarck and would compliment Fitzgerald's alter ego, Amory Blaine, as a "radiant boy" whose education ought not to be entrusted to school or college.

Fay had friends in high places and was a protégé of James Cardinal Gibbons of Baltimore. On a later, wartime mission to Pope Benedict XV, Fay so impressed the pontiff that he was made a monsignor. The promotion delighted the chubby man; his new robes were "too gorgeous for words," he wrote Fitzgerald. "I look like a Turner sunset when I am in full regalia." On his return from Rome, he brought a vast trunk full of ecclesiastical finery. Daisy Chanler remembered a sweltering summer afternoon at Sweet Briar, when the new monsignor put on a fashion show for her and her children, sweeping over the terrace in purple silk with carmine trimmings, looking like nothing so much as an "enormous peony floating about on the hot bricks." High spirited, gayer than the gayest child, the prelate loved to play games and charades and get up in costume for the benefit of the smaller Chanlers. He had a penchant for playing the Pope. Once he even enacted the imaginary flight of the pontiff — in advance of the invading Germans — disguised as Lady Aberdeen, wearing a silver brocade gown and a picture hat trimmed with roses and long, trailing blue ribbons. Fitzgerald, who had not witnessed the performance, was probably quite right when he said that children "adored" the priest.

It was clear that Fitzgerald was deeply moved, even thrilled by Father Fay's gift of outright friendship. His feelings for the priest were deeper than anything he felt for his parents. Everything he wrote about Fay — in his letters and in *This Side of Paradise,* where Fay appears as Monsignor Thayer Darcy — stressed the man's well-being, worldly self-assurance, harmless vanity, and boyish love of adventure and secrecy. Fitzgerald's tribute to Father Fay glows in *This Side of Paradise:* "He was intensely ritualistic, startlingly dramatic, loved the idea of God enough to be a celibate, and rather liked his neighbor." But it was a more profoundly felt emotion that Fitzgerald expressed, late in his career, when he said that, aside from his father, it was Monsignor Fay who had taught him "the few things I ever learned about life."

Both Fay and Shane Leslie, with whom Fitzgerald became friendly during these years, effected something like a religious conversion in Fitzgerald, who was weary of the glum, varnished-oak Irish Catholicism of his St. Paul childhood. They brought to him a sense of a Catholic elite, a society of money and style that moved on a more knowledgeable plane than the provincialism and piety of the Midwest. Fitzgerald would credit the two with making the Church "a dazzling, golden thing, dispelling its oppressive mugginess." Under their guidance, his religion assumed — for a time, at least — "the romantic glamour of an adolescent dream." Leslie had been educated at Eton and Cambridge and knew the young poet Rupert Brooke. He was steeped in Celtic mysticism and the scholastic philosophies of Abelard and Duns Scotus. He knew the latest plays of Synge and Yeats and Lady Gregory. His romantic faith in the cause of Irish nationalism stirred Fitzgerald's interest in his own ancestry. Father

Fay, on the other hand, had a penchant for the novelists and poets of the Decadence — Swinburne, Huysmans, and Oscar Wilde. He particularly admired the French philosopher Henri Bergson, whom he had met in Paris and befriended in America when Bergson lectured at Columbia University. Both Fay and Leslie prodded Fitzgerald to read the novels of Robert Hugh Benson, a popular English writer, a priest, and a prize convert to Catholicism, the son of the archbishop of Canterbury.

It may have been in his final year at Newman that Fitzgerald encountered a rival for the priest's affection in a younger boy, Stephan Vincent Parrott, nicknamed "Peevie." Parrott, slim, golden-haired, and three years younger than Fitzgerald, was the son of wealthy San Francisco parents. As a child, he had been educated abroad. Fitzgerald and young Parrott established a wary friendship under the supervision of Father Fay, who encouraged them to think of themselves as spiritual brothers and as his offspring: "What a thing it is to have charming children! But how could I have anything else?" Fay's letters to Fitzgerald indicate that a healthy rivalry existed between the boys. (Fitzgerald's letters to Fay were destroyed by the cleric's mother after her son's death.) The letters from Fay are chummy and effusive, suggesting that there may have been a homosexual cast to his feelings. "I always think it such a shame," he wrote Fitzgerald, "that your very American training makes it impossible for me to pour out my paternal affection to you like I do to Peevie, for whom I notice you have the truly elder brotherly low opinion. I assure you he is not shallow." It was not unusual for the priest to sign his letters Stephan Fitz Fay, Sr. He clearly hoped that both his "boys" would become priests. But he was especially encouraging of Fitzgerald's literary ambitions, partly because he and his friend Leslie hoped to establish a respectable Catholic intellectual movement in America.

But that sense of encouragement and security which Fitzgerald gained from his friendship with Father Fay developed only gradually, over the months and years after he left prep school and entered Princeton. For the most part he remembered his Newman stay as an unhappy one. Given the simpler autobiographical bent of Fitzgerald's early writings, particularly his first novel, it is not difficult to accept the intense young egotist and snob represented by Amory Blaine as a fairly accurate snapshot of Fitzgerald himself during his two-year stay at Newman:

He was resentful against all those in authority over him, and this, combined with a lazy indifference toward his work, exasperated every master in school. He grew discouraged and imagined himself a pariah; took to sulking in corners and reading after lights. With a dread of being alone he attached a few friends, but since they were not among the elite of the school, he used them simply as mirrors of himself, audiences before which he might do that posing absolutely essential to him. He was unbearably lonely, desperately unhappy.

The emotions, perhaps, have been heightened for dramatic effect, but it is one of the remarkable assets of Fitzgerald's early fiction — and of his first novels, which critics dismiss a bit too readily — that he had achieved such candor in writing about himself. It was a quality that years later, when his work and his professionalism had been worn thin by abuse, still allowed for flashes of true insight and perception.

At Princeton, it was the romantic atmosphere, the prestige, the social life, the opportunities to be a big man on campus, that Fitzgerald remembered and celebrated. He had taken his entrance exams in the summer of 1913 — and had "cribbed" on them, according to his ledger. It was a strange admission, since, in a later testimonial essay, "Princeton," he posed as one of the staunchest upholders of the sacred tradition of the school's honor system. He claimed that he had had no moral struggles over the issue, even though there had been "a dozen times when a page of notes glanced at in a wash room would have made the difference between failure and success for me."

Fitzgerald's preliminary cribbing had done little good. His grades at Newman were poor; his performance on the entrance exams did not pass standards. He was asked to take make-up exams and go through a personal interview. Even then, he did not make the grade. It was only by talking fast to the admissions committee that he was allowed to enter the freshman class, on the condition that he would step up his grades and retake the exams in December. Fitzgerald wired home, announcing his admission and asking that his football shoes and pads be sent immediately. He tried out for the freshman squad, but lasted — so one report had it — through only one day of practice. He claimed that his height and his weight were against him.

From the moment he set foot on campus, however, he was enthralled by the place. In his fiction and in his recollections, it would always be the ultimate university, the American equivalent of Oxford and Cambridge. He could become soppy on the subject: "Only when you tried to tear part of your past out of your heart, as I once did, were you aware of its power of arousing a deep and imperishable love." Even when he criticized it, describing it as a country club in its easy ways, his criticisms were deferential. In Fitzgerald's stories and novels, one can almost determine the nature of a male character by the collegiate background Fitzgerald assigned to him. In *This Side of Paradise,* he offered some fatuous distinctions regarding the Ivy League colleges. "I don't know why," Amory tells Monsignor Darcy, "but I think of all Harvard men as sissies, like I used to be, and all Yale men as wearing big blue sweaters and smoking pipes." Princeton men, by contrast, were "lazy and good-looking and aristocratic." These were not intended to be sly examples of undergraduate attitudes; they were distinctions that Fitzgerald believed in with sophomoric zeal through much of his life. And his devotion to the Princeton football team and its annual games was total. In later years, he became the bane of the Princeton coaches, calling at any hour of the night to propose exciting new plays and offering suggestions.

But what made the strongest impression on him was the ambience of the place itself. His descriptions of the campus took on a special aura: "Suddenly all around you spreads out the loveliest riot of Gothic architecture in America, battlement linked on to battlement, hall to hall, arch-broken, vine-covered—luxuriant and lovely over two square miles of green grass. Here is no monotony, no feeling that it was all built yesterday at the whim of last week's millionaire." For Fitzgerald, Princeton was never simply an American university; it was always a place of the imagination: Camelot rising in the flat midlands of New Jersey.

Although Fitzgerald had been admitted with conditions, he seems to have largely ignored them. His scholastic career, particularly during his first two years, was a sequence of failed exams and extensive cuts in classes. He was active on the social front, vying for election to the right eating club. He made Cottage, one of the more prestigious and social of the clubs. His new acquaintances and friends, mostly the wealthy ones—Townsend Martin, Ludlow Fowler, Alexander McKaig—who were active in the Triangle Club productions or had literary ambitions and worked on the *Nassau Lit* and the *Princetonian*—settled for Quadrangle.

The two most durable and important friendships Fitzgerald made at the university were with Edmund Wilson, class of 1916, the "shy little scholar of Holder Court," as Fitzgerald described him, and the poet John Peale Bishop, a member of his own class, 1917. Wilson, even in college, was a man with extensive and demanding literary tastes. His editorship of the *Nassau Lit,* where he was responsible for publishing the first of Fitzgerald's contributions to the college literary magazine, was the beginning of his own long and distinguished literary career. Slim and amazingly agile—he would suddenly execute somersaults in a burst of good feeling—Wilson was quite different from the portly, Johnsonian figure of his later, more famous years. He became a literary mentor and "intellectual conscience" for Fitzgerald; his dedication to literature was awesome. He pored over the Greek and Latin classics, read widely in English and French literature, kept up with everything of contemporary interest from the novels of Henry James and Edith Wharton to the plays of George Bernard Shaw. Wilson had a lifelong interest in men and ideas. His hero at Princeton was Christian Gauss, then the professor of Romance languages. Wilson thought him a teacher of extraordinary flexibility and range. Gauss deplored routine; when he grew tired of teaching Alfred de Vigny, he launched into Stendhal, bringing to his lectures insights that seemed as fresh as if he were reading the novelist for the first time. Gauss was a professor who guided rather than instructed his students. Though Wilson's habits might suggest someone stiff and overly serious (he did not drink during this period and he never took up smoking), he had a keen sense of fun and a penchant for writing parodies, and produced sketches for the university musical revues. He and Fitzgerald would collaborate on *The Evil Eye,* the Triangle Club's 1915 production.

John Peale Bishop, a young poet from Charles Town, West Virginia, was four years older than Fitzgerald; the pair first met at Princeton. During his adolescence, Bishop had suffered from some form of psychosomatic illness and therefore did not enter college at the usual age. Blue-eyed, intense, stoop-shouldered, Bishop was considered a "Queer bird" and an "awful highbrow" on campus, and Fitzgerald, always concerned about the opinions of colleagues, was not too sure he should be seen too often with the poet. It was from Bishop that Fitzgerald acquired a taste for poetry that was several cuts above the doggerel and humorous verse he wrote for the *Princeton Tiger*. Bishop was fond of Shelley and Swinburne, read Mallarmé and Verlaine, favored the Symbolists, and took a lush, romantic approach in his own verse. He instilled in Fitzgerald a love for Keats's poetry that would be lifelong.

Bishop has left an engaging, mildly sardonic account of his first meeting with Fitzgerald at the Peacock Inn, soon after his arrival on the campus. What started out as a brief, get-acquainted chat lengthened into a suppertime conversation. Bishop's initial impression of Fitzgerald was a familiar one — that of a pert, blond and handsome, brash young Midwesterner who looked something "like a jonquil." The talk turned to books: "those I had read, which were not many, those Fitzgerald had read, which were even less, those he said he had read, which were many, many more." Fitzgerald, Bishop decided, was determined to be a genius at the earliest possible moment, even if it meant trimming his age in order to arrive at the necessary precocity. It was Bishop, evidently, who convinced Fitzgerald that the Princeton English professors were, by and large, inept and incapable of distinguishing between true poetry and bad verse. Fitzgerald promptly took this opinion to class and got into a "series of endless scraps" with his instructors. One of them, Frank Mac-Donald, a gossipy, low-key teacher who had a reputation for inspiring unlikely young men with a love of English poetry, particularly resented Fitzgerald's cockiness in class. When he informed Fitzgerald that he was likely to fail the course, Fitzgerald stood up and asserted, "Sir, you can't flunk me. I'm a writer."

John Peale Bishop had another quality that impressed his close friends. He was a thoroughly successful womanizer whose exploits acquired a legendary and scurrilous interest in his circle. Edmund (Bunny) Wilson, at the time, was virginal and painfully shy about sex. ("When I stayed in hotels, I would dream of amours with complaisant chambermaids," he acknowledged, "but I would not have had the least idea how to initiate one.") His sexual abstinence continued for such a lengthy period that in his final year at Princeton, while reading in his Morris chair, he had an emission and became so worried about it he consulted a doctor to see whether something was wrong with him. Fitzgerald shared Wilson's cautiousness with the opposite sex. One evening when he and Wilson, together with Bishop and Alec McKaig, were walking along Nassau Street, two girls passed them. McKaig immediately announced that they were hookers, and he and Bishop set out after them. Fitzgerald and Wilson continued on their way, down to the lake. Scott announced rather prudishly, "That's one thing that Fitzgerald's never done!"

What became Fitzgerald's principal ambition in his Princeton years was to gain the presidency of the Triangle Club, whose annual productions were written, performed, and produced by the students, and regularly toured the Eastern and Midwestern colleges during winter vacations. Early in January 1914, Fitzgerald began work on a script and libretto for the upcoming Triangle show. The choice of script was determined by the president of the club, Walker Ellis, a Southerner from New Orleans whom Bunny Wilson knew from the Hill School and whom he regarded as showy and brilliant but a bit too adroit at managing anything and everything he set his hand to. Wilson considered him rather unprincipled and not above a little plagiarism in his contributions to the prep school and collegiate literary magazines. Ellis had a knack for choosing the Triangle scripts on the basis of the more exciting female roles, in which he invariably cast himself. When he selected Fitzgerald's *Fie! Fie! Fi-Fi!* for the 1914 production, it was a coup for Fitzgerald, but Ellis proceeded to revise the book and eventually took much of the credit himself. Wilson was surprised that Fitzgerald would sit at the feet of so spurious a character as Ellis. But considering that the year in which Fitzgerald submitted *Fie! Fie! Fi-Fi!* was also the year in which he was angling for election to Cottage, Fitzgerald may have decided to play it cool. Ellis was the president of Cottage. Fitzgerald would at least get billing for his snappy lyrics, and he received favorable reviews for his efforts. One of them even claimed that he could take his place "with the brightest writers of witty lyrics in America" — no mean compliment. But the triumph was mixed with defeat. His failure to pass a make-up exam in geometry precluded his making the annual tour with the Triangle Club show.

He was to be even more disappointed in the following year with the Triangle production of *The Evil Eye,* the book for which was written by Bunny Wilson, with Fitzgerald once again supplying the lyrics. It was to be his grand push for fame at Princeton. He had selected an eye-catching part for himself as a beautiful "show-girl." More important, having already been named secretary of the Triangle Club, he was aiming for the presidency in the upcoming elections. But throughout 1915, Fitzgerald plunged into a round of extracurricular activities, writing anonymous spoofs and articles for the *Tiger,* the college humor magazine, contributing plays and stories ("Shadow Laurels," "The Ordeal") to the *Nassau Lit.* He worked hard on the Triangle show lyrics and was drinking with some regularity. ("Drunk," "Passed out at dinner," "Drunk," the ledger entries read.) He was, it appears, still struggling with his faith, and the drinking seemed to be part of the testing process. Wilson, who claimed that Fitzgerald was the first "educated Catholic" he had met, remembered Fitzgerald's boast: "Why, I can go up to New York on a terrible party and then come back and go into the church and *pray* — and mean every word of it, too!"

He had paid little attention to his courses and once more flunked his make-up exams at the start of his junior year. He was not eligible to take part in the Triangle show tour. His ledger entry reads, "Despair." But what affected him more was that he was ineligible for the Triangle Club presidency. In summing up his junior year, Fitzgerald blamed himself: "Everything bad in it was my own fault." But he held a grudge against the university and against the club membership for not coming to his defense strenuously enough. In the face of his disappointments, Fitzgerald came down sick and was sent to the infirmary. The diagnosis was malaria, but Fitzgerald preferred to think of it as a flare-up of tuberculosis. His grades were so poor that he was required to "withdraw from the University January 3, 1916, for scholastic deficiencies" — so his academic records stated. He returned home to St. Paul before the Christmas holidays to recuperate — from wounded pride as much as anything else. Making a poignant story more poignant, Fitzgerald maintained that he had left Princeton on a stretcher. He nagged the university for a letter stating that he had withdrawn voluntarily because of ill health. (But Dean Howard McClenahan, who did, in fact, send the asked-for letter, also sent a covering note that stated, "This is for your sensitive feelings. I hope you will find it soothing.")

Twenty years later, in one of his "Crack-Up" essays, Fitzgerald wrote about his suspension and the loss of honors as if they were among the crucial failures in his life. He vividly assessed the damage:

> I had lost certain offices, the chief one was the presidency of the Triangle Club, a musical comedy idea, and also I dropped back a class. To me college would never be the same. There were to be no badges of pride, no medals, after all. It seemed on one March afternoon that I had lost every single thing I wanted — and that night was the first time that I hunted down the spectre of wom-

anhood that, for a little while, makes everything else seem unimportant.

The "spectre of womanhood" was Fitzgerald's fancy phrase for a prostitute; failure, in some way, had become associated with the proof of manhood. Certainly it made for a dramatic story. But given Fitzgerald's talents for invention, the details are at least questionable. He had withdrawn from Princeton for poor grades, and he had left late in November, not in the following March during his junior year. It is possible that the episode with the prostitute occurred after February 1916, when Fitzgerald, still an exiled student, paid a disheartening visit to the Princeton campus, as recorded in his ledger account. Still, it was Edmund Wilson's distinct recollection that it was *after* graduation day in the summer of 1916 that Fitzgerald made his dramatic announcement of never having consorted with a whore. Wilson, in fact, reminded Fitzgerald about that episode in a letter written a year later, pointedly recalling how he and Fitzgerald had returned and "sat alone upon the darkened and deserted verandah of Cottage," leaving "the shabby whoring of the Princeton streets" to John Bishop. Fitzgerald's disappointment may not have been quite as traumatic as he had pictured it.

The indignity of his failure was all the greater because Fitzgerald had fallen in love with and had been desperately courting an attractive, dark-haired debutante whom he had met in St. Paul during his 1914 Christmas vacation. She was Ginevra King, of Lake Forest, Illinois, a sixteen-year-old socialite with a bevy of suitors, a schoolmate of Fitzgerald's friend Marie Hersey at Westover, the Connecticut girls' school. Fitzgerald had heard rumors of Ginevra's striking beauty and of her considerable male following, but it was at a party Marie Hersey gave in her honor that he first met her. Fitzgerald asked her for a date on the following day and immediately fell in love. Throughout 1915, he wrote her moony letters and sent her telegrams. The first, which he did not send, was written on the train trip back to Princeton, during which he and Sap Donahoe had gotten drunk on sauterne and Bronx cocktails. Throughout the two-and-a-half-year courtship of Ginevra, Fitzgerald was the ardent and imploring suitor, probably the wrong tactic with a girl who was interested but not that interested. Ginevra King traveled with a different social set, and in the company of her wealthy Lake Forest friends Fitzgerald was made aware — or sensed he was being made aware — that poor boys shouldn't think of marrying rich girls. Ginevra invited him to Westover; she visited him at Princeton. One summer night, on one of her brief transits through New York, Fitzgerald recalled, his dark-haired dream girl "made luminous the Ritz Roof." They attended the theater and went dancing at the Midnight Frolic. It was one of those epiphanies which Fitzgerald would enshrine in his imagination and in his prose. The brief glamour of the occasion was to remain with him for a lifetime.

Fitzgerald had been planning to impress Ginevra with his own success when *The Evil Eye,* on tour, opened in Chicago. It was an odd ambition, since he would be performing in drag. He had already posed for publicity stills for the show in glamorous feminine attire, wearing a lacy picture hat, an off-the-shoulder gown, and a gauzy chiffon scarf, and carrying posies. Even though Fitzgerald was no longer eligible for the tour, his portrait as the entrancing showgirl appeared in newspapers around the country. The look was wistful, the smile was diverting, the pose was modesty itself, despite the bared shoulder. It was too serious to be outrageous or camp; it was Fitzgerald's idea of a beautiful chorine posing for the Sunday supplements.

But Ginevra King, at the time, was more interested in the quantity of her beaux rather than the quality. In her letters, she reported on her gay social life. Fitzgerald gave vent to his suspicions. "Even now," he wrote her, "you may be having a tête à tête with some 'unknown Chicagoan' with crisp dark hair and glittering smile." It is significant that during this period, when his romance with Ginevra was going poorly, Fitzgerald became dissatisfied with his own looks, wishing that he had dark hair and dusky skin, disliking his "fake tenor" voice.

Equally significant was the fact that about the same time, Fitzgerald sent his thirteen-year-old sister, Annabel, an interminable letter that was virtually a charm course on the ways and means of beguiling young men. With total unselfconsciousness, Fitzgerald advised her on such matters as cosmetics and conversation, dress and deportment. "Boys like to talk about themselves — much more than girls. . . ." he informed Annabel. "Here are some leading questions for a girl to use. . . . You've got the longest eyelashes! (This will embarrass him, but he likes it.) . . . I hear you've got a 'line'! . . .

Well, who's your latest crush?" Analyzing the flaws of character and style among the girls he and Annabel knew in St. Paul, he went on, "Margaret Armstrongs slouch has lost her more attention than her lack of beauty. . . . Katherine Tighe is dowdy about her hair lately. Don't I notice it? When Grace's hair looks well—she looks well." He even instructed her on the most effective way of looking at a man: "A pathetic, appealing look is one every girl ought to have. Sandra and Ginevra are specialists at this. . . . It's best done by opening the eyes wide and drooping the mouth a little, looking upward (hanging the head a little) directly into the eyes of the man you're talking to." The advice is startling when one realizes that the prescribed look is eerily similar to the look Fitzgerald bestowed on the photographer taking his publicity stills. His disappointment at the loss of his role as the seductive showgirl must have been quite real. During his winter of exile in St. Paul, Fitzgerald, dolled up in woman's clothes and accompanied by a male friend, attended a fraternity dance at the University of Minnesota. He spent a good part of the evening whirling around the dance floor, presumably giving his partners some of the snappy lines he had suggested to Annabel. The entire incident created a stir.

But there is something more important and revealing about the comic episode than Fitzgerald's urge to play a feminine role or his writing a treatise on etiquette for his sister. The world of fiction is a realm of intriguing possibilities, of amazing transformations. The writer can play and replay a scene from life and make it come out differently, come out "right." He can add and subtract qualities from the characters he has drawn from life. The world of Fitzgerald's fiction is extremely volatile in this respect. It was one of the serious criticisms of his later, major, novel *Tender Is the Night* that his protagonists, Dick and Nicole Diver, begin their fictional lives modeled after Fitzgerald's friends Gerald and Sara Murphy, but end them as substitutions for himself and Zelda. It almost seems that Fitzgerald, in his perpetual quest for a satisfactory identity, was compelled to insinuate himself into each of his major characters.

But there are other, more startling changes in his fictional world, some that seem almost transsexual in nature. Fitzgerald once boasted: "I am half feminine—that is, my mind is. . . . My characters are all Scott Fitzgerald. Even the feminine characters are feminine Scott Fitzgeralds." That insight is borne out by some of the odder events in the tangled history of his fiction. The protagonist in the first versions of *Tender Is the Night,* for instance, was a young film technician, Francis Melarky, who was traveling abroad with a neurotic mother and whose experiences and personality were derived from Fitzgerald's character and career. (Melarky, for example, had been dismissed from West Point for insubordination, a wonderfully economic merger of Fitzgerald's disappointing collegiate and equally disappointing military careers.) But during the lengthy revisions of the novel, Melarky was transformed into a pert young actress, Rosemary Hoyt, modeled after a real ingénue with whom Fitzgerald had had a brief, avuncular affair.

A much earlier instance of such sexual transference occurs in the story "The Ordeal," which Fitzgerald wrote in 1915 at Princeton. The story underscored the growing erosion of Fitzgerald's religious beliefs. In it, a young dark-haired novice, about to be ordained, has a temporary loss of faith. It is accompanied by a sudden, chilling sense of the presence of evil, personified by another novice, who has "fair hair and green-gray eyes that darted nervously around the chapel." Consciously, perhaps—and perhaps sardonically—Fitzgerald may have used the device of bilocation to symbolize the two sides of his ambiguous relationship with the Church: the idealized dark-haired self, still clinging to his faith, and the blond, green-eyed persona who represented a tendency to evil and may even have symbolized the devil.

Five years later, Fitzgerald rewrote this story of the test of faith, calling it "Benediction." In the later version, the blond-haired personification of evil is transformed into the much less malevolent, blond-haired sister of the priest-protagonist. Lois, who has been convent-educated and has not seen her brother for several years (like Annabel), is paying a visit to him in a Maryland seminary. She has begun to have grave doubts about her faith and, moreover, is involved in a love affair with a man who is a determined skeptic. In this version, it is the sister who experiences panic during that chilling moment in the chapel service. She, too, is overwhelmed by a sense of evil. But after struggling with her conscience, she musters up the courage to resume her affair with a man who cannot marry her. It is worth noting that in both versions of the story the male protagonist clings to his faith and adopts a life of celibacy; in the second, the more venturesome woman opts for life and the uncertainties of the future.

IV

It was not until September 1916 that Fitzgerald resumed his college career, though, as he rightly suspected, it was over for him. He did not graduate from Princeton. The principal benefit of his return was that he plunged into writing, producing a spate of unsigned sketches and humorous verses for the *Tiger*. His Keatsian lyrics and a number of short stories that Fitzgerald regarded as the beginnings of his mature work appeared in the *Nassau Lit*. Several of these were revised for commercial publication later or were incorporated into his first novel. Others remained buried in the back numbers of the collegiate magazine, never to be resurrected in his collections. Nevertheless, they sounded themes that occupied him for a lifetime: changing morals, the claims of honor, the challenge of love, the poetry of loss. Fitzgerald made a determined effort to create a literary reputation for himself as a man of letters, writing reviews of current books by E. F. Benson, H. G. Wells, and his friend Shane Leslie. He was especially moved by Leslie's *Verses in Peace and War,* with its themes of English athletes killed in Flanders and its sequence "Epitaphs," written for dead aviators. He noted the "undercurrent of sadness" that gave the poems "a rare and haunting depth."

Fitzgerald's academic standing was no better than it had been before his exile. It was the old story: he was caught up in a whirl of extracurricular activities and paid little attention to his academic studies. Although he could not take part in the Triangle production, he nevertheless wrote lyrics for the upcoming show, *Safety First*. He was still disgruntled with his English professors. Even though he repeated courses he had taken the previous year, he failed half of them and barely escaped flunking out again. His dissatisfaction with the university regulations may have been a factor in his friendship with Henry (Mike) Strater, one of the sophomore ringleaders whose efforts, in the spring of 1917, to boycott the exclusive eating clubs was an embarrassment to the Princeton administration. Strater, tall, hulking, good-humored, but intensely serious, was a reader of Tolstoy, Whitman, and Thoreau, and a dedicated pacifist. He became another of Fitzgerald's heroes, figuring as the campus radical Burne Holiday in *This Side of Paradise*. Fitzgerald gave tacit approval to Strater's rebellion—but calmly and from the sidelines. He tried to be both the snob and the democrat, parodying the rival clubmen and anticlub factions in his contributions to the *Tiger*. But he was always capable of overdramatizing his involvements. After Strater's revolt was quietly suppressed, Fitzgerald said that he had lost his "idealism." It had "flickered out with Henry Stater's anti-club movement at Princeton." But he never, of course, gave up his attachment to his own club, Cottage.

During his Princeton years, Fitzgerald kept up his friendship and correspondence with Father Fay, visiting the priest at his mother's summer house at Deal, on the New Jersey shore, or at Newman, where Father Hemmick was in attendance. One of Fitzgerald's visits occasioned a ledger entry about the priest's "silk pajamas," the emblem of luxury, perhaps. But the adjective coupled with Father Hemmick's name was "unpleasant." Father Fay visited Fitzgerald at Princeton, and the pair made happy excursions to New York, where the priest took him to the Hotel Lafayette, then a haven of wealthy bohemians. They drank claret and sampled the hors d'oeuvres under the eyes of the surly waiters. Afterward, they rode back in style to the hinterlands of New Jersey. There were other, not so sober evenings when Fitzgerald went to New York alone or with college friends, venturing into the popular undergraduate hangouts — Bustanoby's and Shanley's and Jack's — for celebrations that ended with the 5:00 A.M. penance of an uncomfortable train ride back to Princeton.

The binges may have been the result of his rapidly waning romance with Ginevra King. She visited him at Princeton in November 1916 as his guest for the Yale game, but their meetings now were more and more unsatisfactory and frequently ended in bickering. The final break, so Fitzgerald recorded in his ledger book, came in January. But Ginevra lingered on in his imagination for years, undergoing fictional changes, merging with other women, yet remaining the unobtainable "nice" but independent girl. With startling promptness, in fact, she contributed to the character of the selfish, callous heroine of Fitzgerald's play *The Debutante* who outlines her strategies with men for the benefit of a jilted suitor: "Oh, I'll be frank for once. I like the feeling of going after them. . . . Then I begin to place him. Try to get his type, find what he likes; right then the romance begins to lessen for me and increase for him." Since *The Debutante* appeared in the January issue of the *Nassau Lit*, it presumably registered not the actual breakup with Ginevra, but only Fitzgerald's realization that there was not much hope. The bitter recognition that Ginevra had not taken him seriously at all came later, when he asked her to burn his letters and she answered, rather discouragingly, "I'm sorry you think that I would hold them up to you as I never did think they meant anything."

Little wonder that Fitzgerald appreciated the brief glimpse of "a man's world" that he caught one gray late winter or early spring day when he paid a visit to Bunny Wilson, recently graduated and living the life of a man of letters in New York. Fitzgerald was early; quite by chance, from his taxi, he saw his friend striding along a Greenwich Village street into a gathering rain. Not wanting to intrude on Wilson's privacy, he followed along in the cab, observing Wilson swinging his walking stick and forging ahead past the traffic lights. Fitzgerald envied him his new freedom, his New York life.

Wilson, who was working for the *New York Evening Sun*, shared an apartment on West Eighth Street with friends. Fitzgerald recalled the cramped quarers as barricaded with books that helped muffle the nearly perpetual oboe-playing of one of the roommates, Morris Belknap. Another, Larry Noyes, a Yale graduate — certainly a mark against him — had been Wilson's roommate at the Hill School and a traveling companion in Europe. Noyes was from St. Paul, but from a higher social stratum than the McQuillan and Fitzgerald families. Wilson later described Noyes as "the most complete case I have ever known of Eastern-oriented Western snobbery." Nevertheless, he liked Noyes, enjoyed his company, and was unaware at the time that Noyes was homosexual. Fitzgerald, who would always be edgy and often boorish in the company of homosexual men, may not have been aware of Noyes's tendencies, either. He disliked him intensely all the same — but for his social pretensions. The only discordant note of the visit, Fitzgerald claimed, had been "the crisp tearing open of invitations by one man" — Noyes — which he regarded as a show of snobbishness. During vacations at home, Fitzgerald would occasionally socialize with Noyes, but then send caustic reports to Wilson: "Saw your friend Larry Noyes in St. Paul and got beautifully stewed after a party he gave — He got beautifully full of canned wrath — I don't imagine we'd agree on much."

America's entry into World War I, in April 1917, provided a focus for Fitzgerald's growing sense of dissatisfaction. He entertained some thoughts of enlistment and late in the spring signed up for three weeks of military training on the Princeton campus. As a writer, Fitzgerald was extraordinarily sensitive to ambience, to changes in mood and atmosphere, and, at his best, had a knack of finding the right symbol for it in the most trivial detail. In *This Side of Paradise,* Fitzgerald found the perfect symbol for the awakening sense of conflict in the practice drills in the school gym: "Slowly and inevitably, yet with a sudden surge at the last . . . war rolled swiftly up the beach and washed the sands where Princeton played. Every night the gymnasium echoed as platoon after platoon swept over the floor and shuffled out the basket-ball markings." That the image merged the military with the athletic must have added to its potency in his mind.

His friends were joining up. Bunny Wilson, who had been to a military training camp in Plattsburgh, New York, joined a hospital unit and was shipped to France later in the year. Alec McKaig was an ensign in the navy. John Peale Bishop, despite his chancy physical condition, had enlisted in the infantry and was waiting for a commission as a first lieutenant. In July, Fitzgerald spent a "literary month" with Bishop at his home in Charles Town. Bishop was putting together a collection of his poems, to be published under the title *Green Fruit.* His example seems to have spurred Fitzgerald's literary ambitions; he began writing poems at a great rate and was contemplating either a book of verse or a novel in verse form. But life was not all literary; Fitzgerald decidedly romanced one of Bishop's local friends, Elizabeth (Fluff) Beckwith. He invited her to picnics, took her to dances, went horseback riding with her — at some peril to himself, since he was a poor horseman. He teased her with leading questions: "Fluff, have you ever had any 'purple passages' in your life?" She was impressed by the attention but decided that Fitzgerald was more talk than action on a date, and very unlike the aggressive Southern boys she knew. "I'm afraid Scott just wasn't a very lively male animal," she declared. Seemingly inspired, he gave her a copy of a love poem he had written, "When Vanity Kissed Vanity," with the personal dedication "For Fluff Beckwith, the only begetter of this sonnet." It was a pretty gesture. But only a month later, Fitzgerald sent a copy of the poem to Edmund Wilson as a sample of his poetic handiwork. In this case, it was dedicated "To Cecilia," presumably Fitzgerald's favorite cousin, Cecilia Taylor — older than he, and widowed — to whom he was in the habit of regularly sending copies of his poems. Fitzgerald, it seems, was never one to waste a poetic emotion.

From West Virginia, Fitzgerald moved home to St. Paul. There, he drank gin and read philosophy, chiefly Bergson, William James, and the appropriately pessimistic Schopenhauer. He had received word of Ginevra King's engagement to one of the wealthy young men in her social circle. While in St. Paul, he enlisted in the infantry, taking his exams at nearby Fort Snelling, in hopes of a commission. His plans, however, were further complicated by a conspiratorial letter from Father Fay, who had been given a secret diplomatic mission that was nothing less than the "conversion of Russia" to the Church of Rome. The conversion had already begun, according to Father Fay; several millions of the Russian Orthodox had come over to Rome. Fay wanted Fitzgerald to join him in the mission, contending that no matter how Fitzgerald looked at it, whether from the spiritual or temporal point of view, it would be an "immense opportunity" for the young man.

The plan was that Fitzgerald officially would serve as his secretary. (Father Fay had hoped to enlist Peevie Parrott so that all three might be joined in the great cause, but that proved impossible.) The cleric was full of heady plans; he would bring along his Corona typewriter, and he and Fitzgerald would write a book about their experiences. They would also write articles for the *Dublin Review*, which, Father Fay was sure, would be "jolly glad to get anything we send them." He suggested that Fitzgerald brush up on his French. The mission would have to be privately financed, so Fitzgerald should plan on at least $3600 for travel expenses, "as we shall have to keep at least some state."

The secrecy of the mission was obviously enthralling. "Now, in the eyes of the world," the priest wrote, "we are a Red Cross Commission sent out to report on the work of the Red Cross . . . and that is all I can say. But I will tell you this, the State Department is writing to our Ambassador in Russia and Japan, the British Foreign Office is writing to their ambassador in Japan and Russia . . ." No one but Fitzgerald's family should be told of their plans: "As soon as you have read this letter and shown it at home, burn it." For the rest of August, there were plans afoot. There was the matter of Fitzgerald's uniform for the mission. Fay advised that they meet in New York: "Wetzel, military tailor, 2 East 44th Street. . . . He

can measure for the uniform in the morning, try it on in the afternoon and turn it out in three of four days." He advised Fitzgerald
to avoid getting his infantry commission or signing up for the air
force until their secret mission was authorized. For Fitzgerald's benefit he added, "If your summer has had a feminine tinge your winter
is apt to have a distinctly masculine one. Frankly I shall be very
glad when you get back." Apparently Fitzgerald was prey to some
gloomy thoughts, and Fay advised him that he ought to learn how
to spell *death*. "Like all prejudices, of course, it is absurd. I only
mention it in passing since you spelled it 'deth.' "

The Russian Revolution, however, put an end to the great
adventure of the middle-aged priest and the aspiring young writer.
Later in the year, the priest informed Fitzgerald, "We can not go
to Russia because of the new Revolution. Russia has gone to pieces
and we should have spent our winter probably in a German prison."

Fitzgerald returned to Princeton in September, a member of
the class of 1918, waiting for his commission. This time he roomed
with John Biggs, an aspiring writer and an editor of the *Tiger*. In a
frenzy of activity, they often spent nights putting out whole issues
of the humor magazine when it was late for press. Fitzgerald was
also writing regularly for the *Lit*. "Everything around us seemed to
be breaking up," Fitzgerald remembered. But somehow "these were
great days; battle was on the horizon; nothing was ever going to be
the same again and nothing mattered." He sent Wilson reports on
the early casualties in their classes: "Yes — Jack Newlin is dead —
killed in ambulance service. He was, potentially, a great artist."
Newlin had done the Beardsley-style drawings and illustrations for
the *Lit*.

Fitzgerald and Father Fay met with some regularity during
these months. Their initial mission had been replaced by another.
Fay was being sent as a representative of the Church in America to
acquaint the Pope with the views of American Catholics and to report
on a private conversation with President Wilson. But Fay's plan to
take Fitzgerald as his private secretary once more failed. Fitzgerald's
infantry commission as a second lieutenant came through at the end
of October, and within the month he was ordered to report to Fort
Leavenworth, in Kansas.

During one of his fall meetings with Fay, Fitzgerald brought
along Henry Strater, who was impressed by the bouncing and enthusiastic cleric. Fay, it appears, was no less interested in the impres-

sions he created on others than was his protégé, Fitzgerald. "How magnificent Strater is," the priest wrote Fitzgerald. "It gave me a frightful shock when you wrote me he thought me splendid. How can he be so deceived?" Fay went on to assess the qualities that he considered he, Fitzgerald, and Peevie all shared, as in some mystical communion: "We're extraordinary, we're clever, we could be said, I suppose, to be brilliant. We can attract people, we can make atmosphere, we can almost always have our own way, but splendid —rather not." He reported that Shane Leslie considered Fitzgerald the Rupert Brooke of America—not a promising parallel, since Brooke had died two years earlier. The priest did not put much stock in Fitzgerald's gloomy claim that there was no "sentiment" involved in his expecting to die in the trenches. Fay responded, "What is the use of telling me that, when I know well enough what it isn't and what it is, too. It is Romance, spelled with a large R."

Cold thoughts of death in battle also colored Fitzgerald's callous letter to his mother, written just after he had received his commission. But despite his gloomy presentiments about dying on the battlefield, he attended to very practical matters first. The initial order of business was to sign the Oath of Allegiance so that he would be placed on the payroll; the second was a trip to Brooks Brothers in New York to order his specially tailored uniforms. Following these, he wrote to his mother, instructing her on certain questions of rank about which she was obviously ignorant: "I am Second Lieutenant in the *regular* infantry and *not* a reserve officer—I rank with a West Point graduate." Then, in sensible terms, he cautioned her: "Please, let's not have either tragedy or Heroics because they are equally distasteful to me. . . . If you want to pray, pray for my soul and not that I won't get killed—the last doesn't seem to matter particularly and if you are a good Catholic, the first ought to." Being a profound pessimist, he said, he was not depressed about the possibility of danger: "I have never been more cheerful." Just the words his mother must have longed to hear.

With that erratic candor which was one of his better traits, Fitzgerald admitted to being "the worst lieutenant in the whole American army." But during his stint at Officers' Training School at Leavenworth, he at least had the presence of mind to begin writing a novel. At first, he scribbled behind his infantry manuals during study periods—until detected. Then, on weekends, he worked at the officers' club. There, in a corner of the room, in an atmosphere of cigarette smoke, olive-drab conversations, and the rattling of newspapers, he turned out chapter after chapter of a loosely autobiographical chronicle, living, as he said, in the "smeary pencil pages" of his manuscript. He had a title, *The Romantic Egotist,* borrowed, it appears, from Father Fay, who had suggested either "The Romance of an Egoist" or "A Child of the Last Days." (Writing was epidemic in the Stephan Fitz Fay circle; Peevie Parrott had begun a novel but abandoned it, deciding he was too young. Father Fay, too, planned a novel, set in Rome, which would borrow Compton Mackenzie's young hero, Michael Fane.)

In a letter to Edmund Wilson, Fitzgerald announced that the subject of his book would be "the picaresque ramble of one Stephen Palms (Dalius?) from the San Francisco fire thru school, Princeton, to the end where at twenty-one he writes his autobiography at the Princeton aviation school." The book would be a grand farrago of "poetry, prose, vers libres, and every mood of a temperamental temperature"—that is, up-to-date and modern. It would show traces of Tarkington, Wells, Chesterton, and Robert Hugh Benson—authors who were riding high in popularity. Eager for encouragement and approval, Fitzgerald sent progress reports and chapters to his friends. He wrote Leslie that his novel was " a tremendously conceited affair," and the writer answered in encouraging fashion: "Conceit is the soul or germ of modern literature and, of course, 'egotism' is the long-sought synonym for 'style'. . . . Put your utmost into your writing while the furor of youth, its cynicism and indignation, is upon you." Leslie planned to recommend the book to Scribner's, his American publisher.

In his January 1918 letter to Wilson, Fitzgerald boasted that all but five of the twenty-two chapters had been completed. He predicted, "If Scribners takes it I know I'll wake some morning and find that the debutantes have made me famous overnight"—which was exactly on the mark. Aside from the bravado, Fitzgerald also indulged in a little personal confession: "I don't think you ever realized at Princeton the child-like simplicity that lay behind all my petty sophistication and my lack of a real sense of honor. I'd be a wicked man if it wasn't for that."

It was a remarkably frank self-appraisal, and Fitzgerald could, indeed, open up with friends whom he trusted. But he also had a tendency to try on ideas for size, and project images of himself to see how they would be received. In this case, his self-analysis echoed exactly something that Father Fay had written him only a few weeks before. "We have a terrible honesty at the bottom of us that all our sophistry cannot destroy," the priest wrote Fitzgerald, "and a kind of child-like simplicity that is the only thing that saves us from being downright wicked." It is difficult to know, therefore, how much of that confession Fitzgerald actually believed and how much he was simply passing on for effect.

Fitzgerald, especially in his letters, used the truth as a commodity that could be cut and tailored to impress the recipient, to heighten a literary effect, or to dress himself up for a role he wanted to play. Writing to Wilson, for instance, he announced, "Do you realize that Shaw is 61, Wells 51, Chesterton 41, Leslie 31 and I 21? (Too bad I haven't a better man for 31.)" But writing to Leslie, who might do him good at Scribner's, Fitzgerald announced with considerable élan, "Did you ever notice that remarkable coincidence? Bernard Shaw is 61 years old, H. G. Wells is 51, G. K. Chesterton is 41, you're 31, and I'm 21 — all the great authors of the world in arithmetical progression."

Fitzgerald did not complete his novel until February, when he was on leave and staying at Cottage at Princeton. It was, as he had characterized it, a picaresque ramble. His hero, Stephen Palms, did bear some relationship to Stephen Dedalus, the youthful hero of James Joyce's *A Portrait of the Artist as a Young Man,* the book Wilson had urged him to read, claiming it was "another of the best novels of the century." But Fitzgerald had also borrowed from the life of his "spiritual brother," Stephan Parrott, who was born in San Francisco and was a member of a wealthy family. In the early versions of the novel, the connection was even more tangled, because Stephen Palms had a younger brother, Floyd, who may also have been patterned on Peevie Parrott.

Stephen Palms admits to feelings of rivalry that complicate the relationship between the brothers: "I was intensely critical about him and tried desperately to keep him from falling into a severe self-complacency. I succeeded only too well and finally forced him into a state of self-defence where he leaned almost wholly on mother." That might easily have been an accurate account of Fitzgerald and Parrott's relationship with Father Fay, given one of Fitzgerald's transfers of gender. After the publication of the novel, in fact, Parrott stated that he had been the "original" for Amory Blaine. Ted Paramore, a Yale friend of Wilson's, who met Parrott in San Francisco, concurred, saying that Parrott was very much "in character" for the role and acted the part "much better than I should imagine Fitzgerald could."

But the hero is, of course, also a young and ambitious Scott Fitzgerald, who, in the early version, confessed his difficulties with style and structure: "I can't rewrite and all I do is from the vague notes for chapters that I have here beside me, and the uncertain channels of an uneven memory. . . . I'm trying to set down the story part of my generation in America and put myself in the middle as a sort of observer and conscious factor." Fitzgerald's method did not appeal to John Peale Bishop, to whom he sent chapters as they were completed. Bishop would never be an easy critic, even of his friend's efforts, and he clearly decided that Fitzgerald's novel lacked structure, that it failed to trace some crucial development in either the plot or the hero's character. "Don't put in everything you remember," Bishop advised. "Retain only significant events and ride them hard."

Shane Leslie, however, was impressed. Sending the manuscript to Scribner's, he praised it as a vivid portrait of American youth. He noted that it was naïve in places and shocking in others, but suggested that it could be safely pruned without losing the essential sense that Fitzgerald was a prose version of Rupert Brooke. "Though Scott Fitzgerald is still alive, it has a literary value," Leslie informed the publisher, in one of the more unusual recommendations of a book. "Of course, when he is killed it will also have a commercial value." Writing to Fitzgerald, Leslie even offered to make the necessary editorial changes if Scribner's accepted the novel and Fitzgerald was shipped overseas. But Fitzgerald had a long wait before Scribner's made up its mind, and his military career did not end in glory in the muddy ditches of the Argonne Forest.

After his leave, Fitzgerald was sent to Camp Zachary Taylor, outside Louisville, Kentucky. Within a short time, he was transferred twice more, first to Camp Gordon, in Georgia, then to another infantry unit, the 67th, stationed at Camp Sheridan, outside Montgomery, Alabama. It was there that Fitzgerald was made a first lieutenant. Undoubtedly the nattiest officer on the field, in his smartly tailored tunic and highly polished boots, he was a man out of his depth as a "leader of men." The stories of his boondoggled military career are as legendary as the legend. It was said that at Camp Zachary Taylor, while marching his company back from town in a blizzard, he shielded himself from the snow but forgot to take his arm down or to give a snappy salute when the passing general asked for his name. The legend had it that the general ordered the troops to march back to town through the storm. At Camp Sheridan, where he had a conscientious objector in his platoon, his fellow officers gulled him into making "that S.O.B." drill at the point of his .45 — an offense for which Fitzgerald could have been court-martialed. On another occasion, feeling the need to play the strict disciplinarian, Fitzgerald force-marched his platoon in the sweltering heat because some of the men had complained about army food.

There were two versions of a more serious episode regarding a Stokes mortar. One account was that on the practice range, Fitzgerald had lobbed shells, fortunately duds, into a group of soldiers on the other side of a hill. The other version was that a shell became stuck in the mortar that was under Fitzgerald's command and that only the presence of mind of a fellow officer, who tilted the mortar forward and released the shell, averted a damaging explosion. The one valorous act credited to Fitzgerald is the rescue of some men who couldn't swim when an overloaded barge sank in the Tallapoosa River during military exercises.

Fitzgerald, eager to use even the most lusterless of his military exploits, put both incidents into one of his stories, "I Didn't Get Over." Quixotically, he parceled out the episodes between a scapegrace hero, Abe Danzer, who rescues the men from the mortar explosion but is shot while trying to escape from the Leavenworth stockade, and a vindictive officer, Captain Hibbing, who overloaded the barge that sank. Like Fitzgerald, Captain Hibbing is a man who never got overseas. It is impossible to determine, in Fitzgerald's highly ambiguous story, which of these two men Fitzgerald meant to shame or praise. Nor is it possible to determine just what part he played in the actual events on which his story is based.

But after "I Didn't Get Over" appeared in the October 1936 issue of *Esquire,* Fitzgerald received a letter, from a sergeant who had served under him in headquarters company at Sheridan, that casts a harsh light on Fitzgerald's military career. The sergeant had been in the barge just ahead of the one that was swamped, and he wanted to know just how much of Fitzgerald's story was fact and how much fiction. In Fitzgerald's story version of the episode, twenty-two men were drowned; the sergeant had not heard of any deaths resulting from the accident. His recollections of his lieutenant were not what could be called fond. He doubted that Fitzgerald had ever seen the inside of the Leavenworth stockade, but he admitted there were many times "when I consigned you there and beyond—under my breath." The sergeant had a vivid recollection of Fitzgerald "strutting around the camp proud in your new importance as an advance man" before the division was shipped north. "You might even remember me," he suggested; "we seemed to dislike each other. I had heard that you were from Princeton."

A fellow officer of Fitzgerald's recalled that the prevailing attitude toward him was that "if we were given an important task and told he would be assigned to help us, we would prefer to do it alone. This attitude implied no hostility toward Fitzgerald. Indeed most of us liked him." The view of an enlisted man could be quite different.

2

Never the Same Love Twice

IT WAS during the summer of 1918, while he was stationed at Camp Sheridan in Alabama, that Fitzgerald met Zelda Sayre at the country club dance and, as their story has it, relentlessly pursued her. Fitzgerald is said to have rushed her, dating her steadily and calling her almost daily — all of which certainly conformed to his usual technique. Presumably, on hot summer afternoons the pair would sit out on the wide porch of the Sayres' Pleasant Street house, screened from the sun by the thick cover of clematis vines and Virginia creepers that Zelda's mother had trained up on wires. In the cooler Montgomery nights, while the judge read his paper by the light from the window and her mother, "Miss Minnie," sat in her peeling rocker, chatting with callers, Zelda and her Northern suitor sat at the far end of the "gallery," as Miss Minnie called it, swaying together on the creaking swing. In the literature about the Fitzgeralds — and in the literature they created about themselves — there is much about Southern nights and the scent of honeysuckle and the crunch of the gravel underfoot on country club pathways, and there is a heedless girl and a romantic boy and a good deal of heavy drinking. All of it is plausible and appropriate to the setting. And much of it seems to be by way of the truth — if not necessarily true.

But at the time Fitzgerald met Zelda, he was involved with another Montgomery girl, May Steiner. That affair may — or may not — have provided the model for one of the more poignant love relationships in Fitzgerald's fiction, the tawdry little affair between Dorothy Raycroft and the soldier Anthony Patch in *The Beautiful and Damned,* a piece of writing that verifies that when Fitzgerald was not caught up in an atmosphere of spurious glamour, he could be a first-rate realist. During June, while he was courting May Steiner and perhaps dating one or two other Montgomery belles, Fitzgerald was depressed, but, oddly, contemplating marriage at the same time. Monsignor Fay, back from Rome and in full regalia, was plainly concerned about his mood. "You know your letters worry me; you seem so awfully down," he wrote Fitzgerald on June 30. He definitely advised against marriage: "You are now at the most dangerous part of your life with regard to marriage. You might marry in haste and repent at leisure; but I think you won't." He suspected Fitzgerald might suffer "some kind of emotional crisis within the next two years." And he suggested that if Fitzgerald did get leave in August, he should "fly to my paternal arms" at Deal.

Whether May Steiner, slender and curly-haired, was the object of Fitzgerald's marital intentions is not clear. He continued to date her for several months after he met Zelda, and apparently enjoyed sitting on the porch with her, as his ledger book indicates. She fitted the pattern of Fitzgerald's girls; she was popular with the officers and soldiers at Camp Sheridan and Fitzgerald was conscious of her many "visiting bows [beaux]." It appears to have been more than a casual flirtation. When Fitzgerald was discharged from Sheridan, May Steiner fell ill during the Spanish flu epidemic and lost much of her beautiful hair. She expressly planned to visit Fitzgerald in New York when she went north for treatments. Fitzgerald clearly heightened the drama of the little affair in his fictional retelling. In *The Beautiful and Damned,* when Anthony Patch jilts Dorothy Raycroft, she becomes seriously ill. Eventually, she pursues him to New York and tracks him down in a pathetic confrontation.

There is the distinct possibility that Fitzgerald's legendary whirlwind courtship of Zelda was a case of love on the rebound — not, however, because of his relationship with May Steiner, but because he was still wounded by the breakup with Ginevra King, a year and a half earlier. It was a matter of several weeks after his meeting Zelda at the country club dance that Fitzgerald decided he was in love with her. A September 1918 ledger entry reads, "Fell in love on the 7th." But it is certainly significant that only three days earlier, Ginevra King married Ensign William Hamilton Mitchell in Chicago. It is even more significant that the wedding announcement, a full newspaper account of the event ("A gay wedding reception at the Kings' utterly charming house, 1450 Astor Street, followed. Everyone said that there never was a more beautiful bride, or more stunning wedding presents"), and a relic of Ginevra's handkerchief were pasted into Fitzgerald's scrapbook, with a large caption: THE END OF A ONCE POIGNANT STORY. It was symptomatic of Fitzgerald that he made shrines to his love affairs in life and then consecrated them in prose. Ginevra King would trail through Fitzgerald's fiction as the proud, rich, dark-haired, and perpetually unattainable girl.

Ensign Mitchell, an instructor at the naval air station in Key West, Florida, so the columnist gushed, "is as pronounced a blond as [the bride] is a brunette, and a good-looking young aviator he makes." Fitzgerald had known about Ginevra's engagement since June 1917, according to his ledger, but it is not clear whether an earlier entry, in August 1916, connected with one of his Lake Forest visits—"Beautiful Billy Mitchell"—was either a snide or an envious remark about someone he recognized as a rival. But in effect, Fitzgerald's dream girl had married a near-resemblance to one of his heroes.

In August, soon after meeting Zelda, Fitzgerald had a letter from Charles Scribner's Sons, rejecting his novel but suggesting that he rewrite it and submit it again. For a rejection, it was decidedly encouraging: "In fact no ms. novel has come to us for a long time that seemed to display so much originality." Scribner's editors, however, felt that the book was still "crude" and that the plot line did not work up to a satisfactory conclusion: "Neither the hero's career nor his character are shown to be brought to any stage which justifies an ending."

It is not clear at what point Fitzgerald made a hasty revision of his manuscript and returned it to the publisher. Only five chapters of the typescript of *The Romantic Egotist,* the book's original title, survive. These are the chapters that Fitzgerald sent his friend Sap Donahoe, who was in France. It was late October that Fitzgerald received a telegram from Maxwell Perkins, stating that the firm still had not decided whether to take the revised manuscript. Perkins, who would become Fitzgerald's lifetime editor and friend, however, was unable to arouse enough support from the conservative members of the Scribner's editorial board, and *The Romantic Egotist* was rejected for the second time. The telegram, as with most of the evidence of Fitzgerald's defeats and triumphs, was pasted in his scrapbook and received an appropriate caption, "The end of a dream."

Fitzgerald's ledger notes that he had made his hasty revision of the manuscript in August. But that seems questionable, since he had not received word of the first rejection until midmonth. If some of the other ledger notes for August and September are more accurate — "The range," "The range again," "The trench mortar," "War games" — then it would indicate that the stepped-up military activities were in preparation for overseas assignment of his division. And in that case, it seems that he hardly could have completed the revisions in August. Another bit of evidence for a possible later date is fictional. In *Save Me the Waltz,* Zelda notes that her hero had to commute long distances in order to be with Alabama Beggs; David Knight "swore and cursed the collars of his uniforms and rode all night to the rifle range rather than give up his hours after supper with Alabama." And as indicated in a letter from Monsignor Fay, addressed to Fitzgerald at the rifle range, he was engaged in training activities as late as October 19. In his letter, Fay hastened "to send back the parts of your novel which you were good enough to let me read. The more I see of it, the more amazingly good I think it is." The importance of the later date for the revisions is that it offers a clue to Fitzgerald's final disposition of the hero, one that does not survive in manuscript form, but that is indicated in an unpublished preface Fitzgerald wrote. "Finding that I had dragged the hero from a logical muddle into an illogical one," Fitzgerald explained, "I dispatched him to the war and callously slew him several feet in the air, whence he fell not like a dead, but a splendid life-bound swallow . . . down . . . down . . ."

Fitzgerald seems to have arrived at one of those astonishing points in an author's life when circumstances converge to provide him with one of his most potent and persistent symbols — in this case, the aviator and the risk of flight. Ginevra King's marriage to an aviator, Fitzgerald's own thoughts of joining the corps, Zelda's daredevil pilots at Taylor Field, Leslie's poems on the deaths of aviators — all may have contributed to the somewhat punitive death of Stephen Palms in *The Romantic Egotist.* It is possible that Fitzgerald, with his instinct for self-dramatization, in some subconscious manner may have been shooting down his own bright ambitions for the sake of a startling climax. But if the date of Fitzgerald's revisions were later, rather than early, then it is possible that an episode out of life—one he may easily have identified with—had been a determining factor in the death of his hero. On September 26, two days after Fitzgerald's twenty-second birthday, Stephan Parrott's brother Edmund, twenty-two and a Yale graduate, a first lieutenant in the 20th Aero Squadron, was killed in action over Dun-Sur-Meuse, France.

Late in October, on the twenty-sixth, Fitzgerald, acting as supply officer, was ordered north to prepare for the embarkation of his division. Although Fitzgerald later jocularly remarked that "in those days all infantry officers thought they had only three months to live," it is reasonable to expect he had had some sober thoughts of death. His last words to Zelda before he left were characteristically dramatic. "Here is my heart," he said. Zelda would remember that offer till the end of their days.

For very plausible reasons, it is generally assumed that Fitzgerald's sexual affair with Zelda began before his overseas orders, and that it served as the model for Gatsby's seduction of Daisy in *The Great Gatsby*. But that supposition is based on another of those tangles of fact and fiction in the Fitzgeralds' lives. In his remarkably chaste prose style, Fitzgerald recounts how Lieutenant Jay Gatsby, soon to be shipped overseas, "took Daisy one still October night, took her because he had no real right to touch her hand." Fitzgerald's treatment of sex in fiction is always discreet and tasteful; the blackout precedes the bedding-down. For the most part, his heroes are remarkably circumspect, upholding the Victorian code that a kiss was virtually a commitment to marriage. Gatsby's conquest, expectably, leaves him feeling implicated:

> He didn't despise himself and it didn't turn out as he had imagined. He had intended, probably, to take what he could and go—but now he found that he had committed himself to the following of a grail. . . . He felt married to her, that was all.

As a writer, Fitzgerald was deft at adding some new piece of business, some recently experienced detail, to the earlier scenarios of his fictional repertoire. And the scenario for the tender seduction scene in *The Great Gatsby* had existed before he met Zelda and long before he conceived of Daisy or Jay Gatsby. In one of his collegiate stories, "Sentiment—And the Use of Rouge" (1917), a prudish young English lieutenant, Clay Syneforth, whose brother has been killed in the war, is seduced by his brother's former fiancée, Eleanor

Marbrooke. Clay, home on leave and about to return to the front, understandably gives some thought to the possibility of his death. (He, too, is slated for death on the battlefield.) But alone with Eleanor in his bachelor quarters, just before the obligatory fade-out, he muses about the subject of honor:

> Clay was no saint, but he had always been rather decent about women. Perhaps that's why he felt so helpless now. His emotions were not complex. He knew what was wrong, but he knew also that he wanted this woman, this warm creature of silk and life who crept so close to him. There were reasons why he oughtn't to have her, but he had suddenly seen how love was a big word like Life and Death, and she knew that he realized and was glad.

The Armistice intervened before Lieutenant Fitzgerald was able to test himself on the battlefield. Awaiting further orders, he was stationed at Camp Mills on Long Island. It would be one of the irreparable failures of his life — so he judged it — that he had not seen action overseas. As compensation, Fitzgerald devised two contradictory versions of how he had *almost* made it. One was that he had been on a train bound for a Canadian port of embarkation when the Armistice was declared. Another was that he had boarded a troopship in New York but had been marched off again, a week before the war ended, because of an epidemic of influenza. It was a slight variation of the last story that Fitzgerald gave to James Drawbell, a journalist for the *New York World,* who had served in France. The pair met in a bar and indulged in some heavy drinking. The alcohol may well have accounted for the vehemence of Fitzgerald's feelings, as Drawbell reported on them. "God damn it to hell," Fitzgerald complained, "I never got over there. . . . I needed so much to get over. I wanted to belong to what every other bastard belonged to; the greatest club in history. . . . They kept me out of it."

His disappointment was very real; during his time at Camp Mills, he assuaged it with heavy drinking in the New York bistros. One evening he was arrested in the Hotel Astor with a nude girl. The most detailed version of this story, related in Arthur Mizener's biography, *The Far Side of Paradise,* is that Fitzgerald had borrowed the hotel room from a friend and was caught there with a girl by the house detective. Fitzgerald made the situation considerably worse by bribing the detective with a folded one-dollar bill, pretending it was a hundred, and managed to escape with the girl before the hoax was discovered. But the friend had to face the angry detective. If Fitzgerald's commanding officer had not placed him under military arrest at the camp, he would have been turned over to the civil authorities. Fictionally, the soldier-prostitute theme would come in handy. Fitzgerald was probably using this episode from life in his story "I Didn't Get Over." But there, he treated it as farce, employing one of his comic sexual transfers. When the seminude and drunken pair run into the divisional commander in the hotel lobby, the prostitute and the soldier have changed roles: she is wearing his officer's coat, and he is wearing her dress and hat.

In November, Fitzgerald returned to Camp Sheridan to wait out his discharge. In the meantime, however, he was named aide-de-camp to General J. A. Ryan. He was undoubtedly pleased with the assignment, and he certainly looked the part of the snappy and efficient officer, in his jodhpurs and boots. But he was not a very capable horseman. During a parade formation, his horse reared unexpectedly and threw him. The general assigned a sergeant to give him horseback-riding lessons. That story, too, joined the chronicle of his military exploits.

Fitzgerald promptly resumed courting Zelda. They went dancing and drinking together. He took her to the theater, to the vaudeville shows and the touring musical comedies; they held hands, sitting in the gilt and red plush boxes at the Grand Theater. Zelda gave Fitzgerald her diary to read. (He kept it for months and in time made use of it in *This Side of Paradise* and *The Beautiful and Damned*. It was another form of appropriation, possession.) He spent Christmas Day with her in the Sayres' parlor. They walked in the woods.

But Zelda refused to comply with ordinary conventions and would not commit herself exclusively to Fitzgerald. She was being rushed by some of the local wealthy swains, like Peyton Mathis and John Sellers, known as the "Gold Dust Twins," because they were inseparable friends and rivals. They practiced the proper Southern chivalry toward the opposite sex and were disdainful of Northern interlopers. Zelda may not have taken them seriously, but they made Fitzgerald uncomfortable. He and Zelda had simply resumed their former relationship: Zelda, still flirtatious; Fitzgerald, still easily made jealous. It did not help matters that she broke a date with him to attend the governor's inaugural ball with another beau. Their affair seemed poised on some precarious balance point.

Fitzgerald had a habit of making confidantes of his old girl friends, such as Marie Hersey and Alida Bigelow, another of his former St. Paul friends, giving them details about his current affairs, teasing them with bits of gossip. During the course of his romance with Zelda, he had found a new confidante in Ruth Sturtevant, a blond and clever young woman, a schoolmate of Alida Bigelow's at Miss Porter's School in Farmington, Connecticut, whom he took to dances at the Princeton Boat Club, visited in Washington, flirted with on occasion, but confessed he found "disappointing." "My affair still drifts," he wrote Ruth about the uncertain state of his relationship with Zelda. "But my mind is firmly made up that I will not, shall not, can not, should not, must not marry — Still, she *is* remarkable."

And Zelda would recall the uncertainties of an evening when Fitzgerald took her to dinner, perhaps at the officers' club, when the general was away. It was a first dinner engagement for her; before that, she always "just 'had supper.'" She remembered it as a soft, gray night with the scent of pines, "fragrant with the past," and dim lamplight:

> And you said you would come back from no matter where you are. So I said and I will be here waiting. I didn't quite believe it. . . . It was me who said: I feel as if something had happened and I don't know what it is. You said: — Well and you smiled (And it was a compliment to me for you had never heard "well" used so before) if you don't know I can't possibly know. Then I said: I guess nobody knows. And you hoped and I guessed: Everything's going to be all right —

Fitzgerald, it seems, confessed to Zelda his escapade in the Hotel Astor, perhaps to make her jealous. The evidence, however, again is fictional. It occurs in *Save Me the Waltz* but may be autobiographically accurate. When Alabama is told, she has a momentary pang. Then she thinks, "Oh God! . . . Well, I can't help it." And then she provides an excuse that lets them both off the hook: "She said to David that it didn't matter; that she believed that one person should only be faithful to another when they felt it. She said it was probably her fault for not making him care more." The line of reasoning was typical of Zelda, but it is doubtful that it satisfied Fitzgerald.

Exactly what he told Zelda about the episode is not clear. But the version he used in *This Side of Paradise* tranformed it into a heroic deed on the part of Amory Blaine. Fitzgerald produced a pair of connecting rooms in a hotel that was now displaced to Atlantic City. In one of them, Amory, after a night of drinking and gaiety, is sleeping it off; in the other, his friend Alec Connage is entertaining a girl. When the heavy hand of the house detective knocks on the door, Amory sacrifices his reputation in order to save his friend from scandal. He pretends that he had been sleeping with the girl, even to the unusual act of authenticity of slipping into Alec's BVDs. (The point Fitzgerald makes of this is really gratuitous.) Fitzgerald created the girl, Jill—loud and brassy, but vulnerable to the point of worrying that her mother may hear about the incident—with great skill. But the charade of setting up the connecting rooms, of allowing the pair to escape prosecution under the Mann Act (there is no mention of a bribe) by the publication of their names in the newspaper, made it highly improbable. If the Mizener version of the real episode is accurate, then Fitzgerald's fictional version is another of those ambiguous instances in which a painfully real experience is rendered harmless and the guilt shared by the fictional characters. In an ironic way, Fitzgerald's treatment of the episode is proof of his dictum that writing—the saving grace of fiction—was "a back door way out of facing reality." That is, he made it a method of escape rather than confrontation.

Early in January 1919, Fitzgerald received a telegram informing him that Monsignor Fay had died of pneumonia in a New York hospital. The prelate had been thoroughly enjoying his new prestige as a monsignor, and he had burdened himself with too many ecclesiastical activities. Margaret Chanler recalled that Fay had made only one vow for himself: never to refuse any legitimate request for help. The influenza epidemic had struck full force, and Fay had been feeling ill at the time; nevertheless he preached a sermon in the Baltimore cathedral at the request of Cardinal Gibbons and then rushed back to New York to conduct a retreat.

On the night that the monsignor died, January 10, Zelda and Fitzgerald were together. Fitzgerald claimed to have had a sudden fit of trembling; both of them felt something eerie or mystical had happened—a premonition of the monsignor's passing. But it is difficult to verify the authenticity of the experience, considering the passage of time. Soon after, Fitzgerald came down with influenza and was confined to the base hospital. He wrote the headmaster of the Newman School, C. Edmund Delbos, expressing his regrets and saying that he was unable to attend the funeral services. His grief was undoubtedly real, and in attempting to write a few words, his eyes welled up with tears and he found it difficult to continue. "I'll think of the days," he said, "when I came back to school to join his circle before the fire as the happiest days in my life."

He was even more grief-stricken when he wrote Shane Leslie, the same day, and broke off with "Oh God! I can't write." He tried to assess the man and his influence on his own life. Perhaps, out of a sense of identification, Fitzgerald maintained that the dead priest had had a "fear of that blending of the two worlds" — presumably the here and the hereafter or, perhaps, the worlds of good and evil — that caused a "sudden change of values that sometimes happened to him and put a vague unhappiness into the stray corners of his life."

It was not in any happier mood that he wrote Leslie a short time later from the base hospital. "Your letter seemed to start a new flow of sorrows in me," he told him. "I've never wanted so much to die in my life. Father Fay always thought that if one of us died, the other would, and how I've hoped so . . . now my little world made to order has been shattered by the death of one man." The *Liebestodt* pledge probably should be viewed as some form of morbid exaggeration. But it is evidence of a serious emotional loss, and quite probably a greater sense of grief than Fitzgerald would have felt at the death of his own parents. The loss seemed to call up some sense of obligation. "This has made me nearly sure that I will become a priest," he told Leslie. "I feel as if in a way his mantle had descended upon me — a desire, or more, to some day recreate the atmosphere of him."

In the letter, Fitzgerald noted that he planned to move to New York, following his discharge from Camp Sheridan, to "write or something." After his demobilization in mid-February, Fitzgerald took the train to New York in the hope of becoming a journalist, as Bunny Wilson had, and joining the staff of a New York newspaper. He had dreams of trailing murderers by day and writing short stories at night. The departure from Montgomery had not been easy. Zelda had accepted an invitation to a party at Auburn from one of the university's star football players, Francis Stubbs, and she and Fitzgerald had quarreled. (Probably unknown to Fitzgerald, Zelda

was also being rushed by another team player, Pete Bonner, who
sent her a jaunty card: "Have a date with you Saturday P.M. Look
out Stubbs.") Passion was not Fitzgerald's forte, nor was rage; he
seems to have found it easier to treat Zelda as an indulgent father
might treat a child. Zelda was very beautiful and brave, he wrote
Ruth Sturtevant, "but she's a perfect baby." En route to New York,
he sent Zelda a telegram care of Stubbs: YOU KNOW I DO NOT
[DOUBT] YOU DARLING, presumably assuring her he had no
doubts about her fidelity. But considering Fitzgerald's public messages — particularly by wire — there is also the possibility that he
wanted the world, and Stubbs, to know about his prior claim. From
New York, Fitzgerald sent Zelda an even more exuberant message:

DARLING HEART AMBITION ENTHUSIASM AND CONFIDENCE
I DECLARE EVERYTHING GLORIOUS THIS WORLD IS A GAME
AND WHILE I FEEL SURE OF YOU[R] LOVE EVERYTHING IS
POSSIBLE I AM IN THE LAND OF AMBITION AND SUCCESS
AND MY ONLY HOPE AND FAITH IS THAT MY DARLING HEART
WILL BE WITH ME SOON.

Perhaps it was a Fitzgerald invention; billets doux by wire and by
way of every interested third party along the route of delivery.

II

Fitzgerald's confidence in his city of ambition soon wore thin. His
dreams of glory as a cub reporter were quickly dispelled by "seven
city editors" who did not need his services. Fitzgerald accepted a
$90-a-month job writing advertising copy for the Barron Collier
Agency. "We Keep You Clean in Muscatine" was his peppy slogan
for a laundry, one that impressed his employers enough to suggest
that he was an up-and-coming man.

But he was plainly unhappy — living in a drab room on Clare-
mont Avenue, broke much of the time, plodding to work with a
cardboard sole in one of his shoes. Fitzgerald would write of these
months with a gift for self-dramatization that was essential to his
well-being, but that also had an echo of the truth. "I walked quickly
from certain places — from the pawn shop where one left the field
glasses, from prosperous friends whom one met when wearing the
suit from before the war — from restaurants after tipping with the
last nickel." At the Yale-Princeton Club on Vanderbilt Avenue (the

two universities then shared the premises), Fitzgerald took his evening meals. It was also the setting for a meager social life and the starting point of heroic binges, accompanied by announcements that he intended to commit suicide. Alumni members, it is said, became so bored with his sorrows, his unrequited love, that they no longer protested when he threatened to throw himself out a window. Fitzgerald was convinced that only a complete success would win Zelda, and he was far from achieving that goal. His friends, he noticed, were all "launching decently into life." It was during this haze of anxiety and dissatisfaction, he claimed, that he passed "the four most impressionable months of my life."

In March, Fitzgerald met Peevie Parrott in New York. Having first enrolled at Harvard, Peevie was now taking classes at MIT, planning a career in architecture. He and Fitzgerald made an unlikely pair of "spiritual" brothers: both vain, self-conscious, and very much self-involved. It is difficult to imagine that even when the monsignor was alive, his two boys felt much warmth for each other; now that the prelate was dead, the two seemed to be clinging to the relics of an old relationship. Nonetheless, Parrott, who was blond, with cleanly defined features and prominent, somewhat bulging eyes, said there was a similarity between them. "Isn't it strange," he wrote Fitzgerald, "we are both as cold as fishes and yet we do love to be sentimental every now and then." Parrott's letters dwell on himself; they suggest a young man who was overly fastidious, not easily thawed, likely to brood on his own moods and analyze them with great care.

Fitzgerald had given Peevie a manuscript copy of his twice-rejected novel — apparently before Parrott's return to Cambridge. He was obviously eager to have Parrott's report. The long and rambling letter that Parrott sent back, after some delay, discussed all manner of things, including his thoughts on suicide, before it took up the subject of Fitzgerald's novel. "Your conjecture in the letter is quite correct," he told Fitzgerald. "I have been contemplating suicide since I left New York." His intentions were suspect, however, for he was thinking of it in the most dramatic — not to say melodramatic — terms; either by opening a vein or taking an overdose of opium before slipping into his bed on a late summer evening. The former method had the greater possibilities, "because I would naturally do it in a hot tub and my curious hair, long eyelashes (which you very kindly noted) long ashen hands and very white

Renaissance figure would look charming as it was taken out of the tub all dripping blood."

Eventually, in his very narcissistic letter, he broached the subject of Fitzgerald's novel. He was not altogether sympathetic. "I didn't like the beginning," he said. "It was too chopped up and had too many rather animalistic females in it for *my* taste." He conceded that it got more interesting as it went along. But aside from making a few desultory comments, he preferred to wait to discuss it until he and Fitzgerald saw each other again.

Parrott, too, was grieving for Monsignor Fay; he would take down the prelate's biretta and stare at it "until the eyes almost pop out of my head trying to conjure up his presence." Still, his letter was the awkward attempt of one egoist to reach out and touch another. At one point Peevie confessed, "I wish I could see you and talk to you; about your book, and yourself, and myself. I have been thinking so much about you since I left New York."

The awkwardness of the letter may have resulted in part from a discussion that the two men had in New York about a subject — unspecified in Parrott's letter — that had disturbed Fitzgerald. Parrott wrote: "I am so glad that what I told you did not make any difference, and as for your priggish conversation, I did notice it but I did not mind it in the least. It was all news to you and you had to have time to get adjusted, and then, I would stand almost anything from you, why, I can't explain but somehow I would." One can only speculate about the problem discussed. It may have referred to Monsignor Fay's close friend Shane Leslie, since Parrott's next remark is: "I felt exactly about Leslie as you do, but unlike you the next time I go to New York for any length of time, I will religiously call on him and, if all goes well, will be as pleasant as possible." There was, it seems, a disagreeable side to Leslie's character.

Throughout the spring, Parrott and Fitzgerald corresponded irregularly. Fitzgerald seems to have told Zelda about their meeting, and she responded, "I'm glad 'Peevie' is back . . . because I've always thought I'd like him best of all the people you know." And Fitzgerald seems to have told Parrott a good deal about his affair with Zelda, as well as having given him her diary to read. Parrott's response was somewhat oblique: "I wish I could meet a Zelda just now. I feel a horrible desire to fall in love with somebody, I feel so parched and wisely cold like a Babylonian scroll that has been buried for centuries, but the amusing part is that I can't or if I did I can picture myself at thirty with a red camelia in my hand." In a later letter he acknowledged that he had finished reading Zelda's diary and would soon return it: "As you say, it is a very human document, but somehow I cannot altogether understand it. Of course, I have read about love a great deal, but I have experienced it so little that it is very hard for me to picture it anywhere but in a book. However, I envy you greatly; it must be wonderful to be able to indulge in it without horrible pangs of conscience." It was perhaps on those grounds that Fitzgerald and Parrott were similar.

Zelda's diary, that "very human document," had an erratic history. Like some fragment of herself, in the general disorder of her life and in the course of many moves, it was lost. What we know of it is secondhand: the admittedly fictional transcripts Fitzgerald made for his novels; the passing comments of friends who had read it.

Fitzgerald could have received Parrott's commentaries on love only with a certain irony. Throughout the spring, his relationship with Zelda grew worse. She was becoming increasingly restless and provocative; he was becoming desperately anxious. Her letters — "Wild letters," he called them — were calculated to throw him into alternating fits of jealousy and passionate hope. She had kept up with her social life and flirtations, was preparing a ballet for an annual charity event, was glad to be finished dancing in the local vaudeville show. She sent him a bit of news that was sure to keep him off balance: "Some actor with this week's Keiths tried to take me and Livye [Hart] on the road with him — but I — can't ignore physical characteristics enough to elope with a positive APE." She thanked him for sending Compton Mackenzie's *Plasher's Mead,* then announced that she did not like it: "People seldom interest me except in their relations to things, and I like men to be just incidents in books so I can imagine their characters — Nothing annoys me more than having the most trivial action analyzed and explained." It was hardly encouraging news for either an ambitious writer or an aspiring husband.

Over the years, Fitzgerald's views of their affair — his stated public views — would change both subtly and significantly, depending on the circumstances under which he was remembering the events and the people to whom he was telling the story. He would recall being so much in love with Zelda at the beginning that he had no fear of death, even when marching up the gangplank to be shipped overseas. But that was for the benefit of a young apprentice psychiatrist, a woman and a Jungian, in Switzerland. In the privacy of his notebooks — but then, again, with a look ahead to a curious posterity — he would recall, with a mixture of pride and criticism, that "except for the sexual recklessness, Zelda was cagey about throwing in her lot with me before I was a money-maker." Almost anyone would have seemed a better risk to her than "a worker in the arts." And for his daughter's benefit, Fitzgerald would create a poignant fable about his youth, when he had had a great dream and learned to speak of it so that people listened to him, and one day the great dream had divided "when I decided to marry your mother after all, even though I knew she was spoiled and meant no good to me. . . . She wanted me to work too much for *her* and not enough for my dream."

He got little reassurance from letters from Zelda. Although she wrote, "Scott — there's nothing in all the world I want but you — and your precious love. All the material things are nothing," there was, unfortunately, a qualifier: "I'd just hate to live a sordid, colorless existence, because you'd soon love me less — and less." Zelda was young, of course, and she was under silent pressure from her parents. The Sayres did not forbid her romance, but neither did they encourage it. Zelda claimed that Mamma knew that the two of them would get married *someday* but that she also had a habit of leaving, on her pillow, newspaper clippings about "young authors, turned out on a dark and stormy night."

He was equally worried by the breezy accounts she sent him of her flirtations and "scrapes" with local boys. Even more worrisome were Zelda's reports that an Ohio division, returning to Camp Sheridan for demobilization, had already begun a "wild and heated correspondence" with the Montgomery girls even before their arrival. All over the country, men were returning to America for parades and heroes' welcomes — reminding Fitzgerald of his failure. Zelda said she found it "dreadfully peculiar" that she was not at all worried about the return of three or four of her former fiancés. "My brain is stagnating owing to the lack of scrapes," she said.

Very early in their relationship, Zelda realized that Fitzgerald found her popularity an attraction. She took advantage of it, perhaps because of an instinct to be provocative. At a dance, shortly after they had first met, Zelda hurried an escort into a lighted phone booth and kissed him passionately, knowing that Fitzgerald would see them. In *The Great Gatsby,* Fitzgerald would endow his hero with his own response: "It excited him, too, that many men had already loved Daisy—it increased her value in his eyes. He felt their presence all about the house." And Zelda would repeat the same insight, in a later, unpublished novel, *Caesar's Things:* "[He] was proud of the way the boys danced with her and she was so much admired. The glamour of public premium . . . gave [her] a desirability which became, indeed, indispensable to [him]." Zelda, in her uncanny way, seized one aspect of that problematic feature in Fitzgerald's personality: "He had planned his life for story anyway." But there may have been something more to it than Fitzgerald's tendency to live a fictional life. He, at least, sensed that there was something deeper and perhaps subterranean about the urge, some need to find a stimulus in the interest of another man—of other men—in his woman. Twice in his notebooks Fitzgerald grasped at it, like a man grasping at straws. "Proxy in passion," he wrote; and again, "Feeling of proxy in passion strange encouragement." In consequence, there was no way that his relationship with Zelda could be an easy one.

The only bright spot of that spring in New York was the sale of one of Fitzgerald's stories, "Babes in the Woods," to *The Smart Set,* the brash and trendy magazine edited by H. L. Mencken and the drama critic George Jean Nathan. It was the quintessential story of Fitzgerald's early career: a slight sketch about a sixteen-year-old vamp who is considered a "speed" and a handsome young freshman from one of the better Eastern colleges who has a "line" but is not quite sure of himself, an interrupted kiss in a darkened room while the orchestra is playing offstage. The racy style, the up-to-date slang, the snatches of popular songs—"Give me your hand / I'll understand / We're off to slumberland"—would all become trademarks of Fitzgerald's tales of the Jazz Age. Fitzgerald's only regret was that "Babes in the Woods" was a revision of a story he had published in the May 1917 issue of *Nassau Lit.* "The implication," he acknowledged, "was that I was on the down-grade at twenty-two."

With the $30 he earned for the story, he bought himself a pair of white flannel knickers and sent the first of several presents to Zelda. The sequence of the gifts has been altered by time in the versions that Fitzgerald and Zelda committed to print and is not exactly traceable in her undated letters. There was a pair of pajamas:

"They're the most adorably moon-shiney things on earth — I feel like a *Vogue* cover in 'em." Zelda added suggestively, "I do wish yours were touching." There was a magenta (or blue) feather fan: "Those feathers — those wonderful, wonderful feathers are the most beautiful things on earth." And there was a sweater: "I'm going to save it till you come in June so you can tell me how nice I look — It's funny, but I like being 'pink and helpless.' " In March, Fitzgerald sent her an engagement ring that had belonged to his mother. "Scott, Darling," she wrote him, "It really is beautiful. . . . I've never worn a ring before, they've always seemed so inappropriate — but I love to see this shining there so nice and white like our love — And it sorter says, 'Soon' to me all the time." But in the same letter, she also informed him that a visiting ROTC troop from Auburn was in town, livening the social scene. "May's is completely devastated as the result. . . . And every night I get very loud and coarse and then I always wish for you so — so I wouldn't be such a kid." A few days later she wrote him that she had worn the ring in public: "You can't imagine what havoc the ring wrought — A whole dance was completely upset last night — Everybody thinks it's lovely — and I am so proud to be your girl — to have everybody know we are in love." But she also gave him a vivid account of the departure of the Auburn boys: "I have always been inclined toward masculinity. It's such a cheery atmosphere boys radiate — And we do such unique things — Yesterday, when the University boys took their belated departure, John Sellers wheeled me thru a vast throng of people at the station, crying intermittently, 'The lady hasn't walked in five years.' " There was little chance that Zelda would go unnoticed in a crowd.

Although he could hardly afford it on the meager salary he earned at the advertising agency, Fitzgerald made regular monthly trips to Montgomery. They were not always satisfactory. After the first of them, in mid-April, Fitzgerald realized that he knew why princesses had been locked up in towers in the old fairy tales. Unfortunately, he made the mistake of writing this to Zelda, who was finding it difficult to keep up with the regular correspondence Fitzgerald demanded.

> Scott [she responded], you've been so sweet about writing — but I'm so damned tired of being told that you "used to wonder why they kept princesses in towers" — you've written that verbatim in your last six letters! It's dreadfully hard to write so very much —

and so many of your letters sound forced—I know you love me, Darling, and I love you more than anything in the world, but if it's going to be so much longer, we just *can't* keep up this frantic writing.

Zelda could also be provocatively tender. After one of his visits, she sent him a dreamy letter: "Scott, my darling lover—everything seems so smooth and restful, like this yellow dusk. . . . I'm so glad you came—like summer, just when I needed you most." They had been drinking together; he had brought the "best" brand of gin in town, though she preferred the "10¢ a quart variety." She had wanted it, she said, "just to know you loved the sweetness—to breath and know you loved the smell." His presence had not altogether dispelled her feelings of "vague despondency," however, for she went on to describe a visit she had made to a Confederate graveyard, where she had been touched by thoughts of dead loves and dead lovers. The experience was moving, and her feelings were genuine, but she also seems to have wanted to appeal to his literary instincts and probably to demonstrate her own talents along those lines. She asked: "Why should graves make people feel in vain? . . . All the broken columns and clasped hands and doves and angels mean romances and in an hundred years I think I shall like having young people speculate on whether my eyes were brown or blue—of course, they are neither —I hope my grave has an air of many, many years ago about it." She ended, "Old death is so beautiful—so very beautiful—We will die together—I know."

In trying to resolve her uncertainties, Zelda took some unusual steps. She consulted Mrs. Francesca, a local spiritualist, who got a message for her from the Ouija board. (Zelda, who tried it herself, could get only the word *dead,* over and over again.) But Mrs. Francesca's message "told us to be married—that we were soul-mates." By way of explanation, she referred to the beliefs of the theosophists (Minnie Sayre had dabbled in theosophy): that "two souls are incarnated together—not necessarily at the same time but are mated— since the time when people were bi-sexual, so you see 'soul-mate' isn't exactly snappy storyish, after all."

The uncertain love affair, however, came to an abrupt end in June, when Zelda, caught up in a whirl of university proms and commencement exercises, tried to fit Fitzgerald's monthly visit into a very busy schedule. She was going to Georgia Tech ("to try my hand in new fields"), having been invited to the Senior Hop on the sixteenth and to the commencement exercises. She advised Fitzgerald to come before her trip to Atlanta or afterward, around the twentieth, and before the family took a trip to Asheville. She expected to be mighty tired: "They always dance till breakfast." Fitzgerald did not relish riding back with Zelda on the train (as she had suggested) and apparently settled on the later date. He had been celebrating heavily in New York—Sap Donahoe was in town—and had mailed two letters to Zelda without postage, so they were delayed. ("Wild nights and headachy mornings," Zelda surmised.) She wrote Fitzgerald that she was consoling herself with Perry Adair, a young golfer from Atlanta, and that she wouldn't miss the Tech commencement for a million. She would be in Atlanta until Wednesday and hoped that he would come down to Montgomery after that. What proved to be the final straw was that she returned home to Montgomery pinned to Adair. But thinking better of it, she returned the pin with a warm note. Unfortunately—Fitzgerald was never quite sure that it had been a mistake—she put Adair's note in an envelope addressed to Fitzgerald. The letter to Fitzgerald went with the pin to Adair. Fitzgerald, incensed, told her not to bother writing to him anymore. In later years, he embellished the story a bit, telling his daughter that it was a photograph that Zelda had mistakenly sent him, warmly inscribed to Bobby Jones, a world-famous champion at the time he wrote to Scottie. But Jones, who was indeed a freshman at Georgia Tech in 1919, denied that he had ever known Zelda, much less dated her. Nor, responding to some other versions of the story, that he had proposed marriage to her. He was seventeen at the time.

Zelda wrote to Fitzgerald despite the ban, trying to smooth things over, explaining that it had been a simple mistake. Still angry, Fitzgerald made a trip to Montgomery, intent on settling the affair once and for all. The scenario of his visit has become thoroughly established in the literature about the Fitzgeralds' lives. Sitting in the Sayre parlor, he alternately bullied Zelda and begged; both of them wept; she sent him packing. Fitzgerald commemorated the event in a short story, "The Sensible Thing," which he assured Max Perkins was "about Zelda and me. All true." He had a true instinct for describing, in the most economical terms, the wrangling relationships of men and women—in love and war at the same moment—and he managed the break-up scene between George O'Kelly and Jonquil Cary with startling psychological success:

He seized her in his arms and tried literally to kiss her into marrying him at once. When this failed, he broke into a long monologue of self-pity, and ceased only when he saw that he was making himself despicable in her sight. He threatened to leave when he had no intention of leaving, and refused to go when she told him that, after all, it was best that he should.

But that famous rejection scene, which adds such color to the Fitzgeralds' legendary courtship, had already been established in an early story, "The Pierian Springs and the Last Straw." He had written it at Princeton, following his break with Ginevra King. The later version, filled with details from his affair with Zelda, has greater style and maturity. But the collegiate version has its own forcefulness.

In it, George Rombert, an elderly alcoholic writer, tells his nephew, the narrator of the story, that his life really ended on an October evening at sixteen minutes after ten, when he was twenty-one. He was having a passionate and stormy affair with an imperious and handsome girl. They had met at a collegiate dance, and the love affair was immediate and irreparable, full of "ridiculous letters" and "ridiculous telegrams." Rombert knew that the girl was conceited, willful, the "faultiest girl" he had ever met, the "most direct, unprincipled personality" he would ever come in contact with. Still, she aroused in him an overwhelming sense of ambition: "She made me want to do something for her, to get something to show her. Every honor in college took on the semblance of a presentable trophy." At a later dance, they quarreled bitterly because of his jealousy. He stormed out, only to return and abase himself at the fateful hour, and in a manner that was certain to make him despicable in her sight: "I wandered around that ballroom like a wild man trying to get a word with her and when I did I finished the job. I begged, pled, almost wept. She had no use for me from that hour."

Fitzgerald's departure from Montgomery, after his failure, had its comic elements. According to one story, Zelda accompanied him to the station, and Fitzgerald jauntily stepped into the Pullman car, then ignominiously crept into a coach, because he did not have enough money for the luxury fare. Even in abject defeat—or perhaps because of it—he needed to keep up appearances. From New York, he wrote a bitter letter to Ruth Sturtevant: "I've done my best and I've failed—it's a great tragedy and I feel I have very little left to live for. . . . I wish you'd tear up this letter and I know you'll never say what I told you in an hour of depression. Unless someday she will marry me I will never marry."

The inevitable result was a prolonged binge, which lasted about three weeks. He was already assured of consolation from Stephan Parrott, who, knowing his frame of mind, had earlier written him: "I think of you as being unhappy; are you? I know that if we changed places, I should find the drop from the Brooklyn Bridge to the East River very attractive." Fitzgerald took a train to Boston for a short, boozy visit and then returned to New York. The drinking ended with the first day of Prohibition on July 1. Disgusted with himself, unhappy over the affair, Fitzgerald quit his job at Barron Collier and returned to St. Paul. "I was a failure—" he recalled, "mediocre at advertising work and unable to get started as a writer. Hating the city, I got roaring, weeping drunk on my last penny and went home."

III

Fitzgerald's dry train ride to St. Paul provided a negative boost to his writing. He had read one of Hugh Walpole's overfurnished novels, probably *Fortitude,* and decided that it was as bad as possible and that he could definitely do better himself. "After that," he said, "I dug in and wrote my first book." In St. Paul, he settled down to work in a third-floor room in his parents' house, at 599 Summit Avenue. On the wagon, he indulged only in cigarettes and Cokes. The Fitzgeralds, principally his mother, were not supportive of his literary career. During his free time, he made new friends: Father Joseph Barron, dean of students at the St. Paul Seminary, with whom he argued about religious topics, and a young Yale graduate, Donald Ogden Stewart, who was working for the American Telephone Company. Stewart, who later had a highly visible career as a humorist and screenwriter, recalled: "Scott showed me a shoe box, full of handwritten-in-pencil manuscript of a novel called *This Side of Paradise.* Fortunately, I liked it very much, so that our friendship deepened over the years." But that would turn out to be something of a gloss on the truth. Fitzgerald, in fact, did promote Stewart's career with the New York editors he knew, but late in life, Fitzgerald labeled Stewart with the same offensive tab that others had applied to him, that he was a "suck" around the rich. Though Stewart in his later years had a reputation for leftist views, Fitzgerald would claim that the John Hay Whitneys had bought Stewart cheap and "turned him out to grass" on their private golf links.

By July 26, Fitzgerald felt confident enough to send a feeler to Max Perkins, saying he had rewritten the book and that it was no longer a revision of *The Romantic Egotist*. (That was not quite the truth, since a good deal of the earlier material had been incorporated into the new book.) He asked Perkins whether the book could be published in October if he got the manuscript to Scribner's in late August. "This is [a] definate attempt at a big novel," he said, "and I really believe I have hit it."

In mid-August, he was in contact with Edmund Wilson, who had recently returned from overseas. Wilson and another Princeton friend, Stanley Dell, were planning a volume of war stories and asked Fitzgerald for a contribution. "You never got abroad," Wilson wrote, "but *tant mieux!* let us have something about Army life in the States during the war. . . . No *Saturday Evening Post* stuff, understand! clear your mind of cant! brace up your artistic conscience, which was always the weakest part of your talent! forget for a moment the phosphorescence of the decaying Church of Rome!"

Fitzgerald answered that he had just the story for the collection, a tale about an American girl who falls in love with a French officer in a Southern camp. But, he confessed, he hadn't gotten around to writing it yet. He told Wilson that his novel would soon be going off to Scribner's. "Since I last saw you," he wrote, "I've tried to get married and then tried to drink myself to death, but foiled, as have been so many good men, by the sex and the state, I have returned to literature." Only months before, he had been thinking of the priesthood, but now he assured Wilson that his Catholicism was "scarcely more than a memory"—or if anything more than that, he no longer went to mass nor mumbled over his rosary beads. Later, when Wilson asked about his affair with Zelda, Fitzgerald gave him a gloomy reply: "I'll tell you what the situation is now. I wouldn't care if she died, but I couldn't stand to have anybody else marry her."

The torch was rekindled after September 16, when Maxwell Perkins wrote to say that Scribner's had at last accepted his novel, renamed *This Side of Paradise*. (The title was taken from two lines of a Rupert Brooke poem, "Tiare Tahiti": "Well this side of Paradise!/There's little comfort in the wise.") Perkins had pushed for acceptance, believing that Fitzgerald had improved the book enormously: "It abounds in energy and life and it seems to me to be in much better proportion. I was afraid that, when we declined the first manuscript, you might be done with us conservatives. I am glad you are not." His solicitude for Fitzgerald's talent and career was the beginning of a long and legendary author-editor relationship. Since Fitzgerald was a new and untried author, Scribner's offered no advance, only the conventional royalties. But after the defeats of the past year, Fitzgerald was ecstatic. He stopped cars in the street to tell them the good news, wrote his friends buoyantly. "Pretty swell? Eh!" he wrote his Princeton classmate Ludlow Fowler. "Am coming East in November & will call you up and we'll have a supper or two together, wet or dry." To Wilson, who he knew would be an exacting critic, he wrote, "You'll call it sensational but it really is neither sentimental nor trashy."

On the strength of his success, he began writing short stories with new confidence. *Scribner's Magazine,* which he had been trying to break into, now accepted "The Cut-Glass Bowl" and "The Four Fists"; Nathan wrote him that *The Smart Set,* which had already taken his revised collegiate play *The Debutante,* would take his short story "Dalyrimple Goes Wrong" and another of his one-acters, *Porcelain and Pink.* Nathan told him that he had an uncommon gift for light dialogue, and advised him to keep writing plays. "You will do things," he wrote—encouraging words for a beginning author. Recalling that "first wild wind of success," during which it seemed impossible to do anything wrong, Fitzgerald described his feelings in ebullient terms: "That week the postman rang and rang, and I paid off my terrible small debts, bought a suit and woke up every morning with a world of ineffable toploftiness and promise." In his letter of acceptance to Perkins, Fitzgerald pressed hard for early publication, hoping that the book would be out by Christmas or at the latest by early February: "I have so many things dependent on its success—including, of course, a girl."

The girl, in fact, had become as important to Fitzgerald's book as she was to his life. Ironically, when Fitzgerald wrote Perkins that, following his return to St. Paul, his muse had become "an erratic mistress if not a steady wife," he might as easily have been describing Zelda. Zelda—and the failed romance with Zelda—had become the providential focus of the novel. There is no extant manuscript for the complete early version of *The Romantic Egotist,* but in a letter detailing the changes made for the final manuscript, Fitzgerald told

Perkins that the Isabelle and Rosalind of the earlier versions had now been changed into "just Isabelle," and the "new Rosalind is a different person." It is possible that Zelda may have initiated changes in the book at two different stages of its progress. Some time after their first meeting in July 1918, Fitzgerald had sent her a manuscript portion of the novel, with the comment: "Here is the mentioned chapter . . . a document of youthful melancholy. . . . However . . . the heroine does resemble you in more ways than four." It is, of course, also possible that Fitzgerald was merely asking her to acknowledge a resemblance to his earlier heroine. But Amory Blaine's affair with Rosalind Connage, which is definitely patterned after Fitzgerald's affair with Zelda, dominates the second half of the novel. It must have been written during the final revisions of the book, in July and August 1919. That chronology suggests that Fitzgerald may have intended all along to use the experience to bring off his novel. And that perhaps he also planned to use Zelda's letters and her borrowed diary for the purpose. When he later sent a typescript segment of Zelda's diary to Maxwell Perkins, he noted, "You'll recognize much of the dialogue."

But there were other important ways in which Fitzgerald's first novel was, so to speak, cribbed from the life. In his ledger book, he summed up the year as "the most important year of life. Every emotion and my life work decided. Miserable and ecstatic . . ." The experiences served him well. Monsignor Fay was cast in a crucial role in the book, and his character proceeded through several name changes, from Dr. Dudley to Taylor and then Monsignor Thayer Darcy. (Fay, who had been intrigued by his role in the book, had objected to Taylor, preferred Forbes, and offered some changes of dialogue that he seemed to feel were more characteristic of his own speech.) Fitzgerald used the dead cleric's letters, editing them and heightening the style. He used Shane Leslie's account of Monsignor Fay's funeral—which Fitzgerald had not attended—to good effect.

For some reason, perhaps a need to put distance between hmself and Stephan Parrott, Fitzgerald dropped the original name of the hero and replaced it with Amory Blaine. But he borrowed directly from Peevie's lurid suicide letter in an episode in which Amory, drunk and dejected, announces that he plans "to take a room at the Commodore, get into a hot bath and open a vein." Parrott's account of his suicidal intentions had evidently impressed Fitzgerald.

In one of those mystifying changes that all writers deal in and that are more elusive in Fitzgerald than in many other authors, Parrott's first name, with a variant spelling, is given to Amory's father, "an ineffectual, inarticulate man with a taste for Byron and a habit of drowsing over the *Encyclopaedia Britannica.*" In all matters other than wealth, Stephen Blaine is based on Edward Fitzgerald. Fathers, as Fitzgerald recognized (and as Edward Fitzgerald seems to have noticed), were mostly dead before his novels began. Stephen Blaine puts in an appearance on page 1 of *This Side of Paradise* and obligingly dies on page 99, without being mentioned in between. Other than leaving a mismanaged inheritance, Stephen Blaine barely causes a ripple in the plot.

Fitzgerald did, however, provide his hero with a mother. ("Beatrice is a new character," he told Perkins.) Beatrice O'Hara Blaine is more the mother Fitzgerald wanted than the mother he had. She is beautiful, with impeccable taste, has style and verve. Her social distinctions are itemized on page 1 — "known by name as a fabulously wealthy American girl to Cardinal Vitori and Queen Margherita" — and she has access to those upper reaches of society which are known only to the cognoscenti. She is a woman of rather nervous disposition and has a tendency to drink too much. "My nerves are on edge — on edge," she complains to Amory. It is possible that that complaint found a dim echo in the society hostess of T. S. Eliot's *The Waste Land,* published two years after Fitzgerald's novel. ("My nerve are bad to-night. Yes bad . . ." was Eliot's line.) Eliot was a poet who admired Fitzgerald's prose.

As Fitzgerald had intended it to be, *This Side of Paradise* was a novel of a youth's quest, a sequence of allegiances toward enviable men, a series of courtships with desirable women, until, after shedding his illusions one by one, the youth, Amory Blaine, reaches that stage of circumscribed knowledge with which he is ready to confront the world. "I know myself," Amory concludes, "but that is all."

For reasons that have more to do with Fitzgerald's personal life than with his command of fiction, Amory Blaine's infatuations with various men have a curious interest. There is Dick Humbird, who apparently represents one of Fitzgerald's idealized selves — dark-haired, dark-skinned, a boy with aristocratic bearing, a tentative leader of men. "People dressed like him, tried to talk as he did." But Humbird's life ends in drunkenness and a squalid automobile accident. (Strangely, when Amory learns that Humbird's wealth comes from the wholesale grocery business, he has a "curious sinking sensation.")

There is Amory's admiration for the perhaps too highbrow poet
Thomas D'Invilliers (based on John Peale Bishop, though it is Amory
Blaine who is sent into battle and writes letters back to
T. P. D'Invilliers at Camp Gordon, Georgia); and in his socially
minded phase he comes under the influence of Burne Holiday, who
preaches pacifism and spouts the doctrines of Tolstoy. In the novel,
the urbane figure of Monsignor Darcy becomes a kind of mother-
father figure out of pagan mythology. He writes to Amory, "I've
enjoyed imagining that you were my son, that perhaps when I was
young I went into a state of coma and begat you . . . it's the paternal
instinct, Amory—celibacy goes deeper than the flesh." Father Fay
did, in fact, speak too often about "parturition," but the odd doctrine seems to have been Fitzgerald's own.

The novel is also woman- and devil-haunted, from the adolescent seductress Myra St. Clair, whose kiss suddenly repels Amory,
through Isabelle Borgé, who jilts him, and the madwoman Eleanor
Savage, who is fiercely atheistic and self-destructive. Fitzgerald described the hero's relationship with Eleanor Savage as "the last time
that evil crept close to Amory under the mask of beauty." Each of
these relationships was stolen from life: Myra, an amalgam of the
childhood sweethearts whom Fitzgerald chronicled in his "Thoughtbook"; Isabelle from Ginevra King; Eleanor Savage, drawn from an
experience Monsignor Fay had told him about. But was it merely a
sardonic joke that Fitzgerald gave Myra the name of the most famous
brothel in Montgomery, Alabama—Madame St. Clair's? Or was it
simply an illustration of Fitzgerald's theme that for Amory "the
problem of evil had solidified . . . into the problem of sex."

Evil certainly plays a continuous part in the unraveling of his
chronicle. There is the famous and scoffed-at episode in which Amory
is entertained in a cheap room by two chorus girls. (Their names,
Axia and Phoebe, suggest that he was taking a cheap shot at his
mother's favorite poets, Alice and Phoebe Cary.) Amory's eyes are
riveted to a disturbing man in the room; he senses that it is the
devil: "Then, suddenly, Amory perceived the feet, and with a rush
of blood to the head, he realized he was afraid. The feet were all
wrong." He flees the party and is chased by the fiend. When he
turns around to confront him, he sees that the face is that of the
dead Humbird. (Peevie Parrott, reading that scene in the early
manuscript, had similar feelings of revulsion: "I had to stop reading
—I know just what you felt.") But what should one make of the

fact that, as a boy, Fitzgerald had such "Freudian" feelings about his own naked feet? Or what sense can one make of the transformation of the "supernatural" experience he and Zelda had had on the night of Monsignor Fay's death into the episode in which Amory, in the hotel room with the girl on the bed and the detective pounding on the door, senses an unknown presence in the room: "Over by the window among the stirring curtains stood something else, featureless and indistinguishable, yet strangely familiar." Later, he realizes that it was the ghost of the dying Monsignor Darcy. *This Side of Paradise,* in its disorganized way, was an attempt to exorcise the good and evil spirits of Fitzgerald's youth.

Critics would make much of the unwieldy structure of the book, its snippets of prose, poetry, drama, its scraps of undergraduate literary comment, its mishmash of critical opinions of Shaw, Chesterton, Conrad, and Mary Roberts Rinehart. Fitzgerald, with fair accuracy, described the book as "A Romance and a Reading List." And critics, then and now, have pointed out the pervasive influence of Compton Mackenzie's *Youth's Encounter,* one of the quest novels that was much in vogue. Fitzgerald himself, responding to one of his critics, claimed that when he began writing his book in 1917, his literary taste was "so unformed that *Youth's Encounter* was still my 'perfect book.' " Quite naturally, therefore, Mackenzie's influence showed to a "marked degree." But one has to take that claim with a grain of salt, since, in the Donahoe version of *The Romantic Egotist,* Fitzgerald attributed the Mackenzie book to James Barrie. (It is one of Fitzgerald's oddities that in replying to the critic Frances Newman in 1921, he echoed a successful line in the text of *The Romantic Egotist,* one referring to "a book that three people sent me with careful instructions to read it, *Youth's Encounter,* by Barrie." Writing to the critic, he said, "I have five copies of *Youth's Encounter* at present in my library, sent me by people who stumbled on the book and thought that it was an amazing parallel to my own life.") The suspicion is that Mackenzie's influence was not quite so indelible as Fitzgerald claimed on the first version of *This Side of Paradise* but may have occurred during one of the later revisions.

Edmund Wilson, who read the novel in manuscript form, rightly criticized Fitzgerald for fudging the issue of Amory's war service, evading the experience completely by way of an interlude of noncommittal letters. "If you thought you couldn't deal with his military experiences," Wilson pointed out, "you shouldn't have had him go abroad at all." He had targeted what was one of Fitzgerald's real flaws: the need to cut a figure, the need for personal approval, which would sometimes overpower his judgment as an author. But on the subject of the novel's cultural pretensions, Wilson was scathingly cruel: "Your hero as an intellectual is a fake of the first water and I read his views on art, politics, religion, and society with more riotous mirth than I should care to have you know." He did, at least, praise the style: "You have a knack of writing readably which is a great asset. Your style, by the way, has become much sounder than it used to be."

In October, Fitzgerald broke silence and wrote Zelda about the publication of his novel. His letter has not survived; Zelda kept only a few of his early letters, those which she pasted into her scrapbook, along with the many telegrams in which Fitzgerald, in Western Union offices, proclaimed his love or his latest publishing triumphs. Characteristically, Zelda suffered something in the translation. The telegrams arrived addressed to Tilda, Telda, Selda, or Lilda Sayre.

In his letter, presumably, Fitzgerald asked whether he might visit her when he came east in November. He clearly wanted to effect a reconciliation, but, for once and for the moment, he wanted to keep his actions private. He wrote to Ludlow Fowler in New York: "Hope you've guarded well the great secret. God! Lud, I'll never get over it as long as I live. There's still a faint chance. Thank fortune." He planned to visit Zelda in Montgomery, then stop in New York, between the twenty-second and the twenty-sixth.

Zelda's response was not reassuring; she adopted the attitude of independence and nonchalance that Fitzgerald found so difficult to deal with. She wrote, "I'm mighty glad you're coming — I've been wanting to see you (which you probably knew) but I *couldn't* ask you." That much was promising. But at the same time, she made it clear she had not been exactly in retirement since Fitzgerald's departure. "I'm just recovering from a wholesome amour with Auburn's 'startling quarterback' so my disposition is excellent as well as my health." In her boldness and youth, Zelda made no excuses. She asked Fitzgerald to bring a quart of gin; she said she hadn't had a drink all summer. Then she made one of her warm acknowledgments: " 'S funny, Scott, I don't feel a bit shaky and do-don'tish like I used to when you came — I really want to see you — that's all."

At least he was returning to Montgomery a success, a published author with a novel in the works, a series of stories about to break into print in some of the more prestigious magazines in the country, and a literary agent. Grace Flandrau, a St. Paul writer, had put him in touch with a New York agent, Paul Reynolds. The great coup, arranged by Harold Ober, the young Reynolds agent assigned to handle Fitzgerald's work, was the November sale of his story "Head and Shoulders" to *The Saturday Evening Post* for $400. It was a brisk tale about a stuffy young scholar who marries a sassy chorus girl, and it turns on the device of a role reversal. The brainy scholar becomes a star acrobat; the chorus girl becomes a highly successful author. Fitzgerald's mother considered it too racy and suggested that her son use dots in place of words to purify some of the passages. (Fearing the worst, she began buying Fitzgerald religious books.) But it was just the type of peppy yet innocuous story that George Horace Lorimer, the *Post*'s enterprising editor, was looking for to make his magazine, already rich in advertising, as successful with the reading public.

The meeting in Montgomery, however, was disappointing. The relationship returned to what it had been. Although Zelda still loved him, she would not for the moment commit herself. And Fitzgerald felt a sense of loss, realizing — as he would describe it in "The Sensible Thing" — that "there are all kinds of love in the world, but never the same love twice." He had discussed those feelings with Zelda, and she took the sensible view. "Somehow 'When love has turned to kindliness' doesn't horrify me like it used to," she wrote him after his departure. "It has such a peaceful sound . . . and sometimes I'm glad we're not exactly like we used to be." Fitzgerald had given her a manuscript copy of his novel, and much as he appreciated her praise, it must have wounded his feelings to be told "I am very proud of you — I hate to say this, but I don't *think* I had much confidence in you at first." Winning her back, it seemed, would be a matter of increments. When there were delays in the publication of his book, Fitzgerald wrote Perkins with a sense of terrible urgency, saying that he was very "upset": "I explained to you the reasons financial, sentimental & domestic but more than any of these it's for the psychological effect on me."

Fitzgerald's trips to New York while he awaited publication of *This Side of Paradise*—the first in late November 1919 and the next in the following February—were examples of the extravagance that would characterize his later career. The stories about his behavior were like botanical species, subject to local variations. Princeton friends and old acquaintances, visiting him at the Knickerbocker Hotel, for instance, would find him drunk, being bathed by bellboys, or dressed by valets, to whom he dispensed healthy tips. When he left the hotel, he insisted on sticking $100 bills, or $20 or $50 bills, into his pockets so that they were prominently displayed. Friends managed to get the money away from him and leave the $500 or $600 with the hotel cashier. All the versions agree that Fitzgerald generously took his friends to his private bootlegger and provided each with a bottle. And all the stories agree that he once left the bathroom tap at the Knickerbocker running, thereby causing a flood. It is a fact that during his November visit he conducted some sober business, visiting his agent and seeing his editor at Scribner's, and may even have done some editing of the book on this occasion. But he had begun to create for himself the irreversible image of the playboy and the hard drinker.

If Fitzgerald had difficulty distinguishing between fiction and reality in his life, there were sometimes plausible reasons. It was quite possibly the case that during his expedition to New York in late November and early December that he became briefly involved in a wild sexual affair with a young English actress who may have been the real-life reincarnation of his bold chorus girl in "Head and Shoulders." In another coincidence, the actress had the name of his heroine in *This Side of Paradise*. Moreover, Rosalinde Fuller was small and dark-haired and had the pert good looks of Ginevra King. At the time the two met, Rosalinde Fuller was twenty-seven, four years older than Fitzgerald.

The initial evidence for this episode in Fitzgerald's life has, like many events of the past, sifted down into the miscellaneous files of the archives. It can be found in the letter files of the Edmund Wilson papers at the Beinecke Library at Yale. Fitzgerald, it seems, had confided in Wilson about the affair and may have introduced the actress to him at the time. Later in life, Wilson wrote Fuller, perhaps with a bit of gallantry, that Scott had considered his sexual encounter with her to be "his first serious love affair." Another bit of possibly corroborative evidence occurs in an entry in Fitzgerald's ledger, dated November 1919. After the notation "New York," he wrote the name "Rosalind." The general assumption has been that this was a reference to Zelda's sister, but it may well be Fitzgerald's brief remembrance of the English actress.

Rosalinde Fuller first came to the United States in 1913, with two younger sisters, Dorothy and Cynthia, touring the country, singing and playing the folk songs of their Dorset village. The tour was successful enough to merit a performance for President Wilson at the White House.

Then in her early twenties, Fuller was an emancipated and emancipating woman, a believer in free love who practiced what she preached. In New York, in 1916, she had a brisk but meaningful affair with her new brother-in-law, Max Eastman. (Fuller's brother Walter, who had accompanied the sisters on tour, had married Max's sister, Crystal.) Eastman had been struck by Rosalinde's beauty and charms when he saw her in performance, stepping forward from the trio to sing "She's gone with the raggle-taggle Gipsies, Oh!" Unhappily married, separated from his wife, despondent, and ill, he became an eager disciple when the actress, on a visit to his apartment, slipped into his bed, initiating a torrid, two-day affair that released him from his sexual inhibitions and sense of guilt. The affair may have been brief, but the affection was enduring. The two remained friends, corresponded for years, long after the Fuller sisters returned to England in 1917.

It was not until August 1919 that Rosalinde Fuller returned to the United States, alone, determined to make a career for herself as an actress rather than a singer. It could only have been a matter of months after her arrival that she met Fitzgerald. In an unpublished autobiography and in subsequent family letters, Fuller gave a vivid and racy account of her first meeting with Fitzgerald at a party at the Plaza Hotel. Amid the chatter and noise, she became aware of a blond young man with a "gay challenging face," staring at her from across the room. Fitzgerald, she noted, "looked like one of the attendants in allegorical paintings," though she acknowledged that he was a bit smaller than a "god." Introducing himself, he hastily suggested that they leave the party. Rosalinde was a plucky girl and a perennial optimist. ("I have, all my life, lived very consciously in the present and future and have hardly ever looked back," she once

commented.) She immediately agreed. Across from the Plaza, Fitzgerald hired a hansom:

> Scott roused the driver and we got in pulling the rough hairy rug
> round our legs. Scott shut the folding doors as though sealing an
> envelope. We slipped up Fifth Avenue and through the park to
> Riverside Drive. We called the horse Pegasus because we seemed
> to have left the earth and were riding in a circuit of our delight.
> The milky river was very quiet. . . . The clip-clop of the horse's
> hoofs made a background to our discovery of each other's bodies.
> Eager hands feeling in warm secret places under the old rug, while
> the bouncing of the horse's bottom was our only contact with the
> outside world.
>   "You have Egyptian ears," whispered Scott, "and the look of
> a naughty boy."

According to Fuller's testimony, she and Fitzgerald met frequently after that first night. The affair was brief but intensely
sexual. Her recollection is that once they had used Spanish fly, each
standing in a corner of Fitzgerald's hotel room to see what the
"devastating" effect would be. But it only made them feel self-
conscious. Her account, with its romantic flair, gives the impression
of suddenly liberated children exploring the realms of sex. Evidently
she was as effective in demolishing Fitzgerald's sexual inhibitions—
at least for the moment—as she had been with Eastman. There was,
she recalled, "no end to our delight and discovery of one another.
We made love everywhere, in theatre boxes, country fields, under
the sun, moon and stars. We seemed to be riding on some unreal
circus railway, clinging together. . . ."

Fitzgerald took her to speakeasies; occasionally they talked of
writing and of their own dreams of success. Both of them were
restlessly ambitious and self-involved: "We never talked of other
people we were really only interested in ourselves at the particular
time." Fitzgerald seems not to have mentioned Zelda. "I think he
had met her," Fuller recalled, "but she wouldn't marry him until
he had made some money. So when we met we were both trying
our luck at making a living, me in the theatre, he by having his
books published. I think he showed me a writing case full of the
manuscript of his first success."

After that brief interlude of sexual liberation, Fitzgerald, unlike
Eastman, never corresponded with Rosalinde Fuller and evidently

never saw her again. Perhaps he felt some sense of shame at having let himself go so far, in yielding to his physical inclinations. Rosalinde's recollection was that Fitzgerald had gone "back down South to Zelda." She managed to get parts in the John Murray Anderson revues, like *What's in a Name,* and eventually became a lead singer in Anderson's highly popular *Greenwich Village Follies.* It was through her appearance in *What's in a Name* that she met the man with whom she would have a lifelong relationship, Francis Bruguière, an urbane American theatrical photographer who had established a reputation working for *Vogue, Harper's Bazaar,* and the Theater Guild. Rosalinde Fuller never became a spectacular success in New York. Her big break as an actress came in 1922, with the famous John Barrymore production of *Hamlet,* in which she played Ophelia. After a brief stint with the Provincetown Playhouse, and a few more Broadway appearances, Fuller returned to London and enjoyed a lengthy and successful career and far more recognition than she had in the United States.

A minor affair, perhaps—and an odd, rampantly sexual episode in Fitzgerald's life. But with a beautiful, spirited liberated woman who, for all her independence, was aware of others. About Fitzgerald, she remarked: "Sometimes he spoke of writing and the theatre and told me of his disappointment. I felt that he was one of those people who could never be satisfied with life. He seemed to feel there must be something more, that he hadn't gotten and would never get." Given the persistence, in Fitzgerald's fiction, of the role of the ingénue, Rosalinde Fuller assumes more importance. "Our love-affair lasted only a short time," Fuller noted in her autobiography, "but often in his stories I think I can see bits of myself dressed up in other situations."

The nighttime carriage ride through New York, with its sense of warmth and intimacy, in fact, became something of a clue to Rosalinde Fuller's presence in Fitzgerald's fictional world. One of the first instances, probably, is in the story "Myra Meets His Family," a farce about a slightly superannuated vamp who goes after a very reluctant wealthy bachelor, which Fitzgerald had written earlier, but which he revised after his New York expedition. ("I came home in a thoroughly nervous alcoholic state & revised two tales that went the complete rounds of magazines last April," Fitzgerald wrote Max Perkins from St. Paul. "I did 'em in four days & sent 'em to Reynolds.") In the story, the romantic carriage ride that Myra Harper and Knowleton Whitney take up Fifth Avenue in the November twilight may have been the result of his recent experience. It is also very likely that Rosalinde Fuller had some relation to the character of the famous musical comedy star Roxanne Milbank, who marries the doomed author, Jeffrey Curtain, in the 1920 story "The Lees of Happiness." Roxanne is called the "Venus of the hansom cab" in the story. And in a chillingly cruel scene in *The Great Gatsby,* it is during a victoria ride through Central Park that the narrator, Nick Carraway, draws Jordan Baker close to himself and kisses her "wan, scornful mouth" and convinces himself, briefly, that he is in love. In *Tender Is the Night,* it is in a Paris cab that the ingénue Rosemary Hoyt and Dick Diver acknowledge their sexual attraction for each other with a passionate kiss, just before a flawed attempt at love-making in her hotel room.

Back in St. Paul, Fitzgerald wrote Ludlow Fowler on January 1: "I've got several damn strange adventures to tell you when I see you." Perhaps he had his adventures with Rosalinde Fuller in mind. Fitzgerald did, in fact, go south not long after. Providentially, Harold Ober sold "Myra Meets His Family" and another story to *The Saturday Evening Post.* On the proceeds from the sales, Fitzgerald, convinced that he had a touch of tuberculosis and that the St. Paul winter was bad for him, planned to go to New Orleans, stopping at Montgomery on the way. He intended to write and to read the galley proofs of his first novel there.

On the trip down, he did stop at Montgomery to see Zelda, and he made two visits to her during his stay in New Orleans. The two had resumed their relationship and were — unofficially — engaged. They were drinking together and had resumed their sexual relationship. One of the consequences was that Zelda, some time in February, suspected that she was pregnant. Fitzgerald sent her some pills. But Zelda balked.

> I wanted to, for your sake [she told him], because I know what a mess I'm making and how inconvenient it's all going to be — but I simply *can't* and *won't* take those awful pills — so I've thrown them away. I'd rather take carbolic acid. You see, as long as I feel that I had the right, I don't much mind what happens — and besides, I'd rather have a *whole family* than sacrifice my self-respect. . . . I'd feel like a damned whore if I took even one.

She advised him not to do anything until she was certain. It was sensible advice; it turned out that she was not pregnant after all.

Since the beginning of the year, Harold Ober had been pushing Fitzgerald's short stories with great success. He sold four more — "The Camel's Back," "Bernice Bobs Her Hair," "The Ice Palace," and "The Offshore Pirate" — to *The Saturday Evening Post* at fees that rose from $400 to $500. Fitzgerald shared his enthusiasm and good fortune with Zelda. He sent her an expensive platinum and diamond watch. Zelda's response was predictably exuberant: "O, Scott, it's so be-au-ti-ful — and the back's just as pretty as the front. . . . I've turned it over four hundred times to see 'from Scott to Zelda.' " The expensive gift was the occasion for Zelda's telling her mother about their plans: "I thought maybe it might interest her to know, so she sat on the edge of the bed while I told her we were going to marry each other pretty soon. . . . Now that she knows, everything seems mighty definite and nice, and I'm not a bit scared or shaky." In her mind, Zelda thought of herself and Fitzgerald as "very splashy vivid pictures, those kind with the details left out," but she was convinced that their colors would blend. She was in such an obliging mood that she agreed to read the Frank Norris novel *McTeague,* which Fitzgerald had foisted on her. "But you may have to marry a corpse when I finish," she told him. "It certainly makes a miserable start. . . . All authors who want to make things true to life make them *smell bad.*" She hoped Fitzgerald did not intend to become a realist.

Late in February, Fitzgerald sold the movie rights to his *Post* story "Head and Shoulders" to the Metro Studios. He immediately wired the news and the staggering amount — $2500 — no doubt impressing her and the telegraph operators as well. I LOVE YOU DEAREST GIRL, he added. The film version, retitled *The Chorus Girl's Romance,* starring Viola Dana, was produced within the year. The movies represented another of those long and glittering avenues to success that seemed to stretch before Fitzgerald early in his career. And in that volatile world, success bred more success. Within the year, Fitzgerald sold the options for two more stories, "Myra Meets His Family" and "The Offshore Pirate." He also signed a contract with Metro for the film rights on his future stories. Altogether, in 1920 he earned $7425 through film rights and options on stories that he considered commercial, if not wholly meretricious.

It was not until March that their engagement was officially

announced. Fitzgerald sent Zelda an orchid corsage. Some time before that, Zelda had written him an unusually quiet and confident
letter:

> Darling Heart, our fairy tale is almost ended, and we're going to
> marry and live happily ever afterward just like the princess in her
> tower who worried you so much — and made me so very cross by
> her constant recurrence — I'm so sorry for all the times I've been
> mean and hateful — for all the miserable minutes I've caused you
> when we could have been so happy. You deserve so much — so very
> much. . . .

If Fitzgerald enjoyed his phenomenal success, he seems not to
have experienced it with the same sangfroid that Zelda did. For one
thing, he was finding it necessary to justify Zelda to disapproving
friends like Isabelle Amorous, the sister of his Newman classmate
Martin Amorous. "Any girl," Fitzgerald wrote Isabelle, "who gets
stewed in public, who frankly enjoys and tells shocking stories, who
smokes constantly and makes the remark that she has 'kissed thousands of men and intends to kiss thousands more' cannot be considered beyond reproach even if above it. But Isabelle, I fell in love
with her courage, her sincerity and her flaming self-respect." It was,
of course, a courageous defense, a good attempt at judging Zelda
by something other than conventional standards. But, then, Fitzgerald rather spoiled his case with the extraordinary, if not preposterous, claim that Zelda was, in effect, his replacement for the Almighty. "You're still a catholic," he told Isabelle, "but Zelda's the
only God I have left now."

At the back of Fitzgerald's mind, too, there seems to have been
a nagging suspicion that he had bought his bride with his success.
Years later, he would describe his feelings as a bridegroom: "The
man with the jingle of money in his pocket who married the girl a
year later would always cherish an abiding distrust, an animosity,
toward the leisure class — not the conviction of a revolutionist, but
the smoldering hatred of a peasant." Fitzgerald would claim that he
had "never been able to stop wondering where my friends' money
came from, nor to stop thinking that at some time a sort of *droit de
seigneur* might have been exercised to give one of them my girl."
Strong words, but it is best to remember that they were voiced in
the mid-1930s, when strong opinions were fashionable. Fitzgerald,

like many writers of the time, had been sampling the heady waters of Marxism.

It is difficult to know how much emphasis to put on some of the bitter suspicions Fitzgerald seemed to be harboring at the time of his marriage. His disapproval of his own parents appears to have been chronic. But at the time of his marriage he may have been nurturing rather vicious feelings against the equally inoffensive Minnie Sayre. She had had no objections to Zelda's being married in a Catholic church and had encouraged the couple to have the ceremony in New York. "As you know," she wrote Fitzgerald at the time, "Zelda has had several admirers; but you seem to be the only one to make anything like a permanent impression. . . . Your church is all right with me. A good Catholic is as good as any other good man and that is good enough. It will take more than the Pope to make Zelda good: you will have to call on God Almighty direct."

In a bitter time, at the end of his life, when he was a failure, supporting an insane wife who was confined to one asylum after another, Fitzgerald came to believe that Minnie Sayre had been the agent of his unhappiness. In the fall of 1939, in a long, self-pitying letter to Zelda, which charitably he did not send, Fitzgerald accused Minnie Sayre of being a sinister witch. He charged that Zelda had been a notorious drunk when he had first met her, that her mother had forced the marriage on him, and that Zelda had been damaged goods, having slept with other men before he had had sex with her. The implication was that Minnie had encouraged the out-of-town marriage as a means of removing the taint of local scandal.

He wrote that Zelda had been a mere romantic extension of her mother's thwarted ambitions:

> You were to be the stuffed dummy — true or false, screwed or chaste, honest or bogus — on which she was to satisfy her egotism. She chose me — and she did — and you submitted at the moment when your passion for me was at as low ebb as mine for you. . . . I never wanted the Zelda I married.

The rant did not end there but raveled out to even more bitter accusations:

> The assumption is that you were a great prize package — by your own admission many years after (and for which I have [never] reproached you) you had been seduced and provincially outcast. I

sensed this the night we slept together first for you're a poor bluffer
and I loved you—romantically—like your mother, for your beauty
and defiant intelligence, but unlike her I wanted to make it useful.
I failed, as she did, but my intentions were a hell of a lot purer.

If, on the eve of his marriage, Fitzgerald had felt even the mere
beginnings of these suspicions, then, in Zelda's innocent words, their
fairy tale had indeed ended.

PART TWO

3

The Metropolitan Spirit

SINCE HIS CHILDHOOD, according to Fitzgerald, New York had been the mecca of his ambitions. He claimed that he had had his first glimpse of it when he was ten: a moment that crystallized into his symbol of the city—a ferry boat moving slowly from the Jersey shore toward Manhattan in the early dawn. His second vision of it was more reliable: as a Newman boy of fifteen, graduated into long pants, he attended the theater and saw performances by Ina Claire and Gertrude Bryan and felt a "melancholy love" for both, unable to choose: "So they blurred into one lovely entity, the girl. She was my second symbol of New York. The ferry boat stood for triumph, the girl for romance." The third symbol came later, on that gray day when he caught sight of Edmund Wilson, striding along the street full of confidence and energy, seeming to draw strength from the city pavements and some force Fitzgerald could describe only as "that new thing—the Metropolitan spirit."

Throughout Fitzgerald's life, his stories and his notebook entries would register a quickened pace when he described the life of New York. He would speak of its "flashing, dynamic good looks, its tall man's quick-step." Days and nights there would be "as tense as singing wires." Even the monotonous rows of drab apartment buildings would have their moment, turning "darkly mysterious" at night. On crisp autumn afternoons, riding atop a Fifth Avenue bus, he might catch sight of a passing face—"an interested glance, a flash of color"—and it would assume "the proportion of an intrigue." The lights of many battleships, anchored on the dark Hudson, drifted like so many "water jewels," and the image became fixed in his memory. Fitzgerald felt that he could sense the very rhythm of a city weekend — "its birth, its planned gaieties and its announced end." It was a matter of pride with him that he could take "the style and glitter of New York even above its own evaluation." And on that April day in 1920, when he was married, he had returned in triumph with his girl. He was an author at the very edge of success and celebrity, in a city full of dazzling contingencies.

Easter Sunday was the first day of their honeymoon, a holiday they commemorated with an Easter lily, stationed on the dresser in their Biltmore suite, Room 2109. It was a gray day with intermittent showers, but that had not deterred the crowds of worshipers lined up outside the city's many churches. Perhaps it was the sight of the fashionable women along Fifth Avenue that prompted the first of Fitzgerald's official edicts as husband. A few days later, he sent Zelda out in the company of his former St. Paul girl friend, Marie Hersey, to buy a new wardrobe. Zelda had arrived in New York with flouncy organdy dresses that lacked the chic Fitzgerald expected in a sophisticated woman, especially his wife. "You've got to help me!" he told Marie. "Zelda wants to buy nothing but frills and furbelows and you can't go around New York in that kind of thing."

Zelda would remember the shopping expedition with something less than unadulterated pleasure. It was a day of rippling sunlight along Fifth Avenue, and she had bought a stylish Jean Patou suit. Afterward, she and Marie had tea in the Plaza Grill. Fifteen years later, she recalled, with a hint of lingering resentment, that the suit had never been worn, had been stored in a trunk, and was by then the victim of moths. "We are glad — oh, so relieved, to find it devastated at last," she reported with mocking humor. The man who marries, then attempts to remodel his Galatea, can hardly expect thanks for his pains.

Zelda's first impressions of New York were as indelible as Scott's: twilights that hung like indigo washes above the skyline, lights in tall buildings burning hazily and far away in blue nights. Perhaps because of her husband's criticism, she pictured her New York as a world of stylish women. In the orange glow of the Biltmore façade, there were girls with marcel waves, wearing orchids and colored shoes, swarming about the doorman. Under the scalloped portico of the Ritz, women in ermine coats stepped into waiting cabs. She would remember the nickel glitter of the traffic as it flowed down darkening streets. She had an uncanny sensitivity to color and mood.

She would recall "the strangeness and excitement of New York, of reporters and furry smothered hotel lobbies, the brightness of the sun on the window panes and the prickly dust of late spring."

In their suite at the Biltmore, the Fitzgeralds entertained friends. It was there, shortly after the wedding, that Fitzgerald's Princeton colleagues Bunny Wilson and John Peale Bishop met Zelda for the first time. The two bachelors, both on the staff of *Vanity Fair,* had drinks with the newlyweds — a new and fashionable cocktail, the Orange Blossom, made of orange juice and bootleg gin. Unlike several of Fitzgerald's friends, Wilson always felt considerable respect for Zelda, finding her an attractive and interesting personality. On that first meeting, Wilson thought her "very pretty and languid" as she lay on her back on a couch, but suspected she was still embarrassed about the fancy clothes her mother had outfitted her with. They were, Wilson felt, "appropriate for a Southern belle, but not the right thing for New York." Zelda was to regret her mother's taste for some time. Bishop at first thought Zelda beautiful (it was he who described her as a "barbarian princess"), and with Southern chivalry carried on an open flirtation with her in front of Fitzgerald. In later years, however, after a long marriage to an efficient and wealthy wife, Bishop blamed Zelda for Fitzgerald's drunkenness and the waste of his talent. On those rainy days when no one came to call on the Fitzgeralds, they kept to their hotel room, drinking in the company of a wilting Easter lily, and leaned out the window, listening to the hotel band playing show tunes from a new musical, *The Night Boat.*

New York, in the twenties, was a stage on which the theatrical and literary worlds mingled on lively and unapologetic terms. Fitzgerald, stagestruck since youth, was in his element. In the Japanese Gardens of the Ritz, he and Zelda lunched with George Jean Nathan and his current flirtation, Kay Laurell, the Ziegfeld Follies star. Fitzgerald described her as "wistful" — a euphemism, perhaps. Helen Hayes, an ingénue at the time, appearing in *Babs,* knew Laurell a good deal more intimately and described her as a thoroughly practiced gold digger ("the skull and crossbones were right out there on the label for all to see"); nonetheless, she admired the honesty of the glamorous star. At the Montmartre, one of his favorite nightspots, Fitzgerald could catch a glimpse of another Follies queen, Lilyan Tashman, weaving around the dance floor with some highly liquored college boy. At the Midnight Frolic, another popular spot, it was possible to dance elbow to elbow with the dazzlingly untalented Marion Davies, William Randolph Hearst's high-priced mistress. Superfluous as she was, she had an endearing habit of telling off the sycophants who hovered around the wealthy Hearst, "You may be the world to Bill, dear — but you're only a bore to me." Edmund Wilson, who met her at New York parties, neatly summed up her social and dramatic gifts: "common, graceless and dull, with one stiff grimace to express every emotion."

During the first months of the Fitzgeralds' extended honeymoon, the New York theatrical season was in full swing. Ina Claire, Fitzgerald's idol, was appearing at the Lyceum in a brisk comedy, *The Gold Diggers,* and the vamp Theda Bara was installed at the Shubert in *The Blue Flame.* The reigning queen of the season was Marilyn Miller, in *Sally.* (Rosalind Sayre Smith, who had seen the blond star the year before, contended that Zelda could pass for her twin. It agitated Zelda so much that she could do nothing but act and dance for two days. Zelda was as stagestruck as her husband.) For a time, all three of the Barrymores were starring on Broadway. Ethel was appearing in Zoë Akins' *Declassée,* one of her earliest hits, at the Empire; Lionel was in *The Letter of the Law* at the Criterion. John, whose legend would forever be linked with Shakespearean roles, opened in his first, *Richard III,* at the Plymouth. But the producers had strived too much for authenticity; the armor Barrymore donned for the battle scenes became so hot under the lights that the actor steamed inside, and the dressers could not touch it when he came offstage for a change. On the Fitzgeralds' wedding day, the newspapers reported that performances were being cancelled because the actor had had a nervous breakdown.

As devotees of the theater, the Fitzgeralds were a menace. They were quite likely to give more dramatic performances than what was going on behind the proscenium. (It was an old habit with Zelda, who, even when she was "not one bit drunk or disorderly," used to gossip so much with her friends in the Montgomery theaters that the performers stopped the orchestra.) At the performance of *George White's Scandals,* Fitzgerald upstaged the actors by doing the scandalous — undressing in public. He managed to get down to his undershirt before the ushers escorted him outside. At the comedy *Enter Madame,* the Fitzgeralds and their guests laughed at their own jokes instead of the playwright's. Zelda fell off her seat; the actors complained; the management asked them to leave. Zelda stormed out in a huff, trailed by Scott. The Fitzgeralds made splashy appearances in the gossip columns: Zelda later took a plunge in a downtown public fountain. (The legend is divided as to the exact location, whether Union Square or Washington Square.) Fitzgerald, not to be outdone, re-created the event in the chic uptown waters of the Pulitzer Fountain, outside the Plaza Hotel. They soon found themselves the spokesmen for a new generation of gilded youth. Later in his life, in a reminiscence titled "My Lost City," Fitzgerald stated, disingenuously, that the role had been thrust on them and that they found it confusing: "Within a few months after our embarkation on the Metropolitan venture we scarcely knew any more who we were and we hadn't a notion what we were." He had diagnosed the symptoms of their disorder accurately enough.

Caught up in those heady excitements, Fitzgerald — on the surface, at least — seems not to have paid much attention to what was going on in the world beyond the best hotels and the liveliest nightspots. It is unlikely that a week after his marriage he would have noticed an unconfirmed report in *The New York Times* that John Reed, a writer for *Masses* and the American historian of the Russian Revolution, had been executed in Finland. The report was false; Reed had been arrested on charges of smuggling jewelry and money. He was released in June and returned to Russia, where he died of typhus four months afterward. It was not until a decade later, when respectable authors were expected to have political consciences, that Reed became the focus of some of Fitzgerald's belated social views. Fitzgerald claimed that the Jazz Age "had no interest in politics at all." His own "political conscience," he maintained, had scarcely existed then, except as an element of irony in his writing. Lacking a rousing conclusion to *This Side of Paradise,* and being under the spell of H. G. Wells, he had simply turned Amory Blaine into an unconvincing Fabian socialist and left him arguing with a sinister capitalist who wore goggles.

But at the outset of the Jazz Age, Fitzgerald was riding high on good reviews and financial success. Burton Rascoe, in the *Chicago Daily Tribune,* said that the book gave its author "fair claim to membership in that small squad of contemporary American fictionists who are producing literature." He even had kind words for the book's structure, finding it full of "happy influences," such as James Joyce's *A Portrait of the Artist as a Young Man. The New York Times* reviewer thought it a fascinating tale in the "glorious spirit of abounding youth." And H. L. Mencken declared it the "best American novel" he had read of late, "original in structure, extremely sophisticated in manner." Within the year, the book went through nine printings, netting Fitzgerald $6200. And it would bring in only slightly less in 1921.

But it did not take much to bring Fitzgerald down a peg. Heywood Broun, of the *New York Tribune,* surprised by the book's reception, made an astute reference to the hero's formidable self-consciousness: "He sees himself constantly not as a human being, but as a man in a novel or in a play. Every move is a picture and there is a camera man behind each tree." Like many writers, oversensitive to blame but taking praise as their due, Fitzgerald was, for several days afterward, "notably poor company." He invited the paunchy and rumpled critic to lunch, and in a "kindly way" Fitzgerald said that it was a shame Broun had let his life slip away without accomplishing anything. Broun had just turned the corner into his thirties.

Nor was Fitzgerald particularly happy about the errors and misspellings in the text, which became something of a publishing scandal and then a joke after the book appeared. On his honeymoon and on Biltmore stationery, he sent Perkins a list of some twenty-six corrections: "Change Mckenzie to Mackenzie"; "Should be *unimpeachable* instead of *impeachable.*" But then he added to the confusion by offering new misspellings to correct the old ones, changing the name of the popular author Mary Roberts Rinehart to "Rineheart" or suggesting that one of his characters "shimmee entheusiasticly." F. P. Adams, in his *New York Tribune* column, "The Conning Tower," regularly published lists of errors found in the subsequent printings of *This Side of Paradise.* During the summer, the disgruntled Fitzgerald wrote Max Perkins, "F.P.A. is at it again. Here is his latest list."

The Fitzgeralds were not long in New York when they carried their partying beyond the city limits. On the weekend of April 24, Scott and Zelda went to Princeton to chaperone a house party at Cottage. Intending to shock the academic community, he introduced Zelda as his mistress. And in the course of a "rather gay party" that circulated around the campus in a robin's egg blue motorcar, Fitzgerald acquired a black eye. Writing to Marie Hersey about the weekend, Fitzgerald boasted: "We were there three days, Zelda and five men in Harvey Firestone's car, and not one of us drew a sober breath. . . . It was the damnedest party ever held in Princeton and everybody in the University will agree." Their continuous partying at the Biltmore had more direct results: the management asked them to leave, because their antics were disturbing the other guests. They moved to the stuffy but nearby Commodore, where they promptly created another uproar by playing games in the revolving door.

Only a week after the Princeton revels, Fitzgerald returned to the campus for a May Day dinner in honor of former *Nassau Lit* editors. He accompanied Wilson, Bishop, and Stanley Dell in Dell's Buick. Zelda was pointedly left behind, in the company of Dell's wife, Marion. Before the trip, Wilson had written to Christian Gauss that Fitzgerald was reluctant about the return engagement. "I think he will be fairly tame," Wilson commented, "because he is going to leave Zelda at the Commodore. I trust that she will seize the opportunity to run away with the elevator boy or something."

On the trip down, the warm spring day, the liquor, the anticipated reunion, brought out the lyrical vein in the group, and Fitzgerald from time to time exulted, "Isn't it wonderful! Princeton! May! Old friends!" The friends arrived at the campus fairly squiffed. Having bought appropriate stage props in New York—wreaths of gilded laurel leaves, a lyre, pipes of Pan—they proceeded to Gauss's front lawn, crowning him and paying homage in extemporary verses. Fitzgerald, now quite drunk, stumbled his way to Cottage. There, he was informed that his membership had been suspended, because of his disorderly behavior on the previous visit. He was told that he could not stay; a scuffle ensued and he was ejected from the premises. Miffed, he managed to get himself to the railroad station, where he took the seven o'clock train to New York. Wilson, who composed a rambling ode on the Princeton ceremonies, claimed that Fitzgerald, "looking like a tarnished Apollo," had acquired two black eyes on this occasion.

Not long after, Fitzgerald received a letter that added insult to his minor injuries. It was from President John Grier Hibben of Princeton, criticizing the portrait of the university Fitzgerald had painted in *This Side of Paradise.* Hibben complained that Fitzgerald had made Princeton seem little better than a country club, full of young men lounging around in an atmosphere of calculation and snobbishness. Fitzgerald answered, in the tone of a scolded school-boy, that his picture of collegiate life may have been cynical, but that his years at the university hadn't been particularly happy ones.

He agreed that he may have overstressed the country club angle for the sake of reader interest, but he assured Hibben that he loved Princeton "better than any place on earth."

Then, in self-defense, he asserted that he had wasted years trying to fit himself into a curriculum that had been made for the average student. It had tied him down, "taken away the honors I'd wanted, bent my nose over a chemistry book and said 'No fun, no activities, no offices, no Triangle trips — no, not even a diploma if you can't do chemistry.'" There was not the slightest indication that the function of the university might have been educational rather than social. Nor was there any mention of academic abilities when, by way of concession, Fitzgerald listed the virtues of Princeton (and Yale) men over other Ivy Leaguers. Princeton men, he said, were "cleaner, healthier, better looking, better dressed, wealthier and more attractive than any undergraduate body in the country."

Fitzgerald's letter was typical of his performances over the years: truculent on one hand, mollifying on the other. He wanted to be restored to grace, but on his own terms. It is clear that he had been deeply offended by his ouster from Cottage. Given his quixotic loyalty to sometimes sophomoric values, he may not have been overstating the case when he summed up his feelings about his Princeton disgrace: "On that day in 1920 most of the joy went out of my success."

In his diaries of the twenties and thirties, Edmund Wilson is a twentieth-century Samuel Pepys, chronicling the marital, extramarital, conventional, and abnormal sexual manners and mores of the New York literary and theatrical pesonalities of the period. Wilson's accounts of his own affairs with women — the casual pickups and occasional prostitutes, the more serious affairs with the educated women of his circle — have a sensual life, are full of incisive descriptions of women's hair, clothing, undergarments, shoes. So much so, they seem verbal equivalents of the erotic drawings and watercolors of Jules Pascin, the American master of the genre during that same period.

But Wilson's diaries offer more than the graphic look of the time. Aside from their literary worth, they reveal the freewheeling, hard-boiled, and experimental outlook toward sex and sexual practices that became the attitude of the younger generation after World

War I. Unlike Fitzgerald, whose prudishness on the subject was nurtured by a puritanical Irish Catholic upbringing ("A New England conscience — developed in Minnesota," Fitzgerald admitted), Wilson exhibited a candor that was even a bit ahead of his hedonistic times. There was an element of class distinction in all this: Wilson tended to be more open about his affairs with lower-class girls than with women like the poets Edna St. Vincent Millay and Elinor Hoyt Wylie, with whom he was more deeply involved. It had taken him some time, he confessed, to lose his innocence. He frankly recalled the awkward moment when he had waited outside a Greenwich Village drugstore until there were no women present before walking up to the pharmacist to ask for a condom. Unfortunately, the condom, when tested, had burst, and he considered it an ill omen. "I soon got over my shyness with women," he wrote, "but I was a victim of the hazards of sex — from which I might have been saved by previous experience: abortions, gonorrhea, entanglements, a broken heart."

He was a connoisseur of burlesque shows, liked to record the conversations of wisecracking chorus girls, the remarks heard backstage at the Ziegfeld Follies. His diaries are full of sexual snippets, from the suggestive songs of the era, like "Flamin' Mamie" —

> When it comes to lovin' — she's a human oven!
> Awful funny — paper money —

to the gossip of the homosexuals in the Men's Wear Department at *Vanity Fair*. He also set down the randy talk of friends like Ted Paramore, the easygoing Yale graduate who regaled him with stories about the prowess of others, including a mutual friend at the Yale Club: "You couldn't have him in the room with a girl fifteen minutes but you'd find a condom behind the clock."

Paramore, another of the Prohibition-era heavy drinkers, had his own successful formula for seductions: he gave his "more inexperienced girlfriends" a copy of Dr. Robey's sex manual to read, then waited for the ripe plums to fall. His alcoholism and his amiable nature were factors in his conquests; women mothered him or tried to save him from himself. During Paramore's frequent visits to his family in Santa Barbara, he would send Wilson long, bawdy accounts of the heated-up sexual activities on the West Coast. One letter ended, "And yet there are people who say that Fitz and Mrs. Wharton don't know their stuff." But there was, as well, a marvelously comic innocence at work in the musky atmosphere of the twenties. Once, Paramore tried to take a girl friend on a sexual holiday in Mexico. "Oh, Teddy," she moaned, "when we came back, we wouldn't be pure!"

At the time of the Fitzgeralds' honeymoon in New York, Wilson was desperately in love with Edna St. Vincent Millay, the reigning and promiscuous beauty of the postwar generation. It was an impossible three-cornered romance that also included Wilson's friend and fellow editor at *Vanity Fair,* John Peale Bishop. On dates together, the three would indulge in serious petting on a couch, Wilson assigned the lower regions of the poet, while Bishop was entrusted with the top half. Millay complained that the two men managed to keep the romance going without breaking up their own friendship. She referred to them as her "choir boys of Hell." Bishop called her "the Great Queen."

It seems to have been Millay who broke up Wilson's convenient domestic life. After the war, he was once more sharing an apartment with Larry Noyes and the oboe-playing Morris Belknap. Millay, at the time, was living in a dreary cold-water flat. Wilson suggested that she take her baths at his apartment on West Sixteenth Street. "This had, I believe, on Morris and Larry a profoundly shocking effect," Wilson claimed. The result was that he and Ted Paramore decided to share an uptown railroad flat on Lexington Avenue. It was above a furrier's shop and smelled often like wet cat, but there was room enough for each to have separate quarters, where they could invite their girl friends in privacy. The apartment was the scene of a number of boozy parties. Once, having mistakenly carried off some of Larry Noyes's belongings, Wilson had the "bad taste" to send them back with a box of condoms. Noyes archly responded, "I wonder you can spare them."

The odd thing about Wilson's youthful love life is that he seemed to have a penchant for three-sided affairs. During the years he roomed with Paramore, the latter was having a serious love affair with Margaret Canby, a handsome young woman to whom Wilson was obviously attracted. Years later, in the thirties, Wilson married Margaret Canby. Two years after the marriage, which appeared to have been very happy, Margaret Canby died in an accidental fall. Wilson recorded, quite frankly, that he had begun to indulge in homosexual fantasies, some of which involved Paramore. It is doubtful that he had any serious homosexual inclinations; he had seen such relationships while he was in the service and put them down as simple animal satisfaction. And he was inclined to believe that the "cold fishy side" of Plato that he disliked was the result of the Greek philosopher's homosexual tendencies. But Wilson had — and was able to acknowledge — a greater curiosity and greater tolerance for the varieties of sexual experience than Fitzgerald was ever able to manage.

Nowhere in Fitzgerald's notebooks will one find sexual discussions as frank and forthright as those of Wilson's diaries. (Later in life, however, when Fitzgerald was drunk, he could become nasty and abusive toward women in public, referring to them outright as "cunts." And though he considered himself a youthful "connoisseur of kisses" and could write about them comically, as he did in the Myra St. Clair episode in *This Side of Paradise,* Fitzgerald seems to have had moments of repugnance regarding the physical aspects of sex. Amory Blaine, age thirteen, has finally maneuvered Myra into a first kiss:

> Sudden revulsion seized Amory, disgust, loathing for the whole incident. He desired frantically to be away, never to see Myra again, never to kiss any one; he became conscious of his face and hers, of their clinging hands, and he wanted to creep out of his body and hide somewhere safe out of sight, up in the corner of his mind.

When Myra asks to be kissed again, Amory turns virginal and refuses: "I don't want to." That episode, in the Fitzgerald literature, has a marvelous rightness. But the truth is that the many descriptions and occasional perceptions about women in Fitzgerald's notebooks are glowingly romantic and perfectly cerebral.

> She kissed him several times then in the mouth, her face getting big as it came up to him, her hands holding him by the shoulders, and still he kept his arms by his side.

> Her face, flushed with cold and then warmed again with the dance, was a riot of lovely, delicate pinks, like so many carnations. . . .

> Her body was so assertively adequate that someone remarked that she always looked as if she had nothing on underneath her dress but it was probably wrong.

Mae Purley, without the involuntary quiver of an eyelash, fitted the young man into her current dream.

Mae's pale face and burning lips faded off, faded out, against the wild dark background of the war.

Although many of the observations Fitzgerald recorded were certainly intended for his stories—there is the tone of the proper and the publishable about them—one seldom encounters either in the published work or the personal notes the kind of easy, give-and-take sexuality that crops up in Wilson. As far as sex is concerned, Fitzgerald was a moralist in white knickers.

Zelda, on the other hand, had a relaxed attitude toward such matters. She flirted easily; Wilson remembered, appreciatively, "Zelda used to say that hotel bedrooms excited her erotically." And Fitzgerald, in *This Side of Paradise,* evidently meant to praise her in his delineation of certain aspects of Rosalind's character: "She loves shocking stories; she has that coarse streak that usually goes with natures that are both fine and big." But one should remember that Fitzgerald's notions of coarseness probably had a low threshhold at the time. Zelda had an eye for attractive men, and teasingly first—but later in anger—would taunt Fitzgerald with headwaiters in hotels like the Plaza, who were, she said, just as handsome as he was. Other than with the members of her family, Zelda seems to have had few serious or deeply important relationships with women. "Women she detested," Fitzgerald wrote about his heroine. "They represented qualities that she felt and despised in herself—incipient meanness, conceit, cowardice and petty dishonesty. She once told a roomful of her mother's friends that the only excuse for women was the necessity for a disturbing element among men." Quite likely, some of the character flaws were ones that Fitzgerald had added from his own inventory, rather than those Zelda despised in herself. But she certainly did relish the role of the disturber of the peace. It would make men "much more miserable," she once wrote Fitzgerald, "which is exactly what they need for the improvement of things in general."

It was a role she played with gusto among Fitzgerald's Yale and Princeton friends in New York. She flirted openly with Bishop: "John, I like you better than anybody in the world; I never feel safe with you!—I only like men who kiss as a means to an end. I never know how to treat the other kind." It is possible that she intended her remarks as a goad to her husband, who, as a writer, had achieved a reputation for the wonderfully described and passionate kisses in his stories.

She also carried on with Townsend Martin, a Princeton graduate and nephew of the wealthy philanthropist Frederick Townsend Martin. The elder Martin had written a book critical of his wealthy peers, *The Passing of the Idle Rich,* in which he advocated the doctrine of good works. He was regarded as something of a traitor to his class and may have served as one of the models for the crusty old millionaire reformer, Adam Patch, in *The Beautiful and Damned.* Zelda admired the younger Martin's suave good looks and blue eyes. He was an impeccably dressed bon vivant with no intentions of becoming a professional reformer. To women, he had a habit of announcing that he was decended from "a long line of bachelors." He traveled extensively, lived abroad, and was a tiresome name dropper. As a screenwriter, he encouraged Louise Brooks, then a Ziegfeld Follies girl, to take a minor role in *The American Venus,* for which he had written the film script. It launched the dark-haired twenty-year-old actress into the movie career that culminated in her most famous film, *Lulu.* Martin generously shared his spacious apartment with John Peale Bishop. (Bishop dedicated his first book of poems, *Green Fruit,* to Martin.) It became a gathering place for the Fitzgeralds, Wilson, and their friends. Occasionally Martin would return from some exotic trip to find Bishop entertaining in one of his luxurious dressing gowns. Though envious of Bishop's panache, Martin was too much the gentleman to complain.

Edmund Wilson was convinced that Fitzgerald was "neurotically jealous" of Zelda. Like a true Southern belle, she was accustomed to flirting with gentlemen admirers. But it is easy to see that Fitzgerald had cause for his anxieties. At first, Zelda made a great game of kissing Bishop and Martin; Fitzgerald would comment genially, "Oh, yes, they really have kisses coming to them, because they weren't at the wedding, and everybody at a wedding always gets a kiss." But she often pushed things too far, walking into Bishop's bedroom and threatening to crawl into bed with him; cornering Martin in the bathroom and demanding that he give her a bath. In Wilson's words, on those occasions Fitzgerald became "a little worried and even huffy." It is difficult to overestimate the importance of the bathroom, that household retreat, in the fictional and factual lives of the Fitzgeralds. It would be the scene of sensual reveries and relaxation for heroes like Anthony Patch, the setting of suicide attempts by Nicole Diver. In the real lives of Scott and Zelda Fitzgerald, it became the mise-en-scène for pitched battles, lockouts, door stormings, and black eyes that were excused as accidental.

Zelda, a bride among bachelors, later said of her honeymoon, "We did not like women and we were happy." At that stage of her life, the forthrightness and egocentricity had charm. But Zelda, too, would have her critics, often female. Among them was Dorothy Parker, whose barb could be as good as her bite. It was Parker who said that Zelda had a "candy-box face," as well as other traits she did not find terribly engaging. "I never thought she was beautiful," Parker told Zelda's biographer Nancy Milford: "She was very blonde . . . very much on a small scale and there was something petulant about her. If she didn't like something she sulked; I didn't find that an attractive trait." But she did think the Fitzgeralds made a startlingly handsome couple. She recalled that it was Robert Sherwood who had introduced her to the honeymoon pair. Her first glimpse of them was the now famous one of Zelda riding down a New York street on the hood of a taxicab, like some overscaled ornament, while Fitzgerald clung to the roof.

It is possible that Parker was mistaken; even celebrities feel the urge to appropriate a good story when they see one. Edmund Wilson claimed that he had arranged the first meeting between the newlyweds and the Hotel Algonquin wit. According to Wilson, Parker had previously met Fitzgerald and was somewhat "beglamoured" with him. This was not unlikely; Fitzgerald had a Prince Charming act that some women considered irresistible.

Wilson's account of the meeting with Dorothy Parker was circumstantial enough. He and the Fitzgeralds had dinner with her at the Algonquin, all of them sitting at one of the long banquettes with their backs to the walls. Dorothy quipped, "This looks like a road company of the Last Supper." Wilson did not say who was occupying the focal position.

Fitzgerald may indeed have welcomed Dorothy Parker's flattering attention. She was already a New York celebrity, and an attractive one. But Fitzgerald could hardly have been unaware of her poisonous wit. Her theatrical reviews in *Vanity Fair* were considered lethal by the more thin-skinned actresses of the American stage. And her shows of affection were not always to be trusted. She had a habit of warmly embracing what presumably was some old friend, but no sooner would the person leave the room than she might turn to a companion and ask, "Did you ever meet such a shit?" Fitzgerald was evidently acquainted with certain sides of her face. In his notebooks he recorded a joke that may have been going the rounds or that he may have made up. Someone asks whether D.P. has injured anyone. The answer is "No, but don't remind her. Maybe she hasn't done her bad deed for the day."

II

It was a year of "Revelry and Marriage"; it was, so Fitzgerald described it, "the happiest year since I was 18." But strangely enough, the happiest moment of that year revealed a certain ambivalence. "I remember riding in a taxi one afternoon," Fitzgerald recalled, "between very tall buildings and under a mauve and rosy sky. I began to bawl because I had everything I wanted and knew I would never be so happy again." It would be ironic if, as his account suggests, Fitzgerald had been alone at that moment of epiphany.

Yet 1920 was a year in which Fitzgerald accomplished very little in the way of writing. During the first month of his honeymoon, he found it impossible to work in a hotel room. And he and Zelda, in any event, were caught up in a whirl of socializing. On the surface, at least, his career was making a meteoric upward curve. His novel was hitting the best-seller lists around the country. Month after month, his stories, sketches, plays, and poems — some twenty pieces in all — appeared in the pages of *The Saturday Evening Post, The Smart Set, Scribner's Magazine, Metropolitan, Vanity Fair,* and the *Nassau Lit.* The lucrative film adaptations from his stories "The Chorus Girl's Romance" and "The Husband Hunter" were being shown around the country before the end of the year. But that air of energy and productiveness was misleading. Virtually all of the stories had been written before his marriage, many of them during a burst of creativity in late 1919. Several of the pieces written afterward were mere self-promotional essays, like "Who's Who and Why," written for *The Saturday Evening Post,* or, what was worse, mere tossoffs from his talent, like "This Is a Magazine," an imaginary conversation between various types of articles within the covers of an imaginary magazine. The latter appeared in *Vanity Fair,* where the fare generally ranged all the way from the lightweight to the light-hearted.

Even Fitzgerald's several attempts to get down to serious work on a second novel (it would have various titles: *The Demon Lover, The Drunkard's Holiday, Darling Heart*) as well as another project, the ruminations of a "complete literary radical," which he intended to call *Diary of a Literary Failure,* had been declared defunct before his April wedding. (Fitzgerald's most noteworthy attempt at writing on a social theme, "May Day," a story dealing with the May Day Riots of 1919 and the suicide of a sensitive, defeated artist, Gordon Sterrett, written in March, was probably a revision of material from one of his abandoned novels.) It was not until late summer that Fitzgerald began talking seriously to his publisher about his second novel, *The Flight of the Rocket.* There is no denying that his marriage and his tendency to celebrate his good fortune had had a damaging effect on his discipline, already shaky, as a writer. The novel that he promised Perkins would be completed by September was not done until the following spring. And over the next three years, there was only a meager crop of stories.

Fortunately—or unfortunately—his agent, Harold Ober, managed to up the prices Fitzgerald received for his stories from $400 for "Head and Shoulders" to $1500 for "The Popular Girl," written in 1921 and published in the following year. Other than that modest harvest, Fitzgerald produced only book reviews and chatty personal essays.

Romance and marriage were to be the narrow focus of much of Fitzgerald's fiction, and it was not unusual that marriage became the theme of several of the more important stories he wrote during the three or four years following his wedding. But though his marriage may have been happy, there was something a little ominous in his fictional treatment of the theme. In the first of his stories, "The Lees of Happiness," written in the summer of the honeymoon year, the writer-husband, Jeffrey Curtain, has a stroke and lives a vegetable existence for the rest of his life. In a later story, "The Adjuster," Charles Hemple suffers a nervous breakdown. The same fate overtakes the hero of Fitzgerald's second novel: Anthony Patch ends up the ruined shell of a man, pushed along the decks of the *Berengaria* in a wheelchair.

It added to Fitzgerald's problems that Zelda, isolated from

Montgomery and old friends and family life, was restless and dissatisfied. Early in May, the Fitzgeralds bought a secondhand Marmon, vintage 1917, with a view to scouring the countryside for a summer cottage where Scott could work in peace. They had given up any notion of settling near Princeton, where they were not welcome. They decided, after inspection, that Rye, New York, was uninhabitable. They had planned to investigate the Lake Champlain area and even considered a cottage in Maine, but they discovered that swimming was out of the question in either place, because the water was too cold. "That was the shock of our lives," Fitzgerald wrote Ruth Sturtevant, "because if Zelda can't swim, she's miserable."

The problem became acute in mid-May, when the management of the Commodore turned them out — "forcibly," according to Fitzgerald. Their style of living was too disruptive. Packing their bags in the Marmon, they started up the Boston Post Road in search of a home. With the luck of children in a fairy tale, they found just the cottage they were looking for, on Compo Road in Westport, Connecticut. It was a charming gray-shingled two-story house of Revolutionary vintage, called the Wakeman Cottage. For a week or so, until the cottage was available, they stayed in a nearby boardinghouse, where the cooking, Zelda complained, was making her fat.

The setting may have been idyllic, but the two-month marriage began to register signs of strain. Zelda, during the early years, had a view of things that was both sentimental and ironclad at one and the same time. She remembered how they had "quarreled over morals once, walking beside a colonial wall under the freshness of lilacs." Domestic life at the Wakeman Cottage was no more orderly or efficient than it had been in a Manhattan hotel. As a bride, Zelda had little intention of playing housekeeper and helpmate. The dirty laundry piled up in the closets until there was little to wear. Fitzgerald, fussy about dress, became exasperated when there were no clean shirts — and no prospects of any; Zelda hadn't bothered to send them to the laundry.

She seems to have been completely innocent about the details of housekeeping. Not long after their arrival, Zelda wrote to their best man, Ludlow Fowler, who had urged them to move to the country and save money, sending him an offhand invitation: "As soon as we get a servant and some sheets from Mamma, you really must come out and recuperate and enjoy the home you helped so much to get organized." (She also warned Fowler that she might be pregnant, but that proved to be another false alarm.) Considering that her husband would earn $18,850 after agency fees, that first year of marriage, it is clear evidence of Zelda's mismanagement that she had to send home to mother for bed linens.

In mid-June, they hired a diminutive Japanese manservant named Tana, who added a certain exotic flavor to the irregular household. Tana was given to tuneless flute-playing, lengthy conversations, and in his fictional incarnation, planned to reinvent the typewriter. Domestic help did not improve the Fitzgeralds' marital situation. At least, that is what Alec McKaig, Fitzgerald's Princeton friend, observed. McKaig, snub-nosed, with curly hair parted in the middle, a man of brisk charm, was working at an advertising office at the time. He had literary ambitions and, like many of the Fitzgeralds' Princeton and Yale friends, would eventually settle into the theatrical profession. When McKaig first met Zelda at the Biltmore, he had not been impressed. He recorded in his diary: "Called on Scott Fitz and his bride. Latter temperamental small town Southern Belle. Chews gum—shows knees. I do not think the marriage can succeed. Both drinking heavily." His visit to Westport did not change his opinion. "Terrible party. Fitz and Zelda fighting like mad—say themselves marriage can't succeed."

Late in June, or perhaps early in July, Edmund Wilson paid a one-and-only visit to the Fitzgeralds at their rustic retreat. Wilson had been told that "Zelda had decided to change her style and behave like a conventional lady, paying and receiving calls and making polite acknowledgments." As Wilson suspected, the reform was short-lived; but though he left no detailed account of his visit, he was kept routinely informed about the parties at Compo Road. He found it amusing that while the Fitzgeralds were "reveling nude in the orgies of Westport," Van Wyck Brooks, in another part of town and unaware of the Fitzgeralds, was writing a sober plaint "against the sterile sobriety of the country." Wilson turned the irony of the situation into an imaginary dialogue between the two writers in his book *Discordant Encounters*.

Possibly as a holiday from the honeymoon, in mid-July the Fitzgeralds decided to take a sentimental journey in their Marmon to visit Zelda's parents in Montgomery. Typically, they did not bother to warn the Sayres that they were coming. Neither Scott nor Zelda was a careful or competent driver. Zelda, indeed, was positively reckless. Before the trip, she confessed to Ludlow Fowler that she had nearly ruined the car "because I drove it over a fire-plug and completely de-intestined it." It was not strange, therefore, that the journey south turned into a sequence of automotive mishaps—flats, broken axles, and fines for speeding. The first flat occurred outside Philadelphia; just before Washington, a wheel had somehow come off. They managed to put up at the New Willard in the capital, but Zelda's yearnings for Southern breakfasts of hot biscuits and fresh peaches were thwarted. They had a plain breakfast in bed. Zelda recalled the "cindery aroma" of traveling salesmen cruising the corridors. They had come badly prepared financially for the trip and the unexpected garage bills. Fitzgerald sent an emergency letter and personal check to Bunny Wilson—"Touring South. Shy of money." —and asked him to wire the sum ahead to Greenville, South Carolina. "Thanks wads," he quipped.

The farther south they went, the more they became aware of the problem of Zelda's costume. She was wearing a touring outfit of a pair of white knickers to match Fitzgerald's, topped by a schoolboy's jacket and scarf. She looked very jaunty, but managers in the better hotels were reluctant to give the oddly dressed pair a room for the night. In the mornings, at breakfast, women stared. At a garage in North Carolina, the mechanic glared at Fitzgerald and spoke consoling words to Zelda: "It's a pity that a nice girl like you should be let to wear those clothes." At the O. Henry Hotel in Greensboro, North Carolina, Zelda decided to slip a skirt over her knickerbockers. In Georgia, she insisted on stopping at drugstore pay phones to look up some of the phone numbers of boys she had danced with at Georgia Tech, the University of Alabama, and Sewanee. In Athens, where they stayed overnight, there was, she would remember, the "summer whine of phonographs" from open windows and girls walking along shaded streets in billowing dresses: "There were so many smells in the drug stores and so much organdy and so many people just going somewhere."

As they neared Montgomery, the heady atmosphere of the Southern summer filled her with nostalgia. She was overwhelmed by feelings of loss and regret. Fitzgerald, who could write with extraordinary sensitivity about such occasions, described it poignantly: "Suddenly Zelda was crying, crying because things were the same and yet were not the same. It was for her faithlessness that she wept and for the faithlessness of time."

As might almost have been predicted, when they got to Montgomery, they found they were locked out. The Sayres were out of town on a visit. They looked up old friends, partied at the country club, scandalized the natives by wearing their matching outfits on the golf course. An old beau of Zelda's, Peyton Mathis, had his suspicions of Northern vices confirmed. "What's happened to you?" he asked Zelda. "You went away in long skirts and you've come back in short pants."

In Montgomery, realizing that the Marmon would never make the return trip, they sold their car, "Expenso model," to the first prospective buyer. They took a train back to Connecticut. "The joys of motoring," Zelda wrote Ludlow Fowler, "are more or less fictional."

In August 1920, Judge and Mrs. Sayre paid the newlyweds an expected visit in Connecticut. It was not a happy occasion. Although Anthony Sayre, a Southern gentleman, kept his opinions to himself, he was plainly disapproving of the Fitzgeralds' way of life. If one may judge from *Save Me the Waltz,* in which Zelda gives a fictional account of the parental visit, Zelda's feelings about her father had undergone a subtle change. On her honeymoon night at the Biltmore, Alabama Beggs realizes, with a feeling of fright, that with her parents out of the way "no power on earth could make her do anything . . . except herself." But on the eve of her parents' visit, she comes to realize that as much as she resented the judge's ruling hand, "she hadn't been absolutely sure of how to go about anything since her marriage."

Still, writing to Ludlow Fowler, Zelda insisted that the Sayres' visit was a pleasure: "I can't tell you how glad I was to see them." But she was plainly bored in the country and missed the activities of New York: "I feel very festive and I guess it's hardly conventional or according to Hoyle to take one's family on a celebration of the kind I feel in dire need of." As in *Save Me the Waltz,* the judge and his wife cut short their visit. They moved on to Tarrytown to see their daughter Clothilde, with whom Zelda had had a recent quarrel and was not on speaking terms.

In August, Scott and Zelda also had a visit from Stephan Parrott, in the course of which the two men renewed their long talks about Monsignor Fay and Shane Leslie. Fitzgerald duly reported the meeting to Leslie. It may have been during the visit that Fitzgerald gave Parrott a signed photograph of a sketch of himself by the illustrator Gordon Bryant; he inscribed it to "Stephan Parrot [sic] from his brother F. Scott Fitzgerald." The meeting appears to have been pleasant. Parrott later wrote to Fitzgerald from Europe that he had given up any pretense of being a genius. A recent inheritance, it seems, had made it unnecessary. He still hoped to make a career for himself in architecture. And he hoped to enjoy "moderately spaced affairs when the temptation is sufficient and the opportunity satisfactory." Farther down on his itemized list of ambitions was the desire to have an agreeable wife and attractive children. "I am not particularly keen about the wife," Parrott confessed, "but I think that when I am a good deal older, I would thoroughly enjoy children if I could afford them." Fitzgerald, Parrott said, was the only friend he still found stimulating, but he added, "I feel I have not fathomed you and never will." He sent his love to Zelda. Zelda does not seem to have left any comment about Parrott, so it is not clear whether, meeting him in the flesh for the first time, she did like him better than any of the other friends Fitzgerald had told her about.

One of the more frequent guests at Westport that summer was George Jean Nathan. Fitzgerald was definitely courting the Baltimore-based Mencken, who detested New York and New York literary society, confining his visits to the *Smart Set*'s office to a few days a month. Ordinarily he arrived by train on a Sunday, signed in at the Algonquin, and got in touch with Nathan in his suite at the Royalton, across the street. (Nathan maintained his apartment there for fifty years, until his death in 1958.)

The two dined out, usually at Luchow's, since Mencken preferred solid German cooking and beer. An outspoken critic of American society, Mencken served, for a time, as another of Fitzgerald's intellectual mentors. When *This Side of Paradise* was published, Fitzgerald sent the critic one of the early copies, with a flattering inscription that bluntly acknowledged his courtship: "As a matter of fact, Mr. Mencken, I stuck your name in on page 224 in the last proof—partly, I suppose, as a vague bootlick and partly because I have since adopted a great many of your views." He went on to describe his novel as "an exquisite burlesque of Compton Mackenzie with a pastiche of Wells at the end." But that, in fact, was a direct crib from Edmund Wilson, who had written Fitzgerald to the same effect, calling *This Side of Paradise* "an exquisite burlesque of Compton Mackenzie with a pastiche of Wells thrown in at the end."

It is true that reading Mencken had stimulated Fitzgerald's appreciation of the American naturalist writers like Dreiser and the Norris brothers, Frank and Charles, as well as his interest in the hard-bitten philosophy of Nietzsche. And the Baltimore pundit may have turned around Fitzgerald's unfavorable view of Conrad. ("I'm not so cocksure about things as I was last summer," Fitzgerald wrote Max Perkins; "this fellow Conrad seems to be pretty good after all.") Fitzgerald had certainly read Frank Norris' *McTeague* and Charles Norris' *Salt,* but one critic, Robert Sklar, questions whether Fitzgerald had read either Dreiser or Conrad at the time he was discussing them so knowledgeably. And it is not clear whether Fitzgerald's understanding of Nietzschean philosophy had been cut largely from the whole cloth of Mencken's discussions. Fitzgerald's literary opinions were very apt to be handy ones. When, for instance, he wrote to the president of Princeton, "My view of life, President Hibben, is the view of the Theodore Dreisers and Joseph Conrads — that life is too strong and remorseless for the sons of men," he was cribbing directly from an essay by Mencken in which Mencken quoted Hugh Walpole on the subject of Conrad: "Conrad . . . is of the firm and resolute conviction that life is too strong, too clever and too remorseless for the sons of men." Fitzgerald even followed Mencken to the letter by deleting the phrase "too clever" as not being applicable in Dreiser's case. Clearly, Fitzgerald had an eye for topical and well-phrased opinions, but the ability to spot them did not indicate deeply held convictions.

Fitzgerald was far less fawning and more circumspect in his relations with Mencken's colleague George Jean Nathan. An unabashed ladies' man, short in stature, melancholy in mien, a natty dresser, Nathan, unlike his partner, had a taste for French wines and French cuisine. There were always lively parties at his Royalton suite, with smatterings of the literary and theatrical elite of New York. At smaller affairs, he sometimes served absinthe cocktails. His credo was work hard, play to the allowable limit, and pay no attention to the good or bad opinions of others. A self-professed male chauvinist, he preferred that a woman not be overeducated. His way of testing a woman's mental capacities, he maintained, was to ask her the directions to Grand Central Station. If her answer was at

least 50 percent correct, she was intelligent enough for normal use.
Nathan had a penchant for glamorous blond actresses and musical
comedy stars, preferably inches shorter than himself. Their presence
on a stage could often deflect his acid comments on bad plays, which
he otherwise publicly labeled "guano." The tiny Anita Loos, who
had failed in her pursuit of the cerebral Mencken, allowed herself to
be dated by Nathan. She was, for a time, struck by Nathan's "handsome pomposity."

At the time of the Fitzgeralds' friendship with Nathan, the
drama critic was involved with Ruth Findlay, the doll-like star of
The Prince and the Pauper. Zelda, who had a sleuth's eye for minor
bits of circumstantial evidence, noticed strands of Ruth Findlay's
gold hair in Nathan's combs—probably in Nathan's bathroom, since
Zelda had a tendency to take over the bathrooms in apartments she
visited. Nathan, of course, was immediately struck with Zelda and
instituted a humorous courtship, addressing his letters to "Dear
Misguided Woman" and adding coy postscripts: "Why didn't you
call me up on Friday? Is it possible that your love is growing cold?"

On his visits to Westport, Nathan drank heavily, swam at night
with the Fitzgeralds. ("The beach, and dozens of men," Zelda recalled.) He accompanied them to parties at the nearby home of the
theatrical producer John Williams, who always seemed to have an
entourage of young actresses who spoke French when they had had
enough alcohol. At one of the Williams parties, Nathan pointedly
played for Zelda a few choruses of "Cuddle Up a Little Closer" on
the piano. At another of the liquid weekends, while the guests were
disporting on the beach, someone—presumably Zelda, since she
liked to call out the fire engines—pulled a false alarm. When the
hook and ladder arrived and the firemen angrily wanted to know
where the fire was, Zelda pointed to her breast and said, "Here!"
There were angry editorials in the local papers. It was at the same
party that Charles Hanson Towne, a senior editor at *Vanity Fair,*
whom Wilson described as an insipid jokester and "the quintessence
of [his] second-rate generation," completely abandoned himself to
the weekend debauch. On the train back to New York, however,
Towne was so full of "horrified compunction" over his own behavior
that Nathan was not only amused but amazed.

When the Fitzgeralds were bored with the local entertainment
at Westport—the midnight swims, the mad rides along the Post
Road with abrupt stops at roadhouses to replenish the supply of gin

—they transferred the moveable feast to New York. Occasionally, in their cups, the Fitzgeralds missed connections. "Sweet Souse," Nathan wrote Zelda, "what happened to you? Ruth and I got to the Beaux Arts at eleven and sat sucking ginger-ale until midnight. Were you and Scott arrested?" But more often they made the rounds of parties that branched out from Nathan's Royalton suite. At one of these, Zelda, who would take baths — announced and unannounced — in other people's tubs, had a damaging accident. "At present," she wrote Ludlow Fowler, "I'm hardly able to sit down owing to an injury sustained in the course of one of Nathan's parties in N.Y. I *cut* my *tail* on a broken bottle and can't possibly sit on the three stitches that are in it now — the bottle was bath salts — I was boiled — the place was a tub somewhere — none of us remembers the exact locality."

In a late memoir published in *Esquire* in 1958, Nathan recalled a significant event at one of the boozy Westport weekends. According to the account, after Edmund Wilson, John Peale Bishop, and several other members of a gay party had passed out upstairs, Nathan, wandering down into the cellar, discovered Zelda's diaries. He found them fascinating reading. In fact, he suggested publishing portions of them in *The Smart Set*. But Fitzgerald strenuously objected, because he had "gained a lot of inspiration from them and wanted to use parts of them in his own novels and short stories."

There is no doubt that Nathan had seen the diaries. But Nathan's random memories of the fabulous Jazz Age, in which he played an ornamental role, are not free of heavy gilding. Edmund Wilson, while both men were still alive, pointedly denied some of the stories that became part of Nathan's repertoire in print and in private conversation. The *Esquire* tale also related how Wilson, accompanied by Edna St. Vincent Millay, took part in a very drunken party at the Royalton in which Fitzgerald set fire to the rubber bindings of Nathan's sofa pillows. The group of revelers, "all in more or less exalted state," watched with considerable amusement: "Their howls of glee when the rubber started to stench up the place could be heard a block away." In another of Nathan's recollections, Wilson, Bishop, and Fitzgerald stormed the Royalton one morning after a heavy evening out and were wined and dined by the drama critic. In the course of the convivialities, Nathan warned Wilson that a failure to submit articles to *The Smart Set* would be looked on as "a personal affront."

But Wilson denied that he had ever been "wined, victualed, etc." by Nathan at the Royalton—or by Mencken either, for that matter. He had seen Nathan once or twice in the *Smart Set* offices and a few times had run into him at the theater. "I have never seen him or talked to him for more than a few minutes," Wilson said when he heard the Nathan tales. He also denied that he had ever been warned by Nathan to contribute to the magazine. "It may be," Wilson concluded, "that both [Nathan] and Mencken have a certain tendency to think they did more for people and influenced them more than was actually the case."

Alec McKaig was probably the most faithful Boswell of the Fitzgeralds and their activities during their honeymoon year. But McKaig's diaries for 1920 and 1921 are more than a chronicle of youthful dissipations; they are a record of the New York literary life at the outset of the Jazz Age. In particular, they reveal the rivalries, backbiting, emotional entanglements, and quarrels of the literary life, particularly that of the circle of Princeton friends—Fitzgerald, Wilson, John Bishop, Townsend Martin, John Biggs, and McKaig himself—each of whom was eager to make a name for himself.

At first, McKaig had great respect for Fitzgerald's success and his literary gifts: "Mind absolutely undisciplined but guesses right — intuition marvelous. . . . Senses the exact mood & drift of a situation so surely and quickly." But McKaig was also thin-skinned and was hurt when Fitzgerald suggested that he stick to advertising and write on the side. Most of their friends, Fitzgerald assured him, would laugh and boo at him behind his back when be became successful. That had been his own experience. ("Practically everyone of us did boo him, but I never did," McKaig confided to his diary.) When McKaig was with John Bishop, they discussed Bishop and the odd fact that of all their group of friends, only one man had faith in another, and that was Edmund Wilson, who believed in Bishop—mostly because of their friendship in college and not because they had the same literary tastes. When McKaig dined with Wilson, the two discussed the book Wilson and Bishop were writing together, *The Undertaker's Garland,* a collection of poems and pieces on the subject of death. McKaig noted, "I certainly will be glad when this book is finished. I'm sick of having unfinished portions read to me." He and Wilson also discussed Fitzgerald's just published story collection, *Flappers and Philosophers*. Wilson claimed that only he and Millay were aware of Fitzgerald's Byronic tendencies. When Bishop returned from a weekend in Westport, they discussed Fitzgerald's new novel ("sounds awful—no seriousness of approach") and analyzed Fitzgerald's need for success, for flattery, and influence. Bishop and McKaig attributed it to Fitzgerald's coming from a family that was financially and socially on the decline. They were not sympathetic when Fitzgerald complained—as he did—that he could never make more than a hundred thousand a year except by becoming another Booth Tarkington, which meant selling out for popularity.

In such an atmosphere, it is understandable that a man might develop an instinct for self-preservation. That would explain an observation that Fitzgerald once made to Wilson and that Wilson dutifully recorded in his diary. Fitzgerald claimed: "When I'm with John, I say: 'Well, John, you and I are the only real artists,' and when I'm with Alec, I say: 'You and I are the only ones who understand the common man,' and when I'm with Townsend, I say: 'Well, Townsend, you and I are the only ones who are really interested in ourselves,' but when I'm alone, I say: 'Well, Fitz, you're the only one!' "

McKaig, who kept track of the emotional affairs of the little circle, was attentive to the complicated Wilson-Bishop-Millay affair, which was becoming remarkably overheated. He was impressed with Millay, who he thought might be a genius but was also interesting in other ways: "Modern Sappho. Eighteen love affairs and now Bunny is thinking of marrying her." But McKaig grew tired of the frenzy when Wilson passed on some remarks that John Bishop had made about Millay, and Bishop, learning of them, had poured out his grief to McKaig. Bishop, McKaig decided, was "damn stupid—interested only in himself, poetry & women, and loves most the sound of his own voice, & liquor, & adulation (when he can get it.)" He had also begun to find the Fitzgeralds a chore, especially Zelda, and particularly during August and September, when the bored couple were making regular and hurried visits to New York. They were plainly a disruptive force: "Zelda came in & woke me sleeping on couch at 7:15 for no reason. She has no sense of decencies of living." Zelda and Fitzgerald were quarreling often, sometimes on the train trip to the city, and what began on the tracks of the New Haven line, having picked up steam, would continue well into the evening in New York. ("They threatened to put him off, but finally let him stay on," McKaig recounted, "Zelda refusing to give him any money.") It was clear to him that Fitzgerald's dependency on Zelda after only six months of marriage was both emotional and literary. McKaig was plainly disapproving: "Fitz should let Zelda go and not run after her. Like all husbands he is afraid of what she may do in a moment of caprice. None of the men, however, she knows would take her for a mistress. Trouble is—Fitz absorbed in Zelda's personality—she is the stronger of the two. She has supplied him with all his copy for women."

In October, the Fitzgeralds decided against braving the winter isolation of the country without parties and without friends. They rented an apartment in New York, at 38 West Fifty-ninth Street, conveniently located near the kitchens of the Plaza, should they prefer to have their meals sent in. Throughout the fall and winter, McKaig, who was now seeing the pair with great frequency, kept a running account:

October 12:

Went to Fitzgeralds. Usual problem there. What shall Zelda do? I think she might do a little housework—[apartment] looks like a pig sty. If she's there Fitz can't work—she bothers him—if she's not there he can't work—worried what she might do. Discussed her relations with other men. I told her she would have to make up her mind whether she wanted to go in movies or get in with the young married set. To do that would require a little effort and Zelda would never make an effort. Moreover, she and Fitz like only aristocrats who don't give a damn what the world thinks or clever bohemians who don't give a damn what the world thinks. That narrows the field.

October 13:

Fitz made another true remark about himself—draw brilliant picture of Nathan sitting sitting in a chair but how Nathan thinks he cannot depict—cannot depict how any one thinks except himself & possibly Zelda. Find that after he has written about a character for a while it becomes just himself again.

October 16:

Spent evening at Fitzgeralds. Fitz has been on wagon 8 days— talks as if it were a century. Zelda increasingly restless—says frankly she simply wants to be amused and is only good for useless pleasure-giving pursuits: great problem—what is she to do? Fitz has his writing of course—God knows where the two of them are going to end up.

October 18:

Millay's response to F. Scott Fitzgerald's saying he wrote "The Camel's Back" between 8 P.M. and 2 A.M. "Fitz affects all the attributes he believes a genius should have."

October 20:

Fitz is hard up now but Zelda is nagging him for a $750 fur coat & she can nag. Poor devil.

October 21:

Went up to Fitzgeralds to spend evening. They just recovering from an awful party. Much taken with the idea of having a baby. Have just planned a good baby & and a bad baby. . . . Scott hard up for money in spite of fact he had made $20,000 in past 12 months.

October 25

Follies with Scott & Zelda. Fitz very cuckoo. Lost purse with $50.00 & then after everyone in place hunted for it, found it. He did not have enough money to pay check of course. Home 3 A.M.

Lawton Campbell, a Montgomery friend of Zelda's and a Princeton classmate of Fitzgerald's, was an up-and-coming businessman in New York at the time. (Later in the decade, he made a name for himself with two Broadway plays, *The Solid South* and *Immoral Isabella.*) Like McKaig, Campbell suspected that Zelda was the dominant influence on Fitzgerald's writing. He was struck by Fitzgerald's habit of scribbling down Zelda's chance remarks on scraps of paper and the backs of envelopes.

One day, Campbell, having been invited to lunch with the Fitzgeralds, arrived at their apartment at one o'clock. Scott was dressing; Zelda was taking a bath with the door ajar so that she could take part in the conversation. The apartment was a shambles: unmade beds, books and papers scattered everywhere, ashtrays full of stale butts, the breakfast dishes mingling with the leftover drinks from the night before. From the echo chamber of the bathroom, Zelda called out, interrupting and encouraging Fitzgerald in his narrative of their latest spree. This one had ended in the kitchen of the Waldorf, when Zelda, pinching a chef's cap, began dancing on a table, with a resulting crash. They were escorted off the premises by the house detective. Campbell sat through the hour-long narrative until it was too late for lunch.

He also remembered an evening when Zelda and Alec McKaig called on him at his apartment for the purpose of leaving Fitzgerald free to write at home. Zelda, as was her habit, stretched out on the sofa, and with her eyes to the ceiling, related more of her fabulous experiences or dreamed up "cute ideas" she wanted to put into effect. Thinking back on his meetings with her, Campbell was struck by the non sequitur nature of Zelda's conversation: "She passed very quickly from one topic to another and you didn't question her. It wouldn't occur to you to stop and ask her what she meant."

Their lives had become dangerously volatile, a round of partying and drinking. Early on, they had begun to engage in punitive flirtations with others. At some point during the summer Zelda had become "romanticly attached" to Townsend Martin — charmed by those blue eyes, no doubt. That particular worry for Fitzgerald ended when Martin took off on another of his exotic tours, this one to Tahiti. And Zelda became convinced that Fitzgerald, probably in retaliation, had become involved in an affair with "Gene" Bankhead, Tallulah's elder sister. Zelda was familiar, though not friendly, with both Bankhead sisters. They were from Montgomery, where Tallulah had early established a reputation as being even more willful and wild than Zelda. In 1920, Eugenia Bankhead was living in New York, engaged to Morton Hoyt, the brother of Elinor Hoyt Wylie. The couple were married that August in Bar Harbor, Maine, and returned to New York to live. It would never be a happy marriage; the Hoyts were three times married to each other and three times divorced. The problem was Hoyt's alcoholism. A moody and sensitive man, he did occasional writing for *Vanity Fair,* but suspected that he was being high-hatted there by people like Edmund Wilson. He was purported to be a drinking companion of Fitzgerald's, and he eventually became entangled in the Fitzgerald literature in a different way. During an ocean crossing with his wife, Hoyt, despondent, attempted to commit suicide by jumping overboard, but was rescued before he drowned. Fitzgerald used that aborted leap into oblivion in several of the early versions of *Tender Is the Night,* in the character of Curly, a Yale graduate who is the traveling companion of the young actress Rosemary. For structural reasons, or because it seemed so improbable, Fitzgerald dropped the incident after the serialized magazine version, leaving the critics somewhat mystified about the symbolic importance of the episode — or the lack of it. Like much else in Fitzgerald's fiction, it was an incident from life, used and discarded. But names have a talismanic persistence in Fitzgerald's work, and when he assigned a final name to the actress who represented a threat to Dick Diver's marriage, he called her Rosemary Hoyt.

It is uncertain when Zelda's suspicions that Fitzgerald was sleeping with Gene Bankhead were first aroused, whether before or after the Hoyt marriage. She was equally jealous of the attention he was also paying to the blond actress Miriam Hopkins, another Southern girl then in New York. The chronology of Fitzgerald's early romances and sexual relations is problematic. Whether they were premarital or adulterous is not always clear. But they appear to have been brief and not particularly impassioned affairs. They may have occasioned some charming memories for the women involved, but they were not exactly indelible and do not seem to have left any scars. Dorothy Parker, for example, told Lillian Hellman that she had slept with Fitzgerald in "a casual one or two night affair." It does not seem to have had any disastrous consequences in their relationship. Once, years later, when Fitzgerald was in New York, he tried to get in touch with her. Parker wired him back, coyly, from Denver: DEAR SCOTT THEY JUST FORWARDED YOUR WIRE BUT LOOK WHERE I AM AND ALL MARRIED TO ALAN CAMPBELL AND EVERYTHING. She sent him deepest love.

Nathan and Mencken were among the notable visitors to the Fitzgerald apartment that fall. Mencken was still Fitzgerald's "current idol," a fact he would demonstrate in a review of *Prejudices, Second Series,* a collection of Mencken's critical essays. In the review, catchily titled "The Baltimore Anti-Christ" and published in the March 1921 issue of *The Bookman,* Fitzgerald praised Mencken's "brilliant analysis" of the American cultural scene in his essay "The National Letters." But, in typical reviewer fashion, Fitzgerald asserted that there was nothing new in the essay except Mencken's discussion of the American aristocracy. It is clear that Fitzgerald did not quite know what to make of this discussion. Writing to Burton Rascoe, the book review editor of the *Chicago Tribune,* who had praised *This Side of Paradise,* Fitzgerald acknowledged that Mencken was a great man, but said he was a bum critic of poetry. He asked Rascoe: "Why has no one mentioned to him or of him that he is an intolerably muddled syllogism with several excluded middles on the question of Aristocracy. What on earth does he mean by it? Every Aristocrat of every race has come in for scathing comment, yet he holds out the word as a universal panacea for art."

Rascoe, one of the more able and interesting literary critics of the time, soon realized that it was Fitzgerald who was muddled on the subject of aristocracy. He sent Fitzgerald a little pamphlet he had written on Mencken and received in reply a query. With one of his cavalier misspellings, Fitzgerald asked, "Mencken's code of honor springs from Nietche doesn't it? — the agreement among the powerful to exploit the less powerful and respect each other." By then, Rascoe assumed that Fitzgerald's Princeton education had been somewhat lacking, since he appeared to be unacquainted with the old-fashioned classical idea of an aristocracy as being "rule by the best minds." Instead, Fitzgerald had substituted his view of the aristocrat as being the hard-line capitalist who summered at Newport or Bar Harbor and sent his sons to Princeton and Yale.

In one of his letters to Rascoe, Fitzgerald mentioned a recent visit of Mencken to his apartment and said that the critic was "quite entheusiastic about Main Street." Sinclair Lewis' novel, published in October 1920, was a phenomenal success, selling close to three hundred thousand copies in its first year. One reviewer described it as not just a novel but "an incident in American life." Fitzgerald's book, a respectable best seller on the other hand, went through some forty-nine thousand copies in its first year and a half. Lewis' success in taking a hard look at the realities of Midwestern life — the life Fitzgerald had wanted to escape from — must have caused him to wonder about the soft-focus style and glamour of his own subject matter. It is an inescapable fact of the literary life that it is riddled with envy and rivalry, complicated further by a writer's need to be au courant in his field. But even considering the competitive spirit involved, Fitzgerald's views on the Lewis novel were extremely mercurial. Writing to Rascoe on December 7, he declared, "Main Street is rotten." On Christmas Day, writing to James Branch Cabell, the author of *Jurgen,* whose good opinion Fitzgerald was courting, Fitzgerald announced, "I'm all for *Salt, The Titan* and *Main Street.*" A few days later, in a letter to Mencken, he assured the critic, "I agree on Main Street." In January, Fitzgerald wrote to Sinclair Lewis himself: "I want to tell you that *Main Street* has displaced *Theron Ware* in my favor as the best American novel. The amount of sheer data in it is amazing! As a writer and a Minnesotan let me swell the chorus — after a third reading." (Even that brisk encomium may have been an echo of Mencken's views; in his *Smart Set* review, Mencken had praised the novel's brilliant accumulation of detail.) By February, Fitzgerald began to complain that the book was overpraised. In a public letter to Thomas Boyd, the literary editor of the *St. Paul Daily News,* Fitzgerald surveyed the literary scene, predicted a growing split between romanticism and realism among American writers, and carped at the "pleasant sheep" among American readers, those who thought they were "absorbing culture if they read Blasco Ibanez, H. G. Wells and Henry Van Dyke." It was fortunate, he claimed, that these readers, who read what they were told, were now being instructed by "a few brilliant men like Mencken." But he warned: "Even the stupidest people are reading *Main Street* and pretending they thought so all the time. I wonder how many people in St. Paul ever read *The Titan* or *Salt* or even *Mcteague.* All this would seem to encourage insincerity of taste." Boyd published Fitzgerald's letter as "The Credo of F. Scott Fitzgerald" in the February 20, 1921, issue of his paper.

That fall and winter in New York, Fitzgerald's relationship with Nathan began to undergo a chill. "Beginnings of coldness," his ledger records. The reason appears to have been Zelda's flirtation with Nathan, since the next remarks indicate that Fitzgerald was also quarreling with Townsend Martin, who was once more on the scene. Nevertheless, Fitzgerald and Zelda continued to attend the theater with Nathan and his dates, frequently on first nights. The actual break did not come until the following January, with probable cause or causes unknown, except that the event was duly registered in Fitzgerald's ledger book. One rumor had it that Fitzgerald had actually swung a "roundhouse" at the drama critic.

During that winter season, Fitzgerald tried to branch out in his career, having agreed — reluctantly, and at Scribner's urging — to give talks at Wanamaker's and the National Arts Club. Despite his urge to create a distinctive impression at any party, Fitzgerald was noticeably afraid to appear on the public platform, perhaps because of any author's fears that such extemporaneous discussions are likely to expose his or her ignorance and ruin a carefully contrived public image. In any event, Fitzgerald was never eager to repeat such experiences. And when obliged to, his usual recourse was to have several drinks beforehand.

He was also trying to promote what he hoped would be a lucrative film project. Throughout his life, Fitzgerald would be of two minds about the movies, courting offers from the industry in the crassest terms, and at other times, with a bit of condescension, convincing himself that he could bring some needed artistry to the new medium. Earlier in the year, he had boasted to Shane Leslie that he was "living royally" off the film rights to his stories, so the temptation must have been great to solve his economic problems with a movie project. Writing to his uncle and aunt Philip and Lorena McQuillan, he admitted that his intentions were strictly commercial: "I am not averse to taking all the shekels I can garner from the movies. I'll roll them joy pills (the literary habit) till doomsday because you can always say, 'Oh, but they put on the movie in a different spirit from the way it was written!' "

That winter he tried to interest D. W. Griffith in a film story for Dorothy Gish. Fitzgerald and Zelda had recently met both the Gish sisters, Lillian and Dorothy, at a dinner with Nathan and Mencken and the novelist Fannie Hurst in New York. It must have been a boisterous affair. Fitzgerald and Zelda were both talkative; at table, Mencken and Nathan would each start up his own barrage of observations without paying the slightest attention to each other. Lillian Gish was amazed to see the Fitzgeralds, "so beautiful, so blond, so clean and clear," gulp down tumblers of straight whiskey with seemingly no effect.

What Fitzgerald tried to sell Griffith was a movie about movie-making, a story that would revolve around the romance of studio life. According to Fitzgerald, the pioneering director was "immediately contemptuous" of the idea. Griffith's scorn was evidently a match for Fitzgerald's attitude toward movie people. In his letter to the McQuillans, he was not particularly flattering about his prospective star nor her current boy friend, the actor James Rennie, with whom she would elope within the month. "[Dorothy Gish]," Fitzgerald wrote, "is a colorless wench in the life as is her pal." But in later years, Fitzgerald used Gish as a poignant image of the artist isolated in society. He recalled his visit with her in the newly opened Griffith studios in Mamaroneck. "The world of the picture actors was like our own in that it was in New York and not of it. It had little sense of itself and no center; when I first met Dorothy Gish, I had the feeling that we were both standing on the North Pole and it was snowing."

Fitzgerald was, in fact, beginning to feel isolated by his success. He and Zelda were still seeing a good deal of Alec McKaig, though that friendship, too, would suffer in the same way that the relationships with Fitzgerald's other bachelor friends suffered when the men became too involved with Zelda. McKaig's diaries for the closing months of the year, however, continued to record their meetings:

November 13:

Spent evening at Fitzgeralds. Scott told me how he had cried over two of his stories.

November 27:

Fitz making . . . speeches before select audiences. I spent evening shaving Zelda's neck to make her bobbed hair look better. She is lovely — wonderful hair — eyes and mouth.

November 28:

Suggested to Scott and Zelda they save — they laughed at me. Scott said — to go through the terrible toil of writing man must have belief his writings will be eagerly bought forever. Terrific party with two Fitz.

December 4:

Lunch at Gotham. T. [Townsend Martin?], Zelda, Scott & I. Then took Zelda to cocktail party at John Coles and then tea in Biltmore. In taxi, Zelda asked me to kiss her but I couldn't. I couldn't forget Scott — he's so damn pitiful.

It was on that same evening, after attending the theater with the Fitzgeralds, that McKaig returned home to find a message to call Fitzgerald immediately. When he did, he was told that something terrible had happened and that he should come to the Fitzgerald apartment right away — it would be a test of his friendship. When he arrived there, however, he found Fitzgerald talking casually with another friend. Fitzgerald gave him a casual hello and kept talking. McKaig demanded to know what the trouble was. Fitzgerald told him that he and Zelda had had a bad fight and that Zelda had gone into the bathroom, turned on the taps to hide the noise of her footsteps, and left the apartment. Instead of going in search of her, Fitzgerald had merely sat down in the middle of the room and began telephoning all his friends. When, finally, Zelda did call, it was McKaig, not her husband, who went to pick her up. According to McKaig, on the way home, Zelda regaled him with tales of her "many adventures."

One possibility is that Fitzgerald had become suspicious of McKaig and called his apartment to find out whether Zelda was there. Or it is possible that McKaig may not have told the full story in his diary. From that winter of dissipation, Zelda would remember one of their quarrels involving the bathroom, during which Fitzgerald broke down the door and "hurt" her eye. Fitzgerald's ledger notes a bathroom-door incident and a "black eye" as well, but gives it a January date.

McKaig's diary recorded a truce parley in the Fitzgerald wars, following the bathroom skirmish:

December 11:

Evening at Fitz. Fitz and I argued with Zelda about notoriety they are getting through being so publicly and spectacularly drunk. Zelda wants to live life of an "extravagant." No thought of what world will think or of future. I told them they were headed for catastrophe if they kept up at present rate.

But McKaig had begun to entertain some doubts about the authenticity of the Fitzgeralds' public performances. Talking it over with John Bishop a few days later, he wondered whether the notorious scenes were not "all aimed to hand down [the] Fitzgerald legend" to a waiting public and posterity.

In an essay about New York titled "My Lost City," intended for publication in *Cosmopolitan* magazine, but published posthumously, Fitzgerald took a moralistic view of his and Zelda's behavior during their honeymoon year: "Finding no nucleus to which we could cling, we became a small nucleus ourselves and gradually we fitted our disruptive personalities into the contemporary scene of New York. Or rather, New York forgot us and let us stay."

Despite the notoriety and glamour they tried to instill into their days and nights, the Fitzgeralds were living in the midst of an insulating group of college friends and a few literary acquaintances. And their jealousies and quarrels, their difficult public behavior, narrowed the range of friends who would — or could afford to —

keep up with them. Fitzgerald thought this was the case, or, at least, he set down one of the sadder circumstances of their fame: "I remember a lonesome Christmas when we had not one friend in the city, nor one house we could go to."

It may easily have been true. But there was only one Christmas that the Fitzgeralds spent in New York City: that was the Christmas of 1920. And Fitzgerald's ledger note for that December does state "Lonesome Christmas." But considering the way in which the Fitzgeralds, blameless of the actualities, invented and re-invented their lives, believed in a succession of "happiest years," and testified to years of sorrow and snubs, it would be well to set down Zelda's recollections of the Christmas of 1920. Zelda recalled that they had spent that "lonesome Christmas" with the actor Lynn Overmann and his wife.

4

Life, Liquor, and Literature

O
N DECEMBER 31, 1920, Fitzgerald, broke, paid a visit to
his bank, the Chatham and Phoenix at Thirty-third Street and
Fifth Avenue. He hoped to get a loan on two $500 bonds from Fair
& Company that paid 7.5 percent. He learned, unfortunately, that
the bonds were practically worthless for his purposes. He had bought
them on the eve of his marriage as an investment toward his future
security. For the next four years—until he sold them at a $600 loss
—the precious bonds remained a comic hedge against financial disaster. Whenever Fitz was broke, which was often in the years ahead,
he trotted out the bonds in the hope of realizing something on them.
Once, so he claimed, he left them on a subway, and they were turned
in at the transit office. Jokingly, he maintained that the bonds had
acquired "the sacredness of a family heirloom." They had the same
dubious value.

That afternoon, in desperation, Fitzgerald wrote Maxwell Perkins, "I have been pacing the floor for an hour trying to decide what
to do." He owed $600 in outstanding bills and another $650 to the
Reynolds Agency in repayment of an advance against a story he now
found it impossible to write. "I've made half a dozen starts yesterday
and today and I'll go mad if I have to do another debutante [story]
which is what they want."

For the past several months, Fitzgerald had been drawing steadily against the royalties for *This Side of Paradise* that would have been
due him in January 1921. First it was a request for $3000, then
another $1500 when he was hard pressed by Zelda's nagging ("My
family seem[s] to need a fur coat ect," he wrote Perkins); next the

holidays were hard upon him ("If I could have $1000 of it I think I could pay for my Xmas presents"). There was, in fact, nothing terribly wrong with his requests; he had earned the money, and it might just as well have been in his pocket as in the publisher's office. But it established the pattern of his life — running hard on the heels of his earnings, borrowing ahead from his publisher and his agent. He would be on the treadmill for years.

In his year-end emergency, Fitzgerald asked for another $1600 and suggested that Perkins regard it as an advance on his new novel, or that Scribner's lend him the sum at the same interest they would have to pay to borrow it. Finally, Fitzgerald suggested that they make it a month's loan against his next ten books as security. Perkins, as he would for years, came to the rescue.

The novel on which Fitzgerald hoped to secure a further advance was now called *The Beautiful and Damned*. Some months before, Fitzgerald, writing to Charles Scribner II, had outlined his subject as "the life of one Anthony Patch between his 25th and 33rd years (1913–1921). He is one of those many with the tastes and weaknesses of an artist but with no actual creative inspiration. How he and his beautiful young wife are wrecked on the shoals of dissipation is told in the story. This sounds sordid but it's really a most sensational book."

Fitzgerald had had a misguided hope that he would finish the book by November 1. In December, he apologized to Perkins, noting that his attempt to write a movie scenario for Griffith had set him back two weeks. In February, it is true, he had begun to send segments of the manuscript to Edmund Wilson, looking for critical comment. In April he began offering the novel — or early portions of the manuscript — to Carl Hovey, editor of *Metropolitan* magazine, angling for the lucrative serial publication before the novel was published. *Metropolitan* agreed to pay a hefty $7000 for the rights and published an abridged version of the novel between September 1921 and March 1922.

As with his finances, so with his literary capital; Fitzgerald lived hard on his resources, spending them profligately, letting them slip through his fingers on occasion. But he was also one of the more autobiographical novelists of his generation, and from each vaguely defined phase of his life and career he managed to draw a single novel, each one summarizing the lessons of his experience. *This Side of Paradise,* in its brash and self-centered eclecticism, had explored the collegiate enthusiasms and the premature nostalgia of the fledgling writer and undergraduate, his random love affairs and early sorrows. *The Beautiful and Damned,* in hasty fashion, was Fitzgerald's book about marriage, a narrative about the crossfire, the minor and major skirmishes of two egos, the truces and capitulations of love and living together. Oddly, he had begun sketching it out a bare three and half months into his own honeymoon.

Fitzgerald's hero, Anthony Patch, is slim, dark, wealthy. He is a Harvard graduate (which in Fitzgerald's Ivy League parlance means he is something of a sissy). He is also a dandy, with a collection of "silk pajamas, brocaded dressing gowns, and neckties too flamboyant to wear; in this secret finery he would parade before a mirror in his room." Anthony has a tendency to waste his days, lolling about in warm baths under the gaze of framed photographs of Julia Sanderson, Ina Claire, Billie Burke, and Hazel Dawn. Like his later avatar, Jay Gatsby, he is a hoarder of haberdashery; the bathroom wardrobe bulges with "sufficient linen for three men and with a generation of ties." The bathroom, in fact, is his province, his kingdom: "Anthony dressed there, arranged his immaculate hair there, in fact did everything but sleep and eat there. It was his pride, this bathroom." Occasionally, in this sanctum, Anthony gives some thought to his undefined literary ambitions. He plans to become a serious writer and devote his life to a history of the Middle Ages or a volume on the Renaissance popes or something.

Gloria Gilbert is a beautiful, independent, and spoiled Midwestern debutante with a nervous penchant for gumdrops (Fitzgerald had tried to break Zelda of her gum-chewing habit) and an amazing ability to carry on a serious conversation about the precise degree of tan she wants to get on her legs in summer. She has vague thoughts of becoming a movie star. Her father is a dull manufacturer of Celluloid whose Kansas City business is about to be gobbled up by unscrupulous movie producers by means of shady contracts. Mrs. Gilbert is a rattlebrained eccentric who practices Bilphism — Fitzgerald's substitution for Minnie Sayre's theosophy. (The Gilberts' marriage is described as "a war of muddled optimism against organized dullness.")

Gloria is popular, thoughtless, and self-concerned, but she needs news of herself from the outside. "Tell me," she demands when

Anthony says that he had already heard about her before their first meeting. (His Harvard friend Maury Noble told him about his odd conversation with Gloria on the subject of legs and tans.) "I'll believe it," Gloria tells Anthony. "I always believe anything any one tells me about myself — don't you?" The two are a matched pair, ego-seekers in search of identity. "We're twins!" Gloria later tells him and then goes on to explain her mother's doctrine, "that two souls are sometimes created together and — and in love before they're born." It was Fitzgerald's laundered version of one of Zelda's early letters on the subject of "soul-mates" and bisexuality, culled from Minnie Sayre's theosophical doctrines. And it was only one of the several extracts from Zelda's letters and diary notes that Fitzgerald appropriated for the novel.

With more alacrity than usual, Fitzgerald, in *The Beautiful and Damned,* rid the stage of parents. Anthony's mother, a "Boston society contralto," dies when he is five years old; his father, Adam Ulysses Patch, "inveterate joiner of clubs, connoisseur of good form, and driver of tandems," dies suddenly and disagreeably in the best hotel in Lucerne, Switzerland, leaving his eleven-year-old son "wedded to a vague melancholy that was to stay beside him through the rest of his life." Both of Anthony's parents have been removed from the scene by page 6. The Gilberts fare better: Mrs. Gilbert, faithful Bilphist, gives up her "ancient soul" in the Midwest on page 189, allowing Fitzgerald to leave the befuddled Mr. Gilbert — "for the first and last time in his life, a truly pathetic figure" — permanently stranded in Kansas City. The real parental authority, whose shadow stretches across the narrative, is old Adam J. Patch, Anthony's grandfather, the crusty millionaire reformer and philanthropist who disapproves of Anthony's idleness and disinherits him after stumbling into one of his drunken parties at the honeymoon cottage in Marietta. It is on the theme of the Patch inheritance and Anthony's attempts to wrest his grandfather's estate from the hands of the shadowy Edward Shuttleworth, old Adam's secretary and executor, that Fitzgerald strings out the episodes of the novel and the gradual moral and physical degeneration of Anthony and Gloria. Anthony, increasingly alcoholic and bitter, makes a halfhearted attempt to become a foreign correspondent in World War I. (He allows Gloria's selfishness to dissuade him; besides, his dreams of glory were mostly sartorial: "He saw himself in khaki, leaning, as all war correspondents lean, upon a heavy stick, portfolio at shoulder — trying to look like an Englishman.") Instead, he is drafted into the army and stationed in an infantry camp in the South, where he has a pathetic affair with a girl, Dorothy Raycroft, whom he needs to bolster up his ego but toward whom he is condescending. The failure of his marriage with Gloria is symbolized by his departure from Grand Central Station on an October night. She arrives too late to say a proper goodbye: "At the last they were too far away for either to see the other's tears." Gloria drifts into occasional dates, has a minor flirtation with an aviator friend, Tudor Baird, who suffers the usual fate in a Fitzgerald novel: "Afterward she was glad she had kissed him, for next day when his plane fell fifteen hundred feet at Mineola a piece of a gasoline engine smashed through his heart." Anthony and Gloria's reunion after the war is a descent into unhappiness, quarrels, and bickering that erode the last shreds of their love; drunken scenes that lose them friends. Gloria takes a screen test that is a failure; she mourns the loss of her beauty at the age of twenty-nine. "Oh, my pretty face! Oh, I don't want to live without my pretty face! Oh, what's *happened?*" she moans, uncomprehending, in front of the mirror. Anthony spirals down into total alcoholism, badgering friends for money for drinks, getting into fights. As would be the case with most of his novels, Fitzgerald was not quite sure how to dispose of his hero. "Its too obvious to have him go crazy," Fitzgerald wrote to Max Perkins in March. But in the end, Anthony suffers a breakdown and is an embittered shell of a man when the inheritance, after the excruciating wait, comes through — too late to mean anything worthwhile.

The settings and a good many of the characters in *The Beautiful and Damned* had been borrowed from the Fitzgeralds' first year of marriage. The gray honeymoon cottage in Marietta, the Japanese houseboy, the drunken New York friends who take part in the drunken weekend parties. (George Jean Nathan served as the model for the mordant philosopher, Maury Noble; Ted Paramore was clamped into the book without even a change of last name.) The New York scenes and settings, though they represented a somewhat thin slice of American life, were intended to demonstrate Fitzgerald's skills as the social historian of the Jazz Age. It is a world of teas at the Plaza and lunches at the Cascades or the University Club; it is a world of overdue books and smart conversations, and condescending descriptions of the haunts of the bourgeoisie: "There on Sunday nights gather the credulous, sentimental, underpaid, overworked people with hyphenated occupations: book-keepers, ticket-sellers, office-managers, salesmen and, most of all, clerks — clerks of the express, of the mail, of the grocery, of the brokerage, of the bank." Fitzgerald was yielding to the need to demonstrate his social consciousness with a few pot shots at the grubbier occupations: "He tried to imagine himself in Congress rooting around in the litter of that incredible pigsty with the narrow and porcine brows he saw pictured sometimes in the rotogravure sections of the Sunday newspapers." The book suffers at times from the author's straining after effects, a controversial opinion, a bit of sarcasm.

But, strangely, Fitzgerald could turn the weapons on himself. He introduces into the novel his alter ego in the form of Richard Caramel, the author of a runaway best-selling novel, *The Demon Lover* (the title Fitzgerald had once considered for the novel he was actually writing). Caramel is the crass commercial writer, eager for praise and adulation, thin-skinned about critical comment, that Fitzgerald obviously imagined he might himself become. Through Caramel, Fitzgerald would savage even his own attempts at being a social chronicler. Caramel's self-importance is captured in an exchange with Anthony:

> "My publishers, you know, have been advertising me as the Thackeray of America — because of my New York novel." "Yes," Anthony managed to muster, "I suppose there's a great deal in what you say." He knew that his contempt was unreasonable.

Nobody, of course, was more concerned with the advertising copy for his own books than Fitzgerald. Only months before, he had chided Max Perkins because Scribner's failed to use a highly suitable blurb from Sinclair Lewis: "In Scott Fitzgerald we have an author who will be the equal of any young European." Fitzgerald's understanding of the vanity of authors was as accurate as it could be.

If the glamorous life of the smart set, as described in Fitzgerald's novels, is sometimes specious, his grasp of the minor skirmishes of marital life have a deadly accuracy. Fitzgerald had the true novelist's instinct for "the half truths and evasions peculiar to that organ [the heart] which has been famed as an instrument of precision." That aperçu is typical of Fitzgerald, for though the first half has a ringing validity, it would be difficult to think of any serious writer who ever regarded the heart as an "instrument of precision." But in Fitzgerald's fictional world, one has to take the superficial with the substantive; they are as indissolubly wedded as Anthony and Gloria. Fitzgerald's fussiness, his concern for details of dress and deportment, may glitter on the surface of his work, but there is also an undercurrent of psychological acuity that is inescapable. In *The Beautiful and Damned* it is clear that Anthony Patch will never be anything more than a dilettante as a writer, and Gloria anything but an obstacle to his ambitions. Fitzgerald only could have drawn on his awareness of his own weak will and Zelda's selfishness to produce the scathing authenticity of this scene:

> "Work!" she scoffed. "Oh, you sad bird! You bluffer! Work—that means a great arranging of the desk and the lights, a great sharpening of pencils, and 'Gloria, don't sing!' and 'Please keep that damn Tana away from me,' and 'Let me read you my opening sentence,' and 'I won't be through for a long time, Gloria, so don't stay up for me,' and a tremendous consumption of tea or coffee. And that's all. In just about an hour I hear the old pencil stop scratching and look over. You've got out a book and you're 'looking up' something. Then you're reading. Then yawns—then bed and a great tossing about because you're all full of caffeine and can't sleep. Two weeks later the whole performance over again."

One of the odder ironies of the book's characterizations of Anthony and Gloria is that Fitzgerald seldom, if ever, holds back anything in his exposure of Anthony's shifty rationalizations for his behavior. But as author—and perhaps as husband—he admires Gloria's spunkiness and candor, even her selfishness, which he can treat with a quizzical amusement.

> Throughout the previous winter one small matter had been a subtle and omnipresent irritant—the question of Gloria's gray fur coat. At the time women enveloped in long squirrel wraps could be seen every few yards along Fifth Avenue. The women were converted to the shape of tops. They seemed porcine and obscene; they resembled kept women in the concealing richness, the feminine animality of the garment. Yet—Gloria wanted a gray squirrel coat.

Fitzgerald's friends would read *The Beautiful and Damned* as a portrait of Fitzgerald and Zelda's marital life. Edmund Wilson, for instance, having read the earlier portions of the manuscript, wrote Stanley Dell: "I am editing the MS of Fitz's new novel and, though

I thought it was rather silly at first, I find it developing a genuine emotional power which he has scarcely displayed before. I haven't finished it yet, though, so can't tell definitely. It is all about him and Zelda."

It is not clear how much Fitzgerald wanted to reveal about his marital life, or how consciously. He could, it seems, be extremely dense about the connection of his fiction with his own life. H. L. Mencken's friend Charles Angoff remembered an incident in a New York hotel when Fitzgerald, slightly drunk, began outlining the plot for a novel in which a woman who is extremely jealous of her husband—jealous of his achievement in some line in which she also wants to excel—begins to destroy him and the marriage: "Then, I guess she commits suicide—first she does it step by step, the way all people, all women, commit suicide, by drinking, by sleeping around, by being impolite to friends." He hadn't gotten it all down in his head, Fitzgerald said, but he wanted Mencken's opinion. "Well, it's your wife, Zelda, all over again," Mencken suggested. Fitzgerald was irate, calling it "the dumbest piece of literary criticism " he'd ever heard. He had spilled out his guts to Mencken and he answered with "Zelda!" "Of all the times to mention Zelda to me," Fitzgerald went on. "Of all the goddam times to mention her!"

Over the years, apparently, Fitzgerald tended to hedge about how closely he had intended to delineate himself and Zelda in the characters of Gloria and Anthony Patch. While he was working on the novel, he freely admitted the resemblance. The Rosalind of *This Side of Paradise,* he wrote to one correspondent, was really flesh and blood: "I married her eventually and am now writing a very much better & more 'honest' book about her." Presumably one may easily overlook the disclaimer Fitzgerald made in the inscription in the copy of *The Beautiful and Damned* that he presented to his mother: "This book which I feel sure you won't like but which I assure you is not about me." Writing to his daughter, Scottie, years later, he put distance between himself and Zelda and the fictional characters who, in the public eye at least, they had become. "Gloria" he wrote, "was a much more trivial and vulgar person than your mother. I can't really say there was any resemblance except in the beauty and certain terms of expression she used, and also I naturally used many circumstantial events of our early married life. We had a much better time than Anthony and Gloria had."

But the most reliable estimate of Fitzgerald's feelings about the verisimilitude of *The Beautiful and Damned* is a 1930 letter, "Written with Zelda gone to the Clinique," which Fitzgerald may not have sent his wife. It acknowledges the haste with which the book was conceived and his view of its accuracy: "I wish the Beautiful and Damned had been a maturely written book because it was all true. We ruined ourselves—I have never honestly thought that we ruined each other."

In February 1921, Zelda discovered she was pregnant. Throughout the winter, Fitzgerald had been announcing plans for a trip abroad. Now they tried to make up their minds. On the one hand, they thought they should make the trip before Zelda was too far advanced in her pregnancy; on the other, they were thinking of a trip that would take in England and France, with perhaps a lengthy stay in Italy. Fitzgerald, who was still nurturing hopes of becoming a successful film writer, voiced an intention of writing several movies while abroad and continuing to work on his short stories. His failure to interest Griffith did not deter him. But his views on the film industry in general had soured. In an interview published in the January 1921 issue of *Shadowland,* Fitzgerald conceded that "in the old days" he had tried his hand at writing scenarios, but that they had all come back. He had some unkind and oddly inept words about conventional films, saying they were full of "creaky mid-Victorian sugar," a badly mixed metaphor that one hopes was a misquote. Fitzgerald told the interviewer that when he went to the movies, he preferred seeing pleasant flappers like Constance Talmadge or the comedies of Charlie Chaplin or Harold Lloyd. "I'm not strong for the uplift stuff," he said. "It simply isn't life to me."

In March, before they made final plans, Zelda went to visit her family in Montgomery. Fitzgerald, presumably putting the finishing touches on *The Beautiful and Damned,* stayed behind, then joined Zelda in the middle of March, after she had wired him (at the wrong street address) to say that she loved him, missed him, and would he bring her box of Biltmore face powder, her blue fan, and the scrapbook. After their return to New York, they booked passage for May 3, on the Cunard liner *Aquitania.* Max Perkins supplied Fitzgerald with letters of introduction to John Galsworthy, whose books Scribner's published, and to Charles Kingsley, the firm's London representative. On the eve of departure, "very boiled," Fitzgerald wrote to a new friend, Ralph Block, who worked for the Goldwyn Studios in New York, thanking him for an introduction to Aldous Huxley. In a comic twist on his own views about movies, he relayed a story he had recently heard concerning an exchange between George Bernard Shaw and the hardheaded film producer Samuel Goldwyn. Shaw, turning down a film offer, had reputedly said: "The trouble is that you're thinking about art and I'm thinking about money. We never could get together." Fitzgerald asked Block whether the story could possibly be true. Their departure, the following day, came as a surprise to George Jean Nathan. Edmund Wilson, who visited the *Smart Set* offices on May 3, later reported to Fitzgerald that Nathan "seemed a little crestfallen and I think he was sorry that you should have got off without patching up your quarrel."

Scott's ledger mentioned some of the ship's passengers: "Tullocks, Seywards, Engalitcheff." The last was Prince Val Engalitcheff, son of an American mother and the Russian consul in Chicago. A dashing young sportsman, Engalitcheff was a student at Brown University. His suicide, barely two years later, came as a shock to Fizgerald, who used the young man as a character model in his later fiction. Zelda, in a letter to Max Perkins, said that she had gazed "furtively and impressedly" at Colonel E. M. House, friend and adviser to former President Wilson. Otherwise, she had been reduced to monosyllables in response to the horrible dinner partners they had at their table.

Their stay in London was brief, a mere week. They put up at the Hotel Cecil. (There is a snapshot of Zelda in her kimono, queen of disorder, in their hotel room.) She liked the twilights along the Thames and the long files of Indian soldiers in the royal processions. In response to Perkins' letter, the Fitzgeralds were invited to dinner by John Galsworthy at Grove Lodge in Hampstead. The other guests were the Irish playwright and novelist St. John Ervine and his wife. The couple had been to New York the year before for the production of his play *Jane Clegg*. Zelda chiefly noted Ervine's wooden leg. Fitzgerald found Galsworthy what he expected, "a fine quiet reticent English gentleman." But he had started off with one of those rounds of insulting flattery in which he indulged with people he supposedly esteemed. He told his host, "Mr. Galsworthy, you are one of the three living writers that I admire most in the world" — the others being Conrad and Anatole France. When Edmund Wilson, to whom Fitzgerald related the episode later, asked how Galsworthy responded, Fitzgerald admitted, "I don't think he liked it much. He knew he wasn't that good." Wilson assumed that Galsworthy had been put off by "a gross public compliment." He also suspected that Fitzgerald had suffered — or ought to have suffered — from a bad conscience because of his insincerity. It was clear that Fitzgerald had not intended half of what he said. Shortly after the dinner party he wrote to Shane Leslie, "I was rather disappointed in [Galsworthy]. I can't stand pessimism with neither irony or bitterness." Zelda's impressions were gnomic. She told Wilson that Galsworthy's novels were "a shade of blue for which she did not care."

Fitzgerald and Zelda had a more enjoyable time with Leslie, who had them to tea and then took them on a sinister visit to the London docks and slums and the Wapping district. (Zelda, for safety's sake, had donned men's clothing.) Leslie thought Zelda — the "Rosalind" he had heard so much about from Fitzgerald's letters — a lovely thing, as delicate as a toy or a geisha. But over the years, his recollections of the American couple would become a good deal more acidulous.

One of the more exciting events was a luncheon with Lady Randolph Churchill, the famous Jenny Jerome, mother of Winston and Shane Leslie's aunt. Zelda remembered the strawberries, "big as tomatoes," that were served for dessert. The Fitzgeralds met the younger Churchill son, Jack, who at first seemed difficult to talk to, then "turned out to be so pleasant." He took them to a cricket match, from which they left early, evidently bored. But there were other memorable highlights: tea with Charles Kingsley in his home at Richmond ("I liked him mighty well," Fitzgerald wrote Perkins); sharing a bottle of champagne with members of the British polo team; and a visit to Oxford, which Fitzgerald decided straightaway was "the most beautiful spot in the world."

By the seventeenth they were in Paris, staying at the Hotel St. James and Albany. Characteristically, they created a nuisance by keeping an uncured Armenian goatskin in their room and putting ice cream out to melt on the windowsill. Zelda disrupted the service by tying the elevator to her floor with a belt so that it would be available when she finished dressing. They attended the Folies-Bergère, bought a few "dirty" French postcards. One of these, featuring a Cupid and a semiclad woman, was tame enough to send through the mails to Bunny Wilson, who was about to sail for the Continent. "Come on Over," the Fitzgeralds advised him, signing the card,

"Sincerely, Anatole France." Fitzgerald was an admirer of the once iconoclastic but now respected French writer, especially of his *Revolt of the Angels*. He and Zelda kept an hour's vigil outside France's residence on the Villa Saïd, hoping to catch sight of the old man, but were disappointed. Little about France — the country, not the writer — seemed to please them. "France," Fitzgerald wrote to Leslie, "is a bore and a disappointment, chiefly, I imagine, because we know no one here."

They expected better things of Italy and, for a while, were charmed by Venice, where they stopped late in May. One day, with little else to do, they took a gondola out to an American destroyer, the *Sturtevant,* lying in the harbor. Much to their surprise, they discovered that it was named for Ruth Sturtevant's brother. A bronze plaque and a photograph of Albert, so Fitzgerald informed Ruth, commemorated her brother. Zelda "vamped" a young lieutenant named Robbins, with whom she was photographed.

From Venice, they traveled to Florence and Fiesole. "These Wops!" Zelda captioned a photograph of herself, noticeably plump and pregnant, sitting on a stone wall overlooking a deep valley. In Florence, Fitzgerald witnessed a scene that was to color his view of the country: a squad of Italian soldiers roughed up an American woman who refused to give up her train compartment to an Italian colonel. Rome, their next stop, was a mistake. "God damn the continent of Europe," Fitzgerald wrote to Wilson. "It is of merely antiquarian interest. Rome is only a few years behind Tyre and Babylon. The negroid streak creeps northward to defile the Nordic race. Already, the Italians have the souls of blackamoors." His attack of spleen may have been brought on by the fact that he was "drinking, drinking." Nor was it a help that the Grand Hotlel, where they were staying, was flea-ridden. "Men from the British Embassy scratched behind the palms," Zelda observed. Fitzgerald remembered Rome "as the place where Zelda and I had an appalling squabble." Their stay was the beginning of a lifelong distaste for Italy and the Italians.

In Paris, once more, they looked up Edna St. Vincent Millay, living a Left Bank existence but in a first-class hotel. Having escaped from her American suitors, she was now involved with a British journalist, a correspondent for the London *Herald* who complicated matters by having a wife and three children in Saint Cloud. The Fitzgeralds hoped to get in touch, through Millay, with Wilson, who, unknown to them, was staying at the Hôtel Mont-Thabor.

But because of poor planning or lack of foresight, the friends failed to meet. The Fitzgeralds returned to London just in time to catch up on the disappointing English reviews of *This Side of Paradise*. "Of 20 reviews about half are mildy favorable," Fitzerald wrote to Wilson; "a quarter of them imply that I've read '*Sinister Street* once too often' and the other five (including *The Times*) damn it summarily as artificial. I doubt if it sells 1500 copies."

Echoing Mencken's antiwar, Pan-Germanic views, Fitzgerald wrote as scathingly about France as he did about Italy. "France made me sick," he told Wilson. "Its silly pose as the thing the world has to save. I think it's a shame that England and America didn't let Germany conquer Europe." Fitzgerald was convinced that when Anatole France died, French literature would be nothing more than "a silly jealous rehashing of technical quarrels." In twenty-five years' time, he pontificated, New York would be the center of art and literature. "Culture follows money," he said. Still, he had the grace to admit that his reactions were "philistine, anti-socialistic, provincial and racially snobbish." He had come to believe at last, he said, "in the white man's burden."

In London, they shifted from hotel to hotel. They stayed at Claridge's but found their room gloomy and the valet indifferent about whether they stayed or not. They moved to the Cavendish and may have tried the Cecil once more. They celebrated the Fourth of July by dancing at the Savoy ballroom, made another trip to Oxford (this time at the lovely twilight hour), visited Cambridge, and made a sentimental pilgrimage to Grantchester to pay homage to Rupert Brooke, photographing each other standing in the middle of garden paths. (There would never be anything posed or artful about the many snapshots of themselves the Fitzgeralds pasted into their albums; just the blunt fact that they had been at the scene.) They booked passage home on the *Celtic*.

From Paris, Wilson tried to persuade them to return to France. Indeed, he scolded: "The truth is that you are so saturated with twentieth century America, bad as well as good — you are so used to hotels, plumbing, drugstores, aesthetic ideals and vast commercial prosperity of the country — that you can't appreciate those institutions of France, for example, which are really superior to American ones. If you had only given it a chance to sink in!" Wilson sent John Peale Bishop his account of the Fitzgeralds' unhappy tour, but the primary purpose of his letter was to report on Edna St. Vincent

Millay, whom he had visited. Wilson felt that she had arranged the scene very carefully, down to the presence of the big, redheaded, slightly suspicious lover. Millay herself was discovered in a "serious" black dress, seated at her typewriter, surrounded by manuscripts. Wilson claimed that looking at his passionate love now was like staring at an extinct volcano: "I would not love her again for anything; I can think of few more terrible calamities." Still, he admitted, "some glamour and high passion" had passed out of his life.

Bishop, in return, regaled Wilson with a mock-heroic account of the Bastille Day preparations being made for the returning Scott Fitzgeralds. "Goofo and Baby" were expected to dock on the following Sunday. Bishop's letter was one of those cordial and condescending records of the best-of-literary-friendships, a sardonic commentary on Fitzgerald's social ambitions and literary failings. There would be, Bishop noted, a parade down Fifth Avenue, to be reviewed by Mayor John Hylan from a specially erected stand at Thirty-fourth Street (a mistaken reference to the site of Fitzgerald's bank, perhaps?). The streets would be strewn with wrappers from *Flappers and Philosophers* and the numerous typographical errors from the printings of *This Side of Paradise.*

New York, when the Fitzgeralds arrived, was in the midst of a sweltering heat wave. They stayed at the Biltmore for a few days. Fitzgerald, still rankling from his European tour, answered Wilson's letter: "You may be right. Nevertheless, I'm writing a short monograph on the subject and will forward you a copy." He would, in fact, threaten to write a series of twelve articles on his unsatisfactory two-and-a-half-month trip — surely a case of overkill. But for the moment he satisfied himself with a short blast in an article titled "Three Cities," written for Brentano's *Book Chat.* In it, he repeated the opinions about France and French literature that he had vented in his letter to Wilson; he reported on the incident of the *carabinieri* roughing up the Omaha woman; he complained about the flea-ridden hotel in Rome. His anger later cooled enough so that he could admit to Max Perkins that the *Book Chat* article had been an "acidulous (and rather silly) explosion."

As planned, the Fitzgeralds went south to Montgomery — the "Sahara of Bozart," in Mencken's geography — to await the birth of the baby. Bishop duly informed Wilson of the event: "The Fitzgeralds, as you may have heard, have just departed for Montgomery, Alabama, there to establish a family and a plantation. I am inclined to think it may be a very good thing for him as a novelist, because as you remarked, he has at present no social background and his hero and heroine operate in a vacuum." It was, ironically, a queer charge for him to make; he himself would soon take the path of exile.

The South proved unendurably hot, and Zelda found the family style too restricting. She refused to believe that the old-fashioned term *confinement* meant absolute seclusion for a pregnant woman, and she shocked the neighbors and shamed the family by wanting to appear in public in her "delicate condition." Fitzgerald and Zelda also found they could not drink at Pleasant Avenue, since Judge Sayre, bound to uphold the law of the land, respected Prohibition.

In August, they moved again, this time to St. Paul, where friends, Oscar and Xandra Kalman, found them a house at Dellwood on White Bear Lake. Sandy Kalman was one of the few intimate woman friends Zelda had while they lived in the Midwest. Her friendship was all the more welcome, since Zelda seems not have been keen about socializing with Fitzgerald's parents or his sister.

During their stay, Fitzgerald became active in the literary life that St. Paul afforded. He became friendly with Thomas Boyd, who had earlier published Fitzgerald's letter on the American literary scene in the *St. Paul Daily News*. Now, Boyd promptly interviewed the celebrity and urged him to contribute a number of book reviews to his paper. Fitzgerald, who thoroughly enjoyed being the local lion, kept up a high public profile as a writer, contributing reviews of Dos Passos' *Three Soldiers,* Huxley's *Crome Yellow,* and Tarkington's *Gentle Julia.* Boyd was eager, too, to keep Fitzgerald in the limelight. In the following spring, he did a three-part series of articles on Fitzgerald for his paper.

Both Boyd, then twenty-three, and his wife, Peggy, who wrote under the name Woodward Boyd, were aspiring novelists. Fitzgerald, generous toward new authors, campaigned to have Scribner's publish their books. He was especially keen about Boyd's novel *Through the Wheat,* which drew on the young man's experiences as a marine in World War I. Boyd had seen action at Verdun and Belleau Wood and had been awarded the Croix de Guerre. It was the kind of personal experience in which Fitzgerald could take vicarious pride, and when Scribner's published the book in 1923, Fitzgerald, reviewing it, claimed that it was the "best combatant story of the great war," one of the best war books since *The Red Badge of Courage.*

And in the course of the review, he even dissociated himself, in public at least, from some of Mencken's racial theories. "No one," Fitzgerald stated, "has a greater contempt than I have for the recent hysteria about the Nordic theory, but I suppose that the United States marines were the best body of troops that fought in the war."

It was hardly expectable, however, that Fitzgerald would have no complaints about a rival author. When he wrote Perkins about Boyd, he added some qualification about his hero-protégé: "He hasn't a very original mind—that is: he's too young to be quite his own man intellectually, but he's on the right track & if he can read much more of the 18th century—and the middle ages and ease up on the moderns he'll grow at an amazing rate."

Boyd was also a partner in the Kilmarnock Book Store in St. Paul, where Fitzgerald spent free afternoons. It was through the Boyds that he met the novelist and screenwriter Joseph Hergesheimer. The portly, blear-eyed writer was one of the most highly paid authors in America, a man who, having come up the hard way, believed in conspicuous consumption. He wore silk shirts, a coonskin cap, and carried a gold-tipped cane; something of a combination of J. P. Morgan and Daniel Boone. He traveled widely, courted the famous, liked to party with Palm Beach swells, and seemed to thrive in Hollywood. He and his wife, Dorothy, had a luxurious country house in West Chester, Pennsylvania. When Fitzgerald suggested that writing was an uncertain and bitter profession and avowed that he might have been better off as a carpenter, Hergesheimer barked that he had lived for years on hominy grits and black-eyed peas before managing to sell "one God-damned line." He didn't want to be told about the despairs of writers. Fitzgerald described him as a "charming egotist." He clearly envied the older writer his phenomenal success. (Ironically, two decades later Hergesheimer's novels were out of print and he was virtually unknown, living in near poverty in Stone Harbor, New Jersey, and had to be rescued by a Mellon Foundation grant.) Hergesheimer, who appreciated Zelda, promised to give her a big welcoming party at the Algonquin Hotel when she escaped from the wilds of Minnesota. Fitzgerald had little respect for Hergesheimer's writing or his audience. In an unkind moment, he equated the bungalow dwellers who collected first editions of Hergesheimer's novels with people who preferred colored toilet paper.

He was clearly not happy in St. Paul. He had not been able to get down to work and was feeling restless. He wrote to Perkins:

> I'm having a hell of a time because I've loafed for 5 months & I want to get to work. Loafing puts me in this particularly obnoxious and abominable gloom. . . . I should like to sit down with a dozen chosen companions and drink myself to death, but I am sick alike of life, liquor and literature. If it wasn't for Zelda, I think I'd disappear out of sight for three years. Ship as a sailor or something & get hard — I'm sick of the flabby semi-intellectual softness in which I flounder with my generation.

Something of this mood — plus a few new resolves — was evident when Ted Paramore, returning from New York from a "delirious summer" of dissipation in California, stopped off to see the Fitzgeralds in St. Paul. Zelda liked Paramore; she thought him very good-looking and fun to be with. Paramore wrote to Wilson: "Zelda is 8 months and 3 weeks in a state of pregnancy. Scott appears to have swallowed Mencken whole and declares that he is out for the money even if he has to sell bonds to get it. That, I do not need to warn you, is what marriage does to every promising young man."

At the end of September, the Fitzgeralds were asked to leave the Dellwood house; the landlord claimed they were responsible for serious damage to the plumbing system. They moved to the Commodore Hotel in town, near the Summit Avenue area of St. Paul. Their daughter, Frances Scott Fitzgerald, was born on October 26, 1921. With the writer's instinct for detail, Fitzgerald copied down Zelda's remarks as she awoke from the anesthesia: "Oh God, goofo I'm drunk. Mark Twain. Isn't she smart — she has the hiccups. I hope it's beautiful and a fool — a beautiful little fool."

The new parents received peppy telegrams from the New York bachelors. One, signed Townsend, Alec, John, and Ludlow, read: CONGRATULATIONS FEARED TWINS HAVE YOU BOBBED HER HAIR LOVE FROM ALL. Fitzgerald, writing to Wilson, gave a sigh of relief: "I'm glad the damn thing's over. Zelda came through without a scratch and I have awarded her the croix-de-guerre with palm." Such crucial events in life, it seems, would summon up military analogies in Fitzgerald's mind.

While Zelda recuperated, in a house they had leased at 626 Goodrich Avenue, Fitzgerald, with a renewed sense of purpose, rented a downtown office. His principal task was revising and correcting the proofs of *The Beautiful and Damned,* which had been heavily edited and cut for magazine publication. Scribner's planned to bring out the book in March. Perhaps in anticipation of its appearance, Fitzgerald stepped up his writing activities, producing stories, book reviews, a parody reminiscence of Donald Ogden Stewart for the *St. Paul Daily News.* He was contemplating a new play; in the spring he produced a musical revue, *Midnight Flappers,* for the Junior League Annual Frolic. One of the hurried changes on *The Beautiful and Damned* involved a telegram to Perkins stating that Zelda felt the book should end with Anthony's last speech on shipboard: "SHE THINKS NEW ENDING IS A PIECE OF MORALITY." In this case, Perkins felt that Zelda was "dead right" artistically, but he wondered about the popular appeal of a message at the end. Fitzgerald's attempt to round off the story of his beleaguered hero and heroine with a suitably ironic moral was fortunately dropped.

Always sensitive to questions of dress and personal appearance, though, Fitzgerald fussed about the dust-jacket illustrations by W. E. Hill. "The girl is excellent of course," he told Perkins. "It looks somewhat like Zelda, but the man, I suspect, is a sort of debauched edition of me." He complained that in the cover design for *This Side of Paradise* the hero's necktie had been unfashionably "tucked neatly under his collar in the Amherst fashion." But even that would be preferable to the light-haired "bartender" Hill had drawn for the present cover: "He looks like a sawed-off young tough in his first dinner-coat."

Nor was he optimistic about Scribner's promotional efforts. He had been unhappy about their advertising campaign for *This Side of Paradise* and was even more dissatisfied after the success of Floyd Dell's *Mooncalf,* another novel about a sensitive young man who wrote poetry and whispered about lost loves, published by Knopf. Fitzgerald had been badmouthing the book for some time. Writing to Mencken, he called it "the latest spud in the great potato tradition." In his *Book Chat* article about Europe, he had gone out of his way to give Dell's novel a gratuitous slur, saying he had made three "brave attempts" to get through it. But strangely, in mounting his war against Dell's novel, Fitzgerald resorted to cribbing from another writer, this time Edmund Wilson. The weapon was a critical comment Wilson had made about *This Side of Paradise* in a personal letter. Wilson complained that the history of the sensitive young man was "a bum art form," particularly in the case of such British writers as John Davys Beresford and Compton Mackenzie. In their books, it consisted chiefly of "dumping all one's youthful impressions in the reader's lap, with a profound air of importance." Wilson charged, "You do the same thing."

In a letter to Burton Rascoe, Fitzgerald deftly lifted Wilson's criticism, garnished it with some opinions of his own, and applied it to Dell's novel, which he called "a wretched thing without a hint of glamor, utterly undistinguished, childhood impressions dumped into the reader's lap with a profound air of importance and the sort of thing that Walpole and Beresford (whom I abominate) turn out twice a year with great bawlings about their Art." Wilson's well-turned phrase must have seemed particularly serviceable to Fitzgerald, since he lifted it once more, this time in his "Credo" letter, which Tom Boyd published in the *St. Paul Daily News*. Fitzgerald wrote: "This writing of a young man's novel consists chiefly in dumping all your youthful adventures into the reader's lap with a profound air of importance, keeping carefully within the formulas of Wells and James Joyce." *Mooncalf,* Fitzgerald maintained, was a case in point, one that had reached "the depths of banality."

The ultimate irony, however, was that while he was helping himself to Wilson's opinions, Fitzgerald was writing to Mencken, accusing Dell of borrowing "freely from James Joyce and even F. Scott Fitzgerald (cf. the last two pages of *Mooncalf.*)" Mencken seems to have reprimanded him about the plagiarism charges. In his next letter, Fitzgerald apologized: "I'm . . . sorry I said that about Dell and my book. Lord knows I've borrowed freely in my time and again it's only the people I detest like Frank Harris and F. M. Hueffer who quibble endlessly about 'steals.' It was probably my imagination anyhow."

But the *Mooncalf* war did not end there. When, a few months later, an advertisement for Dell's novel extolled it as "the most brilliantly successful first novel of many years," Fitzgerald wrote Perkins a scolding letter and enclosed the ad, marked: "You've let everyone forget that my book once had this title. Knopf's statement goes quite unchallenged." Knopf, he charged, had kept Dell's book in the public eye for a year. Scribner's had failed badly with *This Side of Paradise*—"not *one* newspaper ad, not one *Times* or *Tribune* ad or Chicago ad since *six months* after publication." He obviously wanted to put some iron in the Scribner's sales and promotion departments for his second novel.

Zelda's letters to New York friends dealt with the baby, whom they called Scottie. "She is *awfully* cute," she wrote Ludlow Fowler, "and I am very devoted to her, but quite disappointed over the sex." Nor was she happy about the Minnesota winter. Ironically, before their marriage, Fitzgerald had written one of his more poetic and artful stories, "The Ice Palace," which dealt with a Southern belle who experiences the bleakness of a Midwestern winter on a visit to her fiancé and returns home for good—an unusual theme, the effect of geography on love. Considering that the heroine, Sally Carrol Happer, was based on Zelda, Fitzgerald seems to have had a premonition of that alienation of the spirit which Zelda would feel in frigid St. Paul.

Zelda in the flesh was racier than the rarefied creature Fitzgerald would make of her for the glossy magazines. In her letter to Fowler, Zelda complained: "We are both simply mad to get back to New York. This damn place is 18 below zero and I go around thanking God that anatomically and proverbially speaking, I am safe from the fate of the [brass] monkey."

IV

In mid-March 1922, the Fitzgeralds came east for a week or more of celebration for the publication of *The Beautiful and Damned* and to escape the winter rigors of St. Paul. The official publication date was March 4, but the trip had been delayed when Fitzgerald came down ill. "I've had the pleasure of a three day amour with an Exquisite Case of Spanish Influenza," he wrote James Branch Cabell, "and like all such illicit affairs, it has left me weak and chastened." But Fitzgerald was also having money problems. He had cashed a bad check and had written Perkins and wired Ober for advances amounting to $1600. (He explained to Ober that it was "a raised check by an employee of a club here. I'm trying to trace down the matter.")

In New York, he and Zelda stayed at the Plaza, the "etched hotel, dainty and subdued," which both preferred among the New York hotels. Edmund Wilson, who saw them shortly after their arrival, was surprised by their appearance. He found them changed, "particularly Zelda, who has become more matronly and rather fat (about which she is very sensitive)." Zelda seemed "offended by the cynical indifference of Fitz to the baby; much of her old jazz has evaporated." But Wilson thought her mellower than when he had first met her, and liked her the better for it. As for Fitzgerald, Wilson wrote Stanley Dell, "He looks like John Barrymore on the brink of the grave—chiefly, I guess, because he has just been sick." He found Fitzgerald more intelligent than formerly: "His soul seems to have been somewhat scarified by his trip to Europe combined with the coming of the baby—two events which seem to have gone ill together."

There may have been other reasons for the strained relations that Wilson noticed between the Fitzgeralds. Zelda was pregnant again and did not want a second child so soon after the first. She decided to have an abortion, perhaps with Fitzgerald's approval. The likelihood is that it took place during the March trip to New York. Verification comes by way of an abrupt entry in Fitzgerald's ledger account for March 1922: "Zelda and her abortionist." But it may have been a source of some resentment years later, when Fitzgerald wrote in his notebooks, "His son went down the toilet of the XXXX Hotel after Dr. X——Pills." Zelda, in one of the autobiographical letters in which she detailed the events leading up to her stay in a Swiss mental clinic, specified "pills and Dr. Lackin" during one of her New York visits. Her friend and sometime confidante Sara Mayfield later said that Zelda had had more than one abortion during the course of her marriage.

It would be uncanny if Fitzgerald's fictional treatment of an abortion had preceded the actual event. In *The Beautiful and Damned*, Gloria suspects that she is pregnant, and she and Anthony discuss the possibility of an abortion. Anthony says that he is "indifferent" as to whether Gloria has the child. "That is, I'm neutral. If you have it I'll probably be glad. If you don't—well, that's all right too." In the earlier versions of the novel, he suggests that Gloria get help from some woman friend: "Well, can't you—why can't you talk to some woman and find out what's best to be done. Most of them fix it some way. . . . For God's sake don't lie there and go to pieces."

Zelda's biographer Nancy Milford suspects that the little scene set in Marietta relates to Zelda's suspected pregnancy during the Fitzgeralds' stay in Wesport. If that assumption is true, it tends to confirm the history of several abortions. But the fictional treatment may also have been drawn from the episode shortly before the Fitzgeralds' marriage, when Zelda thought she was pregnant but, with fierce independence, refused to take the pills Fitzgerald had sent her. In *The Beautiful and Damned,* however, Fitzgerald exactly reversed the situation. With fine selfishness, Gloria uses the situation to assert a rather self-serving independence. She is not afraid of the pain, she tells Anthony, but she doesn't want to be forced into the indignity of having a child, the way other women are. And there are reasons of feminine vanity: "Afterward I might have wide hips and be pale, with all my freshness gone and no radiance in my hair." In the novel, the problem is resolved when Gloria learns that she is not pregnant after all. But though it is true that no magazine editor would have been likely to publish a frank treatment of the subject of abortion (the most trenchant part of the discussion was dropped), Fitzgerald's politeness had the effect of turning Anthony and Gloria into a pair of children nonchalantly playing house and deciding against one of the usual options.

The question of a real abortion, however, may well have plunged Fitzgerald into a prolonged binge during their two-week stay in New York. On occasion, it seems, he was by himself during these sprees. Wilson remembered that Fitzgerald showed up very early one morning in a hansom cab "after an all-night party of some kind." Fitzgerald wanted to take him for a drive in Central Park. When he wrote to Wilson later, Fitzgerald conceded that the New York trip had been a disaster. "My original plan was to contrive to have long discourses with you," he told his friend, "but that interminable party began and I couldn't seem to get sober enough to be able to tolerate being sober. In fact the whole trip was largely a failure."

One of the subjects for discussion undoubtedly would have been the lengthy essay about Fitzgerald that Wilson had written for the March issue of *The Bookman.* They had already corresponded about it after Wilson sent Fitzgerald a manuscript copy in January. Wilson's profile was scarcely a gloss on an old friendship. It was full of critical strictures. He noted the easy suggestibility of Fitzgerald's literary values. In college, Fitzgerald had decided that the thing to do was to write an autobiographical novel that ended with a burst of philosophical notions, and produced *This Side of Paradise.* Now, having come under the influence of Mencken, he had written *The Beautiful and Damned,* with the intention of exposing "the meaninglessness of life." If Wilson had been harsh on Fitzgerald's first book ("Not only is it ornamented with bogus ideas and faked literary references, but it is full of literary words tossed about with the most reckless inaccuracy"), he was willing to admit that *The Beautiful and Damned* represented an advance over Fitzgerald's earlier writing. It was more "nearly mature" in its style and the subject more solidly unified in its treatment. Fitzgerald never committed the "unpardonable sin" — dull writing. He had the Celtic gift for turning language "into something iridescent and surprising."

No doubt Fitzgerald was delighted at receiving the first serious critical article on his work. He told Wilson that he had read the review with "uncanny fascination" and didn't see how he could possibly be "offended with anything in it." ("It's no blurb," he wrote Max Perkins, "— nor by a darn sight — but it's the first time I've been done *at length* [by] an intelligent & sophisticated man and I appreciate it — jeers and all.")

Nonetheless, he asked Wilson to make some changes in his personal comments. Wilson had stated that the three most pertinent influences on Fitzgerald's character and writing were that he was from the Midwest and therefore overvalued the glamour and sophistication of the East; that he was Irish ("romantic, but also cynical about romance"); and that he drank heavily. Fitzgerald asked him to drop the references to his drinking habits; the "legend" was widespread anyway, and "this thing would hurt me more than you could imagine — both in my contact with the people with whom I'm thrown — relatives and respectable friends — and, what is more important, financially." Rather preposterously, Fitzgerald claimed that he wasn't Irish on his father's side ("that's where Francis Scott Key comes in"), as if his Irishness and his connections with the Southern gentry were mutually exclusive. He also pointed out that Wilson's catalogue was incomplete: "The most enormous influence on me in the four and a half years since I met her has been the complete, fine and full-hearted selfishness and chill-mindedness of Zelda," one of the more nicely turned and perverse compliments he was to pay his wife.

Fitzgerald had other pressing topics he wanted to discuss as well. During the winter, he had begun work on a comedy — at first called *Gabriel's Trombone;* later, *The Vegetable* — in which a $50-a-week clerk dreams of becoming a postman but is married to a nagging wife who wants him to be a financial success. The second act turns into a political farce when Jerry Frost, in a drunken fantasy, becomes President of the United States and creates havoc, a development that was intended to expose the mindlessness of the political profession. It seems to have escaped critical notice that a postman is a low-profile symbol for a writer (he delivers written messages). That Frost's ambition of being the best postman in the world is thwarted by a shrewish wife is also a farcical commentary on Fitzgerald's own marriage. And that Zelda and he should have "concocted a wonderful idea" for the second act presidential fantasy adds an appropriate irony. Wilson, who read the early versions of the much revised play, not only praised it ("the best American comedy ever written"), but served as an unofficial agent for it among his expanding circle of theatrical friends and connections. Aside from his continuing flirtation with Elinor Wylie (who was, in any case, more serious about John Bishop), Wilson had recently become involved with a bright young actress, Mary Blair, who had made a name for herself in Eugene O'Neill's *Diff'rent*.

Like many of Fitzgerald's friends in the early twenties, Wilson was involved in a number of theatrical projects. He had started work on a three-act play, *The Crime in the Whistler Room*. (It would be produced in 1924 at the Provincetown Playhouse with Mary Blair, then Mrs. Edmund Wilson, in the starring role.) He began writing theater criticism for *The Dial*. And during the tour of the Swedish Ballet in the United States, he served as the troupe's theatrical agent. He worked with the avant-garde composer Leo Ornstein on an ambitious Dada-style ballet, for which he hoped to get Charlie Chaplin to perform a pantomime sequence. And during that spring, when he was enthusiastically pushing Fitzgerald's theatrical project, Wilson and Ted Paramore were planning a comedy burlesque about an expedition in search of a plesiosaurus off the coast of Patagonia. It was prompted by newspaper reports of sightings of some antediluvian monster in those frigid waters.

Fitzgerald had need of someone in New York to look after his theatrical prospects. He had sent copies of the play to the producers William Harris and Daniel Frohman. He had been counting on the help of Alec McKaig, who was an assistant to Gilbert Miller, an associate at the Frohman agency. But during his March vacation in New York, Fitzgerald and McKaig had a bitter quarrel, and it would not be mended for some years. Fitzgerald's reconciliation with George

Jean Nathan during that spring was certainly opportune. "Nathan and me have become reconciled by letter," Fitzgerald had written Wilson earlier that winter. (Zelda sent the drama critic photographs of herself and the baby. "The pictures prove to me that you are getting more beautiful every day," Nathan responded, "but whose baby is it? It looks very much like Mencken.") And early on, Fitzgerald began sounding Nathan out about his play. "I can probably place it for you, if you are unable to do so yourself," Nathan had answered on Valentine's Day.

Fitzgerald was probably counting on Nathan's earlier appreciation of the one-act skits he had written for *The Smart Set*. In *The Theatre, The Drama, The Girls,* published in 1921, Nathan had already gone on record as suggesting that Fitzgerald should try a three-act play: "I feel that he will confect a genuinely diverting comedy. He has a good sense of character, a sharp eye, a gracious humor." *The Vegetable* offered Nathan the opportunity of cashing in on his prophecy. Nor did it harm Fitzgerald's prospects that he had dedicated *The Beautiful and Damned* to Nathan, along with Shane Leslie and Maxwell Perkins. ("A very substantial performance . . . it pleases me to have so good a piece of work dedicated in part to me," Nathan had responded.) And when he was in New York, Fitzgerald dropped in on the *Smart Set* offices, where he found Nathan "his usual self, albeit developing a paunch and losing a bit of his remarkable youthfulness." It seems clear that Nathan approved of the comedy, for Mencken wrote to James Branch Cabell: "Fitzgerald blew into New York last week. He has written a play and Nathan says that it has very good chances." Mencken, however, had some reservations about the Fitzgeralds' way of life: "It seems to me that his wife talks too much about money. His danger lies in trying to get it too rapidly. A very amiable pair, innocent and charming."

Throughout the year, writing and rewriting his play, Fitzgerald entertained glowing hopes of a huge Broadway success. He began by informing Max Perkins that his play was "going to make me rich forever. It really is. I'm so damned tired of the feeling that I'm living up to my income."

He was plainly not encouraged by the sales of *The Beautiful and Damned*. Max Perkins, writing to him on April 17, told him that

he was wrong to be disappointed. Even though the book hadn't sold
in the hundreds of thousands, as they had both hoped, it had by
April reached thirty-three thousand in sales. (Scribner's would print
a total of fifty thousand copies in 1922.) But the critical response,
Perkins suggested, had consolidated Fitzgerald's position in the field.
Fitzgerald was not exactly consoled; he wrote to Wilson that the
sales were "very satisfactory but not inspiring." It had been a mistake
to serialize the book before publication, he felt. He also felt that the
success of Dos Passos' *Three Soldiers* and Hergesheimer's *Cytherea* had
cut into his sales. (Hergesheimer's novel, published in January, went
through seven printings by the end of February.) "*Cytherea*," Fitzgerald told Wilson, "is Hergesheimer's best, but it's not quite."

Many of the reviewers, in fact, did feel that *The Beautiful and
Damned* was an advance over *This Side of Paradise*. That, certainly,
was the case with Wilson, and with John Peale Bishop, who reviewed
it for the *New York Herald.* Bishop thought it better "both in plan
and execution," and added, "If, stylistically speaking, it is not so
well written, neither is it so carelessly written." But, with condescending wit, he put down the author's intellectual pretensions. The
discovery of the meaninglessness of life, Bishop said, had caused
Fitzgerald to realize that his "twilight nymphs were, after all, only
middle-aged chorus ladies." Bishop suggested that the book really
belonged to Gloria rather than Anthony, "not because she is the
more vivid character than Anthony, but because she is the more
vividly imagined, more consistently presented." Bishop's public praise
of Fitzgerald's early work was only tinged with a sense of rivalry.
His private views were a good deal harsher. He wrote enthusiastically
to Wilson that Ben Hecht's *Erik Dorn* was "a marvelous book. So is
Dos Passos' *Three Soldiers*. Both make F.S.F. look like a hack writer
for Zelda's squirrel coat."

Henry Seidel Canby, in the *New York Post,* saw the book in
moral terms as a pathetic story, "the bitter cry of the children who
have grown up in their pleasant vices and found them no longer
pleasant but only expensive habits." He felt that Fitzgerald was too
much of his world to write about it with perfect detachment, but
he compared *The Beautiful and Damned* favorably with Hergesheimer's *Cytherea* as "another picture of a society upset by modernism."
The novel was, Canby contended, a kind of "irresponsible" social
document, "veracious in its way, as photographs are always veracious

in their way, but often untruthful, as photographs are often untruthful." (Fitzgerald was not altogether pleased with the review. He seems to have viewed it as a kind of potty-training effort: "By now you've seen [Canby's] little did in the *Post*," he wrote Perkins.) In *The Atlantic Monthly*, however, Henry Beston praised the truthfulness of the picture. Asking where the secret vitality of the book came from, Beston answered, "It dwells, one imagines, in the shrewd, complete, and quite unequaled picture it renders of the life of the day and the manners and customs of a class."

Among the critics was Zelda, whose review in the Book Page of the *New York Tribune* had been commissioned by Burton Rascoe, now its editor. Rascoe, who conducted a lively feature column about the literary life and personalities of the period, "A Bookman's Daybook," was eager to get provocative articles for his paper. Zelda's review had a zany personal quality that certainly made it different from other reviews. "To begin with," she announced, "every one must buy this book for the following aesthetic reasons: First because I know the cutest cloth of gold dress for only $300 in a store on 42nd Street, and also if enough people buy it, where there is a platinum ring with a complete circlet, and also if loads of people buy it my husband needs a new winter overcoat, although the one he has has done well enough for the last three years." She paid some vague attention to the story line, indicated her preference for the character of Gloria, complained about the author's attempts to "convey a profound air of erudition," which reminded her, suspiciously, of high school essays gotten up from passages in the *Encyclopaedia Britannica*. She also charged the author with stealing passages from her old diary, paraphrasing and editing segments of her old letters. There was a good deal in the book, she said, that seemed vaguely familiar. "In fact, Mr. Fitzgerald — I believe that is how he spells his name — seems to believe that plagiarism begins at home."

Rascoe's ploy in getting Zelda to review her husband's book was a highly successful one and increased his reputation. He and his wife, Hazel, in very short order had established themselves in the literary life of the city. Edmund Wilson was enthusiastic about him:

A most attractive fellow [Wilson wrote Stanley Dell]. I had never cared much for his criticism as I used to get odds and ends of it from the West, but since he has come East, I have got to know him and found him one of the most agreeable and interesting people

I have met in the journalistic business — he is one of the only ones who knows French and German very well and has a genuine enthusiasm for them.

There was a delay in Zelda's payment, so in April Fitzgerald wrote the book editor a coy and amusing letter: "I'm writing you at the behest of the famous author my wife, to tell you that the great paper which you serve is withholding from her the first money she has ever earned. Whatever it be, from a rouble to a talent, prick your clerk into satisfying her avarice — for she has become as one mad." He added, in flattering terms, "You have certainly done wonders with the pages in the *Tribune.*"

But Fitzgerald's attitude toward Rascoe's writing was to change rapidly. "There is something faintly repellent in his manner — in writing I mean," he told Wilson in June. Later he said: "Rascoe is getting worse than Frank Harris with his elaborate explanations and whitewashings of himself. There's no easier way for a clever writer to become a bore." The reasons for this sourness had less to do with Rascoe's style than with the hazards of the literary life in New York. In one of his gossipy columns in the *Tribune,* Rascoe published an anecdote stating that Fitzgerald, while visiting Robert Bridges, the editor of *Scribner's Magazine,* had plucked out six gray hairs from the older man's beard. Fitzgerald immediately wrote to Bridges, apologizing for the story and complaining that every bit of scandalous gossip associated with the new literary generation was being attributed to him. And he wrote Rascoe a tart letter, saying that it was a "silly story" to print and that it put him in an unpleasant position with people he had to work with.

But the real cause of Fitzgerald's anger undoubtedly was Rascoe's unfavorable review of *The Beautiful and Damned* in the May *Bookman.* Rascoe called the book "blubberingly sentimental." Although he said that Fitzgerald had demonstrated more verve and a more promising narrative skill than any recent young author, he suggested that Fitzgerald had collapsed "into the banal and the commonplace," because he had begun to take himself too seriously as a thinker.

Still, the literary life has to move on, whatever the private wounds of an author. Within the month, Fitzgerald was writing to Rascoe to recommend Shane Leslie's novel *The Oppidan,* which Scribner's had just published, and to alert him to an article that Zelda was working on for *McCall's*, with which Rascoe was affiliated. Fitzgerald contented himself with a brief P.S.: "You are all wrong about *The Beautiful and Damned*, but I don't care."

Their last summer in the Midwest was spent at Dellwood, in the White Bear Yacht Club. Zelda devoted much of her time to swimming, playing golf with Sandy Kalman, who remembered that Zelda did not seem to give a damn about clothes or about putting up with people she had no interest in: "I won't say she was rude, but she made it quite clear."

Fitzgerald kept himself busy, revising his play. His hopes for it were still on a rising curve. He wrote only one story during this period, "The Curious Case of Benjamin Button," a puerile allegory about a man who grows younger and younger, ending as an infant. And he wrote a comic account of his and Zelda's Southern tour, "The Cruise of the Rolling Junk." *The Saturday Evening Post* rejected it, but Ober managed to place it eventually with *Motor* magazine, which published it in an abridged form in installments. Otherwise, he made a selection of eleven recent stories for a new collection, *Tales of the Jazz Age*. Though several of them were potboilers, there were one or two important stories, notably "A Diamond as Big as the Ritz" and "The Lees of Happiness." One curious bit of telltale evidence in the lengthy prefaces he wrote for each of the tales was his insistence on the date of his naturalistic story "May Day," published in 1920. "I want to show that it was published before *Three Soldiers*," Fitzgerald explained to Perkins.

Fitzgerald's review of the Dos Passos novel in the *St. Paul Daily News* had its peculiar features. It was another of those evasions or half-truths that indicate how sensitive Fitzgerald was to his not having served overseas. With a kind of borrowed authority, he suggests to the reader that he is thoroughly experienced in what he refers to as "the whole gorgeous farce of 1917–1918." (In his autobiographical essay, "Who's Who—and Why," for *The Saturday Evening Post*, he had practiced an unusually successful elision by mentioning that he had been promoted to first lieutenant, had received his orders for overseas, then fade-out, until, the war over, he is back in New York, knocking on the doors of city editors—all of

which left the impression in the reader's mind that Lieutenant Fitzgerald had gone overseas and was, perhaps, too modest to dwell on
it.)

In his enthusiastically favorable review of *Three Soldiers,* Fitzgerald acts the part of an authentic guide, assuring the prospective
reader that

> he will hear the YMCA men with their high-pitched voices and
> their set condescending smiles. . . . He will see these same obnox-
> ious prigs charging twenty cents for a cup of chocolate. . . . He
> will see filth and pain, cruelty and hysteria and panic, in one long
> three year nightmare and he will know that the war brought the
> use of these things not to some other man or to some other man's
> son, but to himself and to his OWN son.

The high-pitched tone of the review suggests that Fitzgerald, perhaps vicariously, wanted to experience Dos Passos' indignation —
and maybe wanted to heighten it a shade or two.

While Fitzgerald and Zelda summered at the yacht club, they
received full and ribald reports on the upcoming June 17 wedding
of John Peale Bishop to Margaret Hutchins, a wealthy Chicago socialite. The latter was the target of many sour appraisals by Wilson
and his circle. Wilson gave the Fitzgeralds a bleak assessment of the
forthcoming marriage: "I regard it as more or less of a calamity, but
I suppose it was inevitable. She will supply him with infinite money
and leisure, but, I fear, chloroform his intellect in the meantime."
Bishop and his bride intended to honeymoon abroad for a year. "I
think her a prime dumbbell," Wilson wrote, "with nothing much
to distinguish her but an all too strong will which may lead John
around by the balls. A sad, sad business — unless it should turn out
to be a very satisfactory arrangement." Fitzgerald, in reply, expressed
the same ambivalence: "Having the money, she'll hold a high hand
over him. Still, I don't think he's happy and it may release him to
do more creative work."

When Wilson wrote to them about the wedding, he labeled it
"the most amusing piece of buffoonery of the kind I have ever participated in." Bishop seemed "scared into stupefaction." At the end
of the ceremony, the bridegroom was standing on the bride's train,
so she couldn't leave the altar. "His mother and sister were very
skeptical and unreconciled about the whole business and, under the
influence of champagne, became very plain spoken. The bride's father,

under the same influence, became amorous and tried to rape Elinor Wylie and Hazel Rascoe. The younger intellectuals formed a ring and danced round and round in the middle of the room to the jazz orchestra." Fitzgerald's response was bawdy: "Your description of the wedding amused us violently. . . . I wonder if John's penis has drunk its fill at last."

Wilson kept up his randy account to the point of anticlimax and the departure of the newlyweds for Europe. At the moment of sailing, a violent summer storm descended on New York, "as if in portent of some sinister and ominous event. A child with a triple penis was prematurely born in Brooklyn, and a large bright star in the form of the female genital was seen to hover over 53rd Street and Sixth Avenue." Despite the stag-line jokes, Wilson confessed to Fitzgerald that Bishop's leaving had moved him: "It was all very affecting, nearly breaking Alec McKaig's and my hearts." And to Elinor Wylie, Wilson admitted, "I miss him terribly; his going leaves me almost entirely to professional literary people, whom I find very unsatisfactory in some ways."

They were all, it seems, such good friends — and now their crowd was breaking up.

PART THREE

5

Innocence Is No End in Itself

IN SEPTEMBER, the Fitzgeralds were back in New York. They had left the baby in St. Paul while they looked for new quarters in the East. They stayed at the Plaza, but began scouring the countryside once more — both Westchester and Long Island — looking for something suitable. Given their customary extravagance, it is not odd that Zelda felt strangely indebted to the Plaza's headwaiter — "such a handsome head waiter that he never minded lending five dollars or borrowing a Rolls Royce." It was in their secondhand Rolls-Royce that they went house-hunting.

Edmund Wilson saw them soon after they hit town. He was astonished by their good looks and sobriety. "The most extraordinary thing," he wrote John Bishop, "is that they are both in the most wonderful form — partly owing to a summer in the country — and have resolved to begin a new phase of their life. Fitz has not let anybody but me know he is in the city and, though they have been here several days, they have not had one drink!" Both of them looked wonderfully fit — Zelda had lost her fat — and the two were functioning so rationally that Wilson could hardly believe his eyes!

> Fitz goes about soberly transacting his business and in the evening writes at his room in the hotel. I had a long conversation with him last night and found him full of serious ideas about regulating his life. He has hit upon a modus vivendi for preventing Zelda from absorbing all his time, emotion, and seminal juice; they have made a compact for the purpose of obviating the wasteful furies of jealousy, by which each is bound not to go out alone with another member of the other sex. I don't know how long it will last but I

have never seen Fitz present a more dignified appearance. . . . I suppose that when the hyenas find out that he is in town, they will all be on his neck—he has not even told Townsend and Alec. He is busy negotiating about his play.

It was at the Plaza that Zelda and Scott met John Dos Passos, who had told Bishop that the only two reviews of *Three Soldiers* he cared for were Fitzgerald's and his. A mild-mannered, bespectacled young man with a noticeably receding hairline, he was the illegitimate son of a Portuguese-American corporation lawyer. A Choate School and Harvard graduate, he already had acquired considerable urbanity, was well traveled and intensely literary. Gene Markey, a cartoonist for the *New York Tribune,* would caricature the two *"Enfants Terribles"* of the New York literary world as little boys: Fitzgerald in a Buster Brown outfit with limp wrist, smoking a cigarette; Dos Passos in a paper hat, playing with soldiers and shooting a popgun. Fitzgerald, given his predisposition for war heroes, must have envied Dos Passos' service in the ambulance corps, the source of his novel *Three Soldiers.*

In his early years, Dos Passos had fiercely radical views that seemed, to many observers, out of keeping with his soft manners. He suffered from a speech impediment, a decided lisp, that wicked friends like E. E. Cummings would unmercifully ridicule, along with his politics, behind his back. Edmund Wilson remembered a particularly dreadful imitation that Cummings gave of Dos Passos in the bathtub. It ran: "Isn't it dweadful of me to lie here in this luxurious warm bath while human welations are being violated all over the countwy—stwikers are being shot down." Nor was Dos Passos as sexually active as Cummings thought he should be. On a trip through Spain with Cummings, in the spring of 1921, Dos Passos had stymied his friend's every attempt to get him to promenade in the square each evening, prowling for a pickup. Dos Passos stubbornly remained in his room, which, despite his proletarian sympathies, was always in one of the best hotels. When Cummings was awakened every night by unearthly groanings, the result of the vivid nightmares that racked Dos Passos, he decided that abstinence was the cause of his friend's problem. Taking a different tack, Cummings tried to explain that people often had dreams that represented disguised sexual desires. Rather pointedly, he asked Dos Passos to relate his latest dream. Dos Passos answered that he had dreamed he had a bunch of asparagus that he was trying to give to Cummings.

The answer, it was said, "stopped Cummings in his tracks." Elinor Wylie, who saw a good deal of Dos Passos during those early years, complained, with an innocence as impervious as Dos Passos', that there was "something about him that was soft that ought to be hard." But Wilson, who kept up his friendship with Dos Passos for years, even when they disagreed heartily on political issues, thought otherwise. He felt that Dos Passos had a streak of intransigence, an assertion of independence, that was hard to overlook.

Whatever his democratic views, Dos Passos found himself caught up in the Fitzgeralds' legend. Scott had invited him to lunch at the Plaza early in October. Sherwood Anderson was the other guest. The dazzle and glamour of Dos Passos' recollection of the meeting in his memoir, *The Best Times,* may have been inspired by some of the headier passages in Fitzgerald's *The Great Gatsby.* Dos Passos remembered the crisp blue skies, the sparkling New York light. Everything had "the million dollar look," he noted. He found the atmosphere at the Plaza cloying, despite his preference for luxury hotels: the thick carpets, the expensive bouquets in the flower shop, the flashing gold buttons on the elevator man's tunic. Fitzgerald, Dos Passos made clear, was living in style, one of the literary nouveaux riches. The host, opening the door to his suite, scolded Dos Passos for being late, then introduced him to Anderson, who was his usual touseled and unkempt self, shaggy-haired and wearing a "gaudy Liberty silk necktie." Almost immediately, Dos Passos and Anderson, who had seen each other in Paris the year before, plunged into a literary discussion, which they kept up for much of the visit. It may have been in self-defense against the incriminating questions the Fitzgeralds asked new acquaintances.

> Their gambit [Dos Passos wrote] was to put you in the wrong. You were backward in your ideas. You were inhibited about sex. These things might perfectly well have been true but my attitude was that they were nobody's goddam business. Afterward, I used to kid Scott about his silly questions. They were like the true or false lists psychologists used to make up. Even that first time I couldn't get mad at him and particularly not at Zelda; there was a golden innocence about them and they both were so hopelessly good looking.

A glittering lunch table had been set in front of the windows overlooking Central Park; an elderly waiter stood by in attendance. The Fitzgeralds obviously had planned the affair for style. They started with Bronx cocktails and then champagne. "Scott had good bootleggers," Dos Passos claimed, but the meal was not up to the exacting standards of a gourmet like Dos Passos. Fitzgerald had "the worst ideas about food." The lobster croquettes that he had ordered were apparently a bad choice. "But everything you ate at the Plaza was good in those days. There was always the creamiest sweet butter to spread on crisp French rolls."

After lunch, Anderson left and the Fitzgeralds invited Dos Passos to make an excursion with them to Long Island, where they had an appointment with a real estate agent. They had rented a red touring car and chauffeur for the occasion. Perhaps through a sense of competition, Fitzgerald, as soon as they were on the road, started up his own literary conversation, discussing Sherwood Anderson, about whose writing he was both admiring and critical.

> When he talked about writing [Dos Passos noted] his mind which seemed to me full of preposterous notions about most things became clear and hard as a diamond. He didn't look at the landscape, he had no taste for food or wine or painting, little ear for music except for the most rudimentary popular songs, but about writing he was a born professional. Everything he said was worth listening to.

The outing, however, turned sour when they met the real estate agent and began visiting Great Neck estates, largely because the Fitzgeralds ridiculed the man to his face. Dos Passos was disgusted with their behavior and was considerably relieved when they dropped the agent and decided to pay a visit to Ring Lardner. Lardner was one of Fitzgerald's latest literary enthusiasms. He and his wife, Ellis, had recently bought a spacious house on East Shore Road in Great Neck for themselves and their four rambunctious sons. That, too, proved to be a less than happy occasion. Lardner was stupefied drunk and couldn't carry on a conversation. They had drinks with Ellis Lardner in the long, low, and somewhat dark living room and then started back for New York. Zelda's initial impression of Lardner was not especially favorable; she thought him a typical newspaperman with an odd penchant for playing the saxophone; she didn't find him particularly amusing. She was also aware that his binges might last anywhere from "one to x weeks." Quite probably, Lardner's six-foot height and his brooding and morose expression may have been overwhelming to someone as small as she was. She thought Ellis Lardner rather "common," but did like her. Fitzgerald's opinions of the journalist and short story writer were not altogether pleasant, either. On the trip back, sliding into stupefaction himself, Fitzgerald turned condescending about Lardner; he said that every man had his adopted drunk and that Lardner was his. Dos Passos was aware of Fitzgerald's genuine admiration for Lardner as a writer, but he nevertheless thought Fitzgerald's remark was needlessly cruel. Both he and Fitzgerald were in agreement that there was something distinctively American about Lardner's talent. They felt he was a writer of great precision and economy, with a real grasp of the American idiom.

En route to New York, they noticed a carnival. Both Zelda and Dos Passos pleaded to stop so that they could take a few rides. Scott agreed but remained in the limousine, seemingly uninterested, drinking from a bottle he had hidden under the back seat. Dos Passos and Zelda rode in the Ferris wheel, enjoying the flashing colored lights, the misty view of the suburbs from on high, the lilting music of the calliope. Dos Passos tried to explain his sense of excitement to Zelda, but had difficulty communicating with her: "Zelda and I kept saying things to each other but our minds never met."

His description of their evening ride amidst the colored carnival lights suggests a sensual undercurrent in the excitement. About Dos Passos' writing, Zelda would come up with one of her queer comparisons; she said that his books reminded her of impersonal apartments with the Sunday papers strewn around the floors. But she had a more immediate private impression of the man: he was rather like an elongated squirrel but attractive and not an Arrow collar type. "It wasn't that she wanted me to make love to her," Dos Passos explained in his memoir; "she was perceptive enough to know I wouldn't make a pass at Scott's girl. She may have thought it bourgeois but that was the way it was at that time." Dos Passos, in his highly ambiguous account, stated that, circling through the dark, he sensed in Zelda the edge of madness:

> The gulf that opened between Zelda and me, sitting up on the rickety Ferris wheel, was something I couldn't explain. It was only looking back at it years later that it occurred to me that, even the first day we knew each other, I had come up against that basic fissure in her mental processes that was to have such tragic consequences. Though she was so very lovely, I had come upon something that frightened and repelled me, even physically.

Part of that impression may have come from Zelda's desire to go on and on riding the Ferris wheel while Dos Passos, sitting dumbly with her, felt more and more uncomfortable.

The trip back to New York was silent: Zelda sulked; Fitzgerald was sulky drunk. Dos Passos was relieved to leave them outside the Plaza in the nighttime city. Although he would never claim to have been a close friend of the Fitzgeralds, Dos Passos felt that he remained on good terms with them over the years. But he sensed that there was a great divide between his aims in life and theirs. His estimation, based on that early encounter, was harsh but probably accurate: "They were celebrities in the Sunday supplement sense of the word. They were celebrities and they loved it." He recognized that he had as much ambition as the next writer. But he concluded, "The idea of being that kind of celebrity set my teeth on edge." His memoir of that first meeting is clear evidence that the Fitzgeralds had fallen off the wagon rather early after their arrival at the Plaza.

As soon as they found a house in Great Neck — it was a substantial, two-story affair, but with unaccountably small rooms, at 6 Gateway Drive — Zelda returned alone to St. Paul to pick up Scottie. Fitzgerald met his family at the station with a nursemaid, whom Zelda promptly fired. The replacement was little better; she refused to eat with the pair of Swedish servants — "my 14 kt. couple," Zelda called them — the Fitzgeralds had already hired. The result was that the household was in confusion. Nevertheless, by October 13, Zelda was writing to urge the Kalmans in St. Paul to come and visit them in their "nifty little Babbit home." She wrote, "We have had the most terrible time, very alcoholic and chaotic. We behaved so long that eventually we looked up Engalitcheff, which, needless to say, started us on a week's festivity equalled only by ancient Rome *and* Ninevah!" She added, "For the rest, we find ourselves diving into a fountain on the Greenwich Village Follies curtain, getting drunk with Zoe Akins and George Nathan. . . ."

The curtain referred to was another instance of their celebrity. The artist Reginald Marsh had commemorated Zelda's plunge into the fountain as one of the notable events in his drop curtain for the new edition of John Murray Anderson's *Greenwich Village Follies.* Another detail portrayed a truckload of young literary tartars — among them Scott, Edmund Wilson, Gilbert Seldes, John Peale Bishop, Donald Ogden Stewart, and John Dos Passos — speeding down Seventh Avenue. Marsh quite likely got the idea for the latter detail from a recent issue of *Vanity Fair,* which carried a feature

spread with photographs titled "The New Generation in Literature."
Wilson had written the captions for himself and friends. Wilson
took Elinor Wylie to the second-night performance, having thawed
her first with a bottle of port. "The Follies themselves were wonderful," he wrote the still-absent Bishop, "—one of the best reviews
I have ever seen. Bert Savoy [a famous female impersonator] was at
his very best. . . . Doesn't this make you homesick?"

It was a sign that the new literary generation had definitely
arrived.

Throughout the noisy, hopeful decade of the 1920s, the North Shore
of Long Island — the Gold Coast, as it was referred to — was the
haven of millionaires, successful and famous writers, artists, and
theatrical personalities. The region around Great Neck, Zelda declared, "looks like nothing so much as Times Square during the
theatre hour." At one time or another, Eddie Cantor, Ed Wynn,
Jane Cowl, Leslie Howard, Basil Rathbone, and George M. Cohan
had homes there. Gene Buck, a famous songwriter and assistant to
Florenz Ziegfeld, had a home near the Fitzgeralds, designed by
Joseph Urban, the theatrical designer. Zelda liked Buck, who said
"seen" where he ought to have said "saw" and was undoubtedly a
millionaire. She was less approving of Mrs. Buck, a Dulcy-like chorus girl who had very lovely legs. The Bucks were steady drinking
and partying companions of the Fitzgeralds and accompanied them
to the Princeton football games. They were also a source of boozy
quarrels between the two couples; Helen Buck, it seems, had an
unreciprocated crush on Fitzgerald.

The theatrical producers Sam Harris and Arthur Hopkins had
homes in the area. Ring Lardner had an impressive view of the
neighboring estate of Herbert Bayard Swope, executive editor of the
New York World and an inveterate and extravagant party-giver who
liked to get up elaborate treasure hunts with gifts hidden in the
bushes and around the sprawling grounds. Guests, in their cups,
tended to wander into the Lardner "cottage" — Lardner referred to
it more ignominiously as "the Mange" — assuming that it was simply an adjunct of the party across the road. North of the Manhasset
Yacht Club, Clarence Buddington Kelland, one of the most highly
paid short story writers of the slick magazines, had his home. And
on the western shores of Hempstead Harbor, the various members

of the Guggenheim clan and Vincent Astor maintained their baronial mansions.

The Fitzgerald house was very small in comparison with the grand estates of the region, but it became the scene of continuous and expensive weekend partying. In a humorous article for *The Saturday Evening Post,* "How to Live on $36,000 a Year," based loosely on his 1923 earnings (he had in fact earned less; $28,759 after agency fees), Fitzgerald tried to figure out his mysterious finances. He noted that they paid $300 a month rent, $90 a month for Scottie's nurse, $160 a month for a maid-cook and a butler. There were additional fees for a part-time laundress, probably hired in self-defense against Zelda's habit of using closets as clothes hampers, and modest monthly allowances for entertainment, parties, theater tickets. And they had bought their secondhand Rolls, which, like all Fitzgerald cars, would be subjected to cruel and unusual punishment. Somehow, when Fitzgerald concluded his investigation into the higher mathematics of his financial situation, there were $12,000 that could not be accounted for.

On Long Island, the Fitzgeralds were lionized. Scott boasted to friends and relatives that Great Neck was "most amusing after the dull healthy middle west. For instance, at a party last night where we went were John McCormick, Hugh Walpole, F.P.A., Neysa McMein, Arthur William Brown, Rudolf Friml and Deems Taylor. They have no mock-modesty, and all perform their various stunts upon the faintest request so it's like a sustained concert." With a little help from Edmund Wilson on the lyrics, Fitzgerald had perfected his own party number, a comic song sung by a dog-lover, which he would perform with dead earnestness, his jacket tightly buttoned, accompanying himself with appropriate gestures:

> Dog, dog — I like a good dog —
> Towser or Bowser or Star —
> Clean sort of pleasure —
> A four-footed treasure —
> And faithful as few humans are!
> Here Pup, put your paw up —
> Roll over dead like a log!
> Larger than a rat!
> More faithful than a cat!
> Dog! Dog! Dog!

Fitzgerald's drily delivered routine usually occasioned rounds of applause and hilarious laughter, and the song caught on, making the rounds at parties and even turning up in a nightclub act—unattributed to the lyricists.

Fitzgerald himself was in the midst of a welter of theatrical projects, attempting to promote his play, putting it through more revisions. *The Beautiful and Damned* had been sold to Warner Brothers with Marie Prevost and Kenneth Harlan in the leading roles. He was paid only $2500 for the rights, with a promise of a bonus if the movie grossed over $250,000. He considered it poor pay and was embarrassed to have anyone know what the fee was. "And please don't tell anyone what I got for the B&D from the movies," he cautioned Perkins. He was not very pleased with the final results, either; he told Tom Boyd that if he wanted "a good laugh," he should see the film. To Oscar Kalman, he wrote that it was "by *far* the worst movie I've ever seen in my life—cheap, vulgar, ill-constructed and shoddy." He and Zelda, he said, were ashamed of it. In the spring, David Selznick had asked him to write a scenario for Elaine Hammerstein, which was eventually turned down. Later it was offered to Metro for Viola Dana. Famous Players–Lasky Productions were dickering with him for a script for Bebe Daniels, but it did not materialize.

Early in his career, Fitzgerald learned not to be overly sanguine about his film prospects; they had a way of hanging fire for long periods of time, then evaporating suddenly. On the Viola Dana scenario, he told Harold Ober to get an early and definite yes or no; the longer a producer held a property, the more reasons he found for not doing it. Outlook Photoplay Company took an option on *This Side of Paradise* for $3000. There were even suggestions that he and Zelda might star in it, but when the producers failed to pay the option money, the contract was cancelled. He had more success with Townsend Martin, now one of the partners in the Film Guild, who arranged for him to write an original script—for $2000— from which the film *Grit,* starring Clara Bow and a young New York leading man, Glenn Hunter, was made. Hunter was one of the most successful male stars of his time and had been considered for the lead in *This Side of Paradise.* During Hunter's London tour with *Merton of the Movies,* the Prince of Wales turned up so often in front row seats that it started an ugly round of gossip. Fitzgerald, writing to Tom Boyd in St. Paul about working with the young leading man, claimed it was "a pleasant affiliation as he's a nice kid. Paramount are now paying him $156,000 a year and two years ago, he was starving in Central Park." Given the spectacular successes and phenomenal failures, he had good reason to be wary about the lure of the film industry.

One of his minor film projects that winter was writing the "titles" for the silent film version of Edith Wharton's best seller *The Glimpses of the Moon*. Fitzgerald had always claimed to be an admirer of Wharton's work, and when, one day in the spring of 1923, he was in the Scribner's offices and learned that the society novelist was visiting her publisher, Fitzgerald strode in and knelt at her feet — one of his characteristically grand and flattering gestures. Or so the legend had it. Edmund Wilson, reporting to John Bishop, gave a less dramatic account: "By the way, Mrs. Wharton has just left after a brief visit to America; the day she left she met Fitz in Scribner's and they had a rather surprising interview — surprising because he made a great hit with her."

Christmas, that first year in Great Neck, was a season to celebrate. As Zelda confessed to the Kalmans, it began a week before the event and continued for two weeks or more of continuous partying. They attended a very dull New Year's Eve party, which Zelda livened up by tossing people's hats into a bowl-shaped chandelier. And it ended one afternoon, a few days later, at the Famous Players Studios, where they watched a young, balding Canadian-born director, Allan Dwan, filming sequences of *The Glimpses of the Moon*, with Nita Naldi and Bebe Daniels performing. Zelda, predictably, found neither of the reigning vamps attractive. Nita Naldi had a head "full of ozone" and a mouth too full of teeth.

In their season of success and fame, Fitzgerald was feeling flush with rosy prospects. He wrote Boyd to tell him the good news of the resale of the film rights for *This Side of Paradise*, this time to Famous Players: "They paid me fifteen thousand dollars cash for it." He had had an offer from *Hearst's International*, asking for options on his future stories for the coming year. The magazine would pay $1750 apiece. His play *The Vegetable*, for want of a producer, was being published by Scribner's in April. He boasted, "So you see I'm now a purse proud millionaire & as good a business man as Hergesheimer." There was the sound of money in the air. But he added a cautionary note: "No figures in this letter are for publication." It may have been an indirect admission that he had padded the sums a bit. His ledger account gives $10,000 as the fee Famous Players paid for the rights to *This Side of Paradise*.

II

"It was an age of miracles," Fitzgerald would proclaim a bit pretentiously; "it was an age of art, it was an age of excess, and it was an age of satire." Zelda, in more philistine but not inaccurate terms, thinking back on visits to the *Smart Set* and *Vanity Fair* offices, would call it "a collegiate literary world puffed into wide proportions by the New York papers." At the end of the decade, Edmund Wilson, with just the right sense of the important and the negligible, described it as "undisguisably a babel of tongues, a round of disorderly parties, an exchange of malicious gossip and a blather of half-baked opinions." But it did have "its exhilarating qualities of ready response and variety. It was amusing, if nothing else." Yet Wilson would concede that the literary life of the twenties had its undeniable importance: "There *was* something going on in those days. One did feel that great books were being written, that decisive battles were being fought." It was an age of intelligence and wit, though Fitzgerald and Zelda never seemed drawn to the intellectual center of it; only hovered at its edges.

It was also an age of high spirits. At the Algonquin, on West Forty-fourth Street, for instance, the pundits and playwrights of the Round Table, under the watchful eye of the manager, Frank Case, met for lunch on workdays or for the Saturday evening poker games that were held under the auspicious name of the Thanatopsis Literary and Inside Straight Club. The regulars were Dorothy Parker and Robert Benchley, Alexander Woollcott, Robert Sherwood, George S. Kaufman, and Franklin P. Adams, whose "Conning Tower" in the *World* became a kind of clearinghouse for the irreverence and satire of his cronies in the "Vicious Circle." Edmund Wilson, who sometimes dropped in on the group, found them too shallow for his taste: "They all came from the suburbs and 'provinces' and a sort of tone was set — mainly by Benchley I think." They had all been brought up with the same standards of gentility, played the same games, read the same children's books, and were now in the business of mocking their provincial upbringing by way of an acquired New York sophistication. "I found this rather tiresome, since they never seemed to be able to get above it," wrote Wilson. The Round Table wits were frequently accused of logrolling, promoting each other's reputations. The cartoonist John Held, Jr., once did an acerbic little print called "Backscratching at the Algonquin," depicting the various members of the club all engaged in that useful and soothing activity. In addition, the Algonquin group was something of a production-line play factory, with Marc Connelly, Charles MacArthur, Sherwood, and Kaufman turning out the most successful and popular comedies and musical comedies of the period. The actresses associated with the group—Helen Hayes, Peggy Wood, Margalo Gillmore, Ina Claire, Lynn Fontanne, Tallulah Bankhead—starred in the comedies, some of which were written for them. Occasionally, stars and writers married and mingled. Helen Hayes soon married Charles MacArthur; Peggy Wood married John V. A. Weaver, the poet, novelist, and literary editor of the *Brooklyn Eagle* whose initiation into the club was a wrestling match with Ina Claire, in which the slender star threw him flat on his back. When the astonished Weaver quipped, "Listen Mom, put on your glasses and let's fight fair," he was unanimously voted into membership. Occasionally the members of this theatrical cartel would put on an entertainment for their own benefit, like the one-night stand of *No Sirree,* given at the 49th Street Theater on April 30, 1922. Actors, playwrights, and critics all performed: Benchley gave his famous routine "The Treasurer's Report"; Ruth Gillmore did an imitation of Ethel Barrymore; Helen Hayes impersonated an English flapper; Connelly, Kaufman, and Woollcott appeared in parody skits of plays by Eugene O'Neill and Zoë Akins. Despite their usual self-involvement, the Vicious Circle had its idols—an unlikely one in Ring Lardner, who kept his distance from the Algonquin clique, though he did bend sufficiently to collaborate with Kaufman on a comedy, *June Moon.* Wilson, ever suspicious of the Round-Tablers, found it difficult to understand the "enormous reverence" the group had for the morose writer, who certainly didn't reciprocate.

> He never mingled with them. . . . He was somehow aloof and inscrutable, by nature rather saturnine, but a master whom all admired, though he was never present in person. It may be that all any such circle demands is a presiding but invisible deity who is assumed to regard them with a certain scorn.

Edward Fitzgerald with young Scott, ca. 1899

Mary (Mollie) Fitzgerald

Scott at age 2

Zelda in costume
at high school age

Scott at Newman School,
age 16

Scott as the beautiful "show girl"
in the Princeton Triangle Club
production of *The Evil Eye,* 1915

SOME OF FITZGERALD'S FAVORITE ACTRESSES
Rosalinde Fuller (*above left*) at the time of her appearances in *The Greenwich Village Follies;* photography by Francis Bruguière, ca. 1920. James Abbe's *Vanity Fair* portraits of: Lillian Gish (*above right*) in D. W. Griffith's production of *Broken Blossoms,* 1919; Ina Claire (*below left*) in *The Gold Diggers,* 1919; Laurette Taylor (*below right*) in Hartley Manner's play *One Night in Rome,* 1920.

GILBERT SELDES
Formerly American correspondent of the *Echo de Paris*, and now managing editor of The Dial; author of some of the most brilliant critical articles which have appeared in that magazine

JOHN PEALE BISHOP
Princeton, 1917. Author of "Green Fruit," a thin volume of verses; collaborator with Edmund Wilson Jr. on "The Undertaker's Garland"; a contributor of book reviews and other articles to Vanity Fair

DONALD OGDEN STEWART
Mr. Stewart has already received wide recognition on account of his humorous essays and his amusing "Parody Outline of History"

JOHN V. A. WEAVER
Literary editor of the Brooklyn Daily Eagle; author of "In American," a widely read volume of verse in the American language

JOHN DOS PASSOS
A graduate of Harvard, 1916; author of "Three Soldiers," probably the most substantial work yet produced by the younger generation

JOHN FARRAR
Mr. Farrar is now editor of The Bookman and has published two volumes of verse, "Forgotten Shrines" and "Songs for Parents"

STEPHEN VINCENT BENET
At the age of twenty-four Mr. Benét has published three books of poems of which the latest, "Heavens and Earth", divided the prize of the Poetry Society, a successful novel "The Beginning of Wisdom" and has completed a second novel "Young People's Pride"

EDMUND WILSON, JR.
A contributor of brilliant and informed critical essays to The New Republic and other periodicals; one of the authors of "The Undertaker's Garland"

F. SCOTT FITZGERALD
Who found immediate fame on the publication of "This Side of Paradise", written at the age of twenty-two; his second novel is "The Beautiful and Damned"

The New Generation in Literature
A Group of Young Writers Who Have Come Upon Old Age While Still in Their Twenties

"The New Generation in Literature" from *Vanity Fair*, February 1922.
Edmund Wilson wrote the captions for his friends.

Zelda in her traveling
outfit, summer 1920

Nathan and H.L. Mencken
in a photograph taken by
Alfred A. Knopf, 1923

At the honeymoon cottage in Westport, Connecticut, 1920: Tana,
unidentified man, Broadway producer John D. Williams,
Zelda, George Jean Nathan, Scott, Alec McKaig

The *Hearst's International* photo of Scott and Zelda, May 1923.
Collage from Zelda's scrapbook.

A far more sedate literary establishment was the Coffee House at 54 West Forty-fifth Street, where the regulars of the *Vanity Fair* staff and its contributors met. It was more a social and eating club than the Algonquin, and had been started by Frank (Crownie) Crowninshield, the editor of the Condé Nast publication. Wilson called it a "feeder" for contributors to the magazine, probably in both senses, since the rates and salaries at *Vanity Fair* were low. Staff writers, artists, and a few actors met there; everyone sat at a long communal table, though one could bring guests and order a meal, eating in private if one chose.

Fitzgerald's attitude toward *Vanity Fair* was slightly self-serving and chiefly indifferent. His offhand article "This Is a Magazine" was published there, together with a satirical story, "Jemima the Mountain Girl," for which he had received *Vanity Fair's* top fee of $100. Later, while Wilson was serving as managing editor, Fitzgerald contributed an homage to his current idol, Ring Lardner, for one of the magazine's usual features, "We Nominate for the Hall of Fame." His encomium, edited down for the March 1923 issue, read:

> Because he is quite unaware of the approval he is receiving in erudite circles; because he is covered with bruises from representing the Yale football team against his Harvard-bound boys; and finally because with a rare true ear, he has set down for posterity the accents of the American language.

Wilson, when he had first joined the staff, in 1920, had brought in new blood, like his Princeton friends Bishop and Seward Collins, who later became Dorothy Parker's lover and the editor-publisher of *The Bookman*. Wilson had no enthusiasm for the mean-spirited ambience of the *Vanity Fair* office or the dubious charms of its smarmy, gray-haired, bottom-pinching chief editor. Crowninshield talked altogether too much about being a gentleman, Wilson thought. "This has made me suspicious ever since of people who talk much about 'gentlemen.' I think it ought to be a warning to be careful and hold on to one's wallet." Moreover, Crowninshield had a bad habit of offering to lend money to his underpaid staff members and then almost immediately begin badgering them to pay up.

What may well have soured Wilson on the place was that he had gotten the job because of a crisis in the office politics. Dorothy Parker, reviewing a recent performance of Billie Burke in *Caesar's Wife,* a Maugham play, had said the evening seemed "a long and uneventful one." Billie Burke had looked charmingly youthful as the wife and was best in her more serious moments, but she tended to play the lighter scenes "as if she were giving an impersonation of Eva Tanguay." Billie Burke was the wife of Florenz Ziegfeld, one of the regular advertisers in *Vogue,* the lucrative parent publication in the Condé Nast syndicate. Ziegfeld complained; Nast sent word that Mrs. Parker should be fired; Crowninshield obliged. Robert Sherwood and Robert Benchley resigned in protest. The Algonquin trio had constituted an unruly staff-within-the-staff from the beginning. When an edict came down from on high that staff members were not to discuss their salaries with each other, Parker and her two friends wore signs around their necks, announcing how much they got paid.

Wilson had been called in to replace the dismissed staff members. Although Dorothy Parker and Benchley had only jokingly referred to him as a scab, and very kindly showed him the ropes, he nonetheless felt distinctly uncomfortable. For Condé Nast himself, the lean and fastidious publisher, Wilson felt outright scorn: "the glossiest bounder I have ever known." Unlike most of Nast's friends, who regarded him as the sultan of chic and scrambled for invitations to his swank Park Avenue parties, Wilson accused Nast of being "incapable of saying good morning without a formally restrained but somehow obnoxious vulgarity."

Fitzgerald had all along been condescending about Wilson's association with *Vanity Fair.* He welcomed the news that his friend had been offered a job as managing editor of *The New Republic,* commenting, "It always seemed undignified for you to be on *Vanity Fair.*" But he was evidently too much the party-goer or party-giver not to be intrigued by the luxurious parties Nast gave in his thirty-room penthouse at 1040 Park Avenue, with its pink ballroom and glassed-in terraces, its salons furnished by Louis XV out of Elsie de Wolfe. Guests numbered in the hundreds; high society and royalty mixed with show business types, artists, designers, couturiers, and photographers. Each affair afterward would be coded and counted, analyzed for budgetary purposes; the number of invited guests sorted into singles and couples, males and females; the percentage that showed up; the amount of liquor consumed; the number of small tables, gilt chairs, coatracks, hangers, waiters, and dishwashers required; the weather and its effect on attendance. Fitzgerald, who attended at least one of these affairs, thought that they "rivaled in their way the fabled balls of the Nineties."

◁══▷

At *The New Republic*, with which he would be associated off and on for many years, Wilson commandeered articles and reviews by friends and acquaintances like Bishop and Collins, as well as up-and-coming critics and poets like Van Wyck Brooks, Malcolm Cowley, Howard Coxe, Burton Rascoe, Allen Tate — all writers whose intellectual abilities and political views he appreciated. Fitzgerald had promptly congratulated Wilson in fictional terms by clapping him into *The Beautiful and Damned* as Eugene Bronson, "whose articles in The New Democracy were stamping him as a man with ideas transcending both vulgar timeliness and popular hysteria." But Fitzgerald never became a regular or even an occasional contributor to *The New Republic*. The one article he wrote for it, much later, was an obituary notice on Ring Lardner. Quite likely the magazine did not pay well enough to make it worth Fitzgerald's while, but it is also possible that Wilson did not consider him up to the intellectual standards of the publication.

Wilson was one of the most influential vanguard critics of the period, an early champion of T. S. Eliot's *The Waste Land* and James Joyce's banned *Ulysses*. When the smuggled copies of the book were being sold at the Brick Row Book Shop on East Forty-seventh Street, Wilson reviewed it in the July 5, 1922, issue of *The New Republic*. Among his friends, he was the earnest promoter. "It contains some of the most brilliant and some of the dreariest and dullest writing of the age, but it has already been accepted as a sort of divine revelation by the intelligentsia — most of whom have not read it," he advised Stanley Dell. He thought Mrs. Bloom's stream-of-consciousness soliloquy at the end of the book "probably one of the most remarkable things of the kind ever written: I was greatly moved by it." He wrote Fitzgerald that some of the drunken episodes had an uncanny resemblance to the "drunken-vision" scene in his play *The Vegetable*. Fitzgerald, obviously intrigued, managed to get a copy but remained unconvinced. Besides, it reminded him too much of his own middle-class Irish background and made him feel "appallingly naked." Later he commented again, "Am undecided about *Ulysses'* application to me — which is as near as I ever come to forming an impersonal judgment." It was an odd admission, oblique in its way, as if the only things about which he could form an impartial judgment were those which did not touch his ego in some way.

Although he praised Wilson's *New Republic* review of Joyce — "the only criticism yet I could make head or tail of. . . . You are an incomparable egg" — Fitzgerald indulged in some critical back-biting. Writing to his friend Tom Boyd on the subject of Wilson and Joyce, he said:

> I agree with you about Bunny and Mencken — though with qual-
> ifications as to both. Bunny appreciates feeling after it's been filtered
> through a temperament but his soul is a bit *sec* — and in beginning
> the Joyce cult on such an exalted scale he has probably debauched
> the taste of a lot of people — (who of course don't matter anyhow)
> — but these unqualified admirations!

Those were his private views. In public, in a syndicated article, "10 Best Books I Have Read," Fitzgerald listed Joyce's *A Portrait of the Artist as a Young Man* as one of his choices and described *Ulysses* as "the great novel of the future."

It was a time of new beginnings and new social assessments in the magazines of the period. H. L. Mencken, dissatisfied with the trivializing tone of *The Smart Set,* initiated another periodical, *The American Mercury,* once again with Nathan as co-editor. But strangely, in the freewheeling and irreverent age he had helped to usher in, Mencken was becoming censorious. ("It seems that Mencken has studied the anti-smut law so closely," Wilson wrote to Stanley Dell, "that he is now able to see how it could apply to almost anything and is consequently afraid of publishing anything; Rascoe told me some incredible changes he had made in manuscripts.") It was at the poker table of the Thanatopsis Literary and Inside Straight Club that Harold Ross, an enterprising editor, and Raoul Fleischmann, heir of the yeast and baking empire, hatched the idea for the highly successful *New Yorker.* The old political journal *Masses,* defunct since 1918, when it was suppressed by the Justice Department for "con-spiracy against the government," was revived in 1926 with such men as Dos Passos, Mike Gold, Paxton Hibben, and Joseph Freeman on the executive board. Its former editor, Max Eastman, had in the meantime started *The Liberator,* with Floyd Dell, Fitzgerald's bête noire, as literary editor. In November 1922 Wilson wrote to Fitzgerald that Egmont Arens, the former art editor of *Vanity Fair,* was proposing to bring out another edition of his trial magazine *Playboy,* which would contain "drawings and writings by all the more unruly native geniuses." He invited Fitzgerald to a party at the Washington Square Book Shop to discuss the possibilities. Wilson promised that Dos Passos, Seward Collins, and Elinor Wylie would be among the guests. "The idea is to make *Playboy* a sort of mouthpiece for all the bizarre and scurrilous things which people can't publish elsewhere." The magazine never lived up to that ambition; it became a more bohemian version of *Vanity Fair,* with articles by or about the vanguard literary and artistic personalities of the moment, like Georgia O'Keeffe and her photographer husband, Alfred Stieglitz, who, in his gallery, 291, introduced to many Americans the works of Picasso and Matisse, and now kept a stable of new wave American painters, including O'Keeffe, John Marin, and Arthur Dove. There were articles, reviews, and poems by Sherwood Anderson and Wilson and the sculptor Eric Gill. Each of the quarterly portfolios was illustrated with original woodcuts and linoleum prints by artists like Alfred Maurer, Louis Bouché, Rockwell Kent.

But the intellectual, social, and artistic ferment was leavened with a good deal of high spirits and indiscriminate partying. *Playboy,* for instance, held its annual subscription balls at Webster Hall, the lively gathering place of artists and intellectuals on East Eleventh Street. It was an old Village tradition: the early *Masses* crowd had held its yearly fund-raising costume balls there, as well. *Playboy* advertised its subscription balls as "the most elaborate and entertaining events of the Bohemian season," with admissions supposedly limited to "representatives of the Seven Arts (not excluding the Lively Arts) and their friends." They were always boisterous affairs. Ted Paramore, who made it a practice of going to such events as a "vulture"—to hunt for the younger girl friends of older men—had, in the course of one of the *Playboy* dances, stumbled into a kind of stable area in which a dead-drunk "corpse" was laid out in every stall. "It looked like Flanders Field," he said. In late April 1923, Wilson had taken the poet Louise Bogan to one of the seasonal dances and at some point, presumably in the midst of the human debris, she announced, "I feel ready to say 'Blaa!' to the whole world." It was on the same occasion, according to Wilson, that Fitzgerald "blew up as usual, early in the evening, and knocked Pat Kearny unconscious in the lavatory." Probably it was after that evening, or one equally memorable, that Fitzgerald woke up, bleary-eyed, to find himself in the morning headlines: FITZGERALD KNOCKS OFFICER THIS SIDE OF PARADISE. Fitzgerald drily noted, "Successful scrapping not being among my accomplishments, I tried in vain to reconstruct the sequence of events that led up to this dénouement in Webster Hall." He was not being altogether truthful. Increasingly over the years his drinking would bring out a streak of pugnacity; he was to have serious fights with policemen, nightclub bouncers, and taxicab drivers — and receive serious beatings.

Liquor had become an inevitable fact of life in most of the literary and artistic gatherings in New York. Dos Passos, a sometime painter as well as a writer, held an exhibition at the Whitney Studio Club on West Fourth Street. He sent the Fitzgeralds an invitation to his opening — the other artist was Reuben Nakian, the sculptor — that gives an impression of the jaunty and liquid spirit of the times. "Come and bring a lot of drunks," Dos Passos advised. The opening would more than likely be a "tea fight." He added, "Any contestant looking at the pictures or mentioning the syllable art will be declared to have fouled and will be removed from the floor. Consolation prizes (listen to the cocktail shaker, listen to the cocktail shaker, listen to the cocktail shaker singing o'er the grave) will be administered."

It was during this round of New York parties that the Fitzgeralds struck up an intermittent but untroubled friendship with the novelist, critic, photographer, and patron of the arts Carl Van Vechten. Van Vechten was one of the most zealous white promoters of the Harlem Renaissance. Among the guests at the New York parties he gave with his Russian-born wife, the actress Fania Marinoff, were the usual literary and theatrical lights as well as rising black artists and performers like Langston Hughes, Zora Neale Hurston, and Paul Robeson. Tall, stooped, tow-haired, and slack-jawed, Van Vechten was a hulking, gracious host. In other respects, he could be trying. In a bookstore he was an outrageous name-dropper: "I read this book of Cabell's in manuscript"; "Conrad told me that he was not really satisfied with this novel." When the dazed bookseller finally asked who he was, Van Vechten would answer, "Oh, I am Edna St. Vincent Millay." He could also be heavy in hand. Dorothy Parker avoided him at all cost. Once, spotting Van Vechten in a Philadelphia hotel, she fled through the nearest door. It was the entrance to the men's room.

Van Vechten was in his forties when he met the Fitzgeralds; he seemed nonetheless to belong to the younger generation—in the spirit, if not in the flesh. He was a connoisseur of parties; the parties of the Jazz Age, Van Vechten maintained, had good food and drink in abundance and "lots of talk and certainly a good deal of lewd behavior." These were the scenes he painted in his second and highly successful novel, *The Blind Bow Boy,* whose heroine, Campaspe Lorillard, was modeled after the New York saloniste Mabel Dodge. Fitzgerald professed that the novel was better than Huxley's *Antic Hay.* Zelda adopted Van Vechten as a large and shaggy friend, and her enthusiasm for his arch and sometimes outrageous humor was genuine. Van Vechten later put both Fitzgeralds into another of his novels, appropriately titled *Parties.* But he tended to romanticize and glamorize the couple's public squabbles, their dependence, and what appeared to be their devotion: "Rilda and David tortured each other because they loved one another devotedly."

It was at a dinner party in the apartment of the Irish critic and essayist Ernest Boyd, then living on East Nineteenth Street, that the Fitzgeralds met Van Wyck Brooks, the historian of American literature. After two days of continuous partying, they arrived late, after everyone else had eaten. They promptly fell asleep over their soup. Someone picked Zelda up and put her in a bedroom, Brooks remembered. "Scott slumbered in the living-room, waking up suddenly again to telephone an order for two cases of champagne, together with a fleet of taxis to take us to a night-club." Brooks, who was an old friend of Max Perkins', was impressed with the Fitzgeralds' largesse and kept an image of them as romantic lovers. At another party, Fitzgerald, under the misapprehension that Brooks was a dyed-in-the-wool Yankee (he had actually grown up in Plainfield, New Jersey), circled around him and deftly lifted his pants leg, convinced that he would be wearing red longjohns. Fitzgerald's drunken generosity, as Brooks remembered it, was confirmed by Ernest Boyd. Boyd recalled Scott's "embarrassing habit of using his checkbook for the writing of inexplicable autographs in the tragic moments immediately preceding his flight through the weary wastes of Long Island."

It was at a party in Townsend Martin's New York apartment that Gilbert Seldes, the journalist and editor of *The Dial,* met the

Fitzgeralds. It was a lively affair, and Seldes had either had so much to drink or found it so exhausting that he wandered into a bedroom to rest. The newly arrived Fitzgeralds sought him out. "Suddenly," Seldes remembered, "as though in a dream, this apparition, this double apparition, approached me. The two most beautiful people in the world were floating toward me, smiling." The cordiality on the part of Fitzgerald, at least, is surprising, since Seldes, under the pseudonym Vivian Shaw, had written a rather double-edged review of *The Beautiful and Damned* in *The Dial,* complaining that Maury Noble's philosophical speculations sounded like "a résumé of *The Education of Henry Adams* filtered through a particularly thick page of *The Smart Set,*" and suggesting that Fitzgerald had been running so closely on the heels of Edith Wharton's recent novels that he was skirting plagiarism. His praise, on the other hand, was not altogether expansive. The book, Seldes wrote, was important "because it presents a definite American milieu and because it has pretensions as a work of art." Seldes' comment on meeting the Fitzgeralds — "I thought to myself, 'If there is anything I can do to keep them as beautiful as they are, I will do it' " may have been genuine. In the future, his encouragement would sustain Fitzgerald through some hard times.

From some of these parties, Fitzgerald ducked out — solo. It was on one of these occasions that he met the Scots journalist James Drawbell in a speakeasy. The two struck up a lively conversation; Fitzgerald had already been drinking and was "deathly pale." They discovered they had much in common. Drawbell had been a sickly child and as a consequence had a great admiration for athletes, and he was not inclined to be promiscuous in a promiscuous time. He was intensely serious about writing, and his admiration of the celebrated novelist was obviously flattering. Drawbell remembered that as they left the speakeasy Fitzgerald remarked, "Parties are a form of suicide. I love them, but the old Catholic in me secretly disapproves." Fitzgerald suggested they go to a Childs restaurant for some black coffee; instead, the two ended up in Drawbell's seedy room in a West Fifty-fourth Street brownstone, finishing off a bottle of cheap Scotch and carrying on their conversation. Fitzgerald bitterly bemoaned his failure to get overseas, his inability to live up to the men who had the wealth and the social advantages. "I was always trying to be one of them! That's worse than being nothing at all." And they talked about women. "Oh, I've had all the fun," Fitzgerald said, "but in my heart I can't stand this casual business. With a woman, I have to be emotionally in it up to my eyebrows, or it's nothing. . . . When I love, I love. It has to be my life." There was a pause, during which Drawbell expected he would mention Zelda. Instead, Fitzgerald went on, "Silly, isn't it? Look at the fun we miss!" At bottle's end, Fitzgerald left, but not without giving Drawbell the benefit of his advice. Glancing around the drab monastic cell, he said, "You ought to get the hell out of this!"

Quite possibly the most notorious of the New York literary parties in the early twenties was the Dreiser affair. The novelist, not one of the most gregarious of men, had arranged a sedate party to celebrate the publication of one of his novels. As far as Fitzgerald's movements can be determined, early on the evening of the party he encountered Carl Van Vechten, H. L. Mencken, and Ernest Boyd, having dinner at the Brevoort before going to the Dreiser apartment at St. Luke's Place. Fitzgerald, who had not heard of the party, begged to be allowed to accompany them, but no one was willing to risk inviting him. In virtually all of the several accounts of the event, the party is pictured as a glum affair, very like a wake. The guests — mostly critics, writers, and reviewers — were seated in stiff chairs, arranged in a circle, while the host, standing, received his guests in the center. There was little to drink or to break down the starchiness of the occasion other than beer. Mencken tried to leaven the solemnity with a few jokes, which fell flat. Van Vechten, according to Llewelyn Powys, another guest, remained seated in his rigid chair, looking like "an aging madonna lily that had lost its pollen." Fitzgerald, on his own recognizance, wandered into the party late, tipsy and carrying a bottle of champagne, which he presented to Dreiser with a meandering speech about his earnest admiration for the aging novelist's great talents. Dreiser put the bottle on ice and that was the last that was seen of it. After a decent wait, the parched guests, one by one, said their thank yous and good nights and departed. Mencken's version of the story, however, had a soundtrack, in which Fitzgerald, very drunk, introduced himself by saying, "Mr. Dreiser, my name is Fitzgerald. I have always got a great kick out of your works" — a remark not calculated to butter up a defensive author. Sherwood Anderson, present at the occasion, maintained in his memoirs that Dreiser had shut the door in Fitzgerald's face, as Dreiser had once done to Anderson when he showed up, unannounced, to pay homage. Mencken, however, in his copy of the Anderson memoirs emphatically noted, "Another lie! Fitz came in and was treated politely by Dreiser."

A sense of disorientation, a kind of bibulous haze, hangs over a good many recollections of the period. Fitzgerald, trying to be the chronicler of his age, was actually one of its most active participants. Out of necessity, perhaps, or as part of the fictional technique he used in dealing with his life, he picked his way through foggy memories of gay nights and mornings after, of continuous parties that traveled from dimly remembered apartments to vaguely recollected speakeasies. "Even now," he wrote a decade later, in the harsh light of an unhappiness that would not go away, "even now I go into many flats with the sense that I have been there before or in the one above or below." His cool assessment of the lives he and Zelda had lived has an amazing sobriety:

> We had run through a lot, though we had retained an almost theatrical innocence by preferring the role of the observed to that of the observer. But innocence is no end in itself. . . .

III

In the Fitzgerald albums, there is a photograph of a party at Gateway Drive. Crowded into the low-ceilinged small parlor, with its arched windows draped with boldly patterned chintz curtains, are some twenty-six people looking like oversized grownups in a doll house room. The men are mostly in formal wear; the women are wearing evening gowns. The more recognizable or clearly identifiable figures are Sam Harris and Arthur Hopkins, whom Fitzgerald evidently was trying to interest in *The Vegetable,* Peggy Webber, August Thomas, Isabelle Hitchcock, Eva Hopkins, Mrs. Sam Harris, Helen Buck — the attractive blonde in a low-cut lamé gown — and, in a corner, a very glum Ludlow Fowler. (After one of their parties, perhaps this one, Zelda wrote to Fowler: "I'm running wild in sackcloth and ashes because Scott and I acted like two such drunks the other night — Aside from the fact that you were horribly bored, I am sorry because we saw nothing of you.") Zelda, standing at the back of the group, is resolutely turned in profile, her bobbed hair hiding her face. Scott, lounging in the front row on the floor, looks foggy with drink, seated next to the equally foggy Gene Buck. In the center of the group, standing, is a sharp-featured, big-eared, wild-eyed young man, conspicuously labeled "The Mind Reader." He may well have been just that; the Fitzgeralds made the most of special occasions. For dinner parties, Zelda painted place cards of racy chorines for guests like Rube Goldberg and Ring Lardner. For large parties, Fitzgerald would think up surprises; he would hire small bands, magicians, clowns.

The photograph is the bland image of reality. But fiction, in a perverse way, sometimes sharpens the focus. In a remarkably funny, cruel, and perfectly serious imaginary encounter, Edmund Wilson gave a satirical portrait of Fitzgerald himself and of the Alice-in-Wonderland quality of his social life in Great Neck. The ostensible occasion for "The Delegate from Great Neck," published in *The New Republic* on April 20, 1924, was Van Wyck Brooks's winning of the annual *Dial* award. In Wilson's fictional dialogue, Fitzgerald, age twenty-seven, is bringing Brooks, age thirty-eight, a written testimonial from the "younger generation." Fitzgerald, aware that he is hardly the youngest member of the younger generation, explains: "Besides, I'm about the only one who still looks really young. Most of the others are getting old and bald and discouraged. So they picked me out to represent them." After some fatuous remarks about the research Brooks must have done, Fitzgerald comments:

> "Think of it! Reading fifteen or sixteen books just to write a single page! For a book of two hundred and fifty pages that would be—"
>
> Brooks: "They're not all different books, you know. One uses the same books again and again."
>
> Fitzgerald: "I know: but even so—it's perfectly amazing! I suppose you must know more about American literature than anybody else in the world, don't you?"

After reading the testimonial letter, with numerous asides, Fitzgerald then invites Brooks to one of his weekend parties in Great Neck, giving, unintentionally, a hilarious account of a typical Fitzgerald weekend:

> Maybe it would bore you to death—but we're asking some people down who ought to be pretty amusing. Gloria Swanson's coming. And Dos Passos and Sherwood Anderson. And Marc Connelly and Dorothy Parker. And Rube Goldberg. And Ring Lardner will be there. You probably think some of these people are lowbrow, but Ring Lardner, for instance, is really a very interesting fellow—he's really not just a popular writer; he's pretty morose about things.

I'd like to have you meet him. There'll be some dumb-bell friends of mine from the West, but I don't believe you'd mind them. And then there's going to be a man who sings a song called *Who'll Bite Your Neck When My Teeth Are Gone?* Neither my wife nor I knows his name — but this song is one of the funniest things we've ever heard!

Wilson's burlesque gives a sense of the mocking humor of the period and conveys its spirit. But beyond that, it is plausible in most respects: the guest list, for instance, is typical of the hodge-podge of literary and theatrical personalities that might have been at a Fitzgerald party. Both Wilson and Dos Passos were sometime guests at Great Neck. Ina Claire, the actress whom Fitzgerald had "worshipped from afar in 1913," had dined with them. Another actress, Laurette Taylor, had been somewhat stunned at a Great Neck party. Spotting her, Fitzgerald, whose pet term at the time was *egg,* knelt down before her and announced, "My God, you beautiful egg! You beautiful egg!" The frightened actress reported to her husband, the playwright Hartley Manners, "Oh Hartley, I've just seen the doom of youth." Even the dumb song title of Wilson's parody could be matched by some of the Follies' numbers written by the Fitzger-alds' drinking companion Gene Buck: "When the Shaker Plays a Cocktail Tune" and "Wasn't It Nice? Wasn't It Sweet? Wasn't It Good?" Although there is no evidence that Gloria Swanson ever attended a Fitzgerald party, the Fitzgeralds were guests at one or two of hers. A July 1923 ledger entry notes, "Parties at Allan Dwan's. Gloria Swanson and the movie crowd." The superstar was filming *Zaza* at the Paramount Studios in Astoria, Long Island, with Dwan as her director. And there was another occasion when Fitzgerald attended a party given by Swanson at which he got drunk and had a fight with the actor Frank Morgan in the cloakroom. Fitzgerald remained "star-struck" for much of his life, but he also seems to have harbored far less innocent feelings. Only two years later, dis-gruntled with the "movie crowd," he wrote to John Peale Bishop in scatalogical terms: "I'm too much of an egotist and not enough of a diplomat ever to succeed in the movies. You must begin by placing the tongue flat against the posteriors of such worthys as Gloria Swanson and Allan Dwan and commence a slow caressing movement."

What is impressive about Wilson's imaginary dialogue is the manner in which he captured the earnestness of Fitzgerald's approval-seeking and the diffidence that disguised it, the air of disingenuous flattery and ingenuous insult that Fitzgerald lavished on heroes and friends alike. One gets the impression that when Fitzgerald was in an eager-to-please or an eager-to-succeed mood, his opinions could turn on a dime.

During the Great Neck days, the Fitzgeralds struck up new friendships, some casual, some enduring. One was with the Tommy Hitchcocks, who had an estate in nearby Old Westbury. Hitchcock, a star polo player, had been a World War I flying ace, a member of the Lafayette Escadrille who had been awarded the Croix de Guerre. Captured by the Germans, he had made a daring escape by jumping off a moving train. He was ensconced in Fitzgerald's "pantheon of heroes," because he had returned home a national figure but had had the "humility" to enroll at Harvard. Around this same period Zelda and Fitzgerald became friendly with Esther Murphy. Her father, Patrick Francis Murphy, who had turned his leather goods company, Mark Cross, into a lucrative business, had a home at Southampton. Patrick Murphy liked to spend his afternoons at the Southampton Country Club, bounding about the lawns, singing "Sweet Adeline" with his gray-haired cronies, much to the chagrin of his daughter. It would sometimes take three telephone calls to get him home for dinner. Once there, he would promptly ask for cocktails. At the table, his wife, Anna, a morbidly devout Catholic, would air her dark suspicions about the servants, who intimidated her so much that she couldn't fire them. Fitzgerald met Esther Murphy perhaps through Edmund Wilson, who thought very highly of her. She was also a good friend of Alec McKaig's; Wilson suspected the two of them would marry. She was twice married, the second time to a son of President Chester Arthur; her great ambition in life — never achieved — was to write the definitive life of Edith Wharton. Fitzgerald, over the years, had a curious relationship with her; he described it as "an old friendship or a prolonged quarrel that has gone on so long and accumulated so much moss that it is much the same thing."

One of the Fitzgeralds' eminent literary guests was Rebecca West, touring the United States at the end of her ten-year love affair with Fitzgerald's former literary hero H. G. Wells. For once, the intrepid Zelda seemed nervous. "Rebecca West and a rather (not *too*) literary crowd are coming out Sunday for a rather formal party and Zelda's scared," Fitzgerald wrote Tom Boyd. It is not clear whether this was the party that misfired. Fitzgerald, it seems, had promised to pick up West at her New York hotel, but never arrived, and she spent the evening waiting and phoning friends, trying to find out the address. Fitzgerald, forgetting his promise and thinking she had stood them up, painted a face on a pillow, topped it with a plumed hat, and sat it at the dinner table, making insulting comments about the absent guest throughout the dinner. But he and Zelda entertained her on other occasions, despite the mishap. Rebecca West was one of the few acquaintances who did not think Zelda was beautiful at all but had a rather "craggy homeliness" about her. In fact, she thought she detected in Zelda the look one found in Géricault's portraits of the insane.

But Edmund Wilson, who was a weekend guest with his wife, Mary Blair, in the summer of 1923, thought the Fitzgeralds had found a niche for themselves. In a gossipy letter to John Bishop he wrote in detail:

> Fitz and Zelda have struck their perfect milieu in the jazz society of Great Neck, where they inhabit a brand-new suburban house. Zelda plays golf, and Fitz is already acquiring pompous overtones of the successful American householder. They are still one of the most refreshing elements at large, however, and it would take me pages to do justice to their pranks.

One of the pranks, quite possibly, was the set of comic "House Rules" that they made up for their weekend guests: "Visitors are requested not to break down doors in search of liquor, even when authorized to do so by the host and hostess. Week-end guests are respectfully notified that the invitations to stay over Monday issued by the host and hostess during the small hours of Sunday morning must not be taken seriously."

But it was not always laughs at Gateway Drive. John Dos Passos was convinced that Fitzgerald often pretended to be more drunk than he actually was; that he "merely put on disorderly drunken acts, which gave him an excuse for clowning and outrageous behavior, because he had never learned to practice the first principles of civilized behavior." There seems to be some supporting evidence for that observation, although it is also true that there were occasions when Fitzgerald's drunken activities verged on a frightening kind of madness. A Montgomery friend of Zelda's, Eleanor Browder, paid them a visit. She and Zelda went to tea at the Plaza, where they were to meet Scott after his dentist's appointment. Fitzgerald arrived at the Plaza drunk and carrying a bottle of champagne, which he had started drinking to ease the pain of the dentist's work. When the waiter refused to serve him in the Palm Room—he had brought Anita Loos, whom he had met along the way—they had all headed back to Great Neck, Fitzgerald drinking warm champagne from a case he had stowed away. At Gateway Drive, there were cocktails followed by a candlelight supper. An unwelcome woman visitor came to the front door and with difficulty Fitzgerald managed to get rid of her, but when he returned to the table, Zelda made some bitter remark. In the midst of the ensuing argument, Fitzgerald ripped off the tablecloth, sending the plates and glasses in all directions. Zelda merely got up, saying, "Shall we have our coffee in the next room?" The three women stepped over the litter, and Fitzgerald stormed outside to sleep it off.

Anita Loos's version of what may be the same—or a slightly different—episode is a good deal more colorful and ominous. Fitzgerald had picked her up in New York to bring her out to dinner in Great Neck. "I didn't notice he'd been drinking, but we'd only gone a little way when I realized my error. By a miracle, we arrived at their country house without an accident, and, once there, I found to my relief that Zelda was cold sober." Fitzgerald disappeared; a butler in a disheveled uniform "shuffled in" to announce that dinner was served. Soon, Fitzgerald came in and turned the latch on the dining room door, announcing, "Now, I'm going to kill you two!" and proceeded throwing heavy objects—a lighted candelabra, a water carafe, a wine cooler, and a leg of lamb on a platter—at the two women. The butler, who would have seemed the unlikeliest of heroes, came to their rescue, breaking open the door and grabbing Scott while the two women fled to the safety of Ring Lardner's house. Lardner went out in search of Fitzgerald and found him kneeling on the ground, scooping up dirt and cramming it in his mouth. "I'm eating dirt," he explained "to pay for trying to kill those two lovely girls! Those darling girls who never harmed anyone in their lives! And a swine like me tried to kill them!" Much of the story seems to be apocryphal, especially the final detail; but the uncomfortable fact is that Fitzgerald himself, in a later ledger note, records a similar, penitential dirt-eating episode.

In a syndicated interview, "What a 'Flapper Novelist' Thinks of His Wife," circulated that fall, the Fitzgeralds managed to present a more normal and cosy picture of their marital life. The article describes the "charming and brilliant young couple, among the newer lights of the modern literary world," in their "charming country house at Great Neck, Long Island." It is a piece of glossy promotion, pandering to the notion of a carefree marriage, not overly concerned with domestic matters. Zelda discusses her recent attempts at writing stories: "I like to write. Do you know, I thought my husband should write a perfectly good ending to one of the tales, and he wouldn't! He called them 'lop-sided,' too! Said they began at the end." Asked what she would do if she had to earn her own living, Zelda gives a forthright answer: "I've studied ballet. I'd try to get a place in the Follies, or the movies. If I wasn't successful, I'd try to write." Presumably this was her preferred order. Fitzgerald, who took a hand in the interviewing, asks what Zelda would consider an ideal day. Peaches for breakfast, she begins, then golf, then a swim, then just being lazy. For the evening? "A large, brilliant, gathering," she answers. Asked what she would prefer her daughter to be and do when she grows up, Zelda replies, "Not great and serious and melancholy and inhospitable, but rich and happy and artistic." Not, she explains, that money brings happiness, but that the right kind of perfume and a smart pair of shoes are great comforts to the "feminine soul." The article, for all its catchy retorts, has one interesting exchange that rises above the level of celebrity propaganda. Fitzgerald, asked to describe his wife, answers, "She is the most charming person in the world." When asked to expand, he counters, "That's all. I refuse to amplify — Excepting, she's perfect." To which Zelda responds, "But you don't think that. You think I'm a lazy woman." "No," Fitzgerald answers, "I like it. I think you're perfect. You're always ready to listen to my manuscripts at any hour of the day or night. You're charming — beautiful. You do, I believe, clean the ice box once a week."

But life was not the gay time the Fitzgeralds pictured for the newspapers. Fitzgerald was suffering from insomnia. And his monthly ledger entries indicate other problems: "Still drunk," "Tearing Drunk," "Constant drinking. Some golf." Zelda wrote about that climactic season of their lives in disturbing terms: "In Great Neck, there was always disorder and quarrels; about the Golf Club, about the Foxes, about Peggy Webber, about Helen Buck, about everything. We went to the Rumseys, and that awful night at the Mackeys when Ring sat in the cloak room. . . . We gave lots of parties; the biggest one for Rebecca West. We drank Bass Pale Ale and went always to the Bucks or the Lardners or the Swopes when they weren't at our house. We saw lots of Sidney Howard and fought the weekend that Bill Motter was with us. We drank always. . . ."

Fitzgerald's year-end summary was not promising: "The repression breaks out. A comfortable but dangerous and deteriorating year at Great Neck. No ground under our feet."

The most durable, and in some ways the most revealing, of the friendships that Fitzgerald made during that period of loose ends and dissipation was the one with Ring Lardner. Lardner was thirty-seven when the Fitzgeralds moved to Great Neck. Fitzgerald had just turned twenty-six. When sober, Lardner was unusually taciturn; at the start of a drinking spree, he could hold an audience captivated with stories — though never smutty ones; he had an old-fashioned sense of propriety. Since the age of twenty-five, Lardner had been a heavy drinker and in the deeper reaches of a binge would turn incommunicable. By the time that Fitzgerald met him, he was a confirmed alcoholic. He was for the most part, however, able to handle himself much better than Fitzgerald did when consuming large quantities; he took pride in being a "two-bottle" man, where Fitzgerald could turn sullen and nasty after only one or two drinks.

His son Ring Lardner, Jr., in a family memoir, *The Lardners: My Family Remembered,* makes a shrewd assertion that Fitzgerald saw in Lardner his own dissipation farther down the road:

> I think one of the things about Ring that fascinated Scott in the Great Neck days was the image he saw of his own future. He probably felt satisfaction that he could sleep off a drunk and get back to work with much more ease than his older friend, but he must have known he was heading in the same direction. Even the pattern he came to of setting a specific beginning and ending date for going on the wagon was Ring's.

Lardner had been a highly paid sportswriter and journalist who approached sports — especially baseball — as if it were one of the more serious professions in the world. His faith was shaken by the White Sox scandal of 1919 — popularly dubbed the "Black Sox" scandal—in which six members of the team were bribed to throw the World Series game to the Cincinnati Reds. (Ring Lardner, Jr., however, felt that writers and critics have overwritten this as a crisis in Ring's life.) During his years in Great Neck, Lardner had more or less settled down to being a short story writer. He still kept up a highly profitable collaboration with the cartoonist Dick Dorgan on a syndicated comic strip, "You Know Me Al." (It brought him $17,000 a year.) He was an avid theatergoer, liked musical comedies, wrote skits for the Ziegfeld Follies. He was friendly with a number of rising comedians who lived in the Great Neck area at one time or another—Ed Wynn, Eddie Cantor, Groucho Marx. According to his biographer, Jonathan Yardley, in his peak years, whatever his consumption of alcohol, Lardner was earning approximately $100,000 a year. These were terms of success—and self-indulgence—that Fitzgerald must have found encouraging.

Periodically, Lardner went on the wagon, but during the Great Neck years, perhaps because he had found an obliging friend, he entered into a sustained period of drinking. Frequently Lardner and Fitzgerald would sit up to all hours of the night, either at Gateway Drive or on the porch of the Lardner house overlooking the Swope estate, discussing sports and literature. Sometimes, in their intramural partying, they wrote joint letters to absent friends. In his portion of a letter to Oscar Kalman, Fitzgerald reported: "Ring and I got stewed together the other night and sat up till the next night without what he would laughingly refer to as a wink of sleep. . . . This is a very drunken town full of intoxicated people and retired debauchés and actresses." In May 1923, when their literary hero Joseph Conrad was visiting his American publisher, Frank Nelson Doubleday, at Effendi Hill, Doubleday's Oyster Bay estate, the two men, well in their cups, decided to dance a hornpipe on the publisher's lawn. They hoped that Conrad would look out the window and know of their admiration. For their troubles, they were put off the grounds by the caretaker. It was just as well; Conrad was mordantly anti-American, considered it easier to have an intellectual relationship with a "Chinaman" than an American. Selling his books in America, he claimed, made him feel "exactly like a merchant selling glass beads to African natives." If he had caught sight of a pair of drink-crazed Long Island natives prancing on the Doubleday lawn, he would have had his darkest suspicions confirmed.

Ellis Lardner, ordinarily a warm and outgoing hostess, took the

Fitzgeralds cautiously. She was put off by their exhibitionism, and more than likely she regarded Fitzgerald as an encouragement to her husband's drinking. The Lardner children—John, Ring Jr., Jim, and David—liked the Fitzgeralds heartily. They had had brushes with the famous before; Sinclair Lewis, for instance, totally ignored them. Scott took a deep interest in them and their activities. He performed card tricks for them (possibly learned from Bunny Wilson, who was an amateur magician), told them stories, played games with them, and talked to them man to man. But Fitzgerald had a tendency to be too managerial when he played with the boys, making the games too serious, and Ring Jr., seven or eight at the time, seems to have preferred Zelda. She made no great effort to win the boys' friendship, yet all the Lardner boys thought her a beauty and an easygoing companion: "She didn't pay as much attention to us as Scott did, but we were used to that from visiting children, and that was how we thought of her, as another child, free and impulsive in saying or doing whatever she felt like."

If Lardner was Fitzgerald's adopted drunk, he was also his special literary project. Almost immediately, Fitzgerald began promoting him to Max Perkins, and he badgered Lardner into putting together a collection of his stories to be published by Scribner's. Lardner seemed to be so indifferent about the project that Fitzgerald had to get copies of the stories from the local libraries. ("My God, he hadn't even saved them!") And he was stunned by what he regarded as Ring's callousness toward his craft—"the worst editor of his own stuff who ever turned up in a big way of the writing line, with the possible exception of Theodore Dreiser." He even came up with the title for the book, *How to Write Short Stories*. The entire project, in fact, was carried out by Fitzgerald and Max Perkins with little help from the author. But in the summer of 1923, the three men met to discuss the terms over dinner in a local restaurant, René Durand's near Manhasset, and the meeting became another item in the Fitzgerald mythology. After a liquid discussion, Lardner went off in his car. Fitzgerald, taking Perkins home to Great Neck, unfortunately turned left instead of right and drove the car into the shallow end of a pond. Perkins, who told the story in New York for months afterward, somehow thought they had barely escaped drowning in a lake. The story rippled out in publishing circles until it came to rest three years later in an article in *The New Yorker*. But the reality was brought home to Perkins a good deal earlier. A year after the episode, when he was having lunch with Lardner at the same restaurant, he watched with some amazement as the owner's dog waded across what was, in actuality, a very small and very shallow lily pond. It was, he reported to Fitzgerald, "a disillusioning afternoon."

Fitzgerald's promotion of Lardner's reputation in elite publications like *Vanity Fair,* his concern that Ring's better stories, like "Champion" and "The Golden Honeymoon," make up the volume of collected stories, his efforts to get Scribner's to bring out a uniform edition of Lardner's work, were certainly acts of generosity from one writer to another in the highly competitive literary profession. But there also may have been something personal in the urgency he brought to his efforts. The impetus may have come from that sense of proxy which Fitzgerald recognized in his own behavior on occasion. He may have needed to prove that, like Lardner, he too — a highly successful writer for the commercial magazines — was deserving of praise and consideration in intellectual quarters.

There was, it appears, some reciprocity in Fitzgerald's literary relationship with Lardner. Fitzgerald introduced the older writer to the work of Gertrude Stein, specifically *Three Lives,* the book that Edmund Wilson had first introduced him to. It may well have been the "Melanctha" story, written in a kind of black dialect, that Fitzgerald wanted Lardner to read. And Lardner, it seems, introduced him to Dostoievski's *The Brothers Karamazov* (and possibly Dickens' *Bleak House*), a book that Fitzgerald would claim was an important influence on his writing. Fitzgerald later told Mencken that he had resorted to its "masculine" influence in writing *The Great Gatsby,* rather than the feminine one of Henry James's *The Portrait of a Lady.* Fitzgerald's admiration for Lardner's talents was genuine, as Edmund Wilson would testify:

> Scott was always lost in admiration at Ring's ability to find out about different kinds of people and would ask him how he managed it. Ring would tell him just to enter into conversation with anybody that he happened to be sitting next to on the Long Island railroad. Scott was incapable of this: his way of trying to document himself was to ask ill-mannered leading questions of a kind that would shut up anybody like a clam: "How much money did your family have?" "Do you still sleep with your wife," etc. It seemed to him a miracle that Ring could understand enough about such people as the couple in "The Golden Honeymoon" to write a story about them.

But there was, too, an element of condescension in Fitzgerald's feelings about Lardner—a rather odd case, but typical of Fitzgerald's sophomorisms. He found it difficult to understand Lardner's interest in baseball. Fitzgerald considered it far inferior to collegiate football, which for him had glamour and importance. Specifically, he wondered how Lardner could have wasted so many years reporting on baseball:

> During those years when most men of promise achieve an adult education, if only in the school of war, Ring moved in the company of a few dozen illiterates playing a boy's game. A boy's game, with no more possibilities in it than a boy could master, a game bounded by walls which kept out novelty or danger, change or adventure.

How Lardner felt about Fitzgerald one must largely infer from the long, humorous letters he sent, detailing the gossip of Great Neck and America, when the Fitzgeralds were abroad. In one of them he complained, "2,500 words, and I'm not getting a nickel for it." There is of course his famous quip "Mr. Fitzgerald is a novelist and Mrs. Fitzgerald a novelty." Like his sons, Lardner had a particular affection for Zelda, whom he courted in insidious verses that ran along the following lines:

> Of all the girls for whom I care
> And there are quite a number.
> None can compare with Zelda Sayre
> Now wedded to a plumber.

Zelda's initial dislike of Lardner seems to have softened under such comic onslaughts. But she could still be amazingly cool in her assessments of the lives of others. "Ring is drinking himself to an embalmed state so he'll be all ready for the grim reaper," she wrote a friend. "I don't think he'll have long to wait if he keeps on. His wife is worried sick."

During that summer in Great Neck, there were spells of such sweltering heat that Zelda, jokingly, began to wonder whether she was already experiencing "the after life." They spent days at Long Beach, waiting for the cool relief of evening. But despite the heat, despite the still-distracting hopes for the production of his play, despite the rounds of parties and the trips to and from New York along the heat-shimmering highway, past slums and ash heaps, Fitzgerald had begun to feel a stirring of the imagination, some sense of the undercurrents beneath the surface of uneventful days and stalled opportunities.

There were impressions, chance impressions. One evening, on a "not-forgotten summer night," an acquaintance from one of the Great Neck golf clubs, Robert Kerr, had told him about an experience from his youth. As a fourteen-year-old boy, he had warned a wealthy yachtsman, Major Edwin Gilman, that his yacht could be damaged in the running tides of Sheepshead Bay. As a consequence, Kerr was hired by Gilman and lived on the yacht for three years. The true-to-life fable about the largesse of a prince who lifts a young boy out of the ordinary life lodged in Fitzgerald's mind. He would recall the story about Gilman, the "mysterious yachtsman whose mistress was Nellie Bly." There was a Great Neck neighbor, Max Gerlach, a man with a characteristic turn of speech that would linger in Fitzgerald's memory, like some offhand, nagging tune. During that summer, Gerlach was off on a trip; he came across a newsphoto of the Fitzgeralds in some local paper. The celebrities were shown sitting on their lawn at Great Neck, with Scottie in a frilly sunbonnet. The caption was bland, routine journalese: "THE BEAUTIFUL AND DAMNED DOES NOT LOOK ALL OF THAT: F. Scott Fitzgerald, his wife and their 2-year-old daughter 'Scotty,' at their summer home on Long Island. Mrs. Fitzgerald is the heroine of her husband's successful novel, 'The Beautiful and Damned.' " Gerlach sent the clipping with a rapidly scrawled note, equally unimportant: "Enroute from the coast — Here for a few days on business — How are you and the family Old Sport?" There is nothing to indicate that that casual act of an acquaintance would have any consequence in Fitzgerald's work, or that Gerlach's characteristic expression, "Old Sport," would acquire a resonance all its own. Zelda, late in life, when asked about the model for Jay Gatsby, remembered their neighbor "Von Guerlach," who supposedly had some connection with General Pershing and had been in trouble because of bootlegging.

There was also a meeting with a shady gambler, Arnold Rothstein, a friend of the Swopes, who had been involved in some way with the White Sox scandal that had made such an impression on Ring Lardner. Rothstein and a girl friend, Dorothy King, were later found murdered; the case went unsolved. Somehow the lives of these three men, strange and shadowy, would merge for Fitzgerald into an image of sinister glamour. There were other stray impressions that came together in Fitzgerald's mind during that Great Neck season of his career; the carnival along the highway when he had sat drinking in the chauffeured automobile while Zelda and Dos Passos rode the Ferris wheel, the dazzle of wealth and fame at the Swope and Dwan parties, the unremitting heat, the dim memories of New York apartments would hover about the composition of *The Great Gatsby.*

But the long approach to the novel had begun earlier, in St. Paul, when he informed Max Perkins that his third novel would be set in the Midwest and New York, and that it would have "a catholic element." In the dissolute summer at Great Neck, he had once more taken up work on it, but with a noticeable seriousness. Zelda complained to the Kalmans: "Scott has started a new novel and retired into strict seclusion and celibacy. He's horribly intent on it and has built up a beautiful legend about himself which corresponds somewhat to the old fable about the ant and the grasshopper. *Me* being the grasshopper." The strange feature of the letter is not the familiar complaint about her laziness, but her remark about Fitzgerald's self-imposed "celibacy." It puts an odd emphasis on Edmund Wilson's earlier letter to John Bishop about Fitzgerald's having hit on a "modus vivendi for preventing Zelda from absorbing all his time, emotion, and seminal juice." But the truth is that for some years past Fitzgerald seems to have had rather subterranean thoughts on the subject of sex and celibacy, ambition and the lure of the flesh, and the role of the priesthood.

In the unpublished preface to *This Side of Paradise,* written four years earlier, Fitzgerald admitted to having deleted some "awe-inspiring half-lines" from the earlier versions of his first novel. One of these romantic phrases, "the dark celibacy of greatness," gives a sinister cast to his own drives toward becoming one of the great writers of his time. If Fitzgerald thought the phrase too purple, he evidently considered it too important for the wastebasket and used it in his preface. And the theme of sexual abstinence would, in fact, recur in the novel itself in the personification of Monsignor Darcy, who, in a letter to Amory Blaine, advises his protégé, "Celibacy goes deeper than the flesh," a mystic doctrine that was intended to explain the priest's notion that he had fathered Amory in some platonic fashion.

Fitzgerald did not invent such notions out of the whole cloth; they bore a certain family resemblance to the ideas of Monsignor Fay, who, in one of his letters to Fitzgerald, took up the question of Fitzgerald's religious worries and sexual inhibitions. "The fear of God," Fay wrote Fitzgerald, "is your greatest frustration—as it is mine, nor would you rid yourself of it if you could—it will always be there. As to women—it is not a convention that holds you back as you think, but an instinct that if you once begin—you will run amuck —I know whereof I speak." In another letter, with wonderful inno- cence he made a connection between Fitzgerald's creative impulses and his procreative ones. Diagnosing Fitzgerald's depression after he had completed the first draft of *The Romantic Egotist,* Monsignor Fay explained: "Of course you shot a tremendous bolt in your book. A great part of yourself has gone out from yourself in a kind of intellec- tual parturition, and it will take you some time to make up the void." Comic as that explanation may seem, Fitzgerald's ambivalence toward sex, his odd notions about celibacy and greatness and the problems of identity, did converge at this point in his life, during the writing of a story that had intricate connections with his new novel.

Although Great Neck provided the setting for much of *The Great Gatsby,* Fitzgerald did not complete his novel there. His in- tention of providing a Catholic element in his novel, though it seems to have been worked at on Long Island, was later discarded. But out of the husks of that material, Fitzgerald did shape a story, "Abso- lution," that dealt with the experiences of a young boy, Rudolph Miller, and an aging priest, Father Schwartz, a man of obvious sensitivity and sensuality, who would pay a great price for his cel- ibacy. Father Schwartz is driven to madness by his dreary isolation in a Midwestern parish. In an offhand admission to a little-known critic and admirer, John Jamieson, Fitzgerald explained the origins of his hero Gatsby:

> He was perhaps created on the image of some forgotten farm type of Minnesota that I have known and forgotten, and associated at the same moment with some sense of romance. It might interest you to know that a story of mine, called "Absolution" . . . was intended to be a picture of his early life, but that I cut it because I preferred to preserve the sense of mystery.

"Absolution" is one of the most crucial and beautiful stories in Fitzgerald's work, a story in which the details, the imagery, work flawlessly. The imaginative boy, who does not believe he is the child of his dull parents, who invents a new personality for himself,

"Blatchford Sarnemington," who has random ambitions of being a baseball player, an actor, a navy officer, is obviously drawn from Fitzgerald's childhood. Rudolph is troubled by an awakening sexual awareness and "the ebony mark of sexual offenses upon his soul"; he once listened intently when he heard another boy and a girl saying "immodest things" to each other while playing in a barn loft: "He could not tell Father Schwartz how his pulse had bumped in his wrist, how a strange, romantic excitement had possessed him when those curious things had been said." But he is in terror, because, under the seal of the confessional, he has told the priest an outright lie — that he has "never" lied — and he is sure he will be struck dead when he receives communion.

The priest, too, is tormented by sensual temptations: "Sometimes, near four o'clock, there was a rustle of Swede girls along the path by his window, and in their shrill laughter he found a terrible dissonance that made him pray aloud for the twilight to come." Even the sweet scent of cheap toilet soaps from the drugstore assails him when he passes on Saturday evenings after hearing confessions, "and he grew careful to walk on the other side of the street so that the smell of the soap would float upward before it reached his nostrils as it drifted, rather like incense, toward the summer moon." It is possible that some element of Father Schwartz's descent into madness may have been patterned after that sense of morbid inclinations Fitzgerald felt he detected in Monsignor Fay on rare occasions.

Everything about the story — the boy's guilt in the midst of his terrible small sins, the priest's fall from sanity, even the sweltering afternoons, the torpor of summer lying over the wheatfields — seems to converge in the final paragraph, which is raised above the story like some monstrance, a pure invention, a symbol of life's irreverence and fecundity. It is an image of Swedish girls with yellow hair walking "sensuously along roads that bounded the fields, calling innocent, exciting things to the young men who were working in the lines between the grain. Legs were shaped under starchless gingham, and rims of the necks of dresses were warm and damp. For five hours now hot fertile life burned in the afternoon." The story ends with certain knowledge that "it would be night in three hours, and all along the land there would be these blonde Northern girls and tall young men from the farms lying out beside the wheat, under the moon."

Despite its masterly restraint, "Absolution" is one of Fitzgerald's most faultlessly sensual stories. But before the final epiphany, the priest delivers an awesome message. With the frightening poetry of madness, he summons up the symbol of an amusement park in all its glamour and tawdriness:

> It's a thing like a fair, only much more glittering. Go to one at night and stand a little way off from it in a dark place — under dark trees. You'll see a big wheel made of lights turning in the air, and a long slide shooting boats down into the water. A band playing somewhere, and a smell of peanuts — and everything will twinkle. But it won't remind you of anything, you see. . . .

Out of that vision, the priest calls up a terrible lesson, one that Fitzgerald had already learned — the need to distance oneself from reality: "But don't get up close . . . because if you do you'll only feel the heat and the sweat and the life."

The great disappointment that fall — a sobering disappointment — was the failure of his play *The Vegetable*. From the very beginning, he had entertained unrealistic hopes for its success in a Broadway production. "My play is the funniest ever written and will make me a fortune," he had written Harold Ober at the outset, perhaps a bit facetiously. During revisions, made in St. Paul and Great Neck, he had been buoyed up by the enthusiasm of Edmund Wilson and George Jean Nathan. He still was looking ahead to that rosy future. When it was being turned down by one producer after another — Frohman, Hopkins, the Theater Guild — his anticipations remained high. When, for lack of a producer, he decided to publish it with Scribner's in April, he hoped that his name would stir the necessary interest. He had continued to promote it through the summer with Sam Harris, and he was not discouraged when a deal with his Westport friend, the producer John Williams, fell through. He acknowledged that the reviews of the published version were not at all that favorable (a number of them mentioned that the play had been turned down by three New York managers); the critics' predictions that the play "would flop on the boards" only made him "violently anxious for a big success." Even so, it must have come as a surprise that Sam Harris finally agreed to produce it, with tryouts in Atlantic City before the New York opening.

Throughout much of October, he was busy in New York, attending rehearsals. His busy schedule interrupted work on his novel. He wrote to Perkins: "I have been coming every day to the city to rehearsals and then at night writing and making changes on the last act and even on the first two. It's in shape at last and everybody around the theater who has seen it says it's a great hit." He was once again in need of money, because he had invested in the production and had not done much writing during the summer, other than the intermittent work on the novel. He tried to get an advance on the royalties, on the grounds that the play was in rehearsal — but without success. "I'm at the end of my rope," he wrote Perkins, asking whether he could assign the play's future royalties to Scribner's, to whom, he figured, he was now in debt by about $3500: "If I don't in some way get $650 in the bank by Wednesday morning, I'll have to pawn the furniture." He had various schemes for repaying the publishers. His parting shot was glum: "I don't even dare come up there personally but for God's sake try to fix it."

The Vegetable opened for a week's run at the Nixon Apollo Theater in Atlantic City on November 19. The author's theater party included the Lardners and Allan Dwan. The opening-night performance was attended by Mayor Hylan of New York. "It was a colossal frost," Fitzgerald wrote, punning on the name of his henpecked hero, Jerry Frost. "People left their seats and walked out, people rustled their programs and talked audibly in bored impatient whispers. After the second act, I wanted to stop the show and say it was all a mistake, but the actors struggled heroically on." One legend has it that after the second act Fitzgerald and Lardner had cornered Ernest Truex, the lead, and suggested that he forget the rest of the play and join them in the local bar. Zelda, writing to Sandy Kalman, was blithely amusing:

> In brief, the show flopped as flat as one of Aunt Jemima's famous pancakes — Scott and Truex and Harris were terribly disappointed. . . . The first act went fine, but Ernest says he has *never* had an experience on the stage like the second. . . . People were so obviously bored! And it was all very well done, so there was no use trying to fix it up. The idea was what people didn't like — Just hopeless!

The play folded in Atlantic City. Writing to Ober, Fitzgerald conceded, "The whole thing has already cost me about a year and a half of work so I'd rather let it drop. It's honestly no good."

Despite the jaunty air, Fitzgerald was shaken by his theatrical failure. Like many a writer before him, he had pinned a good many hopes on a theatrical success. The experience seems to have taken the ground out from under him, undermining his confidence. Over the years, he would regard the failure of *The Vegetable* as the emblem of defeat. The snapshots pasted into a scrapbook — photos of Zelda huddled in a fur coat, buttoned up against a blustering wind on the Atlantic City Boardwalk — are probably the appropriate images of Fitzgerald's chilling failure as a playwright.

But the defeat did send him back to work with a new sense of seriousness. Between November and the early spring, he retired to his room above the garage and produced ten salable stories, the most important of which was "The Sensible Thing," based on his failed courtship of Zelda and their reconciliation. He was watching his drinking, sustaining himself on coffee. In retrospect, he would write to Bunny Wilson about his frustration and his sense of defeat, "I really worked hard as hell last winter — but it was all trash and it nearly broke my heart as well as my iron constitution." Wilson and Mary Blair spent Christmas Day with the Fitzgeralds. The other guests were Esther Murphy, Gilbert Seldes, and Dos Passos. Wilson reported to John Bishop on the new air of sobriety in the Fitzgerald household: "Scott's play went so badly on the road that it was taken off before it got to New York, thereby causing them a great deal of chagrin. Since then, Fitz has entered upon a period of sobriety of unexampled duration, writing great quantities of short stories for the popular magazines. He is doing a new novel." Wilson added, "I like Zelda better and better every year, and they are among the only people now that I am always glad to see." But the convivial gathering seems to have brought to mind the absence of Alec McKaig, and Wilson gave Bishop a commission: "Alec and they are still at outs and I wish that for heaven's sake when you get back, you would try to reconcile them. I have attempted it in vain. It all dates from that terrible time they came to New York in March, I think, two years ago and stopped at the Plaza." It was a time when old ties, old friendships, were becoming the casualties of a career.

Wilson's letters and diaries give another glimpse of the Fitzgeralds at the end of their Great Neck stay. It was in the spring, and the Fitzgeralds, weary with Long Island, were on the eve of departing for Europe. Scott's era of sobriety was obviously over. Wilson spent a long, dispiriting evening with the couple, one that underscored their dissatisfaction with their lives: "Fitz said he was going abroad because his reputation was diminishing in America and he wanted to stay away till he had accomplished something important and come back and have people give him dinners." The drinking that evening was heavy, and when they finished off the liquor at Gateway Drive, the party migrated to the Lardners', farther up East Shore Road. Lardner insisted on supplying each of the guests with a small bottle of Grand Marnier, and when those were depleted, they moved on to the Scotch.

Zelda, earlier, had been disagreeable when Fitzgerald, in a tutorial mood, brought out some charts he was keeping on the Middle Ages, so the party was uneasy for the moment. Lardner, Wilson, and Fitzgerald got into a lengthy discussion of George Meredith's *The Egoist,* and Fitzgerald became huffy when Lardner corrected him on the title of the book, which Fitzgerald referred to as *The Egotist.* Fitzgerald tried to convince Lardner that the Meredith work was a poor one, because of some critical revelation he had, but in his drunken condition he badly mangled his explanation. Lardner, also high and in one of his expansive moods, began to read out the rules of the local golf club in a cold and sober voice, full of disdain, that "conveyed his disgust with his successful suburban life."

The party then wended its way back to Gateway Drive, where both Fitzgerald and Zelda fell fast asleep while Lardner and Wilson began a lengthy discussion that started off with a recent oil scandal and then moved on to "baseball, Heywood Broun, Lardner's writing, the Americanized *Carmen,* the Rascoes, etc."

Wilson's account of that long-winded evening, which ended in a wearisome dawn, is a kind of photographic record of a night in the dark, leafy wasteland of Long Island:

> Deep blue patches appeared at the windows. I couldn't think at first what they were — then I realized it was the dawn. The birds tuned up one at a time. It grew light. It was seven o'clock. Scott asked what we had been talking about. Lardner said we had been talking about him — "I suppose you analyzed me ruthlessly." Zelda was sick and had to have the doctor and apologized profoundly for her "rudeness."

A typical evening among the young literary set. But for the Fitzgeralds, it was the beginning of a long morning after.

6

A Consciously Artistic Achievement

DESPITE their previous unhappy visit to the Continent, the Fitzgeralds sailed for France early in May. Fitzgerald, hoping to finish his novel, planned an extended stay. They took with them seventeen pieces of luggage, a hundred feet of copper screen ("against the mosquitoes"), a newly bought set of the *Encyclopaedia Britannica* (for which Fitzgerald still owed Scribner's $700), and an eight-stanza farewell poem to Zelda written by Ring Lardner, which offered to rescue her from an insensitive husband:

> So dearie when your tender heart
> Of all this coarseness tires,
> Just cable me and I will start
> Immediately for Hyères.
>
> To hell with Scott Fitzgerald then!
> To hell with Scott, his daughter!
> It's you and I back home again,
> To Great Neck where the men are men
> And booze is ¾ water.

They spent only nine or ten days in Paris, where they arrived in mid-May, interviewing prospective nannies for Scottie, seeing the sights, spending an evening in Montmartre, and visiting the Bishops, whom they had not seen since their marriage two years before. They hired a "wonderful English nurse" named Lillian Maddock, who seems to have had the efficiency and the skills of coercion needed to manage the badly disorganized lives of the Fitzgeralds. Within half an hour, Miss Maddock could turn a Parisian hotel suite or the cabin of an ocean liner into a cosy English parlor by ordering the staff and crew about, sending them in search of the necessary items.

They lunched with the Bishops at an expensive restaurant in the Bois. Fitzgerald later sent Wilson a report on their meeting: "Yes, John seemed to us a beaten man—with his tiny frail mustache—but perhaps only morally. Whether or no he still echoes the opinions of others I don't know—to me he said nothing at all. In fact, I remember not a line (I was drunk and voluble myself though.)"

It was in Paris that the Fitzgeralds first met Gerald and Sara Murphy, through Gerald's sister Esther. Gerald, eight years older than Scott, had refused to go into the family business and instead opted for the life of an expatriate, planning to become a landscape architect. One day in Paris, having seen works by such painters as Braque, Picasso, and Gris in the Rosenberg Gallery, he suddenly decided that painting was what he wanted to do. He made friends with Picasso and Fernand Léger, and studied under the Russian émigré painter Natalia Goncharova. In time, he became an estimable painter in his own right, in a precisionist style of flat images—usually of homely objects, such as cigar-box tops, American safety razors—a style that somewhat presaged the Pop Art style of the 1960s. His contribution to modern art was minor; he stopped painting in 1929. But Murphy received recognition several decades later, when the American modernist painters of the twenties and thirties were rediscovered.

Where Gerald Murphy had a quicksilver temperament and was given to occasional black moods, Sara Murphy's approach to life was calm and unflustered, sensible and not especially profound. She had a stunning and reposeful kind of beauty; the Murphys' friend Archibald MacLeish once described her as being "like a bowl of Renoir flowers." When MacLeish first met the couple, he thought them strikingly "well-laundered" and was eager to know them. If the Murphys had been slightly older, they might well have passed for Fitzgerald's ideal parents. They were wealthy, well-bred, and handsome. Their cultural interests ranged far more widely than his own; they appreciated the vanguard compositions of Les Six and the musical comedies of their friend Cole Porter, and introduced Negro spirituals to their French friends. They had distinctive good taste when it came to wine and food; everything they did had style—whether it was serving cocktails, furnishing a house, or giving a party. Their three children—Honoria, Baoth, and Patrick, ranging from six to four years old—were extraordinarily beautiful and exceptionally well mannered. The youngest, Patrick, had a tendency to seriousness; Picasso once dubbed him *"un monsieur qui est par hasard un enfant."* They were a storybook family.

At the time the Fitzgeralds met them, the Murphys had taken a house in Saint Cloud, and Gerald had a studio on the rue Froidevaux in Paris. Like everything else about them, their house was special; it had once belonged to Gounod. And they had recently bought a villa at Cap d'Antibes that was in the process of being renovated by architects. As much as anyone, the Murphys would be credited with making the French Riviera fashionable in the summer. It had always been considered strictly a winter resort; the wealthy residents traditionally fled the region for Trouville and Deauville on the Atlantic coast, leaving it to the natives and straggling English pensioners. It was considered unhealthful after May.

Both the Murphys and the Fitzgeralds took to each other on very short acquaintance and planned to meet again in the summer. The Murphys may have been a bit wary at first. Scott and Zelda had a habit of turning up in the middle of the night outside the house in Saint Cloud, calling up to the windows in the hope of being invited to come in.

From Paris, the Fitzgeralds moved down to Hyères, where they stayed at Grimm's Park Hotel. Looking up the hill from their room, they could see Edith Wharton's Château Ste. Clair. They had just missed the American author, who had left for Paris. "Not that I care," Fitzgerald wrote Tom Boyd, "except that I met her in New York and she's a very distinguished grande dame who fought the good fight with bronze age weapons when there were very few people in the line at all." The description, oddly, made her seem like an old war-horse.

When Fitzgerald wrote to Boyd, he was in a relaxed frame of mind. He and Zelda were sitting in the Café l'Univers, both "a little tight and very happily drunk" under a silver Mediterranean moon. Fitzgerald was feeling unusually confident about his work and pleased with his isolation: "I hope to God I don't see a soul for six months. My novel grows more and more extraordinary; I feel absolutely self-sufficient and I have a perfect hollow craving for loneliness." He boasted, in fact: "I shall write a better novel than any novel ever written in America and become par excellence the best second-rater in the world."

Zelda, reporting to Max Perkins, said that Fitzgerald was reading nothing but the lives of Byron and Shelley. She didn't like the "forced atmosphere of picturesqueness and beauty" at Hyères. It was suitable, perhaps, for English watercolor sketches. "But I always suspect any place that isn't blatant — Venice, to me, is perfect."

They did not stay there long, however. Instead, they rented an elegant villa at Valescure, just above St. Raphaël, and farther up the coast toward Cannes. Hyères was dreadfully hot, and Zelda had not liked the food (she was sure she had been served goat's meat), and the bathing beach wasn't satisfactory. But perhaps there was another reason for their departure from the little out-of-season resort town. One day Fitzgerald saw a twelve-year-old girl whose face seemed like an enormous scab with slits for eyes and a mouth; her features had been miserably distorted by congenital syphilis. "It rather spoiled the streets for me," Fitzgerald confessed.

The Villa Marie at Valescure was a "clean, cool villa" perched high on a hillside above the town. From his window he could see nearby Fréjus, with its Roman aqueducts. The villa had "a summerhouse and a sandpile and two bathrooms and roses for breakfast." There was a gardener, who called Fitzgerald "Milord." They planned to stay till November 1. For convenience, they had bought a little Renault for $750.

It was in that romantic setting, with the flat blue Mediterranean and its sky hanging like a theatrical curtain in the distance, with the waves lapping on curved beaches and in sheltering coves, with pink and white and yellow villas nestling in the hills, and gardens abloom with the papery white flowers of bougainvillea, that Fitzgerald settled down to work on his novel. He also kept regularly in touch with Harold Ober, asking to be informed about a flurry of offers for film rights to his recent stories. He was planning to write a sequel to his *Saturday Evening Post* article "How to Live on $36,000 a Year," this one dealing with his efforts to economize on the French Riviera. In a burst of enthusiasm, he wrote to Tom Boyd, "Everything's idyllic and for the first time since I went to St. Paul in 1921 (the worst move I ever made in my life) I'm perfectly happy."

Zelda, however, was restless. She had none of the chores of motherhood. Three-year-old Scottie was in the hands of the overly competent Miss Maddock. If Zelda interfered, Nanny went to Scott to complain. The house was staffed with servants, though Fitzgerald suspected they were padding the grocery bills. Zelda tried to keep herself occupied, reading Henry James novels and Carl Van Vechten's latest book, *The Tattooed Countess*. With a French-English dictionary at hand, she tackled Raymond Radiguet's *Le Bal du Comte d'Orgel*. She spent a good deal of time at the beach, getting a rich brown suntan. In *Save Me the Waltz,* her fictional account of that pivotal summer in their marriage, Zelda suggests something, perhaps ominous, hovering in the very lushness of the scenery: "The Riviera is a seductive place. The blare of the beaten blue and those white palaces shimmering under the heat accentuates things. . . . The Riviera afternoons are long and still and full of a consciousness of night long before evening falls."

They visited the Murphys, staying once more at Antibes while their villa was being renovated. They began to meet people and, in the evenings, gave parties. They had taken up with a group of lively young bachelors, aviators from the nearby airfield at Fréjus and their friends. The names, misspelled, were set down in Fitzgerald's ledger "Josanne and Silve . . . Bobby Croirier." Zelda's impressions of two of the young men — fictional — hint at perverse undercurrents. René Silvy is described as "the artistic son of a Provençal avocat. His eyes were brown and consumed by the cold fire of a Tintoretto boy." Bobbé, the older friend (Zelda's Bobbie), "had been in the war and his eyes were as gray and desolate as the churned spaces about Verdun — during that summer, René painted their rain-washed shine in all the lights of that varied sea." She hints at something sexual, something conspiratorial in the behavior of the two men: "René and Bobbie protruded insistently from their white beach clothes and talked in undertones of Arthur Rimbaud. Bobbie pulled his eyebrows and his feet were flat and silent butler's feet." As a writer, Zelda was, in certain respects, like some species of night-flying moth, palpae fluttering, alert to the subtlest stimuli.

But it was the third of the group, Edouard Jozan, a twenty-five-year-old aviator, stationed at Fréjus, who served as the catalyst for one of the major disturbances in the Fitzgeralds' marriage. In Zelda's novel, he appears under the florid name Jacques Chèvre-Feuille (honeysuckle in French), an ingratiating and personable young officer in a starched white uniform, one of the band of gilded youths whom David and Alabama Knight become friendly with on the Riviera. It is not clear whether it is a matter of truth or fiction that Jozan, like the daring young aviators of Taylor Field, swooped low over the roof of Villa Marie in a noisy tribute to Zelda. In the novel, Jacques Chèvre-Feuille does.

But the whole episode, which is central to the story of the Fitzgeralds, is so woven round with a cocoon of fiction and fantasy that it is impossible to know what is authentic and what is invented. To begin with, the hero of the affair might have come straight from the central casting office of Fitzgerald's imagination or from his rivals in the past, a reincarnation of the handsome naval officer who had married his sweetheart Ginevra King, or a French version of one of the daring pilots who had courted Zelda before their marriage. Only the scantiest details provide the factual core of the episode: a few scattered entries in Fitzgerald's ledger book; a dim apology in one of Zelda's later letters; the vague recollections of friends like the Murphys, recounted years later, the denials of Jozan himself. The rest is largely invention, the changing stories the Fitzgeralds spun out about themselves.

How serious the affair was is difficult to tell. At first it must have seemed only a mild summer flirtation. With Fitzgerald busy at work on his novel, Jozan and Zelda were often together on the beach or dancing together at the casino in the evenings. The aviator and his friends were invited to dinners at the Villa Marie. That Zelda was attracted to the lithe young aviator with the strong hands is clear from her fictional account of Jacques and Alabama dancing. "He was bronze," Zelda wrote, "and smelled of sand and sun; she felt him naked underneath the starched linen. She didn't think of David."

The Murphys, who were seeing a good deal of the Fitzgeralds, were conscious that something was happening between Zelda and Jozan. Sara was surprised that Scott was so unaware, considering that everyone else knew. Gerald felt that Scott was partly to blame: "I don't know how far it really went, I suspect it wasn't much, but it did upset Scott a good deal. I wonder whether it wasn't partly his own fault."

According to Fitzgerald's ledger, the affair came to a head in mid-July: "The Big Crisis — 13th of July." It was some five or six weeks — perhaps even less — since they had met Jozan and his friends. The circumstantial evidence suggests that, whatever its nature, the affair must have been brief, Fitzgerald's awareness of it early, and the showdown not long in coming. As late as June 23, for instance,

Fitzgerald was writing Tom Boyd in ecstatic terms about the idyllic life he and Zelda were living on the Riviera. So his suspicions, quite likely, were aroused some time after that date, a matter of two or three weeks before the actual crisis. Nor does anything after the date of the crisis suggest that there were further problems serious enough for Fitzgerald to note them in his ledger. "A sad trip to Monte Carlo" suggests an emotional aftereffect, perhaps. "Zelda swimming every day. Getting brown," is rather routine. Otherwise, the notes for the remainder of July indicate that they gave a dinner party, that they took one or more trips to Ste. Maxime, and that Ring Lardner's book was a "big success."

The Jozan affair has been studied and restudied for its impact on the Fitzgeralds' marriage, but it remains shadowy at best. There is, however, one overlooked clue to what may have been Fitzgerald's emotional state during the weeks immediately preceding and following the crisis. During the first two weeks of July, he was working on his travel piece about life on the Riviera for *The Saturday Evening Post*. And only a few days after the Big Crisis, he wrote to Harold Ober that the article was finished and in the hands of a typist at Nice. He assured his agent that the article would "positively" be mailed on the following Monday, July 21 — a week after the crisis. And on July 24, he wrote Ober that the article had been sent.

Under the circumstances, "How to Live on Practically Nothing a Year" must be considered a triumph of style over personal anguish. For the benefit of the readers of *The Saturday Evening Post*, Fitzgerald created a picture-postcard view of an American family abroad. It was his family. The article is full of sun-drenched color, self-consciousness, minor barbs at tourists, and an assortment of ironies. It is rambling, funny, unperturbed — hardly the article of a supremely unhappy husband. His "distinguished looking young man, accompanied by a young lady," are pictured lounging on a sandy beach in France:

> Both of them were burned to a deep chocolate brown, so that at first they seemed to be of Egyptian origin, but closer inspection showed that their faces had an Aryan cast and that their voices, when they spoke, had a faintly nasal, North American ring. Near them played a small black child with cotton-white hair who from time to time beat a tin spoon upon a pail and shouted, "*Regardez-moi!*" in no uncertain voice.

Out of the casino near by drifted weird rococo music — a song dealing with the non-possession of a specific yellow fruit in a certain otherwise well-stocked store. Waiters, both Senegalese and European, rushed around the bathers with many-colored drinks, pausing now and then to chase away children of the poor, who were dressing and undressing, with neither modesty nor self-consciousness, upon the sand.

The conversation of Fitzgerald's two Americans is instructive:

"Hasn't it been a good summer!" said the young man lazily. "We've become absolutely French."

"And the French are such an aesthetic people," said the young lady, listening for a moment to the banana music. "They know how to live. Think of all the nice things they have to eat!"

"Delicious things! Heavenly things!" exclaimed the young man, spreading some American deviled ham on some biscuits marked Springfield, Illinois. . . .

"The trouble with most Americans in France," he remarked sonorously, "is that they won't lead a real French life. They hang around the big hotels and exchange opinions fresh from the States."

"I know," she agreed. "That's exactly what it said in the New York Times this morning."

Fitzgerald's glossy account of his first two months in France demonstrated his virtues and flaws as a writer. There was the necessary projection of a glamorous image of himself and family, offset by their American attitudes; there was the picture of a luxurious way of life, chastened by a not too chastening glimpse of the local poverty. The priggish reference to the European custom of undressing at the beach and the introduction of American products and popular American songs were authentic.

But what is astonishing about Fitzgerald's *Post* article is his final description of the visit of the French aviators to the Villa Marie. It has Fitzgerald's Riviera mood — the sense of time stopped, of warm still nights, an incomparable air of romance. Edouard Jozan does not figure in this account, but Fitzgerald treats René and Bobbé with the charm that he reserved for admired and envied heroes. And there is the added touch of near identification with René, who has missed the war and has literary ambitions:

It is twilight as I write this, and out of my window darkening banks of trees, set one clump behind another in many greens, slope down to the evening sea. The flaming sun has collapsed behind the peaks of the Estérels and the moon already hovers over the Roman aqueducts of Fréjus, five miles away. In half an hour René and Bobbé, officers of aviation, are coming to dinner in their white ducks; and René, who is only twenty-three and has never recovered from having missed the war, will tell us romantically how he wants to smoke opium in Peking and how he writes a few things "for myself alone." Afterwards, in the garden, their white uniforms will grow dimmer as the more liquid dark comes down, until they, like the heavy roses and the nightingales in the pines, will seem to take an essential and indivisible part in the beauty of this proud gay land.

Whatever the emotional impact of Zelda's betrayal, it clearly had had little effect on Fitzgerald's professional verve. In fact, his aplomb seems rather chilling.

The aftermath of the affair seems to have been devoid of further crises. Early in August, Gilbert Seldes and his bride, Amanda, on their honeymoon, spent several days with the Fitzgeralds. There were trips to the beach and to Monte Carlo. Seldes saw no signs of marital troubles. The most noteworthy event he could recall — other than the hair-raising drives with the Fitzgeralds along the narrow, winding coastal road — was a very quiet one. On one of the blue Mediterranean mornings when everything seemed fresh and starched and new, he opened the window and saw Scott, on the balcony outside his bedroom, gazing calmly out toward the sea. Catching sight of Seldes, Fitzgerald called the news that Conrad was dead. Fitzgerald's ledger entries for the remainder of August suggest a return to normality. There were frequent trips to Antibes, where John Dos Passos, following a walking trip through the Pyrenees, was a guest of the Murphys at their hotel. There were further "rows" with Miss Maddock. Fitzgerald also noted, "Good work on novel. Zelda and I close together."

Like much else about the Fitzgeralds' lives, the Jozan affair seemed made for literature. If it had peaked and subsided rather rapidly that summer on the Riviera, in time it grew to dramatic — even tragic — proportions in the uses the Fitzgeralds made of it in their stories and novels and in the later accounts they gave out to family and friends. The wilder, personal versions all suggest the Big Crisis. Fitzgerald told a relative that one day Zelda came to him and confessed her love for Jozan and asked him for a divorce. Fitzgerald, in a rage, insisted that Jozan come to him personally and, in front of Zelda, ask for the divorce. But Jozan did not respond, and the confrontation never took place. Still, Fitzgerald locked Zelda in her room and made her swear that she would never see the aviator again. However, Fitzgerald's laconic July entry in his ledger book—"Zelda swimming every day. Getting brown"—seems to contradict that story.

In a later variation, Fitzgerald told Sheilah Graham, his mistress at the time, that there had been a confrontation and that it had been dangerous. Graham wrote: "He told me he was so furious that he challenged Jozan to a duel and bought a pistol. According to Scott, they each fired a shot but neither harmed the other." Graham concluded, "While he was telling me this, I had the feeling that the whole episode was to provide material for his book." It had; Fitzgerald was giving her a slightly altered version of the scenario for an illicit love affair and a duel that he had written into his novel *Tender Is the Night.*

Inevitably, the tale of the Jozan affair turned tragic and the fallen aviator who had died for the love of Zelda was resurrected from the Montgomery speedway and plunged to his death once more —but in a Riviera setting. Fitzgerald would tell Ernest Hemingway several versions of this story. Hemingway, drily, admitted a preference for the earliest one: "This first version that he told me of Zelda and a French naval aviator falling in love was truly a sad story. . . . Later he told me other versions of it as though trying them for use in a novel, but none of them was as sad as this first one." Hemingway's first wife, Hadley, a reputable source, remembered the Fitzgeralds' concert version of the story. "It was one of their acts together," she told Nancy Milford. "I remember Zelda's beautiful face becoming very, very solemn, and she would say how he had loved her and how hopeless it had been and then how he had committed suicide. Scott would stand next to her looking very pale and distressed and sharing every minute of it. . . . It created a peculiar effect."

In reality, Zelda did apologize for the Jozan episode. "Then there was Josen and you were justifiably angry," she wrote Fitzgerald in a later autobiographical letter, characteristically misspelling her lover's name. (Is it, perhaps, a queer confirmation of their marital fidelity that neither of them ever learned to spell the name of the alleged adulterer?) But fiction makes stern demands on the truth, and Zelda, in *Save Me the Waltz,* treated the affair with greater plausibility. In the novel the couple do not reach the stage of having sex together, and Jacques does not die in a plane crash but is sent off to Indo-China, leaving Alabama with a letter in French (which she cannot read) and a photograph (which she tears up) and a lesson learned from experience: "Whatever it was that she wanted from Jacques, Jacques took it with him. . . . You took what you wanted from life, if you could get it, and you did without the rest." In her novel there is a plane crash, but it is a mere false alarm and does not involve Jacques. Quite probably, Zelda realized that it was inadvisable to have two fatal crashes involving her heroine. (In the first, one of Alabama's wartime beaux has an accident in which the mechanic is killed.)

Edouard Jozan did not die in a plane crash. He went on to a prestigious career in the French navy, was a decorated hero who took part in the Dunkirk evacuation of World War II, and saw duty in the Far East. When Nancy Milford succeeded in tracking him down for her 1970 biography, *Zelda,* Jozan was a retired vice-admiral. In reply to her written queries, he denied, whether out of truthfulness or gallantry, that there had been an affair. He admitted to having been caught up in the glamorous lives of the two Americans — as were his other bachelor friends. Jozan thought Fitzgerald a bit of an intellectual, more sophisticated than any man he had yet met. Zelda, he said, was extremely attractive but not a complicated woman. Her pleasures seemed to be simple ones: sunning on the beach, rides along the coast, informal dinners. Jozan said that he was totally unaware of the domestic scenes that may or may not have taken place at the Villa Marie. After he left Fréjus in October, he neither heard from nor saw the Fitzgeralds again. Fitzgerald's ledger recorded the departure of his misspelled rival: "Last sight of Josanne."

Zelda's friend Sara Mayfield interviewed Jozan in Paris for her 1971 biography, *Exiles from Paradise.* But, though aware of the admiral's still obvious charm, she came to the conclusion that the affair had been largely a summer flirtation — "romantic, decorous, and slightly comic"; that is pretty much the story as Zelda told it in *Save Me the Waltz.* Jozan's analysis, written to Milford, is worth recalling: "But they both had a need of drama; they made it up and perhaps they were victims of their own unsettled and a little unhealthy imagination."

Nothing about the Fitzgerald legend is simple, and little is definitive. One bit of contradictory evidence that suggests that the affair was totally serious comes from the Murphys. They recalled that one morning, around three or four, Fitzgerald pounded at their door. He was green and trembling, carrying a candle. Zelda, he said, had taken an overdose of sleeping pills. They returned with him, and Sara walked Zelda back and forth, back and forth, to keep her from falling asleep. When she tried to get Zelda to take some olive oil, Zelda made the eerie remark "Sara . . . don't make me take that, please. If you drink too much oil, you turn into a Jew."

However, Sara Mayfield, whose biographical treatment of Zelda tends to be overprotective in most respects, dismisses the entire episode of the suicide attempt on the not unreasonable grounds that Fitzgerald would hardly have left Zelda to drive the fifty-two kilometers to Cap d'Antibes to summon help. Another discrepancy also suggests itself: In a presumably well-run establishment like the Hôtel du Cap, where the Murphys were staying, would it have been possible for someone to show up unannounced at the Murphys' door? And why the candle? It is highly unlikely that the Murphys would have invented such a drastic story. But it is possible that they may have misremembered by a year. In the summer of 1925, the Murphys moved into their renovated Villa America, and in August of that year the Fitzgeralds were staying in Antibes. The possibility that the overdose had been taken in the summer of 1925 becomes all the more plausible when one finds the following entry in Fitzgerald's ledger for August 1925: "Zelda drugged."

Still, whether Zelda's "affair" with Jozan was only a simple flirtation, or another attempt to make her husband jealous because she was restless or bored and he was preoccupied with his work, it may have had serious consequences. Well before the meeting with Jozan, Fitzgerald's critic-friend Ernest Boyd had been surprised by Fitzgerald's old-fashioned Catholic attitude about marriage: "Upon the theme of marital fidelity, Fitzgerald's eloquence has moved me to tears. . . . Where so many others are conscious only of sex, he is conscious of the soul. His Catholic heaven is not so far away that he can be misled into mistaking the shoddy dream of a radical millennium as a substitute for Paradise." Even a scoffer like Hemingway acknowledged Fitzgerald's "strange mixed-up Irish catholic monogamy" where Zelda was concerned. In the far stricter Catholic doctrine of Fitzgerald's time, to feel the urge or even entertain the wish to commit adultery was only slightly less sinful than committing the sin itself. Given Fitzgerald's morbid jealousy, Zelda's pseudo-affair must have shaken his confidence. Later in life, he commented, "That September 1924, I knew something had happened that could never be repaired."

Besides, it had a queer similarity to the Ginevra King affair: the competition with a dashing naval pilot — the active, athletic type he envied and wanted to be. Something about the train of events that summer seemed to call up subterranean thoughts of identifying himself with another man. In his notebooks, Fitzgerald — in hindsight, it is true — gave the following sequence of recollections:

> The going to the Riviera . . . The table at Villa Marie. The attempt at adjusting swimming time. The aviation field. The garden in the morning. The Seldes. Night in Ste. Maxime. *Feeling of proxy in passion strange encouragement.* . . . He was sorry, knowing how she would pay. [Italics added.]

Zelda, when describing that summer in fictional terms, found the precise psychological metaphor to fit the relationship of the two men involved:

> "Do you think he actually *is* a god?" Alabama whispered to David. "He looks like you — except that he is full of the sun, whereas you are a moon person."

The sun that rules by fiat and the moon that shines by proxy, in a reflected light.

II

Fitzgerald had come to France determined to reshape his career. Before leaving Great Neck, he sent Max Perkins one of the most sober and self-possessed letters of his life. He was full of grand ambitions. His new book, he told Perkins, would be a "consciously artistic achievement"; it would involve the "sustained imagination of a sincere and yet radiant world"; it would not be dependent on "the trashy imaginings" of his commercial stories. He made his excuses for not having finished his novel: "Much of what I wrote last summer was good, but it was so interrupted that it was ragged." He was now approaching the book "from a new angle," and that meant that he had had to discard a good deal of what he had already written. Looking back over the two or more years since the publication of *The Beautiful and Damned,* Fitzgerald reckoned that he had written only about a hundred words a day, a sorry record. "If I'd spent this time reading or traveling or doing anything—even staying healthy—it'd be different, but I spent it uselessly, neither in study nor in contemplation but only in drinking and raising hell generally." He asked Perkins to be patient: "Trust me that at last, or at least for the first time in years, I'm doing the best I can." He acknowledged that he had gotten into dozens of bad habits, a few of which he enumerated:

1. Laziness
2. Referring everything to Zelda—a terrible habit, nothing ought to be referred to anybody until it's finished
3. Word consciousness—self doubt
            ect. ect. ect. ect.

For all his doubts, Fitzgerald ended his letter on a note of self-confidence that was rare and promising: "I feel I have an enormous power in me now, more than I've ever had in a way, but it works so fitfully and with so many bogeys because I've *talked so much* and not lived within myself. . . . Also, I don't know anyone who has used up so much personal experience as I have at 27." He assured Perkins that if he ever again had "the right to any leisure," he would not waste it as he had over the past few years.

Throughout the summer at the Villa Marie, Fitzgerald sent Perkins regular progress reports. "We are idyllicly settled here & the novel is going fine—it ought to be done in a month," he wrote in June. In July he admitted, "I'm not going to mention my novel to you again until it is on your desk. All goes well." Late in August he announced, "The novel will be done next week. That doesn't mean, however, that it'll reach America before October 1st, as Zelda and I are contemplating a careful revision after a week's complete rest." (It seems unlikely that he and Zelda were calmly working together on revisions if the Jozan affair had stirred up deep and bitter feelings of resentment.) Fitzgerald's letter was full of chatty items; there was only one allusion to recent troubles: "Its been a fair summer. I've been unhappy but my work hasn't suffered from it. I am grown at last." He was enthusiastic about his book, modestly announcing, "I think my novel is about the best American novel ever written. It is rough stuff in places, runs to about 50,000 words."

Early in October he was writing Edmund Wilson in exuberant terms: "My book is wonderful, so is the air and the sea." He assured Wilson that he was fully recuperated from all the physical problems resulting from his winter of hard work the year before: "I have got my health back — I no longer cough and itch and roll from one side of the bed to the other all night and have a hollow ache in my stomach after two cups of black coffee." A few days later, around October 10, he assured Max Perkins that the novel would be sent in five days and that he was awaiting the visit of Ring and Ellis Lardner. The Lardners, who were staying at the Beau Rivage in St. Raphaël, were invited to dinner and encouraged to take a trip in the Renault to Cannes and Nice and Monte Carlo. Lardner, familiar with Fitzgerald's driving, suggested that they hire a car and chauffeur so that they could all sit back and enjoy the scenery en route. Fitzgerald, however, insisted on driving. According to Lardner's comic account of his European trip, "The Other Side," written for *Liberty* magazine, the only marital blow-up in the Fitzgerald ménage took place at the hotel in Monte Carlo while they were dressing for dinner. From the Fitzgeralds' suite, he heard Fitzgerald raising a storm, "mentioning prominent Biblical characters," when he discovered that the maid had forgotten to pack his new dinner jacket.

The Lardner visit seems to have caused a further delay. It was not until late in October that Fitzgerald took his manuscript to his typist in Nice and then mailed it to Max Perkins, on the twenty-seventh. He was still undecided about the title. (There had been several choices during the course of writing it: *Among Ash-Heaps and Millionaires, The Great Gatsby, Gold-Hatted Gatsby, Trimalchio,* and *The High-Bouncing Lover.* And he would be uncertain up to the very publication date.) But he still felt a surge of confidence: "I think that at last I've done something really my own, but how good 'my own' is remains to be seen."

He was feeling sad — and old, even at the age of twenty-eight. He and Zelda had planned to spend the winter in Italy, now that the book was completed. (It was Zelda's idea; she had been reading Henry James's *Roderick Hudson.*) Something of Fitzgerald's end-of-summer mood had crept into his novel. That was the gist of a letter he sent Ludlow Fowler, who was also feeling the passage of the years. "I feel old too, this summer —" Fitzgerald wrote. "I have ever since the failure of my play a year ago. Thats the whole burden of this novel — the loss of those illusions that give such color to the world so that you don't care whether things are true or false as long as they partake of the magical glory."

◁━━━◁

The Great Gatsby begins with a father's advice and ends with a father's false illusions. It is the father of Nick Carraway, the narrator, who sets the tone of wealth and noblesse oblige that opens the novel. "Whenever you feel like criticizing anyone," Nick is told, "just remember that all the people in this world haven't had the advantages that you've had." As a consequence, Nick has learned to postpone making judgments of others. "Reserving judgments," Nick claims, "is a matter of infinite hope."

It is Jay Gatsby's lower-middle-class father who subscribes to the Great American Dream. Having come east for his son's funeral, he maintains the ultimate fiction: "If he'd of lived, he'd of been a great man. A man like James J. Hill. He'd of helped build up the country." Hill, a nineteenth-century capitalist, entrepreneur, railroad magnate, was also the idol of Rudolph Miller's father in "Absolution" — another connection between that preliminary story and the novel. In real life, James J. Hill, who had built a grand mansion on Summit Avenue and was one of the benefactors of St. Paul, was the hero of the McQuillan clan. His mention establishes a link between Jay Gatsby, who is dissatisified with his family's lowly origins, and his creator, Scott Fitzgerald, who is equally dissatisfied with his ineffectual father and his inescapable "black Irish " heritage. Moreover, *The Great Gatsby* is the only novel of Fitzgerald's in which a father survives a protagonist son. It is undoubtedly the novel Fitzgerald had in mind when he claimed that, to please his own father, he "once had a father stagger in and out at the end of the book." Edward Fitzgerald, so his son reported, "was far from flattered."

Despite Fitzgerald's reputation as the chronicler of the Jazz Age, the writer who had done most to establish the myth of a glamorous decade of waste, extravagance, and self-indulgence, he was, in his way, one of the most circumstantial of American authors. The blue lawns and the Georgian gardens, the swank parties and the yellow cocktail music, the premature moons that were produced, like the suppers, "out of a caterer's basket," were all derived from Fitzgerald's residence in Great Neck. Late in his life, in the endpapers of his copy of André Malraux's *Man's Hope,* Fitzgerald was at pains to set down the circumstances of *The Great Gatsby* that had been drawn from his life and those which were matters of pure invention. In the early chapters he had used the glamorous lives of the Hitchcocks and Rumseys to produce the atmosphere of opulence and the "magical glory." (Charles Cary Rumsey, a daredevil horseman, polo player, and sculptor, was married to the heiress Mary Harriman.) Gatsby's lavish parties were modeled after similar parties Fitzgerald had attended at Herbert Bayard Swope's estate. And it seems nearly certain that Fitzgerald's carefully prepared vignette of the movie director and his star, "a gorgeous, scarcely human orchid of a woman," was prompted by a scene witnessed at some party given by Allan Dwan and Gloria Swanson:

> They were still under the white-plum tree and their faces were touching except for a pale, thin ray of moonlight between. It occurred to me that he had been very slowly bending toward her all evening to attain this proximity, and even while I watched I saw him stoop one ultimate degree and kiss at her cheek.

In life, Fitzgerald could be ribald about the pair when writing to John Peale Bishop; but in literature, he remained the romantic.

Bob Kerr's story of the millionaire yachtsman was undoubtedly the origin of Jay Gatsby's wealthy alcoholic patron, Dan Cody, the man who lifts young Jimmy Gatz out of a life of mediocrity, hiring him in some "vague personal capacity." Fitzgerald's hazy recollections of boozy parties in cheap Manhattan apartments, his blistering rides past Flushing Meadows in the summer heat, furnished the mise-en-scène for the seedy orgy in the apartment of Tom Buchanan's mistress, Myrtle Wilson, and for the novel's most potent image, the Long Island wasteland of ash heaps over which the oculist's sign, the eyes of Dr. T. J. Eckleburg, preside like an all-seeing God. Memories of Ginevra King's wedding provided the details for Daisy Fay's marriage to Tom Buchanan. And Zelda's breaking-off of their engagement and her romance with Edouard Jozan provided the motivation for Daisy's two betrayals of Gatsby: first when he is a young infantry officer in France, then in the confrontation scene in the Plaza. In that climactic scene, Gatsby insists that Daisy deny the past, that she tell her husband "that you never loved him—and it's all wiped out forever." Daisy backs down, saying the sensible thing: "I can't help what's past. . . . I did love him once—but I loved you too." The purely invented parts of the novel, as Fitzgerald itemized them, were Gatsby's reunion with Daisy in Nick Carraway's cottage, Gatsby's murder by George Wilson, who has been led to believe that Gatsby had run his wife down in the roadside accident, and Gatsby's funeral.

In one of the novel's more famous passages, Fitzgerald lists the preposterously comic names of the guests who attend Gatsby's extravagant parties:

> Clarence Endive was from East Egg, as I remember. He came only once, in white knickerbockers, and had a fight with a bum named Etty in the garden. From farther out on the Island came the Cheadles and the O. R. P. Schraeders, and the Stonewall Jackson Abrams of Georgia, and the Fishguards and Ripley Snells. Snell was there three days before he went to the penitentiary, so drunk out on the gravel drive that Mrs. Ulysses Swett's automobile ran over his right hand. The Dancies came, too, and S. B. Whitebait, who was well over sixty, and Maurice A. Flink, and the Hammerheads, and Beluga the tobacco importer, and Beluga's girls.

It is a neat Joycean or Freudian merger of the Social Register and the telephone directory, but a bit too full-blown, running to two pages. More ironic, perhaps, are the names and characterizations, drawn from personal connections, that Fitzgerald assigned to the central figures of his novel. His heroine's maiden name, Fay, is taken from Monsignor Fay—a curious gender reversal. Daisy's friend Jordan Baker, a champion golfer—"incurably dishonest" and with a professional scandal buried somewhere in her brief past—had a connection with Zelda's Montgomery life. According to Sara Mayfield, during Fitzgerald's courtship of Zelda, Jordan Prince, one of Zelda's girl friends, had invited her as a companion on a midterm date at Sewanee, and Fitzgerald had been jealous. But Jordan Baker had, as well, a connection with the other unfaithful woman in Fitzgerald's past, Ginevra King. Fitzgerald wrote Max Perkins, "Jordan of course was a great idea," and then informed his editor that the character had been drawn from that of a championship golfer who had been a classmate of Ginevra's at Westover. Even the name of Gatsby's drunken patron, Dan Cody, had a link with Zelda's past and her infidelity. Again according to Sara Mayfield, Dan Cody, the son of a well-to-do Montgomery banker, was one of Zelda's suitors and Fitzgerald's worrisome rivals. An extensive doctoral thesis, in fact, could be done on Fitzgerald's tendency to pick up the names of friends, heroes, recent acquaintances, and promptly install them in his stories and novels. Much of it was a smart-aleck performance or a form of private joke, but in some cases it appears to have been a method of pillorying rivals and enemies by means of fictional characterizations.

Nearly all of Gatsby's shady connections with bootlegging, sports scandals, and stock swindles were related to unnamed but clearly identifiable Great Neck residents. One person involved in Gatsby's shady dealings was a Great Neck neighbor, Edward M. Fuller, a wealthy stockbroker who, with his partner William F. McGee, was indicted for illegally gambling with customers' funds. Another was the gambler Arnold Rothstein, the man who had been implicated in the 1919 Chicago White Sox scandal. In the novel, Rothstein became Meyer Wolfsheim. But Fitzgerald, who occasionally liked to give his heroes some daring or romantic criminal taint, seems to have played down that element in *Gatsby*. Or at least, in ambivalent fashion, claimed to have done so. In a letter to a friend, he maintained: "In *Gatsby,* I selected the stuff to fit a given mood or 'hauntedness' or whatever you might call it, rejecting in advance in *Gatsby,* for instance, all of the ordinary material for Long Island, big crooks, adultery theme and always starting from the *small* focal point that impressed me—my own meeting with Arnold Rothstein for instance."

Fitzgerald was, indeed, one of the most opportunistic of American novelists, the most alert to the winds of change, whether of literary style or public opinion. Every scrap of experience, his own or borrowed from others; every insight, earned or overheard, was considered usable knowledge for his fictional pursuits. In his antic honesty, Fitzgerald once boasted to Zelda that he had one quality that he had found "almost as valuable as positive originality"; that was the ability to "make a few paragraphs from Marx, John Stuart Mill, and *The New Republic* go further than most people can do with years of economic study. That is one way to grow learned, first pretend to be—then have to live up to it." In *The Great Gatsby,* evidently sensing some change in the political weather, Fitzgerald seems to have discarded the theories of Nordic supremacy he had picked up so handily by reading and misreading H. L. Mencken. At least, he attributes such ideas to a patent racist like Tom Buchanan, who has read a book "by this man Goddard" titled *The Rise of the Colored Empires.* Civilization, he feels, is going to pieces: "It's up to us, who are the dominant race, to watch out or these other races will have control of things." Daisy, winking at Nick Carraway, mocks her husband. "We've got to beat them down," she says. But Tom's rant is an echo of Fitzgerald's own distempered letter to Edmund Wilson about Europe and the threat of the negroid streak creeping "northward to defile the Nordic race."

Where Fitzgerald was capable of dropping old opinions effort-lessly, he was also gifted at trying out new possibilities. At the first of Gatsby's parties, the orchestra plays a vanguard composition by the composer Vladimir Tostoff, "Jazz History of the World," which had created a big sensation at Carnegie Hall. Fitzgerald had little interest in classical or avant-garde music, nor did his character Nick Carraway, who confesses that "the nature of Mr. Tostoff's compo-sition" eludes him, and turns his attention to his host. But in earlier versions of the novel the piece is attributed to a composer named Leo Epstein, and Fitzgerald struggled manfully to give it some sym-bolic importance in the novel: "But what struck me particularly was that just as you'd got used to the new discord business there'd be one of the old themes, rung in this time as a discord, until you'd get a ghastly sense that it was a preposterous cycle after all, pur-poseless and sardonic." Fitzgerald must have been trying to approx-imate the music of Leo Ornstein, though it is not clear whether he had ever attended a concert of Ornstein's music. But certainly he had heard abut the composer through Edmund Wilson, who was collaborating with him on their ballet. Fitzgerald's decision to elim-inate the descriptive passage of "Jazz History" probably had struc-tural reasons, but it was also a confession that he had not been able to carry it off with sufficient authority. He wrote Max Perkins that he thought the whole episode was "rotten" and pointedly asked, "Did you? Tell me your frank *reaction — personal*. Don't *think*! We can all think!"

Not long before he finished his manuscript, Fitzgerald sensed that there was something focally wrong in the book. Early in Sep-tember, he wrote to Max Perkins that he had put the book in storage so that he could come back to it fresh "and see what I've left out — there's some intangible sequence lacking somewhere in the middle and a break in interest there invariably means the failure of a book." Still, he was confident about his novel: "It is like nothing I've ever read before."

Once the manuscript had been delivered, both Fitzgerald and Max Perkins recognized that the problem was Gatsby himself: his origins, his past, his shadowy persona. Perkins wrote Fitzgerald that among the more carefully etched characters in the book, "Gatsby is somewhat vague. The reader's eyes can never quite focus upon him, his outlines are dim." Although it was all right to leave Gatsby's profession mysterious, there ought to be some discreet way of making it apparent that it was somehow criminal.

Fitzgerald, writing from Rome in December, acknowledged the problem: *"I myself didn't know what Gatsby looked like or was engaged in* & you felt it. If I'd known & kept it from you, you'd have been *too impressed with my knowledge to protest.* This is a complicated idea but I'm sure you'll understand." He was now convinced that, with his editor's suggestions, he could make the book "perfect." Incredibly, however, he claimed that his first instinct was to let Gatsby go and make Tom Buchanan the dominant male figure in the book. About Buchanan, Fitzgerald bragged, "He's the best character I've ever done — I think he and the brother in 'Salt' and Hurstwood in 'Sister Carrie' are the three best characters in American fiction in the last twenty years, perhaps and perhaps not." Fortunately, Fitzgerald did not surrender the book to Buchanan, who, however well depicted, represented the usual proxy-hero of Fitzgerald's imagination — the aggressive, athletic, self-sufficient all-American male. "But Gatsby sticks in my heart," he told Perkins. "I had him for awhile then lost him & now I know I have him again."

It was inevitable that Gatsby would create a problem in the book, one that Fitzgerald never really resolved. Gatsby remains the flaw at the center of the diamond. Like his creator, Gatsby is a man of assumed identities. In his letter to Perkins, Fitzgerald's "complicated idea" — hardly *that* complicated — was that authority was a matter of recognizing what one was and what one knew in order to be able to carry off a performance or command a situation. But Gatsby, like his creator, was a man of conflicted and conflicting identities, a series of personal inventions, many of which had some grain of truth or circumstance. He was not, as he implied, a graduate of Oxford, though he had spent time there. It is doubtful that he merited the medals he displays with such theatrical modesty. The swank parties, the wanting to belong, are all an admission that he is the outsider trying to buy his way into the closed circle of wealth and social approval. The obsessive dream of his love for Daisy is brought down to reality by Daisy's callousness and betrayal. Tom Buchanan shatters the Gatsby myth when he announces that he has no intention of sitting back and letting "Mr. Nobody from No-where" make love to his wife. As Fitzgerald brutally summarized it, Gatsby's pretensions had broken up "like glass against Tom's hard malice."

Jay Gatsby, in fact, was never the son of wealthy parents from San Francisco, as Stephan Parrott was. (Fitzgerald's envy could last a lifetime.) Gatsby was the poor farm boy Jimmy Gatz, who had dreams of "ineffable gaudiness" at night while the clock ticked on the washstand and the moonlight slipped over the tangled mass of clothes on the bedroom floor. Fitzgerald makes it clear that Gatsby was a creature of invention; he even knows the exact hour when he invented himself. He had become Jay Gatsby at the decisive moment that he borrowed a rowboat and pulled up to Dan Cody's yacht with the warning about the dangerous winds. Typically, in Fitzgerald's imagined world of success, Gatsby's change of status is marked by a change of dress. Cody takes the young boy to Duluth and buys him a blue coat, six pairs of white duck trousers, and a yachting cap. In one of the most striking passages of the book, Fitzgerald describes Gatsby's moment of self-creation:

> I suppose he'd had the name ready for a long time, even then. His parents were shiftless and unsuccessful farm people — his imagi-nation had never really accepted them as his parents at all. . . . So he invented just the sort of Jay Gatsby that a seventeen-year-old boy would be likely to invent, and to this conception he was faithful to the end.

Both Nick Carraway and Fitzgerald grant Gatsby absolution in that moment when Nick, turning to catch sight of the defeated hero in his "gorgeous pink rag of a suit," standing on the white steps of his preposterous mansion, calls out: "They're a rotten crowd. . . . You're worth the whole damn bunch put together." (It will never be pos-sible to know the degree of bitterness and triumph Fitzgerald put into those words.) But Gatsby, of course, pays the price for "living too long with a single dream." Lying in his swimming pool, he sees the vague, ashen form of George Wilson gliding forward to put several bullet holes through his illusions about the world.

Gatsby had believed that he could recapture the past, recreate an old love. "Can't repeat the past?" he assured Nick Carraway. "Why of course you can!" Gatsby's creator, however, saw that it was a futile enterprise. So, too, was the attempt to invent a new future for oneself in order to escape the past. It was part of Fitzgerald's vision that the past was changeless, that at the end of each day, as the landscape darkened, the present day joined the past. The past consumed life and was inescapable. The past, like one's parentage, was forever.

Fitzgerald's coda to the novel is a justly famous piece of writing. On his last night in the East, Nick Carraway pays a visit to Gatsby's empty house and reflects on Gatsby's fate:

> He had come a long way to this blue lawn, and his dream must have seemed so close that he could hardly fail to grasp it. He did not know that it was already behind him, somewhere back in that vast obscurity beyond the city, where the dark fields of the republic rolled on under the night.

Fitzgerald includes himself and Gatsby among the pursuers of the dream: "So we beat on, boats against the current, borne back ceaselessly into the past."

<hr />

Rome was not the perfect choice; it was a Holy Year and the city was full of pious tourists. At first, they looked for a house or an apartment, then put up at the Quirinale, which they did not like — the air was stale, the sitting rooms were full of middle-aged English. Finally, they settled in the Hôtel des Princes, near the Piazza di Spagna. It proved to be little better: the sheets were always damp; at night they could hear the snoring of the guests in the next room. They were paying $525 a month for the privileges, including meals and tips.

Fitzgerald once more began writing stories; "Love in the Night," "The Adjuster," "Not in the Guidebook" were written or begun in Rome. But he was becoming increasingly dissatisfied with his commercial efforts and considered them poor or "no good," cheap and lacking even the spontaneity of his earliest stories. "Love in the Night" was a frothy, sentimental tale about young love lost and found. For its hero, Val Rostoff, Fitzgerald had appropriated the family background of his friend Val Engalitcheff, who had committed suicide — an American mother and a father who was a Russian prince. It is part of Val's dashing image that he has fought a duel with a man four years older than he, and that he bears a scar on his head. (Fitzgerald, who did not fight a duel with Edouard Jozan, was

four years older than his rival.) But the real importance of "Love in
the Night" is that its lush Riviera setting and the duel are rehearsals
for Fitzgerald's next novel, *Tender Is the Night.* "Not in the Guidebook" and "The Adjuster" continue Fitzgerald's vein of stories about
disabled marriages. In the first, Jim Cooley, a bogus war hero,
deserts his young wife in France, stealing her meager inheritance.
In "The Adjuster," a drudge of a husband, Charles Hemple, has a
nervous breakdown, trying to satisfy his thoroughly spoiled and
selfish wife, Louella. She, too, confronted with an invalid husband,
having to manage the household and the help—and then suffering
the sudden death of her infant son—nearly has a breakdown. But
she is taught the lesson of resignation from the mysterious Dr. Moon,
who is both a psychoanalyst and a symbol of passing time. He advises
her:

> "We make an agreement with children that they can sit in the
> audience without helping to make the play," he said, "but if they
> still sit in the audience after they're grown, somebody's got to work
> double time for them, so that they can enjoy the light and glitter
> of the world."

It seemed to be a lesson Fitzgerald was trying to convey to Zelda.

Fitzgerald's correspondence with Perkins during the winter was
taken up with suggesting changes in the novel, asking for advice,
pleading for money, questioning the suitability of each of the several
titles he had thought up for the work. He had been extremely
anxious about Perkins' reaction to the book. "I won't get a nights
sleep until I hear from you," he had written his editor when he sent
the manuscript, "but do tell me the absolute truth, *your first impression of the book.*" Perkins' response was magnanimous: "I think the
novel is a wonder. . . . It has vitality to an extraordinary degree,
and *glamour.* . . . It has a kind of mystic atmosphere at
times. . . . And as for sheer writing, it's astonishing." Two days
later, after a second reading, Perkins was even more enthusiastic:
"It is an extraordinary book, suggestive of all sorts of thoughts and
moods. You adopted exactly the right method of telling it." He was
particularly impressed by Fitzgerald's symbolic use of the oculist's
sign: "In the eyes of Dr. Eckleburg various readers will see different
significances; but their presence gives a superb touch to the whole
thing: great unblinking eyes, expressionless, looking down upon the
human scene. It's magnificent!"

Fitzgerald's response was heartfelt, but it took an oddly financial metaphorical turn: "Your wire & your letters made me feel like a million dollars—I'm sorry I could make no better response than a telegram whining for money. But the long siege of the novel winded me a little & I've been slow on starting the stories on which I must live." He was once more on the treadmill. But despite his financial problems, he turned down an offer of $10,000 from *College Humor* for the serial rights to *Gatsby*. It had previously been offered to the Hearst syndicate and *Liberty* and been turned down; *Liberty* felt that the story was "too ripe" for its readership, too full of mistresses and adulteries. And though he would have accepted $20,000 if *College Humor* had upped its offer, he still did not want to postpone publication of the book. Besides, he considered the magazine "a lowsy sheet" and was afraid that publication there would create a poor impression of the book and kill sales as well. So he declined. "It makes me weep," he confessed to Harold Ober.

The winter in Rome turned sour. Fitzgerald was drinking, and he came down with a siege of the grippe. More important, Zelda underwent an operation, supposedly to facilitate pregnancy, and got an infection that would not clear up. They went sightseeing, but preferred not to use a guidebook; took in the night life of the city; visited the Campagna. According to Zelda, they were moved to tears by the sight of the Pope. Galsworthy, Fitzgerald informed Perkins, was visiting Rome, but he seems not to have tried to see the English novelist. Despite his earlier and obvious flattery, Fitzgerald was not sympathetic to Galsworthy's work, most of which left him "cold." He thought the subject matter of *The Forsyte Saga* stuffy. Fitzgerald suspected that Galsworthy had had some unfortunate idyllic love affair locked away in his past and that it was only when he touched on that that his writing came alive. Typically, where Fitzgerald felt some sense of identification, he was approving.

For a while, the Fitzgeralds got caught up in the busy life of the cast and crew members of the Metro-Goldwyn-Mayer Company, in Rome that winter to film *Ben Hur* with Ramon Novarro and Carmel Myers. Fitzgerald started a mild but public flirtation with the young blond movie star. (In Hollywood, later, he inscribed a copy of *The Great Gatsby*, "For Carmel Myers from her corrupter, F. Scott Fitzgerald.")

Christmas, like every holiday, was an important event in the

Fitzgeralds' calendar of celebrations; they had a tree in their hotel room, hung with silver bells. But it seemed they expected so much from such occasions that they were inevitably disappointed, drank too much, and spoiled it for themselves. Christmas in Rome was no exception. At the Christmas ball for the *Ben Hur* cast at the Hotel Excelsior, something unpleasant happened. Zelda, who had not wanted to go, either became upset or sick and asked Howard Coxe to take her home. Coxe, a Princeton graduate, a journalist and novelist, and a reviewer for *The New Republic,* was another of the attentive bachelors who entertained amorous feelings toward Zelda. She playfully referred to him as "Hungary" Coxe, an all-round Joycean pun. Coxe genuinely admired Fitzgerald, but he later made a serious mistake. One evening when they were drinking together in a bar, Coxe boasted or blurted out, "I could sleep with Zelda any time I wanted to." He was astonished at himself for having said it, but the damage was done. Coming soon after the Jozan affair, it was bound to make Fitzgerald touchy and resentful. Coxe later told the story to Edmund Wilson. Wilson's private comment was that "Zelda was not so loose nor Howard so dangerous. . . . He was envious of Scott, I suppose, and the drinks had brought this to the surface."

The most damaging experience Fitzgerald had in Rome was one that permanently soured his impressions of the Eternal City and of Italy and the Italians. He was convinced that the Italian taxi drivers cheated, and one night he refused to pay the fare asked. His relations with drivers in most nationalities, it seems, tended to be abusive. Sara Mayfield later recalled a legendary ride in Paris when Fitzgerald, drunk, had commandeered a funeral hearse, with a pair of leftover prostitutes in mourning, and prodded the driver with his cane and orders in Franglais, *"Plus vite, plus vite,* you son of a bitch." But this time the consequences were serious. A surly crowd gathered around the argument; Fitzgerald appears to have taken on a plain-clothes detective who had arrived on the scene, and he then became insulting when the *carabinieri* showed up. He was thrown in jail and badly beaten up. With an air of blamelessness, he said it was "just about the rottenest thing that ever happened to me in my life." And though he was often groggy about the details of the episode, he would remember, "through the dim midst of blood," that Howard Coxe and Zelda came to get him out of the jail.

It is quite possible he used the incident in "Not in the Guidebook," in describing Jim Cooley's drunken brawl with a pair of French soldiers: "There was a rushing, crashing noise in his ears as fists and then feet struck at him, and the world seemed to close like water over his head." Certainly he would make it one of the crucial episodes in the moral deterioration of Dick Diver in *Tender Is the Night*. And more than likely it was the cause of an outburst in a letter to Harold Ober, who had been pressing him to write an article about his Roman stay. Fitzgerald's reply was definitely not for the guidebooks: "I hate Italy and the Italians so violently that I can't bring myself to write about them for the *Post* — unless they'd like an article called 'Pope Siphilis the Sixth and his Morons' or something like that."

In mid-February the Fitzgeralds fled to Capri. Fitzgerald had more or less finished reading the galley proofs of *Gatsby* and making substantive changes. All along, he had been concerned that Gatsby was too elusive a character, and that the disappearance of Tom and Myrtle into the bedroom of Myrtle's apartment may have been too risqué. (The word *orgastic* also worried him; he assured Perkins it was "not a bit dirty.") He and Zelda had hated Rome, he told Perkins. On the resort island, they took a suite in the Tiberio Palace Hotel, with a sunny balcony looking out over the Mediterranean. Zelda was fascinated by the rabbit-warren houses, the dark meandering streets and alleys, the "Rembrandt butcher shops and bakeries." She was still recuperating. Fitzgerald wrote to John Bishop, back in New York and attempting to make a living in the publishing field, "Zelda's been sick in bed for five weeks, poor child, and is only now looking up." His letter began with the admission "I am quite drunk" and, toward the end, the complaint "Oh Christ! I'm sobering up!" He asked for news of Ludlow and Alec and Bunny and wanted to know whether Townsend Martin's first picture had gotten good reviews. But principally he was angling for Bishop's opinion of his forthcoming novel — unnamed. (He seems to have been still undecided about the title.) "I think it's great. . . ." he assured Bishop. "To me it's fascinating. I never get tired of it."

"This place is full of fairies," Fitzgerald wrote to Max Perkins, as if the island were the resort for migrant butterflies. Over the years he would become more and more inquisitive about such sexual habits. But it did not seem to cloud his literary opinions. "One of them, a nice young man my own age, is a writer of promise and performance on the Aldous Huxley type," he told his editor. "I like his books . . . and suggested that I send some to you as you are shy on young English of recent years, but Knopf had signed him up three weeks before." In a letter to Bishop, Fitzgerald announced: "Dodo Benson is here. I think he is (or was) probably a fairy." E. F. Benson, the brother of Robert Hugh Benson, whose novels Fitzgerald had read at the urging of Father Fay and Shane Leslie, was the author of *Dodo* and the *Lucia* novels. What makes Fitzgerald's insistence on tallying "fairies" so odd is that he himself could be outrageously campy on the subject. In a recent letter, full of mangled French, he had informed Bunny Wilson, "I have just been reading the advertisements of whore-houses in the French magazines. I seethe with passion for a 'bains-massage' with *volupté* [for] oriental delights (*tout un*) in a Hotel Particular, or else I long to go with a young man (intell. *bonne famille, affectueux*) for a paid amorous weekend to the coast. . . . Deep calling to deep." It was an old habit in his correspondence with Wilson. Once during World War I, when he had sent some photographs of himself to Wilson, serving in France, he suggested, "Give one to some poor motherless Poilu fairy who has no dream."

It was on Capri that Fitzgerald finally met one of his former literary heroes, Compton Mackenzie. He wrote Bishop about that "historic" moment: "I sat up (tell Bunny) half the night talking to my old idol Compton Mackenzie. Perhaps you met him. I found him cordial attractive and pleasantly mundane. . . . The war wrecked him as it did Wells and many of that generation." When Fitzgerald later told Wilson about his meeting, it was clear that he had been as tactless as he often was on such occasions. Probably he was weary of the comparisons between Amory Blaine and Mackenzie's Michael Fane. "I asked him," Fitzgerald told Wilson, "why he had petered out and never written anything that was any good since *Sinister Street* and those early novels." It was Fitzgerald's uninformed private theory that "the trouble with Mackenzie" was that he had missed the great experience of the war. Mackenzie, who was physically disabled, had nevertheless had a long and dangerous connection with the British Secret Service and later wrote about it in his memoirs. Wilson, who maintained that Mackenzie's influence on Fitzgerald "can't be over-estimated," also suspected that Zelda's style had been influenced by the English author, though he was not sure whether the influence came by way of Fitzgerald or from reading Mackenzie's books.

Fitzgerald later gave an odd summing-up of his state of mind at the end of his island visit:

> The cheerfullest things in my life are first Zelda and second the hope that my book has something extraordinary about it. I want to be extravagantly admired again. Zelda and I sometimes indulge in terrible four-day rows that always start with a drinking party, but we're still enormously in love and about the only truly happily married people I know.

As the publication date for *The Great Gatsby* approached—April 10, 1925—Fitzgerald became increasingly nervous and hopeful. He knew he had written an extraordinary book, and he wanted it to stand on its own merits, without endorsements. "I don't want any signed blurbs on the jacket," he wrote Perkins, "not Mencken's or Lewis' or Howard's or anyone's. I'm tired of being the author of *This Side of Paradise* and I want to start over." His hopes for the success of the book were on a rising curve, though he hedged a bit at first: "If my book is a big success or a great failure (financial—no other sort can be imagined, I hope) I *don't* want to publish stories in the fall. If it goes between 25,000 and 50,000, I have an excellent collection for you." Spurred on by Perkins' enthusiasm, Fitzgerald grew more optimistic: "Anyhow, I think (for the first time since *The Vegetable* failed) that I'm a wonderful writer and it's your always wonderful letters that help me to go on believing in myself." A bit later, he revised his figures upward: "My guess is that it will sell about 80,000 copies, but I may be wrong." The upward revision may have been the result of Max Perkins' dangerous habit of reporting to Fitzgerald on the sales figures of other Scribner's authors. *The White Monkey,* by Galsworthy, Perkins had written him, sold seventy-five thousand copies, even though it had come out late in the season. (Fitzgerald had labeled the book "stinko.") He was still fussing about the title of his book. Twice in March, he cabled the editor with suggested title changes—*Gold-Hatted Gatsby,* once again, then *Under the Red, White and Blue,* which he said he was "crazy" about. Perkins managed to discourage him both times. On March 31, Fitzgerald confessed, "As the day approaches my nervousness increases." He told Perkins that he planned to leave for France some time at the end of April. "If the book prospers, I'll expect some sort of cable before I leave for Paris."

On April 10, he was thrown into a fit of depression:

The book comes out today and I am overcome with fears and fore-bodings. Supposing women didn't like the book because it has no important woman in it, and critics didn't like it because it dealt with the rich and contained no peasants borrowed out of *Tess* in it and set to work in Idaho? Suppose it didn't even wipe out my debt to you — why, it will have to sell 20,000 copies even to do that! In fact, all my confidence is gone — I wouldn't tell you this except for the fact that by the [time] this reaches you the worst will be known. I'm sick of the book myself. . . .

On the spur of the moment, Fitzgerald decided to book passage on the S.S. *President Garfield* for the trip from Naples to Marseille. They had to transport their Renault back to France, and Zelda did not feel up to making the long overland journey from Italy to Paris; they planned to drive north from Marseille. Somehow, the bad news he had been anticipating managed to reach him en route. Perkins cabled him: SALES SITUATION DOUBTFUL EXCELLENT REVIEWS.

Fitzgerald answered from Marseille: "Your telegram depressed me. I hope I'll find better news in Paris and am wiring you from Lyons." He still suspected that if the book failed, it would do so because of the title and the lack of an important woman character. He didn't think that the unhappy ending mattered particularly. Perkins, in a follow-up letter, tried to analyze the problem. He thought it was the small size of the book — only 218 pages; some of the big distributors had cut back on their orders because of that. It was futile, he realized, to explain "that the way of writing which you have chosen and which is bound to come more and more into practice is one where a vast amount is said by implication." He also had to acknowledge that it seemed to be "over the heads" of even the people who felt its "enchantment." Some of the private comments were good; people like Van Wyck Brooks and John Marquand thought it was Fitzgerald's best book. And Gilbert Seldes, who would be reviewing it, was "quite wild about it." Perkins was enormously sympathetic: "I know fully how this period must try you: it must be very hard to endure, because it is hard enough for me to endure."

The trip to Paris did not help matters. At Lyon the car broke down and was badly in need of repair. Zelda was feeling too indisposed to make the remainder of the journey by car. So they left the Renault in a Lyon garage and went on by train. By the time they reached Paris and found an apartment at 14 rue de Tilsitt ("from May 12th to January 12th, eight months, where I shall do my best. What a six months in Italy! Christ!"), he had had time to read some of the early reviews and take stock of his failure. Ruth Hale, Heywood Broun's wife, had written a devastating review of it in the *Brooklyn Eagle,* saying there was no "chemical trace of magic, life, irony, romance or mysticism in all of 'The Great Gatsby.' " And a brisk report, unsigned, in the *New York World* was headlined F. SCOTT FITZGERALD'S LATEST A DUD. Even the praises in Isabel Paterson's review in the *Herald Tribune* Book Page were tempered with serious qualifications. She thought Fitzgerald's virtuosity was amazing: "He gets the exact tone, the note, the shade of the season and place he is working on; he is more contemporary than any newspaper." But she added, "He has not, yet, gone below that glittering surface, except by a kind of happy accident."

The personal letters from friends and critics whose judgment he respected ought to have bucked up Fitzgerald's ego considerably. Edmund Wilson wrote him: "It is undoubtedly in some ways the best thing you have done — the best planned, the best sustained, the best written. . . . You have succeeded here in doing most of the things that people have always scolded you for not doing." Wilson, however, found the characters unsympathetic. Mencken wrote him: "I think it is incomparably the best piece of work you have done. Evidences of careful workmanship are on every page. . . . My one complaint is that the basic story is somewhat trivial — that it reduces itself, in the end, to a sort of anecdote. But God will forgive you for that." Unfortunately, Mencken was not so forgiving; he began his syndicated review of *The Great Gatsby* by stating that it was "in form no more than a glorified anecdote, and not too probable at that." Gilbert Seldes wrote Fitzgerald with ready enthusiasm: "It's so good, Scott; so satisfying, and so rich in stuff. And written; and by the Lord, composed." Seldes' review in *The Dial,* which did not appear until August, was unequivocal. Fitzgerald, he stated, "has mastered his talents and gone soaring in a beautiful flight, leaving behind him everything dubious and tricky in his earlier work, and leaving even farther behind all the men of his own generation and most of his elders." It was high praise.

But there were some friendly criticisms that rankled him, chiefly those of Ring Lardner, who had read the book in page proof and pointed out a number of inaccuracies: "On Page 82, you had the guy driving his car under the elevated at Astoria, which isn't Astoria, but Long Island City. On Page 118, you had a tide in Lake Superior." Lardner admitted that his points were trivial, but pointed out they were just the things that critics liked to pick on. He said he like it "enormously," but the praise was disappointingly thin: "The plot held my interest . . . and I found no tedious moments. Altogether I think it's the best thing you've done since Paradise." Fitzgerald, his hackles rising, passed on the remark to Perkins: " 'The best since Paradise.' God! If you knew how discouraging that was."

Like many an author with a book in print, Fitzgerald curried favor. He wrote Mencken that he was "tremendously moved" by his letter, and "as you know I'd rather have you like a book of mine than anyone in America." And he told Wilson that his letter had compensated him for the fact that of all the reviews "not one had the slightest idea what the book was about and for the even more depressing fact that it was, in comparison with the others, a financial failure (after I'd turned down fifteen thousand for the serial rights.)" Even with an old friend like Wilson, Fitzgerald found it necessary to puff up his fees.

There was no avoiding that the book was a financial failure. Scribner's had made an initial printing of twenty thousand copies and a second of three thousand in August. But the book did not sell out, and the result was far below Fitzgerald's hopeful estimate of eighty thousand. His royalties from *The Great Gatsby* managed to clear up his indebtedness to his publisher. The failure of *The Vegetable,* much as it had depressed Fitzgerald, could be considered negligible. The failure of *The Great Gatsby* was one of the crucial defeats in Fitzgerald's professional life. He had counted heavily on its success so that he could gain a new footing in his career. He had worked hard and carefully on the manuscript to bring it to perfection; he had wanted, at last, to be recognized for the serious writer he intended to be. His bitterness was understandable. But, strangely, he seems to have anticipated his failure at the very outset, and made plans accordingly — plans that were tinged, perhaps, with resentment and self-pity. In the letter he wrote to Perkins from Marseille, he said:

> In all events I have a book of good stories for the fall. Now I shall write some cheap ones until I've accumulated enough for my next novel. When that is finished and published I'll wait and see. If it will support me with no more intervals of trash, I'll go on as a

novelist. If not, I'm going to quit, come home, go to Hollywood and learn the movie business. I can't reduce our scale of living and I can't stand this financial insecurity. Anyhow there's no point in trying to be an artist if you can't do your best. I had my chance back in 1920 to start my life on a sensible scale and I lost it, and so I'll have to pay the penalty.

As early as May, Fitzgerald seems to have conceded defeat, but not without savaging his critics. "I think all the reviews I've seen, except two," he wrote Perkins, "have been absolutely stupid and lowsy. Some day, they'll eat grass, by God! This thing, both the effort and the result, have hardened me and I think now that I'm much better than any of the young Americans *without exception.*"

His remark is all the more odd, since he had just met a young American writer who was on the verge of a success that would far outdistance his own.

7

Just a Real Place to Rough It

E RNEST HEMINGWAY'S account of his first meeting with Scott Fitzgerald has the truth of the survivor. It is given in his memoir, *A Moveable Feast,* written in the late 1950s, when Fitzgerald was nearly twenty years dead and Hemingway himself was edging toward the dementia that would end his life in suicide. Hemingway's story of his stay in Paris spared few of his contemporaries, least of all Gertrude Stein, who, in her imperturbable egotism, had adopted the handsome young correspondent for the *Toronto Star* as one of her favorites. Hemingway was particularly vicious on the subject of Alice B. Toklas, Stein's lifetime companion, watchdog, typist, and, eventually, widow. But the cruelest portrait in *A Moveable Feast* was of Fitzgerald, whose major offense — aside from his tedious bad habits when drunk — was that he was a rival writer whose stature nearly matched that of Hemingway. The acid portrayals of Fitzgerald and Zelda in the memoir are surpassed only by some of the random passages about the couple in Hemingway's posthumously published letters.

One gets the impression that the truth for Hemingway was a matter of contingencies. In *A Moveable Feast,* and more noticeably in the letters, the stories about himself and others that Hemingway told, retold, revised, and revamped over the years — and more precisely his personal attitude toward them — depended on the audience to whom he was addressing himself and to the image of himself or others that he wanted to convey at a particular moment. Hemingway's recollections are rather like constructions in Lincoln Logs: the parts and details are sturdy and solid, but they are easily dismantled and readily reassembled for different versions on different sites. His easy manner with the plausible facts could be a subject of embarrassment or defensiveness on the part of his friends. Janet Flanner, the bright and snappy Paris correspondent for *The New Yorker,* was one of Hemingway's more loyal friends. She once prefaced an interview by stating, "If you're going to ask me if Ernest was a liar, I won't answer any of your questions."

A Moveable Feast is a superbly written book, concise, highly styled, evoking charming images of idyllic happiness in the Paris of the expatriates following World War I. But is is populated with sacred monsters of Hemingway's making. The married couples — Gertrude and Alice, Scott and Zelda — are meant to provide just the right contrast for the idealized love of the poor but happy Hemingways — Ernest and his bride of three years, Hadley Richardson. Hadley, seven years older than her husband, had a small income, which allowed for occasional trips to Spain and Italy, skiing excursions to Austria, so the romantic poverty of the hero and heroine of *A Moveable Feast* is somewhat questionable. It is also sobering to recognize that the love affair which Hemingway chronicled with such tenderness is a bit suspect. When Fitzgerald first met him, Hemingway had already been introduced to Pauline Pfeiffer, the wealthy young woman on the staff of the Paris edition of *Vogue* who would become the second Mrs. Hemingway. Little more than a year later, in fact, Hemingway separated from Hadley. There is sufficient reason, then, for heeding Hemingway's cautionary advice in the preface of *A Moveable Feast:* "If the reader prefers, this book may be regarded as fiction."

Fitzgerald was aware of Hemingway's reputation and quite probably had read his writings even before meeting the author. But it is not clear why he began a promotional campaign in Hemingway's behalf well before they became acquainted personally. Late in October 1924, Fitzgerald wrote Max Perkins in a burst of enthusiasm, "This is to tell you about a young man named Ernest Hemmingway who lives in Paris, (an American) writes for the transatlantic Review & has a brilliant future." In the issue of *The Dial* of that same month, Edmund Wilson wrote a brief but highly favorable review of Hemingway's *Ten Stories and Three Poems* and *In Our Time,* the latter a series of vignettes that established Hemingway's reputation as a writer with a terse journalistic style. It may well have been the Wilson review that prodded Fitzgerald into action on behalf of the author.

But he would later claim that it was Wilson who had shown him the little pamphlet with Hemingway's brief sketches, meaning that he had read them before sailing for Europe; so it is not clear why he waited until October to alert Perkins to Hemingway. In his letter to his editor, Fitzgerald suggested that Perkins get hold of a copy of *In Our Time:* "I haven't it here now but its remarkable & I'd look him up right away. He's the real thing."

Perkins had difficulty getting a copy of the book and was slow in contacting Hemingway; his first letter went astray. By the time Fitzgerald and Hemingway met in Paris, Horace Liveright had already drawn up a contract with Hemingway, agreeing to publish *In Our Time* in America and securing an option on Hemingway's next three books. Fitzgerald communicated the news to Max Perkins in a letter dated May 1, 1925. As nearly as can be determined, the two writers met some time late in April, soon after the Fitzgeralds arrived in Paris and before their move to the rue de Tilsitt apartment. A bit later, in May, Fitzgerald wrote Perkins about the twenty-five-year-old author, still misspelling his name. "Hemminway is a fine, charming fellow and he appreciated your letter and the tone of it enormously. If Liveright doesn't please him, he'll come to you, and he has a future. He's 27."

Hemingway's account of the meeting at the Dingo Bar on the rue Delambre, written more than thirty years after the event, is a well-calculated affair; all the reasons for their later break are established at the beginning. Hemingway was at the bar with some "completely worthless characters" when Fitzgerald arrived, already quite drunk. Fitzgerald was with a friend, Duncan Chaplin, a celebrated pitcher from the Princeton baseball team, whose virtuous masculinity provided the foil for Fitzgerald's self-indulgence. Hemingway's descripton of Fitzgerald, written in the compressed style for which he was justly famous, is a marvel of economy and innuendo:

> Scott was a man then who looked like a boy with a face between handsome and pretty. He had very fair wavy hair, a high forehead, excited and friendly eyes and a delicate long-lipped Irish mouth that, on a girl, would have been the mouth of a beauty. . . . The mouth worried you until you knew him and then it worried you more.

But on this occasion, that beauty was marred by Fitzgerald's dissipated and puffy appearance. His apparel came in for a good deal of scrutiny in Hemingway's account: a Brooks Brothers outfit with a button-down oxford shirt and a Guards tie that had been bought in Rome. The description of Fitzgerald's preppy American stylishness was a subtle form of put-down; even Hemingway's disreputable friends knew that it was a breach of dress code to wear a Guards tie. Hemingway even suggested that Fitzgerald's ignorance might be the cause of a fight should any Englishmen happen into the bar. Scott also broke another unwritten rule by extolling Hemingway's talents as a writer. Hemingway held to the view that "praise to the face was open disgrace." It is not impossible that Fitzgerald may have subsequently adopted the same code. Following his meeting with the young author, there were one or two incidents in which Fitzgerald regarded compliments, however genuine, as insults.

Fitzgerald then launched into his usual obnoxious questioning: Did Hemingway sleep with his wife before they were married? He even became insistent when Hemingway refused to answer. But fortunately the champagne overtook Fitzgerald, who suddenly began to sweat, then turned the color of a wax candle, and passed out. Hemingway and Chaplin got him into a cab and sent him home. The great discrepancy in this seemingly authentic and detailed episode is that Dunc Chaplin — "the extraordinarily nice, unworried, relaxed and friendly" Dunc Chaplin — was not present. Matthew Bruccoli, whose *Scott and Ernest* offers the most detailed account of the Hemingway-Fitzgerald relationship, learned from Chaplin himself that he had not been present at the meeting of the two men; in fact, had not been in Europe at all in 1925. The marvel of Hemingway's stories, with their seemingly indisputable detail, with Hemingway's uncanny ear for authentic dialogue (one can hear the needling insistence and peremptoriness of Fitzgerald's questioning about Hemingway's marital habits) is that they are all made up of plausible elements.

In Hemingway's account, when he and Fitzgerald met again a few days later at the Closerie des Lilas, Fitzgerald was completely charming and ingratiating, with no symptoms of drunkenness, even though he belted down a couple of whiskies. And he was totally blank about their previous meeting, though he did have some vague recollections that Hemingway's friends had been rude. On the later occasion, the two discussed literary matters, and Scott spoke slightingly of the commercial stories he wrote for *The Saturday Evening Post*. He was unhappy about the sales reports Max Perkins was sending him on *The Great Gatsby* and eager to have Hemingway read the book "as soon as he could get his last and only copy back from someone he had loaned it to." In one of those quotations which add immeasurably to the credibility of a Hemingway story, Hemingway noted: "To hear him talk of it, you would never know how very good it was, except that he had the shyness about it that all non-conceited writers have when they have done something very fine." That is one of the quintessential ploys in Hemingway's literary strategy: we are meant to feel fine about Fitzgerald's modesty—the sign of a real writer—and fine about Hemingway's recognition of Fitzgerald's talent and fine about Hemingway's grasp of the real values in life. The meeting of the two men in the Closerie des Lilas turned out so well ("He was cynical and funny and very jolly and charming and endearing, even if you were careful about anyone becoming endearing") that Hemingway agreed to accompany Fitzgerald, at Fitzgerald's expense, to Lyon to pick up the Renault and drive it back to Paris.

But all that good feeling was a mere preamble to a masterly exercise in retrospective revenge. No doubt the excursion to Lyon had its tiresome episodes. But Hemingway manipulated his account to expose every fault in Fitzgerald's character: his unreliability and self-pity, his morbid hypochondria, his foolish dependency on Zelda, his patronizing and exasperating habits when drunk. And all of these flaws are neatly contrasted with Hemingway's sensible manly behavior and forbearance.

To begin with, Fitzgerald does not show up at the station as scheduled. Hemingway, the poor and struggling writer, pays his fare to Lyon, where he puts up at an expensive hotel, awaiting Fitzgerald. He makes an expensive phone call to Paris, leaving a message with the Fitzgeralds' servant, who informs him that Zelda is ill and still sleeping. (The implication is that she is either lazy or sleeping off a hangover.) Hemingway has an inexpensive supper in a cheap Algerian restaurant. And for the first time in three years he sleeps in the unaccustomed luxury of a big hotel. He lulls himself to sleep reading Turgenev's *A Sportsman's Sketches*. (He knows how to make the best use of his time, enjoy the pleasures that come his way.) His resentment at wasting money he and Hadley had saved

for a trip to Spain and the summer bullfights in Pamplona subsides:
"I was delighted that I had used up the anger at the start and gotten
it over with. It was not a trip designed for a man easy to anger."

Scott shows up at the hotel the following morning with only
perfunctory excuses; insists on an expensive breakfast at the hotel,
rather than a quick bite at a café as Hemingway urges; demands that
the hotel put up a picnic lunch for them that costs four or five times
what they would pay if, as Hemingway suggests, they pick up some
bottles of wine and something from a charcuterie along the route.
When they get to the garage, Hemingway is astonished at the condition of the car; the roof has been removed at Zelda's insistence.
The garage mechanic takes Hemingway aside and pleads with him,
as one knowledgeable man to another, to have Fitzgerald take proper
care of the vehicle, specifically, to have new piston rings put in and
to run it with sufficient oil and water. The mechanic, like Hemingway, has a sense of métier. Fitzgerald, we learn, is as careless of the
vehicle as he is of his talents. Naturally, since there is no roof and
neither of them has a raincoat, it begins to rain a mile north of the
city. It is a wet journey, and they are forced to seek shelter under
trees and in cafés along the way. Although Fitzgerald is an experienced drinker, amazingly he seems never to have experienced the
pleasure of drinking wine straight from the bottle. We are given a
sardonic account of this: "It was as exciting to him as though he
were slumming or as a girl might be excited by going swimming
for the first time without a bathing suit."

The remainder of the journey is pure Molière farce. Soaked to
the skin, from inside and out, Fitzgerald becomes convinced that he
has come down with pneumonia, and at the hotel where they stop
overnight he gives a performance of Camille on her deathbed. Bravely,
he tells Hemingway that he would not mind dying of congestion of
the lungs in some forsaken hotel if he could be sure that someone
would take care of his wife and daughter. He insists that Hemingway
find him a thermometer. The only one available is a bath thermometer, which Hemingway convinces him should be placed under the
arm. Through some mumbo-jumbo that Fitzgerald is too fatuous to
recognize as such, Hemingway assures Fitzgerald that his temperature is normal. At this, the patient brightens a bit, certain that he
has great recuperative powers. During the darker moments of his
illness, he has told Hemingway the deeply tragic story of the French
aviator's love affair with Zelda. Now he insists that he must call her

in Paris; he tells Hemingway that he has never been separated from his wife for a night since their marriage. (A lie, obviously — but whose?) After the call, the two have dinner in the hotel dining room, where Fitzgerald passes out at the table. The whole of Hemingway's account is deadpan, except for one brief moment when he remarks, "I was getting tired of the literary life." On the following morning, a beautiful day, the two make the drive to Paris. En route, Fitzgerald tells Hemingway the plots of Michael Arlen's best-selling novels.

Every detail of the account may easily have been true; every character habit — the hypochondria, the drunkenness, the self-pity — could be attested to by other Fitzgerald stories, equally demeaning. Hemingway's scathing retrospective account, however, bears little resemblance to the report he sent Max Perkins at the time: "We had a great trip together driving his car up from Lyon through the Cote D'Or." And he added approvingly, "I've read his Great Gatsby and think it is an absolutely first rate book. I hope it is going well." Nor did Fitzgerald, evidently, sense any undercurrent of sourness. Writing to Gertrude Stein, to whom he had been introduced by Hemingway just before the trip, Fitzgerald reported: "Hemingway and I went to Lyons shortly after to get my car and had a slick drive through Burgundy. He's a peach of a fellow and absolutely first-rate." They seemed destined to become the best of friends.

❧ ➤ ❧

It was in the nature of things that Hemingway became Fitzgerald's principal hero. He fitted the pattern perfectly: six feet tall, burly, handsome, dark-haired, and with a ruddy complexion. He had served overseas in an ambulance corps and had been seriously wounded at Fossalta, in northern Italy, and subsequently decorated for his heroism in rescuing an Italian soldier. He was modest about each of the four Italian decorations he received, acknowledging that one of them had been given mistakenly for an action that he hadn't participated in, since he was in the hospital at the time. Like Fitzgerald, he was a Midwesterner; he had grown up in Oak Park, Illinois. And he had played on the local football team and was a fervent sportsman. His father, Clarence Hemingway, was a general practitioner and a knowledgeable sportsman, whom Hemingway worshiped but also felt shame for because he allowed himself to be henpecked by his wife. But there the family similarities ended. Where Mollie McQuillan Fitzgerald was mildly eccentric, Grace Hall Hemingway was the domineering and assertive woman against whom Hemingway rebelled for much of his adult life.

It was one of the fortunate accidents of Fitzgerald's life that Zelda disliked Hemingway from the beginning. Had she flirted with his new idol as she had with Fitzgerald's Princeton classmates and with Jozan, the result would have been devastating. As it was, the relationship between Zelda and Hemingway became something of a tug of war over Fitzgerald's allegiances. It is not difficult to understand why she considered the intensity of Fitzgerald's dedication to the young writer to be a threat.

The first meeting between Zelda and Hemingway apparently took place shortly after the trip to Lyon. Hemingway and Hadley were invited to lunch at the Fitzgeralds' apartment on the rue de Tilsitt. The apartment itself was stuffy and uncomfortable, crowded with gilded Louis XVI furnishings bought at the Galeries Lafayette. One visitor described it as looking like a furniture show window. Zelda's first impression of Hemingway was that he was "bogus." Later she regarded him as "phony as a rubber check." She seems to have resented his masculine swagger and once remarked that nobody could be "as male as all that." She also cast a cold eye on the Hemingway marriage, and once, within Hemingway's hearing, remarked to Hadley that she noticed that in the Hemingway household Hadley always did what Hemingway wanted. Hadley admitted that this was true; Hemingway did not like the observation at all. For the Hemingways' part, the Fitzgeralds would always be difficult friends; they had more money at their disposal. Moreover, the Fitzgeralds had a bad habit of showing up unannounced, at odd hours of the day and night, at the Hemingways' modest second-floor apartment on the rue Notre Dame de Champs, overlooking a noisy sawmill. (The Hemingways' means, however, were not so modest that they could not afford a *femme de ménage*.)

At the first meeting, according to Hemingway, Zelda was formally pleasant and agreeable to both him and Hadley. She and Scott, at her insistence, had been partying the night before, and she was suffering from a hangover. It was Hemingway's contention that Fitzgerald was trying to cut down on his drinking and had become serious about his work, but Zelda was restless, bored, and jealous of Fitzgerald's writing. She was persistent in her attempts to encourage him to party and drink, quarreling with him and calling him a spoilsport and killjoy. At the lunch, Fitzgerald, nervous but hospitable, made a point of bringing out his ledger book, with its detailed, year-by-year accounts of the stories he had written and the rising fees he had been paid. The Hemingways were also introduced to little Scottie, not quite four, blond and healthy and speaking English with a "strong Cockney accent." Scott explained that they had hired an English nanny because he wanted his daughter to speak like Lady Diana Manners when she grew up. The emphasis on the child's accent, of course, is one of Hemingway's triumphant put-downs, meant to expose both Fitzgerald's social pretensions and his ignorance of real class.

Hemingway was always a master of the understated detail. He claimed that he knew from the beginning that Zelda was crazy, if not yet "net-able." The moment of recognition came when Zelda, with the air of having a profound secret, once asked him, "Ernest, don't you think Al Jolson is greater than Jesus?" But Gerald Murphy, too, said that Zelda had asked him precisely the same question — and that he had been too embarrassed to pursue the topic.

Hemingway's rancorous attitude toward Zelda, however, is hardly noticeable in his letters of the period. During the early years of their acquaintance Zelda was often sick, suffering from one complaint or another, possibly as a result of the infection from her Rome operation. Hemingway, writing to Fitzgerald, always asked after both Scottie and Zelda. Occasionally, he even demonstrated some minor concern for Zelda's health. "Pain's such an awful thing," he once wrote. "It's such a rotten shame for her to be sick." But the truth is that during those early years, his queries are mostly perfunctory: "And how is Zelda?" "Best love to Zelda." "Regards to all yr. family."

If Hemingway valued Fitzgerald's attention and enthusiasm in the early years — and he seems to have done so — he assumed a much more measured attitude in later life. After Fitzgerald's death, he said that he had never had any respect for Fitzgerald himself, only for his "lovely, golden, wasted talent." Writing to Arthur Mizener, Fitzgerald's first biographer, he gave a sour assessment of his former friend and literary sponsor: "He was romantic, ambitious, and Christ, Jesus, God knows how talented. He was also generous without being kind." The latter remark may have been accurate: there was often something calculated about Fitzgerald's attempts to promote other writers; one gets the impression that he viewed the efforts as desirable things to do, not as the direct result of spontaneous feelings of warmth or good will. Yet in any comparison of their respective virtues along those lines, Fitzgerald had insights as shrewd as Hemingway's. "Ernest," Fitzgerald noted, "would always give a helping hand to a man on a ledge a little higher up."

Fitzgerald's attempts to promote his new protégé were sometimes awkward. On a Riviera beach, he cornered Glenway Wescott, the young author of a much talked-about novel, *The Apple of the Eye,* which Fitzgerald regarded as "pretty much the old stuff." Fitzgerald insisted that Hemingway was "the one true genius" of the decade and that *The Apple of the Eye* and *The Great Gatsby* were "rather inflated market values" at the time. Therefore, Wescott should help launch Hemingway by writing a laudatory essay. Wescott was touched and flattered that Fitzgerald should take so much for granted: "It simply had not occurred to him that unfriendliness or pettiness on my part might inhibit my enthusiasm." On another occasion he turned belligerent on Hemingway's behalf. When Michael Arlen, whose novel *The Green Hat* was a huge success both as a book and in its stage version, voiced some criticism of Hemingway's meager reputation, Fitzgerald, drunk, accused him of being "a finished second-rater that's jealous of a coming first-rater." There was an element of desperation in Fitzgerald's promotional efforts.

Hemingway groused about Fitzgerald's propensity to put him on a pedestal. "He was a charming cheerful companion when he was sober, although a little embarrassing from his tendency always to hero-worship." Early in their acquaintance, it was clear that Fitzgerald had installed Tommy Hitchcock, Gerald Murphy, and Hemingway himself as his current idols. "He probably had others that I don't know about," Hemingway maintained, "but in those three he certainly played the field." Hemingway evidently sensed some subtle connection between Fitzgerald's hero-worshiping tendencies and his failures of ambition and will power, for his next remark was telling: "Above all he was completely undisciplined and he would quit at the drop of a hat and borrow some-ones hat to drop. He was fragile Irish instead of tough Irish." From the beginning he was certain that Fitzgerald was getting no help from Zelda. She was encouraging him to drink and with a secret pleasure that Hemingway said he could read in her eyes whenever Fitzgerald took up a glass of wine. On the days following the binges and quarrels, Hemingway took long walks with Fitzgerald while the latter sweated out the alcohol from the most recent party. The two discussed writing. Hemingway complimented the older writer on the fine novel he had just written and encouraged him to believe in his own talent. Fitzgerald seemed convinced that Paris — their social life in Paris — was the problem and that if he and Zelda could get away to the Riviera, he would be able to work well.

Still, it was during that difficult spring and summer in Paris — and with Hemingway's encouragement, as he claimed — that Fitzgerald managed to complete a solid and significant piece of work. "The Rich Boy," which appeared in *Redbook* magazine the following year, was one of the most carefully controlled and accomplished stories in Fitzgerald's fiction. It is little wonder that Hemingway singled it out, for the style is Hemingwayesque in its direct and declarative manner. But the evidence for such an influence is indecisive, depending on how well acquainted Fitzgerald was with Hemingway's scantly published writings before he began to promote the younger author and before they met in Paris. Fitzgerald had actually begun work on the story on Capri in April of 1925. He continued working on it in Paris and was still revising it in late July or early August, when he and Zelda went south to Antibes. Anson Hunter, the rich boy of the story, was based on Ludlow Fowler, Fitzgerald's well-to-do Princeton friend, and in one of the more famous passages of the novella-length story, Fitzgerald announces: "Let me tell you about the very rich. They are different from you and me. They possess and enjoy early, and it does something to them, makes them soft where we are hard, and cynical where we are trustful. . . . Even when they enter deep into our world or sink below us, they still think that they are better than we are."

Fitzgerald wrote to Fowler about his intentions: "It is in large measure the story of your life, toned down here and there and simplified. Also many gaps had to come out of my imagination. It is frank, unsparing but sympathetic and I think you will like it — it is one of the best things I have ever done." For the most part, that was a truthful assessment of the completed story. (Fowler requested some changes, which were made before "The Rich Boy" appeared in Fitzgerald's collection *All the Sad Young Men.*) But it was not exactly a sympathetic portrait of the protagonist: Anson Hunter drifts through casual and ineffectual relationships, hovers around club rooms and the more expensive nightspots, and has little that would pass for a purposeful connection with life. At one point, in his muddling and self-righteous meddling, he precipitates the suicide of his aunt Edna's lover. The story, which is masterly in its cumulative detail, ends as inconclusively as the life it describes, with Anson Hunter striking up one more transitory relationship, this time with an attractive young woman aboard ship en route to Europe. He is much preoccupied with the fact that he is thirty years old, and the implication is that this latest affair will end as all the others have. As the narrator-friend explains at the end of the story: "I don't think he was ever happy unless someone was in love with him, responding to him like filings to a magnet, helping him to explain himself, promising him something. What it was I do not know." Like his creator, Anson Hunter is in search of confirmation from the outside for something superior in himself—some gift, some quality, that he cherishes but cannot quite define.

It is highly probable that during the course of his walks and talks with Hemingway in Paris, Fitzgerald was being influenced by something more than the virtues of Hemingway's literary style. His encounter with the self-assured young writer produced a noticeable hardening in Fitzgerald's opinions about the American literary establishment, which included his old friends and protégés.

Hemingway, at the outset of his literary career, had drawn a bead on anyone who ventured into what he considered his literary terrain. However modest he appeared as a war hero, he was devastatingly critical of anyone who wrote on the subject of men in battle. His most unlikely target was Willa Cather, whose Pulitzer Prize−winning novel, *One of Ours,* included some battle scenes. In a scathing letter to Edmund Wilson, Hemingway said that they had all been "Catherized," episode by episode, from D. W. Griffith's movie *Birth of a Nation.* "Poor woman," Hemingway explained, "she had to get her war experience somewhere." The crime of the literary critic Laurence Stallings, evidently, was that he had written a war play, *What Price Glory?,* in collaboration with Maxwell Anderson, and that it had become an incontestable Broadway hit during the 1924−1925 theatrical season. That Stallings had been seriously wounded in World War I ("It seems Stallings is a great critic because he lost a leg in the war") only heightened Hemingway's scorn. Stallings' critical taste, Hemingway declared, "could be roused to enthusiasm by exclamation points, mentions of the quatz arts bal or the omission of verbs or other things that at once point a masterpiece to Mr. Lawrence Stallings."

It is not clear whether Hemingway was aware of Stallings' favorable review of *The Great Gatsby* in the *New York World*. Stallings had called the novel "the first authentic book, from the civilized point of view, upon the scene it surveys." In his review, titled "Great Scott," he declared that *The Great Gatsby* represented a remarkable advance over the author's previous work. Fitzgerald, certainly, had been grateful for Stallings' early and favorable notice; he called it "the only intelligent review so far." He thanked God for Stallings, he told Max Perkins: "I had begun to believe no one was even glancing at the book." Yet, strangely, at the end of the year and at the same time that Hemingway was fulminating at the critic, Fitzgerald was echoing Hemingway's opinion, numbering Stallings among the "boys who find a new genius once a week and at all cost follow the fashions."

Fitzgerald's attitude toward his St. Paul protégé, Tom Boyd, had always been somewhat ambivalent. But in the spring, he had written to Max Perkins, praising Boyd's collection of war stories, *Points of Honor*, saying they were "great." He wrote to Boyd himself that he was "crazy about *Points of Honor*"; that it and Boyd's war novel, *Through the Wheat*, were practically his "favorite modern books." He added, "Feeling the war, as one still does over here, they grow in stature."

But in June, after meeting Hemingway, Fitzgerald, in a long letter to Perkins, began mounting an offensive against Boyd, his new farm novel, *Samuel Drummond*, and what Fitzgerald perceived as the threat of the whole native-son-and-soil movement that was taking shape in American writing. He wrote: "I haven't an enormous faith in Tom Boyd either as a personality or an artist—as I have, say, in E. E. Cummings and Hemingway. His ignorance, his presumptuous intolerance and his careless grossness which he cultivates for vitality . . . have always annoyed me." He accused Boyd of "dressing up a few heart throbs in overalls" and expecting to produce literature. Boyd had now joined the ranks of writers like Glenway Wescott and Burton Rascoe who were "going to tell us mere superficial 'craftsmen' like Hergesheimer, Wharton, Tarkington and me about the Great Beautiful Appreciation they have of the Great Beautiful Life of the Manure Widder." For once, Fitzgerald may have been in the vanguard of a critical assault. It was only later in the year that Hemingway wrote to Fitzgerald, asking, "Did you ever read [Knut Hamsun's] *The Growth of the Soil?* And then for Christ sake to read Thom Boyd." Hemingway, too, voiced his disdain for the people who are "getting stirred up over Main Street, Babbitt and all the books your boy friend Mencken has gotten excited about just because they deal with the much abused Am. Scene." Mencken — "that shit," as Hemingway labeled him — would remain one of Hemingway's permanent enemies, along with Gilbert Seldes — presumably because he had not recognized his talents from the beginning.

In Paris, that spring, Hemingway and Fitzgerald seem to have launched a two-man war against the American critical establishment, its values, its spokesmen, and fellow travelers. At times, the attacks became scatalogical. In the summer of 1925, Hemingway and Hadley were in Spain, together with Donald Ogden Stewart, a former protégé, and Lady Duff Twysden, Pat Guthrie, and Harold Loeb, Hemingway aficionados who would figure in his novel *The Sun Also Rises.* From Burguete, on July 1, Hemingway wrote Fitzgerald a randy letter on his view of heaven. It would be a big bull ring with choice seats for himself and a trout stream outside that no one else could fish in. He would have two lovely houses: one for his wife and children, the other for his nine beautiful mistresses. In both establishments, Hemingway intended to put certain American periodicals to good use: "One house would be fitted up with special copies of the Dial printed on soft tissue and kept in the toilets." In the other, *The American Mercury* and *The New Republic* were to serve the same useful purpose.

Fitzgerald's idea of heaven, Hemingway maintained, would be "a beautiful vacuum filled with wealthy monogamists, all powerful and members of the best families all drinking themselves to death."

II

"This city is full of Americans," Fitzgerald complained in a letter to Edmund Wilson, " — most of them former friends — whom we spend most of our time dodging, not because we don't want to see them but because Zelda's only just well and I've got to work." He was disgusted with Americans in general and with American women in particular — "these preposterous, pushing women and girls who assume that you have any personal interest in them, who have all (so they say) read James Joyce and who simply adore Mencken." If he had had anything to do with creating the manners of the contemporary American girl, he confessed, "I certainly made a botch of the job." He and Zelda, he ended, "think we're pretty good, as usual, only more so."

The summer of 1925 was to be a summer of "1000 parties and no work." Esther Murphy was in town, and the Fitzgeralds toured Les Halles, the market district, with the Murphy clan. Teddy Chanler, who had known Father Fay, had tea with them at the rue de Tilsitt. Zelda's sister Rosalind and her husband, Newman Smith, visited, as did the Ordways, St. Paul friends of Fitzgerald. At parties, they encountered the actresses Eva Le Gallienne and Mary Hay, the latter estranged from her actor-husband Richard Barthelmess, their Great Neck neighbor. From that summer of dissipations, Zelda remembered rides in the Bois de Boulogne and an all-night party at the Ritz at which they played puss-in-the-corner. Fitzgerald met old Princeton heroes. He partied with Sap Donahoe. "Sap was great," he later wrote Ludlow Fowler, "but he and I have grown apart in some things." One day, on a Paris street, he caught a glimpse of the "romantic" Buzz Law, a former football idol, who was "looking by no means distinguished."

Fitzgerald was getting notices of *The Great Gatsby* that gave him personal satisfaction. Gilbert Seldes sent him an advance copy of a review that was to appear as the "New York Chronicle" in T. S. Eliot's London magazine, *The Criterion*. Seldes praised the book and the author, claiming that Fitzgerald "has certainly the best chance, at this moment, of becoming our finest artist in fiction." Fitzgerald wrote to thank him: "I believe I'd rather [have] your discriminating enthusiasm than anyone's in America (did I tell you this before?)." Little wonder that Fitzgerald was concerned about repeating himself: he had written the same thing to Mencken only a month or two earlier and to Perkins even before that. Seldes' praise, he said, made him feel "exciting" and believed-in once more. But he admitted that *Gatsby* was not selling as well as he had hoped it would. "I may go to Hollywood and try to learn the moving picture business from the bottom up," he threatened. He and Zelda, he said, were planning to drive down to Antibes — the baby and nurse would go by train — to spend a month getting brown and healthy. "God, I'm wild for the Riviera," he wrote.

There was also warm and discriminating praise from Gertrude

Stein. Hemingway had taken Fitzgerald and Zelda to meet the American writer at her famous studio on the rue de Fleurus, where the walls were hung with paintings of her vanguard painter-friends, Picasso, Matisse, Juan Gris. They represented the first phase of her career—that of the pioneering collector of modernist art. Now the doughty fifty-one-year-old writer and the waspish Alice B. Toklas were the center of a celebrated literary salon that attracted such habitués and visitors as Sherwood Anderson, Ford Madox Ford, Robert McAlmon, Edith Sitwell, Robert Coates, and Janet Flanner.

The Fitzgeralds' friend Carl Van Vechten, another of the hostages to Stein's fame, served as the American agent for her difficult-to-place experimental poems and plays. Hemingway was her current favorite.

When Fitzgerald met them, Stein and Toklas were on the eve of leaving Paris for their annual summer vacation in the Haute-Savoie. Fitzgerald presented Stein with an inscribed copy of *The Great Gatsby*. From Belley, on May 22, she wrote him a warm and complimentary letter. She had liked the "melody" of Fitzgerald's dedication to the book: "Once Again to Zelda." It showed, Stein told him, "that you have a background of beauty and tenderness." Another of his virtues, she said, was that he wrote "naturally in sentences." She went on, "You are creating the contemporary world much as Thackeray did his in *Pendennis* and *Vanity Fair*." Evidently she was already aware of Fitzgerald's touchiness in the face of open praise, for she stressed that this was not "a bad compliment." In her run-on style, she went even further: "You make a modern world and a modern orgy strangely enough it was never done until you did it in *This Side of Paradise*. My belief in *This Side of Paradise* was alright. This is as good a book and different and older and that is what one does, one does not get better but different and older. . . ."

Fitzgerald, answering, assured her that no part of her letter was a "bad compliment." "My wife and I," he said, "think you a very handsome, very gallant and very kind lady." That may not have been Zelda's opinion at all. At the rue de Fleurus, it was the custom for Alice B. Toklas to take charge of the women visitors while the gentlemen were allowed to talk to the star attraction, a custom Zelda may have resented. According to Sara Mayfield, Zelda considered Stein's conversation "sententious gibberish." It is possible that Zelda may have felt uncomfortable in the Stein household, with its lesbian tinge. Edmund Wilson, one of the few major critics who took Stein's writing seriously and thought her a stimulating conversationalist, was put off by something "creepy" about the Stein-Toklas relationship. He once described it as "the most complete example of human symbiosis I have ever seen." But Zelda, who had taken up painting while on Capri, was decidedly impressed with the Stein Picassos hanging on the walls: large and glowing Rose Period nudes, barbarous studies for Picasso's raw masterpiece the *Demoiselles d'Avignon,* a series of imperturbable Cubist still lifes. In general, she believed Picasso's work more "idea" than painting, but she thought the Stein Picassos were "the only ones worth having."

Fitzgerald was impressed with the woman herself, though the obsequious terms in which he wrote to her raise a few suspicions. "You see," he said, "I am content to let you, and the one or two like you who are acutely sensitive, think or fail to think for me and my kind artistically (their name is not legend but the word like it)." He was, he said, a very "second rate person compared to first rate people," but it honestly made him shiver to know that Stein had attributed such significance to *This Side of Paradise:* "It puts me in a false position, I feel. Like Gatsby, I have only hope." Since Fitzgerald had only recently been complaining about the praise he was forced to endure for his first novel in comparison with his third, there is some reason for believing his response to Stein's compliments was a bit less than 100 percent heartfelt.

That summer in Paris, Fitzgerald also received compliments from another expatriate American writer and celebrated saloniste, Edith Wharton. There could scarcely have been anything more different from the Stein ménage than the aristocratic salon that Edith Wharton presided over in her garden estate, the Pavillon Colombe in St. Brice-sous-Forêt, a dozen miles north of Paris. Mrs. Wharton's circle consisted of academicians and ambassadors, upper-crust novelists like Paul Bourget or the society painter Jacques Emile Blanche, with occasional appearances by Paul Valéry and André Gide. The two women represented the polar opposites of American life and culture. Stein, raised in San Francisco, came from the new-moneyed, Jewish-immigrant, egalitarian stock that rose to prominence after the Civil War. Wharton was the personification of the old guard, New York – Newport – Bar Harbor Eastern establishment wealth. Where Mrs. Wharton, staid and stayed in fashionable couturier gowns, dazzled her guests, Stein, uncorseted, took the democratic approach, and appeared in what were described as "strange steerage clothes."

Despite their many years in France, the two American women never met. The one thing they had in common, it seems, were the occasional visits of Jean Cocteau, a man who managed to walk the boundary line between two very different social worlds.

On June 8, Edith Wharton wrote to thank Fitzgerald for a presentation copy of *The Great Gatsby:* "I feel that to your generation, which has taken such a flying leap into the future, I must represent the literary equivalent of tufted furniture and gas chandeliers." She thought the book a considerable advance over his prevous work. But she had a criticism: "My present quarrel with you is only this: that to make Gatsby really Great, you ought to have given us his early career (not from the cradle—but from his visit to the yacht, if not before) instead of a short summary of it. That would have situated him, and made his final tragedy a tragedy instead of a *'fait divers'* for the morning papers." She had been especially impressed with Fitzgerald's account of the "seedy orgy" at the Buchanan flat, with the dazed puppy looking on.

On July 2, she sent a note inviting Fitzgerald and Zelda to tea on the following Sunday. Zelda did not go with her husband. In one version of what happened, Zelda declared that "she was damned if she would go forty or fifty miles from Paris just to let an exceedingly proper and curious old lady stare at her and Scott and make them feel provincial." This first version, related in Arthur Mizener's biography, came by way of Richard Knight, a lawyer-friend of the Fitzgeralds. In it, Fitzgerald, nervous about the meeting, went alone and proceeded to fortify himself along the way, so he had arrived at the Pavillon Colombe rather drunk. In a belligerent state of mind, he attempted to shock the hostess and her guests with a story about himself and Zelda having lived in a bordello for two weeks when they first arrived in Paris. Instead of being shocked, Mrs. Wharton listened with great interest to his fumbling recital, then commented, "But Mr. Fitzgerald, you haven't told us what they did in the bordello." The defeated Fitzgerald fled back to the rue de Tilsitt, where, after a few more drinks, he put his head down on his arms and, pounding on the table with his fists, confessed, "They beat me! They beat me! They *beat* me!"

Andrew Turnbull gives a different version, gathered from Teddy Chanler, who had also been invited—his mother, Daisy Chanler, was a longtime friend of Mrs. Wharton's—and who accompanied Fitzgerald on the drive out to St. Brice-sous-Forêt. Again, along the route

Fitzgerald stopped for several bracers while Chanler remained in the car. At the Pavillon Colombe, there was another guest, Gaillard Lapsley, an American-born Cambridge don. Fitzgerald, attempting to break the ice, asked permission to tell "a couple of—er—rather rough stories." He launched into a tale about a naïve American couple who had spent three days in a Paris bordello, thinking it was a hotel. Mrs. Wharton's comment in this version was "But Mr. Fitzgerald, your story lacks data." When Fitzgerald left, Edith Wharton remarked to Lapsley, "There must be something peculiar about that young man." Lapsley explained that Fitzgerald was drunk. But some years later, Chanler gave another Fitzgerald biographer, Matthew Bruccoli, a rather different, somewhat laundered account of the famous Wharton tea party. While acknowledging that Fitzgerald had had one or two drinks before arrival, Chanler said he was by no means drunk. The occasion, he explained, was stiff and formal, and Fitzgerald had obviously tried to liven up the event with his bordello story. "On the way back to Paris," Chanler maintained, "[Fitzgerald] showed no sign of feeling squelched, or that the failure of the occasion was due to him rather than to Mrs. Wharton." Chanler suspected that Fitzgerald's soul-wrenching "They beat me!" was an invention. But Fitzgerald's breakdown after the event may not have been a pure invention: Zelda was aware of some desperate need Fitzgerald had to acquit himself well at social functions, then "go out and get drunk when it's over."

According to Sara Mayfield, the Mizener version of the affair was confirmed in her presence, during one of Scott and Zelda's quarreling sessions. Fitzgerald complained that Zelda was in the habit of snubbing his friends, especially Hemingway, and that she had refused to accompany him to the Pavillon Colombe. Zelda's retort was "That was better than going and making an ass of yourself as you did, telling her we lived in a brothel in Paris when all we did was to go to The House of All Nations one night." (The House of All Nations was a famous pornographic tourist attraction in Paris.)

Whatever the actual event—the grass has grown up tall around it, over the years—the one certifiable report is Edith Wharton's terse diary note: "To tea, Teddy Chanler and Scott Fitzgerald, the novelist (awful)."

In August, they went to Antibes, where the Murphys had moved permanently into their renovated villa. The spot was one that haunted

Fitzgerald's imagination. Eventually, he repossessed it for Nick and Nicole Diver in *Tender Is the Night.* The fourteen-room Villa America stood on high ground that sloped down to the beach of La Garoupe, which Gerald Murphy had meticulously cleared of seaweed to make it suitable for swimming. The villa was in the Moorish style, beige stucco with yellow shutters, and a flagstone terrace, shaded by a linden tree, where the Murphys gave their dinner parties. It was decorated in the *style moderne:* white walls, floors of waxed black tile, not a period piece in sight, the chairs covered in black satin. The terrace furniture was metal, painted with silver radiator paint. The gardens were punctuated with palms and eucalyptus, cedars of Lebanon and mimosa. There were orchards of tangerines and lemons and olive trees. Sara had an herb garden. Gerald had a separate studio for painting; there was an old Provençal farmhouse, which was used for guests; the Murphys' seven-year-old daughter, Honoria, had her own playhouse.

It was from Antibes that Fitzgerald wrote Max Perkins another of his optimistic letters about his progress on a new novel. For the moment, it was titled *Our Type;* later it would be called *The Boy Who Killed His Mother.* It was to be "about several things, one of which is an intellectual murder on the Leopold-Loeb idea." Fitzgerald was planning to have the hero of this early version of *Tender Is the Night,* the young Hollywood film technician, Francis Melarky, kill his domineering mother. But in his letter to Perkins, Fitzgerald also noted, "Incidentally it is about Zelda & me & the hysteria of last May & June in Paris. (Confidential)."

But if Fitzgerald had been hoping to escape into solitude where he could work, he did not find it on the Riviera that summer. Judging from a letter he sent to John Peale Bishop, only the Hemingways (away in Spain) were missing from Fitzgerald's name-dropping inventory. "There was no one at Antibes this summer," he wrote, "except me, Zelda, the Valentinos, the Murphys, Mistinguet, Rex Ingram, Dos Passos, Alice Terry, the MacLeishes, Charlie Brackett, Maude Kahn, Esther Murphy, Marguerite Namara, E. Phillips Oppenheim, Mannes the violinist, Floyd Dell, Max and Crystal Eastman, ex-Premier Orlando, Etienne de Beaumont. . . ." It is not clear what Fitzgerald felt about the screen idol Valentino. On the basis of Valentino's screen appearances, he had once meanly described him as a "pretty young man with machine oil on his hair." His impressions of Archibald MacLeish were highly favorable, though,

like Bishop, he felt MacLeish had been too clearly influenced by
Eliot. He "liked Archie MacLeish enormously. Also his poem, though
it seems strange to like anything so outrageously derivative. *T.S. of
P.* was an original in comparison."

Fitzgerald's list of the famous, and the soon-to-be famous, at
Antibes, most of them sporting on the Murphys' beach, was a sign
of the invasion by the cultural elite that would, in short order, turn
the Riviera into an international playground. "Just a real place to
rough it," Fitzgerald informed Bishop; "an escape from all the world."
Fitzgerald would remember that he had been happy at Antibes, but
that Zelda had been ill much of the time. One benefit of the summer
was the growing friendship between the two couples. When the
Fitzgeralds left in September, Gerald Murphy wrote Fitzgerald the
kind of letter, overflowing with sentiment, that Fitzgerald himself
often wrote.

> There *really* was a great sound of tearing heard in the land as your
> train pulled out that day. Sara and I rode back together saying
> things about you both to each other which only partly expressed
> what we felt separately. . . . Most people are dull, without dis-
> tinction and without value, even *humanly* . . . you two belong so
> irrevocably to that rare race of people who are *valuable.* As yet in
> this world we have found four.

Murphy's letter mounted in its enthusiasm of the discovery of new
friends:

> We four communicate by our presence rather than any means: so
> that where we meet and when will never count. Currents race be-
> tween us regardless: Scott will uncover for me values in Sara, just
> as Sara has known them in Zelda through her affection for Scott.
> Suffice it to say that whenever we knew that we were to see you
> that evening or that you were coming to dinner in the garden we
> were happy. . . . My God. How *rare* it is. How rare.

It was a remarkably generous letter and equally remarkable testimony
to the aura the Fitzgeralds could create around themselves — most
often, early in a friendship. Murphy's letter is rather like a monu-
ment that rises about the later debris of the Fitzgeralds' lives.

That rush of mutual feeling carried over through the end of the
month, when the Murphys stopped in Paris for a week on their way
to the United States. The Fitzgeralds saw them almost daily. Writing to Marya Mannes, who, with her father, the concert violinist

David Mannes, had been among those at Antibes that summer, Fitzgerald recalled a moment of "glowing peace" the two had shared when the moon was rising over the Murphys' garden. "No one ever makes things in America," he wrote the young woman, "with that vast, magnificent, cynical disillusion with which Gerald and Sara make things like their parties." He had obviously begun the process of transformation by which the Murphys, as well as he and Zelda, would become Dick and Nicole Diver. Despite his sending Perkins encouraging reports that his new novel would be great and that it was progressing slowly and carefully because he was revising heavily, despite his prodding Ober to begin negotiations for the sale of the serial rights, Fitzgerald's October letter to Marya Mannes suggests that he was only at the beginning: "My new novel is marvelous. I'm in the first chapter. You may recognize certain things and people in it."

But, more important, Fitzgerald's letter to the young woman was a long and reasoned scolding about the values of gilded youth, precisely the audience to whom his books presumably appealed. Mannes had mentioned being "thrilled" by New York. "I doubt you will be after five more years," Fitzgerald answered, "when you are more fully nourished from within. I carry the place around the world in my heart but sometimes I try to shake if off in my dreams." The young people of America, he told her, were brilliant with a "second-hand sophistication" they had inherited from their betters in the war generation: "They are brave, shallow, cynical, impatient, turbulent and empty. I like them not." In one of his most evocative sentences, Fitzgerald wrote: "America's greatest promise is that something is going to happen, and after awhile you get tired of waiting because nothing happens to people except they grow old, and nothing happens to American art because America is the story of the moon that never rose."

"The moon that never rose" was the perfect image for that promissory view of American success—and its ironic failure—which Fitzgerald had explored in *The Great Gatsby*. It was the story of Gatsby himself. But the perfect phrase was, in fact, another man's phrase. Fitzgerald had picked it up from the critic Paul Rosenfeld, who had coined it in an essay about Fitzgerald himself. The essay was in Rosenfeld's book *Men Seen,* published earlier in 1925. Rosenfeld was not the most venturesome of the New York critics, but he was one of the most sensitive to nuance. His essay was written before the appearance of *The Great Gatsby,* but even so, Rosenfeld had sensed in Fitzgerald's earlier work an "almost glacial impersonality," which allowed the young author to create "a curious atmosphere of mixed luxury and rottenness of the heart." He suggested that Fitzgerald ought to take a new direction in his work. He thought Fitzgerald was mistaken in believing that "the field of his vision is essentially the field of 'youth.' " There were deeper themes in American life that Fitzgerald was capable of dealing with. Fitzgerald ought to break his mold, Rosenfeld argued, even though it would mean a loss of his current popularity. The story he would then tell would be a pathetic story: "the legend of a moon which never rose; and that is precisely the story a certain America does not wish to hear."

In his letter to Marya Mannes, it appears that Fitzgerald had taken Rosenfeld's message to heart and was passing it on to a younger generation.

It is indicative of Fitzgerald's relationship with Hemingway that his first surviving letter to his protégé, a letter postmarked November 30, 1925, should be one in which Fitzgerald apologizes for his drunken behavior on a visit to the Hemingways' small flat on the rue Notre Dame de Champs. Fitzgerald makes light of the episode but confesses that he is quite ashamed. "However," he goes on, "it is only fair to say that the deplorable man who entered your apartment Saturday morning was *not* me but a man named Johnston who has often been mistaken for me." Zelda, too, had been in bad shape. Evidence to the contrary, Fitzgerald claimed, Zelda "was not suffering from lack of care but from a nervous hysteria which is only relieved by a doctor bearing morphine. We went to Belleau Wood next day to recuperate." Perhaps Fitzgerald intended his remark as a joke. But Zelda remembered that winter in Paris as a time when she was ill and under a doctor's care: "Dr. Gros said there was no use in trying to save my ovaries. I was always sick and having *piqûres* [injections]."

Fitzgerald's letter to Hemingway also mentioned a trip he and Zelda had made made to London; apparently he'd already spoken of it to Hemingway in the Saturday morning appearance. During the London sojourn, he had visited his English publishers. Chatto & Windus were planning to publish *The Great Gatsby* in the spring. They had also visited Tallulah Bankhead, who was appearing as Iris March in Michael Arlen's *The Green Hat.* The play was a hit; Bankhead's reviews were mixed, though she seemed ideally cast as the daredevil heroine. Zelda's insouciance was a match for Tallulah's. "We went to London to see a fog," she later wrote to young Scottie, "and saw Tallulah Bankhead, which was, perhaps, about the same effect." There had been a round of swank parties with the Mountbattens and with Tallulah's friend the Marchioness of Milford Haven. Fitzgerald felt it necessary to retract some of the more glowing reports he had given Hemingway about their "English orgy." Lady Milford Haven, he conceded, "was very nice — anything else I may have added about the relations between the Fitzgeralds and the house of Windsor is pure fiction."

He also wanted to correct a slight fabrication that he had told Hemingway: that he was now getting $3000 apiece for his stories. "For some reason I told you a silly lie — or rather an exaggeration. . . ." Fitzgerald admitted. *The Saturday Evening Post raised me to $2750 and not $3000, which is a jump of $750 in one month."* But how conscience-stricken Fitzgerald was, is debatable. Comically, he simply replaced the original lie with a less expensive one. In truth, as his ledger entries indicate, the *Post* was paying him $2500 for his stories (before agency commissions), and that represented a $500 advance.

Fitzgerald was anxious about one other item of his drunken meeting: the "garbled version" he may have given Hemingway about rescuing their mutual acquaintance Robert McAlmon "from a beating he probably deserved." Whether the incident happened in London or in Bricktop's Parisian nightclub, Le Grand Duc, where Fitzgerald and McAlmon may have had another exchange, is not clear. McAlmon was married to the British heiress Winifred Ellerman, who wrote under the name of Bryher. It was strictly a marriage of convenience. McAlmon was homosexual, and Bryher had wanted independence from her upper-class family. McAlmon was a notorious alcoholic; he also had a sharp tongue and a pugnacious disposition. A gifted writer himself, he generously set up a small vanguard press in Paris, subsidized largely by his wealthy father-in-law. Under his Contact Press imprint, he published the works of such contemporaries as William Carlos Williams, Djuna Barnes, and Nathanael West. His efforts on behalf of jealous and temperamental colleagues did not save him from the usual backbiting and bitchiness of the literary life. The fact that he had published Hemingway's first volume, *Three Stories and Ten Poems,* did not earn him any gratitude from the author. "McAlmon is a son of a bitch with a mind like an ingrowing toenail," Hemingway wrote Fitzgerald, in response to his report. "I'm through defending that one." Nor did McAlmon s undertaking the heavy burden, financially and typographically, of publishing Gertrude Stein's elephantine novel *The Making of Americans* in 1925 assure him of her continued good will. Stein, plainly optimistic about what she regarded as her masterpiece — comparable in her mind to Joyce's *Ulysses* and Proust's *Remembrance of Things Past* — was plainly dissatisfied with McAlmon's promotional efforts. The two had a serious quarrel that was never mended. Fitzgerald, who had been wildly enthusiastic about the Stein novel when it began appearing serially in the *transatlantic review,* urged Perkins to publish an American edition of the book. But by the end of 1925, he conceded, "Its good you didn't take up my advice about looking up Gertrude Stein's new book. . . . Only the first parts, the parts published in the Transatlantic are intelligible at all."

Much of that winter in Paris, Fitzgerald was caught up in a very dedicated effort to make Hemingway a Scribner's author. Largely through the efforts of Sherwood Anderson and Dos Passos, Hemingway was under contract to Boni & Liveright, which was publishing the American edition of his stories and sketches, *In Our Time.* But by November, partly, it seems, irritated by the continual linking of their names, Hemingway turned against his benefactor to the extent of writing a burlesque of Anderson's novel *Dark Laughter.* It was only one of the many disservices Hemingway felt obliged to perform for people who had helped him along the way. In clodhopper strides Hemingway parodied Anderson's style and his rural characters. For good measure he included a few digs at H. L. Mencken and Scofield Thayer (the current editor of *The Dial*). He also commented scathingly on Willa Cather's purported wartime experiences, a lunch date with John Dos Passos, and a visit by F. Scott Fitzgerald, who showed up tipsy and sat down in the fireplace. One section was titled "The Passing of a Great Race and the Making and Marring of Americans," so Stein, too, in an oblique way, figured in his text.

The satire was called *The Torrents of Spring,* and Hemingway read passages from it to Dos Passos one afternoon at the Closerie des Lilas. Dos Passos had one or two laughs but advised Hemingway against publishing it. He felt Anderson didn't deserve such treatment. Fitzgerald, however, loved it; he told Perkins that it was "almost a vicious parody" of Anderson and his imitators. But he doubted that it would sell. Sixty years later, one wonders what the fuss was about. *Torrents* is now a rather pointless satire. Its principal interest derives from the fact that Hemingway's hero, Scripps O'Neill, is married to an elderly waitress who fears that she is about to lose her husband because he has developed a lech for a younger waitress. If one considers a waitress one of Hemingway's tropes for a wife, the book may have been unintentionally prophetic.

"I agree with Ernest," Fitzgerald wrote Perkins, "that Anderson's last two books have let everybody down who believed in him — I think they're cheap, faked, obscurantic and awful." Though he and Hemingway would deny that it was a matter of planned strategy, nonetheless *The Torrents of Spring* proved to be the vehicle for Hemingway's move to Scribner's. Boni & Liveright were eager to publish Hemingway's still incomplete novel about the Parisian expatriates, *The Sun Also Rises,* which was much talked about in publishing circles. But Hemingway had decided to send them, instead, his satire on Anderson, figuring that if they turned down the manuscript, he was free to move to another publisher. Since Anderson was one of Boni & Liveright's star authors, and it was unlikely that they would offend him, Hemingway's gamble was a very safe one. Fitzgerald advised Perkins to send Hemingway a "strong wire" — the Hemingways were vacationing in Schruns, Austria — offering to publish *The Torrents of Spring* and, following that, to negotiate for the novel as well. "He and I are very thick," he advised Perkins, "& he's marking the time until he finds out how much he's bound to Liveright." The situation was particularly urgent, since Harcourt, through the expatriate American writer Louis Bromfield, was offering to take the satire, sight unseen, in order to get the novel. Fitzgerald was sure he could get Hemingway to give the novel to Scribner's, but he warned Perkins not to tell Hemingway anything about his part in the discussions. He did, however, collaborate with Hemingway to the extent of writing to Boni & Liveright, praising *Torrents of Spring* to the skies — "about the best comic book ever written by an American" — and then blatantly admitting that he hoped they would turn it down: "Frankly, I hope you won't like it — because I am something of a ballyhoo man for Scribner's and I'd some day like to see all my generation (3) that I admire rounded up in the same coop." But his attitude toward Hemingway remained condescending. As he later wrote to Perkins, "To hear him talk you'd think Liveright had broken up his home and robbed him of millions — but that's because he knows nothing of publishing, except in the cucoo magazines, is very young and feels helpless so far away." The remark suggests Little Red Riding Hood defending a very inexperienced wolf.

Christmas that year was the Christmas of the famous photograph. Fitzgerald, Zelda, and little Scottie, beaming with health and prosperity, are strung out in a chorus line before the tree in the apartment on the rue de Tilsitt. It is a picture of the carefree life. Zelda, each year they were abroad, packed and unpacked the fragile Christmas ornaments. She and Nanny had decorated the tree; it was strung with silvery garlands and decorated with Christmas baubles: birds with spun-glass tails were perched on the branches, little cardboard houses glittering with snow were tucked away in crevices. Under the tree were a toy automobile, a doll's vanity dresser, a xylophone, among the noticeable gifts. The Fitzgeralds sent the photo as Christmas greetings to friends like Ring Lardner, who were suitably impressed. "We agree that Scotty is the second best looking one in the outfit or shebang, to use the colloquial," Lardner wrote back.

In the photo, all three look buoyant and happy in the low-ceilinged parlor, the walls lined with bookshelves. Fitzgerald had every reason to be happy. *The Saturday Evening Post* had raised its fees for his stories, though he hadn't written many that year. The New York playwright and theatrical producer Owen Davis had taken an option on *The Great Gatsby,* and it was scheduled for production early in the coming year. He had earned $18,333 for his literary work that year, only $2000 less than he had made in 1924. He had a new collection of stories coming out, *All the Sad Young Men,* which Max Perkins assured him was "notable"; the stories all had "depth and diversity." When one considered the collection together with the *The Great Gatsby,* there was no telling what Fitzgerald might yet do. And even though he was working on his novel in only desultory fashion, Fitzgerald somehow found it very promising.

Yet there are times in life when unhappiness settles in like a season of discontent; there are places in which misery seems to gather in the corners. Zelda would describe that winter in the rue de Tilsitt as "a terrible winter in a Paris flat that smelled of a church chancery because it was impossible to ventilate." In *Save Me the Waltz,* she would describe her hero and heroine, David and Alabama Knight, as trapped during a winter of rain in an apartment that was "a perfect breeding place for the germs of bitterness they brought with them from the Riviera." In her personal recollections, she gave an equally grim appraisal: "I was sick again at Christmas when the MacLeishes came. . . . I was always sick."

Fitzgerald had his own morbid spells, as is clear from a letter he wrote to Perkins shortly after the Christmas festivities:

I write to you from the depths of one of my unholy depressions. The book is wonderful — I honestly think that when it's published I shall be the best American novelist (which isn't saying a lot) but the end seems far away. When it's finished I'm coming home for awhile anyhow though the thought revolts me as much as the thought of remaining in France. I wish I were twenty-two again with only my dramatic and feverishly enjoyed miseries. You remember I used to say I wanted to die at thirty — well I'm now twenty-nine, and the prospect is still welcome. My work is the only thing that makes me happy — except to be a little tight — and for those two indulgences, I pay a big price in mental and physical hangovers.

In the letter, Fitzgerald mentioned that Zelda was "not entirely well yet. We're going south next month." At the recommendation of Zelda's physician, Dr. Gros, in January they went to a health resort at Salies de Béarn in the Pyrenees. Zelda's ailment was diagnosed as colitis — the "disease of that year," as Fitzgerald described it. They stayed for nearly two months at the Hôtel Bellevue in a bland, white-pine room with a view of misty streets and the nearby casino, its boarded-up windows splattered with bird-droppings. It was definitely out of season and unfashionable. Fitzgerald called it an "out-of-the-way hole," and maintained that the only other inhabitants were "two goats and a paralytic." Zelda remembered that she and Scott were "a little discouraged about everything." The only relief were the once-a-week excursions to Biarritz and Pau and Lourdes.

There was, however, good news from New York. The Owen Davis adaptation of *The Great Gatsby,* with James Rennie and Florence Eldridge in the leading roles, opened on February 2, 1926, at the Ambassador Theater under the direction of George Cukor. It received generally favorable reviews and ran for 112 performances. The Lardners caught a matinee performance, and Ring sent laconic congratulations: "We thought the show was great and that Rennie was just about perfect. . . . Every now and then one of Scott's lines would pop out and hit you in the face and make you wish that he had done the dramatization himself." Max Perkins, who had seen the out-of-town tryout at Stamford ("You need not feel ashamed of the play. . . . Far from it"), sent copies of the reviews. There was a favorable one from Franklin P. Adams, who had, years before, pilloried all the typographical and grammatical errors in *This Side of Paradise*. His notice of *The Great Gatsby* produced an explosion of rancor at Salies de Béarn. "Think of that horse's ass F.P.A. coming around to my work after six years of neglect," Fitzgerald wrote back to Perkins. "I'd like to stick his praise up his behind. God knows it's no use to me now."

The play's successful run inevitably sparked a bid for the screen rights. Famous Players offered $50,000, with 10 percent taken from the top by a West Coast agent. Fitzgerald promptly cabled Ober to accept. The picture, starring Warner Baxter and Lois Wilson, was produced within the year. The money was split between the playwright, Owen Davis, the play's producer, William Brady, and Fitzgerald, who, after paying his own agency commission, ended up with $13,500. Even in Europe, Fitzgerald managed to pick up trade gossip and learned that Theodore Dreiser had supposedly been paid $90,000 for the film rights for *An American Tragedy*, so the success was relative. Later, Zelda, with editorial supervision from Fitzgerald, wrote a lively memoir about the hotels at which they had registered during their restless travels in life, "Show Mr. and Mrs. F. to Number ———." Fitzgerald in his editorial additions telescoped the events somewhat, heightened the fragility of their lives at Salies de Béarn, and lofted the Hollywood offer: "We had a play on Broadway and the movies offered $60,000 but we were china people by then and it didn't seem to matter particularly."

While at the Hôtel Bellevue, Fitzgerald performed one more friendly service for Hemingway by writing a review of the American edition of *In Our Time* for the May 1926 issue of *The Bookman*. Titled "How to Waste Material: A Note on My Generation," the review provided Fitzgerald with a double opportunity. It was a chance to promote his friend, and it was the occasion for him to take up the cudgels—this time in print—against the vogue for farm novels and Main Street epics and their writers, whom he described as "a family of hammer and tongs men—insensitive, suspicious of glamour, preoccupied exclusively with the external, the contemptible, the 'national' and the drab." By now he was fixing the blame on Mencken's criticism and Sherwood Anderson's homespun novels—Hemingway's current targets. After due consideration of Hemingway's stories, the best of which he thought was "Big Two-Hearted River," Fitzgerald concluded, "Many of us who have grown weary of admonitions to 'watch this man or that' have felt a sort of renewal of excitement at these stories wherein Ernest Hemingway turns a corner into the street."

I V

Early in March, the Fitzgeralds met Hemingway in Paris. They were making arrangements to go to the Riviera for the spring and summer, planning to drive to Nice in a rented limousine. Hemingway, just back from New York, where he had negotiated a contract with Maxwell Perkins, was en route to Schruns to rejoin Hadley and their son, John, known as Bumby. No doubt, Hemingway told him at length about his literary activities in New York and his impressions of the stage version of *The Great Gatsby*. He thought the adaptation was "pretty darn close to the book" and gathered that it was considered a hit in New York. But writing to Louis Bromfield, he confessed, "I had to pay to get in. Would have paid to get out a couple of times but on the whole it is a good play."

For his part, Fitzgerald was delighted with Hemingway's move to Scribner's and rather proud of his matchmaking. Writing to Perkins about the Paris meeting, he boasted: "I'm glad you got Hemmingway. I saw him for a day in Paris on his return and he thought you were great. I've brought you two successes (Ring and Tom Boyd) and two failures (Biggs and Woodward Boyd) — Ernest will decide whether my opinions are more of a hindrance or a help."

Hemingway did not return to Schruns immediately; as he phrased it in *A Moveable Feast,* he did not take the first train or the second or the third. Instead, he had started his affair with Pauline Pfeiffer, and he was, so he said, filled with remorse because of the "unbelievable, wrenching, killing happiness, selfishness and treachery" of everything he and Pauline did. When he returned to Schruns and found Hadley and the baby waiting for him at the station, he was overcome with guilt, wishing that he had died before loving anyone but Hadley — as he asserted in his memoirs. Presumably when Dos Passos and the Murphys arrived at Schruns a few days later for a week's skiing expedition, Hemingway found their company a great relief from his guilty conscience. Neither Dos Passos nor Gerald Murphy was a practiced skier. Dos Passos made no pretense about it; when the slopes became too steep, he simply sat down on his skis, turning the run into a toboggan ride. Murphy tried to live up to Hemingway's standards of perfection. According to Murphy's recollections, Hemingway asked him whether he had been scared, and Murphy admitted he was. Hemingway told him that that was what courage was, "grace under pressure." Murphy recalled, "It was childish of me, but I felt absolutely elated." But Gerald Murphy had a capacity for invention nearly equal to Fitzgerald's, and the circumstances surrounding Hemingway's famous phrase may have been somewhat different. Apparently Fitzgerald, who had heard the idea first, told it to Murphy in the course of discussing Hemingway's romance with bullfighting. At Schruns, Murphy may have repeated it to Hemingway, who was far from pleased. Writing to Fitzgerald, Hemingway scolded: "It makes no difference your telling G. Murphy about bull fighting statement except will be careful about making such statements. Was not referring to guts but to something else. Grace under pressure."

According to Dos Passos, the vacation in Schruns was the "last unalloyed good time" that he spent with Hemingway and Hadley. They devoured quantities of trout, drank beer and wine, and slept like dormice. They were, it seemed, all on the best of terms and parted like brothers and sisters. Hemingway even read aloud for them passages from *The Sun Also Rises,* and the Murphys were both thrilled and impressed. Sara Murphy, in fact, felt an unquestioned affection for Hemingway and for years would not allow anyone to speak ill of him. Both of the Murphys were struck by his brilliance as a writer, even more impressed with Hemingway than with Fitzgerald. The feelings seemed to be mutual all around. But years later, in *A Moveable Feast,* Hemingway gave a vicious account of how an unnamed rich couple (the Murphys) had induced him to read the manuscript. "It's great, Ernest," they told him. "Truly it's great. You cannot know the thing it has." And Hemingway had performed like a bird dog, wagging his tail with pleasure when he should all the while have been wondering, "If these bastards like it what is wrong with it."

If the Murphys fared badly in Hemingway's recollection, Dos Passos did no better. He is described as the unnamed "pilot fish" who had steered the rich sharks onto Hemingway, after which nothing could ever be the same.

> The pilot fish leaves of course. He is always going somewhere or coming from somewhere, and he is never around for very long. He enters and leaves politics or the theater in the same way he enters and leaves countries and people's lives in his early days. . . . He

has the irreplaceable early training of the bastard and a latent and long denied love of money. He ends up rich himself.

The remarkable suppleness of the prose manages to tone down the crazy rancor of Hemingway toward his one-time friends. But the most remarkable feat of all is that the cozy self-righteousness makes the reader overlook the point that this diatribe against the rich was written by one of the wealthiest of American writers.

"I'm happier than I've been for years," Fitzgerald wrote Perkins from the Riviera in mid-March. "It's one of those strange, precious and all too transitory moments when everything in one's life seems to be going well." His new novel was "growing absorbing," he assured the editor. He was sending the same good news to Harold Ober, claiming that the novel was about one-fourth done and that he could deliver it for possible serialization by the following January. "It will be about 75,000 words long, divided into 12 chapters, concerning, tho this is absolutely confidential, such a case as that girl who shot her mother on the Pacific coast last year." On the strength of the reports, Ober began negotiating an agreement with *Liberty* magazine.

It was less than the happy time Fitzgerald claimed. The Villa Paquita, which they had rented in Juan les Pins, was uncomfortable. Zelda was often sick. Fitzgerald could not work, because his room was too damp. He and Zelda began looking for another house. Still, from the Villa Paquita, Fitzgerald sent further glowing reports to Perkins: "My book is *wonderful.* I don't think it'll be interrupted again. I expect to reach New York about December 10th with the ms. under my arm." But for nine years, Fitzgerald would be bogged down with one variation and another of the novel that became *Tender Is the Night.*

Early in May, they moved to another house, the Villa St. Louis, close to the beach and the casino at Juan les Pins. The mistral began raging soon after they moved in, and Fitzgerald confessed to Perkins that the idea of writing was "anathema" to him. Nevertheless, he said that there was "every prospect of a marvelous summer" ahead. He had written Hemingway in very similar terms, maintaining that he had started on his novel, was working hard and seeing no one, that he had stopped drinking. But as was often the case with Fitzgerald, the need to broadcast some windfall was a symptom that he could not get down to work. Rather fatuously, he told Hemingway that he had received his $15,000 advance on the film rights to *Gatsby,* and with it, he probably would be able to manage through Christmas. Fitzgerald's supposedly straitened circumstances did not impress Hemingway; sardonically, he offered to have his own royalty checks sent to Scott. Fitzgerald also wrote Perkins ("This is confidential") that *Liberty* was offering $35,000 for the serial rights to his new novel, sight unseen. And he promptly told the same thing to Archibald MacLeish, who was renting a villa near the Murphys. MacLeish passed the good news on to Hemingway. By this stage, the new novel, more of a hope than an actuality, was renamed *The World's Fair.*

The Hemingways and Bumby were expected at Antibes later in the summer, having been invited by the Murphys, who offered them their small guest house. Hemingway, from Paris, wrote Fitzgerald a progress report on his own novel, which had been sent off to Perkins. He told Fitzgerald he would bring a carbon copy with him to the Riviera; he would appreciate Fitzgerald's advice. In the meantime, he offered a comic précis of the plot: "The hero, like Gatsby, is a Lake Superior Salmon Fisherman (There are no salmon in Lake Superior)" — a small jibe at Fitzgerald's ignorance about Lake Superior, which had no clams, no salmon, and no ebb tides, as Fitzgerald had written in *Gatsby.* Then Hemingway launched into a spoof on the matricide theme of Fitzgerald's new novel. The action of *The Sun Also Rises,* Hemingway noted, "all takes place in Newport R.I. and the heroine is a girl named Sophie Irene Loeb who kills her mother. The scene in which Sophie gives birth to twins in the death house at Sing Sing . . . I got from Dreiser, but practically everything else in the book is either my own or yours. I know you'll be glad to see it."

In May, Hadley and Bumby arrived; Hemingway was making a three-week trip to Spain before joining his family. Unfortunately, Bumby was still suffering from the whooping cough he had contracted in Paris and the Murphys, worried about their own children, called in their English doctor. Hadley and Bumby were quarantined. The Fitzgeralds offered Hadley the vacant Villa Paquita until their summer lease expired.

It was to be a summer in which many things came apart. The troubles began with Hemingway's arrival. The Murphys, visibly taken up with their new protégé, made it the occasion for a welcoming party at the casino. Champagne and caviar were ordered; Fitzgerald began by making derogatory remarks about the bill of fare, calling it the height of affectation. The group, which included the MacLeishes and Hemingways and a few others, was seated at a big table in the casino. Fitzgerald turned his chair to stare at a beautiful young woman with an older man at a nearby table, and he continued to stare so persistently that the couple called for the head waiter. Next, Fitzgerald began tossing ashtrays around. "He really had the most appalling sense of humor," Gerald Murphy said; "sophomoric and — well, trashy." Murphy became so annoyed, in fact, that he got up and left his own party. Fitzgerald muttered that he had never seen Gerald so silly and rude.

Sara Murphy sent Fitzgerald a frank and disapproving note on the following day. She and Gerald, she said, considered themselves friends of his, but they were past the age when they wanted to be bothered with the kind of behavior Fitzgerald had displayed the night before. If Gerald had been "rude" in getting up and leaving a party that had become quite bad, then he must have been rude to the Hemingways and MacLeishes as well. She suspected, Sara said, that she and Gerald had been caught up in some fictional pursuit of Fitzgerald's and confessed that they both found it distinctly uncomfortable: "You can't expect anyone to like or stand a *Continual* feeling of analysis & sub-analysis & criticism — on the whole unfriendly — Such as we have felt for quite awhile." She had her doubts as to whether Fitzgerald was concerned about their *"Manners"* — again she capitalized and underlined. It was, more probably, "some theory you have — (it *may* be something to do with the book). But *you ought to know at your age* that you *Can't have Theories about friends."* She ended by assuring Fitzgerald that she and Gerald were fond of both him and Zelda, adding, "And so — *for God's sake* take it or leave it — as it is meant — a straight gesture, *without* subtitles — Yr. old and rather irritated friend."

Sara Murphy's letters give the impression of a woman who is sensible rather than profound in her approach to life; a woman who had the assurance of money and was satisfied with her opinions once they were formed. But she seems to have grasped one of the besetting problems of Fitzgerald's character: his tendency to fictionalize life, to make intense literary demands on it. Zelda would characterize this trait of Fitzgerald's in the character of Jacob, the bored husband in her unfinished novel, *Caesar's Things*. Jacob cannot stand the grit of life; he dislikes sitting on a Riviera beach in a wet bathing suit; he hates the taste of sand. He seems compelled to remake life rather than transform it into art. (He is a painter.) In her ruminative late style, Zelda wrote that Jacob was "exhaustive in his way of making the stories of people fit into his impetuous pre-conclusions about them. He kept nagging and asking and third-degreeing his acquaintances till it all made acceptable continuity with what he thought it ought to be dramatically."

Given the complicated fate of the Murphys' fictional image during the long siege of writing that *Tender Is the Night* underwent, it seems probable that Fitzgerald had fixed on them the same annoying scrutiny, the same yearning to know — to appropriate — another life or lives that he subjected Zelda to. In life, the Murphys were an ideal couple — wealthy and stylish, exemplars of good taste — the parents that Rudolph Miller, Jimmy Gatz, Scott Fitzgerald *ought* to have had. In the novel, they served as the initial alter egos for the more dramatic personas Fitzgerald would contrive for himself and Zelda. The Murphys were a considerate couple, generous with friends, and one has the impression that they preferred politeness and good breeding in their relationships — the gentleman poet Archie MacLeish rather than the troublesome Fitzgeralds. (Their involvement with the social issues of the time was largely a checkbook liberalism, serving the causes of more radical friends.) Little wonder, then, that Gerald and Sara Murphy wanted to shed the responsibility of becoming role models for Fitzgerald. And little wonder that Fitzgerald, sensing the shift in their loyalties, their growing appreciation of Hemingway as a writer, their displeasure with his own behavior, became stubbornly jealous and drunkenly sophomoric.

But there was another factor that contributed to Fitzgerald's desperate behavior during the summer of 1926. Hemingway had brought with him the promised copy of the manuscript of *The Sun Also Rises*. Fitzgerald read it promptly. He wrote to Perkins that he liked it, but with "certain qualifications." He gave Hemingway the impression that he was quite excited about the book, but in a detailed letter he spelled out all his qualifications. Any writer who receives the kind of letter Fitzgerald wrote would know that he was being addressed *de haut en bas* and probably for posterity. Fitzgerald began, "Dear Ernest: Nowadays when almost everyone is a genius, at least for awhile, the temptation for the bogus to profit is no greater than the temptation for the good man to relax. . . ." There was much that was overbearing in the letter, and there was a good deal of sound literary advice. Fitzgerald pointed out that there were too many "sneers, superiorities and nose-thumbings-at-nothing," which marred the text. At times, Fitzgerald said, Hemingway had "done a lot of writing that *honestly* reminded me of Michael Arlen." Some of the criticisms were niggling ("Quarter being a state of mind, ect. This is in all guide books"); others could only have been wounding ("I can't tell you the sense of disappointment that [the] beginning with its elephantine facetiousness gave me. Please do what you can about it in proof"). He made some sound suggestions in recommending that Hemingway cut out the biographical accounts of some of the major characters at the beginning of the book. Hemingway agreed with him and was even more ruthless; he simply dropped the first fifteen pages of the text. And there was some unqualified praise in Fitzgerald's comment "God! the bottom of p. 77 *jusque* the top of p. 78 are wonderful." Fitzgerald recognized that Hemingway might be ready to tell him to take his criticism and shove it — "But remember this is a new departure for you, and I think your stuff is great. You were the first American I wanted to meet in Europe — and the last."

And Fitzgerald had one complaint that seemed to devolve more from his own state of mind than from Hemingway's. He was particularly insistent on the shadowy subject of Jake Barnes's emasculating wound, suffered in the war, and of Lady Brett's failed attempt to seduce the hero: "The heart of my criticism beats somewhere upon p. 87. I think you can't change it though. I felt the lack of some crazy, torturing tentativeness or insecurity — horror, all at once — that she'd feel — and he'd feel — maybe I'm crazy. He isn't *like an impotent man. He's like a man in a sort of moral chastity belt.*"

Impotence seems to have been on his mind. He had had a similar complaint and a similar response to the subject in another book, Van Wyck Brooks's *The Pilgrimage of Henry James,* a study of the American author who, in his youth, reputedly had had a mysterious injury in the groin that left him impotent. "Why didn't you touch more on James impotence (physical) and its influence?" he complained to Brooks. "I think if [he] hadn't had at least one poignant emotional love affair with an American girl on American soil he might have lived there twice as long, tried twice as hard, had the picaresque past of Huck Finn and yet never struck roots." Fitzgerald seems to have felt a sense of identification with the fastidious James: "Novelists like he (him) and in a sense (to descend a good bit) me, have to have love as a main concern since our interest lies outside the economic struggle or the life of violence, as conditioned to some extent by our lives from 16–21." Fitzgerald's queries suggest that the impotence which often accompanies alcoholism—and its sense of humiliation and frustration—may have become a problem for him. Zelda recalled that he was drinking heavily throughout the summer.

The partying with the Murphys and Hemingways was cut short in June by Zelda's illness. She and Fitzgerald left for Paris and the American Hospital at Neuilly, where Zelda had an appendectomy. Zelda's Montgomery friend Sara Mayfield happened to be in Paris at the time and encountered Fitzgerald at the Ritz Bar with some girls from Westport and a bunch of Princeton boys. It was on this occasion that Fitzgerald argued with Michael Arlen on the merits of Hemingway as a writer and took the surrealistic ride in a French hearse. He invited Mayfield to dinner with him, intending to pay a visit to Zelda in the hospital. But first he stopped at Harry's New York Bar to find out news about the Hemingways, who, along with Pauline Pfeiffer and the Murphys, were in Pamplona. But there he became so drunk, and the whole evening so disorderly, that Mayfield never got to the hospital. (She was convinced that the appendectomy was really a euphemism for another of Zelda's abortions.) The Princeton boys loaded Fitzgerald into the hearse and took Mayfield to her hotel in a taxi.

In Paris, Fitzgerald also ran across the actor James Rennie, who had starred in the play version of *The Great Gatsby*, and his wife, Dorothy Gish. The couple visited Zelda at Neuilly, and Rennie, a heavy drinker himself, went the rounds of the French bistros with Fitzgerald. Rennie was appalled by the size of the tips Fitzgerald deposited during the course of their drinking and surreptitiously pocketed most of the money. On their last evening out, Rennie confessed to his deception and turned over the tips to Fitzgerald, who at first was miffed but then smiled: "This is wonderful. . . . Let's go somewhere quickly and spend it."

Back in Juan les Pins in mid-July, Fitzgerald was once more involved in a round of parties while Zelda recuperated. Anita Loos, visiting Antibes with her boy friend, the screen director John Emerson, remembered a dangerous night, soon after the Fitzgeralds' return, when Zelda was supposed to remain in bed and sober until her stitches were removed. But one night Scott returned from a party to find her missing, an empty gin bottle beside the bed. She had had a temperature of 104 degrees and felt that a swim might cool her off. Zelda's later recollections of that summer were of loneliness and unhappy times: "I wanted you to swim with me at Juan les Pins but you liked it better where it was gayer at the Garoupe with Marise Hamilton and the Murphys and MacLeishes." There were nights when Fitzgerald did not come home at all; there were mornings when she came downstairs and found the living room full of strangers. "You left me lots alone. . . ." she complained to Fitzgerald. "I swam with Scottie except when I followed you, mostly unwillingly." But in a letter to Maxwell Perkins, Zelda maintained — somewhat ambiguously, it is true — that it had been a fine summer, full of gay and decorative people who somehow gave Antibes a "sense of carnival and impending disaster." She noted that Hemingway had been there as a "sort of a materialistic mystic," and Rebecca West, "looking like an advertisement for cauliflower ears and entirely surrounded by fairies — male." Gilbert Seldes was down the road, writing detective stories about Monte Carlo, and the place was full of "Broadway snobs," whom she was quite fond of and very glad to see leave.

One of the less successful Broadway lights was Fitzgerald's former Princeton idol, Walker Ellis, the impresario of the Triangle shows. Fitzgerald had last seen him in New York during the casting sessions for *The Vegetable,* when Ellis auditioned for a role in Fitzgerald's play. The only part Fitzgerald could offer him was that of a newspaper boy, who walked on stage, shouting "Wuxtry, Wuxtry," a bit part that was later written out of the play. Ellis declined it. He next tried out for a role in Somerset Maugham's *The Camel's Back,* scheduled to open that November. But the playwright, in New York for the production, made Ellis a rather different proposition, offering to set him up in style — a proposal that Ellis also turned down. Fitzgerald was gleeful. "Think of Walker," he told Edmund Wilson, "looking for a job and getting an offer to be a harlot!"

Sara Mayfield paid a visit to Antibes, staying at the Hôtel du Cap. When she asked Zelda what Hemingway's new novel was about, Zelda frankly characterized it as "bullfighting, bullslinging and bull——." Fitzgerald cut her short with "Don't say things like that." Zelda countered, "Why shouldn't I?" "Say anything you please,"

Fitzgerald answered, "but lay off Ernest." The chief bit of important news that summer was that Hemingway and Hadley had decided to separate. Both of the Murphys took Hemingway's side. Sara, in fact, thought that Hadley had made a big mistake in confronting Hemingway with her suspicions that he was in love with Pauline; she thought it put the idea in Ernest's head and made him feel guilty at the same time. The Murphys offered Hemingway Gerald's studio on the rue Froidevaux in Paris. Later Gerald Murphy deposited $400 to Hemingway's account to help him over the bad time. Despite their own old-fashioned views on marriage, they considered Hemingway's decision a matter of his personal and artistic integrity. Hemingway wrote them later, seemingly in gratitude for their concern, saying he was as happy as an average empty tomato can: "However, I love you both very much and like to think about you and will be, shall we say, *pleased* to see you." Sara responded, "In the end, you will probably save us all — by refusing — to accept any second rate things. Bless you, and don't ever budge." Zelda, however, had a rather different opinion. According to Sara Mayfield, she claimed that Hemingway had turned Catholic in order to annul his marriage to Hadley and then marry Pauline Pfeiffer.

Every account of that summer, among the several the Fitzgeralds spent on the Riviera, depicts it as a summer of gaiety, amusement, dissipation, and frequent quarrels. Grace Moore had taken a villa at Antibes and awoke each morning to find dirty words scrawled on the garden walls. She scrubbed them off, only to find worse on the following morning. The remarks were part of a Dada-type film with a preposterous or nonexistent plot that the playwright Charles MacArthur, Fitzgerald, and others were making, with many of the summer residents cast in the various roles. It was a summer of incidents that developed into legends which grew more elaborate with each telling; of nude swimming parties at the beach, from one of which Alexander Woollcott, rising from the sea like some overweight Venus, wearing only a straw hat, strode up to the hotel desk, asked the clerk for his key, and, unabashed, proceeded through the lobby to his room. It was the summer in which the plump and aging love goddess of dance, Isadora Duncan, encouraged Fitzgerald, in a restaurant in St. Paul de Vence, to sit at her feet while she stroked his head. (It was not so impressive an honor that Fitzgerald remembered her name. In his ledger, he set it down as Eleanora Duncan, then rectified the mistake. But it impressed Zelda enough that in a jealous fit she flung herself down a steep stairway, almost plunging off a cliff.) It was the summer in which Fitzgerald, in a fit of drunken rancor, encountered an old woman (an old man in some versions) carrying a tray of sweetmeats (nuts in other versions) and gave it a swift kick, sending the contents all over the ground. In some versions, Fitzgerald paid the woman for this bit of nastiness; in others, it was Gerald Murphy who made amends. Zelda's recollection was that it had happened at Nice, early in the spring, and that Fitzgerald, in a fit of ill-temper, had bought a whole wagonful of roasted chestnuts and perversely scattered them everywhere. It was the summer in which Fitzgerald and the boisterous Charlie MacArthur (evangelist's son turned alcoholic) herded a band of musicians into the Villa St. Louis and locked them in, to play for the evening's party, dragged a waiter to the edge of a cliff, promising to push him off, and threatened to saw a waiter in two, claiming there was no danger since it was a "musical" saw. It was the summer in which the Fitzgeralds drove home from a party and turned off on a railroad trestle and parked and went to sleep (and would have been demolished if a peasant hadn't wakened them in time); it was the summer in which Zelda, drunk, lay down in front of their car, daring Scott to run over her — and Scott would have, if friends hadn't stopped him. It was the summer in which Zelda, in a crowded nightspot, stood up on a table and began an eerie dance, slowly raising her skirts above her head, to the delight of the male members of the audience.

But it was, too, the summer in which the Fitzgeralds gave a party for Scottie and her guests, the Murphy children. There was a papier-mâché castle with a tower in which a beautiful princess was imprisoned; Zelda had made the castle and the costumes. There were two contending armies (from Scott's collection of toy soldiers) and a moat with toy ducks and a prince and a dragon (a local beetle). Fitzgerald, on his knees, marshaled the rescuers while Zelda, offstage, provided the cries of the princess in the tower and the shrieks of the witch who held her captive. Honoria Murphy, with a child's recollections of the dazzling couple, remembered: "I couldn't wait for them to come to dinner because they always had a wonderful plan afoot. He was sensitive and delicate looking and she wore spangles and shimmering 20's kinds of dresses in lovely shades of salmon and bright pink."

More and more that summer, Fitzgerald tested the patience of the Murphys. At a dinner party in their garden, given in honor of the Princess Chimay, Fitzgerald pursued a young man around the dance floor, asking him if he was a homosexual — and then was abashed when the boy said he was. But that offense had to be surpassed; during the dessert course, he threw a ripe fig down the back of the princess's décolletage. (She merely stiffened her back and ignored the incident.) Next, he began throwing Sara Murphy's prized Venetian glasses, full of liquor, over the garden wall, ruining her prize tomatoes. When told to stop by Archibald MacLeish, Fitzgerald swung at the poet. (Another version has it that MacLeish took him outside and punched him.) Fitzgerald was banished from further parties at the Murphys', though they seem to have been rather lenient, limiting the prohibition to only two or three weeks. But Fitzgerald had his revenge; he showed up one evening and tossed garbage into the cocktail party the Murphys were giving on the other side of the wall.

Under the tyranny of alcohol, something turned coarse in Fitzgerald's nature, and there was a self-pitying unhappiness and bitterness in his letters. Writing to Hemingway later in the fall, he invented a parody version of one of Hemingway's *In Our Times* vignettes: "We were in a back-house in Juan-les-Pins. Bill had lost control of his sphincter muscles. There were wet Ma Fins in the rack beside the door. There were wet Eclaireurs de Nice in the rack above his head. When the King of Bulgaria came in, Bill was just firing a burst that struck the old limeshit twenty feet down with a *splat-tap.*

"At this point in my letter," Fitzgerald added, "my thirtieth birthday came and I got tight for a week." It was a curious letter to send, considering that it was in response to Hemingway's announcement that he and Hadley had definitely split up. "Your letter depressed and rather baffled me," Fitzgerald added in a brief personal note. "Have you and Hadley permanently busted up, and was the necessity of that what was on your soul this summer?" He reported on the slow, whining end of his summer. The Murphys had left. But he and Zelda had seen them before their departure and gotten stewed at one of their parties:

> That is we got stewed and I believe there was some sort of mawkish reconciliation. However, they've grown dim to me and I don't like them much any more. MacLeishes, too, have grown shadowy — he's *so* nice, but she's a club woman at heart and made a great lot of trouble in subtle ways this summer.

Swimmings almost over now. We have our tickets for America, Dec. 10th on the *Conte Biancamano* — we'll spend the winter in New York. Bishop was here with his unspeakably awful wife. He seems anemic and washed out, a memory of the past so far as I'm concerned.

His letter was an indictment of summer acquaintances, summer betrayals. Zelda, writing to Maxwell Perkins, gave a different appraisal of their final weeks: "Scott is working and still brooding about the war. . . . It's heavenly here when its burnt and dusty and the water crackles in the fall. Scott's novel is going to be excellent."

They left the Riviera and traveled to Genoa, where they caught the Italian liner for New York. Zelda became so sick, she later recalled that she "almost died." It seems to have been a preliminary episode of the excruciating asthma attacks she suffered when she had her breakdown. But Scott appears to have been oblivious of her suffering or anxieties. Writing to Hemingway from on board the *Conte Biancamano,* he said: "I go back with my novel still unfinished and with less health and not much more money than when I came, but somehow content, for the moment, with the motion and New York ahead and Zelda's entire recovery — and happy about the amount of my book that I've already written." He offered to look out for Hemingway's interests at Scribner's while he was in New York. His most important message in the letter was a genuine one. He confessed to Hemingway, "I can't tell you how much your friendship has meant to me during this year and a half — it is the brightest thing in our trip to Europe for me."

Ludlow Fowler and his bride, Elsie Blatchford, of Winnetka, Illinois, were among the passengers on the return trip to America. At the dinner table, Fitzgerald would lead discussions on such subjects as "Is there any man present who can honestly say he has never hit his wife in anger?" And Zelda would take Fowler aside and tell him confidentially, "Now Ludlow, take it from an old souse like me — don't let drinking get you in the position it's gotten Scott if you want your marriage to be any good."

Her later recollections of the crossing struck a solemn note: "And we were back in America — further apart than ever before." An abyss as wide as the Atlantic was opening between them.

PART FOUR

8

Weekends at Ellerslie

EVER SINCE the failure of *The Great Gatsby*, Fitzgerald had been threatening to go to Hollywood to learn "the movie business." By way of Ring Lardner, he had heard of the lucrative offers that Lardner had been offered (and had turned down) and the attractive $7500 fees the Metro-Goldwyn-Mayer "people" had paid to John V. A. Weaver and Marc Connelly for their scriptwriting services. On December 30, two weeks after his return to America, Fitzgerald himself received his call from the ministry of glamour: a telegram from John W. Considine, Jr., a Yale graduate and an admirer of Fitzgerald, and the president of his own production corporation, Feature Productions. Considine wanted a "FINE MODERN COLLEGE STORY" for Constance Talmadge, the film to be produced by United Artists.

The offer came at a hectic time; he and Zelda and Scottie had spent Christmas with Zelda's parents in Montgomery and planned to visit Fitzgerald's mother and father, who were living in Washington. In need of money, and probably flattered by the proposal, Fitzgerald did not take long to make up his mind. In fact, he didn't bother to consult his agent; he settled for a $3500 initial fee and an additional $12,500 if the script was accepted. On January 4, he wired Max Perkins, GOING TO COAST FOR THREE WEEKS CONFIDENTIAL ADDRESS FIRST NATIONAL PICTURES HOLLYWOOD HAPPY NEW YEAR.

Leaving Scottie with Fitzgerald's parents, the couple took the Twentieth Century Limited to the West Coast. For Zelda it was something of an adventure, traveling under skies streaked with red

279

and purple. But she had an eye for odd effects, and the landscape looked to her strictly provisional, like the setting for a toy train: green and brown hills with houses that were "on probation," a sudden dark tunnel, tiny brick stations. At El Paso, Fitzgerald suddenly became ill. ("Daddy got so nervous he thought he had an appendicitis," Zelda informed Scottie.) They had to get off the train and spend a night at a hotel, where Fitzgerald quickly recovered. That Fitzgerald, in a state of anxiety or apprehension, should suffer from precisely the same ailment which had hospitalized Zelda earlier that year suggests there was something symbiotic in their dependence on one another.

In Los Angeles, they took a suite in one of the "bungalows" at the Ambassador Hotel. It was exciting to see the stars, Zelda wrote Scottie. Their bungalow was "just between the leading vamps of the cinema: Pola Negri on one side and John Barrymore on the other." Barrymore's "ducky little girl," Diana, was in New York, but the actor's walls were covered with pictures of her, an example of parental devotion that Zelda felt she and Fitzgerald ought to follow. There were other more familiar guests at the Ambassador — Carl Van Vechten and Carmel Myers, their friend of Roman days. Van Vechten, whose novel *The Tattooed Countess* had been made into a film, found himself chronicling Hollywood society — or the lack of it — for *Vanity Fair,* using the usual Hollywood superlatives. Words like "incredible, fantastic, colossal" came to mind, the premise being that there was simply more of everything and anything in Hollywood than one was likely to encounter elsewhere on the American continent. More money, sunlight, distances, jewels, oil wells, fur coats ("in a climate where they are not required"), work, poverty, bad luck. And more flowers: "A young man unable to come to a tea party I attended apologized for his absence by sending the hostess five dozen orchids." Buildings were so skimpily constructed that it was possible to kick a hole through "the average domicile." The Hollywood attitude was equally hollow, Van Vechten noted, "but I never found the occasion to kick a hole through it."

Zelda, at first enchanted, soon began to recognize the air of improbability; the squares of green grass that were as fresh as wet paint, trapped between walkways of brand-new concrete; the sudden torrential rains that rushed down the gutters like hot brown molasses candy; the highway toward Long Beach, with its unbroken line of automobiles "weaving along under the vast sky, like an invasion of beetles." On one of their first evenings there, she and Fitzgerald went dancing in a nightclub full of artificial palm trees and a ceiling with moving clouds and blinking stars. There was an artificial waterfall, and in the fake trees were stuffed monkeys with eyes that lit up. "Hollywood," she wrote Scottie, "is not gay like the magazines say but very quiet. The stars almost never go out in public and every place closes at mid-night." They had been to see a screening of *The Great Gatsby,* she wrote: "It's ROTTEN and awful and terrible and we left." Mostly, she was bored and resorted to swimming in the hotel pool and taking lessons for the new dance craze, the Black Bottom. "There's nothing on earth to do here but look at the view and eat," she complained. "You can imagine the result since I do not like to look at views."

Fitzgerald, too, noted the implausibilities of the scene: the cramped bungalows, the apartments decorated in 1920 Moorish, the desperate Sunday social life — a continuous round of dull afternoon teas and cocktail parties and buffet suppers on the stars' one day off. But he sensed, or thought he sensed, something more significant beneath the surface of the life, something more emblematic: Hollywood was a place that wasted beauty and dreams. As he wrote his cousin Ceci: "This is a tragic city of beautiful girls — the girls who mop the floor are beautiful, the waitresses, the shop ladies. You never want to see any more beauty." Carl Van Vechten had similar notions: Hollywood was a place of police dogs, heartbreak, Italian villas, Spanish houses, and beautiful girls. It had become the capital of insouciance and bad taste, of flashy marriages and casual adulteries. Girls with good looks and savvy mothers — like the Talmadge sisters, Norma and Constance — married the big-money producers or held off for brief affairs and long lives of good times, expensive clothes, and stunning jewels. Others, including Lillian Gish, had serious ambitions of achieving high art and were considered aloof by the rest of the artificial little community that grew up around the new industry. Hollywood, in the twenties, was a makeshift colony peddling dreams and romance, intent on avoiding boredom and finding amusements of a nonintellectual kind. The mistakes and the scandals were removed like bad odors — with the same ease with which Norma Talmadge got rid of the cigar smoke from the all-night poker games of her husband, Joe Schenck, by spraying the area liberally with Shalimar perfume.

If Fitzgerald had intended to keep his Hollywood stint a secret, he plainly had made a bad job of it. A Montgomery newspaper carried a squib about his assignment and departure for the coast. And the studio press agents were busy grinding out advance releases even before his arrival. It was variously reported that Fitzgerald, billed as "one of America's foremost young short story writers and novelists" had joined "the Hollywood game of authors" and would fashion "one of his blonde, reckless, wilful and irresponsible girls" for Constance Talmadge. Fitzgerald arrived in Los Angeles in a flurry of hype and clichés. Once there, he gave interviews to the local press and the movie magazines. Gossip columnists said that he was "working like a dog" in his Ambassador suite. Margaret Reid scooped up his opinions on the reigning cinema queens for a lengthy article in *Motion Picture* magazine: Clara Bow, "impudent, superbly assured . . . briefly clad and 'hard-berled' as possible"; Joan Crawford, "doubtless the best example of the dramatic flapper . . . dancing deliciously, laughing a great deal with wide, hurt eyes"; Colleen Moore, "the young collegiate—the carefree, lovable child who rules bewildered but adoring parents with an iron hand." The praise for his prospective star was overwhelming and slightly suspect: "Constance Talmadge is the epitome of young sophistication. She is the deft princess of lingerie—and love—plus humor. She is Fifth Avenue and diamonds and Cattleya orchids and Europe every year. . . . She is the flapper *de luxe*."

They went to parties at Carmel Myers' and teas with Ronald Coleman. They visited Richard Barthelmess on a movie set; they were photographed with Wallace Beery and the fashionable illustrator Harrison Fisher. They were introduced to Lady Diana Manners, appearing in *The Miracle*. ("She is the prettiest lady I have ever seen," Zelda assured Scottie, "and I have been kissing the cross you sent me every day to try to turn into a lady like her.") They were twice invited to Pickfair, the estate of America's sweethearts, Mary Pickford and Douglas Fairbanks. In an ebullient mood, Fitzgerald cashed a hundred dollars into change and threw it up against the hotel windows, shouting, "It's money, it's money, it's money! It's free!" At one party, he and Zelda collected all the ladies' purses and, sneaking into the hostess's kitchen, cooked them up in a savory tomato soup.

James Montgomery Flagg, the originator of the World War I poster of Uncle Sam ("I Want You"), remembered an unsavory expedition with the young Fitzgeralds to visit the legendary screenwriter John Monk Saunders, who had a reputation as a very effective lady's man. It was in the middle of the night when the Fitzgeralds roused their victim. He came down dressed in pajamas and his Sulka dressing gown to give the unexpected visitors drinks. Zelda sat next to him on the sofa, inhaling deep breaths from his manly chest and exclaiming how lovely he smelled. Then she picked up a handy pair of shears and offered to "perform a quick operation" that would put an end to all his earthly troubles. En route back to the hotel, Fitzgerald kept turning back to Flagg and exclaiming, "God! But you look old!" The illustrator's feelings about the Fitzgeralds — "These charming young people" — were understandable: "If I had [never] seen them again, it would have been too soon." Townsend Martin's friend, the actress Louise Brooks, fresh in Hollywood and under contract to Paramount, had a rather different but equally vivid impression of the pair when she met them in their Ambassador suite: "They were sitting close together on a sofa, like a comedy team, and the first thing that struck me was how *small* they were." She had come to meet the famous writer, "but what dominated the room was the blazing intelligence of Zelda's profile. It shocked me. It was the profile of a witch."

They attended a famous costume party, given by Samuel Goldwyn for the Talmadge sisters. Uninvited, they simply turned up at the door on hands and knees, barking to be let in. Once admitted, Zelda swept upstairs to the bathroom, ran the water, stripped, lounged in the tub, rose, dried her hair, and went downstairs to join the crowd. The actress Colleen Moore, about to leave when the Fitzgeralds arrived, was astonished by Zelda's aplomb and waited through the whole performance. "Even in Hollywood the Fitzgeralds were unique," she maintained. But Zelda had been frankly bored at a party at Colleen Moore's, where the guests had all sat around glumly sizing up one another. All she could remember was "the aura of House-detective that pervaded the gathering."

Zelda was often bored in Hollywood. "I am trying to make 'ole Massa' let me come east alone *now* — This very minute — but NO is all I get in answer," she wrote Scottie. "If we ever get out of here I will *never go near* another moving picture theatre or actor again." She preferred to be in Paris or even New York, where "there's enough mischief for every-body." One reason for her feeling out of it, perhaps, was an attractive young starlet, Lois Moran, with whom Fitzgerald was carrying on a flirtation. Moran, only seventeen and a protégée of Sam Goldwyn's, had made her debut in *Stella Dallas*. A newspaper column, a typical piece of Hollywood press agentry, pasted into a Fitzgerald scrapbook, shows a pert young face, bright eyes, and an authentic Hollywood smile. The accompanying text indicates that she is a dedicated actress with intellectual interests. Her favorite authors are listed as "Romain Rolland, F. Scott Fitzgerald, Frederick Nietzche [*sic*] and Rupert Brooke." She is interested in philosophy and swimming, likes to wear "backless evening clothes," and collects wristwatches, which she always manages to break.

The reading list and the article itself suggest that Fitzgerald may already have taken a hand in her literary education and her public relations propaganda. That he was decidedly interested in the girl herself is clear from his prompt use of her in one of his short stories, "Jacob's Ladder," written a few months after the Hollywood excursion. The heroine, Jenny Delehanty, is depicted as a beautiful, hoydenish shop girl ("It was the face of a dark saint with tender, luminous eyes") whom the thirty-three-year-old hero, Jacob Booth, molds into a movie star. Lois Moran was obviously flattered by Fitzgerald's attentions. She even went so far as to suggest that Fitzgerald take a screen test so that he could appear in a film with her. But Fitzgerald did not pursue the opportunity any further than making the test. Zelda, writing to Scottie, was disappointed: "Daddy was offered a job to be a leading man in a picture with Lois Moran!! But he wouldn't do it. I wanted him to, because he would have made so much money and we could all have spent it, but he said I was silly."

Fitzgerald's flirtation with Lois Moran, it seems, did not go very far and never became an affair. Like many youthful starlets in Hollywood—among them the Talmadge sisters and Norma Shearer —Lois Moran had a mother who served as both an unofficial agent and a moral watchdog. Mrs. Moran, who apparently encouraged the relationship with Scott, was always present at their meetings. Even so, Zelda became bitterly jealous of the time Fitzgerald spent with the young actress, and the two had frequent and bitter quarrels. Later, Zelda accused him of engaging in "flagrantly sentimental relations with a child" while forbidding her to go out on her own dates: "You said you wanted nothing more from me in all your life, though you made a scene when Carl [Van Vechten] suggested that I go to dinner with him and Betty Compson." In the course of one of their arguments, Fitzgerald scornfully told Zelda that at least Lois

Moran was doing something useful with her time and her talents. It was a bitter indictment for Zelda, who was feeling out of place and unnecessary. ("Everybody here is very clever and can nearly all dance and sing and play and I feel very stupid," she wrote to Scottie.) One evening when Fitzgerald had taken the Morans out to dinner, Zelda burned her clothes in the hotel bathtub. If, as Nancy Milford indicates in her biography, Zelda burned the clothes that she had designed and made, then it was more than an act of retaliation. It also represented a kind of remorseless self-destruction, refuting Fitzgerald's accusations by totally destroying the one creative effort she had been able to make and that he had failed to appreciate.

The Hollywood trip was to result in other forms of bitterness. At some point Fitzgerald quarreled with Constance Talmadge, and that seems to have been a factor in the studio's decision to drop the script Fitzgerald wrote. However, both the premise of the story and the scenario he had written for Talmadge were weak. *Lipstick* was a familiar reprise of the college boy and the streetwise girl that he had used in "Head and Shoulders," only this time it dealt with a girl who was unfairly jailed and a boy from a college much like Princeton. She is given a magic lipstick that makes every man want to kiss her and eventually wins the snooty college boy away from the debutante. It was a slight and improbable idea, and the scenario aimed at clever writing that was hardly practical for the film medium: "School was over. The happy children, their books swinging carelessly at a strap's end, tripped out into the Spring fields — Wait a minute, that's the wrong story."

If Fitzgerald had gone to Hollywood fired up to show the industry a thing or two, he failed badly. As he later admitted, he had gone there "confident to the point of conceit." He still believed in himself as a man of the world. But he experienced a failure of nerve: "I woke up in Hollywood no longer my egotistic, certain self but a mixture of Ernest in fine clothes and Gerald with a career — and Charlie McArthur with a past." Anyone who could restore his faith in himself, as Lois Moran did, was "precious" to him. The Hollywood experience proved to be a costly one; the money he was paid did not cover the expenses of their trip, and there was no $12,500 payment forthcoming. Although Harold Ober tried to place the screen treatment of *Lipstick* elsewhere, it was never produced.

What Fitzgerald had gained, however, was an acquaintance with two Hollywood figures who would play important parts in his subsequent novels. The first was Lois Moran, whose role as the ingénue starlet was to figure first in several of Fitzgerald's short stories and eventually come to rest, along with her mother's, in *Tender Is the Night*. The second was Irving Thalberg, in 1927 the boy wonder of the film industry, who would be transformed into the tragic hero, Monroe Stahr, of Fitzgerald's unfinished novel, *The Last Tycoon*. Thalberg, twenty-seven at the time, was small, dark, physically frail, suffering from a congenital heart condition. He had a reputation as a wizard who commanded box office successes without the loss of artistry — precisely the role Fitzgerald had intended to play both as a novelist and screenwriter. It was Thalberg, as a youthful second vice-president and supervisor of production, who promoted some of Hollywood's most glamorous women (Garbo, Joan Crawford, and his wife-to-be, Norma Shearer), who had saved the floundering Roman production of *Ben Hur* from financial disaster by bringing it home to Culver City and making a proper spectacle of it, with chariot races and a cast of thousands, who cannily championed directors like King Vidor against the conservative studio heads.

Fitzgerald was never to forget the one brief meeting he had alone with the legendary producer, held in the Metro-Goldwyn-Mayer studio cafeteria. Thalberg, with immense self-importance and the ponderous egotism of his youth, delivered one of the lengthy parables about the perils and loneliness of leadership that he customarily gave to authors, stagehands, and crewmen.

> Scottie, supposing there's got to be a road through a mountain — a railroad and two or three surveyors and people come to you and you believe some of them and some of them you don't believe; but all in all, there seems to be half a dozen possible roads through those mountains. . . . Now suppose you happen to be the top man, there's a point where you don't exercise the faculty of judgment in the ordinary way, but simply the faculty of arbitrary decision. You say, "Well, I think we will put the road there," and you trace it with your finger and you know in your secret heart and no one else knows, that you have no reason for putting the road there rather than in several other different courses. . . . But when you're planning a new enterprise on a grand scale, the people under you mustn't ever know or guess that you're in doubt because they've all got to have something to look up to. . . .

Fitzgerald took the long-winded sermon to heart and recalled it in detail some twelve years later, when be began making notes for *The Last Tycoon*. Thalberg also had a reputation for keeping screenwriters waiting hour after hour for conferences. Anita Loos, who had a saucy attitude toward the industry, devised a scheme of knitting a scarf —like Madame Defarge—while cooling her heels in Irving's outer office. It was twice her diminutive height when she was finished, and at her salary of $2500 a week, she calculated that it had cost Metro-Goldwyn-Mayer $20,000.

They had planned to stay for three weeks, but it was eight before the Fitzgeralds left Hollywood. As a memento of their stay, they piled up the furniture in their hotel room and crowned it with their unpaid bills. Lois Moran sent a parting telegram, which they received en route: BOOTLEGGERS GONE OUT OF BUSINESS COTTON CLUB CLOSED ALL FLAGS AT HALF MAST. . . . BOTTLES OF LOVE TO YOU BOTH. But a letter addressed to "Darling Scott" was more provocative. "I miss you enormously," she wrote. "Life is exceedingly dull out here now. . . . I'm wondering what sort of trip you had—You must have spent all your time filling out telegraph blanks, judging from the numerous and hectic wires Carmel, John [Barrymore] and I received." Fitzgerald had obviously taken the young girl's education in hand, concerned as he was about her intellectual development. He was once more playing Pygmalion and had given her some assigned readings. She thanked him for David Garnett's *The Sailor's Return* and Hemingway's *The Sun Also Rises*. "The first," she commented, "was so tragically real and the second caught that feeling of unrest very perfectly."

On the train trip east, Fitzgerald and Zelda had another bitter quarrel about Lois Moran. But she went the young starlet, with her battered wristwatches, one better. Zelda reportedly threw out of the train window the expensive diamond and platinum watch Fitzgerald had given her during their courtship. Certainly that would fit the pattern of Zelda's destructive acts turned against herself and whatever she considered valuable. But Zelda's Montgomery confidante, Sara Mayfield, maintained that the wristwatch story was an invention; Zelda had carelessly left the watch on a bathroom commode and it had accidently been brushed into the toilet and flushed down the drain.

It was not long after the Fitzgeralds' return east that they received a scatological welcome home note from H. L. Mencken:

Thank God you have escaped alive! I was full of fears for you. If Los Angeles is not the one authentic rectum of civilization, then I am no anatomist. Any time you want to go out again and burn it down, count me in.

⌐▰◢▬◣▱

Within the year, Fitzgerald wrote two stories based on his Hollywood excursion and his "flagrantly sentimental relations" with a teen-age starlet. "Jacob's Ladder," written a few months after his departure from the film capital, appeared in the August 20, 1927, issue of *The Saturday Evening Post;* "Magnetism" was completed by the end of the year and was published in the March 3, 1928, issue of the same magazine. The hero of the earliest and probably most significant treatment of his recent experiences, Jake Booth, exemplified one of Fitzgerald's youthful ambitions: "Once he had possessed a tenor voice with destiny in it." But Jake has lost his gift by abusing it. Now, he has made a fortune in real estate. He is a restless Pygmalion of the brash sixteen-year-old shop girl, Jenny, whom he promotes to stardom — tutoring her on the management of her career, buying her the proper clothes, cautioning her against drinking and promiscuity. He pushes Jenny's career so successfully with a Long Island film director that she is given a Hollywood contract. When Jenny leaves for the West Coast — in one of those characteristic gender reversals of Fitzgerald stories — Jake sends her a telegram that is the echo of the one Lois Moran sent him: NEW YORK DESOLATE . . . THE NIGHT CLUBS ALL CLOSED BLACK WREATHS ON THE STATUE OF CIVIC VIRTUE. . . . For Fitzgerald, however, fiction quite often served as a redress against life. The action in "Jacob's Ladder" is the reverse of life: Jenny heads toward success, whereas Fitzgerald had quit Hollywood in defeat.

One of the principal problems in dealing with Fitzgerald as a writer is that one's knowledge of his dissipated life may obscure one's perception of his striking talents as a writer — his eye for telling detail, his sense of the undercurrent of an occasion. "Jacob's Ladder" is not one of his major stories, but it is one of the more revealing examples of how much Fitzgerald was able to grasp as a writer, no matter how badly he might be behaving as a man in the midst of an event. In the story, Fitzgerald not only gives a convincing portrayal of Jenny's coming-of-age, of her mild flirtations with leading men, of her difference from the run-of-the-mill starlets in the Hollywood colony, but it is clear in his account of Jake's visit to the West Coast that he had understood a great deal about Hollywood social life. He describes one of the aimless and protracted Sundays:

> At the first tea, Jacob noticed that there was an enormous preponderance of women over men, and of supernumeraries — lady journalists, cameramen's daughters, cutters' wives — over people of importance. A young Latin named Raffino appeared for a brief moment, spoke to Jenny and departed; several stars passed through, asking about children's health with a domesticity that was somewhat overpowering. Another group of celebrities posed immobile, statue-like, in a corner. There was a somewhat inebriated and very much excited author apparently trying to make engagements with one girl after another.

At the final party, a buffet supper:

> The totality of the cocktails Jacob had swallowed was affecting him pleasantly, but try as he might, the plot of the party — the key on which he could find ease and tranquillity — eluded him. There was something tense in the air — something competitive and insecure. Conversations with the men had a way of becoming empty and overjovial or else melting off into a sort of suspicion. The women were nicer.

Although it was intended for the commercial market, "Jacob's Ladder" is a highly commendable tale. What Fitzgerald effectively created is a tender story of mismatched sexual desires, of lost opportunities. In New York, Jenny, in her gratitude, makes a fumbling advance toward the man who has befriended her. But Jake is not responsive:

> Hesitating tentatively, he kissed her and again he was chilled by the innocence of her kiss, the eyes that at the moment of contact looked beyond him out into the darkness of the night, the darkness of the world. She did not know yet that splendor was something in the heart; at the moment when she should realize that and melt into the passion of the universe he could take her without question or regret.

Jake is another of Fitzgerald's moralistic lovers. Unfortunately, his moment never comes. Later, when he is caught up in the glamour of Jenny's success, jealous of her attention to handsome actors, Jake convinces himself that he is in love with her. With Fitzgerald, it is never quite clear whether he is repeating a successful fictional ploy or rendering a different version of an urgent theme. In "Jacob's Ladder" he repeats the magical refrain that Gatsby had so wanted Daisy to say to Tom Buchanan—"that you never loved him." There, it was meant to be a moment of scathing truth. But this time it has the aura of romance. Jake Booth, lying awake, conjures up an image of Jenny, "an image that would endure as long as love itself, or even longer—not to perish till he could say, 'I never really loved her.' " What Jake is left with is the overblown image of the movie screen, the kind of promissory image that stirs the imagination of Jake's chauffeur and the frisky bellboys at the Plaza, when Jenny, having fallen in love with a film director, comes to New York to seek Jake's approval. There are touches of mawkishness at the end of the story, but there is a genuinely affecting final moment, when the abandoned Jake, walking down Broadway, sees Jenny's name in lights on a theater marquee and, like the other consumers of dreams, buys his ticket and walks down the aisle to sit in "the fast-throbbing darkness."

What is ironic in this short story is that Fitzgerald appears to have appropriated the theme of love balked by impotence from Hemingway, whom he had so roundly criticized for mishandling it in *The Sun Also Rises*. Strangely, too, the model for his heroine was Lois Moran, the starlet to whom he had given Hemingway's novel. Whether it was a case of professional rivalry, an intentional gambit, or some form of unconscious imitation is not patently clear. But there is one bit of minor evidence that Fitzgerald had had Hemingway in mind while writing "Jacob's Ladder." Fitzgerald's hero is named Jake Booth, and Hemingway's is Jake Barnes.

"Magnetism" is a much more contrived short story. The hero is George Hannaford, a handsome, thirty-year-old film actor who has the magnetism that Fitzgerald felt he lacked. Not only Hannaford's adoring fans, but his studio script girl and his Mexican maidservant dream wasted dreams of affairs with him. George is besieged by women but remains politely aloof. Perhaps he is the morally fastidious film idol Fitzgerald imagined he would himself have been if he had seriously considered the idea of a film career.

Hannaford and his wife, Kay, a former Ziegfeld Follies showgirl, are considered the ideal Hollywood couple, but their marriage, in fact, has grown stale. Lately, George has begun to entertain vague and dreamy thoughts about an eighteen-year-old ingénue, Helen Avery. Helen, though young, is too ambitious and uncertain about her career to risk any scandal. The would-be lovers, however, come to a quiet recognition of their feelings for one another. But Helen has the kind of humor with which Fitzgerald endowed his feminine characters, though seldom his stuffy males. She laughs and admits, "Oh, we're such actors, George—you and I."

The plot is a hodgepodge. Kay, out of jealousy, flirts with another man. The rejected script girl tries blackmail and then attempts suicide. There is a reconciliation of sorts between George and Kay. The Mexican girl, Dolores, having staved off the imploring telephone calls of Helen Avery (who has changed her mind), receives condescending praise from the kindly George. At the end, Dolores is left sitting on the stoop, watching the thin, pale California moon as it rises.

It could hardly have escaped Zelda's notice that in both stories Fitzgerald exonerated himself of having had any serious affair with Lois Moran. Nor could she have overlooked Fitzgerald's making use of the brief flirtation, as he had once used their courtship and her diaries and letters in creating different versions of his heroine, the girl with a talent. Perhaps she recognized in "Jacob's Ladder" some element of her husband's attraction to his young protégée in Jake Booth's response: "He rode away in a mood of exultation, living more deeply in her youth and future than he had lived in himself for years." And perhaps she read in "Magnetism" some reprimand to herself in Fitzgerald's description of Kay Hannaford, a minor entertainer saddled with a child (and an English nanny), as being "one of those people who are famous far beyond their actual achievement."

Zelda, too, would write about their Hollywood episode, in a story titled "The Millionaire's Girl," which appeared in the May 3, 1930, issue of *The Saturday Evening Post.* The heroine is a sixteen-year-old aspiring entertainer who has some touch of scandal in her background. Caroline is a free spirit: "Her story, to date, was short and hysterical—a runaway marriage—annulled immediately—a year in small parts on the New York stage, and the scandalous journalism that followed that affair of Brooklyn Bridge." Caroline is something of a gold digger. When she meets Barry, "the heir to fantastic millions," she sets her sights on him and is successful. But Barry's family disapproves of their forthcoming marriage and attempts to buy her off. She accepts an expensive car and a sizable check, rather disingenuously treating them as gifts. Caroline and Barry have a very public and very bitter quarrel in Ciro's restaurant

—with a good deal of attendant publicity—and Barry heads for Europe and Caroline for the West Coast, where she plans to make a career for herself in the movies.

Certain elements in Zelda's story—the Brooklyn Bridge scandal, the quarrel in the restaurant—may have a topical significance that is not readily recoverable. In the sequence of stories about modern women that Zelda wrote for *College Humor* magazine, Zelda borrowed bits and pieces of personal history from the careers of movie stars and debutantes like Mary Hay and Josephine Ordway, whom she had met or read about, to fill out the lives of the heroines in stories like "The Girl with Talent" and "The Girl the Prince Liked." It was probably a ficitional device she had picked up from Fitzgerald, who regularly borrowed the names and lives of friends and professional acquaintances in order to give an air of authenticity to the fictional alter egos he created for himself and Zelda.

Zelda's heroines may have professional résumés and personal histories that differ from hers, but they all have one thing in common: the desperate ambition to be something, to be someone other than "Miss Alabama Nobody." In "A Millionaire's Girl," Zelda wrote herself into the role of the young film actress, as is clear from her description of Caroline: "She learned to accentuate a slight defect in her lovely face with heavy make-up, so that her wide cheek-bones gave her a Tatar look under the thick, creamy powder." But part of her motivation may have been the desire to make it evident that her ingénue was a more forceful and tragic figure than either the well-mannered Lois Moran or her fictional counterpart, Jenny Prince. Zelda's narrator, encountering Caroline on her transcontinental train ride to California after the break with Barry, describes her as follows:

> She was royalty in exile. From the slope of her shoulders to the eloquent inactivity of her hands her whole person cried out, "This is the way I am, and I'm going to stick by it." Now I knew that Caroline had not a bit of that fading-violets closing-episode note of the minor lyric poet that makes people run from things in her erstwhile personality. . . .

Zelda had a flair for the ironies of a situation, if not for the complications of plot. She describes Caroline's rise to dubious stardom: "People knew her by name; her career was getting underway. She drank little and spent the mornings having herself pummeled and pounded into a nervously receptive state that was, for film purposes, the equivalent of dramatic ability." At the same time, it is both an indulgent fantasy about, and a caustic put-down of, a Hollywood career.

On the night that Caroline's big movie has its première, Caroline learns from a newspaper headline that Barry plans to marry a wealthy woman in Paris. She attempts suicide, upstaging both her own opening and Barry's engagement. Her dramatic action, however, brings the couple together again, and they marry. But Zelda avoids the nostalgic, faded-flowers type of ending—the note of the minor lyric poet or of her husband's two stories. Caroline gives up her film career, but the conventional happy ending is soured:

> She married him, of course, and since she left the films on that occasion, they have both had much to reproach each other for. That was three years ago, and so far they have kept their quarrels out of the divorce courts, but I somehow think you can't go on forever protecting quarrels, and that romances born in violence and suspicion will end themselves on the same note; though, of course, I am a cynical person and, perhaps, no competent judge of idyllic young love affairs.

Zelda wrote her story three years after her husband had indulged in just such an "idyllic" love affair with Lois Moran. But what is most significant about the three stories that grew out of that episode in their lives is that they illustrate one of the more unusual features of the Fitzgerald marriage. They were able to use their fictional stories to send each other signals, warnings, provide excuses and justifications for their behavior. Could Fitzgerald have missed the message of Zelda's final paragraph—that their marriage was in trouble?

II

"It is in the thirties that we want friends," Fitzgerald would write. "In the forties we know they won't save us any more than love did." Fitzgerald was thirty, that spring of 1927 when he rented Ellerslie, a Greek Revival mansion on the banks of the Delaware River near Wilmington. He wanted to get away from New York, though not *too* far away, in order to finish his overdue novel, but it was an exercise in self-defeat. During the two years that the Fitzgeralds lived in Ellerslie, there were frequent trips to New York to escape the isolation of Wilmington, and many long weekend parties at Ellerslie to which Fitzgerald summoned his friends. "Deluxe service, hot & cold water, American bar," he promised Edmund Wilson, trying to entice him to visit.

It was Fitzgerald's former Princeton roommate, John Biggs—now a practicing lawyer in Wilmington and a sometime writer, whose novel, *Demigods,* Fitzgerald had encouraged Scribner's to publish in 1926—who found the house for him. They leased it for $150 a month. It was a sprawling establishment with so many rooms, they were never sure of the exact count. A huge portico with Doric columns faced the great stretch of lawn punctuated with old chestnut trees. The view beyond the yard stretched over sand flats toward a buoy station with bright red roofs. Zelda remembered the remnants of an antebellum garden blooming with violets when they arrived —and, later, hedges of white roses and climbing yellow roses that were as blowsy as crumpled tissue paper. Decorating the large, high-ceilinged rooms on the first floor was a challenge, and Zelda designed oversized furniture that had to be made in Philadelphia. With her flair for the unusual, she painted the garden furniture with maps of France.

Zelda's urgent decorating and housekeeping activities, her attempts to make the huge ark livable, were undoubtedly a refutation of Fitzgerald's claims that she wasted her time and talents. But Ellerslie was a house that required servants. They had Marie, a gawky black maid, and Ella, another black, who sang spirituals in the kitchen and was terrified of the fierce lightning storms that were frequent in the region. For the first few months after the move to Ellerslie, they still had Nanny to take care of Scottie. When she left, they hired "Mademoiselle," who, according to Zelda, reeked of sachet and had large brown eyes that "followed a person about like a mop." Writing to Carl Van Vechten, Zelda confessed that Mademoiselle was unnerving: "She is a great trial, but I find her philosophy so uplifting and her tongue so sharp that I am afraid to fire her—I will surely have to go to France to get rid of her."

SNAPSHOTS: In the photos taken in front of the mansion—snapshots of the most banal kind—the little group stands clustered together on a bright day with a ruffling wind. It is the weekend of

May 21 and the Fitzgeralds' first large house party. The guest of honor is Lois Moran, down from New York and chaperoned by her mother. The other guests are Ernest Boyd, the critic and friend of Mencken, and Teddy Chanler. Carl Van Vechten has also been invited.

In the snapshots, Lois Moran is dressed in prim fashion, in a light-colored dress buttoned up to the neck, with a demure little collar. She wears light-colored stockings and light shoes and looks more like a nurse on her day off than a Hollywood starlet. Fitzgerald, looking dapper and avuncular, offers his arm. He is wearing a light jacket and trousers, white shoes. He is beaming like a child on his birthday, full of high spirits and fun. Boyd, like Chanler, is formally dressed, with a wing collar and black tie, looking jaunty as he stands on the rough-chopped grass. He was a man with a refreshing sense of Irish irreverence. In his Dublin youth, he had modeled as the figure for Christ for a church window, and in his later years he liked to claim a resemblance to the Master. Once, he sent Anita Loos a postcard of this window-portrait of himself with the message "Anita, what a friend you have in Jesus!" Fitzgerald, when he read Boyd's profile of him in *Portraits: Real and Imaginary,* claimed that he was "honestly delighted." But in his usual fashion, he wrote to Max Perkins that he found Boyd's critical writing very plausible and very dead.

There is a photo of Mrs. Moran with the group (Scott is absent, presumably taking the picture; Zelda does not appear). She looks amazingly like an older version of her daughter: the same prissy outfit, hairdo, the same squinting smile in the too-bright, unflattering sunlight. Both have that upward glance that Fitzgerald considered so appealing in women. Lois Moran, recalling the visit years later, remembered no unpleasantness nor any undercurrent of jealousy on Zelda's part. What she did recall from that weekend was the thrilling news of Lindbergh's landing at Le Bourget airport. There was a picnic on the river bank, and for a moment the whole party stood silent, looking eastward toward the sky. Zelda had rather different recollections of the party. Her account of the young starlet has some acid touches: "She had no definite characteristics of her own save a slight ebullient hysteria about romance. She walked in the moon by the river. Her hair was tight about her head and she was lush and like a milkmaid."

Zelda's correspondence with Van Vechten suggests that there was a good deal of heaving drinking that weekend and some kind of emotional disturbance.

> From the depths of my polluted soul [she wrote Van Vechten a week later] I am sorry that the week-end was such a mess. Do forgive my iniquities and my putrid drunkenness. This *was* such a nice place, and it should have been a good party if I had not explored my abysses in public — Anyhow, please realize that I am sorry and contrite and thoroughly miserable with the knowledge that it would be just the same again if I got so drunk.

It is difficult to know just how genuine her act of contrition was. Two days later, she was writing Van Vechten in her usual bantering style to thank him for a gift of a cocktail shaker: "You were very sweet to make such a desirable contribution to the Fitzgerald household." Then she added, archly, "It's such a nice one that I have been looking about to see what damage you must have done." Other gifts followed: bootleg recordings by black singers, including one by Bessie Smith. "I love 'Squeeze Me' so much," Zelda wrote, "that it has distracted me from being taken up by Philadelphia society." As for another of the "hot" selections, Zelda warned that it was doing "something biological to me by degrees. You are an angel of a very colored God to send them." In return, she offered to give Van Vechten an oddly phallic present, "a shining sword which collapses like a rubber dagger."

Fitzgerald seems to have enjoyed Van Vechten's company, though in the privacy of his journals he referred to him as a "pederast." It is not always clear how genuine he was in his praise of Van Vechten's competent but frothy novels. But even late in his career, Fitzgerald tried to promote Van Vechten's reputation as a discoverer of new talent — to a doubtful H. L. Mencken. Mencken wrote back: "Carl is a great fan for literary oddities, and whenever he happens upon delicatessen of that sort he starts beating the drums. To be sure, he has thus made some propaganda for really first-rate authors, but I think it is only fair to say that he has also whooped up some duds."

Zelda's comic friendship with Van Vechten was never clouded by any taint of literary rivalry. And her letters to him from Ellerslie are among the liveliest, giving him reports of developments on the bank of the Delaware, and of their growing menagerie — a cat named Chat and two dogs from a local pound: "One of them is splotchy but mostly white with whiskers although he is sick now, so his name is Ezra Pound. The other is named Bouillabaisse or Muddy Water or Jerry. He doesn't answer to any of them so it doesn't matter." Her feelings for him were evidently genuine. In a clinical autobiography written for her psychiatrists, Zelda later spoke of an untroubled appreciation: "Carl is divine. . . . He is an experimentalist and connoisseur. . . . [He] saved my letters and collects first editions in friends whom he vivisects with rapt interest. He's a dramatist at heart. Our relations were very impersonal but Carl was a fine friend."

Despite the teasing implications of their letters, there was clearly no question of any sexual attraction between the two. But that seems not to have been the case with another of the party guests, Teddy Chanler, whom Zelda described, oddly, as "an instrument of our lost republic." Evidently that weekend they paid a visit to a local amusement park that the Fitzgeralds often frequented when they were in a partying mood. (Once they brought home the fortuneteller in order to exorcise the reputed Ellerslie ghost. But the fortuneteller turned out to be as convivial as her host and hostess and began reciting Vachel Lindsay, which did not have the desired effect.) According to Zelda, Chanler "could understand why an amusement park is the best place to be amorous — it's something about the white-washed trees and the smell of peanuts and the jogging of the infernal machines for riding." Her description seems to corroborate John Dos Passos' suspicions about the ride he and Zelda had taken together on the Ferris wheel a few years earlier.

Fitzgerald's preoccupation with Lois Moran did not end with the housewarming party. He saw her on a few more occasions during visits she made to New York. Nor was Zelda the only person affected by his infatuation with the girl. At some point, Fitzgerald had words with John Barrymore on the subject of Moran. It is not clear when the argument occurred, nor what the precise cause was. But Barrymore had come east in the early spring for the New York première of his film *Beloved Rogue*, based more than loosely on the life and loves of François Villon. It was written by his wife, Michael Strange, the popular novelist and playwright, from whom he was separated. (Barrymore, it is said, thought even less of his performance than the critics. Watching a screening, he called out from the rear balcony, "Call yourself an actor? My God, what a ham!")

Fitzgerald evidently blurted out the details of his squabble with Barrymore, some time late in June, during the course of an extended cocktail hour with a new acquaintance, Charles Green Shaw, that began at the Meadowbrook restaurant and ended at the Plaza, where the two men met Zelda. As usual, after such sessions of boozy personal revelation, Fitzgerald had second thoughts. He wrote Shaw afterward:

> Dear Charlie, Its occurred to me, and worried me, that I may [have] given you a false impression in that Barrymore matter, of having interfered in Lois's affairs. I didn't. We were both pretty tight; he made this remark and I simply called him on it that was all. The whole incident didn't take a minute & was probably aggravated by the fact that we'd had words when he was rude to Zelda the week before. Anyhow please treat the thing as confidential.

Shaw, whom Fitzgerald probably met that summer of 1927, was one of those attractive, wide-ranging New York personalities of the period, a minor writer and journalist, a friend of Nathan, Mencken, and Anita Loos. Tall, husky, and handsome, with dark, sleeked-down hair — his Yale classmate Cole Porter called him "Big Boy" — he was an avid theatergoer, a connoisseur of New York nightspots, a regular guest at Mrs. Vanderbilt's Christmas Eve parties, and a summer resident of Newport. He wrote articles and interviews for *Vanity Fair* and *The New Yorker,* and later, during the forties, became an abstract painter of serious reputation. Fitzgerald offered Shaw some mild praise and astute critical advice on his first novel, *Heart in a Hurricane.* He called it "a damn good piece of humorous writing from end to end." But he added: "I wish you'd try something with a plot, or an interrelation between two or more characters, running through the whole book. Episodes held together by an 'idea,' in its fragilest sense, don't give the opportunity for workmanship or for really *effective* effects."

On the basis of their brief meetings, Shaw wrote a chatty sketch about Fitzgerald that appeared in his book *The Low-Down,* which was published the following year. Oddly, but aptly, he described Fitzgerald as a "congenitally shy" man who managed to conceal the fact. The sketch was one of those celebrity studies that concerns itself even with the subject's shirt labels. Fitzgerald, Shaw noted, wore "green or mauve" suits made by Davies & Son ("19–20 Hanover Street, London, W.1") and shirts from Hilditch & Key, also of London. His principal dislikes were "Sunday, Washington, D.C., cold weather, Bohemians, the managing type of American woman, avarice and dullness." Perhaps with a stroke of perversity, Fitzgerald informed Shaw that André Gide was currently his favorite author.

There is some significance, considering the marital cold war between the Fitzgeralds, in Fitzgerald's describing an ideal woman as someone who more closely resembled Lois Moran than Zelda: "His preference in women is a not-too-light blonde, who is intelligent, unopinionated and responsive." Fitzgerald's greatest interests were listed as "scandal touching upon his friends, everything about the late war, discovering new men and books of promise, Princeton and people with extraordinary charm." As for politics, Shaw informed the reader, Fitzgerald "is an autocrat in theory but a socialist in practice, and with respect to the Younger Generation, he says, he feels like an old man."

Shaw touched briefly on Fitzgerald's professional habits; "When writing, he is usually nervous and irritable and will engulf, during his labors, innumerable cups of Coca-Cola. He writes entirely in pencil and makes from two to four drafts, depending upon the class of work involved. While so engaged, he will consume about half a carton of Chesterfield cigarettes."

Portrait of the author at age thirty.

But for the first ten months of his residence at Ellerslie, the author wrote very little. Fitzgerald seemed incapable of settling down to work, whatever his usual routine: "He ordinarily rises about eleven o'clock and does most of his work from 5. P.M. to 3:30 A.M." he had informed Shaw. Little or nothing was accomplished on his novel, *The Boy Who Killed His Mother.* Considering that "the managing type of American woman" was a subject on his mind during that first year at Ellerslie, the title has an added significance. During that year, he wrote only two important stories — "Jacob's Ladder" and "Magnetism" — and four minor ones — "The Love Boat," "A Short Trip Home," "Outside the Cabinet-Maker's," and "The Bowl" — as well as an article, "Princeton," his tribute to his alma mater, written for *College Humor.*

In July there was a flurry of excitement when he wired Ober with a hot idea, an article to be called "Sissy America," dealing with the overeducated American woman and her domination of the generally ineffectual American male, who managed to be successful only in the line of business. Fitzgerald maintained that he would not propose any remedies nor put blame anywhere but on the man for letting the control slip from his hands. But it would be nonetheless "A BITTER AND SENSATIONAL ARRAINMENT OF CONTEMPORARY MALE." He suggested that Ober take it up with *The Saturday Evening Post*.

He was not surprised that the *Post* was wary of the subject and preferred to see a two- or three-page description before making a decision. So Fitzgerald told Ober that he would go ahead with the article anyway, if there were any prospects of his selling it elsewhere. But when the *Post* declined, Fitzgerald delayed, promising Ober throughout July and August that the article was finished or nearly finished, until finally, on September 1, he admitted in a wire that the article was "ROTTEN" and that he was working on a two-part "SOPHISTICATED FOOTBALL STORY," which he expected to complete in a week. He asked Ober to see whether the *Post* could schedule it for one of the fall issues, during the football season.

Throughout that summer and fall, Fitzgerald's telegrams to Ober promised that stories would be completed tomorrow or on the following day, that they were finished but in the hands of a typist, or that he would bring them to New York on the Tuesday of one week or the Thursday of the next. The telegram about "The Love Boat" read, WILL BE UP WITH STORY FRIDAY FITZGERALD. But Ober's scribbled note was "He didn't come!" When Ober wrote, asking him to send at least part of the proposed football story, for which the *Post* was waiting, Fitzgerald wired him a long-winded excuse and then, three days later, wired him again, confessing that the story was "JUST AN AWFUL MESS" and that he had better tackle something else. In the end, the football story was rewritten as "The Bowl," but not until December, too late for the current season.

The terrible irony of Fitzgerald's situation was that his income was peaking during the latter years of the decade while his professional discipline was sliding toward its nadir. He would earn $29,737 in 1927, certainly the measure of a highly successful writer for the time. *The Saturday Evening Post* was now paying him $3500 for each of his stories. Yet despite the rosy economics, there were signs that should have worried the man: $5752 of the money he earned was an advance against his stalled novel. The royalties from his published books and collections of short stories, according to his ledger, amounted to only $169 — not any great compensation for a writer who would be struggling for another seven years on a long and complex novel. He wired Ober every few days, or at least once a week, asking for advances of $1000 or $800 or $500 for stories he proposed and then dropped or promised delivery of but never completed. The only conditions under which Fitzgerald could support his way of living was writing for the popular magazines. It was a task he had begun to dislike and one that, in his most pessimistic moods, he regarded as demeaning for a serious writer.

It is difficult to know what real problems underlay the repeated requests for money, and how genuine the recurring apologies and excuses for the delays were. He seemed to be a man chasing after every distraction. Certainly the Fitzgeralds' expenses continued in unremitting fashion. There was the rental on the mansion, the salaries for the staff. There were the usual weekend parties and guests. (Sometimes Fitzgerald made special trips to New York to pick up the bootleg wine and liquor for his parties.) And there was a series of summer excursions. In July, they went to Virginia Beach and then to Norfolk to visit Scott's favorite cousin, Cecilia (Ceci) Taylor, and her family. In August, there was a trip to Long Island to see the Rumseys and the Hitchcocks; it was the height of the polo-playing season. It was also the peak of the hysteria surrounding the Canadian tour of the heir apparent to the British throne, Edward Albert, "the indestructible Dancing Drinking Tumbling Kissing Walking Talking and Sleeping — but not Marrying — idol of the British Empire," as *Vanity Fair* described him. Fitzgerald wrote young "Teah" Taylor, Ceci's daughter, "Zelda prays nightly that the Prince of Wales will come down from Canada." (Zelda's later story, "The Girl the Prince Liked," was about a young married socialite whose boringly routine life is irrevocably changed when she is singled out at a party by "the most famous young man in England.") Afterward, the Fitzgeralds paid a visit to Daisy Chanler at Sweet Briar Farm.

Both at home and abroad, the Fitzgeralds were quarreling regularly. "I don't blame either of you," Fitzgerald wrote to Gilbert and Amanda Seldes after one of their New York excursions, "for being disgusted with our public brawl the other day — but the manhole is on again; we are sober and almost the nicest people I ever met." The "difference of opinion" that had caused the fight, Fitzgerald confessed, had been going on for two weeks before they got to New York. The drinking was beginning to take its toll. Early in September, Zelda wrote to Carl Van Vechten that they were unable to accompany him on a visit to the MacLeishes "on account of pursuing pursuits about here — Scott is digging gold. . . . We have got away from it all so often this summer that the trail of our escapes binds us very tightly — There is scarcely a pullman on the N.Y. Central in which we have not been taken drunk and Scott simply has to work."

Zelda was pursuing her own pursuits with frenetic energy. "I am painting again," she wrote Van Vechten, "and will have to work if I am to turn two apples and a stick of gum into an affair of pyramids and angles and cosmic beauty before the fall." She was also making a strenuous effort to become a ballerina, taking lessons three times a week at the Philadelphia Opera School of Ballet with Catherine Littlefield, a pupil of Mme. Lubov Egorova, who had been Honoria Murphy's teacher in Paris. At first, Fitzgerald seems not to have taken the lessons very seriously, but he soon began to balk at the inconvenience of Zelda's weekly train trips to Philadelphia and the general disorder in household affairs that resulted. "You did not like it when you saw it made me happy," Zelda later accused him. "You were angry about rehearsals and insistent about trains." Fitzgerald's uneasiness — it would be too dramatic to call it panic — at Zelda's drive for independence was to become another source of argument in the family.

In a desultory way, she was also striving to become a writer. In Hollywood, she had written an "Editorial on Youth" for *Photoplay* magazine. At Ellerslie, during 1927, she wrote two more articles, "The Changing Beauty of Park Avenue," for *Harper's Bazaar,* and "Looking Back Eight Years," for *College Humor.* None of the articles appeared under Zelda's independent byline. *Photoplay* did not publish the "Editorial on Youth" at all, and when it appeared in *The Smart Set,* under the title "Paint and Powder," it carried only Fitzgerald's name. The reason, apparently, was a bit of finagling on his part. Although the article is credited to Zelda in his ledger account, Fitzgerald, in order to get the magazine to pay up, wrote the Reynolds agency, claiming that the article was his and saying that a representative of *Photoplay* had "stood over me in person until I handed it to him." His bland explanation for not sending the article through the agency in the first place was that "it was so small & simple a matter that I didn't refer it to you." When Ober placed the article with *Smart Set* later, he evidently did not want to tell them it was Zelda's. The two remaining articles appeared in 1928, bylined F. Scott and Zelda Fitzgerald, and were also the subject of necessary explanations to the agency. Writing to Harold Ober on this occasion, Fitzgerald said that the pieces hadn't been sent to him because they had both been written "entirely" by Zelda. "The editors knew this but insisted my name go on them with her." But there is a real question as to whether "Looking Back Eight Years," which dealt with the changed viewpoint of the younger generation, then reaching the age of thirty, was not written chiefly by Fitzgerald himself. It lacks any evidence of Zelda's brilliant offbeat style and is heavily larded with what look like Fitzgerald's views on the issues confronting a generation of former war heroes. "The men who at twenty-one led companies of two hundred must, it seems to us, feel an eternal let down from a time when necessity and idealism were one single thing and no compromise was ever necessary. That willingness to face issues, a relic of ten years ago, is perhaps the explanation of some of the unrest and dissatisfaction of today."

Another of Zelda's creative projects that fall was the decoration of an elaborate doll house, intended as a Christmas gift for Scottie. The work was conducted in secret in a third-floor room of Ellerslie. The project may have represented something more than the making of a Christmas gift; maybe it was also a pleasant sublimation of Zelda's own yearnings for a house of her own. In several of the letters she wrote to Scottie from Hollywood at the beginning of the year, she had playfully mentioned that she was buying "lots of magazines about houses," trying to pick out just the house she would like. "I am *crazy* to own a house," she wrote Scottie. "I want you to have a lovely little Japanese room with pink cherry-blossoms and a ducky little tea-table and a screen—would you like it?" Now, with a litter of wallpaper fragments and snippets of material, she was creating for her daughter just such an environment.

That pre-Christmas project also provided the inspiration for one of Fitzgerald's gentler stories of the period, "Outside the Cabinet-Maker's." In the story, a father and his six-year-old daughter are waiting in a car outside the shop. The father invents a fairy tale about the people on the street and about a princess who is being kept prisoner by an ogre in one of the drab houses. Inside the shop the mother is arranging to have the doll house made. (From the father's prior instructions, in French, that the doll house should be at least as large as the Murphys', it is clear that the family is the

Fitzgerald family.) On one level, the story is a parable about the writer's ability to instill a sense of magic into the dingy routine of ordinary life. But it is also a story about loss — the writer's inability to believe in the fiction he has created for someone else. "The man was old enough," Fitzgerald wrote, "to know that he would look back to that time — the tranquil street and the pleasant weather and the mystery playing before the child's eyes, mystery which he had created, but whose luster and texture he could never see or touch any more himself."

"Outside the Cabinet-Maker's" is one of the first indications of Fitzgerald's growing interest in the themes of childhood innocence and times past — themes that would take him back to his own childhood in St. Paul in an attempt to recover his personal past.

<hr>

PARTIES: Whatever Zelda may have said about the need of serious purpose and work, in her letter to Carl Van Vechten she was plainly trying to seduce him down to Ellerslie for a "party of sorts" that she was planning for the weekend of September 24, the weekend of Fitzgerald's thirty-first birthday. Her intended guest list was comic: President Coolidge and his wife, the bathtub girl from Earl Carroll's *Vanities*, the Indian guide who was a principal in a current murder case, and the Sistine Madonna — "good simple people and all my intimate friends." Van Vechten, however, was unable to come.

The party, given in honor of the visiting Teah Taylor as well as Fitzgerald, was not an altogether happy event. One of the guests was John Dos Passos, who could hardly have been in a festive mood, embittered as he was by the execution of Sacco and Vanzetti the month before. He had worked hard in the defense of the two anarchists and was disappointed in friends like Wilson (and presumably Fitzgerald), who had not taken the case as seriously as he had. It may have been for this reason that Dos Passos told Wilson the weekend at Ellerslie had been "a regular wake." But he later told Nancy Milford that it had been one of the Fitzgeralds' typical "delirious parties." At Ellerslie, Dos Passos said, "dinner was never served." He had had to go to Wilmington, some miles away, in search of a sandwich. It was "a wild time."

Another of the guests was Richard Knight, the New York lawyer with whom Zelda had become especially friendly. He did not add to the occasion. Before setting out for Delaware, Knight had gone to the New York City morgue to give a positive identification of his brother. He talked about the event with a chilling lack of grief. Knight was an enigmatic figure, short and stocky, with an overly large head. Zelda was charmed by his "magnetic voice," but he was unpredictable in his behavior; at one Ellerslie party, he flung a pot of mustard at the dining room door. Edmund Wilson, who knew him, disliked Knight intensely, thought him a bounder, and described him as a "supernatural apparition." Knight, who was later disbarred, died under questionable circumstances.

Fitzgerald was — and remained — jealous of Zelda's friend. It is not clear, from the Fitzgeralds' disorderly chronicles of their lives, precisely when Zelda had first given him cause. She recalled "one lost afternoon" at a cocktail party in a New York apartment, when she and Knight sat on a stairway together, "oblivious with a kind of happy desperation. . . . We would have made scenes but there was trouble." She also remembered another occasion when Fitzgerald had gone to New York expressly to meet Lois Moran. At a party given in honor of Paul Morand, the French diplomat and writer of travel books, Zelda encountered Knight, and the two had acted so friendly that Fitzgerald forbade Zelda to see Knight again. He was also "furious" about a letter Knight had written her, even though, as Zelda maintained, Fitzgerald was still "thoroughly entangled sentimentally" with Lois Moran.

They all appear, this strange conglomeration of people, in a sequence of snapshots commemorating the birthday weekend at Ellerslie — people in captured moments, frowning in the blank sunlight on the portico steps. Dick Knight lounges against a pillar, with Scottie peering from behind him. (Ironically, Scottie later described Knight as one of the more colorful figures her parents knew.) Zelda stands next to the beaming Dos Passos and Teah. In another, captioned "War Pictures," Dos Passos is reclining on a mattress covered with a plaid blanket and Teah holds the slide viewer for the war photographs, with their scenes of battle and mutilation, with which Fitzgerald insisted on entertaining his guests.

It was in the nature of the Fitzgeralds' floating entertainments that the party did not end at Ellerslie but moved on to New York, where the Fitzgeralds took Teah on visits to speakeasies and the theater. On the return trip to Wilmington they stopped at Philadelphia so that Zelda could take her ballet lesson. Fitzgerald, however, had no intention of waiting in the studio; he took Teah off for drinks. By the time of departure, Fitzgerald was quite drunk, and Zelda completely ignored him. Teah was left to manage Fitzgerald for the remainder of the trip, and when it was over, it was only with the aid of a conductor that she got him into a taxi for the drive to Ellerslie.

Early in October, Fitzgerald managed to induce Maxwell Perkins and his wife, Louise, to come for a visit. Perkins was reluctant; he suspected it would be a weekend of "cocktails, made-up girls, cigarette smoke and talk." Presumably, the Fitzgeralds were on their best behavior, and Perkins was agreeably surprised. The weather was superbly mild, with a light breeze blowing in through the windows. An early riser, Perkins even managed to have a quiet Sunday morning breakfast for himself. He thought Ellerslie had "more quality of its own" than almost any other house he had been in. But Fitzgerald was extremely nervous, with noticeably trembling hands — the effect, Perkins suspected, of too much drinking and too many cigarettes. He advised Fitzgerald to cut down on the alcohol, to smoke only Sano cigarettes, and to start on a regimen of exercise. He worried that Fitzgerald was close to a breakdown; it only confirmed his suspicions when, a short time later, Fitzgerald came to New York to work for a while in the Scribner's office. Fitzgerald began fidgeting nervously, complained that he needed to go for a walk, and badgered Perkins into coming out to have a drink with him. When Perkins agreed, but on the condition that he have only one, Fitzgerald became huffy: "You talk to me as if I were Ring Lardner."

That fall there was a parade of guests and a round of parties at Ellerslie. Later in October, Townsend Martin and Ludlow Fowler came. For that occasion, Fitzgerald organized a game of croquet-polo with borrowed plow horses from a neighbor's farm. In a snapshot, Martin and Fowler are mounted on the nags, with the beaming and bespectacled Fowler holding out a minuscule silver trophy. Charlie MacArthur was another of the guests, which suggests that it was a bibulous affair. MacArthur improvised a session of skeet shooting on the front lawn, using some of the Fitzgeralds' dinnerware for targets.

Not all the parties were so convivial. When drunk, Fitzgerald could become a tiresome bore. That seems to have been the case at a party he hosted for Thomas Lineaweaver, a Princeton friend, and his wife, Eleanor — quite probably in the fall of 1927, considering that the conversation was about Fitzgerald's current topic, the domineering American female. After the party, Fitzgerald wrote Linea-weaver one of those letters which seem a model for all such Fitzgerald letters — part abject confession and part roguish humor:

> I'm afraid I was the world's greatest bore last night. I was in the insistent mood — you know the insistent mood? I'm afraid I irritated both you and Eleanor, and I wanted to please you more than anyone there. It's all very dim to me but I remember a lot of talk about fairies and the managing kind of American woman, whatever that means. It's possible that I may be apologizing to the wrong people — anyway if I was lousy, please forgive me. . . . Tell Eleanor I love her and I want to marry her. Does that fix everything?

Zelda, writing to Carl Van Vechten in mid-October, confirmed the need for reform. "It seems that life went to pieces. . . ." she said. "Guests came and every-body has been so drunk in this country lately that I am just finding enough chaos to pursue my own ends in, undisturbed, again. . . . We've given up hope that you'll ever come back to Ellerslie — and now that we've got delirium tremens we are going to sit here and brood until Christmas." Fitzgerald made some dubious claims to full sobriety in a later letter to Maxwell Perkins, assuring his editor: "I have been on the absolute wagon since the middle of October. Feel simply grand. Smoke only Sanos. God help us all."

He did, however, admit that the prohibitions were not enforced during the Christmas holidays — the festival of the year that the Fitzgeralds most looked forward to. The Christmas of 1927 was planned to be a more or less quiet affair, with a few friends and the unveiling of Scottie's doll house, on which Zelda had expended so much time and care. But somehow, there were unexpected guests — a drunken newspaper man and a theatrical agent who socked his mistress. And at the height of the general melee, a group of village carol singers arrived and were invited in to add to the festivities. The next morning the house was in minor chaos and Scottie was crying. Fitzgerald, with some nonchalance and evidently a considerable hangover, surveyed the wreckage and said, "Just think — it's like this now all over the country."

Late in February 1928, Thornton Wilder, one of Fitzgerald's newer literary enthusiasms, came for a weekend. Fitzgerald had admired

the thirty-three-year-old author's first novel, *The Cabala,* sent him
a complimentary letter about it, and received a flattering one in
return. "I have been an admirer, not to say a student, of The Great
Gatsby too long not to have got a great kick out of your letter,"
Wilder responded. He was teaching at the Lawrenceville School,
near Princeton, and hoped they would have a chance to meet. They
did, some weeks later, when Fitzgerald, against his better judgment,
agreed to speak at a Cottage Club dinner at Princeton. An informal
afternoon talk to undergraduates had gone well enough, but Fitzgerald became increasingly nervous about the evening ordeal and
started drinking. When the time came, he was barely able to get
out a few incoherent remarks, and mumbling to himself "God, I'm
a lousy speaker!" he sat down. Wilder sent a consoling note: "Don't
brood about your speech in the evening; your speech in the afternoon
was a raring wow and the audience wants more."

Fitzgerald invited him down for the weekend of February 25.
Making an occasion of it, he also asked Edmund Wilson, Gilbert
and Amanda Seldes, and Esther Murphy. Since Zoë Atkins was in
Wilmington for the tryouts of her play *The Furies,* with Laurette
Taylor in the leading role, Fitzgerald offered to send his car for the
two women after the performance, if they cared to come to a "small
revel Saturday night."

Fitzgerald's invitation to Wilson was a comic production: "All
is prepared for February 25th. The stomach pumps are polished and
set out in rows." He promised, "There will be small but select
company, coals, blankets, 'something for the inner man.' " After
further rigamarole, he concluded, "Pray gravity to move your bow-
els. It's little we get done for us in this world. Answer."

It turned out to be one of the more awful Fitzgerald parties.
But Wilson, writing about it in a later reminiscence, "A Weekend
at Ellerslie," thought that it had begun in promising fashion. At
the Wilmington station, while waiting for the Fitzgerald car to pick
him up, he met Thornton Wilder for the first time. He hadn't yet
read any of Wilder's books, but the two had a lengthy discussion
about Proust, whose final novel, *Le Temps Retrouvé,* they had both
just finished reading. Wilder asserted that in the final volume, Proust
had pulled too many homosexuals out of the closet; that the revelations about Charlus would have been enough. Wilson commented
on Proust's mastery of the theme of time; how the opening sequence

had begun with the word *"Longtemps"* and the novel had ended with the phrase *"dans le temps."*

Wilson was impressed with Ellerslie; he had never seen the Fitzgeralds in such a "magnificent setting." Scott, living up to his image as the country squire, met them at the door—immensely proud—and proceeded to take them on the grand tour. He also had another motive. He had hidden a butler behind one of the bedroom doors to play the role of the Ellerslie ghost, rattling chains and groaning lugubriously. But owing to the noise and confusion, the arrival of new guests, the ghost was barely audible, and Fitzgerald kept repeating, "Don't you hear something strange?" Fitzgerald was a host who believed in planned activities at parties, perhaps as a hedge against the chaos that would inevitably follow once the drinking began. The guests were next given a choice of listening to a new recording of Stravinsky's *The Rite of Spring* or looking through Scott's album of gruesome war photos. Drinks were served, and soon the structure of the late afternoon dissolved; somehow everyone was out on the darkening lawn in the chilly February air, playing a game of diabolo.

Next, predinner drinks were being served in a large salon to Wilson, Wilder, the Seldeses, Esther Murphy, and the newly arrived John and Anna Biggs. Fitzgerald took Wilson aside to complain about an old grudge that he had been harboring—something to do with Wilson's having been rude to him and Zelda. It did not bode well for the weekend. Wilson managed to head off what might have been an unpleasantness; still, he wondered why he should be getting a lecture on manners from Fitzgerald, of all people. Then Zoë Atkins and several members from the production staff of *The Furies* arrived, including a moody stage designer.

Dinner started out affably, with liberal amounts of wine. Wilson was seated next to Zelda, who was fortunately at "her iridescent best." Wilson always had a high opinion of Zelda's conversational talent: "She had no readymade phrases on the one hand and made no straining for effect on the other." Wilder, who remained visibly "non-soluble" throughout the weekend, was engaged in a lengthy conversation of the subject of Colette's novels with his dinner partner, Esther Murphy. Even though he might be slipping off into an alcoholic haze, Fitzgerald was still the observant host; he later apologized to Wilder for saddling him with Esther Murphy and her "tragedienne's voice"—though Wilder, having discovered that he and Esther Murphy shared the same enthusiasms, could have kept up the conversation for years. The only unhappy moment at the table came when Zoë Akins—an actress with something of the grand manner—began reciting passages from Shakespeare. Fitzgerald and Zelda, having planned to shine at their own party, sulked. When Akins and her entourage left for the theater, Fitzgerald grumbled, "All that memorized Shakespeare!" Then, suddenly, both he and Zelda announced that they were going to bed, leaving their guests to their own devices. Wilson, who had grown weary, too, went to bed as well. But Fitzgerald, deciding that he wanted to show Thornton Wilder something, took his guest up into the attic, where, stumbling over a gun, he picked it up, waved it around, and accidentally shot if off; the bullet lodged in the wall perilously close to Wilder. Although Fitzgerald blanked out the whole episode and was suitably remorseful when it was recalled the following morning, to Wilder it was one of the more vivid recollections of his Ellerslie visit.

There had, however, been a second act to the Saturday night party. Following the evening performance of *The Furies,* the theatrical group, minus Zoë Akins, returned, ready to continue the party. That is, all except the little set designer, who took himself off into one of the empty rooms and, in a Hamlet-like pose, leaned against the marble mantle. Zelda, revived and fresh from her nap, found him there and tried to start up a conversation. The designer responded by telling his hostess, "Please go away. I'm thinking and I don't want to be disturbed." Out of the blue, Zelda shot back, "Oh, you're not really thinking, you're just being homogeneous!" —a remark that set the young man off in a huff. He gathered his friends, claimed he had been insulted, and insisted that the Fitzgerald car be brought around to take them all home.

Fitzgerald, having slept through the whole incident, did not learn about it until later. When Wilson and Seldes encountered him the morning after, he was lounging in his bathrobe. Wilder had left Ellerslie early in the morning, a move Wilson wished he had made also, for he found himself growing more irritable as the day wore on. Fitzgerald proposed reading the two men a segment from his novel. It included a "dazzling" description of a group of young girls on the beach or in a room; the passage distinctly impressed Wilson.

He was amazed later when he could find nothing vaguely resembling it in the final version of *Tender Is the Night* and assumed that Fitzgerald had destroyed it.

Later that morning, when Zelda got up, she related her little set-to with the designer. Fitzgerald was extremely disturbed; he insisted that they must search out the young man and make proper apologies. It was a matter of the honor of the household. Summoning the chauffeur, he dragged along Wilson and Esther Murphy for moral support and set out in quest of the offended party. Only a masochist — or a writer — would be so intensely concerned about what other people thought of him. Fitzgerald gave the chauffeur the third degree about what was said during the angry drive to Wilmington the night before. The chauffeur obliged: "Why, the little fellow said, 'Fitzgerald thinks he's got a swell place there, but an uncle of mine's got a house that makes that house look like a dump!' " Fitzgerald's spirits darkened; still, he pursued the matter, even though Wilson and Esther Murphy suggested he drop the subject. Fitzgerald countered, "It's only very seldom that you get a real opportunity to hear what people say about you behind your back." Turning to the driver, he asked, "Didn't anybody have anything good to say about me?" The driver mentioned that one member of the party had tried to speak up, but that the others had held him down on the floor of the car with their feet on him.

A gloomier Fitzgerald began to wonder about the usefulness of his mission. When he discovered that not every member of the theatrical troupe was staying at the hotel — and suspecting, perhaps, that his apology would be more of an embarrassment than he expected — he suggested that Wilson and Esther Murphy return to the house. He would try to round up the guests and bring them back to Ellerslie so that he and Zelda "could be nice to them."

Wilson later commented, "The aftermath of a Fitzgerald evening was notoriously a painful experience." It was so on this occasion. He was himself in a disagreeable mood, and for no discernible reason he picked a fight with Esther Murphy, who, in consequence, told him that he had an "intellectual arrogance" that was very trying for his friends. Wilson's rule was that when a Fitzgerald party began to founder, it was best to desert the sinking ship. He decided he could not spend another night at Ellerslie. But the suitably moral conclusion of his little drama was that he needed to cash a personal check in order to buy his ticket back to New York, and the only person on the premises with cash to spare was Esther Murphy. He got the $10 from her.

The comic — or not so comic — aftermath of the party, Wilson learned from Gilbert Seldes. Fitzgerald, still dissatisfied with the performance of the Ellerslie ghost, decided to play the role himself. With a sheet over his head, he crept into the Seldeses' bedroom in the dead of night and commenced a mournful groaning as he hovered beside the sleeping couple. The ghost, unhappily, had decided to smoke beneath his shroud and the sheet caught fire. The blaze was speedily put out, but not without a few moments of panic.

The day before his February 25 weekend party, Fitzgerald had wired Harold Ober that a story he was working on would be delayed; he would try to get it to Ober by Monday night. Only a few weeks before, Fitzgerald had tapped a new and promising vein of literary material — what would eventually be a series of short stories on the youthful adventures and coming-of-age of Basil Duke Lee, a conceited and opinionated boy who grew up in the Midwest but longed for the glamour of Eastern schools and was attracted to the mecca, New York. Within the year, Fitzgerald wrote a sequence of eight of these tales, detailing his brisk young hero's life from the age of fourteen to his first year at Yale. (A ninth story, unpublished during Fitzgerald's lifetime, carried Basil back to his childhood and a kissing party at the age of eleven.) Ober promptly sold the first story, "The Scandal Detectives," to *The Saturday Evening Post* for $3500, and the magazine was particularly eager to have a second, since they had an opening for a lead story in one of their upcoming issues.

The initial inspiration for Fitzgerald's sequence may have been Booth Tarkington's highly popular and successful Penrod and Sam tales. Fitzgerald, however, brought something fresh, less sentimental, and more up-to-date to the depiction of his fatherless young adolescent, whose exploits, general girl-craziness, and overweening egotism were patently drawn from his own personality and his experiences growing up in St. Paul. "The Scandal Detectives" was based on the club he had founded at the age of fourteen in the Ames yard (transformed into the Wharton yard in the story), which had been the gathering place for him and his friends. The Basil stories were, in effect, Fitzgerald's remembrance of things past. Proust was very much in the air for him at the time; a March 1928 entry in his ledger indicates that he was reading the French novelist's works. Quite probably, it was the enthusiasm of Wilson and Wilder that had prompted him.

"The Scandal Detectives" was evocative in its descriptions of locale, especially of the Wharton yard: "It had a child's quality — the thing that makes young people huddle inextricably on uncomfortable steps and desert the houses of their friends to herd on the obscure premises of 'people nobody knows.' " Max Perkins, on reading it, was especially impressed with Fitzgerald's "account of how the boys and girls met in a certain yard at dusk. That was beautifully done. That magical quality of summer dusk for young boys I have never before seen evoked." Fitzgerald gave the stories a distinct feel of the thin, unexamined decencies of Midwestern society; he also had a flair for the snappy dialogue of youth in the new century. His look at childhood was racier than Tarkington's, though it was a good deal more innocent, less Freudian, than Proust's.

But after the first story, Fitzgerald seems to have hesitated, faltered in determining the proper sequence of the succeeding stories. "The Freshest Boy," originally the second story, was moved back to make way for another, "A Night at the Fair." It is possible that his reading of Proust had encouraged him to tackle something more ambitious, thematically and structurally. One bit of telltale evidence of the influence of Proust is the appearance, in a later story, of a teen-age vamp named Ermine Gilberte Labouisse Bibble, a droll American echo of Proust's Gilberte. The fully extended name was probably Fitzgerald's sly acknowledgment of Midwestern pretensions to class.

That Fitzgerald placed some special value on his attempt to recover the personal past is clear from a sentence in a letter he wrote to a friend in St. Paul that "The Scandal Detectives," in which he paid tribute to the Ames back yard, would be appearing in an April issue of the *Post:* "Please clip it and save it for your children, for sooner or later time will wipe out that pleasant spot." But over the years, Fitzgerald's view of history, even personal history, would darken considerably. The past acquired an awesome finality for him; he would refer to "that terrible door into the past through which we all must go." Nor, despite the popularity of his Basil stories, would Fitzgerald ever be anything but ambivalent about them. They were "a mistake," he told one correspondent, a case of "too much good material being shoved into a lousy form." In one way or another, it seems, Fitzgerald's childhood remained unsatisfying for him.

Certainly, he did not rush his new effort into print. Needless to say, he did not complete a second Basil story during the weekend party at Ellerslie. He wired Ober on the following Tuesday, February 28:

> CAN YOU DEPOSIT THREE HUNDRED TODAY OR TOMORROW STORY UP WEDNESDAY SURE.

But the story was not completed even then. On March 10, he wired again:

> BRINGING MANUSCRIPT UP TODAY CAN YOU LUNCH WITH ME.

That, too, was a false alarm. It was followed by another wire on the next day:

> SENDING STORY OFF THIS MORNING CONSIDERABLY IMPROVED IN FACT I THINK IT IS NOW VERY GOOD CAN YOU POSSIBLY DEPOSIT CASH INSTEAD OF CHECK THIS MORNING.

A week later, the story not finished, Fitzgerald sent a desperate plea for help:

> DEAR HAROLD MY INCOME TAX CHECK IS DUE IN NEW YORK TOMORROW MONDAY CAN YOU POSSIBLY DEPOSIT THREE HUNDRED FIFTY DOLLARS TO KEEP ME OUT OF JAIL STOP ALSO COULD I COUNT ON ABOUT TWELVE HUNDRED BEING DEPOSITED SAY WEDNESDAY OR HAD I BETTER SAY THURSDAY STOP WORKING ON STORY AND WILL TRY TO GET IT TO YOU THIS WEEK STOP YOURS IMPROVIDENTLY AS USUAL F SCOTT FITZGERALD.

It is not altogether certain whether Fitzgerald actually delivered the second story in the Basil series to Ober before he, Zelda, and Scottie, as planned, sailed for Europe on April 21. There were at least three more wires asking for money and promising delivery of a manuscript. The story written third in order, "A Night at the Fair," was definitely mailed from Paris.

III

There was an element of desperation in Fitzgerald's flight to Europe. He planned to stay three months but remained for five. No doubt his having managed to complete *The Great Gatsby* while abroad may have encourage him to think that he would be successful there with his stalled novel.

Before their departure, they had paid visits to Long Island: "Ring looking bad," Fitzgerald noted in his ledger. And he had had his usual farewell glimpse of New York City from the roof of the Plaza Hotel. He also had meetings with Ober and with Max Perkins, who lunched with Fitzgerald and the Seldeses at the Plaza. Perkins, reporting to Hemingway, then in Key West, noted that Fitzgerald had entirely gotten over his "nervous attacks." These may have been "the Stoppies" mentioned in the ledger several months before ("Terrible incessant Stoppies begin," "Stoppies now reached its height"), perhaps referring to episodes of the jitters. Perkins was not optimistic about the trip; he found Fitzgerald extremely depressed, maybe as a result of a party with Ring Lardner the night before. It was clear that he would have to make some kind of change, and Perkins had hoped he would stay in America for a long time, "but after seeing him the way he was, I am glad that he won't. He seemed to have no resilience at all, which is most unusual in Scott. He has made no progress with his novel for a long time, always having to stop to write stories."

Hemingway, in his reply to Perkins, was sympathetic about Fitzgerald's nervous troubles — he offered to send a cable to Scott on the *Paris*. But he was not overly sympathetic as far as Fitzgerald's writing problems were concerned. Fitzgerald, he said, was using his work on his commercial stories as an excuse "to keep from having to bite on the nail" and finish his novel. He was stuck on the notion of having to write a very important novel, because the critics had said such fine things about *Gatsby*. Hemingway added: "But critics like Seldes etc. are poison for him. He is scared and builds up all sorts of defences like the need for making money with stories. . . . He could have written three novels in this length of time — and what if two of them were bad if one of them was a Gatsby."

There had been an ominous incident before the Fitzgeralds' departure. "Black eyes in the Jungle," Fitzgerald noted in his ledger

—a reference, it seems, to a disastrous beating he had received in a New York speakeasy. The actual source of the episode is Lawton Campbell, though Fitzgerald's biographers have misdated it as occurring just before Scott and Zelda's first trip to Europe. Campbell had met the Fitzgeralds by accident at the Jungle Club. Scott was having an argument with a determined bouncer, who refused to let him have another drink at the bar. Campbell managed to get Fitzgerald to sit with him. But Zelda, appearing at the door to the bar, insisted that Fitzgerald come back with her. "No so-and-so bouncer," she announced, "can prevent Scott from going anywhere he pleases." Fitzgerald, all grace under pressure, followed her back, and the bouncer once more refused to let him take a seat. Fitzgerald took a few wild swings; the bouncer pushed him away with so much force that Fitzgerald crashed into a table. Campbell, coming to his aid, persuaded him to leave the club and take a taxi home. Zelda, arriving on the scene, berated Campbell and once more insisted that Fitzgerald accompany her back into the speakeasy. The result, according to Campbell, was that Fitzgerald was so badly beaten that he was bedridden the next day, sporting black eyes, bruises, and bandages on his head. He couldn't remember what had happened the night before.

Their friends worried about them. Zelda had begun to interpret the symptoms of their desperate voyaging, their living always at the edge of their emotions. In one of her later stories, "A Couple of Nuts," she depicted her hero and heroine, a pair of nightclub entertainers, Larry and Lola, as attractive, ruined by success, indulging in extracurricular romancing out of bored experiment or retaliation:

> In those days of going to pieces and general disintegration it was charming to see them together. Their friends were divided into camps as to whose stamina it was that kept them going and comparatively equilibrated in that crazy world of ours playing at prisoner's base across the Atlantic Ocean.

Despite Hemingway's contention that Fitzgerald was "prolific as a Gueinea pig (mis-spelled)," Fitzgerald had written only three of the Basil stories when he sent the manuscript for "A Night at the Fair" to Harold Ober early in May. And he would write only two more

—possibly three—by the time he returned to America in October. Early in June, he also cabled Ober that he had completed two more chapters of his novel. Although he assured Max Perkins that he was "on the absolute wagon and working on the novel, the whole novel and nothing but the novel," and that he would return in August "with it or on it," he was making only meager progress. Later, he would call on the sacred example of James Joyce, whom he had recently met at a dinner party. Joyce, Fitzgerald told Perkins, did not expect to finish his next novel (*Finnegans Wake*) for another three or four years, "and he works 11 hours a day to my intermittent 8." His own novel, he promised, would "be done *sure* in September." The dinner party, which became one of the twenties' legends, was given by Sylvia Beach, proprietor of the Parisian bookstore Shakespeare & Company and the ill-paid publisher of Joyce's banned prose. Fitzgerald, who drew a little sketch of the event, showing himself kneeling in front of the haloed Irish writer, titled it "Festival of St. James." With his usual dubious flattery, he heightened the drama of the evening by threatening to jump out of a fourth-floor window in proof of his admiration for Joyce's genius.

Zelda was completely indifferent to the Irish writer, which rankled Fitzgerald, though he had his own explanation: she was too caught up in her ballet lessons. She had begun training in earnest under Mme. Lubov Egorova, former dancer with the Diaghilev troupe and mentor of her teacher in Philadelphia. She was a highly respected dance instructor. Zelda had become obsessive about her lessons, leaving Fitzgerald to his own devices, and Scottie—that trundled child of their marriage—with the governess, Mlle. Delplangue. Zelda would speak of that summer on the rue Vaugirard with bitterness: "You were constantly drunk. You didn't work and you were dragged home at night by taxi-drivers when you came home at all. You said it was my fault for dancing all day. What was I to do?" Even given the honed edge of Zelda's self-justifications, it is still clear that their marriage was coming apart, that Fitzgerald was not on the wagon, and that he was not working. His own ledger account confirms that it was a summer of partying, drinking bouts, and destructive episodes. In July, he noted a "first trip to jail" and in August a second. There are other bits of damaging evidence: "Drinking & general unpleasantness," "general aimlessness & boredom."

Paris was crowded with friends and new acquaintances. John

Peale Bishop and his wife were in town frequently that summer, waiting for the renovations on their château at Orgeval to be completed. Fitzgerald would never entertain friendly feelings toward Margaret Bishop, whose verbosity he disliked. ("There *can't* be that many words," Sara Murphy commented about Margaret Bishop's conversation—a remark Fitzgerald salvaged for his notebooks.) And it may well have been during this summer that Fitzgerald wrote on Margaret's dress with a lipstick, an act not calculated to endear him to any woman. But that summer he did make a decided effort to get Bishop to produce a volume of stories, one of which, a novelette dealing with the Civil War, particularly impressed him; "Its right up to Bierce & Stephen Crane," he told Perkins, "beautifully written, thrilling and water tight as to construction & interest." But the literary profession is stony ground for gratitude. Bishop, writing Bunny Wilson late in the summer, acknowledged Fitzgerald's persistence in planning a volume of stories. But he was condescending about Fitzgerald's admiration for the novelette: "Scott professes great enthusiasm for the finished tale, giving it, I think, rather more value than it deserves."

As he generally did when he was abroad, Fitzgerald discovered new talent that he tried to encourage Perkins to publish. On his earlier trip he had recommended Raymond Radiguet's *Le Bal du Comte d'Orgel*—a perceptive choice, in light of Radiguet's later reputation. But Perkins was never a venturesome editor where the vanguard was concerned, and he was even more timorous about writing that bordered on frankness, to say nothing of the salacious. (With Hemingway's upcoming novel, *A Farewell to Arms,* there were certain words that he could not bring himself to pronounce when consulting with his publisher, Charles Scribner. Instead he chose to write one out on a slip of paper. The elderly Scribner, donning his pince-nez, inspected the word—it was *cocksucker*—and turning to his editor asked, "Perkins, do you think that Hemingway would respect you, if he knew that you were unable to say that word?")

This time, Fitzgerald was urging a safe choice, André Chamson, whose novel *Les Hommes de la Route* was being much talked about. He had met the twenty-eight-year-old reporter and novelist through Sylvia Beach. Chamson, Fitzgerald wrote Perkins, was "head over heels the best young man here, like Ernest and Thornton Wilder rolled into one." Perkins would be making a mistake if he didn't take the book. "Radiguet was perhaps obscene—Chamson is absolutely *not.*" Scribner's published the book under the title *The Road* in 1929.

Not content with promoting Chamson's novel with Scribner's, he also talked up the book with King Vidor, the film director, who was in Paris at the time. Vidor eventually made a movie based on it. It was also through Fitzgerald's good offices that Vidor, planning to make an all-black movie — *Hallelujah!* — hired Gerald Murphy as a consultant on the music. But there were occasions when Fitzgerald's friendship could be embarrassing. Once, visiting the Chamsons in their sixth-floor apartment on the rue Thouin, Fitzgerald, rather than making threats of leaping from the heights, climbed out on a balustrade and, balancing himself at the edge of the violet Parisian twilight, shouted: "I am Voltaire! I am Rousseau!" — names that came more from his freshman course in French literature than from any resemblance between himself and the writers.

Fitzgerald's ledger notes give a staggering list of friends and acquaintances he and Zelda met in Paris during their five-month stay. They saw the Murphys with some regularity. Esther Murphy was also in town. There were visits from Powell Fowler, Ludlow's brother, and from the Gene Bucks and Richard Knight. There was Blanche Knopf and Cole Porter. And Sandy and Oscar Kalman. He had met Harold Stearns and, "feeling drunk and Christ-like," suggested that Stearns write an article about living in Paris, which he would attempt to sell for him. (Stearns complained about the meager $100 fee *Scribner's Magazine* paid for it. Fitzgerald's own opinion was that it wasn't very much, but that it wasn't much of an article either.) Thornton Wilder and his traveling companion, the prizefighter Gene Tunney, a man with an intellectual bent, were in Paris that summer. (Fitzgerald had met Tunney earlier that year in New York; according to one account, he was so euphoric after meeting the champion that in an act of generosity he bought up all the newspapers from a newsboy he encountered on the street.) In Paris, he met Wilder and Tunney for lunch at the Racquet Club.

He and Zelda ate out frequently — sauerkraut at Lipp's, Pouilly and bouillabaisse at Prunier's — "in a time of discouragement," according to Fitzgerald's recollections. And there were "desolate" trips to Versailles, to Rheims, to the battlefields of World War I — to escape their growing boredom and dissatisfaction. They were storing up grievances against one another, artillery for later years and later arguments.

Fitzgerald:

Somewhere in there I had a sense of being exploited, not by you
but by something I resented terribly, no happiness. . . . I remember wondering why I kept working to pay the bills of this desolate
menage. . . . During all this time, remember, I didn't blame anyone but myself. I complained when the house got unbearable but
after all I was not John Peale Bishop — I was paying for it with
work, that I passionately hated and found more and more difficult
to do. The novel was like a dream, daily farther and farther away.

Zelda:

You made no advances toward me and complained that I was un-
responsive. You were literally eternally drunk the whole summer.
I got so I couldn't sleep and I had asthma again. You were angry
when I wouldn't go with you to Mont Matre. You brought drunken
under-graduates in to meals when you came home for them, and it
made you angry that I didn't care any more. I began to like Egorova.

They quarreled frequently that summer — about the poor servants, about the bad apartment. Fitzgerald spent many evenings
alone, sitting in the Closerie des Lilas, remembering the happier
times with Hemingway and Hadley, with Dorothy Parker and Robert Benchley. Or he drank at the Ritz, "where I got back my self
esteem for half an hour, often with someone I had hardly ever seen
before." Those evenings usually ended with Fitzgerald so drunk, he
had to be taken back to the rue Vaugirard by a cab driver.

His birthdays had become reminders of wasted time. Fitzgerald
spent his thirty-second birthday in Paris. His ledger book carried
the notation "Thirty-two years old (And sore as hell about it)." It
was probably on this occasion that Fitzgerald paid a visit to Gertrude
Stein and Alice B. Toklas at the rue de Fleurus. Alice Toklas remembered that Fitzgerald was extremely restless. She recalled his
saying, "You know, I am thirty years old today and it is tragic.
What is to become of me, what am I to do?" Gertrude Stein answered
that he shouldn't worry; he had been writing like a man of thirty
for many years. She told him that he should go home "and write a
greater novel than he ever had." Since Fitzgerald had spent his
thirtieth birthday at Juan les Pins in September 1926, and since
John Dos Passos recalled that it was Fitzgerald's thirtieth birthday
that he had celebrated at Ellerslie in 1927, and Alice Toklas recalled
that it had been woefully celebrated at the rue de Fleurus in 1928

—there is, at the least, a distinct suspicion Fitzgerald had been playing the pitiful thirty-year-old author some two years past its term. In the privacy of his ledger book, however, Fitzgerald acknowledged the beginning of his thirty-third year with the admission: "Ominous. No Real Progress in *ANY* way & *wrecked myself with dozens of people.*"

A bit more accurate, perhaps, was his account of the strange compulsion that had brought him to Paris in the first place. "Anything to be liked," he noted, "to be reassured not that I was a man of a little genius but that I was a great man of the world. At the same time I knew it was nonsense — that part of me that knew it was nonsense brought us to the Rue Vaugirard." Unfortunately, the attempt to put distance between himself and the follies of his life in America had failed.

On the first of October they sailed on the liner *Carmania*. It was a stormy crossing and an unhappy one. They were accompanied by Scottie's Mademoiselle and a new servant, Philippe, a former taxi driver and boxer whom Fitzgerald hired as a butler, chauffeur, companion, and general factotum. On the trip back, vague worries preyed on Zelda's mind. She told Fitzgerald she was worried that maybe there was something "abnormal" about her devotion to Egorova, but Fitzgerald dismissed it with a laugh. On October 7, when the *Carmania* docked in New York, Max Perkins was waiting at the pier to meet them. Fitzgerald, of course, had not completed his novel, but, a bit tipsy, he clutched at a briefcase as if the manuscript were inside. He later promised to send Perkins two chapters at a time, month by month, and at least kept the promise to the extent of sending the first two chapters in November. It was not an auspicious return of the native. And there may have been something even more ominous — given his penchant for odd acts of penance — in his ledger notation: "Dirt eating at hotel."

I V

Earlier, in the summer, Fitzgerald had written Hemingway from Paris to tell him that he had twice called on Hadley but had missed seeing her. He had, however, seen Bumby and reported, "Think he's the best kid I ever saw by 1000 miles." (Hemingway was a father once again: Pauline had given birth to a boy, whom they named Patrick. The new parents spent most of the summer and fall in Wyoming.) Fitzgerald in his letter noted that he had been seeing "a good deal of Joyce" — not substantially true, though Joyce and his wife, Nora, had been to the rue Vaugirard for dinner. Fitzgerald also noted that he and the Murphys were friends again. He suggested that Hemingway send a story to George Horace Lorimer of *The Saturday Evening Post*.

For his troubles, Fitzgerald received, on his arrival home, a joking-insulting letter from Hemingway: "Send Lorimer a story, hell. I'm letting you send Lorimer stories for both of us." Maxwell Perkins, it seems, had passed on to him the news that Scott was reputedly working eight hours a day on his novel. It inspired one of Hemingway's heavy-handed put-downs:

> Well Fitz you are certainly a worker. I have never been able to write longer than two hours myself without getting utterly pooped — any longer than that and the stuff begins to become tripe, but here is old Fitz whom I once knew working eight hours every day. How does it feel old fellow?

Jokingly, he added, "You dirty lousy liar to say you work (write) eight hours a day." What followed next appears to have been a little salt for Fitzgerald's wounds. Hemingway noted that he had finished the first draft of his "bloody" novel a month ago. "God I worked hard on that book. Want like hell to start rewriting but I know I ought to wait a while still." Hemingway obviously suffered from no writer's block; he had energy to spare.

From creative functions, Hemingway moved to the procreative with considerable ease. His son Patrick, he told Fitzgerald, was "built like a brick shithouse." He was thinking of hiring himself out as a stud: "Since the age of fourteen [Mr. Hemingway] has been embarrassed by a succession of perfect Little Ones. Now he has decided to make this great gift available to All." He cautioned prospective clients, however, against the services of Mr. Fitzgerald, who was known in the profession as a one-time performer. "Mr. Fitzgerald it is true is the father of a very perfect child with, we must admit, a delightful English accent (a thing Mr. Hemingway cannot guarantee his clients.)" Mr. Dos Passos, however, was "practically sterile" and a poor choice.

He asked Fitzgerald where he expected to be around the end of October. "How's to get stewed together Fitz? How about a little mixed vomiting or should it be a 'stag' party." He concluded by saying that he was glad Fitzgerald and the Murphys were friends once again.

There was no mention of Zelda in Hemingway's letter. He saved his observations about her for a letter he wrote to Max Perkins two days later. There he was explicit: 90 percent of Fitzgerald's problems could be assigned to Zelda's influence: "Almost every bloody fool thing I have ever seen or known him to do has been directly or indirectly Zelda inspired. I'm probably wrong in this. But I often wonder if he would not have been the best writer we've ever had or likely to have if he hadn't been married to someone that would make him waste *Everything.*" The shift to the past tense indicates that Hemingway already considered the problem past remedy. "I wish to god," he went on, "he'd write a good book and finish it and not poop himself away on those lousy Post stories. I don't blame *Lorimer* I blame Zelda." He made it clear that he didn't want Fitzgerald to know that he thought so.

Interestingly enough, the "lousy" stories Fitzgerald was currently wasting his time on were the Basil stories he had been contributing to the *Post* — the only stories, in fact, that he had been writing lately. Hemingway's earlier Nick Adams stories were also concerned with a young man's coming-of-age in the Midwest, but Fitzgerald's stories were acceptably sophisticated and polite enough for the *Post* audience. There was no denying that they lacked the raw vigor, the cuss words, and fornication that had announced Hemingway's arrival on the literary scene.

The return to Ellerslie was a downhill slide. Fitzgerald completed the two chapters of the novel he had promised Perkins. And that accomplishment brought a stirring of the old pride and enthusiasm. "It seems fine to be sending you something again." Fitzgerald wrote. He went on at some length about the manuscript. Chapter 1 was good he felt; Chapter 2 had caused him some trouble — but it had been twenty-seven thousand words initially. He did not want Perkins to comment on the book until he had seen the complete manuscript, but Fitzgerald was clearly hoping for some encouraging word. "Remember novel is confidential, even to Ernest," he warned, a sign that Hemingway's taunts had found their mark. Perkins was enthusiastic: the first chapter was "excellent"; the second contained "some of the best writing you have ever done — some lovely scenes, and impressions briefly and beautifully conveyed." He had some criticisms but would reserve those until he had the completed book in hand. He pushed for early publication; he hoped it would be in the spring.

But Fitzgerald was past such encouragement. He wrote two more Basil stories — with the usual delays and requests for advances from Ober. And he completed another short story, "The Last of the Belles," reverting to his earlier theme of the Southern belle and the soldier, and indicating that he was still capable of wringing a sense of poignance and loss from earlier material. But his novel proceeded no further than the two chapters he sent Perkins.

Zelda, too, was working. She resumed her ballet lessons in Philadelphia with a crazed energy. She also took on a new instructor, Alexandre Gavrilov, a former dancer with the Diaghilev ballet, and the maître of a ballet troupe, the Ballet Moderne, that performed in New York. (Gavrilov had at least the tinge of greatness; he had been the stand-in Nijinsky used to choreograph *The Afternoon of a Faun*.) At Ellerslie Zelda practiced daily in front of a huge mirror she had bought in Philadelphia — she called it her "whorehouse mirror" — to the insistent scratching of the gramophone. She danced continually when she was alone; she danced when there were guests. John Biggs claimed that he had heard "The March of the Toy Soldiers" so often at Ellerslie that the tune was engraved on every organ in his body. Fitzgerald, obviously piqued by Zelda's dedication, was feeling as estranged as he had been in Paris. In the evenings he went out to drink with Philippe, and the two of them had scrapes from which they had had to be rescued by Lawyer Biggs. At home, Philippe was the butler, an arrangement that had its comic aspects, since the Fitzgeralds had fastened a French car horn to one of the dining room chairs to summon Philippe from the distant kitchen. Zelda thought him "stupid and insubordinate," but she was intimidated by his insolence. To add to the manic disorder of the household, Mademoiselle was infatuated with the butler and frequently became "hysterical" about him. Zelda and Fitzgerald were quarreling often; the subject of Lois Moran was once more in the air. "He left me so much alone," Zelda would say, "that I was very ashamed of wanting him once. . . . He was thinking of the actress; he said so. I said I wanted to leave him but he wouldn't let me go. We fought."

It is possible that in remembering their final season at Ellerslie, Zelda was distorting the past. And it is possible that out of a growing sense of alienation, she had actually put herself in situations that were dangerous. She later described an episode involving Gavrilov that had the quality of a nightmare:

> My dancing teacher was a protégé of Nijinsky. I ate lunch with him at [Reuben's] and went with him to his apartment. There was nothing in the commercial flat except the white spitz of his mistress and a beautiful collection of Leon Bakst. It was a cold afternoon. He asked me if I wanted him to kill me and said I would cry and left me there. I ran to my lesson through the cold streets. I always wore white. . . .

She had become, it seems, a bride on new thresholds.

But the real nightmare that season was an actual event, at Ellerslie: the November 17 weekend visit of the Hemingways. It has come down to posterity in several hearsay versions, full of discrepancies, distortions, and personal prejudices. On those grounds, it is perhaps as hallucinatory an event as one of Zelda's visions.

It was the weekend of the Princeton-Yale game at Palmer Stadium. It began casually enough: the Hemingways, accompanied by Henry (Mike) Strater, met the Fitzgeralds at Princeton. (Scott and Zelda had stayed at Cottage.) Strater, who had been one of Fitzgerald's heroes at Princeton — he was the Burne Holliday of *This Side of Paradise* — was now a practicing artist. He had done his stint in Paris, had been befriended by Joyce and Pound, and had painted early portraits of Hemingway and Hadley. A tall, hulking man with an eye for women (a friend dubbed him Henry Satyr), he thought Zelda was "a lovely person, a lovely, lovely person," and was in agreement with many others that Fitzgerald's drinking "was out of control."

Fitzgerald remained sober during the game, but on the train to Philadelphia he proceeded to get drunk. Hemingway was to give more than one version of the unhappy occasion. In an unpublished section of *A Moveable Feast*, he describes Fitzgerald as becoming insulting on the train ride and repeatedly referring to another passenger, a medical interne, as a clap doctor. At the Philadelphia station, they are met by Philippe with the Fitzgerald Buick. En route to Ellerslie, Philippe complains that Fitzgerald will not allow him to put oil in the car because American automobiles do not need it. Just before the narrative ends, Fitzgerald and Zelda have an argument about the correct route to Ellerslie.

Sara Mayfield gives a different version of the weekend in *Exiles from Paradise:*

> To add to Zelda's troubles, the Hemingways arrived for a visit. Ernest was immensely pleased by his title for his new book, *Men without Women,* because he thought it would sell well to the "gay" boys and the old Vassar girls. His jokes with Scott about pederasty, anal eroticism, and other forms of perversion annoyed and frightened Zelda. And to judge from Ernest's unpublished letters to Scott, she had reason to be alarmed. Fitzgerald and Hemingway went on a bender, got in a fight, and landed in jail. Zelda was further outraged when she learned that Ernest had borrowed a hundred dollars from Scott before he left.

How much of this version is accurate is debatable. It is, of course, highly likely that Zelda told Sara Mayfield some elements of the story and about her feelings toward Hemingway. It is certainly true that Fitzgerald and Hemingway liked to write bad-boy letters to each other and often bantered about their titles. (Hemingway: "THE SUN ALSO RISES [LIKE YOUR COCK IF YOU HAVE ONE]: A greater Gatsby." Fitzgerald: " This tough talk is not really characteristic of me — it's the influence of *All the Sad Young Men Without Women in Love.* . . . 'Now I Lay Me' was a fine story — you ought to write a companion piece, "Now I Lay Her.' Excuse my bawdiness but I'm oversexed.") It is quite possible that in the course of a boozy weekend the two made a schoolboy attempt to be raunchy and blasé on any subject, including pederasty, particularly if they succeeded in getting a response from Zelda or the other guests. And if Zelda had begun, as she recalled, to have anxieties about her attachment to Egorova, she would have felt threatened.

It was true, however, that Fitzgerald had had some kind of episode at the train station, following the Hemingway visit to Ellerslie. In a note written from aboard the Spirit of St. Louis, Hemingway offered the conventional thank-yous: "We had a wonderful time — you were both grand — I am sorry I made a shall we say nuisance of myself about getting to the train on time." There is no indication that the two men fought, but there is a mention of some mysterious encounter with a policeman. "When you were in the hands of the Cop," Hemingway wrote, "I called on the phone from our platform and explained you were a great writer — the Cop was very nice — He said you said I was a great writer too but he had never heard of either of us." Ellerslie mansion, Hemingway noted, "is the most cockeyed beautiful place I've ever seen." Clearly, their brush with the law, whatever its nature, was nothing too serious.

Another, and much more derogatory account of that weekend, given by Hemingway, is reported in *Papa Hemingway* by A. E. Hotchner. In this version, which has its inaccuracies, the setting is a mansion outside Baltimore, and there is no indication that Pauline was with Hemingway. The car has become a custom-made Hotchkiss (an automobile Fitzgerald never owned), and the coachman is named Pierre. At the dinner table, Fitzgerald has uncorked six bottles of Burgundy, knowing Hemingway's preference. The most searing part of the story is Fitzgerald's behavior during the meal, which was served by a Negro maid. In a thoroughly drunken state, Fitzgerald says to her, at least ten times, "Aren't you the best piece of tail I ever had? Tell Mr. Hemingway." And there is a last, nightmarish account of the ride to the railroad station on the following day. Fitzgerald is so drunk and so irritated by Hemingway's leaving that he kicks his foot through the windshield and is cut and bleeding. Hemingway, knowing that the act is a device to make him miss his train, insists that the chauffeur drive to the station before taking Fitzgerald to the doctor. Zelda is sobbing in the back seat; Fitzgerald becomes so abusive and hysterical that Hemingway is forced to slap him. After such an episode, it seems hardly likely that Hemingway would have been capable of writing the bland bread-and-butter note that he did.

The only eyewitness to this apocalyptic — or apocryphal — episode in the lives of the Fitzgeralds is Henry Strater, the surviving guest of the party. Strater left early in the morning, before the Hemingways' departure. Badgered by historians and biographers, determined not to be "Hemingwayed to death" or become an appendage to the legends of the Fitzgeralds and Hemingways, Strater prefers to be remembered for his own achievements as a painter. He refuses to discuss the Ellerslie weekend, except to say that when he

got to the station the next morning, he hoped he would never see
Fitzgerald or Hemingway again. "Those two," he has said, "they
were really awful. They brought out the worst in each other."

The Ellerslie lease was up in March 1929. Fitzgerald had accomplished nothing further on his novel. Once more they decided to
leave for Europe, and booked passage on the *Conte Biancamano,* bound
for Genoa. Early in March, on the eve of his departure, Fitzgerald
sent Perkins a note:

> Dear Max, I am sneaking away like a thief without leaving the
> chapters — there is a weeks work to straighten them out & in the
> confusion of influenza & leaving, I havn't been able to do it. I'll do
> it on the boat & send it from Genoa. A thousand thanks for your
> patience — just trust me a few months longer, Max — its been a
> discouraging time for me too but I will never forget your kindness
> and the fact that you've never reproached me.

9

A Country Where Many Things End

THEIR RECOLLECTIONS of their last trip abroad would become a litany of their unhappiness: accusations, recriminations, rationalizations, bitter reproaches. Zelda remembered that on the crossing Fitzgerald struck up his own friendships. She was "very unimaginative" with a dark-haired man who thought it was nice that he had a brown jacket and she had a blue one. There were champagne parties in their cabin; she vaguely recalled that she wanted to show the dark man a new nightgown she had bought. She also remembered that she and Scott slept together in Genoa:

> On the boat coming over you paid absolutely no attention of any kind to me except to refuse me the permission to stay to a concert with whatever-his-name-was. I think the most humiliating and bestial thing that ever happened to me in my life is a scene that you probably don't remember even, in Genoa.

Fitzgerald, in his escape from his stillborn novel, looked forward to carefree times — and was disappointed:

> Another spring — I would see Ernest whom I had launched. Gerald and Sara who through my agency had been able to try the movies. At least life would be less drab; there would be parties with people who offered something, conversations with people with something to say. Later swimming and getting tanned and young and being near the sea. . . . By the time we reached the beautiful Riviera I had developed such an inferiority complex that I couldn't [face] anyone unless I was tight. . . . You were gone now — I scarcely remembered you that summer.

Strangely, Zelda remembered that they were happy at Nice. She was back to her ballet lessons again. She and Scott were happy walking in the bright sunlight, watching a frog swallower on the promenade, taking in the awful comedies at the casino:

> We drank apéritifs at a blue café in front of the Jetée and I loved walking to the hotel from my dancing. The sapphire twilight was deep and mysterious and I hummed the songs that the old man played, mostly Strauss waltzes. . . . The studio piano was out of tune. The hotel bedroom was red plush and the bed was brass and the rooms were on the sea and I loved [Scott] very much.

In personal relationships there are no certifiable truths: the happiest times blend into the landscape; the unhappy times are mired in the search for self-justification, excuses, mitigating circumstances. Fitzgerald was drinking, and his memories were probably clouded by alcohol. Zelda's recollections were written during bouts of lucidity in one mental institution or another. They were trying to trace the breakdown of their marriage, fix the blame. Even from the distance of a decade, they remembered every grievance in detail. Fitzgerald's bill of particulars was steeped in self-pity. Zelda's, full of reproaches and charges of indifference, nonetheless stressed each moment of happiness — spots of bright color — as if every personal defeat might have its special geography, its own locale.

The promptness with which Fitzgerald sent Harold Ober "The Rough Crossing," a short story, was unusual. Late in March, he mailed it from the Hôtel Beau Rivage in Nice. Considering the excuses and delays of the past year, it may be that the recent crossing with Zelda provided the inspiration for the new story. Fitzgerald was extraordinarily sensitive to the impact of an experience, but one often has the suspicion that, plagued as he was by the need for quick money, he tended to capitalize on his material too soon, before it had ripened into the kind of deeper significance that would have made even his commercial stories more important.

Many of the details and some of the atmosphere of "The Rough Crossing," to be sure, could easily have been drawn from any of the boozy crossings the Fitzgeralds had made on one ship or another, passing from America to Europe or on a return voyage. (The storm quite likely was derived from their last trip, on the *Carmania*.) But a brief entry in Fitzgerald's ledger, "Zelda's Beau," indicates that the 1929 crossing on the *Conte Biancamano* provided the setting for Fitzgerald's story of an archetypal couple, Adrian and Eva Smith, whose disintegrating marriage undergoes further stress during the course of a transatlantic voyage. Both Smiths become involved in pointless affairs, the playwright husband with a brassy young girl who pursues him, dazzled by his fame. The jealous wife drinks so much during the course of the voyage that the captain refuses her any more liquor (a gender reversal of the situation in the Jungle Club). Eva has a flirtation with an obstreperous young man who becomes her champion against the pampered husband. Inevitably both lovers are dumped before the end of the trip. The Smiths enter into a conspiratorial agreement, denying that anything has really happened. It must have been, they say, two other Smiths who were involved, there being so many Smiths in the world. It is a clever ending, but one that leaves Fitzgerald's characters unchanged, as nonchalant as they were at the beginning of the story.

Nice, Zelda remembered, was "brittly cold," but somehow, along the Promenade des Anglais, people seemed to be walking at a summer tempo. She was working strenuously at the ballet, studying with another Russian, Nevalskaya, though she disliked the studio. Fitzgerald had begun to fancy himself something of a gourmet; he and Zelda drove to Villefranche to sample salade Niçoise and a special bouillabaisse. He promised Ober "the best dinner procurable in France" if Ober would make the trip abroad. "I've become something of a connessieur," he announced with his typical misspelling. As proof of the claim, he sent the agency a brief skit on gourmandise, intended for *The New Yorker,* a publication he was courting. Titled "A Short Autobiography (With Acknowledgments to Nathan)," it was a year-by-year inventory of memorable meals and supposedly proper wines, ranging from 1913 to 1929 ("Chambéry Fraise with the Seldes on their honeymoon. . . . Kirsch in a Burgundy inn against the rain with E. Hemingway"). *The New Yorker* published it in its May 25 issue. Zelda, not to be outdone, later wrote an article on the same topic for the same magazine. But with perverse ingenuity, her skit, titled "The Continental Angle," depicted an American couple dining in a French restaurant, recalling dinners in Broadway chophouses and pancakes at Childs.

Fitzgerald was spending much of his time drinking or gambling at the casino. His ledger acknowledges the usual consequences. Philippe, his drinking companion, had trouble in a speakeasy. There is a notation, "The Prison at Nice," which suggests that he had another of his run-ins with the law. Still, he informed Ober, "I'm happy to be back here."

It was still too early in the season for the regulars to have moved down to the Riviera, so the Fitzgeralds moved north to Paris at the beginning of April. While hunting for an apartment, they took rooms in a cheap hotel whose name they could not recall later, but that evidently was so new that the cement was barely dry. It was a pointless economy, since they took their meals out every night. Zelda did not like the starchy table d'hôte at the hotel.

It was another of their stints of renewing acquaintances with old friends and meeting new ones in a Paris that was abloom with spring. They saw John Bishop often, but avoided Margaret whenever possible. In addition to their château at Orgeval, the Bishops had an apartment in Paris, fashionably near the Etoile. Bishop craved literary company and enjoyed it, but his comfortable life was somewhat resented by his friends. Nor did he work hard enough at his writing, they felt. The poet Allen Tate later wrote, "John is like a man lying in a warm bath who faintly hears the telephone ringing downstairs." Bishop, writing to Bunny Wilson during the full tide of that spring, noted "Cummings is here . . . Fitzgerald, Hemingway, all of which makes Paris pick up even more than the chestnut blooms and the May sun."

Townsend Martin and Teddy Chanler were in Paris. They saw Esther Murphy, who was soon to be married to John Strachey, the political writer. Fitzgerald found the Kalmans, Oscar and Sandy, a disappointment, especially Oscar. Writing to Sinclair Lewis, also a friend of the Kalmans, Fitzgerald complimented Lewis on his new novel, noting, "Dozens of people have become 'Dodsworth' for me within the last fortnight (Oscar Kalman among others)." It was during that spring in Paris, too, that they met the English art critic Clive Bell, whose avant-garde ideas, if not his bumptious personality, made an impression on Zelda.

But it was not the happy and relaxed time Fitzgerald had anticipated. Zelda resumed her rigorous dance lessons with Mme. Egorova. Fitzgerald was still drinking—"almost always," Zelda claimed. Sara Mayfield, in Paris to check the couturier collections, had been warned by mutual friends to avoid Fitzgerald because of his recent antics. His latest had followed an evening of heavy drinking at

Ciro's, when he swiped a baker boy's tricycle and pedaled past the cafés along the Champs-Elysées, thumping the Russian doormen with a long loaf of bread. On one of the few occasions that Mayfield met the couple, at the Deux Magots, they were at the tail end of a party that had been going on for days and were surrounded by disreputable types they had picked up along the way. Fitzgerald and Zelda had gotten into an argument on the subject of Hemingway, Zelda referring to him bitterly as "a pansy with hair on his chest."

The friendship with Hemingway had begun to go sour, and Fitzgerald, rather than letting it slide, became defensive about it. The Hemingways were now living at 6 rue de Ferou, in an apartment for which Hemingway hoped to get an extended lease. When he learned, earlier in the spring, that Fitzgerald would be coming to Paris, Hemingway pointedly wrote to Maxwell Perkins, asking him not to give Fitzgerald his address. The last time Fitzgerald was in Paris he had gotten Hemingway kicked out of his apartment by insulting the landlord, pissing on the front porch, and trying to break down the door in the small hours of the morning, around 3 and 4 o'clock. He preferred to meet Scott in public places, Hemingway said. He was very fond of Scott, but he would beat him up before he let him come and get them ousted from the new apartment. It had nothing to do with friendship, Hemingway went on—that implied obligations on both sides—but when he heard that Fitzgerald would be in Paris, it gave him the horrors.

The prohibition against Fitzgerald's visiting the rue de Ferou did not hold up long; both Scott and Zelda recalled visits there. They once were invited to dinner, but Fitzgerald's comment was "Certain coldness." Hemingway's action could hardly have been taken as anything but an unfriendly gesture, and Fitzgerald was becoming a connoisseur of slights and snubs. At a later date he registered them all in his notebooks. "Ernest apartment" was duly recorded, as was "Ernest taking me to that bum restaurant. Change of station implied." Hemingway was not the only offender. A rather lengthy list included the Hotel O'Connor, John Barrymore, Constance Talmadge, a Tallulah Bankhead telephone call, and the University of Chicago.

It is more than likely, too, that Fitzgerald considered it a snub that Hemingway did not let him read *A Farewell to Arms* before it was set up in galley proofs for its serial appearance in *Scribner's Magazine.* Athough he regarded it as a superior book, it did not deter him from sending Hemingway an officious letter suggesting

all sorts of cuts and corrections. From the numerous criticisms it is
clear that Fitzgerald wanted to appear the professional author confronting a serious job of work, untroubled by considerations of
friendship or tact. "114–121 is slow and needs cutting—" he told
Hemingway; "it hasn't the incisiveness of other short portraits in
this book or in yr. other books. The characters too numerous and
too much nailed down by gags. *Please* cut!" Hemingway's heroine,
Catherine, was not all she should be: "talks too much physically. In
cutting their conversations cut some of her speeches rather than his.
She is too glib." "Remember," he noted, "the brave expectant il-
legitimmate mother is an OLD SITUATION and has been exploited
by all sorts of people you won't lower yourself to read." There were
genuine compliments. The account of the retreat from Caporetto was
"marvelous," and Fitzgerald concluded, "A beautiful book it is!"
But he was aware that he may have overstepped his bounds: "Our
poor old friendship probably won't survive this but there you are—
better me than some nobody in the Literary Review that doesn't care
about you and your future."

Hemingway's response was blunt and private. "Kiss my ass
E.H.," he wrote at the bottom of Fitzgerald's letter. Although he
seemed to accept the criticism with a certain amount of equanimity,
the rancor did not dissipate. Over the years, his anger, like a well-
corked bottle of wine, matured with age. In 1951, he told Fitzgerald's biographer Arthur Mizener that Fitzgerald's letter of advice,
with its fifty or more suggestions, was "one of the worst damned
documents I have ever read and I would give it to no one."

Fitzgerald aimed to be helpful in other ways as well. Hemingway was already tangling with Max Perkins on the subject of the
strong language in *A Farewell to Arms,* and he was already irate
because Perkins had given a copy of the manuscript to Owen Wister,
who admired the novel but was distressed about the four-letter words,
and recommended changes. And because Robert Bridges, the editor
of *Scribner's,* was making editorial changes. Fitzgerald had already
warned him that the word *cocksucker* would get the book suppressed
and confiscated within two days of publication. Eager to be of service,
he gave Hemingway a copy of Erich Maria Remarque's *All Quiet on
the Western Front,* a war novel that had had a phenomenal success in
Germany and England and was due for publication in America. It
contained a number of four-letter words that Hemingway could use
in his own defense. Of course, there is no greater service that one

friendly author can render to another than to alert him to a best-selling book on the same subject that is likely to steal his thunder. ("Ernest's last letter a little worried, but I don't see why," Fitzgerald wrote Perkins in bland innocence. "To hell with the toughs of Boston. I hope to God *All Quiet on the Western Front* won't cut in on his sales. My bet is the book will pass 50,000.") But it was clear that Hemingway was worried: he enumerated the four-letter words in the Remarque novel, suggested that Perkins print the most offensive word as c——s——r (readers might think it meant *cocksure*), and gave vent to one of his real concerns: "The trouble is Max that before my book will be out there will be this All Quiet on the Western Front book . . . and I hate to kill the value of mine by emasculating it."

At times Fitzgerald was no less frank in his dealings with other writers. That spring he met the young Canadian writer Morley Callaghan, whom Hemingway had known on the *Toronto Star*. Perkins had recently taken him on as a Scribner's author, publishing a book of Callaghan's short stories, *A Native Argosy*. Perkins considered the twenty-six-year-old Canadian's work the "genuine thing" and wrote Fitzgerald that Callaghan was very eager to meet him. Callaghan and his wife were visiting Paris for the first time. Perkins had already assured Callaghan that he need not stand on ceremony in calling on Fitzgerald. It proved to be the wrong advice. Both Scott and Zelda were cold in their reception; they made it evident that they were "tired" after an evening at the theater. Nor did Callaghan get an enthusiastic response from Fitzgerald on the not yet published novel, *It's Never Over,* he had asked him to read. "Your frank opinion of the book is honestly appreciated," Callaghan wrote afterward. "It was what I wanted. If I had caught you at any other time I would have been the poorer for it." Somewhat lamely he added, "Please don't think that I resent the way you told me the novel was rotten. It would have been much easier for you, I am sure, to have said that it was a nice piece of work, and so I am grateful to you."

Although, as Callaghan relates in his memoir, *That Summer in Paris,* he saw the Fitzgeralds frequently, Fitzgerald seems never to have warmed to the younger man. Part of the difficulty, perhaps, was that Callaghan was not quite deferential enough to either Fitzgerald or Hemingway. At one of their earlier meetings, Fitzgerald read aloud a passage of Hemingway's novel that impressed him. He was annoyed when Callaghan described it as a bit "too deliberate."

Zelda, too, maintained that Hemingway's style was "pretty damned Biblical."

But the event that most damaged the relationship of the three men, that summer in Paris, was the boxing match between Callaghan and Hemingway in the gymnasium of the American Club. The match was scheduled for five in the afternoon, but Hemingway and Fitzgerald had dined so well at Prunier's that Hemingway was afraid he would be too groggy to box well, so the match was pushed ahead an hour or so. Fitzgerald served as the official timekeeper. In one of the early rounds Callaghan landed a punch that split Hemingway's lower lip, causing it to bleed profusely. Hemingway, in response, began to move in more aggressively. Callaghan somehow landed a punch that caught Hemingway off guard and sent him sprawling backward on the floor.

At just that moment, Fitzgerald, realizing that he had passed the two-minute period, exclaimed, "Oh, my God! I let the round go four minutes." Hemingway swore, then bent a furious eye on Fitzgerald. "All right, Scott," he said. "If you want to see me getting the shit knocked out of me, just say so. Only don't say you made a mistake." He strode off to the shower room to stop the bleeding. "My God," Fitzgerald complained to Callaghan, "he thinks I did it on purpose. Why would I do it on purpose?" For the remainder of the match Fitzgerald was ashen-faced and miserable.

There were to be several versions of the Hemingway-Callaghan bout, in which the circumstances and the time of the rounds varied considerably. In one of Hemingway's later accounts the miscalled round stretched to thirteen minutes. But the essence of the charge was that Fitzgerald had deliberately let the round go on too long. Fitzgerald would never quite exonerate himself—in his own mind at least, and probably not in Hemingway's—of having wanted to see Hemingway beaten. The version of the story that Hemingway sent to Max Perkins was that Fitzgerald had let the round go on too long because he was "so interested to see if I was going to hit the floor!"

It made matters only worse that, in one of the later rounds, Callaghan accidentally tripped and fell to one knee. In his eagerness to make amends, Fitzgerald called out too hurriedly, "One knockdown to Ernest, one to Morley." By that point, both Callaghan and Hemingway despised the timekeeper.

To Morley Callaghan the Fitzgeralds were a remarkably handsome and, on first acquaintance, a remarkably sophisticated couple. But he was surprised at the peremptory way that Fitzgerald treated Zelda on occasion, and at the meek way that Zelda accepted his commands. Whenever Zelda became too excited or keen — though much of the time she seemed moodily silent — Fitzgerald would tell her she was tired and send her home to bed. Afterward, Fitzgerald would explain that Zelda's dancing lessons were strenuous and that she needed rest.

On a later occasion, when the two couples were having dinner together, Zelda made a point of letting it be known that she was a writer, too, and that she wrote quite well. Callaghan noticed that she had a disconcerting habit of laughing to herself when there seemed no real occasion for it. She was noticeably restless. Once, in an animated mood, Zelda suddenly suggested they go roller-skating, an idea that seemed like fun to the Callaghans. But Scott was visibly reluctant. When it became apparent that everyone else wanted to go roller-skating, he abruptly grabbed Zelda by the wrist and, like a father dealing with a child, told her that she had to go home. It was one of those instances when Fitzgerald decided to exercise authority over his wife, but Callaghan's account suggests there may have been an element of desperation in Fitzgerald's behavior. When Callaghan asked about Zelda's compulsive attraction to dance, Fitzgerald explained that Zelda wanted to "have something for herself, be something herself."

Dancing in Paris that summer, Zelda claimed, was like "living in a dream." She began to feel like a priest about her work. She had found an "impersonal escape" into a world in which she could express herself. In the mornings she took dance class; in the afternoons, private lessons. Sometimes, she spent the evenings at practice and Sundays as well. Mme. Egorova had become the focus of her days. Out of gratitude, Zelda felt she should do something for the woman in return for her kindness and patience. It was important to Zelda that she be the first at the studio in the morning in order to show her dedication. Because the studio on the rue Caumartin was hot and steamy, she brought lemonade. She bought gardenias for Egorova, because they were white and cool and beautiful like Madame. In her watchfulness, Zelda fixed on any sign of disapproval or disappointment in her teacher, any slackening of interest. Once she cried for two hours because Madame told her to work with another student, a girl whom Zelda considered far less accomplished than she was. She was beginning to experience the most intense sensations when she danced—as if everything had turned red, or, oddly, as if everything were drained of color. She began to avoid the blank stare of the studio windows. But if she looked out them and into the street, she saw people looking like ants in a bottle.

Her friends, her husband, realized that Zelda had started too late; that she was too short, too old; that she lacked the suppleness of youth demanded by ballet. Fitzgerald first indulged her and then grew annoyed. The Murphys, invited to watch her at the training school, were embarrassed and sat through the performance unhappily: Zelda was awkward, her legs were too muscular, there was something about her intensity when she danced that made her look grotesque.

When Scott showed any interest in Egorova, Zelda became jealous. Once when he agreed to go to dinner at Egorova's studio, he passed out drunk in front of Madame; for Zelda that was practically an act of blasphemy. On another occasion, they took Egorova to an expensive dinner at the George V; Scott pulled his Prince Charming act, and the dance teacher enjoyed herself. (Faced with Zelda's abject devotion, Egorova may have found Fitzgerald's gallantries a relief.) It may have been at Zelda's urging that Fitzgerald had even tried to "place" Egorova's son.

Scott, by way of explaining his drinking, complained that he worked all day and wanted to relax at night but that Zelda was always too tired. She had become more and more an "egotist and a bore." Zelda's long monologues on ballet, on dance steps, had pushed him into drinking. Whenever he tried to start a conversation on some other topic, Zelda's response was glazed eyes. Her industry and perseverance may have irritated him—perhaps even frightened him. She had reached a stage where she hated taking money from him for her lessons. That was one of the reasons that she had made such a dedicated effort to write that summer.

The opportunity, in fact, had come earlier—in the late winter, at Ellerslie, when H. N. Swanson, the editor of *College Humor*, suggested that Zelda do a sequence of stories on different types of women for his magazine, though he expected that Fitzgerald would look over the stories and edit them and that they would be published under both names. Swanson wanted the pieces to be stories, not philosophical discussions, and he hoped that each of the girls—city debutante, young married woman, Southern belle, country club girl, for instance—would have a name. The project had not begun under the happiest circumstances. The first story, "The Original Follies Girl," apparently was the cause of a fight between Zelda and Fitzgerald. Presumably it was the story she had finished in the Philadelphia library one afternoon, after which she went out with some of the girls from the dance school and got drunk in an Italian restaurant. Fitzgerald was furious. It was certainly the story that Fitzgerald delivered to Ober, in place of one of the Basil stories that he could not finish, just before they left for Genoa. "This is a poor substitute . . ." Fitzgerald claimed, "tho it is a beautifully written thing." During the summer in Paris, Zelda ground out several more stories, all of which received high praise from Swanson. And at Fitzgerald's insistence, she was paid higher fees. When they reached Paris, Fitzgerald had mailed Zelda's "Poor Working Girl" to Ober. In June, it was followed by "Southern Girl," and within the next several months Zelda completed three more: "The Girl the Prince Liked," "The Girl with Talent," and "A Millionaire's Girl." The two or three stories Fitzgerald completed during the summer— "Majesty," "At Your Age," "The Swimmers," and the gourmet piece for *The New Yorker*—were preceded by the usual cablegrams of apology and requests for advances, but it is possible that Zelda's example may have goaded Fitzgerald into making a more serious effort with his own writing.

With the exception of "A Millionaire's Girl," all of Zelda's stories appeared in *College Humor* under the byline Swanson had insisted on: "By F. Scott and Zelda Fitzgerald." But they were, as Fitzgerald acknowledged, almost entirely written by Zelda, although Fitzgerald edited them and pointed them up before mailing the manuscripts to Ober. When it became apparent that Swanson thought highly enough of the stories to feature them, Fitzgerald prodded Ober into asking for more money, first upping the price to $500. Next, he suggested that if *College Humor* was not willing to pay more than $500, then "it seems to me Zelda's name should stand alone." Swanson eventually agreed to pay $800. With scrupulous honesty, Fitzgerald noted in his ledger Zelda's authorship of the stories and the fees she received. It was not only a matter of principle; it was a necessity for income tax purposes. But for all his promotional efforts on Zelda's behalf, it is probable that he was beginning to feel a bit overlooked in the light of Zelda's newfound success. When he sent Ober "The Girl with Talent," he said that it should be worth $1000. The stories were all "pretty strong draughts on Zelda's and my common store of material," he maintained. "This is Mary Hay for instance and the 'Girl the Prince Liked' was Josephine Ordway both of whom I had in my notebook to use." In other words, he had been sacrificing his material for Zelda's benefit.

Fitzgerald had always been aware of Zelda's special gifts as a writer, certainly of her flair for description. She was, he conceded, "a great original in her way, with perhaps a more intense flame at its highest than I ever had." But with the shrewd accuracy of a writer, he also pointed out: "She isn't a 'natural story-teller' in the sense that I am, and unless a story comes to her fully developed and crying to be told she's liable to flounder around rather unsuccessfully among problems of construction." The prime example of her lack of inventiveness in plot and narrative was "Southern Girl." Lacking those elements, Zelda simply appropriated the narrative situation of Scott's brilliant story "The Last of the Belles," published in a March issue of *The Saturday Evening Post,* a bare two months or more before she wrote "Southern Girl." Like Scott's tale, Zelda's is the story of a popular Southern belle who is jilted by a Northern soldier. In depicting the hero, Zelda chose a few details from Fitzgerald's military career: Dan Stone just misses being sent overseas. And for good measure, she borrowed aspects from another of Fitzgerald's prize stories, "The Ice Palace," in which the Southern heroine visits her lover in the Midwest and is forced to recognize that she does not fit in. But, as if to de-emphasize the comparison, Zelda has her Southern schoolteacher, Harriet, visit Dan Stone in midsummer.

Fitzgerald may have been unconsciously aware that Zelda was following very closely in his footsteps. The evidence is a rather peculiar slip of his pen. In the summer of 1929, Harold Ober wrote Fitzgerald, asking him to select one of his stories for inclusion in an anthology being edited by the *Literary Digest.* Inadvertently, Fitzgerald proposed "Southern Girl" as one of his choices. In his next letter to his agent, he corrected the error: "When I suggested story for Lit Digest I accidentally said *Southern Girl* meaning *Last of the Belles.*"

But the most important of the stories Zelda wrote for the *College Humor* series was "A Millionaire's Girl." It was the best of her stories, the one that most nearly approached Fitzgerald's standards. It was also the most controversial in terms of the Fitzgerald legend. To begin with, it was Zelda's well-considered rebuttal to Fitzgerald's fictional treatment of the Lois Moran affair. And the suspicion is that it was intended, all along, to be the climactic story of her "Girl" series. Throughout the sequence the narrator's name and sex remain unidentified. In "A Millionaire's Girl," when Caroline and Barry drive out to Long Island to annouce their engagement to their narrator-friend, Caroline asks, "Is this Fitzgerald's roadhouse?" — the nickname of the Great Neck cottage — revealing that the narrator is either Zelda or Scott, but leaving it uncertain as to which it is.

The controversy surrounding "A Millionaire's Girl" revolved around what is regarded as Fitzgerald's and Harold Ober's high-handed treatment of what was admittedly Zelda's story but was published in *The Saturday Evening Post* under Fitzgerald's name alone. Whatever the actual guilt or blame, now difficult to settle, it seems to have begun as an honest mistake. Fitzgerald ordinarily sent type-script copies of both his and Zelda's stories to Ober, with last-minute corrections in his handwriting. When Ober received "A Millionaire's Girl," he believed it was one of Scott's stories and sent it to the *Post*, where it was promptly accepted. Writing to Fitzgerald when he received the manuscript, Ober commented, "I like it a lot and some of your lines about California are very amusing, indeed." Within a few days, the error was discovered, and Ober cabled Fitzgerald that the *Post* would pay $4000 for it but on condition that Zelda's name be dropped from the byline. Fitzgerald, presumably with Zelda's acquiescence, agreed. At this stage, the rationalizations took over. Ober wrote to Fitzgerald, "I really felt a little guilty about dropping Zelda's name from that story . . . but I think she understands that using the two names would have tied the story up with the *College Humor* stories and might have got us into trouble." The excuse Ober offered was that it was "much too good a story" for *College Humor*. It had so much of Fitzgerald in it, Ober claimed, "that I am sure it would have been recognized as your story no matter under what name it was published." It was all right to let Swanson have short sketches, he noted, "but as I wrote you some time ago, I think it is a great mistake to waste good ideas on Swanson for such a low price." But he asked Fitzgerald to tell Zelda that it was "a mighty good piece of work." The chief consideration, it appears, for Fitzgerald and Ober and perhaps for Zelda, was the difference between $800 and $4000.

"Zelda," Fitzgerald answered Ober, "was delighted with your compliments." The stories, of course, had brought her welcome attention and praise—and some modest amounts of money. At their worst, the "Girl" stories are a superior travel and hotel guide, or a manual on interior decoration in the twenties, a catalogue of haute couture and hair styles, written in a vividly descriptive style that would have made Zelda one of the important feature writers for *Vogue* or *Harper's Bazaar* or *Vanity Fair,* if she had written for those publications rather than *College Humor.* As fictional exercises, however, they had a more important role: through the guise of other lives (based often on women she knew or read about in the society columns), she found an opportunity to explore and imagine her own feelings, herself superimposed on the invented lives of others. She may even have been sending signals to Fitzgerald about her muddled interior life, her aspirations, her dangerous pyschological state. That certainly must have been the intention of a lengthy passage about the heroine, Gay, the dancer in the earliest of the stories, "The Original Follies Girl." And it seems to have been a message that Fitzgerald let pass unheeded, or recognized only when it was too late:

> At this time she was making an awful struggle to hang onto something that had never crystallized for her — it was the past. She wanted to get her hands on something tangible, to be able to say, "That is real, that is part of my experience, that goes into this or that category, this that happened to me is part of my memories." She could not correlate the events that had made up her life, so now when she was beginning to feel time passing she felt as though she had just been born; born without a family, without a friendly house about her, without any scheme to settle into or to rebel against. The isolation of each day made her incapable of feeling surprise and caused her to be wonderfully tolerant, which is another way of saying that she was sick with spiritual boredom.

II

In July 1929 they were once more on Scott's "beloved Riviera," having rented the Villa Fleur des Bois in Cannes. Scott assured Harold Ober, from whom he had been drawing heavy advances, that he would be keeping a "really inexpensive menage." He was damned tired, he said, of the delays on his novel; he looked forward to two solid months of work on it and was hopeful of having it completed by September. His letter to Max Perkins was equally promising: "I am working night & day on novel from new angle that I think will solve previous difficulties." The last words were an indication that he was once more involved in another of the novel's substantial revisions and was not likely to meet any deadline. Late in August he sent a rosy report to Hemingway, who was touring the bullfights in Spain. "I've been working like hell," Fitzgerald wrote, "better than for four years, and now am confident of getting old faithful off before the all-American teams are picked." There was some truth in the report, for during that summer Fitzgerald worked up a fifty-page section that developed a new theme for the book, dropping the one of matricide. This one involved a movie director and his wife, Lew and Nicole Kelly, who, on shipboard traveling to Europe, encounter an aspiring young actress named Rosemary. All the personae would figure in *Tender Is the Night.* (The Kellys, however, would be dropped from the book but would serve as the protagonists in a story, "One Trip Abroad.") For once, there is supporting evidence, other than Fitzgerald's letters to Perkins and Ober, that he had really begun to work. A September entry in his ledger reads, "Work on novel. Stenographers."

Hemingway, however, was not buying such tales. His warm congratulations were tainted with suspicion. "I cant tell you how glad I am you are getting the book done," he wrote. Then, skeptically, he added, "Of course, all this may be premature and you may not be finishing your book but only putting me on the list of friends to receive the more glowing reports." Scott's problem, Hemingway wrote him, was the laudatory review of *The Great Gatsby* that Gilbert Seldes had written for *The Dial.* "After that you became self conscious about it and knew you must write a masterpiece." But Scott should realize that "nobody but Fairies" could write masterpieces as a conscious effort. "Anybody else can only write as well as they can."

All the documentary evidence — the mere fifty pages of a new attempt, the ledger notes, Fitzgerald's letters to Hemingway, his and Zelda's bickering recollections of the summer at Cannes — indicates that it was not a time conducive to writing. It was a period of unhappiness and irreversible estrangements in their marital life, a time of parties spoiled by Fitzgerald's drunkenness and of angry quarrels over Zelda's dancing lessons. "It was a nightmare," Zelda remembered. "I worked every day in Nice, largely to escape."

Fitzgerald's August letter to Hemingway is sardonic testimony of their unhappy stay: "It's been gay here but we are, thank God, desperately unpopular and not invited anywhere." On the average of once a week or so, he claimed, they saw the Murphys and their guest, Dorothy Parker. Fitzgerald felt a comradely sympathy with Parker, whose drinking problems and depressions were as serious as his own. He even tried to do her a favor by recommending the novel or novelette she was supposedly working on to Perkins, knowing that she was not getting good prices from publishers. But he was miffed that she seemed so unsympathetic to his own emotional problems. Evidently he had watched, with an edge of meanness, the hospitality the Murphys were lavishing on their guest. They had "given their whole performance for her this summer and I think, tho she would be the last to admit it, she's had the time of her life," he told Hemingway. Gerald Murphy, Fitzgerald noted, was "older, less gay, more social, but not so changed as many people in five years."

There were parties with the Murphys and the visiting playwright Philip Barry and his wife, who had a villa in Cannes. There were trips on the Murphys' yacht, *Honoria*. (The merriment apparently concealed the Murphys' worries about their son Patrick, who was ill all summer with what would later be diagnosed as tuberculosis.) Fitzgerald's behavior must have been particularly trying under the circumstances. "You disgraced yourself at the Barrys' party, on the yacht at Monte Carlo, at the Casino with Gerald and Dotty," Zelda remembered. Fitzgerald's ledger corroborated his sins and added others: "Being drunk & snubbed." And there were other strange entries: "Fairies Breakdown."

In periods of stress and self-justification or self-pity, Fitzgerald had recurrences of the tuberculosis fears he had had in his youth. He was examined by a radiologist at Cannes; the x rays revealed old lesions but no current infection. Fitzgerald remained unconvinced; it became part of his martyrdom.

Apparently when drunk he felt the need to prove that he was a working writer to the acquaintances he brought home with him on his sprees. One morning, after such a night, Zelda found his manuscript strewn all over the floor. She was retreating more and more into herself, even to the point of avoiding Scottie, because, she said, she couldn't stand the newest governess, Mme. Bellois. Fitzgerald, although he disliked her as much, nonetheless took some kind of perverse pleasure in carrying on interminable conversations with her about French politics. By now, Zelda had taken a place on his list of enemies: "You were simply one of all the people who disliked me or were indifferent to me. I didn't like to think of you." His ledger impressions were blunt: "Zelda dancing & sweating. Rows & indifference."

He sent a testy and defensive letter to Hemingway, stating that during the two and a half months he had been on the Riviera, he had written one short story and twenty thousand words of his novel. He had taken another chapter to the typist. (At the most he had written only some fifty pages of manuscript, about half the word count he claimed.) Nevertheless he played the hard-working author, insisting:

> I've paid for it with the usual nervous depressions and such drinking manners as the lowest bistro (bistrot?) boy would scorn. My latest tendency is to collapse about 11:00 and, with the tears flowing from my eyes or the gin rising to their level and leaking over, tell interested friends or acquaintances that I haven't a friend in the world and likewise care for nobody, generally including Zelda, and often implying current company—after which the current company tend to become less current and I wake up in strange rooms in strange palaces.

He was trying to work, brooding a good deal, reading detective stories. He realized that "anyone in my state of mind, who has in addition never been able to hold his tongue is pretty poor company." But when he was drunk, Fitzgerald boasted, "I make them all pay and pay and pay."

He apologized for the "gloomy letter." But as a parting shot, he added: "Here's a last flicker of the old cheap pride: the *Post* now pays the old whore $4000 a screw. But now it's because she's mastered the 40 positions—in her youth one was enough." This time, he was truthful about the fee.

In the fall, they took an apartment at 10 rue Pergolèse in Paris. The ménage included themselves and Scottie, who would soon be enrolled in school, a new governess, Mlle. Serez, who mercifully proved to be more agreeable than the departed Mme. Bellois, a *bonne à toute faire,* and a little terrier named Adage, whom they had bought in the spring. Presumably Fitzgerald had given him the name in honor of the old adage about man's best friend; he needed the dog to replace the friends he was alienating. Adage was not housebroken, adding another complication to the household.

Zelda was back to her dance lessons with Mme. Egorova, working with even greater fervor. Fitzgerald was attempting to resume work on his novel. "I've sworn not to come back without the novel which is really drawing to a close," he assured Harold Ober, who had recently quit the Reynolds agency to set up his own firm. He was equally optimistic in his letters to Perkins. "For the first time since August," Fitzgerald wrote his editor in mid-November, "I can see my way clear to a long stretch on the novel, so I'm writing you as I can't bear to do when it's in one of its states of postponement."

Unfortunately, they had not been long in Paris when the social life began in full swing. The Bishops promptly invited them to a dinner party at their Paris apartment to meet Allen Tate, the Southern poet, and his wife, the novelist Caroline Gordon. (The Hemingways had also been asked.) Tate was on a Guggenheim fellowship, and he and his wife had just returned from a summer in Brittany. The Fitzgeralds arrived late. Zelda immediately came forward to be introduced to Tate. "Not a beautiful woman," Tate thought, "but immensely attractive, with the Southern woman's gift for conversation that made people feel that she had known them for years." Zelda insisted that Tate must have danced with her at one of the proms at Sewanee. Tate regretfully informed her that he had gone to Vanderbilt.

Fitzgerald was nowhere to be seen. When Tate asked his host, Bishop told him that Scott was no doubt hiding his gin bottle in the kitchen and that, during the course of the evening, he would make frequent trips there to replenish his martini. When Fitzgerald finally did join the party, he immediately started giving Tate the usual third degree: Did Tate enjoy sleeping with his wife? To which Tate answered that it was none of Fitzgerald's business. Tate was also put off by Fitzgerald's persistent questions about what teen-age girls thought about America or whether they had read *The Beautiful and Damned*. Tate, who had no interest in what teen-age girls thought, decided that Fitzgerald was overly concerned with his public image. But Fitzgerald's interest was more than mere vanity. He had been commissioned by *McCall's* magazine to write an article on the "present day status of the Flapper" and was no doubt conducting a bit of easy, offhand research. Despite that not too promising beginning, and other meetings at which Fitzgerald was a nuisance, Tate liked

Fitzgerald better than he liked Hemingway, even though Fitzgerald was not as good company. Fitzgerald, writing to Edmund Wilson, said, "Met your friend Allen Tate, liked him and pitied him his wife."

Fitzgerald's ledger for that fall and winter was an inventory of parties with the Bishops and Caroline Dudley, the theatrical agent who introduced Josephine Baker to France, meetings with Janet Flanner, *The New Yorker's* peppy Paris correspondent who wrote under the name Genêt, with Margaret Anderson, founder of *The Little Review,* and Padraic and Mary Colum, the Irish writers and New York literary critics. At one of the Dudley parties, Fitzgerald and Zelda were introduced to Jules Pascin, the urbane painter of nudes and women in charming dishabille.

In the midst of this turmoil, Fitzgerald managed to write only two stories, "Two Wrongs" and "First Blood." The latter was the first in a series about a teen-age vamp, Josephine Perry, who ends up an emotional bankrupt. He also wrote a rather flimsy sketch for *The New Yorker,* titled "Salesmanship in the Champs-Elysées," about buying an automobile in Paris.

Things were not going altogether well with his writing. In mid-November he learned that *McCall's* had turned down his flapper article, "Girls Believe in Girls," and he was irate. The editor's excuse was that the piece was too serious: "I feel that the same ideas might have been expressed in the vernacular and found greater welcome among our readers." The rejection obviously stung Fitzgerald a great deal more than his earlier rejections, when he was a novice. He sent Ober a barrage of letters and cablegrams, telling his agent to bring suit against *McCall's.* It was only gradually that Ober persuaded him to let *Liberty* publish the article and to forget about the legal action. Even then, Fitzgerald's anger was not assuaged. He threatened to expose the editor who had commissioned the piece in the first place, by sending the entire correspondence to the Authors' League *Bulletin* and asking them to publish it.

Everything about Fitzgerald's life seemed to exasperate him. The apartment was "rotten"; the maid "stank." Zelda was caught up in her frenzied obsession with dance. He accused her of spoiling a story he was writing because she insisted on their taking Mme. Egorova out to dinner. His bitterest feelings seemed directed toward Zelda: "You were going crazy and calling it genius—I was going to ruin and calling it anything that came to hand." But it was another of those odd instances in which Fitzgerald had to take the outside view, to see himself and Zelda from the perspective of others before he could grasp the reality of their lives: "I think everyone far enough away to see us outside of our glib presentation of ourselves guessed at your almost meglomaniacal selfishness and my insane indulgence in drink. Toward the end nothing much mattered."

That fall and winter in Paris there was trouble between Fitzgerald and Hemingway that marked the beginning of the end of their friendship, though the two men continued to see each other on infrequent occasions. For Fitzgerald, the relationship was becoming degrading, and he was both apologetic and belligerent by turns. With unerring accuracy — the kind of accuracy that Hemingway could seldom muster when assessing his own character — Fitzgerald analyzed himself in relation to the author who represented his ideal of brusque masculinity. "With Ernest," Fitzgerald wrote, "I seem to have reached a state where when we drink together I half bait, half truckle to him."

The trouble had actually begun brewing earlier in the year over the question of Hemingway's rue de Ferou apartment. He had paid $3000 on a sublet, with the assumption that it would be a permanent base for him. The arrangement had been made through Ruth Goldbeck de Vallombrosa, an attractive socialite and a member of the international set. But one day, while Hemingway was working, a group of people arrived, wanting to look over the apartment. Hemingway was furious and vented his anger to Fitzgerald, but made him promise that he would not mention the incident to Ruth Goldbeck.

On the Riviera that summer, Fitzgerald did just that, informing Hemingway that "Ruth Goldbeck Voallammbbrrossa" had no intention of throwing him out but had promised *"on her own initiative"* to speak to the woman who owned the place, and that she was not deserving of Hemingway's "nervous bitterness."

Hemingway blew up:

> But you seem to have damned well forgot my coming around the next day to tell you that I thought Ruth Goldbeck Vallambrosa was a fine girl, had always admired her and told you for gods sake never to let her know that I had cursed about the Apt. *She* did not know I was sore and the only way she would ever find out would be through you. You said you understood perfectly and for me not to worry you would never mention it to her.

Fitzgerald, by way of self-exoneration, explained: "Incidentally I thought you wanted a word said to Ruth G. if it came about naturally—I merely remarked that you'd be disappointed if you lost your apartment—never a word that you'd been exasperated."

Next, with honorable intentions no doubt, Fitzgerald tried to arrange for Harold Ober to act as Hemingway's agent, something that he had recommended earlier but that had been complicated by Ober's connection with the Reynolds agency. His letters to Ober, in fact, were somewhat scolding: "I think it was foolish to let him slide so long as he was so obviously a comer." On the other hand, he preferred that Hemingway did not know of his behind-the-scenes maneuvering. He warned Ober, "*Please* don't in any correspondence with him use my name—you see my relations with him are entirely friendly & not business & he'd merely lose confidence in me if he felt he was being hemmed in by any . . . *coalition.*"

At the same time that he was attempting to bring Hemingway around to Harold Ober, Fitzgerald was being solicitous—overly solicitous—about the sales of Hemingway's novel, *A Farewell to Arms,* about which Max Perkins was keeping him regularly informed. Perkins' reputation as a masterly editor, based on his recognition and support of the most important authors of his time—is now an article of faith. And certainly with his three stars—Fitzgerald, Hemingway, and Thomas Wolfe—he was a model of concern, patience, and lifelong dedication. But there were contemporaries, like Edmund Wilson, who could become apoplectic on the subject of Scribner's niggardliness toward more dependable authors. (Wilson once tried to borrow $75 and once asked the firm to sponsor a bank loan for him, and was unsuccessful each time.) When Perkins was foolish enough to chide him for having gone to a different publisher, Wilson exploded, "You wouldn't do anything for me . . . at a time when you were handing out money to Scott Fitzgerald like a drunken sailor—which he was spending like a drunken sailor." Scribner's cavalier attitude toward texts was also a subject that could raise Wilson's temperature by several degrees. "Max Perkins," Wilson maintained, "couldn't spell himself and couldn't be made to take proofreading seriously."

Perkins' gossiping with Fitzgerald—not always a reliable confidant—about the sales prospects of *A Farewell to Arms* had expectable results. Just after the stock market crash in late October, Perkins wrote Fitzgerald, saying that Hemingway's book was a remarkable success, having sold about thirty-six thousand copies, and that the only obstacle "to a really big sale" was the effect of the market's collapse on the publishing industry. Good friends are sometimes eager to bring bad news; Fitzgerald stopped by Hemingway's apartment but learned that he was in Berlin with a friend, following the bicycle races. As soon as Hemingway returned, Fitzgerald managed to worry the author enough so that he badgered Perkins for news.

In the roundabout fashion in which he dealt with his authors, Perkins wrote Fitzgerald, "Ernest has cabled me several times to report on the sales, but it is hard to do it because there are always complications." He was, he said, eager to avoid overstatement. "In reality, between ourselves, the sale must now be 50,000, and perhaps more." When Hemingway learned that his worries had been unnecessary, he apologized to Perkins, indicating that Scott had precipitated the crisis:

> Came home from Berlin feeling fine and found Scott had been here with some alarm. I went over to see him and he showed me something you had written about the book going well and the only thing to watch was the market slump. I thought there was nothing alarming in what you had written but he knows so much more about the financial side of writing than I do that I imagined he did not show me the whole letter, but only the part referring to the book, that there was some contingencies I did not know about. Also he seemed so alarmed.

Chronology is important in human affairs, and although it is still not possible to fix the precise date of the events, there was a period of from two to three weeks — from the end of November through early December — in which the Hemingway-Fitzgerald relationship suffered a series of blows from which it was unlikely that even the most hardened friendship could survive. The culprit in this instance was not Hemingway but Fitzgerald, whose meddling, nagging, petulant, and erratic behavior would have tried even the patience of a saint.

The first episode in this bizarre sequence was a Wednesday evening party at Gertrude Stein's. Hemingway had had his notable falling-out with Stein over his parody of Sherwood Anderson in *The Torrents of Spring*. But after his return from Berlin, he met Stein on the street, and she soon issued an invitation to him to appear at the rue de Fleurus. Reluctant to pay the visit, Hemingway urged the Tates and the Bishops to come with him. He wrote Fitzgerald as well, saying that Gertrude had asked for him: "She claims you are the one of all us guys with the most talent etc. and wants to see you again."

Two letters that Hemingway wrote Fitzgerald within days of each other — one before the party, the other just after — have previously been assigned dates in late October. Internal evidence, however, indicates that this dating is a mistake. In the first letter, Hemingway asks Fitzgerald about his suit against *McCall's*. Since Fitzgerald did not learn that the magazine had turned down "Girls Believe in Girls" until late in November and promptly cabled Ober, on November 20, to sue *McCall's* if necessary, the Stein party could not have taken place until late November. Other circumstances in that time period suggest that the party could not have taken place before Wednesday the twenty-seventh. Ordinarily, whether it had occurred in October or November would be of no grand importance. But the cumulative evidence of Fitzgerald's three-week onslaught on Hemingway's patience is impressive.

Allen Tate, in an acerbic little memoir, "Miss Toklas' American Cake," depicts what was evidently the same Stein party, though he dates it in early December. It was, he notes, the occasion of Hemingway's reconciliation with Stein; he quotes Hemingway's assertion "Gertrude has taken me back into favor." But the real purpose of the evening was a lecture on American literature that was given by Gertrude herself. The men sat in one corner of the salon; the wives and unattached women were clustered around Alice B. Toklas' tea table. The subject of Stein's lecture was the gift for abstraction of American writers, beginning with Emerson, proceeding through Henry James (whom Stein, according to Tate, regarded as a "sad case" of misplaced allegiances), and ending with — "the entelechy towards which all American literature was striving" — Gertrude Stein. Tate noticed that Hemingway had positioned himself at the rear of Gertrude's audience and throughout the evening he had not exchanged so much as one word with his hostess.

But some words must have been exchanged, for this is almost certainly the same evening party that Alice B. Toklas describes in her memoir, *What Is Remembered*. Toklas was no admirer of Hemingway; she was jealous of Gertrude's attention to her young protégé and instinctively doubtful of his loyalty and sincerity. She describes an evening when Hemingway and Fitzgerald had visited the studio, following the publication of *A Farewell to Arms*. She was pleased to see that Fitzgerald was not above "giving Hem a little dig" now and then. Fitzgerald had sidled up to her, saying that he was sure she would want to know how Hemingway achieved "his great moments" in writing. Toklas reported:

> And Hem said rather bashfully, What are you up to Scotty? He said, You tell her. And Hem said, Well, you see, it is this way, When I have an idea I turn down the flame, as if it were a little alcohol stove, as low as it will go. Then it explodes and that is my idea.

Toklas remembered that Fitzgerald had pointedly turned his back on this. She managed to give Hemingway, however, one of the few compliments she would tender him, telling him that the retreat from Caporetto had been "well done."

It was the respective merits of the "flames" of the two writers that became the source of antagonism that evening. Gertrude complimented Fitzgerald to his face and in Hemingway's presence. For some inexplicable reason, Fitzgerald took offense and behaved so badly that on the next day he felt apologies were necessary. Hemingway, with a forbearance that was unusual, now found himself in the queer position of apologizing to Fitzgerald for the compliments that Stein had paid Fitzgerald. In answer to Fitzgerald's note, he wrote:

> I was not annoyed at anything you said. (You surely know by now, I've written it often enough, how much I admire your work). I was only annoyed at your refusal to accept the sincere compliment G. Stein was making to you and instead try and twist it into a slighting remark. She was praising her head off about you to me when you came up she started to repeat it and then at the end of the praise to spare you blushes and not be rude to me she said that our flames (sic) were maybe *not* the same — then you brood on that —

Anyway, Hemingway stated, compliments and comparisons of hypothetical "flames" were "pure horseshit." Still, he found it necessary to add more reassurances: "I cross myself and swear to God that Gertrude has *never* last night or any other time said anything to me about you but the highest praise. That is absolutely true. The fact that you do not value or accept it does not make it any less sincere." The problem, Hemingway concluded, was that "you're getting touchy because you haven't finished your novel — that's all — I understand it and you could be a hell of a lot more touchy and I wouldn't mind."

Fitzgerald's anger at the Stein compliment was not an isolated incident. A short while later, he was just as disagreeble with the poet and novelist Robert Penn Warren who, inadvisedly, had had a good word to say about Fitzgerald's work. The episode followed a dinner party at the Bishops' apartment that Tate and Gordon also attended. The Fitzgeralds had been invited, but only Scott came. After dinner the guests and Bishop (Margaret was pregnant at the time) adjourned to a café. Fitzgerald, in a fidgety state, said he wanted to get Zelda. Warren recalls the incident graphically:

> Turning to me he said, "Red, come with me." We had a very animated conversation until we approached the door of his apartment house, when he fell into a kind of abstract, or sullen, silence. I started to wait in the street, but he said, "Come along." I can't remember whether he lived on the second or third floor of the apartment house, but as we approached the level of the floor on which he did live, he turned suddenly and said, "Wait here." There I was, stuck. I couldn't help but see Zelda's feet as she let him in the door, and couldn't help but hear the frightful hissing quarrel, well laced with obscenities, which went on between them. Finally, he slammed the door and came down to join me, saying, "Let's go." He was absolutely silent until we got back to the café. A short time later, after the conversation had become general, I made some complimentary remark about *The Great Gatsby*. To my understandable surprise, he said, "Say that again, you son of a bitch, and I'll knock your block off (or head, or something)!" I replied, "Call me a son of a bitch again, and I'll knock yours off," and got up from the table. He made no motion, so after a moment I went over to the coat rack and put on a blue overcoat — which happened to be John Bishop's. They were both blue, and we were of the same build, and I went out.
>
> The next morning I got a *pneumatique* from Fitzgerald, full of apology, saying he had been under great strain and drunk besides, and asking me to dinner when he got back from a trip he was taking. . . . I had had, of course, no warning of the strained condition Fitzgerald was in and his frantic worries about the new book and Zelda. So all was a great shock to me. Particularly after the warmth and cordiality of the early part of our acquaintance.

For understandable reasons, Hemingway wrote Max Perkins, "Am damned fond of Scott and would do anything for him but he's been a little trying lately." Then, early in December, within a matter of days, the gossip of the literary world stirred up two more crises in the Fitzgerald-Hemingway friendship. Robert McAlmon, in the course of a visit to New York in October, had used the occasion to spread a number of vicious stories about Hemingway around New York and to Max Perkins. The irony is that it was Hemingway who had sent McAlmon to Perkins in the first place, with the idea that Scribner's might take on McAlmon as one of its authors. To Perkins' amazement, when he took McAlmon to dinner, the supposed friend began making libelous remarks about Hemingway as a man and a writer. Perkins wrote Fitzgerald about the incident, but cautioned him to keep the story confidential. "This is absolutely between you and me," he said.

Fitzgerald, replying, was only too happy to enlarge on McAlmon's slanders:

> McAlmon is a bitter rat and I'm not surprised at anything he does or says. He's failed as a writer and tries to fortify himself by tieing up to the big boys like Joyce and Stein and despising everything else. Part of his quarrel with Ernest some years ago was because he assured Ernest that I was a fairy — God knows he shows more creative imagination in his malice than in his work. Next he told Callaghan that Ernest was a fairy. He's a pretty good person to avoid.

For several weeks, Fitzgerald was the soul of honor and kept the Perkins story to himself.

But when drunk, Fitzgerald had a loose tongue, a flaw he freely acknowledged. Invited to dinner at the Hemingways' on December 9, he got drunk and relayed McAlmon's gossip. Hemingway was enraged, and Pauline, not very helpfully, said it was Hemingway's fault for associating with such people. Hemingway, in an angry letter to Perkins, said he knew most of McAlmon's slanders: that Pauline was a lesbian, that he was a homosexual, and that he had beaten Hadley, thus causing the premature birth of Bumby. He threatened physical violence, a threat he carried out later in Paris, when he calmly beat up McAlmon outside Jimmy's Bar, growling, "Now tell that to your God-damn friends!" But in another of his extraordinary displays of patience, Hemingway told Perkins not to blame Fitzgerald for revealing a confidence; Fitzgerald, he said, was an honorable man when sober, but irresponsible when drunk.

The McAlmon affair, it seems, did not anger Hemingway as

much as a gossipy story by the columnist Caroline Bancroft that appeared first in the *Denver Post* and was repeated in the *New York Herald Tribune;* it claimed that Morley Callaghan had knocked Hemingway out during their boxing match in Paris. Egged on by the irate Hemingway, Fitzgerald sent Callaghan a collect cablegram: HAVE SEEN STORY IN HERALD TRIBUNE ERNEST AND I AWAIT YOUR CORRECTION SCOTT FITZGERALD.

Callaghan, having seen the story earlier, in Canada, had already written the *Tribune,* denying the incident. But when he received Fitzgerald's cable, he sent off an angry letter to Paris. By the time the smoke cleared and the three men, through the agency of their editor, Perkins, managed to communicate with one another, they were none of them on the friendliest terms. Hemingway wrote Callaghan, absolving Fitzgerald of having initiated the cablegram and offering to meet Callaghan in the States to settle the matter honorably, as long as it was some place where there was "no publicity attached."

Once more, Fitzgerald worked up a grievance against Hemingway, and once too often, it appears, Hemingway was obliged to write a reassuring letter:

> I know you are the soul of honor. I mean that. If you remember I made no cracks about your time keeping until after you had told me over my objections for about the fourth time that you were going to deliberately quarrel with me. . . . I was so appalled at the idea of you saying that you were going to deliberately quarrel with me that I didnt know (just having heard this vile stuff from McA. and C. which I thought I should have heard a long time sooner, if I was to hear it. . . .) where the hell I stood on anything.

It is evident from Hemingway's letter that Fitzgerald was in one of his nagging moods, returning again and again to the topic, and that Hemingway once again was put on the defensive, denying that he was angry — only irritated because Fitzgerald's carelessness had allowed Callaghan to make his "lying boast" in the first place. He believed in Fitzgerald implicitly, he said: "I only wish to God you didnt feel so bum when you drink. I know it's no damn fun but I know too everything will be fine when your book is done."

It was characteristic of Fitzgerald that he could so completely overlook the role that his drinking and meddling had played in the end of his uneasy friendship with Hemingway. In his notebook, he preferred to ascribe it to other, outside causes. Obviously referring to Hemingway, he wrote, "I really loved him, but of course it wore out like a love affair. The fairies have spoiled all that."

Fairies, to Fitzgerald, were the enemies of life, the enemies of promise. Throughout his life, he seems to have had a strictly puritanical attitude toward that form of sexual activity, believing that it was both a sinful and an unnatural practice. It was, perhaps, another vestige of his early Catholic training. Fairies, Fitzgerald declared in one of his random notes, were "Nature's attempt to get rid of soft boys by sterilizing them." Another of his notes, obviously a suggestion for a story, reads, "Fairy who fell for wax dummy." Nowhere in his notes or letters did Fitzgerald deal with homosexuality other than in completely disparaging terms. It became an article of faith that homosexuality was damaging to the creative writer, giving his work a peculiar slant: "Apropos of Cocteau — perverts love of perverted children." André Gide, Fitzgerald commented, "lifted himself by his own jockstrap so to speak — and one would like to see him hoisted on his own pederasty." Of an unnamed writer, Fitzgerald said: "He had once been a pederast and he had perfected a trick of writing about all his affairs as if his boy friends had been girls, thus achieving feminine types of a certain spurious originality. (See Proust, Cocteau and Noel Coward.)" The sole touch of wit that issued from Fitzgerald's nearly botanical study of fairies, fags, pederasts, sodomists, and lesbians was this: "The great homosexual theses — that all great pansies were pansies."

It was not that he disowned homosexual writers; some of his best friends, including the "pederast" Carl Van Vechten, were so inclined. But in private discussions about writers and in promoting likely candidates for the Scribner's list, Fitzgerald made a point of red-tagging any homosexual preferences. René Crevel, he wrote Perkins, was a great, great talent: "I am opposed to him for being a fairy but in the last *Transition* (number 18) there is a translation of his current novel which simply knocked me cold with its beauty." For his part, the Dadaist poet, having met the Fitzgeralds on the Riviera, was similarly perplexed. Writing to Gertrude Stein in Franglais, he commented: "Curious and poor fellow. A boy. He has a wonderful wife, you know her, I think, but what this young, charming and spirituel people has in the hed (tête)? I cannot say."

In Fitzgerald's stories, the scenes of passion are likely to involve little more than a smoldering kiss and a Hollywood fade-out. He was never tempted to describe the graphic sexual episodes Hemingway resorted to as a means of testing the censorship of publishers and the prudery of editors and of asserting his image of masculinity. And in those terms, certainly, he was closer than Hemingway to meeting Max Perkins' standards of editorial propriety. Even in his private notebooks, in a brief segment titled "Rough Stuff," Fitzgerald could not bring himself to an outright private reference to squirrels fucking; instead he calls it "yincing." But oddly, when he spoke of himself in disparaging terms, it was in disparaging feminine terms—his boast to Hemingway, for example, that the "old whore" was now being paid $4000 a screw by *The Saturday Evening Post.* That seems to have been a different version of a more forceful remark he noted in his "Rough Stuff" pages: "My mind is the loose cunt of a whore, to fit all genitals."

Given Fitzgerald's lifelong distaste for homosexuality, McAlmon's rumors must have had a devastating effect. They came at a time when his self-esteem was being eroded by his drinking habits, by his inability to complete his novel, and his recognition that even with his commercial stories, he was not producing his best work. Morley Callaghan, in *That Summer in Paris,* describes a grim incident. Fitzgerald, drunk, had instinctively reached for Callaghan's arm when crossing a street. Then, sensing some coldness on Callaghan's part, dropped it. "It was like holding on to a cold fish," Fitzgerald remarked later. "You thought I was a fairy, didn't you." Under the circumstances, there was something a bit perverse in Hemingway's ragging Fitzgerald on the subject—such as his remark that only fairies wrote masterpieces. Later, he sent Fitzgerald a handsome photograph of himself inscribed, "To Scott from his old bedfellow, Richard Halliburton." Halliburton was a Princeton graduate with whom Fitzgerald had a bantering correspondence. He was famous for his highly popular travel books, like *The Royal Road to Romance,* in which, in gushing prose, he described his feats of derring-do: climbing the Matterhorn, putting an infant lama to bed in a monastery high in the Himalayas, taking a clandestine moonlight dip in the nude in the alabaster pool in front of the Taj Mahal. (He liked to illustrate his books with photographs of himself in exotic garb.) Hemingway and Fitzgerald regarded him as a homosexual, a fey version of the Hemingway adventurer.

What is also significant is that Fitzgerald was having sexual difficulties with Zelda at this point — and may have had them for some period of time. His alcoholic intake, of course, would have been a factor in his poor sexual performance. But it is also possible that the rancorous atmosphere of the marriage — Fitzgerald's repressed anger — may have been a contributing factor as well. It was at this nadir of his self-esteem, evidently, that Fitzgerald had turned to Hemingway, his ideal of manhood, for advice. Hemingway's account of the episode in *A Moveable Feast* is unintentionally comic and deliberately demeaning. It is not clear on what date Fitzgerald met Hemingway at Michaud's restaurant and confessed his problem. But it could not have been, as Hemingway claimed, just after Zelda's first breakdown, since Hemingway was not in Paris at the time. More likely it was either in the early summer of 1929 or after the Fitzgeralds had returned to Paris from the Riviera that fall. Pitifully, and in all innocence, it seems, Fitzgerald told Hemingway that Zelda had complained that his penis was not large enough.

There is a good deal of insinuating condescension in Hemingway's account: the old pro teaching the poor sexual novice. He takes Fitzgerald into the lavatory to inspect his problem and reassures Fitzgerald that there is nothing wrong with its size. (In later years, after Fitzgerald's death, Hemingway, who had become something of an expert on matters of masculinity, would tell correspondents that Fitzgerald simply didn't know the proper method for measuring a penis.) Fitzgerald claims that he has not slept with any woman other than Zelda since his marriage (an admission that must have aroused Hemingway's scorn in any event). Hemingway suggests that Fitzgerald pick up some easy French girl; he gives him advice about the use of a pillow and the right angle of approach. Except for the fact that two grown men are involved, it all has the air of a schoolboy event, part social experiment, part braggadocio behind the barn — a "Matter of Measurements," as Hemingway titled the episode. Hemingway's final judgment is blunt: "Zelda is crazy. There's nothing wrong with you. . . . Zelda just wants to destroy you."

With bizarre appropriateness, Zelda, too, was having problems with her sexual identity. She had already begun to worry that there was something abnormal about her intense feelings toward Egorova. Fitzgerald apparently had dismissed her confession as nonsense. But it is clear, from one of his notebook observations, that he regarded his wife as a pawn in a contest for domination. "I've seen that everytime Zelda sees Egrova and me in contact," he wrote, "Egrova becomes gross to her. Apart, the opposite happens." In *A Moveable Feast,* Hemingway wrote that Zelda threatened Fitzgerald with her lesbian affairs: "This spring she was making him jealous with other women and on the Montmartre parties he was afraid to pass out and he was afraid to have her pass out." Hemingway's severest critics view this as a canard. Certainly, as is the case with some of Hemingway's recollections, the chronology is suspect. Hemingway said that this happened in 1925, when he first met the Fitzgeralds. But early in their marriage, Zelda had few women friends and did not seem to court any; she was much more involved with flirting with Fitzgerald's male companions or comely headwaiters. Hemingway's account more accurately should have been dated the summer of 1929, when one of Fitzgerald's ledger notes reads, "Zelda & Dolly Wilde." Dolly Wilde, a niece of the great Oscar's, was a celebrated lesbian who wore exotic make-up. She was a regular user of cocaine, though no one knew how she afforded it; her finances were a mystery to her closest friends. At a party, Wilde made a pass at Zelda, who was very drunk, and Fitzgerald was furious. It is possible that Zelda, in her growing alienation, may have tried to make Fitzgerald jealous with women as she had done with men.

But she would recall that summer and Dolly Wilde and Emily Vanderbilt, another frequenter of Natalie Barney's lesbian salon, in rather different terms. "In all that horror," Zelda wrote, "Dolly Wilde was the only one who said she would do anything to be cured — How did Emily suddenly seem to represent order and independence to me? Last summer when we went with her to Natalie Barney's I was sorry for her, she seemed so muddled and lost in the grist mill." The problem, or the anxiety, had reached down deeper into some subterranean region of her mind. In a later letter to Fitzgerald, written during one of her episodes of madness, she exhorted him to acknowledge "the Beauty of homosexuality as our marital relationship." God willed it as a means of requiting "the second of our sexual functions," she said. "Thus there will no longer be any necessity for the use of catatonic and homosexual controls which have sold too many of us into bondage."

Their unhappiness, that year in Paris, came to a climax one night when Fitzgerald had been out drinking with Hemingway. After stumbling home, he crawled into bed. Half-asleep, he murmered, "No more, Baby." Zelda took this as a revelation that Fitzgerald and Hemingway were involved homosexually. She would list it among the causative incidents in her breakdown: "We came back to the Rue Palatine and you, in a drunken stupor told me a lot of things that I only half-understood; but I understood the dinner we had at Ernest's." Fitzgerald, miserable about the accusations, admitted, "The nearest I ever came to leaving you was when you told me you thot I was a fairy in the Rue Palatine."

I I I

She went for days without eating; she could not bring herself to talk to the servants, much less scold them. The cook pampered the dog and paid no attention to her little girl. She was sick, she knew, sinking—but when she went to her husband with her problems, he sat in the bathroom singing, "Play in Your Own Back Yard." He blamed her because the servants were bad, because the apartment smelled, because he could not work. But the servants had no respect for him. How could they, when they found him, morning after morning, fully clothed, sleeping off the drunk from the night before.

She suspected that she loved Madame. (Of course it was wrong to love her teacher when she should have loved her husband, but she hadn't had him to love for a long time.) And Madame was beautiful—and thoughtful; Madame was a good woman; Madame had lost everything and therefore worked hard. In Madame's steps, she could read all the frustrations of a mind that was searching for its place.

She was aware of strange experiences; there were times when everything hovered at the edge of some new significance. The façades of buildings, streets, the Métro stations, stood out so clearly. Colors seemed infinite, part of the air; they escaped free of the forms they identified. There was music beating behind her head or falling deep into the pit of her stomach, as if from some high parabola; sad Chopin mazurkas or the turning, turning, turning of Liszt. There were frightening times when everything turned vaporous and uncertain. People looked like one-dimensional cutouts; buildings turned tremulous at the edges. She couldn't tell whether what she saw was real or an optical illusion. Her head throbbed and roads disappeared. She had headaches. She could jump higher than ever—but next day she would be sick. She was becoming dependent on Madame; if she didn't have her lesson, she could not walk in the street; she could not go into a department store. She was afraid she was becoming too sentimentally involved.

Twice that winter, she went to him and asked whether they could start all over again. He sang her a song about gigolos. But if that was what she had in mind, there were other opportunities — her hairdresser, the whole studio. Something was going wrong in her head. Why didn't he see fit to explain to her or try to help her? If only he had helped that night when they had had dinner with John Bishop and gone to the fair and she had suddenly become hysterical. (Wasn't it the obligation of those who understood to explain, she thought; the blind out of necessity needed to be led.) It astonished her that she was beginning to look on him with unfriendly eyes. He belittled the few friends that she could trust.

That winter was a winter of visits and artists and many women. She and her husband seemed to be always setting out on trips to inaccessible apartments up endless flights of stairs through tangles of cobwebs. (Artistic people with money liked cobwebs, she thought.) At Gertrude Stein's the atmosphere was hazy and oracular; a young poet vomited out of sheer emotion. They met John Dos Passos' wife, Katy, who was very pretty and had a kind of excited restraint in her voice, the voice of a primitive woman. There was Janet Flanner and her shock of gray hair. And there was the pasty effeminacy of Kenneth Macgowan, the film producer, who had a face like an old bartender and was very antagonistic toward her. They went to an exhibition of Picabia paintings and met the artist — very handsome, with a big possessive wife. The wife, she thought, explained the falseness, the pathological quality of Picabia's paintings. But Brancusi, when they met him, had a magnificent robustness. There were quantities of tall women with unpigmented eyes and no eyebrows who she assumed were contributors to *The Dial*. They seemed to have special nightclubs. But that winter she had been mostly lost in illusions — expensive illusions.

In February she had bronchitis — so bad that she had to be cupped every day. For two weeks she had a fever, but she kept up with her lessons because she couldn't exist without them. She didn't understand what she was doing. She didn't know what she wanted.

To forget the bad times, they took a trip to North Africa. She had never seen a continent so full of eyes. The Arabs seemed to be fermenting in the vastness. Everywhere she could smell the smell of ants. People looked infinitely small, seemed suspended in time. At

Bou Saada, they saw the moon come up, dead white, stumbling over the sandy hills. The Ouled Nail girls were clean-cut and brown, perfect instruments for sex, jangling gold bracelets to savage tunes. In Biskra, he photographed her on a camel, going up, up, up (they were off on a visit to the sculptor Claire Sheridan). It was a wobbling ride down glaring streets past bedraggled palms. It was hot; the streets ran through the town like white lava. Arabs were selling nougat and little cakes that were a poisonous pink. At the Gorge of Constantine she was cold and unhappy. Once, on a bus trip, tearing through the desert past bleak hills, she felt nervous. But the nights were like thick velvet and there were soft muted cries in the dark. She was restless, desperately impatient to get back to her dancing. She wrote many letters to Madame. On the boat coming back she was seasick. An annoying Englishwoman called out "Cheerio" every time the ship pitched and rolled. She stayed in her room, too sick to move. She thought the ship was sinking.

In Paris, she brought her gifts to Madame: a bandanna filled with perfumes and enough green silk for a dress. In Paris, she tried to make up with her husband again. But twice he left the bed, saying, "I can't! Don't you understand!" But she hadn't understood. He was drinking too much, and when she tried to get him to come home, he told her to go sleep with the coal man. Once he told her that he had coughed up a cup of blood. She cried all night; the next day he told her that it wasn't true. Work was the only thing that made her feel safe. She hated his friends who didn't work. (They were her friends once.) She felt contemptuous of them. She spent her money on flowers for Madame: black tulips and white lilacs and deep red roses and threatening sprays of gladioli and flowers that seemed as carnivorous as the flowers in Van Gogh paintings. She was superstitious about her dance lessons, full of presentiments: What if it should rain? Would it be sunny? She stayed after her classes, not wanting to go home.

Something, quite likely, was going wrong in her head; people looked at her strangely. Once, when John Bishop came to lunch, she was sure that Bishop and her husband were talking about her; she watched to see whether she could catch them at it. Once, her husband had said very pointedly that Lucienne had been sent away. She didn't understand what that meant, though it seemed to mean that something had gone wrong. And once when the Kalmans came to lunch at the apartment, she suddenly became terrified that she would miss her lesson and got up from the table and hurried out. Kaly had followed her and rode with her in the cab. But she was so worried that she began changing into her practice clothes. In her panic, she jumped out of the car and ran all the way to the studio. Kaly had called her husband, and they both came for her. And one afternoon, when she came home from class, Michael Arlen was there, drinking with her husband. She liked him, and when he saw how upset she was, he suggested that she go to a clinic. But she made a scene because her husband obviously preferred to spend his time drinking with Arlen, even though she needed him. And then it was Eastertime and she wanted to do something for her little girl, but she was afraid to go into the shops, and Madame had to help her. And then, one day, the world between her and the others stopped —just stopped.

They took her to a clinic at Malmaison, outside Paris. She did not want to go. The doctors diagnosed her case as a *petite anxieuse;* she was worn out by her obsession with dance. She kept repeating: "It's frightful, it's horrible, what's going to become of me. I must work and I no longer can, I must die." She told them about Madame: "comparable to sunlight falling on a block of crystal, to a symphony of perfumes, to the most perfect strains of the greatest masters in music." The doctors claimed that she had indulged in heavy drinking and that she was slightly drunk on arrival. They noted that there had been several suicide attempts, which had not, however, been pushed to the limit. They said she had fears of homosexual tendencies, particularly with regard to her teacher. But that could hardly be true, because she flirted "outrageously" with the doctors. Her anxiety attacks, the doctors said, seemed to occur around nightfall.

She did not stay long at Malmaison; against the doctor's advice, she left early in May. It was a short reprieve. She wanted to resume her dance lessons, but that was no longer possible. Madame came to bring her a present and she knew she would not dance again and she was heartbroken when she said goodbye to Madame. Her husband was no help. He was drinking too heavily—for more than a week when Ludlow Fowler's brother, Powell, was married in Paris. There was a round of parties from which he never sobered up. It frightened her.

Later in May, they took her to a Swiss clinic, Val-Mont, near Glion. She did not want to go; she told the doctors that she had been brought there by force. She said she was not sick. When her husband tried to reason with her, she became violent and abusive; she accused him of being homosexual. She wanted to get back to Paris. She told the doctors she was losing precious time. They asked her about her daughter, but she told them that that was all over now. She wanted to do something else. She told them that the most precious things in the world were being taken away from her—her work, her lesbian tendencies.

At Val-Mont, she felt dizzy; the noises in her ear got louder and louder; she could feel vibrations from the people she met. She realized that she was very dependent on her husband, but there was nothing for her in his life except physical comfort. She wanted to arrange her life so that she could be free. They brought in another doctor, a specialist in nervous disorders from the Rives de Prangins. He said he wanted to treat her there. That evening she agreed, but in the morning she changed her mind and would not go. Her husband and her brother-in-law took her to Prangins all the same. The specialist said that her husband would not be allowed to visit until her treatment was established.

She wrote him accusing letters. Why, instead of sending her vague reassurances, didn't he write her what he really thought? Since he had always had such sympathy for other people forced to start over in life, why couldn't he be generous enough to help her? He was wasting time and effort and money, taking away the little they had left. If he thought he could return her to Alabama or if he thought she was going to spend the rest of her life roaming from one sanatorium to another, he was mistaken. Every day it was getting harder to think and live. She couldn't understand the purpose of wasting the dregs of her life here, alone, full of devastating bitterness.

She seemed queer to herself. You have to come and tell me how I was, she wrote him. Now she saw odd things: people's arms were too long or their faces looked stuffed and they seemed tiny and far away or out of proportion. "Please explain," she wrote him.

She wrote him that it was no use trying to write him, because if she wrote something one day, she thought something else immediately. She had a feeling of coming disaster. Why didn't he come to see her and at least give her some assurance that would counteract the abuse he had given her in Lausanne when she was so sick? She was thoroughly and completely humiliated and broken, if that was what he wanted.

Scott, Zelda, and Scottie in Paris, Christmas 1925

Fitzgerald's editor at Scribner's,
Maxwell Perkins, as a young man

His agent, Harold Ober, in a
portrait by Willard H. Ortlip

Ernest Hemingway—
photograph with comic inscription
for Fitzgerald

The Fitzgeralds aboard ship,
ca. 1928–1931

The Hemingways—Ernest, Pauline, and Patrick—
en route to France, April 1929

Laura Guthrie in her Gypsy
fortuneteller's outfit,
Asheville, North Carolina, 1935

Fitzgerald at Chimney Rock,
North Carolina, summer 1935

Sheilah Graham
in Hollywood

Scott and Zelda
attending the theater
in Baltimore, 1932

Ballerinas (1938), a painting by Zelda Fitzgerald in the collection of the Montgomery Museum of Fine Arts, Montgomery, Alabama

She wrote him that his letters were just noncommittal phrases of the kind he might write Scottie, but they did not help to unravel the infinite psychological mess she was in. Now she watched the nurse's attitude each day and then looked up what symptoms she had in Dr. Oscar Forel's book. Why, she wanted to know, had her ignorance on a medical subject that was never particularly interesting reduced her to the mental status of a child?

She wrote him, asking that he write Madame to see whether she could still have a career as a dancer. But the doctor and her husband had decided that her obsession with dancing had been a cause of her breakdown. They did not encourage her. When her husband sent Madame's letter, it was a bitter disappointment. It said that she could never be a first-rate dancer, because she had started too late, but that she could be a very good dancer who might perform lesser roles in repertory companies. It was not what she had hoped to hear.

She came down with eczema and was invalided for weeks. She wrote him about the torture of it and her bitter feelings. She asked him, out of charity, to get Dr. Forel to let her out of the treatment. She had been living in bandages for a month; her head and neck were on fire. She hadn't slept for weeks. Bromides and morphine hadn't helped. She was suffering all this because no one had taught her to play tennis. If he knew how miserable she was, he could write lots more stories, light ones to laugh about. Her dancing had been taken away from her. She couldn't read; she couldn't sleep; she wished she were dead.

She wrote him that the panic had settled into a persistent gloom, that she had moments of hysteria, that she still had the foul eczema—but she was impatient to see him, if he would only come. Did he still smell of pencils and sometimes of tweed? Yesterday, she played some gramophone records, and it reminded her of other days at Ellerslie. She wondered why they had never been very happy and why this had happened to them. It was much nicer a long time ago, when they had each other and the space around the world seemed warm. Couldn't they get it back—even by imagining? He couldn't be very happy in a hotel room. They had been awfully used to having each other around.

She wrote him angrily that she had begun to realize that sex and sentiment were not the same thing; that she knew in her heart that it was a godless dirty game, that love was bitter and all that there was. . . . The rest was for emotional beggars and people who stimulated themselves with dirty postcards.

When she had a relapse, they transferred her to the Eglantine, the house for the people who had to be physically restrained.

Friends wrote her and she answered. Her letters were blurred with strange images, odd trains of thought. Edmund Wilson, who had had a nervous breakdown himself, wrote her a consoling and encouraging letter. She thanked him for the gesture. She said that she assumed she was almost cured of the fanaticism of her last three years. But nothing had ever cost her so much cerebral clarity as the Russians. If she emerged from her troubles, the cold flame of segregation would have a devout worshiper. The modern world might be moving toward the Orient on the Dollar Line, but it would be a pity that so many of them wasted so much time in sanatoriums. She still liked perspective in pictures and abstractions in emotions: American Colonial. She related the only gossip she knew — the gossip of Paris before she had been sent to the hospital: meetings with Dos Passos and his wife, with John Bishop and Gertrude Stein; the fact that Americans no longer seemed to be in vogue anymore. She apologized that her letter seemed a bit curious at times. He should attribute it to her five months of isolation.

Her husband visited her now, and she was well enough to go on picnics and outings. In between times, in lucid moments, she wrote him letters in which she tried to analyze their problems. What a disgraceful mess they were in — but if it stopped their drinking, it would be worth it. He would be able to finish his novel and write a play and they could have a house somewhere with friends for Scottie and there would always be Sundays and Mondays that were different one from the other. There would be Christmases and winter fires and her life wouldn't lie up the back stairs of music halls and his wouldn't trail down into the gutters of Paris. If it would only work and she could keep sane and not become a bitter maniac.

And she wrote him letters brimming over with affection and half-offered sexual enticements. She had woken up that morning and the sun lay on the table like a birthday parcel out of which happy things fluttered — love for her Doo-do and memories of mornings in which their skins felt cool against each other. She was happy because he had phoned her. She had walked on the telephone wires for two hours, using his love like a parasol to balance her. The moon was now slipping behind the mountain like a lost penny. She wanted him near so that she could touch him in the autumn stillness like a lost echo of summer. She loved the velvet nights. She could never tell whether the night was a bitter enemy or a grand *patron*. Was he feeling sort of aimless and surprised, having finished one of his stories, or like someone who had ridden hard with a message to save the army and found the enemy had decided not to attack? Or was he like a darling little boy with a holiday on his hands in the middle of the week — the way he sometimes was — or was he organizing and dynamic and mending things — the way he always was? She ended her letter with:

> Dear —
> Good-night —
> Dear dear dear dear dear dear dear
> Dear dear dear dear dear dear dear
> Dear dear dear dear dear dear
> Dear dear dear dear dear dear
> Dear dear dear dear dear dear . . .

She was remembering other times and other places and wrote him saying she would like to be in Provence again, with the white glare of the country roads and the colorless oblivion of its rotating summer. She thought of Avignon, too, and the wide quiet of the Rhone. She wished they could be having lunch once more at Chateauneuf-du-Pape, looking out over the valley with its tiered vineyards and the Palace of the Popes shimmering like a mirage in the summer heat.

And what would he like? she asked. Not work, she knew, and not lonely places. Would he like to be in New York with a play in rehearsal, or to have decorative people around him, or to be reading Spengler, or what?

But then her mood darkened and her letter trailed off into dangerous territory. Old suspicions, old hints of homosexuality rose to the surface. She couldn't believe, she said, that he would like to be back in the old hurry and disorder of the Ritz Bar and Montmartre. She couldn't believe, she said, that he wanted to return to the highly excitable scenes of the party they had gone to with Macgowan and where, she said, he had passed so much of his time recently.

IV

His princess was in the tower. But Zelda's imprisonment in her insanity, in the "iron maiden" of eczema, in the institutions to which he had taken her that summer — Malmaison, Val-Mont, Prangins — could hardly have afforded Fitzgerald any sense of security.

Now, in her lucid moments, Zelda sent him letters that made him feel bitter and guilty. Her accusations shamed him. When she was at Prangins, he sent her a tortured, self-pitying letter. He had a photograph of her: "The photograph is all I have; it is with me from the morning when I wake up with a frantic half-dream about you to the last moment when I think of you and of death at night."

"The rotten letters you write me," he told her, "I simply put away under Z in my file. My instinct is to write a public letter to the Paris Herald to see if any human being except yourself and Robert McAlmon has ever thought I was a homosexual. The three weeks after the horror of Valmont when I could not lift my eyes to meet the eyes of other men in the street after your stinking allegations and insinuations will not be repeated." He was willing, he said, to take his full share of the responsibility for their tragedy. He tried to reason with her, to show her that if he had failed her, it was just possible that she had failed him, too. But he was afraid, he said, that she would read over every line of the letter, trying to wring some slant or suggestion of his homosexuality in it. "I love you with all my heart," he concluded, "because you are my own girl and that is all I know."

The dialogue of self-justification that had coursed through their stories, acted out by their fictional characters, surfaced in their letters. Zelda refused to feel guilty. "Please don't write to me about blame," she told Fitzgerald. "I am tired of rummaging my head to understand a situation that would be difficult enough if I were completely lucid. I cannot arbitrarily accept blame now when I know that in the past I felt none. Anyway, blame doesn't matter." In another letter she reminded him that he had always told her she had no right to complain as long as she was materially cared for; now, she told him, he was free to construct whatever self-justifications he pleased. "This is not a treatise of recriminations," she went on, "but I would like you to understand clearly why there are certain scenes not only toward the end which could never be effaced from my mind."

They were casting back over their lives, and in autobiographical letters they inventoried their grievances, the imagined and imaginary slights, the failures of communication. Mostly, their letters were exercises in self-justification. Fitzgerald's undated letter—"Written with Zelda Gone to the Clinique," a purely pitiful aside—may not have been sent, but was saved for posterity. He began it with the journey from Capri to Paris, five years earlier, claiming that these had been among the happiest days of his life. He seems to have confused his elation at completing *The Great Gatsby,* his realization that he had written a great book, and the praise it brought him with the actual circumstances: Zelda had been sick at the time. And it was, as he acknowledged, the aftermath of her affair with Jozan—"your heart betraying me," as he euphemistically described it, though perhaps it was no more than that. Even the more recent events in their lives became part of the indictment. Zelda had spoiled his story in order to take Madame to dinner; she had poisoned the trip to Africa. There were bills, the ballet always before his eyes, her indifference. He preferred to see these as the results of malice rather than madness. He saw themselves still as competitors. "For all your superior observation and your harder intelligence," he wrote, "I have a faculty of guessing right, without evidence even with a certain wonder as to why and whence the mental short cut came." It was an argument carried on with a woman who was trying to climb up from insanity. Just possibly, it was more useful than pity; it gave her a hard rung to grasp on to.

Zelda, in a long autobiographical letter written at Prangins, was more detailed and far more descriptive of the people and the events in their lives, from their marriage in New York to her institutionalization in Switzerland. It is in itself an extraordinary act of remembrance, the recollection of the sights and sounds, the summer hotels, the Riviera nights, reaching back for a decade. But Zelda tended to attribute her difficulties to other facts: that Fitzgerald had repudiated her sexually; that he had failed to understand her deepening alienation; that his drinking was ruining their life together; that his drinking was the reason he could not write and could not finish his novel. Nowhere did she acknowledge that she had offered little real encouragement to his professional career, or that her selfishness and boredom had held him hostage, that her obsession with dancing had played its part in tearing them apart, that her independence — the quality that had attracted him in the first place — constituted a threat to a threatened man.

Out of the hazy episodes of the past few months, Zelda recalled an incident at Val-Mont: "I was in [torture] and my head closed together. You gave me a flower and said it was 'plus petite et moins étendue' — We were friends — Then you took it away and I grew sicker, and there was nobody to teach me." She resented his still being able to make some literary use of her life. With bitter civility she commented that she was glad he had found in her situation the material for another of his Josephine stories. She was equally glad that he had developed a new interest in sports. (Fitzgerald was taking lessons from a tennis pro.) Her circumstances were very different, however: "Now that I can't sleep any more, I have lots to think about, and since I have gone so far alone, I suppose I can go the rest of the way." In a fragmentary letter to her brother-in-law Newman Smith, she begged that he come and get her and take her back to France. Fitzgerald, she said, had shamefully neglected her: "What with his drinking and tennis I suppose he hadn't time — so there's no good my asking him for help or pity." To Fitzgerald, she wrote sarcastically, "If you want to know what it's like, you might pass up your next tennis game."

In a postscript to one of her letters, she asked whether he had stopped drinking. Dr. Forel had asked, so she asked, she said. (Forel believed that Fitzgerald's heavy drinking was one of the precipitating factors in Zelda's breakdown.) Fitzgerald was incensed; it was one more stone in the tower of blame that Zelda seemed to be constructing. He countered by writing Forel a long, whining letter about his inability to give up drinking at this point in his life. He thought it grossly unfair that he should be expected to. "My work," he told the psychiatrist in a fit of underlining, *"is done on coffee, coffee and more coffee, never on alcohol."* (Not altogether true, since he had admitted to friends that at Ellerslie he had sometimes resorted to drink for inspiration.) At the end of five or six hours of this regimen, he informed Forel, he got up from his desk *"white and trembling and with a steady burn in my stomach, to go to dinner."* Dedication of that sort inevitably resulted in an inability to relax and be gay with his wife. It was Zelda who had urged him to have wine at dinner. They had been on hard drinking parties "sometimes" before, but the reg-

ular use of wine and apéritifs was something he had "dreaded"—
but that Zelda had encouraged, because it made him more cheerful
and allowed her to drink more. Zelda also drank at lunchtime, which
he did not, Fitzgerald pointed out, sanctimoniously. It was he who
had urged Zelda to take up dancing in order to stop her drinking
habits, which had become so destructive that she had already made
several attempts at suicide. It was then that he had begun to drink
more—from unhappiness.

He told Forel that when he and Zelda gave up drinking (they
had made several attempts, he assured Forel), he immediately got
"dark circles" under his eyes and was "listless and disinclined to
work." During the course of a recent medical examination for *"a
large insurance policy"* (a gratuitous detail added to impress Forel), he
discovered that he had low blood pressure. A pint of wine with each
meal made a great difference in the way he felt. The dark circles
disappeared; the coffee no longer gave him eczema. (Fitzgerald seems
to have had sympathetic reactions to Zelda's ailments; when she had
had appendicitis, he soon after believed he had it. Now that she had
eczema, he had begun to experience the symptoms.) When he had
a little wine with his meals, his head no longer throbbed all night,
and he looked forward to his dinner instead of staring at it.

Much of the letter reads like a documentation of sibling rivalry.
He clearly wanted to improve his image with the doctor. Quite
probably he was concerned about the stories Zelda may have been
telling Forel in the course of her treatment. Fitzgerald had his own
bitter commentaries on Zelda. He obviously wanted to absolve himself from any damaging claims of homosexuality. He told Forel that
he had given up women for Zelda; now she was dragging him—
"of all people"—into her homosexual suspicions. Life with Zelda
had become a hopeless grind; he was supporting a woman whose
tastes were daily diverging from his. Zelda no longer read or knew
anything or liked anyone "except dancers and their cheap satellites."
People respected Zelda, he wrote, "because I concealed her weaknesses, and because of a certain complete fearlessness and honesty
that she has never lost."

His ambition, he told Forel, was to become part of English
literature. It was true that he had lived hard and had ruined his
"essential innocence." He had abused liquor and would have to pay
for it with suffering and death. But the renunciation of liquor was
something else. It was as illogical as giving up sex permanently

because he had caught a venereal disease. (He hastily assured Forel he never had.) The issues that Fitzgerald raised in his letter were certainly serious and his circumstances were deserving of sympathy, but his self-righteousness verged on the ludicrous. It was as if he had had to mount all the rhetorical grandeur of the Declaration of Independence to justify his pint of wine with his meals. "Give up strong drink permanently I will. Bind myself to forswear wine forever I cannot." A pint of wine at the end of a day's work was "one of the rights of man."

In his efforts to become instrumental in Zelda's treatment, Fitzgerald suggested that giving up his drinking would only convince Zelda that she had been right in blaming it for her illness. Worse, it would constitute proof for her relatives. He was particularly concerned that Zelda's condition be attributed to any cause other than his alcoholism. Nowhere was this more evident than in the reports he sent friends and his in-laws. He informed Perkins, for example, that the doctors had advised him that Zelda would not be able to drink again, and added, "not that drink in any way contributed to her collapse." Then, perversely, he noted that her treatment would involve a sacrifice on his part: "I must not drink anything, not even wine, for a year, because drinking in the past was one of the things that haunted her in her delirium."

In September, with Zelda into her fifth month of treatment, Fitzgerald wrote Edmund Wilson to congratulate him on his recent marriage to Margaret Canby and commiserate with him on his breakdown the year before. Confronted by Zelda's illness, he had been encouraged to learn that Wilson had survived his ordeal. (He had undergone hydrotherapy, electric shock, and near-addiction to paraldehyde in an upstate New York sanatorium.) Fitzgerald wrote Wilson that Zelda was almost well, "which is to say the psychosis element is gone. We must live quietly for a year now and to some extent forever. She almost went permanently crazy." He blamed the dancing: "four hours' work a day at the ballet for two years, and she 27 and too old when she began." He was relieved, now, that the ballet was done with, "as our domestic life was cracking under the strain and I hadn't touched my novel for a year."

He told Wilson that he had seen no one for months, except John Bishop in Paris, who seemed more concerned about building a well on his property than with his writing. Also he had met Thomas Wolfe, whom he considered "a fine man and a fine writer."

Wolfe, who tended to be paranoid on several matters, was not so kindly disposed toward Fitzgerald, who he felt was dissipated and a social climber. Worse, he suspected Fitzgerald of trying to sabotage his work and his peace of mind by acting as a spy for his abandoned mistress, Aline Bernstein, the New York stage designer, whose desperate letters and cablegrams followed him from Paris to Montreux. Unaware of Wolfe's dark suspicions, Fitzgerald complained to Wilson about other matters. Paris, he wrote Wilson, had been swarming with fairies, and "I've grown to loathe it and prefer the hospital-like air of Switzerland where nuts are nuts and coughs are coughs."

He was not on the best terms with Zelda's family — most especially with Rosalind Smith, who was living in Brussels with her husband. Fitzgerald had no great love for his sister-in-law; he claimed that Rosalind was "always hiding in closets till the battle is over and then coming out to say, 'I told you so' " — which was not what he needed. When Zelda became ill, Rosalind had written him a letter that he considered insulting. There is a draft of a reply that he presumably sent and that was unusually bitter. For three agonizing months, he told her, he had given all his time to trying to pull Zelda out of the mess they were in. "The matter is terrible enough without your writing me that you wish she would die now, 'rather than go back to the mad world you and she created for yourselves!' " He was well aware, he said, that Rosalind disliked him; nonetheless he had both Scottie and Zelda to think about and simply could not stand to be upset and harassed still further.

When, later in Zelda's first year of treatment, Fitzgerald felt that she was not making sufficient progress, he brought in Dr. Eugen Bleuler, the pioneering Swiss psychiatrist who had invented the term *schizophrenia*. Fitzgerald had acted on a "sort of American hunch" that the Prangins doctors were not as effective with Zelda's case as they might be. In any event, he at least wanted Forel's diagnosis confirmed. Bleuler, whom Zelda diagnosed as "a great imbecile," felt that the treatment had been correct, but recommended that Zelda remain in the clinic rather than undergo the risk of a journey to America. Fitzgerald, writing to Judge and Mrs. Sayre about that decision, made it plain that he was spending heavily for Zelda's recovery. (Which was true: Bleuler's fee was $500; Zelda's confinement at Prangins would mount to about $13,000.) He passed along Bleuler's opinion that Zelda's was a case of *"skideophranie, a sort of borderline insanity, that takes the form of double personality."* According to Bleuler's diagnosis, Zelda's case presented no unusual features, which could be taken as a sign of a good prognosis. Allaying his own sense of guilt, Fitzgerald told the Sayres that Zelda's illness had begun about five years ago and that Bleuler had assured him that he was not responsible. Although he might have retarded Zelda's condition, he could not have prevented it.

In January 1931, Fitzgerald's father died in Washington, at the age of seventy-nine. Leaving Zelda in Prangins and Scottie in their Paris apartment, Fitzgerald sailed home on the *New York* to attend the burial at Rockville, Maryland. Zelda wrote him a somewhat formal but not unfeeling letter — the kind of letter one might send a remote friend. Once he was in America, she told him, the loss of his father would affect him more deeply than it did in Europe. Reliving the scenes of his youth would be a painful affair. She offered him what little comfort there was in the knowledge that "someone who is close to you" appreciated the feeling that some part of his life was now definitely over. A "neurose," she said, was not much good in times of distress. It was difficult to "extract solace from the past." She sent him her "profoundest sympathy."

Fitzgerald had never been close to his family. He tended to regard his father as little more than a gentle failure, though a somewhat romantic one. His father's Civil War stories, his ancestral connection with Francis Scott Key, provided a link with the American past. In her letter, Zelda seems to have echoed, or tried to reinforce, Fitzgerald's attitude. She advised him not to feel sorry for his father's lot in life. "By the time the failures of his middle years had grown far enough away . . . he was already old and tired." By then, with money enough, Edward Fitzgerald had been spared "the great scramble for a place in the world." Fitzgerald would write about the experience of returning for his father's burial in a story first titled "Home to Maryland" and then "On Your Own." But he would change the gender of the protagonist and cast it as a shipboard romance between the wealthy George Ives and an American actress, Evelyn Lovejoy, who is returning home for the burial of her father in Maryland. It was an ill-fated tale and another of the warning symptoms of Fitzgerald's declining popular reputation. For five years, Harold Ober tried to place it with a number of magazines, without success. It was never published during Fitzgerald's lifetime. But

Fitzgerald salvaged the burial scene, reversed the gender once more, and ascribed the experience to Dick Diver in *Tender Is the Night*.

How much Fitzgerald's ambivalence toward his father contributed to the story's failure is not easy to determine. But there is a definite flaw in the conception of the story, which was written shortly after his return to Switzerland. In his hasty treatment of the subject, he merged two incompatible personal experiences—the death of his father and his shipboard flirtation with one of the women on the *New York,* Bert Barr, a lively extrovert who at first convinced him that she was a professional cardsharp. The conflict between the poignancy of the father's death and the conventional nature of the romance—in the old, peppy Fitzgerald manner—is never resolved.

In "On Your Own," the father is an old country doctor laid to rest among his ancestors in the churchyard cemetery. Evelyn Lovejoy, standing by the graveside, reflects: "All these dead, she knew them all, their weather-beaten faces with hard blue flashing eyes, their spare violent bodies, their souls made of new earth in the long forest-heavy darkness of the seventeenth century."

As she leaves, Evelyn remarks, "Goodbye then Father, all my fathers"—a recognition, as Zelda had warned, that a significant part of Fitzgerald's life had ended.

In Switzerland, if for no other reason than economic necessity, Fitzgerald returned to writing his commercial stories. But they were stories that tended to draw on his recent experiences—Zelda's madness, his alcoholism—stories that were different from the madcap antics of the Jazz Age. Probably, as consolation to Zelda for her renunciation of the dance lessons, he also tried very hard to promote the stories she wrote while she was hospitalized. Three of them, written, as he said, "in the dark middle of her nervous breakdown," he recommended to Max Perkins, expecting that Perkins would push for publication in *Scribner's Magazine.* "I think you'll see that apart from the beauty & richness of the writing, they have a strange haunting and evocative quality that is absolutely new," he told Perkins. He went even further: "In my opinion they are literature tho I may in this case read so much between the lines that my opinion is valueless."

Perkins thought they showed an "astonishing power of expression," but thought they were for a more selective audience than the

Scribner's readership. Despite his caution, he was sensitive to the special quality of the stories: "Descriptively, they are very rare, and the description is not just description. It has a curious emotional content in itself." Fitzgerald was, of course, disappointed, but he acknowledged that they might be elusive for the reader "who doesn't know from what depths of misery and effort they sprang." Writing to Ober, he suggested he try the *Century* or, better still, Edmund Wilson at *The New Republic,* with the title, "Stories from a Swiss Clinique," accentuating the psychiatric angle. Although Wilson held the stories for a considerable time, he was unable to use them, and they were never published and appear to have been lost.

Fitzgerald, too, had begun to tap the less glamorous aspects of his personal life for his fiction, and two of the stories, "One Trip Abroad" and "Babylon Revisited," were among the best he produced in the later stages of his career. The first was adapted from one of the false starts on his novel, the Kelly version. In the story, he chronicles the moral deterioration of Nelson and Nicole Kelly, recently married. Having inherited a half-million dollars, the pair are traveling through Europe. Both have had lonely youths and "now they wanted the taste and smell of the living world; for the present, they were finding it in each other." Both are vaguely interested in the arts. Nelson paints a little (like Gerald Murphy, he has painted a picture of a smokestack in the modern style). Nicole intends to study singing. But neither of them has the force of character or perseverance for such a career.

The underlying theme of "One Trip Abroad" is the blind force of destruction set loose in the world and in personal life. (It is very coolly suggested by a symbolic plague of locusts in the opening paragraph.) And it is one of Fitzgerald's more important stories of a disintegrating marriage. In the course of their experiences abroad—in North Africa, on the Riviera, and in Paris—and in their descent into dissipation, the Kellys encounter a young couple whose marriage is breaking up in rancorous public scenes.

Eventually, in broken health and spirits, the Kellys settle into a clinic in Switzerland, "a country," so the narrator observes, "where very few things begin, but many things end." There, the Kellys find, much to their surprise, that their Doppelgängers, the other couple, are also patients. Out of some sense of apprehension, however, they avoid meeting them. The dénouement of the story comes in the course of a lightning storm, when the Kellys catch sight of the shadowy couple in the rain-soaked garden. They are both physically shaken. In Fitzgerald's earlier story, "The Rough Crossing," written the year before Zelda's breakdown, Adrian and Eva Smith refuse to acknowledge their disintegration; they claim it must have been some other Smiths who had behaved so poorly on the voyage. In "One Trip Abroad," written the year after Zelda's breakdown, the Kellys cannot avoid the shock of recognition. Nicole cries out, "They're us! They're us! Don't you see?" Like the Fitzgeralds, the Kellys had been forced to see themselves.

"Babylon Revisited" drew upon another instance of personal failure and family bitterness, Scottie's stay with her aunt Rosalind Smith in Brussels. The theme is a father's dissipation and his inability to live down the reputation as an alcoholic that he established for himself in the boom days of the twenties. Rosalind Smith served as the model for the neurotic sister-in-law who refuses to give up her guardianship of Charles Wales's daughter, Honoria. (As a cruel family joke, Fitzgerald gives the sister-in-law's address in Paris as the rue Palatine, the setting in which Zelda had accused her husband of homosexuality. In the story, too, Charles Wales's wife, Helen, after a married life of drunken scenes, quarrels, and recriminations, is dead, fulfilling Rosalind's wish that Zelda would die rather than return to the wild life she and her husband had lived.) But it is Wales who has been in the sanatorium and who is shakily putting his life together again to make a home for his daughter. He is a man who has lost a good deal of money in the Crash but lost everything he wanted in the boom that preceded it. In the end, thwarted by his sister-in-law, he resolves not to give up: "He would come back some day; they couldn't make him pay forever."

It was one of the unfortunate circumstances of Fitzgerald's career that the market where he had made his reputation was so little interested in the stories in which he dropped the brittle glamour and attempted to deal honestly with the more complex problems of his experience. The editors of *The Saturday Evening Post* accepted a recent story, "The Hotel Child," but complained that the expatriate life and the characters Fitzgerald depicted were a bit more "shady" than they liked. They were even less happy with the next three stories — "Flight and Pursuit," "A New Leaf," and "Indecision" — all of which were set in Europe and drew on Fitzgerald's personal life. They pointedly asked Ober to relay their dissatisfaction, even though they accepted the trio. They preferred that Fitzgerald write "some American stories — that is stories laid on this side of the Atlantic." They also felt that the stories were lacking in plot. Ober, when he wrote Fitzgerald in May 1931, was apologetic:

> I think it is probably a mistake for me to write you this letter but the Post have definitely asked me to tell you how they feel. Although these last stories of yours may not be as good as some you have done, they are so much better than most of the stories that I read, that it makes me a little angry with the Post.

Ober suggested that Fitzgerald tear up the letter and write his stories as he wanted.

But he made an urgent request that Fitzgerald get to work on his novel so that "without fail" they could have it out in 1932. He suggested that Fitzgerald hide away somewhere beyond the reach of his friends. "I realize that you are having a tremendous lot of expense for Zelda and that must of course worry you a great deal." He wondered whether it wasn't time for Fitzgerald to return home, where Zelda could be treated by American doctors. He offered his personal encouragement: "I believe, and others who are much more competent judges than I, believe that you ought to go further than any American writer and I think now is the time for you to get down to hard work and finish the novel."

Still, there may have been an undercurrent of disapproval in Ober's letter, a hint that he was becoming exasperated by delays and excuses. More ominous were the signs that the winds of taste were changing in the magazines for which Fitzgerald had written so profitably. They were becoming more conservative, more chauvinistic. But Fitzgerald was trying to branch out into new territories in his fiction. Slowly, his once unassailable reputation was being eroded — by the Depression mentality, by the slackness of his professional habits. It was another of the items in the inventory of his failure.

In the summer of 1931, Zelda was well enough to take an extended vacation from Prangins. For two weeks she and Scottie and Fitzgerald managed to have one of the rare occasions in their family history — a relaxed and happy time together. It was spent at the lakeside resort of Annecy, in the Haute-Savoie. It proved to be the ideal spot: a broad and sparkling lake with scudding sailboats, green and shady parks bordering the water, an old quarter with cobbled streets and canals, old shops, houses decorated with windowboxes bright with flowers.

At first, they put up at the Beau Rivage on the western shore of the lake; then they moved to the east bank at Menthon. "The water was greener there," Zelda recalled, "and the shadows long and cool and the scraggly gardens staggered up the shelved precipice to the Hôtel Palace." They played tennis and fished, drove into the countryside, took excursions to the spa at Aix-les-Bains. It was at Annecy that they celebrated Zelda's thirty-first birthday with a party.

In the full glare of summer, they bathed in the lake, breathed in the piny smell of the bathhouses redolent in the heat. "We walked at night towards a café blooming with Japanese lanterns, white shoes gleaming like radium in the damp darkness." On other nights, they danced Viennese waltzes in the hotel ballroom and "simply swep' around." Zelda sent reassuring cards to her father, noting that Annecy was so blue that it tinted the air and made you think you were living inside an aquarium. "It is as peaceful inside its scalloped mountains as a soup-ladle full of the sky."

There were other brief excursions during that last summer abroad, for Zelda was to be released from Prangins in another two months — trips to Caux and Munich. ("The young Germans stalking the ill-lit streets wore a sinister air — the talk that underscored the beer-garden waltzes was of war and hard times.") Thornton Wilder took them to a famous restaurant where the beer was deserving of the silver mugs it was served in. They visited the Murphys in the Austrian Tyrol, where young Patrick was being treated for tuberculosis. In Vienna, they dined at the Widow Sacher's while a more illustrious diner, one of the Rothschilds, was hidden behind a leather screen. On their return trip they stayed a few days at Vevey Palace on Lake Geneva.

But Annecy was that special time in their lives — a time out from the wars of the self. When Zelda, later, pasted their snapshots in her album — photographs of the Fitzgeralds beside their six-cylinder Renault in front of the Hôtel Palace, the white-aproned servants in attendance; the three of them in the merciless sunlight of the hotel's scruffy tennis court; Scottie and Zelda inspecting the menu in a hotel dining room; the three of them in a motor launch, wearing bathing suits, smiling as if they were the most ordinary and happy family alive—she wreathed the page with cutouts of flowers. The stay at Annecy, in fact, was their last happy time abroad.

They would remember it with particular vividness. "It was like the good gone times when we still believed in summer hotels and the philosophies of popular songs."

In September, they returned to America on the *Aquitania*. Stopping in New York for a few days, they decided to be economical and put up at the New Yorker Hotel. Fitzgerald noticed that the customs officials were politer than he had remembered. New York itself seemed like an echoing tomb, although a few "wraiths" were still carrying on the old party habits of the days before the Crash. It had always been his habit, when leaving the city, to bid it farewell from the top of the Plaza Hotel, his symbol of elegance and luxury. But now, the Empire State Building, constructed by Governor Alfred Smith during Fitzgerald's two-and-a-half-year absence, offered a greater vista.

In "My Lost City," his homage to New York, written not long after his return, Fitzgerald described the oddness of his new perception. New York had been his city of ambition and power, the center of success. Now, looking out over it from the world's tallest structure, he realized that the city, like the ambitious country that had failed with the stock market crash, had limits. But he saw that it merged into the country on all sides, into an expanse of green and blue that was limitless. It was, after all, a city and not a universe. The dream had been part of a larger and more complicated reality, all along.

That sense of a broader context also brought home to him a few political realizations that did not necessarily engage his own sympathies. Bunny Wilson, he noted, "had gone over to Communism and frets about the wrongs of southern mill workers and western farmers, whose voices, fifteen years ago, would not have penetrated his study walls." He was forced to realize that time had brought changes as irrevocable as those he had experienced abroad. His mood was nostalgic, but the prose in which he described the city that had once been his splendid mirage was slightly tinged with the rhetoric of Thomas Wolfe. "Come back," he called, "come back, O glittering and white!"

Politics and the economy were also the topics of an interview published in the *Montgomery Advertiser* on October 8, the day after they arrived in Alabama. He and Zelda decided to settle close to the Sayres so that he could work on his novel and Zelda would have the family nearby. They stayed at the Greystone Hotel. Judge Sayre was ill, and Fitzgerald, in any case, did not want to live with his in-laws. Eventually, they found a spacious and fairly modern house at 819 Felder Avenue.

In his interview with a reporter, Walling Keith, Fitzgerald expressed surprise that Montgomery showed fewer signs of the Depression than any of the cities he had visited. "I'm going to like it here in Montgomery, I know," he told the reporter. "It's a relief to spend a few hours in a city where I'm not met with talk of depression." In the East, he said, at the parties he went to, the subject came up even before he had had a chance to become acquainted with the guests. The topics he seemed most eager to discuss were Prohibition and communism, his recent meetings with Hemingway and Ring Lardner in New York. Hemingway, he noted, was at work on a new novel; Lardner was "seriously ill." Prohibition, he maintained—speaking purely as a fiction writer and not "an earnest student of political science"—was nonsense, and most of the people he knew who were concerned about human welfare just laughed at it. He was surprised that no one in Montgomery seemed especially fearful of communist activities. "It seems foolish for an American to be afraid of any communistic revolution in this country, right now," he said, "but I heard so many conjectures of possible reactions here, while in Eastern cities, that at times I felt myself becoming concerned with the question."

He said: "In ideals, I am somewhat of a communist. That is, as much as other persons who belong to what we call 'the arts group'; but communism as I see it has no place in the United States . . . and the American people will not stand for its teachings."

That he made this announcement with a deferential laugh, according to the interviewer, perhaps indicates his ambivalence about current political issues. But Fitzgerald had always been sensitive to the example of his colleagues. He must have been impressed by the political activism of friends like Wilson and Dos Passos. His political conscience had evidently been stirred.

There is no way of knowing when Fitzgerald entered one of the more significant items in his notebooks: "They went to sleep easily on other people's pain." And there is no way of knowing whether he intended it as a description—or a criticism—of his and Zelda's former insouciance and selfishness.

PART FIVE

10

The Invented Part

F OR YEARS, Fitzgerald thought of Hollywood as punishment both for him and his public. In 1925, realizing that *The Great Gatsby* was a financial flop, he threatened to give up writing novels and go to Hollywood to learn the movie business. During his stay in Europe in 1930–1931, with Zelda ill and his novel stalled, his stories not meeting with success, he once more began thinking about his punitive exile.

Both Max Perkins and Harold Ober had been urging that if he could not complete his novel in time, perhaps he should consider bringing out a collection of his Basil Duke Lee stories. Fitzgerald was against it; he wrote to Perkins that he had seen too many writers —Tom Boyd and Michael Arlen, among many others—"fall through the eternal trapdoor of trying [to] cheat the public, no matter what their public is, with substitutes"; better to let another four years go by before bringing out his novel. *"I know what I'm doing*—honestly, Max," he pleaded. The *Post* stories, Fitzgerald told Ober, were all right *"in* the *Post*," where they were no spot on his reputation. "They're honest and if their *form* is stereotyped people know what to *expect when* they pick up the *Post*." If he brought out a collection of minor stories now, he might just as well "get tickets for Hollywood immediately."

Late in October, by way of Harold Ober, Fitzgerald had his ticket. Metro-Goldwyn-Mayer offered him $750 a week plus railroad fare to do a screen adaptation of Katherine Brush's successful novel, *Red-Headed Woman*. Fitzgerald claimed that he didn't want to go "for a damn," but on Ober's advice he held out for more money, and the studio reluctantly agreed to pay him $1200 a week. Since the assignment was expected to last only six weeks, it was an opportunity for Fitzgerald to clear up his debts and buy time for work on his novel. An added inducement was that he would be working under Irving Thalberg.

With his family settled in at Felder Avenue (Mademoiselle was still with them, and there were two black servants, Freeman and Julia, to look after the household), Fitzgerald left for the West Coast in early November. Unfortunately, he and Zelda quarreled at the station, and Scottie cried on the way home. Zelda attempted to send a wire to one of the stops along the way, but it was returned. "It's unbearable to think that I was mean to you . . . " she apologized. "Goofo, *please* love me." During the weeks he was away, she wrote him regularly. On Armistice Day, four days after his departure, she told him that the bereft family looked like "a lot of minor characters at table waiting for the entrance of the star." There had been a parade, she said, but she hadn't gone: "I love the still desertion of the back streets when men are marching." She was keeping the light burning on his desk at night so that she would think he was there when she got up in the mornings. She was reading his early story "The Offshore Pirate," she said. "You were younger than anybody in the world once." Later, when she came to "The Sensible Thing," the story of their courtship days, she felt like crying. "Reading your stories," she wrote, "makes me curious more than ever about you. I don't suppose I really know you very well."

She, too, was writing stories. There was a murder story, "All About the Downs Case," which proved to be unsalable and was never published. And she was still awaiting word from Harold Ober, who was trying to place her story "A Couple of Nuts." She was afraid she was just "writing for myself." During Fitzgerald's absence, she seems to have begun work on a novel, as well. But she confessed to having literary problems: "I can't seem to get started writing. I haven't got that inner happiness or desperation that leaves a person free in the external world of imagination, but just a sort of plugging along feeling." She reported on the family news: she was playing tennis every day with her niece Noonie, Marjorie's daughter; Scottie was taking riding lessons. Her father, she wrote, was sinking rapidly, so the doctors said. She went every day to Pleasant Avenue, but the judge was mostly unconscious and didn't recognize anyone. She took her mother for long drives to get her out of the house.

She had had a disturbing nightmare: Fitzgerald had come home from Hollywood with a great shock of white hair. It had turned suddenly from his worrying about being unfaithful. "That was an awful dream — awful dear. I didn't want to live and you were only formally sorry." Zelda was still concerned about her husband among glamorous Hollywood stars. It didn't help when Fitzgerald mentioned meeting Lily Damita and Constance Bennett at parties.

The dream factory to which Fitzgerald reported on November 11 was an incongruous hodgepodge of buildings painted a banal gray, rising on the former salt flats of Culver City, outside Hollywood proper. There, for the next several weeks, Fitzgerald worked for the "Great Little Master," Irving Thalberg. The movie executive was even more of a phenomenal success than when Fitzgerald had met him in 1927. He was now married to Norma Shearer, had grown thinner and more frail, wore his trimly tailored business suits with padded shoulders to give himself an appearance of substantiality.

It was not a congenial assignment. The script that Fitzgerald had been picked to work on had already been gone over by several screenwriters and was unsatisfactory. Fitzgerald, however, was the first choice of Samuel Marx, the youngish story editor at MGM, who had been an admirer of Fitzgerald's writing since the twenties. But Fitzgerald's immediate supervisor was the Rumanian-born director Marcel de Sano, who was a favorite at the front office, particularly with Thalberg's assistant, Albert Lewin. Fitzgerald regarded him as a studio hack. The whole Hollywood system of revision after revision, time-consuming conferences, long waits for appointments with Thalberg, and still new revisions proved discouraging. In his gloomier moods, Fitzgerald felt the film industry simply failed to use his qualities as a writer. Collaboration was the key, but he was stuck with a director he didn't like or respect. Nor did he have the jaunty confidence he had brought to Hollywood the previous time. He was, in fact, plainly jittery, and consequently began drinking more than he should have at a welcoming party at his hotel with King Vidor and his wife, Eleanor Boardman, and Samuel Marx and his wife. According to Marx, after only a drink or two Fitzgerald began to slur his speech, and within a very short time he was past the stage of going out to dinner with his guests. To make matters worse, within a few days after his arrival de Sano was spreading the word that Fitzgerald got drunk from merely sniffing the cork on a wine bottle. Fitzgerald evidently wrote Zelda about his unhappiness. She tried to be consoling. "I'm sorry your work isn't interesting," she answered. "I had hoped it might present new dramatic facets that would make up for the tediousness of it. If it seems too much drudgery and you are faced with 'get to-gether and talk-it-over' technique — come home, Sweet. You will at least have eliminated Hollywood forever." She added, "My mind stumbles about the shadows of your room and thinks of nothing at all except that you were there a week ago."

If Fitzgerald was unhappy, he must have been even more anxious when, on November 18, Zelda wrote him that her father had died the night before. The family had waited until the next morning to tell her. "The struggle is over and this is the end of another brave uncompromising effort to preserve conceptions," she wrote him. Of course, she attended the funeral: "The Capitol flag is flying at half-mast and old gray-headed men seem terribly sad. But Daddy seems young and beautiful and somehow master of everything. He looks very little in his clothes." Fitzgerald got the impression that she was coping with the situation much better than he had expected. Zelda had some somber reflections not long after, on the day when she went to clean out the judge's office and found a big butterfly pinned to a map, shirt samples in a drawer, a copy of Josephus: "It's just the little personal things we care about in people. . . . And all of us care that we will never hear a certain chuckle again or see the fingers meet a certain way." There was not another living soul, she complained, except Fitzgerald with whom she could have the slightest communion. Fitzgerald, equating the two deaths in the family — his father's and Judge Sayre's — observed a similarity: "Our fathers died. Suddenly in the night they died and in the morning we knew."

His sense of uneasiness and dissatisfaction prompted him to cut loose and make a nuisance of himself at the parties that were as much a ritual of Hollywood Sundays as a weekend church service. And he often went to gay parties with Carmel Myers and with the Vidors. He met David Selznick again — this time with his new wife, Irene, the daughter of Louis B. Mayer, Thalberg's boss and competitor. And he chummed around with Dwight Taylor, whom he and Zelda had known during their New York partying days, when Taylor was an aspiring writer and young man about town. Now, he was a screenwriter at MGM. He and Taylor were invited to an elite affair given by Thalberg and Norma Shearer in honor of the visiting British playwright Freddie Lonsdale.

Actually, it was a party to which people were "bidden" rather than invited. Fitzgerald, nervously hoping to make a good impression, did as badly as possible. At first he turned down the martinis circulating around the room on silver trays, but then wandered off, out of Taylor's sight, and had one or two. His initial faux pas was to insult Robert Montgomery, who had asked expressly to meet him. Montgomery, unfortunately, had come to tea very well turned out in a polo outfit. It gave Fitzgerald the opportunity to ask, snidely, why Montgomery hadn't brought his horse. Next, after a few more surreptitious martinis, he decided to perform his old party song, "Dog," the one that he and Bunny Wilson had made such a hit with years ago. Ramon Novarro was commandeered to play the piano, Miss Shearer's pet poodle was fetched, and Fitzgerald cradled it in his arms. With the confidence of a few drinks, Fitzgerald started off with the opening verse which, in Taylor's recollected version, was a dull echo of the earlier song:

> In Spain, they have the donkey
> In Australia, the kangaroo
> In Africa, they have the zebra,
> In Switzerland, the zoo.
> But in America we have the dog —
> And he's a man's best friend.

The crowd gathered around the piano was mildly tolerant and vaguely amused. But as one vapid verse piled on another, with the same limp refrain, people stood fixed and stony-faced and began looking about for some excuse to escape. When it dawned on Fitzgerald that his performance was a flop, the beads of perspiration began to break out on his forehead. But he seemed locked into continuing, verse after verse. Taylor, watching in embarrassment, decided that the song itself had been an awful mistake — certainly for the crowd at a Hollywood party; it would have been amusing to a freshman at college perhaps, or to someone sufficiently drunk. Thalberg, standing at the far end of the room, his hands thrust deep in his pockets, surveyed the scene. Then, from the edge of the crowd, there came a loud and insistent hissing sound, like steam escaping from a radiator. Lupe Velez and John Gilbert were rendering their verdict. It was one of those ineradicable human nightmares, but it was hap-

pening in broad afternoon. Everyone was frozen, unable to move.
Only Norma Shearer seemed capable of keeping up an encouraging
smile. Taylor felt a glum kind of horror, recognizing that Hollywood
society actually had no social leadership. There was no malice in
people's faces, nor any sense of fun either; they simply waited while
Fitzgerald's little entertainment fell flat in front of them. Taylor,
taking Fitzgerald's arm, said, "Come on, Scott. We're going home."

The next day, Fitzgerald received a telegram from his hostess
that may have been some consolation to his frayed pride: I THOUGHT
YOU WERE ONE OF THE MOST AGREEABLE PERSONS AT OUR
TEA. But Fitzgerald got the real verdict when, at the studio, he
asked Dwight Taylor how he had done, and Taylor answered, "Not
so good." Fitzgerald looked down at the floor, saying that the job
meant a good deal to him. "I hope," he said, "I didn't make too
much of a jackass of myself." The two went to the studio commissary
for lunch; Fitzgerald was nursing a hangover. Metro-Goldwyn-Mayer
was, at the time, filming a horror movie called *Freaks,* with a cast
made up of side-show attractions from the Barnum & Bailey Circus,
most of whom ate in the cafeteria. When a pair of Siamese twins,
the Hilton sisters, sat down on a single chair at Fitzgerald's table
and cheerily began studying the menu, Fitzgerald turned pea-green
and bolted for the door.

Zelda, who evidently was not told about Fitzgerald's performance at the Thalberg tea, wrote him in high spirits about the
publication of her story "Miss Ella" in the December issue of *Scribner's.* It had made a "sensation" in Montgomery. "People seem to
like it," she said. It was one of her Southern stories about a spinster
whose former fiancé had shot himself in her garden, in front of an
old playhouse, on the day she was to marry another man. Zelda had
first written it at Prangins. It had her particular virtues—the oddly
intense psychological perception; and her vices—the flashy style that
called attention to itself, the cluttered descriptive passages. Zelda
maintained that she was afraid to read it herself, but she sent a copy
to Dr. Forel in Switzerland out of sheer vanity. "I *wish* you could
teach me to write," she told Fitzgerald.

It was around this time that Scott's nemesis, Dick Knight,
turned up in their lives once more. Zelda wrote Fitzgerald about
"Dick's telegram" to her, which she had unfortunately lost but which
she paraphrased for him: " 'Am moanin' low over your story. You
are the swellest short-story writer living as I have just found out

from Scribner's'—words to that effect—I was very tickled about the story, naturally." She told Fitzgerald that she had visited Daddy's grave on the side of an old and sinking hill; she was lonesome for Fitzgerald, she said, because she hadn't anyone to trust and talk to about intellectual things: "There's no use asking anybody else's opinion because I don't care what it is." She was planning for Christmas and Fitzgerald's homecoming and a possible visit from her mother-in-law, whom Fitzgerald had urged to spend Christmas in Montgomery. The house, Zelda wrote, was as fresh as "a candy-store" in preparation: "The curtains are washed and starched to paper and the rugs are cleaned and bright, owing to hap-hazard animal excretions." Felder Avenue had become a menagerie, with a cat named Chopin and a dog named Trouble. Zelda was also tending Polly, the house-keeper's parrot, until Christmas. Polly could say "Aw go to hell" and sing "Yes Sir, That's My Baby," and Zelda desperately wanted a parrot of her own. Scottie, she told her husband, was disillusioned on discovering that there was no Santa Claus.

Molly Fitzgerald, it appears, had decided not to spend Christmas with them. Zelda was sympathetic. Old people, she said, were tragic gestures left over from the days when they felt desire and had unconscious responses to others. They had "all those placative phrases with which they've managed to piece the rents and tears of the current of life and patch away the meaning of things." Her letters were full of little oddities of expression that probably meant nothing; on the other hand, they may have carried warning signals. She was having attacks of asthma that kept her awake at night. There were minor recurrences of eczema.

In Hollywood, the mean gossip was that Fitzgerald's behavior at the Thalberg tea was one of the reasons he was dropped from working on the *Red-Headed Woman.* Fitzgerald, however, claimed that he had been gypped out of command by de Sano, who took it on himself to rewrite Fitzgerald's script. He wanted to complain to Thalberg directly, but was "erroneously warned" that it would be considered bad form. Later, with an air of grievance and apparent satisfaction, he referred to de Sano as "a bastard . . . since a suicide." His version of his Hollywood failure was that the studio had, after all, approved the script but wanted him to remain for rewrites, and he had been eager to get back east to Zelda. The studio had regarded this as "running out on them." At the end of five weeks, he signed an agreement abrogating his contract. He was free to return home.

On December 15, the day before Fitzgerald was told that he could quit Hollywood earlier than planned, Anita Loos was in town, ready to take over Fitzgerald's assignment. Thalberg had contacted her several days earlier. At her first meeting in Thalberg's office, the producer informed her that he wanted her to give *Red-Headed Woman* the kind of sex and humor she had given *Gentlemen Prefer Blondes.* He wanted the audience to laugh with—and not at—Lil Andrews, the hard-boiled heroine who sleeps her way into marriage with her boss. "Scott," Thalberg told Loos, "tried to turn the silly book into a tone poem!"

After the Christmas holidays in Montgomery, Fitzgerald and Zelda took a brief vacation together in St. Petersburg, Florida. From there, Fitzgerald wrote Perkins with his old jauntiness, flush with his Hollywood earnings, which had wisely been paid to Harold Ober in weekly installments. "At last," he told Perkins, "for the first time in two years and a half I am going to spend five consecutive months on my novel. I am actually six thousand dollars ahead." He had changed the plan for his book; he intended to keep "what's good in what I have" and add forty-one thousand words. Then it would be ready for publication. "Don't tell Ernest or anyone—let them think what they want," he cautioned Perkins; "you're the only one who's ever consistently felt faith in me anyhow." His admiration for Irving Thalberg, apparently, had not been tarnished in any way by his recent experience. In fact, he seems to have appreciated the producer's decisiveness. Advising Perkins to take a proper vacation, he counseled, "When you come back cut off an empty head or two. Thalberg did that with Metro-Goldwyn-Mayer."

Nor did Fitzgerald regard his Hollywood stint as wasted time. Writing to Ober, he maintained that he was not sorry, "because I've got a fine story about Hollywood which will be along in several days." "Crazy Sunday" would be one of the ill-fated minor masterpieces in Fitzgerald's career. It was indeed a story about the bleak Hollywood social life, but it was also one in which Fitzgerald transformed an embarrassing personal defeat—his performance at the Thalberg tea—into a brilliant work of art. In it, Joel Coles, a young screenwriter, is invited to a "top-drawer" party at the home of the film director Miles Calman and his wife, the actress Stella Walker. Calman is one of Fitzgerald's artist-heroes. He "had never made a cheap picture though he had sometimes paid heavily for the luxury of making experimental flops." He is clearly patterned after Thalberg, as Stella Walker is modeled on Norma Shearer. He is a man struggling to maintain his integrity in a corrupting profession. But Calman is an alter ego of Fitzgerald, the genuine artist who has had an experimental flop, *The Great Gatsby,* and paid heavily for it.

Except for the dénouement, the incidents in "Crazy Sunday" are drawn from Fitzgerald's experiences in Hollywood. Coles, who knows that Calman disapproves of heavy drinkers, sneaks too many cocktails and decides to give a burlesque imitation of a noted Jewish producer whose "cultural limitations" and malapropisms suggest a parody of Louis B. Mayer and Samuel Goldwyn. Coles gets the same chilly reception from the guests and receives the same consoling telegram from his hostess that his creator did. Even the side-show freaks—"the sad, lovely Siamese twins, the mean dwarfs, the proud giant from the circus picture"—turn up in the story. But they provide a symbolic contrast to the equally freakish actresses, "pretty women, their eyes all melancholy and startling with mascara, their ball gowns garish in full day." "Crazy Sunday" is a story set in a world of make-believe, but a world in which reality and illusion have a working relationship. Strangely, the one element of fantasy in the story that was not derived from Fitzgerald's actual experiences was the climactic one, when Coles sleeps with Stella Walker on the night that her husband, away from Hollywood, is killed in a plane crash.

But there was an even odder confrontation between art and life in Fitzgerald's story. Dwight Taylor, when he read "Crazy Sunday," was both amazed and amused to find that Fitzgerald had performed a switch. Taylor, whose mother was the actress Laurette Taylor, found himself cast in the role of the alcoholic young continuity writer whose mother was a famous actress. And it was Taylor, as Coles, who had the humiliating experience of being booed at the producer's party; Fitzgerald assigned himself the role of the Good Samaritan, the older, more highly paid screenwriter, Nat Keogh, who takes Coles home at the opportune moment.

Even more important, Taylor had somehow sensed in Fitzgerald's fictional sleight-of-hand something that Fitzgerald had confided in the privacy of his notebooks, that "feeling of proxy in passion," the need to appropriate the more turbulent experiences of others. Taylor described the dénouement of Fitzgerald's story, the one-night affair of Coles and Stella Walker, in terms of a mythological fantasy that served a psychological purpose for its author.

> Just as Jupiter is said to have taken on a variety of disguises — Amphitryon, a bull, a swan, even a shower of gold coins — in order to gain access to a woman, so did Scott project himself into the skin of others in an attempt to enjoy himself without the concomitant of guilt.

Fitzgerald had moderate hopes for "Crazy Sunday" when he mailed it to Harold Ober from Florida in mid-January. But his agent found considerable trouble in placing it. The editors of *The Saturday Evening Post* thought it was probably an accurate picture of Hollywood, but they felt the final tragedy was not adequately prepared for. *Redbook* turned it down flat. Ober ruled out most of the women's magazines, because they would consider the ending immoral. *Cosmopolitan,* a Hearst publication, also declined it. One of Hearst's policy men said they didn't dare use it because it might offend the movie people with whom the publisher was affiliated. Fitzgerald claimed that he had mixed up the characters so thoroughly that no one in Hollywood would recognize himself or herself. But later he capitalized on the rejection by claiming that *Cosmopolitan* was afraid of offending Thalberg, Norma Shearer, John Gilbert, and Hearst's mistress, Marion Davies, all of whom were presumably identifiable. In the end, "Crazy Sunday" was published in *The American Mercury* for the lowly fee of $200. For Mencken's benefit, Fitzgerald hyped up the story of the story, claiming it had been written specifically for *Cosmopolitan* but was banned "on the ground that it discussed well-known figures in Metro."

II

But Fitzgerald had far greater problems than the failure of a story. During the Florida vacation, Zelda began to show disturbing signs of a relapse. And on the return trip to Montgomery, she got hold of Fitzgerald's flask and drank all the contents. Her old delusions that her physical ailments were being caused by other people in connivance with her husband reappeared. Fitzgerald, worried, wrote to Dr. Forel and then, as Zelda grew worse, took her, with her consent, to the Phipps Clinic at the Johns Hopkins University Hospital in Baltimore. Zelda was admitted on February 12, 1932. Fitzgerald's overriding fear was that she would turn against him as violently as she had in Paris. She was put under the care of Dr. Adolf Meyer, a Swiss psychiatrist, considered one of the leading authorities in the diagnosis and treatment of schizophrenia. Neither Fitzgerald nor Zelda recognized that her frenetic activities — her grinding out one story after another, seven of them (most of them unsalable), her work on the novel (which she felt was going badly) — and her complaints of eye trouble and the eruption of the eczema were pointing toward a breakdown. Fitzgerald returned to Baltimore, completely discouraged, waiting for further word from the doctors. It was all the more disheartening because he and Zelda had managed to convince themselves that she was gradually improving.

Zelda wrote him a plaintive letter from the clinic: "It seemed very sad to see you going off in your new shoes alone. Little human vanities are somehow the most moving poignant things in people you love." Life was becoming intolerable, she wrote him in another letter. Every day she developed some new neurosis: "Now it's money: We must have more money. To-morrow it will be something else again: that I ran when Mamma needed me to help her move, that my hips are fat and shaking with the vulgarities of middle-age." "O Darling! My poor dear," she wrote him, "watching everything in your life destroyed one by one except your name. Your entire life will soon be accounted for by the toils we have so assiduously woven — your leisure is eaten up by habits of leisure, your money by habitual extravagance, your hope by cynicism and mine by frustration." Freud, she claimed, was the only human being, outside the Baptist church, who took man seriously.

Evidently she was well enough to be taken out on excursions. She reported that she had seen the movie *Freaks*. It gave her the horrors. She launched into a kind of evangelical sermon: "God! the point of view of sanity, normality, beauty, even the necessity to survive is so utterly arbitrary. . . . We are all seeking the absolution of chastity in sex and the stimulation of sex in the church until sometimes I think I would loose my mind if I were not insane." Her letter was even more revealing for one of its grim self-images, one that she said she had told Fitzgerald about on other occasions:

> I am that little fish who swims about a shark and, I believe, lives indelicately on its offal. . . . Life moves over me in a vast black shadow and I swallow whatever it drops with relish, having learned in a very hard school that one cannot be both a parasite and enjoy

self-nourishment without moving in worlds too fantastic for even
my disordered imagination to people with meaning.

But the message of that analogy was that if she was the dependent
pilot fish, then it followed that Fitzgerald had been cast in the role
of the shark.

It is one of the most remarkable — and unremarked — features of
Zelda's stay at the Phipps Clinic that within a month of her admission
she had completed work on a novel, begun barely three months
earlier, that was considered publishable by a very demanding author-
husband and a canny editor of one of the country's major publishing
firms. To Fitzgerald, totally unaware of the startling progress Zelda
had made on her book, it came as a shock. The preliminary news of
it he had had from one of her letters from the clinic, written some
time in early March. "I am proud of my novel," she wrote, "but I
can hardly restrain myself enough to get it written. You will like it
— It is distinctly École Fitzgerald, though more ecstatic than yours
— Perhaps to much so." The announcement carried a comic aside
that must have gotten a rise from Fitzgerald. Having been unable
to avoid the usual "said" for dialogue, she had emphasized it "à la
Ernest much to my sorrow." Hemingway, she noted, was a very
determined writer, "but I shall also die with my boots on." Shortly
afterward, Fitzgerald had the real shock. The writing had gone so
well that she mailed a copy to Max Perkins without so much as
informing her husband. She told him blithely, "It's an amusing book
which I will mail to you Monday." Her letter to Perkins was cagy;
Scott, she said, was absorbed in his own book, but as soon as Perkins
wired her that he had received her manuscript, she would mail a
copy to Scott.
    Fitzgerald, as soon as he received his copy, was in a rage. He
fired off a letter to Dr. Mildred Squires, the psychiatrist with whom
Zelda was working in treatment. It was not only, he said, that Zelda
was familiar with his novel and had imitated a whole section of it,
but that she had taken two important episodes on which his book
would turn and reduced them to anecdotes. Zelda's own material —
her childhood experiences, her affair with Jozan, her observations
about Americans in Paris, the "fine passages" about the death of her
father — Fitzgerald would criticize only in an impersonal and profes-

sional manner. But Zelda had also lifted the name of the hero of his first novel, Amory Blaine. "Do you think," he asked Dr. Squires, "that his turning up in a novel signed by my wife as a somewhat anemic portrait painter with a few ideas lifted from Clive Bell Leger ect could pass unnoticed?" It put him in an absurd position and Zelda in a ridiculous one. If Zelda had chosen to examine their life together in some inimical fashion, he could do nothing but answer in kind or remain silent. "But this mixture of fact and fiction," he wrote Dr. Squires, "is simply calculated to ruin us both or what is left of us and I can't let it stand." Zelda's use of the name of his character would put "intimate facts in the hands of the friends and enemies we have accumulated *en route* — My God, my books made her a legend and her single intention in this somewhat thin portrait is to make me a non-entity." In his outrage, Fitzgerald was openly concerned about the image of himself and of their marriage that Zelda was conveying to the public at large. He seems to have forgotten that he, too, in borrowing from Zelda's diaries and letters, had put Zelda's life and character up for public scrutiny. And he seems to have overlooked the point that the merger of fact with fiction was a technique he had used often enough, most recently in "Crazy Sunday." But considering Zelda's furtiveness about the whole affair, Fitzgerald was absolutely correct. She knew in advance that he would resent it. "That's why she sent the book directly to New York," Fitzgerald wrote Dr. Squires. For each of them, fiction was a form of retribution.

What irked Fitzgerald at the outset of Zelda's treatment at Phipps was that he sensed that Dr. Meyer did not take him seriously as a writer, did not recognize him as the professional who supported the ménage. The doctor had never bothered to compare their work; nor was it likely, since he was caught up in his own generation and his own "cerebral world," that he would have caught "the counter-implications or the nuances" in either case. This was the nearest Fitzgerald would ever come to hinting at the transactional nature of his and Zelda's writing, the private dialogue of exoneration and blame, image and counterimage, evasion and fact, that they resorted to in their otherwise fictional enterprises.

Zelda, having learned of his anger and hurt by way of Dr. Squires, tried to rationalize. Rather lamely, she explained that she had purposely not sent him the manuscript first, "knowing that you were working on your own and honestly feeling that I had no right to interrupt you to ask for a [serious] opinion." She was sure that Perkins would not want the book; she was in a rush to get it off her hands ("You know how I hate brooding over things once they are finished"); she wanted to have both his and Scribner's criticisms to use in her revisions.

Zelda next tried to placate him: "Scott, I love you more than anything on earth and if you were offended I am miserable." They had always shared everything, but she had come to feel she had no right to inflict all her needs on him. "*I was also afraid*," she admitted, "*we might have touched the same material.*" This was precisely the cause of Fitzgerald's anger.

In a second letter, Zelda was not quite so submissive. She did agree to delete an episode about General Pershing which Fitzgerald had accused her of stealing. (In *Tender Is the Night,* the character Abe North pretends to be General Pershing in the lobby of the Paris Ritz.) It occupied only one line, she said, and would not be missed. Because the early draft of Zelda's novel is lost, along with Fitzgerald's letters demanding revisions, there is no way of knowing how closely she had followed Fitzgerald's book. In *Tender Is the Night,* the Pershing incident occupies only a few lines — and would not have been missed, either. Zelda, however, stood firm on other questions. She wanted it understood, she said, that her revisions would be made on an esthetic basis: "*that the other material which I will elect is nevertheless legitimate stuff which has cost me a pretty emotional penny.*" But her letter was also a plea that he understand her needs: she had no friends — there were only the people who sought Fitzgerald's stimulus and fame, ate her dinners, and invited "the Fitzgeralds."

In his anger, Fitzgerald fired off a barrage of telegrams to Perkins. On March 16 he told Perkins not to judge or even consider Zelda's novel until he had gotten a revised version. A little more than a week later, he informed the editor that Zelda's novel could safely be placed on Scribner's spring list, but "CERTAIN SMALL BUT NONETHELESS NECESSARY CHANGES" had to be made. He advised Perkins to send the manuscript back to Zelda on the pretext that he hadn't read it yet. He told Perkins that he thought it was "A FINE NOVEL." Three days later, he wired Perkins to read the novel if he hadn't sent it back, but told him that the name of the hero and the title would have to be changed. (Zelda eventually chose a new title from a Victor record catalogue, *Save Me the Waltz.*)

The revisions, he thought, would take only two weeks, but the whole middle section of the book would have to be radically rewritten.

At the end of March, Fitzgerald went to Baltimore and worked with Zelda on the revisions. He kept Perkins informed of their progress. "Zelda's novel is now good, improved in every way," he wrote late in April. "It is new. She has largely eliminated the speak-easy-nights-and-our-trip-to-Paris atmosphere" — a trenchant comment on one of Zelda's failings as a writer. In fact, the novel might be even better than he had thought. But he cautioned Perkins that if he liked the book, he should not wire Zelda to that effect. He was afraid that too much praise would start up the obsessional behavior she had displayed toward her dance lessons. But it would also be best not to treat her as an invalid and try to cheer her up. "I'm not certain enough of Zelda's present stability of character to expose her to any superlatives. If she has a success coming she must associate it with work done in a workmanlike manner for its own sake. . . . She must not try to follow the pattern of my trail which is of course blazed distinctly on her mind."

Save Me the Waltz is not so much an invented fiction as a novel plotted from the life. David Knight, Zelda's renamed hero, is patterned after Fitzgerald and his fictional hero Amory Blaine, though cast in the not too convincing role of an artist. Alabama Knight's history recapitulates Zelda's family relationships, her ambivalence toward her father, her marriage to Fitzgerald, her affair with Jozan, and her obsession with dance. The comic relief of the story, and one of Zelda's best touches, is the characterization of the English nanny and her meddling ways of dealing with the two adults in the family rather than with her charge, who is named Bonnie in the novel.

A kind of decalcomania, however, covers parts of the book, as if Zelda were wreathing certain episodes with floral motifs — as she had done with the Annecy pages of her scrapbook. The descriptions are startling and varied. There are the spring blooms of Alabama's courtship of David: "Spring came and shattered its opalescent orioles in wreaths of daffodils. Kiss-me-at-the-gate clung to its angular branches and the old yards were covered with a child's version of flowers: snowdrops and primula veris, pussywillow and calendula. David and Alabama kicked over the oak leaves from the stumpy roots in the woods and picked white violets." There are horrible couturier versions of the natural: "nasturtiums of leather and rubber and wax gardenias and ragged robbins out of threads and wires. They manufactured hardy perennials to grow on the meagre soil of shoulder straps and bouquets with long stems for piercing the loamy shadows under the belt." There are the ambiguous flowers that Alabama, in her obsession with dance, brought to the studio each day for Madame, her dance teacher: "deep-red roses like a Villon poem," "malignant parrot tulips," "threatening sprays of gladioli," "gardenias like white kid gloves."

It is a novel of showy brilliance, full of overwritten metaphors that the editors failed to prune and of glaring errors—"orioles" for "aureoles," for instance—that they overlooked. But it was also a book about the hard lessons Zelda said had cost her a pretty emotional penny. For Alabama the lessons are drawn from her two involvements: the conspiratorial relationship with her husband ("They had evolved a tacit arrangement about waiting on each other's emotions, almost mathematical like the trick combination of a safe") and the experimental love affair or, more accurately, the flirtation with the aviator Jacques Chèvre-Feuille. In the novel it never becomes sexual, just as, fictionally, Fitzgerald's affair with Lois Moran was depicted as the flirtation of an older man with a younger girl. Alabama's response when Jacques leaves her with nothing but a photograph and a letter in a foreign language that she cannot read is poignant: "There wasn't a way to hold on to the summer, no French phrase to preserve its rising broken harmonies, no hopes to be salvaged from a cheap French photograph." The stiff resolution was perhaps more fictional than factual, a hope rather than the actuality in Zelda's life: "You took what you wanted from life, if you could get it, and you did without the rest." But the truth was that neither she nor Fitzgerald had been successful at playing the role of the marauder in life, nor was either willing to do "without the rest" —the life of summer hotels, vivid parties, New York nights. There was some truth in Zelda's claim in one of her apologetic-assertive letters to Fitzgerald: "the story of myself versus myself. That is the book I really want to write."

From the beginning, there was never any question as to whether her book was publishable, and every evidence indicates that both Fitzgerald and Perkins knew it was. And although Perkins had agreed not to write Zelda about it at first, he admitted that in not writing her, "I have not been showing anything like the interest we feel in her novel." He plainly did not want to discourage her from sending the manuscript back to Scribner's. The unanswered—and perhaps, unanswerable—question is how mad Zelda was when she was admitted to Phipps Clinic. The implication is that she could hardly have been in any deep psychotic state; otherwise she could hardly have achieved what she did. The further implication is that her hospitalization had provided her with a safe retreat, a sanctuary in which to complete her book within a month's time. That possibility seems reasonable when one learns that on entering the hospital, Zelda, in response to one of the doctor's queries about the reasons for her breakdown, answered that with her husband away in Hollywood, she had found it impossible to function: "I was left alone with my daughter and it was just too much." Instinctively, Fitzgerald too may have sensed that Zelda's retreat from the problems of reality had been a bit opportune; at least that would explain his anger at having to cope with the burdens of a household and a child while Zelda had the luxury of painting and writing at his expense.

It is one of the ironies of Zelda's quarrels with Fitzgerald over *Save Me the Waltz* that when she chose a new name for her hero, she picked David Knight. Probably she had taken the first name from Carl Van Vechten's recently published novel, *Parties,* in which the Fitzgeralds appeared as David and Rilda Westlake. More probably, the hero's last name was a form of revenge, for she took the name of Fitzgerald's nemesis, Dick Knight. That name came up in her discussions with the doctors at the Phipps Clinic during March, and she acknowledged Fitzgerald's jealousy. An added bit of confirmation of Fitzgerald's resentment of Knight—and his possibly tangential relationship to *Save Me the Waltz*—crops up in a testy letter that Fitzgerald wrote to the New York lawyer on the subject of Zelda's book and of Knight's encouragement of Zelda's ambitions. It is a letter of controlled anger—and quintessential proof of Fitzgerald's jealousy where Zelda was concerned. But it is, as well, a remarkable summing-up, on Fitzgerald's part, of his realization of what their previous life had cost the two of them. "That was swell praise you gave Zelda," Fitzgerald wrote Knight after a recent and probably unpleasant meeting, "and needless to say delighted her and set her up enormously. She revised the book so much that she lost contact with it and yours is the first word that gives it public existence." Fitzgerald then apologized: "I'm sorry I used the word fairy and that

you found it offensive. I have never in my wildest imaginings supposed you were a fairy. . . . It is a lousy word to anyone not a
member of the species." He excused himself on the grounds that he
had been half-asleep when Knight arrived and then was "subsequently a little tight."

But he rather frankly admitted that he had some intention of
wounding his visitor:

> You annoyed me — specifically by insisting on a world which we
> will willingly let die, in which Zelda can't live, which damn near
> ruined us both, which neither you nor any of our more gifted friends
> are yet sure of surviving; you insisted on its value, as if you were
> in some way holding a battlefront, and challenged us to join you.
> If you could have seen Zelda, as the most typical end-product of
> that battle, during any day from the spring of '31 to the spring of
> '32 you would have felt about as much enthusiasm for the battle as
> a doctor at the end of a day in a dressing station behind a blood
> battle.

Fitzgerald next acknowledged that most of his antipathy toward
Knight was the result of Knight's liking for Zelda, although "the
sincerity of your feeling toward her shouldn't offend anybody except
the most stupid and churlish of husbands." Zelda, he wrote, now
had to live on a regimen of "Teutonic morality." "When you city
fellows come down you can't put ideas in the heads of our farm girls,
without expecting resistance."

If Fitzgerald's grasp of their situation was real, his sense of the
chronology of his experiences was somewhat cloudy. The "any day
from the spring of '31 to the spring of '32" that encompassed the
period of Zelda's worst ordeal also included the nine months that
preceded her second breakdown and that, in a letter to Zelda's psychiatrist Dr. Meyer, Fitzgerald claimed as "the happiest of my life
and I think, save for the agonies of her father's death, the happiest
of hers." His truths were provisional truths, adopted for the moment
and the audience.

In May, when it was clear that Zelda would be in treatment
for a lengthy period, Fitzgerald rented an old Victorian country
house, La Paix, in Towson, Maryland, outside Baltimore. He struck
up a friendship with his landlady, Mrs. Margaret Turnbull, nine
years older than he, a minister's daughter, and a member of the
Maryland gentry, to whom he regularly lent copies of Proust,

D. H. Lawrence, and Rilke from his library. He was apologetic about Hemingway's *The Sun Also Rises,* acknowledging that there was "a streak of vulgarity in it," but he knew that Hemingway used it as a protest against censorship. His discussions with Margaret Turnbull about marriage and child-rearing, literature and politics, frequently resulted in morning-after letters that picked up the argument anew, with apologies for his being dogmatic the night before: "Of course, I don't believe in the double standard—I believe it's disappearing anyhow—I only meant that it was possible for a man to be far from a saint and yet be wildly jealous of his wife, as I am." Or, on a different occasion, "I simply meant that for me the test of human values is conformity to the strictest and most unflinching rationality, while in your case it is based on standards of conduct." Fitzgerald developed a warm interest in the three Turnbull children, the two daughters, Frances and Eleanor (the latter became Scottie's special friend), and eleven-year-old Andrew, whom he took under his wing, encouraged to play football, and enchanted with stories about his alma mater, Princeton. It was Andrew who eventually became Fitzgerald's biographer. Although Fitzgerald seems not to have had a very cordial relationship with Margaret's husband, Bayard Turnbull, a Baltimore architect, he did persuade Turnbull to fix up a grass tennis court that proved useful in keeping up a program of physical exercise for himself and for Zelda when she was released from Phipps.

Fitzgerald was still ambivalent about the subject of Zelda's novel. When he sent the revised manuscript to Perkins in May, he commented, "It is a good novel now, perhaps a very good novel— I am too close to it to tell." Then, rather oddly, he asked Perkins specifically not to mention it to Hemingway at all. Hemingway, he said, had once told him that he would never publish a book in the same year that one of Fitzgerald's books was scheduled to come out. After twenty years in the profession, Perkins must have noticed "the streaks of smallness in very large personalities." Not that there could be any conflict between Zelda's book and anything of Hemingway's, "but there has always been a subtle struggle between Ernest & Zelda." That spring, writing to H. L. Mencken, Fitzgerald mentioned Zelda's "rest cure" at Hopkins, adding that she was "just finishing a fine novel." And in a letter to Dr. Forel, he noted the autobiographical tenor of the book, asserting it was "excellent," but expressing his worries that the writing of it may have "raked up a lot of the past." The Phipps doctors, Fitzgerald noted, described Zelda as tense and driven by nervous energy while she was writing it.

At La Paix, Fitzgerald had tried to resume his own career. He hired a secretary, Mrs. Isabel Owens, who brought some stability to the household. But during that spring he managed to write only three stories—"Family in the Wind," "The Rubber Check," and "What a Handsome Pair!" The last dealt with an embattled marriage between a competitive husband and wife. Stuart Oldhorne is a former Yale athlete, a polo player and golfer. His wife, Helen, has outstripped him as an amateur golfer and is now winning the prizes in tournaments. The story, in other words, is a commentary on Zelda and her novel. Oldhorne hopes that "instead of feeding her egotism, the actual achievement would make things easier between them"— clearly the sentiments Fitzgerald was harboring. But the more accurate testimony to his feelings was this summary one: "He hated the conflict that had grown out of their wanting the same excellences, the same prizes from life."

In his letter to Forel, Fitzgerald had outlined his plan for easing Zelda back into domestic life. Now they followed it. At first, she spent mornings at La Paix, returning to the clinic in the afternoon; then in June she was released from Phipps, under her husband's care, but with continued supervision by Dr. Meyer. At regular intervals throughout the summer, both Fitzgerald and Zelda returned to the clinic for conferences.

In a letter to John Peale Bishop, Zelda described the twenty-eight-acre Turnbull estate in somewhat sardonic terms as a "nice Mozartian hollow disciplined to elegance by imported shrubbery." Scott, she said, liked it better than France, and she liked it fine. Scott was reading Marx; she was reading the cosmological philosophers. "The brightest moments of our day are when we get them mixed up." Fitzgerald, who had hired an aging tennis pro, was taking lessons. He played frequently with Scottie and young Turnbull. "I'll perforate you, Andrew!" was his usual threat as he crouched to receive a serve. Zelda, too, was taking lessons, but Fitzgerald waited each day for the moment when she would throw the racquet at Mr. Crosley, the tennis pro. Mostly Zelda was uncommunicative, spending hours in her room, playing and replaying "Valencia" on the gramophone. Occasionally, she swam in the quarry that the

Turnbull children used. Andrew remembered her as she sat on the raft, smoking, basking in the sun, her short, tawny hair water-slicked. Though there were occasional holiday visits and afternoon teas with the two families, Mrs. Turnbull never quite warmed to Zelda, who was aloof in return. Margaret Turnbull thought of her as "a broken clock."

It was true, as Zelda had written Bishop, that Fitzgerald was reading Marx, probably *The Communist Manifesto*. On a trip to New York, he had phoned Dos Passos to tell him that he was in touch with the communists in Baltimore. Hemingway, who learned of the call, commented, "Just too late." He told Dos Passos sardonically that Fitzgerald would "now go back to Baltimore and tell the communists he went to N.Y. and got in touch with Dos Passos." In Baltimore, Fitzgerald had taken up with a young Marxist whom he invited out to La Paix to discuss politics and serve as a sparring partner. The two would square off on the front lawn, wearing big squashy gloves. "The Community Communist," Zelda informed Max Perkins, "comes and tells us about a kind of Luna Park Eutopia." She, however, was reading Tolstoy's *War and Peace* and thought it "magnificent." Her sickness had not ruined her piercing sense of humor nor her wonderment at some of Fitzgerald's enthusiasms. She added: "I have taken, somewhat eccentricly at my age, to horse-back riding which I do as non-committally as possible so as not to annoy the horse. Also very apologeticly since we've had so much of communism lately that I'm not sure it's not the horse who should be riding me."

Perhaps it was only coincidence—Zelda had signed a contract with Scribner's in June and was reading galley proofs of *Save Me the Waltz* during that summer—that in August Fitzgerald noted in his ledger that he had begun work on his own book: "The novel now plotted & planned, never more to be permanently interrupted." He had worked out a lengthy outline, called his General Plan, for the book, which he now referred to as *The Drunkard's Holiday*. He had dropped the matricide theme, and though he still retained elements of the Kelly story he had made into "One Trip Abroad," he struck off in a new direction. The most important element of the plotting was the theme of the psychiatrist who marries one of his wealthy patients. He manages to cure the heroine by pretending to an emotional stability that is not real. (He is a secret drinker.) At this early stage, Fitzgerald also gave the novel a political slant. The psychiatrist pretends to believe in the social order, but he is, in fact, "a communist-liberal-idealist, a moralist in revolt."

The ages and backgrounds of his hero and heroine were elaborately worked out—then, in an addendum, he gave their names as Dick and Nicole and their parentage in terms of the real-life models he planned to draw from. "For his external qualities," Fitzgerald noted of Dick Diver, "use anything of Gerald, Ernest, Ben Finney, Archie Mcliesh, Charley McArthur or myself. He looks, though, like me." The hero's vices, however, are derived largely from Fitzgerald: "the weakness such as the social-climbing, the drinking, the desparate clinging to one woman, finally the neurosis." Nicole's character is a good deal more focused: "Portrait of Zelda— that is, a part of Zelda." Zelda's breakdown seems to have been the motivating force behind the novel. It may also have rescued the narrative from Fitzgerald's enchantment with the Murphys, his social ideals. Fitzgerald's delineation of the hero—and the early political emphasis of his story—is instructive:

> Show a man who is a natural idealist, a spoiled priest, giving in for various causes to the ideas of the haute Burgeoise, and in his rise to the top of the social world losing his idealism, his talent and turning to drink and dissipation. Background one in which the liesure class is at their truly most brilliant & glamorous such as Murphys.

There is, here, the bare suggestion that his idealizations of other enviable selves hid more than a trace of resentment. The hero may be an enemy.

Time was not kind to either writer. Zelda's novel, published in October, received damaging reviews, and the sales were negligible. The *New York Herald Tribune* reviewer saw it as the "last will and testament" of a departed era and attributed the exaggerations of the literary style to the fact that it was a first novel. *The New York Times* found the book "a curious muddle of good psychology and atrocious style." Dorothea Brandes, in *The Bookman,* scolded the publisher for not having curbed the "ludicrous lushness" of the language, but even more for not having seen fit to give the book "the elementary services of a literate proofreader," thereby making the book a "laughing-stock." Zelda wrote Maxwell Perkins that she was sorry she had asked to see the reviews. Since the proofreading was his responsibility, Perkins in his consoling letter may not have been so consoling: "Many reviewers did object to the figures of speech, and I think their objection to them prevented them from penetrating to the real heart of the book. You write so very well [when you write] simply that you do not need the similes much."

Nor did Fitzgerald begin work on his novel so readily. He was in a very agitated and quarrelsome mood. On a three-day trip to New York, he went on a "terrible bat" and fought with both Edmund Wilson and Hemingway. He wired Wilson his apologies and invited him down to La Paix. Later, he wrote him a mollifying letter:

> We had a most unfortunate meeting. I came to New York to get drunk and swinish and I shouldn't have looked up you and Ernest in such a humor of impotent desperation. I assume full responsibility for all unpleasantness. . . . Making trouble between friends is the last thing I had ever thought myself capable of. Anyhow, plenty of egotism for the moment.

But then, he proceeded to needle Wilson about politics. He reported that Alec McKaig had visited him at the Plaza, where he had been laid out, recuperating from his hangover and an attack of pleurisy.

> He [McKaig] told me to my amazement that you had explained the fundamentals of Leninism, even Marxism, the night before, and Dos tells me that it was only recently made plain thru the same agency to *The New Republic*. I little thought when I left politics to you and your gang in 1920 you would devote time to cutting up [Woodrow] Wilson's shroud into blinders! Back to Mallarmé.

It was, no doubt, an impolitic approach to Wilson's politics, which had veered more sharply to the left than even Dos Passos'. Wilson was becoming more and more certain that capitalism was past reformation. He may also have been in a state of shock and grief over the death of his wife, Margaret, a few months before. Fitzgerald, however, repeated his invitation to Wilson to visit La Paix when he went to Washington to cover the inauguration of Franklin Roosevelt. But he pleaded with his friend, "Please not a word to Zelda about anything I may have done or said in New York. She can stand literally nothing of that nature."

Fitzgerald also wrote to Perkins about the New York binge, apologizing for not having called on him. He was going on the water wagon, he said, but asked: "Don't tell Ernest because he has long convinced himself that I am an incurable alcoholic. . . . I am *his* alcoholic, just like Ring is mine and do not want to disillusion him, tho even Post stories must be done in a state of sobriety." He reported that Bunny Wilson was in a gloomy frame of mind. "A decision to adopt Communism definitely, no matter how good for the soul, must of necessity be a saddening process for anyone who has ever tasted the intellectual pleasures of the world we live in." Wilson's dilemma, then, was the crux of the political and moral conflict that Fitzgerald planned to introduce into his own novel.

Wilson did, in fact, stop off at La Paix on his way back from the Roosevelt inauguration. He was mildly enthralled by the house, with its "balconies and bulges," its varnished-oak interiors, carved bedsteads, wainscoting, jigsaw fretwork, the Victorian clock with its comforting motto "Our Times Are in His Hand." Zelda, he thought, looked "cute" in her blue sweater and light tan riding breeches, but she had developed a bad habit of biting the side of her mouth, and she mumbled at times. Fitzgerald, pretending to be on the wagon, gave him one cocktail for lunch. At dinner, Fitzgerald had a little wine — one glass to Wilson's two. But he disappeared into the kitchen often enough to replenish his glass. He would bring back a little thimbleful of wine for Zelda (supposedly on her "Teutonic" regimen). "A little treat, honey, in honor of Bunny," he would say. At lunch on the following day, when Wilson decided not to have anything to drink, Fitzgerald was a bit put out: "It seems so puritanical somehow, breaking off entirely like that!" Once more, he began snitching drinks for himself — but would bring out another little thimbleful for Zelda. When he took Wilson to the train station, he asserted, rather coolly, that he was having a hard time with Zelda, because she had begun to steal drinks on the sly.

Throughout the spring, Fitzgerald was engaged in a minor skirmish with Zelda's doctors at Phipps — Dr. Meyer and Dr. Squires and a young psychiatrist, Dr. Thomas Rennie. There were the regular joint sessions at the clinic, but Fitzgerald had taken to writing long, pleading letters to Dr. Meyer. He was plainly suspicious — and concerned — about what Zelda may have said about him during the course of her treatment. He wrote that Zelda had even convinced Dr. Forel that he was "*a notorious Parisien homo-sexual.*" But what was uppermost in his mind was the need to establish his authority over Zelda, who needed a strong hand. Week by week, Zelda was regressing to the point where they were now "back to the agonizing cat and dog fight of four or five years ago." Dr. Meyer had given him no real authority in dealing with Zelda when she was *"persistently refractory."* Zelda was writing and painting, but "under a greenhouse which is my money and my name and my love." She tended to cross over the line and spend too much time at both occupations, and he incurred her ill will when he tried to exercise some control over her hours. What he needed was some weapon for dealing with Zelda at these times — something other than brute force. Meyer had essentially foisted Zelda on him, wanting to keep her out of the hospital. But Fitzgerald wanted the authority to tell Zelda, when necessary, to pack her bag and to send her to the clinic "to spend a week under people who can take care of her." It disturbed him that his outbreaks of temper and lack of self-control tended to make the doctors side with Zelda. But he warned, half-jokingly, "I will probably be carried off eventually by four strong guards shrieking manicly that after all I was right and she was wrong, while Zelda is followed home by an adoring crowd in an automobile banked with flowers, and offered a vaudeville contract." He and Zelda, it is clear, were involved in a contest of proving their credibility to the doctors. What also disturbed him was that Meyer tended to discount his judgments on Zelda's case because he drank heavily. He countered by stating, "During the last six days I have drunk *altogether* slightly less than a quart and a half of weak gin, at wide intervals."

The real gist of Fitzgerald's dissatisfaction with Meyer's handling of Zelda's treatment was the poor image of him that Meyer had formed. For the benefit of one of Zelda's later psychiatrists, Fitzgerald aired his grievances, claiming that Meyer "could never seem to appreciate that my writing was more important than hers by a large margin because of the years of preparation for it, and the professional experience, and because my writing kept the mare going, while Zelda's belongs to the luxury trade." It was, again, a question of image and self-image, the need for some external confirmation. Meyer had given him a certain ignominious status in relation to Zelda, because he had "never really *believed* that I worked very hard, had a serious reputation or made money."

He was a man going downhill, whose authority as a husband and as a professional was being challenged by a woman trying to climb out of madness by asserting her right to her own life, to her independence. Fitzgerald was, in effect, living the novel he was writing.

⊟ ▬◢ ⊟

Their confrontation came to a head in one of the clinical conversations that Fitzgerald thought were "barren" and unfair to him. This one was conducted at La Paix between himself and Zelda, with Dr. Rennie serving as a moderator. It was recorded by a stenographer.

Fitzgerald claimed that he was a different sort of person from Zelda, that his equipment for being a writer, for being an artist, was different from hers. . . . He knew she was a drunkard the first time he met her. . . . She was spoiled. She was made the pet of the family and was told she had no obligations. Like all women, she ceased being the prettiest person in the world, ceased to be so at twenty-five, though she still was, to him, the most sexually attractive woman in the world. . . . Writing is a struggle; it was a struggle for him. He was aware that nobody cared about anything anymore. But it was a perfectly lonely struggle that he was making against other finely gifted and talented writers. She was a third-rate writer and a third-rate ballet dancer. . . . He was a professional writer with a huge following. He was the highest paid short story writer in the world.

She said that he was making a rather violent attack on a third-rate talent. . . . Why in the hell was he so jealous? If she thought that about anybody, she wouldn't care what they wrote.

He said that she was poaching on his material at all times. It was as if a good artist came into a room and found that some mischievous little boy had drawn on his canvas.

Well, she said, what did he want her to do?

He said he wanted her to do what he told her to do. That was what he wanted her to do. The doctors and he had agreed that it was extremely inadvisable for her to write any novels that dealt with her insanity or discussed insanity. But one day he had given her a clipping about Nijinsky, and immediately she had decided to write a novel about insanity. She had been sneakingly writing it for several months. It was for her sake that he didn't want her to write a book on the subject and because she knew there was certain psychiatric stuff in his books. She picked up the crumbs that he dropped at the dinner table and stuck them into books. She wanted to write a novel against everybody's advice. . . . Everything that they had done was his — if they made a trip, it was his material. He was the professional novelist and he was supporting her. It was all his material. None of it was her material. . . .

He said that these were bad times, things were hard and tough. . . . He had all the worries that everyone else had — of making a living — and he found that he had an enemy in the family, treachery behind his back, or what he considered treachery.

She said that he thought it was personally all right for him to feel that way, for him to accuse her of everything in the world — with having ruined his life, not once, but over and over again.

And when, he asked, did that first happen?

She said that it was last fall. That he had sat down and cried and cried. That he had been drunk and said that she had ruined his life and that he did not love her, that he was sick of her and wished he could get away. He said it again when he came back from New York, drunk again — and that, she said, was the kind of life she was expected to live with him, making whatever adjustments she could.

What, he asked, did she think had caused those two episodes?

She said it was impossible to live with him. She would rather be in an insane asylum — where he would like to put her.

What, he repeated, did she think caused those episodes?

She said that it was his drinking. That was what she thought was the cause. She was perfectly willing to put aside the novel, but she would not have any agreement or arrangements, because she would not submit to his neurasthenic condition and be subjected to these tortures all the time. She could not live in that kind of a world and she would rather live in any insane asylum. That was her last word on the subject.

He said that their sexual relations had been very pleasant until he got the idea that she was ditching him. They were all very nice till then, weren't they? he asked her.

Well, she said, she was glad he considered them satisfactory.

He said he wanted her to stop writing fiction. . . . Whether she wrote or not did not seem to be of any great importance.

She said that nothing she did seemed to be of any great importance.

Then why, he asked, didn't she drop it?

Because, she said, she didn't want to live with him. Because she wanted to live some place where she could be her own self.

Would she like to go to law about it? he demanded.

She said, Yes, she would. . . . The only thing was to get a divorce, because there was nothing but ill will on his part — and suspicion.

He said that he was perfectly determined to take three or four drinks a day. . . . If he should stop drinking, her family would always think that he was acknowledging that he was responsible for her insanity — and so would she. And it was not so.

She said that the problem was that he had not written his book and that if he would ever get it written, then he wouldn't feel so miserable and suspicious and mean toward everybody else.

He said that it had to be unconditional surrender on her part. That was the only promise he could accept. Otherwise he would rather go to law, because he didn't trust her. . . . The unconditional surrender was that she would have to give up the idea of writing anything. . . . She was only to write when, under competent medical assistance, he said that she could write. That might sound awfully egotistical, but that was the only way he could ever organize his life again.

She said that she wanted to write and she was going to write. She was going to be a writer — but she would not do it at his expense if she could possibly avoid it. She would agree not to do anything he did not want — a complete negation of self — until his book was out of the way, because the thing was driving her crazy as it was. . . .

He told the doctor that she always claimed that she was working to get away from him. That was the thing that stuck with him.

She told the doctor that it wasn't true. . . . The truth of the matter was that she always felt some necessity for the two of them to be on a more equal footing than they were. . . . She simply could not be completely dependent on him, when he did not care anything about her and reproached her all the time. . . . When he said something that was not so, then she wanted to do something so good that she could say, That is a goddamned lie — and have something to back it up. . . .

Now, he said, we have found rock bottom.

What is our marriage anyway? she asked. It had been nothing but a long battle ever since she could remember.

He said he didn't know about that. He said, We were about the most envied couple in America around 1921.

She said, I guess so — we were awfully good showmen.

He said, We were awfully happy.

III

Throughout the fall of 1933, Fitzgerald was working on his novel under a self-imposed deadline and on borrowed money (advances from Ober, a loan from Scribner's at 5 percent against the possible screen rights to the book, and small loans from his mother). He promised delivery of the manuscript to Perkins by November 1, and for once was a few days in advance of his promised date. It could hardly have been a happy period in his life nor an easy working schedule to maintain. There had been a fire at La Paix in August, which Zelda caused when she tried to burn papers in an unused fireplace on the second floor. There was considerable smoke, and Fitzgerald's collection of war books had been damaged. The Baltimore papers had photographed the couple on the lawn, surrounded by their salvaged possessions. Fitzgerald asked the Turnbulls to delay the repairs on the house so that he would not be disturbed until he completed his novel. For the next two months, he worked on, surrounded by water-stained walls and woodwork. In November, with the novel finished and the prospects of a glum winter ahead, he and Zelda moved to a townhouse in Baltimore, at 1307 Park Avenue.

During that period, Fitzgerald was still drinking heavily, and for four days in early September he had himself admitted to the Johns Hopkins University Hospital for treatment. It was one of his later regrets that he hadn't finished the book in sobriety. "A short story," he maintained, "can be written on a bottle, but for a novel you need the mental speed that enables you to keep the whole pattern in your head and ruthlessly sacrifice the sideshows. . . . I would give anything if I hadn't had to write Part III of *Tender Is the Night* entirely on stimulant."

Late in September, Ring Lardner died of a heart attack, at the age of forty-eight. His health had been failing rapidly over the past years as a result of heavy drinking and bouts of tuberculosis. In spite of his deadline, Fitzgerald took time out to pay homage to Lardner in an obituary essay for *The New Republic*. Fitzgerald pictured Lardner in the hospital setting in which he had last seen him, two years before: "It was terribly sad to see that six feet three inches of kindness stretched out ineffectual in the hospital room. His fingers trembled with a match, the tight skin on his handsome skull was marked as a mask of misery and nervous pain." It was a very different image from that of the man he had known in Great Neck, the boon companion of drinking sprees and all-night conversations, the Lardner whose reputation was riding high and whose interests were broad: "people, sports, bridge, music, the stage, the newspapers, the magazines, the books." Looking back on those years, Fitzgerald was surprised to recognize that "the impenetrable despair" that had dogged Lardner for the remainder of his life had begun even there.

But Fitzgerald's praise began to take a curious turn toward condemnation that may have been tinged with some unconscious self-condemnation of his own. "Whatever Ring's achievement was," Fitzgerald wrote, "it fell short of the achievement he was capable of, and this because of a cynical attitude toward his work." Those were charges Fitzgerald made easily enough about his strictly commercial stories when he referred to himself as an old whore in the trade.

When he sent the article to Edmund Wilson, Fitzgerald apologized for the final paragraph, which he said had given him "private shame. The tears obscured me eyes and time was pressing!" The paragraph had opened with "A great and good American is dead," a clause Wilson objected to on the grounds that it "didn't seem to meet the case exactly." When Fitzgerald pressed him to say why Lardner wasn't a great and good American and asked who was, Wilson replied that the remark sounded too much like something from a political speech. "Besides," he added, "Lardner, though a first-rate writer, wasn't exactly great, was he? — and, though personally likable, his chief claim to distinction was a gift for Swiftian satire based on hate." Wilson took a darker view of Fitzgerald's hero: "He always seemed to me to be desperately irked by his family, his associates, and himself." Wilson was delighted to hear that Fitzgerald's book was finished. "Now is your time to creep up on Hemingway," he added.

But it was not long after Wilson's November 4 letter that he and Fitzgerald had another quarrel in New York — nearly on the anniversary of their spat the year before. It came about, partly, because of Fitzgerald's habit of needling his friends, after which he lavished them with praise, which Wilson found equally annoying. Recently, however, he had started indulging in another, more irritating practice, that of pointing out highly uncomplimentary passages in his writings and saying that these were based on Wilson. The two had a falling out, but on this occasion, Wilson wrote apologetically: "I'm sorry about the other day, but you are sometimes a hard guy to get along with and I'm told I'm not wonderful in this respect either. What I object to is precisely the 'scholar and vulgarian,' 'you helped me more than I helped you' business." Wilson acknowledged that this wasn't a role Fitzgerald had foisted on him, but one he had partly created himself. "But don't you think," he asked, "at our present time of life we might dispense with this high-school (Princeton University) stuff? I've certainly laid you under contribution in the past in the concoction of my literary personae and I don't blame you or object a bit if you do the same with me. But just don't make yourself disagreeable about it after asking me to lunch, you mug."

Tender Is the Night was serialized in four installments in *Scribner's Magazine,* from January through April 1934. Fitzgerald particularly admired the Edward Shenton woodcuts used in the serial version. "I've gotten very fond of the illustrations," he wrote Perkins, suggesting that they might be used as chapter headings for the hard-cover edition, to be published in April. They might give the book "a certain distinction," he said.

The earliest and kindest responses to the novel came from friends who read the serial version or who had received advance copies of the book and knew of the personal struggle it had involved. Louis Bromfield wired Fitzgerald promptly, JUST READ SECOND INSTALMENT NOVEL WONDERFUL, and was even more gratifying about the hard-cover version. "There are certain pages," he wrote Fitzgerald, "which are unforgettable and there is a beautiful *quality* about the whole performance. It is I should think permanent." Archibald MacLeish wrote a brief note: "Great God Scott you can write. You can write better than ever. Believe it. Believe It— not me." Thomas Wolfe, who had read proofs of the final installments in the Scribner's office, sent some cautious praise: "I thought you'd be interested to know that the people in the book are even more real and living now than they were at the time I read it. It seems to me you've gone deeper in this book than in anything you ever wrote." John Peale Bishop, though he quibbled about Fitzgerald's choice of names, was full of admiration: "The first installment of the novel confirms what I have long thought, that your gifts as a novelist surpass those of any of us. It is so skilful, so subtle, so right that I have only praise for it. You get the whole romance of that period, which is now like history."

Edmund Wilson's "mild criticism" of the book had been given during the course of another of their touchy meetings in New York. But Fitzgerald claimed to have been more elated than otherwise by his remarks: "If the characters got real enough so that you disagreed with what I chose for their manifest destiny the main purpose was accomplished." Wilson had read the magazine version, and though he felt that some of the characters were "cockeyed," he thought that Fitzgerald had gotten something "real" in the marital relationship. But one of his principal complaints was that Fitzgerald did not give any real sense of Diver's professional abilities. It was unlikely that if Diver was a brilliant psychiatrist he would fade out in obscurity; more likely he would end up as a shyster alienist with a fashionable practice in New York. Years later, writing to Malcolm Cowley on the subject, he maintained, "Except for the movies, Scott never had any kind of organized professional life" — his explanation for Fitzgerald's failure to establish Diver's professional credibility. "It is, of course, a remarkable book just the same," he concluded.

Fitzgerald regretted that he had allowed the serial publication, because he made a considerable number of changes for the book publication. In editing the serial version, of course, he had cut the more sensitive sexual episodes. He wrote to Wilson, "I could wish that you, and others, had read the book version." The last half of the book, he said, now had "a *much* more polished facade," and he had cut "such irrelevancies as Morton Hoyt's nose dive." His feelings must have been confirmed when John Dos Passos wrote him, saying that he had gotten an entirely different impression from reading the book than he had from the serial version: "It's so tightly knit together that it cant be read in pieces. The layout and construction of the damn thing is enormously impressive, all building up to a final paragraph that'll certainly be quoted in all the future textbooks."

From the beginning, the critics treated *Tender Is the Night* as a flawed novel. They praised its distinctive style, its depiction of the now suspect expatriate life. But they faulted the book on its characterizations. In *The Saturday Review,* Henry Seidel Canby complained, "The central figures change, the focus of the plot shifts, the story rambles, the style drops to the commonplace." He felt that it ought to have been a more impressive achievement, that it failed in its handling of the central relationships. Any "second-rate English society novelist" might have written the story better than Fitzgerald, Canby said, "though not one of them could have touched its best chapters." J. Donald Adams, in the Sunday *New York Times* Book Review, called it a "disappointment." It had Fitzgerald's "most engaging qualities," to be sure, but it also had his weaknesses in "ineradicable" measure. The book lacked the firmer grasp of life one might have expected; it was "clever and brilliantly surfaced" but not the "work of a wise and mature novelist."

Once again, unfortunately, Max Perkins' slackness about editorial standards added to the impression of failure. The critics were not so harsh as they had been in dealing with *Save Me the Waltz,* but Canby had asked, obliquely, "Is it laziness, indifference, a lack of standards, or imperfect education that results in this constant botching of the first-rate by American novelists?" Clifton Fadiman, reviewing the book for *The New Yorker,* listed the misspellings in French and English, in the names of psychiatrists, physicians, and medical diagnoses (*schizzoid* for *schizoid,* for instance), composers, place names, and types of liqueurs, and made the most pertinent case against the sloppy proofreading and editorial supervision. "It would be picayune indeed to list these proofreader's oversights were it not that the inhabitants of Mr. Fitzgerald's world, who pride themselves on their impeccability, should never arouse in the reader's mind the slightest suspicion of their competence in fields — such as liquor, resort geography, and mental disease — that are staked out as their very own."

John Chamberlain, in one of the more sympathetic reviews, written for the daily *Times,* noted that the rumors of Fitzgerald's continued difficulties with the book had created expectations of failure. "We now know that the gossip was — just gossip," he wrote. "Mr. Fitzgerald has not forgotten his craftsmanship, his marvelous sense of what might be called social climate, his sheer writing ability." Chamberlain did, however, feel that the opening segment of the book — Rosemary's view of the little colony of Americans on the Riviera — was a "false start." But he felt Fitzgerald had more than succeeded in his handling of the marital theme, which became the focus of the book: "The story is the story of the Divers, husband and wife, how they came together and how they parted. As such, it is a skillfully done dramatic sequence."

Ironically, Chamberlain claimed that *Tender Is the Night* was not a story of "post-war degeneracy" and that, though many American playboys figured in the novel, it was not about the famous "lost generation." But the fact was that the whole theme of social relevance had been taken up wholeheartedly by American reviewers, including liberal-minded and sophisticated reviewers in the general press as well as the critics on the left. The harshest criticism that Fitzgerald received—along political and social lines—was Philip Rahv's review in the *Daily Worker*. Although he recognized that Fitzgerald no longer wrote about "expensive blondes and yachting parties, lavish surroundings and insane love-affairs from the same angle of vision as in the past," Rahv chided the author, in routine Marxist style, for not having realized "how near the collapse of his class really is." He saw the book as a "fearful indictment of the moneyed aristocracy," which the author himself hadn't quite recognized because he was so caught up in its specious glamour. Rahv, rather ingeniously, theorized that there was a perhaps unconscious connection between the psychiatrist-hero and the author: "The truth is that Nicole can be understood as a symbol of the entire crazy social system to which Fitzgerald has long been playing Dick Diver." As a parting shot, he gave the author a bit of personal advice: "Dear Mr. Fitzgerald, you can't hide from a hurricane under a beach umbrella."

Though Rahv's review must have been nettling, Fitzgerald may have been more wounded by Malcolm Cowley's review of the book in the June 6 issue of *The New Republic*. Cowley had been a guest at La Paix a year earlier, when Fitzgerald was getting down to work on his novel. It had been an awkward evening. Cowley had a brief encounter with Zelda, who was not well enough to come to dinner. But he saw her later and had a glimpse of her paintings, which he found emphatic and interesting but lacking in craftsmanship and proportion—the problems that he felt had marred *Save Me the Waltz*. During most of that evening, Fitzgerald had paced around the room with a glass in his hand, which he explained was filled with water, though he kept slipping out of the room to replenish it with gin. It was a kind of ghostly atmosphere, in the creaking, overlarge, uncarpeted house, with Fitzgerald going on and on about Zelda's past life, her popularity as a Southern belle, her talent, her beauty, her family. "Sometimes," he told Cowley, "I don't know whether Zelda and I are real or whether we are characters in one of my novels."

Fitzgerald had sent Cowley a copy of *Tender Is the Night*, suggesting that he not review it himself but put a young man on it.

But Cowley preferred to do the review, "rather than pass it along to one of the young guys who would ask why you weren't a proletarian novelist." Cowley's review, all the same, raised the political issue, though with a good deal more sympathy and perspicacity than Rahv's had. "Fitzgerald," Cowley wrote, "has always been the poet of the American upper bourgeoisie; he has been the only writer able to invest their lives with glamour." Then he touched on what he considered Fitzgerald's ambivalent loyalty to the class he wrote about: "It is as if he had a double personality. Part of him is a guest at the ball given by the people in the big house; part of him has been a little boy peeping in through the window and being thrilled by the music and the beautifully dressed women." But Cowley also noted that it was a hardheaded little boy who wanted to know how much it all cost and where the money came from. He quoted Fitzgerald as saying, "There is a streak of vulgarity in me that I try to cultivate." He also quoted Fitzgerald as saying that *Tender Is the Night* was intended to be his farewell to the members of his own generation. "I hope he changes his mind," the critic added. "He has in him at least one great novel about them, and it is a novel that I want to read." Fitzgerald, who had seen an advance copy of the review, took to referring to the critic as "Malcolm Republic, c/o *The New Cowlick.*"

For years, Fitzgerald had been asserting that he was a socialist at heart. But, then, he was distrustful of the rule of the people: "Freedom has produced the greatest tyranny under the sun." Now that he had come out of the closet, so to speak, and was, in his view, a progressive, it must have been a source of embarrassment that he was being rebuffed in liberal quarters. He began to have second thoughts about the politics of the left. In August, he wrote his cousin Ceci that he had given up politics:

> For two years I've gone half haywire trying to reconcile my double allegiance to the class I am part of, and the Great Change I believe in. . . . I have become disgusted with the party leadership and have only health enough left for my literary work, so I'm on the sidelines. . . . Their treatment of the Negro question finished me. This is confidential, of course.

Fitzgerald's remarks are somewhat ambiguous. But his defection was not unusual. At the time, the Communist Party line on the "Negro question," made in Russia, was one of separation and

self-determination in the Black Belt, proposing a kind of independent nation-within-the-nation in those Southern regions where
there were black majorities. It was a policy many American communists—black and white—found difficult to support. The leader
of the opposition, Jay Lovestone, one of the founders of the party in
the United States, had been read out of the party for his stand against
the Comintern on this and other issues. Fitzgerald had entertained
Lovestone, "the Opposition Communist," one Saturday night in
Baltimore. But he was uncomfortable in the company of either the
party faithfuls or the party renegades. About Lovestone, he wrote
Max Perkins that he hadn't "quite made up my mind what I think
of him."

But judging from Fitzgerald's published stories and his letters
and journals, it would be difficult to believe he was a real advocate
of civil rights for blacks. In his private notes, more often than not,
he referred to them as niggers.

⌾▬◁⌾

What the critics must have sensed, whatever their political biases,
was that Fitzgerald's novel had had no core to sustain it over the
eight-year period in which it was continuously revised and reshaped.
The plot lines had shifted from the early matricide theme involving
Francis Melarky, who, in a fit of rage, was going to murder his
domineering mother; the shipboard chapters of the Kelly version,
which would probably have covered the theme of middle-aged adultery between Lew Kelly and the young actress named Rosemary; and
finally the theme of marital breakdown and insanity. The strongest
element of the final version of the novel was the double helix of
Diver's corruption and decline under the influence of the Warren
family money and Nicole's recovery and independence with the breakup
of the marriage. There, the situation from life gave the narrative a
needed structure. But Fitzgerald had lost his way in the book; when
the political winds shifted—he had, after all, been working at it
from the period of boom through bust, with all the social changes
that implied—he had attempted to give it a political and social
emphasis, despite his uncertain political stance. He had evidently
sensed some dim or vague connection between his private life and
the social crisis of the moment. In his ledger, he noted it: "*The
Crash! Zelda & America.*"

But the most noticeable problem with the book was the problem of characterization, the restless fugue of shifting identities, changing moral attitudes, chance experiences, that were tried out and dropped, only to surface once more and be dropped again. Fitzgerald may have gotten his models from real life: the Murphys, Ring Lardner, Charlie MacArthur, Tommy Hitchcock, Lois Moran. But during the eight years it took to write the book, the names of the dramatis personae and whatever experiences had converged about their names (for whatever strange or unconscious associations) were transformed. Abe North became the end product of unspecified personal associations — a combination of Lardner and Charlie MacArthur. Rosemary Hoyt, as Fitzgerald admitted, was based on Lois Moran and perhaps Mary Hay, though in time he intended for her to grow coarse, rather like Lupe Velez. Sometimes the characters bore the mark of the author's fluctuating animus. Nicole's sister, Baby Warren, was made up of elements borrowed from Fitzgerald's disapproving sister-in-law Rosalind Smith, and from Sara Murphy's sister Hoytie, a woman with a sharp tongue and a bad case of anglophilia.

At various stages in the composition of the book, Fitzgerald, with a combination of fascination and disgust, investigated the more abnormal forms of sexual identity. There were lesbian scenes, prompted, perhaps, by Zelda's exploits in Paris. In the final version, without adequate psychological preparation for the reader, he attributed the practice to Mary North, who became sexually involved with a notorious English lesbian after the death of her husband. One homosexual scene — a lengthy set-piece that took place in a gay bar in the Hotel of Three Worlds, in Lausanne, a brilliant and scathing catalogue of different types of fairies — had originally been written for the Melarky version. Fitzgerald had considered using it in the later, Dick Diver version, then dropped it — for the good reason, perhaps, that it went on too long and would have weighted the book on the topic of homosexuality. But significantly, the Lausanne episode ended with a refrain that echoed the graveside address he had used in the story "On Your Own" and that he used once more in Tender Is the Night when Dick attends his father's burial in Virginia. In the deleted Lausanne episode, however, it was an odd recitative addressed to the homosexuals: "Goodby, you unfortunates. Goodby, Hotel of Three Worlds."

The flaw in Tender Is the Night, one suspects, was Fitzgerald's search for a suitable identity among the various scrapped idols of his life, the discarded ideals, the roles that had been played and that, in the end, had proven unsatisfactory. He had tried to get through his life without confronting his drunkenness, the breakdown of his marriage, his guilt about Zelda's insanity, his anger at the burdens it had brought him. He had tried to work out the psychoanalytical background — but, as he acknowledged in his General Plan, it was necessary to cover up his lack of expertise by faking it, "being careful not to reveal basic ignorance of psychiatric and medical training yet not being glib. Only suggest from the most remote facts." Quite rightly, he had not wanted to end "with a novelized Kraft-Ebing." But he elected to play the role of a psychiatrist — and husband — the role he had wanted to play with Zelda's doctors. It was, in life and in the book, a role he wanted to assume.

The problem with *Tender Is the Night* is that Fitzgerald tried to solve in literary terms the problems he could not resolve in private life.

Fitzgerald had to wait for word from Hemingway; he did not hear from him during the serialization in *Scribner's Magazine*. Finally, on May 10, a month after the publication of *Tender Is the Night,* Fitzgerald wrote, asking: "Did you like the book? For God's sake drop me a line and tell me one way or another. You can't hurt my feelings. I just want to get a few intelligent slants at it to get some of the reviewers' jargon out of my head."

What he got from Hemingway was a long psychological critique of Fitzgerald's relation to his work, his professional attitudes, his personal involvement with the Murphys (to whom Fitzgerald had dedicated the book: "To Gerald and Sara, Many Fêtes"), and of his marriage to Zelda. Hemingway began by saying he both liked *Tender Is the Night* and didn't like it. He admired the marvelous description of Sara and Gerald with which Fitzgerald had started out. "Then," he commented, "you started fooling with them, making them come from things they didn't come from, changing them into other people and you can't do that, Scott. . . . Goddamn it you took liberties with peoples' pasts and futures that produced not people but damned marvellously faked case histories." His blunt opinion was that Fitzgerald had cheated with the book and that it had been unnecessary. Fitzgerald was too caught up in the good opinions of people like Gilbert Seldes, which had "nearly ruined you," and too caught up in his family problems. "Forget your personal tragedy," he advised. "We are all bitched from the start. . . . But when you get the damned hurt use it—don't cheat with it." For all the savage insensitivity of his letter, Hemingway had hit the mark.

"I'd like to see you and talk about things with you sober," Hemingway added. "You were so damned stinking in N.Y. we didn't get anywhere. You see, Bo, you're not a tragic character. Neither am I. All we are is writers and what we should do is write." Then Hemingway settled into a diatribe against Zelda: "Of all people on earth you needed discipline in your work and instead you marry someone who is jealous of your work, wants to compete with you and ruins you." From the first time he met Zelda, he said, he thought she was crazy, and Fitzgerald had complicated the problem by being in love with her. Of course Fitzgerald was a rummy, but so were Joyce and other good writers. Hemingway now claimed that he had not been that keen about *The Great Gatsby* when they first met. But he told Fitzgerald, "You are twice as good now as you were at the time you think you were so marvelous. . . . All you need to do is write truly and not care about what the fate of it is." He was "damned fond" of him, Hemingway said, by way of softening the blows.

In time, Hemingway's opinion of *Tender Is the Night* would change. More than a year later, in passing, he wrote to Fitzgerald that it was a better book than he had first thought: "This may irritate you but it's the truth." Five years later, while in Cuba, he wrote Max Perkins, asking him to pass on the word to Scott that he was amazed at how "*excellent*" much of it was. Hemingway admitted to Perkins that he had always had "a very stupid little boy feeling of superiority about Scott—like a tough little boy sneering at a delicate but talented little boy." Rereading *Tender Is the Night*, he discovered that much of it was so good that "it was frightening." But by then his friendship with Fitzgerald had been so eroded that the two were communicating with each other largely through Perkins.

Fitzgerald's answer to Hemingway's initial criticism was measured and surprisingly cool. He disagreed with Hemingway's assessment of his characterizations, especially with regard to the Murphys. Hemingway, he said, was hardly the detached reader: "If you had never met any of the originals then your opinion would be more convincing." Composite characters hadn't honestly hurt the book; they had hurt it only for Hemingway. "To take a case specifically,

that of Gerald and Sara. I don't know how much you think you
know about my relations with them over a long time, but from
certain remarks that you let drop, such as one 'Gerald threw you
over,' I guess that you didn't even know the beginning of our relations. In that case you hit on the exact opposite of the truth."

From somewhere — clearly not anything Hemingway had said
in his letter — Fitzgerald had gotten the impression that Hemingway
felt he disliked Pauline, "or that I didn't like her as much as I
should." He assured Hemingway that this was not the case. He
jokingly put on the cloak of Christian charity, perhaps as a dig in
response to Hemingway's uncharitable remarks about Zelda. "My
temporary bitternesses toward people," Fitzgerald said, "have all
been ended by what Freud called an inferiority complex and Christ
called 'Let him without sin — ' I remember the day he said it."

The Murphys did not like *Tender Is the Night,* either. "I hated
the book when I first read it," Sara said, "and even more on rereading. I reject categorically any resemblance to ourselves or to
anyone we know." Fitzgerald was not on the best of terms with the
Murphys that spring after the publication of the novel. He had
picked a quarrel with them during one of his New York visits. Sara's
dissatisfaction with the author may have crept into a scolding letter
she wrote to him:

> . . . consideration for other people's feelings, opinions or even time
> is *Completely* left out of your makeup — I have always told you you
> haven't the faintest idea what anybody else but yourself is like —
> & have never (yet) seen the slightest reason for changing this opin-
> ion, "half-baked" as you consider it! You don't even know what
> Zelda or Scottie are like — in spite of your love for them.

Gerald Murphy was well aware of the struggle that the book had
cost. He reportedly had seen Fitzgerald take one of the earlier drafts
out in a rowboat and systematically tear it up, page by page, scat-
tering it in the Mediterranean. But he also claimed that Scott "never
did really understand our life." He did, however, have praise for the
uncanny descriptive passages and the power of some of the emotional
scenes. He, too, would change his opinion of *Tender Is the Night.* In
December 1935, months after his son Baoth, at the age of sixteen,
died of spinal meningitis and while his son Patrick was wasting away
with tuberculosis, Gerald wrote Scott: "I know now that what you
said in 'Tender is the Night' is true. Only the invented part of our

life — the unreal part — has had any scheme any beauty. Life itself has stepped in now and blundered, scarred and destroyed."

Among Fitzgerald's friends, Murphy seems to have been the only one who recognized how desperately Fitzgerald had tried to live within the fiction — and make something imperishable out of it.

Zelda had not been allowed to read the manuscript version of *Tender Is the Night*. As she acknowledged earlier to Max Perkins, "We wait now till each other's stuff is copy-righted since I try to more or less absorb his technique and the range of our experience might coincide." When Zelda began reading the *Scribner's Magazine* installments, she was in the hospital once more. On February 12, 1934, she was admitted to the Phipps Clinic for a period of three or more weeks, in a hostile mood and without encouraging signs of improvement. She told the doctors there that she was upset by Scott's characterization of her in his novel: "What made me mad was that he made the girl so awful and kept on reiterating how she had ruined his life and I couldn't help identifying myself with her because she had so many of my experiences." From Phipps, she was transferred to Craig House, in Beacon, in upstate New York, a sanitarium recommended by Dr. Forel. It was expensive — $175 a week — and at first Zelda found the country club atmosphere congenial, with its gardens and tennis courts, its views of rolling hills and pastures. Reading the serial at Craig House, she was more communicative. The third installment was fine, she wrote Fitzgerald: "It's a swell book." She made some odd and extended observations about Gerald and Sara: "It seems very careless of the Murphys to have got old; like laundry in the corridors of a pleasure-resort hotel. They could get tragic, or join a curious sect . . . but to expose the mechanics of the glamour of life in slowed-up motion rings of indecency." But it is not altogether clear whether she meant the real Murphys or the fictional Murphys of the novel. When she got to the episode of Rosemary in Rome, she was more emphatic: "It makes me very sad — largely because of the beautiful, beautiful writing." She chided him for not having sent her a copy of the hard-cover edition: "You seem afraid that it will make me recapitulate the past; remember, that at that time, I was immersed in something else. . . . Of course it is a haunting book — everything good is haunting because it calls to light something new in our consciousness." As if to prove that the book evoked pleasant memories, she wrote him again that she was thinking about it "and it haunts me." She reminisced about the past, wishing they could spend July by the sea, "browning ourselves and feeling water-weighted hair flow behind us from a dive . . . and it would be nice to smell the starch of summer linens and the faint odor of talc in blistering bath-houses. Or we could go to the japanese gardens with Kay Laurel and waste a hundred dollars staging conceptions of gaiety." There was often a cutting edge to Zelda's recollections.

The ban had been lifted on her own writing, but she seemed uncertain as to whether Fitzgerald really meant it: "*Please say what you want done,* as I really do not know." And she was painting but felt uncertain about that as well. "Dear: I am not trying to make myself into a great artist or a great anything. Though you persist in thinking that an exaggerated ambition is the fundamental cause of my collapse . . ." Nevertheless, through a young friend named Cary Ross, Fitzgerald had arranged for an exhibition of Zelda's paintings and drawings that spring. He and Zelda had met the young Yale graduate and would-be poet in Europe, and Fitzgerald had accompanied him on drinking bouts in low dives. He was another of the protégés that Fitzgerald had recommended to Max Perkins, on the basis largely of some maudlin poems. Ross had been inspired by a vision of the two Fitzgeralds on a summer beach to write his free-verse impressions of them:

> Carved forms like golden heads
> pedestalled
> Immortally above the moving sea.

Ross had tried for one or two years to interest New York dealers in showing Zelda's work, among them Alfred Stieglitz, the art dealer–photographer, and his wife, Georgia O'Keeffe, with whom Ross had stayed at Lake George in the summer of 1932. But O'Keeffe was not interested in the drawings Ross had shown her. "Except for Picasso, Marin and herself, I think she is not interested in any living artist," he wrote Fitzgerald. Finally, he persuaded Fitzgerald to let him give the exhibition in his studio on East Eighty-sixth Street. It included some thirteen paintings and fifteen drawings and ran from the end of March through April. Ross seemed eager to capitalize on the success of a recent exhibition of Nijinsky's painting, though he assured Fitzgerald that he would not mention that most of Zelda's work had been done in a sanitarium. Still, the catalogue carried the motto *Parfois la folie est la sagesse* (Sometimes madness is wisdom). Zelda, released from Craig House to attend the opening, stayed with Scott at the Algonquin. The press was less interested in the work than in the resurrection of a legendary figure from the Jazz Age. The attention it gave was rather degrading. *Time's* coverage of the show carried a grim photograph of Zelda, looking a wreck in an ugly pose and very unattractive dress, and looking more like a patient on release from an asylum than a former flapper beauty. Few of Zelda's paintings were sold, and those mostly to friends. Dorothy Parker bought a painting of a cornet player; the Murphys bought *Chinese Theater,* a picture of acrobats. One of the paintings was an odd portrait of Fitzgerald as Christ with a crown of thorns. Whether it was some bizarre image Zelda had invented out of her sense of Fitzgerald's suffering or had picked up from Fitzgerald's self-pity at the time, it did have a queer fictional precedent in Fitzgerald's *The Beautiful and Damned.* After Anthony's departure for the army, Gloria writes him a letter "full of confused sentiment," then spends a sleepless night. The image that comes to her mind is a likeness of her husband "akin to some martyred and transfigured Christ."

In May, Zelda was transferred to the Sheppard and Enoch Pratt Hospital, near Baltimore and adjacent to the Turnbull estate. According to Fitzgerald, she was in a catatonic state. When she came out of it, she tried to commit suicide by strangling herself. And once, when she was considered well enough to walk with Fitzgerald on the grounds at La Paix, she suddenly tried to throw herself in front of a train that crossed through the estate. Fitzgerald managed to restrain her just in time, but he began to despair of Zelda's ever recovering completely. He later wrote, "I left my capacity for hoping on the little roads that led to Zelda's sanitarium."

Earlier in 1934, during his trips to New York while he was working on the magazine proofs of *Tender Is the Night,* Fitzgerald struck up a friendship with a twenty-nine-year-old admirer, the writer and reporter John O'Hara. The two men had begun a correspondence some years earlier, and at this point in his career O'Hara was in a low mood. He was recently divorced from his wife, had been fired from a magazine job in Pittsburgh, and had encountered a block halfway through his first novel, *Appointment in Samarra.* Fitzgerald, as usual with a young and up-and-coming talent, offered O'Hara the encouragement of recognition. O'Hara, in return, became a devotee of *Tender Is the Night,* which he read in proof. Nevertheless, he was aware of the flaws of characterization in the novel, which he put down to Fitzgerald's having been more interested in the life, rather than the lives, of his protagonists. Still, he remained convinced that it was a far better book than *The Great Gatsby,* which years later he characterized in a letter to Gerald Murphy as "greasy kid stuff." (Having met real mobsters in New York, O'Hara was convinced that Gatsby wouldn't have lasted a week with gangsters, let alone taken control.) The problem with Dick Diver, he told Gerald Murphy, was the problem with much of Fitzgerald's writing: sooner or later, "his characters always came back to being Fitzgerald characters in a Fitzgerald world." Dick Diver had ended up as "a tall Fitzgerald."

O'Hara was a writer with faith in the four-letter word, and he was mildly bemused by Fitzgerald's fastidiousness in that respect. He thought that such prudishness was a liability for a writer. Writing to Fitzgerald to thank him for the encouragement he needed to finish *Appointment in Samarra,* O'Hara announced, "My message to the world is Fuck it!" Fitzgerald, proud of the letter, pasted it in his scrapbook but carefully blue-penciled the word. There was, in fact, something about the grittier, starkly unromantic side of O'Hara's talent that Fitzgerald disapproved of. In his notebooks, he wrote, "John O'Hara is in a perpetual state of just having discovered that it's a lousy world." And he repeated the remark of the screenwriter Nunnally Johnson, that O'Hara was "like an idiot to whom someone has given a wonderful graflex camera and he goes around with it not knowing what to snap."

All the same, O'Hara's admiration for the older writer survived his having seen Fitzgerald in one or two of his grubbier moments. Once, in New York, he and Fitzgerald were out drinking with Dorothy Parker and O'Hara's former wife, Helen, and Fitzgerald, in his cups, began making boozy passes at Helen, evidently intent on making a conquest in front of her former husband. When Parker remarked to O'Hara, "He's awful, why didn't you punch him?" O'Hara countered that Helen seemed to be enjoying it and, in any event, they were divorced. O'Hara was more outspoken about a later occasion, when he had driven to Baltimore to visit Fitzgerald. It was a Sunday, and Zelda had been allowed out of the clinic for the day. When it came time to take her back, Fitzgerald, already drunk, insisted that he had to have more gin and nagged so persistently that O'Hara stopped at a pharmacy and after considerable trouble managed to persuade the druggist to part with a quart. "I wanted to kill him. Kill . . ." O'Hara said of the drive along one of the back roads to Zelda's sanitarium; "he kept making passes at her that could not possibly be consummated. . . . I wanted to kill him for what he was doing to that crazy woman, who kept telling me she had to be locked up before the moon came up." That was the last time O'Hara saw Zelda.

Fitzgerald's capacity for work had begun to show dangerous signs of slipping, and his professional judgments were becoming hasty and poorly planned. He had had great hopes of selling the film rights to *Tender Is the Night* (he had borrowed money from Scribner's on those hopes), and when they came to nothing, he decided to make an adaptation himself, with the assistance of a somewhat inexperienced young Baltimore playwright and director he had recently met, Charles Marquis Warren. When the script was completed, young Warren took off for Hollywood, armed with letters of introduction to the directors, actresses, and studio executives Fitzgerald knew. Fitzgerald bombarded Carmel Myers, George Cukor, Richard Barthelmess, the MGM story editor, Samuel Marx, and Thalberg's assistant, Al Lewin, with letters and phone calls. One night, at two o'clock, he telephoned Marx to get Thalberg's private number, hoping to persuade the producer to take on the book as a vehicle for Norma Shearer in the role of Nicole. As it happened, Marx recalled, Thalberg was looking for a film property for his wife, so he reluctantly gave Fitzgerald the number, though he realized that Fitzgerald was drunk. Much to his chagrin, he learned that Fitzgerald had called Thalberg that very night.

When it became evident that he could not be bailed out by Hollywood, Fitzgerald turned back to writing his commercial stories — but on one of the most ill-advised subjects he could have picked. He decided to write a serial about a ninth-century French knight, Philippe, Count of Villefranche, a paragon of manhood who was to be patterned after Ernest Hemingway, still his hero. It may have been some subconscious pugilistic association that led Fitzgerald to give the name of his former chauffeur, drinking companion, and sparring partner to his many-talented protagonist, Philippe. The stories were so improbable and poorly written that after the initial magazine publication, only one of them has ever been reprinted. In

order to avoid some form of made-up medieval speech, Fitzgerald
decided to update the language to modern slang: "Sister," Philippe
asks, "where'd you get that swell horse that's tied around behind
the house?" The sequence became a kind of medieval Western. Even
so, Fitzgerald's name commanded enough respect for Ober to sell
the stories to *Redbook* magazine, which published the first three
installments and then held the fourth. Fitzgerald planned to make
a novel of the completed series; it was to deal with a young man's
recovery of his father's territory from the invading barbarians. Its
symbolic content was more interesting than anything the plot had
to offer.

For more than a year, Fitzgerald's incredibly patient agent,
Harold Ober, had been worrying about Fitzgerald's professional attitude. Fitzgerald had been writing fewer and fewer stories, and these
were too hastily written. When, in August 1933, the *Post* turned
back Fitzgerald's latest story, "What to Do About It," Ober wrote
his author a letter of advice. He thought it was a mistake, he said,
to "let the Post feel that you were rushing out stories in order to
get some money." Ober proposed a new regimen so that both would
be sure that the stories were "just right," and then he would see
that they were properly typed before sending them to any magazine
editor. "I want to try to create the impression," Ober wrote at the
time, "that I am sending them a Scott Fitzgerald story, that it is a
fine story and that I don't care whether they take it or not. I am
sure it is a mistake for the Post to feel that you are uncertain about
a story and anxious to know whether or not they like it."

Unfortunately, in December 1934 Ober was confronted with
other problems. Fitzgerald had been failing to meet the deadlines
for his Philippe stories for *Redbook*. Ober, plainly discouraged, decided to lecture Fitzgerald. Putting a better face on the situation
than was the case, he said that two or three years before, when
Fitzgerald promised that a story would be in, he would have been
as certain of its arrival as he would that the sun would rise the next
day. "As far as it concerns myself," Ober wrote, "I do not mind
this. I know that life has been very difficult for you, that you have
been working under pressure." Now, however, Fitzgerald had taken
to calling and writing editors directly and promising delivery and
not producing the manuscript — and this was decidedly a mistake.
In passing, Ober noted, it was also a mistake to call and write movie
directors as readily as Fitzgerald had been doing. "Sometimes," Ober

said, "I think it would be better if you would take the telephone out of your house entirely." Fitzgerald, he said, was too apt to use the phone "when you are not in your most rational state of mind and when you do call anyone up in that way it only adds to the legend that has always been ready to crop out—that you are never sober."

At first, Fitzgerald maintained that he did not resent Ober's letter a bit. But after brooding over it, he allowed his irritation to show. He became suspicious that Ober and Max Perkins had gotten together and decided that he needed disciplining. He understood their good intentions, he said. "Nevertheless," he charged, "the assumption that all my troubles are due to drink is a little too easy." He couldn't decide which was the hen and which the egg when it came to his domestic problems and his self-indulgence. But his failure to get his manuscripts out on time had coincided with his problems with Zelda and his family troubles. What bothered him most was that, except for his *Post* readers, his literary reputation was "at its very lowest ebb. I was completely forgotten and this fact was rubbed in by Zelda's inadvertently written book." His chief concern then had been to get his book published at any cost and still manage to survive. No sooner had he finished the proofs on his book than he had had to take up his *Post* stories, without time for recuperation. It left him, he said, "in the black hole of Calcutta, mentally exhausted, physically exhausted, emotionally exhausted, and perhaps, morally exhausted." His "apologia," which he admitted could be considered a whine, broke off, incomplete.

In 1934, after thirty years as an expatriate, Gertrude Stein returned to America and, accompanied by Alice B. Toklas, made a highly publicized lecture tour. In November, Stein wrote Fitzgerald that she would be in Baltimore over the Christmas holidays and hoped to see him. In her run-on fashion, she also told him, "I liked a lot of Tender is the Night, and I am sure that you will do some more." On Christmas Eve, the two women paid a visit to 1307 Park Avenue. Zelda had been allowed home from Sheppard and Enoch Pratt Hospital for an overnight stay. During the course of the visit, she showed Stein some of her recent paintings. When Gertrude expressed an interest in them, Fitzgerald immediately told her to choose any two that she liked. She did so, but Zelda balked, and Fitzgerald tried to convince her that Stein would hang them in her salon and make her famous. Besides, he said, Gertrude had been kinder to him than almost anyone. Zelda's answer was "If she has been as kind to you as my doctor has been to me, you should give her everything you own, but she can't have those paintings." Gertrude chose one picture, a different one.

Fitzgerald and Stein talked about literary subjects, Stein maintaining that a good sentence should be like good plumbing. Fitzgerald asked for an example. She chose his dedication in *The Great Gatsby*, "Once Again to Zelda," cupping her hands and saying that it was complete, it held together — "it doesn't leak." Fitzgerald remembered the remark, a few days later, when he wrote to Stein, apologizing for being "somewhat stupid-got with the Christmas spirit." He had enjoyed "the one idea that you *did* develop and, like everything else you say, it will sing in my ears long after everything else about that afternoon is dust and ashes." It had meant so much to Zelda, he said, "giving her a tangible sense of her own existence, for you to have liked two of her pictures enough to want to own them." His guests had all felt that their Christmas Eve had been well spent in the company of her "handsome face and wise mind — and sentences 'that never leak.' "

I V

In April 1935, Fitzgerald learned, through newly taken x rays, that his tuberculosis was once more active, and he arranged to spend the summer recuperating in Asheville, North Carolina. Zelda was still at Sheppard and Enoch Pratt, and Scottie was scheduled to go to a summer camp and spend some time with Harold Ober and his family in Scarsdale, New York. Ostensibly, at Asheville Fitzgerald was under the care of a specialist, Dr. Paul Ringer, but he managed to convince the doctor that any publicity about his being hospitalized would be detrimental to his career, so he was allowed to stay at the Grove Park Inn.

It was at the inn that Fitzgerald met an engaging, somewhat stolid woman who reminded him of Sara Murphy, except for her rather loud, sharp voice. Laura Guthrie, who was also under treatment with Dr. Ringer, was waiting for a divorce. She had ambitions of becoming a writer and, at the moment, was working at the inn as a fortuneteller, complete with the Gypsy costume, bandanna, and earrings. Fitzgerald started up a mild flirtation, calling her his Dollar Woman (the price of a palm reading), but she was too hesitant to become deeply involved. Fitzgerald later hired her as his part-time secretary and confidante. Mrs. Guthrie kept a diary of her meetings and conversations with Fitzgerald during that summer. (Lengthy excerpts from it were published in *Esquire* after Fitzgerald's death.) Its principal interest is in its reports of Fitzgerald's occasional literary discussions and its chronicle of Fitzgerald's passing but hectic affair with a young married woman, Beatrice Dance, who was staying at the inn with her sister, Eleanor, who was recovering from nervous troubles. Beatrice Dance's husband, "Hop," a wealthy businessman and sports enthusiast, was at home in Texas.

There was a second historian of Fitzgerald's adulterous summer in North Carolina. Fitzgerald had met another aspiring young writer, Tony Buttita, the proprietor of the Intimate Bookshop in the George Vanderbilt Hotel in Asheville. Always responsive to young writers who were aware of his work and reputation, Fitzgerald took Buttita into his confidence. Buttita scribbled down Fitzgerald's comments and commentaries on love, fame, literature, and politics in the end-pages of the books he was reading. Later, he used them in a devastating memoir, *After the Good Gay Times*. In it, Buttita gave other details of Fitzgerald's affair with Beatrice Dance that more or less corroborated Laura Guthrie's recollections.

If the love affair had not been quite so depressing and destructive in personal terms, the events of that summer in Asheville might be read as a light comedy or a hotel farce. At the outset it was Beatrice Dance, impressed by Fitzgerald's fame and romantic reputation, who pursued a reluctant author. According to the man-to-man story Fitzgerald gave Buttita, Beatrice had bribed a bellhop at the inn to let her into Fitzgerald's room, where she greeted him in the nude, lying on his bed, when he returned. Fitzgerald had not taken advantage of her on this occasion. In fact, it was not until he discovered her reading *The Great Gatsby* in the hotel writing room that he allowed himself to be seduced. The two lovers, rather daringly, had used her sister as a blind. When Beatrice's husband arrived in North Carolina for a brief visit, he was put up in a hotel in Highlands, two counties away. Eleanor's illness served as a convenient excuse for Beatrice to remain behind at the Grove Park Inn. The telephone operators had been alerted to tell the husband, if he should call, that Mrs. Dance was with her sister, who was too ill to

be disturbed at the moment. A bellhop then warned the lovers in
Fitzgerald's room. At the Grove Park Inn, it was hardly a clandestine
affair. And Beatrice's sister, well aware of what was going on, became
increasingly distressed and progressively resorted to liquor and Luminal.

The tension only increased Fitzgerald's drinking. He had given
up hard liquor, presumably, and was drinking beer—between twenty
and thirty bottles a day, the empties mounting up in his closet. He
ate little. He was also suffering from insomnia and was alternating
between doses of Amytal and Luminal, which caused him to break
out in a rash. Trying to escape from his purgatory of love, he moved
from one hotel to another, or some nearby resort town, registering
under an assumed name. (Once he used Amory Patch, borrowing
from two of his fictional characters; another time, he selected Francis
Key.) But from these retreats, he would contact Beatrice Dance or
leave messages for her with Laura Guthrie, starting all over again.
During the breaks in the affair, Beatrice would write him passionate
letters. Never overly discreet, Fitzgerald gave them to Laura Guthrie
to read and file, asking for her views and advice on how to conduct
his adultery. Inevitably, she was drawn into the frantic affair and
became a kind of central relay station for messages and letters, telegrams and telephone calls, from the suspicious husband, the anxious
sister, and the occasionally parted lovers. Each morning, Fitzgerald
and his secretary would rehash and discuss the events of the evening
before. The only immediate retreat for the philandering lover and
his harried secretary was the local movie theater, which, appropriately enough, seemed to be having a festival of Shirley Temple films.
For longer periods of escape, Fitzgerald made trips to Baltimore or
New York; sometimes he escaped to a few days of sanity with his
friends Nora and "Lefty" Flynn at nearby Tryon, North Carolina.
Their home was a haven of sobriety. Nora was a Christian Scientist
who tried to persuade Fitzgerald to take the cure; Lefty was a Yale
graduate and former movie star (he had been one of the guests at
the Goldwyn party in Hollywood at which Fitzgerald and Zelda had
created a stir) and a reformed alcoholic.

As if to complicate his already overcomplicated sexual life that
summer, Fitzgerald also became involved with a classy prostitute
who worked the luxury hotels in Asheville. He met her through
Buttita, who, in his memoir, gave her name as Lottie, noting that
she came to his shop often to get books, which she seldom read.

Lottie carried them under her arm when she walked her two French poodles, giving an air of distinction to her profession. According to Buttita, Fitzgerald was at first put off by the fact that Lottie was a whore, then intrigued, and eventually he became sexually involved with her—though not without first requiring that she show him a clean bill of health. As he did with many women, Fitzgerald decided to further Lottie's education; he recommended books for her to read —*Gatsby* and *Lady Chatterley's Lover* among them. He recited Keats's "Ode to a Nightingale" for her, and gave her lectures on the life of John Reed, whom he had come to admire, and suggested that Lottie study Reed's *Ten Days That Shook the World.* According to Lottie, who discussed the affair with Buttita, Fitzgerald also opened up during his sex-time conversations, revealing how hurt he had been by Zelda's charges about his sexual inadequacies. The prostitute felt that he was continually seeking confirmation of his sexual virility, though she plainly found his boozy and tearful queries a nuisance.

The climactic moment of that disorderly summer occurred when the suspicious husband, accompanied by the family doctor, flew up from Texas in response to Beatrice Dance's worries about the mental condition of her sister. Fitzgerald thought that a confrontation with the husband was in order and had even armed himself with a pair of beer-can openers. But the two men did not discuss what really concerned them; only college careers and the military profession. Fitzgerald aired his views about psychological help for Eleanor. Still, he felt he had acquitted himself so well that he boasted to Laura Guthrie, "I held [Hop] with my eyes and kept the conversation on whatever I wanted." He was so impressed with his own performance that he persuaded Laura Guthrie to pay a visit with him to the Dances' hotel bedroom that evening. Beatrice was in bed, having been given a sedative; the husband was in his bathrobe and pajamas. Fitzgerald had two beers' worth of general conversation, sitting on the husband's bed, then asked the wife if he might kiss her good night, a question she answered with a radiant "Of course." As Fitzgerald and Laura left, the husband slammed the door shut and noisily turned the key. When Fitzgerald, in hazy innocence, asked Laura whether she thought it had been a good idea to visit the couple, she answered that the husband did seem to be upset. The setting was not the Riviera, with its velvet nights, but Asheville, in the steamy summer. The scenario, including doctors, neuroses, invalids, heavy drinking, and resort hotels, however, suggested a comic replay of *Tender Is the Night.*

Fitzgerald appears to have collaborated with the Dances' family physician, Dr. Cade, in securing his release from the love affair. After one or two interviews with Fitzgerald, Dr. Cade managed to convince Beatrice that both she and Fitzgerald were headed for breakdowns if the pressures did not end. The husband, wayward wife, and the distraught sister left hurriedly for the West. One of the more decisive contributions Fitzgerald made to the end of the affair was a scolding letter he wrote Beatrice not long afterward. He reminded her that there were various "half truths" that, on occasion, men, and especially women, had to live by. "The utter synthesis between what we want and what we can have," he told her, "is so rare that I look back with a sort of wonder on those days of my youth when I had it, or thought I did." In pontificating fashion, he told her that she had to develop a sense of priorities in life, a sense of comparative values: "This comes first — This comes second. *This is what you, Beatrice, are not doing!*" Her attractiveness to men depended on what Ernest Hemingway had called "grace under pressure." When she failed to exercise control over her luxuriant emotions, she became "just another victim of self-indulgence."

The oddest feature of Fitzgerald's letter — what he called "the tough part" — was that, for Beatrice Dance's edification, he enclosed one of Zelda's intimate letters to him. The purpose was to administer a needed "sharp shock of a *fact*" in the midst of the emotionalism. In the past, Fitzgerald had used Zelda's letters and intimate diaries in novels and short stories; now he used one to justify his conduct in a love affair. This particular letter, it seems, was especially serviceable. Earlier he had sent it to Harold Ober — "on an impulse," he claimed — to verify for Ober's benefit the "awful strangling heart-rending quality" of the tragedy he and Zelda had been living for the past six years.

Zelda's letter is one of the more authentic documents of human misery and regret:

> Dearest and always Dearest Scott: I am sorry too that there should be nothing to greet you but an empty shell. The thought of the effort you have made over me, the suffering this *nothing* has cost would be unendurable to any save a completely vacuous mechanism. Had I any feelings they would all be bent in gratitude to you and in sorrow that

of all my life there should not even be the smallest relic of the love and beauty that we started with to offer you at the end.

You have been so good to me — and all I can say is that there was always that deeper current running through my heart: my life — you. . . .

Now that there isn't any more happiness and home is gone and there isn't even any past and no emotions but those that were yours where there could be any comfort — it is a shame that we should have met in harshness and coldness where there was once so much tenderness and so many dreams. Your song.

Fitzgerald used Zelda's letter for self-serving ends, but he well understood its message. He drew the implications for Beatrice Dance: "There are emotions just as important as ours running concurrently with them — and there is literally no standard in life other than a sense of duty."

It was no doubt a guilty conscience, and a suspicious rash, that gave Fitzgerald, in mid-August, the idea that he had syphilis, presumably contracted from Lottie. With dread, he began to imagine the consequences if he had given it to Beatrice and if she had given it to her husband. He wrote to Dr. Cade, asking what he should do if, in fact, he was "tainted." And he entertained vague thoughts of suicide, including jumping off a boat — "no one near, and you need never speak to anyone again." Fitzgerald went out of state for his Wassermann. Three days later, he called for the results from downtown Asheville rather than from his hotel. But curiously, when he learned the test was negative, he experienced a let-down from the high drama he had imagined. Pacing the floor of the bookshop, he told Buttita, "I was all keyed up for action, not sticking around. It means I'll have to face the whole damn mess all over again."

According to Tony Buttita, it was over the issue of politics that he and Fitzgerald had a rancorous break. Buttita was a young activist who wrote on such subjects as the proletarian novel. He and his friends held lively discussions in the bookshop on Karl Marx and the American Communist Party and its current concerns. Fitzgerald seemed to take a lively interest in the discussions and even joined in, apparently enjoying debates with young radicals just out of college. And during one boozy session in Fitzgerald's hotel room, in

which he was trying to sweat out a cold with a bottle of gin Buttita
had brought on request, Fitzgerald touched on his own efforts at
coming to terms with the politics of the "Great Change" and his
decision to stick to the sidelines. From Buttita's account — a biased
one — one gets the impression that Fitzgerald's political persuasions
were another form of self-image, an attempt to assume an identity
that was suitable for the times.

It was some time later that the break came. Fitzgerald had
stopped by the bookshop and, while leafing through a copy of Nancy
Cunard's anthology of Negro writers, began baiting Buttita, re-
marking that Cunard, a sponsor of the Harlem Renaissance, had had
black lovers. Buttita, according to his memoir, let this pass. But
then Fitzgerald began ranting against liberal and Marxist critics,
some of whom, like Burton Rascoe and Tom Boyd, had been early
friends of his. He was particularly virulent about Rascoe, whom he
labeled "a stinking parlor pink who will jump off the radical band-
wagon when the wind changes." But it was on the subject of Negro
rights and equality, according to Buttita, that Fitzgerald became
most exercised, calling it "gibberish." It was the party's support of
such causes that had decided him against joining. "It's the thing
they were yapping about most that made me pull out of the League
against This and That," Fitzgerald said. "And it's time you came
to your senses before going the way of all our Tom Boyds. You seem
to have some of his vitality and stubbornness, if not his talent, so I
doubt if this will seep through that skull of yours." Buttita, now
angry, suggested that the reason Fitzgerald hated Rascoe's guts was
that Rascoe had panned *The Great Gatsby* and praised "the barnyard
boys" like Boyd.

Fitzgerald's Asheville encounters came to an end soon after, and
the occasion was Fitzgerald's last meeting with Lottie. Enraged by
his argument with Buttita, he was abusive on the subject in front
of Lottie, asserting that it was because Buttita had been sold a bill
of goods by the Communist Party that he was championing the
black cause. Lottie, so she told Buttita, listened carefully. "He talked
like a dyed-in-the-wool Southerner, thinking I was on his side."
Fitzgerald began harping about radicals wanting to mix the races.
It was then, she said, that she decided to spell it out for him; she
told him that she was only three-quarters white herself. Fitzgerald
went into a rage, slamming around the room, opening drawers,

looking for a drink. Then he broke down and bawled, "Oh, God, what's happened to me? What's happened to me?" Lottie tried to console him by saying that in her years in the South, everyone knew that "a white boy wasn't a man till he smoked, got stinko under the kitchen table, and had himself a nigger gal in the barn." She told Fitzgerald that he had now made it in style.

II

Too Much Anger, Too Many Tears

O F COURSE all life is a process of breaking down," Fitzgerald wrote in the first of three articles he published in *Esquire*, beginning with the February 1936 issue. "But," he went on, "the blows that do the dramatic side of the work—the big sudden blows that come, or seem to come, from outside—the ones you remember and blame things on and, in moments of weakness, tell your friends about, don't show their effect all at once." Several months before, in November 1935, he had returned to North Carolina, where he stayed at the Skyland Hotel in Hendersonville, living in a state of partial poverty, existing on potted meat and Uneeda Biscuits, rationing his beer, doing his own laundry. He found it amusing that the hotel clerks were unaware that he was thousands of dollars in debt. He had hit bottom; having bought the American Dream early in his life, he was forced to weigh its value for him at the moment. When his income tax came due in December, he wrote to Ober, asking for the needed $300 and for additional money for Zelda's and Scottie's expenses and $50 for himself. About his taxes, Fitzgerald was mildy sardonic: "What a typically modern joke this is—me, with $11 in the bank at the moment."

The Crack-Up, as Fitzgerald's *Esquire* series was eventually called, is a genuine American document of the period, a chronicle of the boom-to-bust road Fitzgerald had traveled, of his personal breakdown and the breakdown of his generation. It had taken longer for Fitzgerald to feel the effects than the man on the street. He was still coasting on his reputation, still commanding reasonably high prices for his stories, although the *Post,* in keeping with the hard times, was paying him $1000 less for the stories it accepted. Unfortunately, that number was diminishing with the years, because the plots were going stale and the writing was rushed. More and more frequently, Ober returned the manuscripts, requesting changes and suggesting revisions. But in the confessional articles he was writing for Arnold Gingrich, a young editor at *Esquire,* for a meager $250 each, he had tapped a vein of honesty, self-reproach, and ironic bitterness that was new to his writing. "The Crack-Up," "Pasting It Together," "Handle with Care," are some of the most incisive and important writing of the period. Working from his own experiences, without glamorizing the facts or dramatizing himself—and without too much of what he called "the tin cup of self-pity"—Fitzgerald described the times in which he lived, or, at least, that corner of those times which he knew well. He had become the sociological reporter whose role he had been playing for years.

He looked back at his blithe acceptance of early success: "Life was something you dominated if you were any good. Life yielded easily to intelligence and effort." That had been his formula at the time. It was romantic to be a successful author in those years. He had lived hard; the big problems in life seemed to solve themselves. But then, suddenly, prematurely, at the age of thirty-nine, he had cracked.

Yet even in his moments of disarming honesty, Fitzgerald could not quite give up the old lies, the old exaggerations. He assured the readers of *Esquire* that he had not cracked because of his drinking; he said he had been on the wagon for six months prior to his breakdown, not drinking even so much as a bottle of beer. No, his crack-up had simply been a nervous reflex to a period of "too much anger and too many tears." Next, he dramatized his plight, saying that just before his collapse he had received "a grave sentence" from a great doctor. But it was highly questionable that the flare-up of tuberculosis had been quite as serious as he depicted. He had been abusing his health for years. His drinking and carrying on in Asheville during the summer after that "grave sentence" does not suggest any real concern for his health at the time. There were very few references in Laura Guthrie's diary account to any serious course of treatments under Dr. Ringer. She reportedly told Tony Buttita later that Fitzgerald's claims were largely a "myth," that Scott thought he could convince people that he had tuberculosis—even Dr. Ringer. "But the doctor was disgusted with the hoax and told me so," she informed Buttita. The lesions were real enough, no doubt, but medical crises were a strategic weapon Fitzgerald used in his letters to others.

In many ways, the "Crack-Up" essays were meant to be an act of dismissal for the outworn moral values he had been brought up to believe in and still clung to. He had always preached the importance of professionalism; now he recognized that "I had been only a mediocre caretaker of most of the things left in my hands, even of my talent." He was also ready to admit, with some frankness, "that every act of life from the morning tooth-brush to the friend at dinner had become an effort." For a long time he had not liked people and things, "but only followed the rickety old pretense of liking. I saw that even my love for those closest to me was become only an attempt to love, that my casual relations — with an editor, a tobacco seller, the child of a friend, were only what I remembered I *should* do, from other days."

He itemized the things he no longer felt it necessary to like or give lip service to: "All in the same month I became bitter about such things as the sound of the radio, the advertisements in the magazines, the screech of tracks, the dead silence of the country." He had become "contemptuous at human softness, immediately (if secretively) quarrelsome toward hardness." He offered a strategic lie: "Like most Middle Westerners, I have never had any but the vaguest race prejudices." Then he told a strategic truth, giving an inventory of all the assorted hatreds that had risen to the surface of his despair: "I couldn't stand the sight of Celts, English, Politicians, Strangers, Virginians, Negroes (light or dark), Hunting People, or retail clerks, and middlemen in general." He hated all writers and avoided them carefully, "because they can perpetuate trouble as no one else can." He was a man who wanted to turn his back on life.

He had been forced to rethink his life. It came as a surprise that for years he had left his thinking to others: to Edmund Wilson, who had become his "intellectual conscience"; to Hemingway, who was his "artistic conscience." His political conscience had barely existed for several years. He had become a man without an identity:

> So there was not an "I" any more — not a basis on which I could organize my self-respect — save my limitless capacity for toil that it seemed I possessed no more. It was strange to have no self — to be like a little boy left alone in a big house, who knew that he now could do anything he wanted to do but found that there was nothing that he wanted to do. . . .

He had become a man of borrowed qualities; a man estranged, complaining in a hotel room, while his wife was spending years wandering down the corridors of mental asylums.

It was not, Fitzgerald recognized, solely his personal tragedy. As early as his 1931 essay "Echoes of the Jazz Age," he had begun to notice how his contemporaries were disappearing "into the dark maw of violence." A classmate had killed his wife and himself on Long Island; another had tumbled "accidentally" from a skyscraper in Philadelphia; a third had jumped purposely from a building in New York. One of his acquaintances had been killed in a speakeasy in Chicago; another had been beaten in a New York speakeasy and crawled home to die at the Princeton Club. There was another who had had his skull crushed in by a maniac's ax in an insane asylum where he had been confined. These were not catastrophes he had gone out of his way to look for; they had happened to friends, the people he had met at parties.

Five years later he could have expanded the list of the casualties and the disabled of the Jazz Age. Edmund Wilson's manic-depressive phases had taken him to the clinic at Clifton Springs in New York. When Zelda was at Prangins, Wilson had written Fitzgerald, recommending Jung, who had treated their college friend Stanley Dell two years earlier. Two years after Zelda was released from Prangins, James Joyce's deranged daughter, Lucia, who had had an obsession with dance and studied under Egorova, was briefly committed to Prangins under the care of Dr. Forel. Later in the thirties, there was Fitzgerald's friend Alec McKaig. (John Bishop, writing to Wilson, reported: "He is hopelessly and completely insane. It sounds like paresis. He is unable to receive any communication and only sporadically and uncertainly recognizes visitors.") Lives had come to full stops; careers seem to have ended in rest homes for alcoholics and asylums for the insane. The nurse and the white-coated attendant had become presences in the literary life.

By 1936, when the "Crack-Up" articles were published, Fitzgerald was aware of the number of his contemporaries who had given thought to what he called "the idea of the Big Out." His brother-in-law Anthony Sayre had had a nervous breakdown and plunged out of a hospital window in Mobile. Dorothy Parker, after unhappy love affairs and an abortion or two, had attempted suicide on several occasions, slashing her wrists, taking overdoses of Veronal; but wisely she took the precaution of alerting friends or a hotel desk clerk, or calling a nearby restaurant to have a meal sent up, and was rescued in time. Jules Pascin, the lively Bulgarian American painter the Fitzgeralds had met at a party in Paris, had been more effective; he slashed his wrists and hanged himself, leaving a message in blood on his studio wall. Fitzgerald's friend Emily Vanderbilt shot herself on a lonely Montana ranch one summer day in 1935. And over the course of a harrowing decade, Van Wyck Brooks slipped into deep depressions and mental institutions, troubled by feelings of guilt and unworthiness, overwhelmed by suicidal impulses. Left unattended, he swallowed the shattered crystal to his watch and tried to throw himself under moving vehicles. He had a fantasy that special laws had been passed stipulating that he be buried alive for his sins.

And there were others, whom Fitzgerald knew only slightly or heard about secondhand: the playboy and publisher of the Black Sun Press, Harry Crosby, who with his mistress made a well-publicized exit in a murder-suicide pact in a borrowed apartment in the Hotel des Artistes in New York in December 1929. (Hemingway, who knew Crosby only slightly, nevertheless claimed a deep friendship with the man during the height of his troubles with Fitzgerald in Paris. Crosby's death was one more reason, he said, that he did not want to lose Fitzgerald's friendship, especially over a useless squabble.) Ralph Barton, the celebrated illustrator of New York theatrical life, committed suicide because he had failed to appreciate his former wife, Carlotta Monterrey, who divorced him to marry Eugene O'Neill. (His bizarre farewell letter, "If the gossips insist on something more definite and thrilling as a reason, let them choose my pending appointment with my dentist. . . ." was much quoted at the time.) The poet Hart Crane, wrecked by years of alcoholism, took what Fitzgerald seems to have considered the cleanest way out of life: in 1932 Crane either jumped or fell from a ship plying between Mexico and New York. And there would be the suicide Fitzgerald did not live to see: Hemingway, shooting himself on a summer morning in 1961 in Ketchum, Idaho.

Confronting the Depression years and the fate of his generation, Fitzgerald decided that his response would not be the old-fashioned one of marching ahead, bloody but unbowed. Instead, in "Handle with Care" he announced that he had given up the man he had hoped to be; now he intended to be the writer, solely the writer. He would cultivate a sardonic attitude and a hypocritical smile. He was working on the smile, he said, and it would combine "the best qualities of a hotel manager, an experienced old social weasel, a headmaster on visitors' day, a colored elevator man, a pansy pulling a profile." Everything, in other words, that was false or fawning. He had given up his illusions; he was no longer the man who believed in starlit nights and Riviera mornings, in dancing at the roof garden at the Ritz. "The natural state of the sentient adult," he said, "is a qualified unhappiness." He would manage to live under a new dispensation. "And just as the laughing stoicism which has enabled the American Negro to endure the intolerable conditions of his existence has cost him his sense of the truth — so in my case there is a price to pay." He would be a different social animal. "The sign *Cave Canem* is hung permanently just above my door. I will try to be a correct animal, though, and if you throw me a bone with enough meat on it I may even lick your hand."

Fitzgerald's "Crack-Up" essays were the costliest bit of honesty and irony in his professional career. On one level, at least, Fitzgerald had written them to shed the tiresome public image he had created for himself; he revealed the angry man behind the literary playboy. Harold Ober regretted them from the start. "Remember," Fitzgerald told him, "it was written last November when things seemed at their very blackest." Max Perkins, who disapproved of them, nonetheless decided that "in some deep way," they were a cause for hope, since a "hopeless man" would scarcely write such articles. Perkins, who was keeping Hemingway regularly informed about Fitzgerald's condition, thought that Scott "may have lost that passion in writing which he once had, but he is such a wonderful craftsman that he could certainly make out well if he were able to control himself and be reconciled to life." That Fitzgerald was well aware of what he was doing seems evident in a letter he wrote to a despondent author: "The writing of the articles helped me personally but rather hurt me professionally."

In the course of the next several months, Fitzgerald received chiding letters from friends and former friends. John Dos Passos was probably the most tactless, caught up as he was, for the time being, in his own political concerns. "Christ man," he wrote Fitzgerald, "how do you find time in the middle of the general conflagration to worry about all that stuff? . . . We're living in one of the damnedest tragic moments in history — if you want to go to pieces I think its absolutely o.k. but I think you ought to write a first rate novel about it (and you probably will) instead of spilling it in little pieces for Arnold Gingrich." He did, at least, have the grace to ask Fitzgerald to forgive the locker-room pep talk. Hemingway's opinion of the "Crack-Up" essays went to Max Perkins. He thought Fitzgerald took too much pride in the "shamelessness of defeat" and thought the *Esquire* pieces were miserable. "I always knew he couldn't think— he never could—but he had a marvellous talent and the thing is to use it—not whine in public." Edmund Wilson seems to have remained silent; he later decided that he had "hated" the essays when they were first published. But after Fitzgerald's death, he admitted, "There was more truth and sincerity in it, I suppose, than we realized at the time." Oddly, Sara Murphy wrote him one of the more understanding letters he received, at least to the extent that she realized Fitzgerald needed to get something off his chest. "*Do* you feel better?" she asked. But she took him to task for believing that he could run things, could control his life by just wanting to. "Even if you meant your *own* life it is arrogant enough—but life!"

One of the most sympathetic responses came from a figure out of the past, John V. A. Weaver, the former critic and novelist, now a broken-down screenwriter in Hollywood. Weaver's letter, too, was another genuine document of the period. "I can't express to you how excellent, and how disturbing those articles . . . in Esquire are to me," Weaver wrote him. "They say for me what has happened to me. But I didn't know it had happened to you." The years of defiance had caught up with him, Weaver admitted. He was practically an invalid, not allowed a drop to drink; but he would be damned if *that* would beat him. He painted a grim picture of his life in Hollywood: "I try to hack here in this abbatoir of the intellect, where anybody who can write his name on a contract and can remember gags and situations becomes a 'writer.' But even hacks have to be wanted, and unless one is News, it's not so easy to be even a whore." He had a few consoling words for Fitzgerald; he assured him that he would come out of the pit, since "you always had a certain integrity, and a delicacy with words." But Weaver put the blame for what had happened to him and to Fitzgerald and a good many other talented people of the twenties on history: "What threw the whole thing out was quite simply and vulgarly the overturn of the economic scheme—the crash. It killed me, because, knowing that

I was a fool, I went for its dough — and then lost all the price of my sell-out."

Early in April 1936, Fitzgerald transferred Zelda to the Highland Hospital in Asheville. He wrote Sara Murphy that, though Zelda was no better, the suicidal cloud had lifted. Sara had recommended Christian Science as a remedy for his alcoholism, and Fitzgerald said that he had visited a practitioner but found it "about as effectual as the candles my mother keeps constantly burning to bring me back to Holy Church." Besides, at the moment, Zelda claimed to be in direct contact with Jesus Christ, William the Conqueror, Mary Stuart, and Apollo. ("*Won't* you say your prayers?" Zelda wrote him on one occasion. "God is surely not closed to legitimate appeal; and after all we've done a lot of work from time to time.") Fitzgerald admitted that Zelda's hallucinations were hardly funny, but compared to the time when she had tried to strangle herself, the present phase of her illness was preferable. There was never a sober night now that he didn't think about her for an hour in the darkness. "In an odd way," he added, "perhaps incredible to you, she was always my child (it was not reciprocal as it often is in marriages), my child in a sense that Scottie isn't, because I've brought Scottie up hard as nails."

At Highland, Zelda was under the care of Dr. Robert Carroll, whom Fitzgerald came to regard as the most understanding and capable of Zelda's psychiatrists. With Zelda in a hallucinatory phase, Fitzgerald became more and more convinced that she would never be capable of functioning in the world — at least without a companion. It was presumably that discouraging time in his life which he referred to in a notebook entry: "The voices fainter and fainter — How is Zelda, how is Zelda — tell us — how is Zelda." There were times when he took her for outings (to Chimney Rock, which she had been to as a little girl with her family), and the cloud seemed to lift and he would be hopeful — but only for a few moments. Zelda had reached a phase in her treatment where she was often restless, more often bored — where she alternated between pleading sweetly for little treats, little luxuries, and angrily demanding them when they weren't forthcoming. If she read in a magazine about a trip to Guatemala, she wanted to go.

It was not a happy year. Fitzgerald had planned to spend Zelda's birthday with her, but he dislocated his shoulder doing a swan dive. He was hospitalized and placed in a cast that extended from his waist to his shoulder, with his arm extended at shoulder level. In the midst of his troubles, he was trying to arrange for Scottie's admission to the Ethel Walker School, in Simsbury, Connecticut, but at a reduction in rates, because he could not afford the regular tuition. (Gerald Murphy had recommended it as one of the top-flight girls' schools in the country.) Next, he had a bad fall in the bathroom while still in his cast. He had lain there for hours without help. He developed an arthritic condition that kept him in bed for seven weeks.

The August issue of *Esquire* carried his "Afternoon of an Author," an essay-story about a failed and failing author in a routine day of work. But the same issue also carried Hemingway's story "The Snows of Kilimanjaro," in which a writer dying of gangrene on the plains of Africa reflects on the corrupting influences of the rich, including his wife. Hemingway's hero, Harry, thinks back on "poor Scott Fitzgerald," who was in awe of the rich and once began a story, "The very rich are different from you and me." And someone — patently Hemingway — had answered, "Yes, they have more money." It would become the literary retort of the decade. In what appears to be Hemingway's response to Fitzgerald's "Crack-Up" essays, Hemingway's hero remarks that Fitzgerald thought the rich were a special glamorous race: "When he found they weren't it wrecked him just as much as any other thing that wrecked him."

In measured terms, Fitzgerald wrote Hemingway a brief note asking that he lay off him in print. "If I choose to write *de profundis* sometimes it doesn't mean I want friends praying aloud over my corpse." He asked Hemingway to drop his name from the story when it was reprinted. "Riches," he told Hemingway, "have *never* fascinated me, unless combined with the greatest charm or distinction." Hemingway's answer is lost, but Scott told Max Perkins it was a "crazy letter" in which Hemingway said he was a Great Writer and that he loved his children. "To have answered it would have been like fooling with a lit firecracker," Fitzgerald said. No matter what Hemingway did, Fitzgerald still loved the man, but another crack like that, and Fitzgerald would have to throw his weight with the gang that was laying for Hemingway. "No one," Fitzgerald said, "could ever hurt him in his first books but he has completely lost his head."

Writing to Beatrice Dance about the confrontation, Fitzgerald said that he was proud of the way he had handled the situation. Hemingway had written him, saying that since Fitzgerald had so "shamelessly" exhibited his private life in *Esquire,* he felt it was open season. The letter Fitzgerald had written in reply — "a hell of a letter" — would have meant sudden death for somebody the next time they had met. But he had decided not to send it. He considered that a sign of maturity on his part. Hemingway, he wrote Beatrice, was "quite as nervously broken down as I am but it manifests itself in different ways. His inclination is toward megalomania and mine toward melancholy."

In the three-sided correspondence between Hemingway, Fitzgerald, and Perkins, in which Perkins served as a kind of clearinghouse, Hemingway had already told Perkins that Fitzgerald's letter surprised him, considering that he had written "those awful things about himself" in *Esquire.* He said that he told Scott that for five years he had refrained from writing about people he knew because he was sorry for them, but he was now going to stop being a gentleman and return to being a novelist. It was evidently meant to be a snide paraphrase of the attitude that Fitzgerald said he was adopting in the last of his "Crack-Up" articles.

Although he had been feeding Hemingway reports on Fitzgerald's personal life that were bound to prompt Hemingway's scorn, Perkins thought that Hemingway's remarks in print were contemptible. He did not say so to Hemingway, of course — in fact, he had complimented the writer on "The Snows of Kilimanjaro." Like Arnold Gingrich, who had first published the story and had seen the letter Hemingway wrote to Fitzgerald (he described it as "brutal"; said it was written in language "you'd hesitate to use on a yellow dog"), Perkins did not want to alienate Hemingway. But he bared the real story behind the story in a letter to a cousin. Perkins and Hemingway and the literary critic Mary Colum had been lunching together when Hemingway made a passing remark about his wealthy acquaintances: "I am getting to know the rich." And it was Mary Colum who had made the famous rejoinder that the only difference between the rich and other people was that the rich had more money.

Considering the circumstances, Perkins' letter to Fitzgerald was rather bland: "As for what Ernest did, I resented it, and when it comes to book publication, I shall have it out with him. It is odd about it too, because I was present when that reference was made to the rich and the retort given, and you were many miles away."

In the early evening of September 2, 1936, Fitzgerald's mother died. She had been in a hospital, terminally ill. Her death was no shock and seems not to have precipitated any crisis in Fitzgerald's life. But, anticipating it, he had actually written what turned out to be a preliminary obituary for her in the form of one of his fictional-factual essays, "An Author's Mother," which happened to be published in the September issue of *Esquire*. The description of the "halting old lady in a black silk dress and a rather preposterously high-crowned hat that some milliner had foisted upon her declining sight" was clearly the Mollie Fitzgerald of her son's photograph albums. "An Author's Mother" is not a cruel characterization, though it has comic touches. Fitzgerald gives a sly account of "Mrs. Johnston's" relations with her son, who is a successful author:

> She had by no means abetted him in the choice of that profession but had wanted him to be an army officer or else go into business like his brother. An author was something distinctly peculiar — there had been only one in the middle western city where she was born and he had been regarded as a freak. Of course if her son could have been an author like Longfellow. . . .

Mrs. Johnston's preference is for poets like Alice and Phoebe Cary, and for the more popular novelists, like Mrs. Humphrey Ward, and her current favorite, Edna Ferber. (This was Fitzgerald's sly dig at Ferber, who, in a symposium in *Vanity Fair*, called "The Ten Dullest Authors," had listed F. Scott Fitzgerald among her choices.) It is while visiting a bookshop in search of a volume of the Cary sisters' poetry that Mrs. Johnston collapses and is carried off to the hospital.

There is, perhaps, some inkling of Fitzgerald's sentiments about his mother in the essay and in a letter he had written to his sister, Annabel, earlier in the summer. Fitzgerald had had to arrange for his mother's transferral to either a hospital or a nursing home and for putting her belongings into storage.

> It was sad taking her from the hotel [he wrote Annabel], the only home she knew for fifteen years, to die — and to go thru her things. The slippers and corset she was married in, Louisa's dolls in tissue paper, old letters and souvenirs, and collected scrap paper, and diaries that began and got nowhere, all her prides and sorrows and disappointments all come to nothing, and her lugged away like so much useless flesh. . . .

But there is at least a suspicion that he had revealed his lack of any deep feeling for his mother by writing and arranging for the publication of his obituary story before the event; he had hustled the old lady off the scene in advance of her actual exit.

Mollie Fitzgerald left her son approximately $23,000, his half of the estate minus the money he had borrowed from her over the past few years. Her legacy, Fitzgerald wrote Beatrice Dance, was "the luckiest event of some time." It seemed a special providence. "She was a defiant old woman, defiant in her love for me in spite of my neglect of her, and it would have been quite within her character to have died that I might live." But like much good fortune, it was not immediately accessible. Under Maryland law, Fitzgerald had to wait six months before he could claim his inheritance, and in the meantime Maryland banks would not lend him money with his inheritance as collateral. He was in dire need of cash — to pay bills, keep up his life insurance, pay for his accident and Zelda's treatment and Scottie's schooling. He pressed Annabel, who was handling the estate matters, to convert the inheritance to cash as soon as possible. It was another of those situations in which, during recent years — and with what bitterness and subdued hostility it is hard to tell — he found it necessary to explain the status of his drinking to family, friends, his editor, his agent, Zelda's psychiatrists. Writing to Annabel, he said that he needed six or eight weeks free of worry about anything and free from the pressures of writing. He was becoming a nervous wreck at the age of forty.

> There is no use of reproaching me for past extravagances [he wrote], nor my failure to get control of the liquor situation under these conditions of strain. During this time I have been in a night club exactly three times and have used the liquor for purposes of work or of accomplishing some duty for which I no longer have the physical or nervous energy. I am completely on the spot.

The well-favored might move with ease in the world, but a man like Fitzgerald, who had so publicly ruined himself, now had to face in the mirror the daily reminder of his excuses, his lies, his evasions. In the end, the law did not move quickly enough. Fitzgerald was forced to send desperate telegrams to his old friend Oscar Kalman and to Max Perkins, asking for loans against his legacy.

Then, on his fortieth birthday, while he was still recovering from his accident, he had another shaming experience. A reporter from the *New York Post,* Michel Mok, came to interview him at the

Grove Park Inn in Asheville, where he was now living, under the care of a nurse. It could hardly have been unexpected—considering the revelations of his "Crack-Up" articles—that the reporter carefully observed every feature of his behavior. Mok noted his frequent trips to the drawer in a highboy where Fitzgerald had a bottle and the frequent pouring of a drink into the measuring glass on the bedside table and the expectant look at the nurse, with Fitzgerald saying, "Just one ounce?" He noted the trembling hands, the twitching face—the anatomy of failure. Fitzgerald later said that the reporter had pieced together his remarks from the "Crack-Up" articles and that he had said none of them during the interview. But Mok recorded that awful mixture of boasting and whining that characterized Fitzgerald's alcoholic performances. "A writer like me," he told Mok, "must have an utter confidence, and utter faith in his star. It's an almost mystical feeling. . . ." Thomas Wolfe and Ernest Hemingway both had that characteristic quality, he said. "I once had it. But through a series of blows, many of them my own fault, something happened to that sense of immunity and I lost my grip."

In an expansive mood (he was now countering the nurse's disapproving look, each time he took a drink, by saying, "Much against your better judgment, my dear") he began telling Mok about exploits during his army days, the episodes of Camp Mills, the dubious story of his commandeering a train to Washington. In the wake of his mother's death, he talked about his father and his father's Civil War stories, adding, "My father lost his grip and I lost my grip. But now I'm trying to get back." Much of the information that Mok reported could never have been scratched up by research. Fitzgerald maintained that his comeback had begun with the *Esquire* articles: "Perhaps they were a mistake. Too much *de profundis*"—using the same phrase he had written to Hemingway. "My best friend, a great American writer—he's the man I call my artistic conscience in one of the *Esquire* articles—wrote me a furious letter. He said I was stupid to write that gloomy personal stuff."

However disparaging the Mok interview may have been, it strikes one as extremely accurate reportage. Fitzgerald had never learned to keep his mouth shut when drunk. Toward the end, there was even that sense of growing belligerence that characterized Fitzgerald at his worst moments. Mok, clearly baiting the author on controversial issues, asked about politics. Fitzgerald replied, "My views? Well, in a pinch, they'd still be pretty much toward the left." Asked about his Jazz Age contemporaries, he said: "Why should I bother myself about them? . . . Haven't I enough worries of my own? You know as well as I do what has happened to them. Some became brokers and threw themselves out of windows. Others became bankers and shot themselves. Still others became newspaper reporters." After that sally against his interviewer he added, "And a few became successful authors." Fitzgerald then stumbled over to the highboy for another drink, saying, "Successful authors . . . Oh, my God, successful authors!"

The article appeared in the *Post* on the following day, September 25, under the headline THE OTHER SIDE OF PARADISE: SCOTT FITZGERALD, 40, ENGULFED IN DESPAIR. The story was picked up by *Time* and given even wider circulation. In his anguish, considering himself ruined, Fitzgerald took an overdose of morphine, but fortunately vomited it up almost immediately. "The nurse came in & saw the empty phial & there was hell to pay. . . ." Fitzgerald wrote Ober, "afterwards I felt like a fool." Strangely, he turned to Hemingway, sending him a telegram that mentioned the Mok article and saying, IF YOU EVER WANTED TO HELP ME YOUR CHANCE IS NOW. Then he sent a second: WIRED UNDER IMPRESSION THAT YOU WERE IN NEW YORK NOTHING CAN BE DONE AT LONG RANGE AND ON COOLER CONSIDERATION SEEMS NOTHING TO BE DONE ANYHOW THANKS BEST ALWAYS SCOTT. It was becoming a life spelled out in newspaper headlines and in block letters on telegrams.

He had been glad "to say goodbye to the most calamitous year" of his life. It had ended during the Christmas holidays with a tea dance given for Scottie at the Hotel Belvedere in Baltimore. Fitzgerald had made elaborate plans for it with Margaret Turnbull and one or two other hostesses. He had positively vetoed Scottie's idea of a swing band and a guest list of ninety. "If I had thought that the Ethel Walker School was going to give you a peculiar idea of what your financial resources are, it would have been far, far better to send you to a modest school here in the Carolina mountains. You are a poor girl, and if you don't like to think about it just ask me." His plans were very definite. He wrote her, "Remember that I expect you and your crowd to dance by the hurdy-gurdy during the whole afternoon, quietly and slowly and without swing music, just doing simple waltz dancing." He seems to have lost touch with the younger generation, children of fifteen and sixteen. But as a concession, he said that Scottie might bring in some of her "choice" friends to dance to the swing orchestra that he had hired for the adults.

The party, held on December 22, started well, but Fitzgerald took to visiting the bar and then, not too steady on his feet, began dancing with the young girls. Some looked "scared or embarrassed"; others giggled behind his back. Mostly, Andrew Turnbull noted, "those who realized what was happening tried to pretend he wasn't there." Abruptly, Fitzgerald told all the guests to go home. He paid the orchestra to stay on, however, took a seat, put a bottle of gin on the table, and sat there drinking—the lonely celebrant at a party that was over.

Scottie spent Christmas with her friend Peaches Finney and her family, then went to Asheville to visit her mother. Fitzgerald went to the Johns Hopkins University Hospital for several days of drying-out and recovery from a case of the flu with a temperature of 104 degrees. On January 2, he wrote Harold Ober, "I'm all right now —(back on the absolute wagon, by the way.)"

I I

Since August 1936, Harold Ober had been trying to sell Fitzgerald to Hollywood. "I think those confounded *Esquire* articles have done you a great deal of harm and I hope you won't do any more," he told his author. He had tried to convince Edwin Knopf, the story editor for MGM, that Fitzgerald was perfectly capable of serious work. But Fitzgerald's accident had precluded any move to the West Coast, and Knopf, in any event, seems to have had difficulty in persuading the reluctant studio officials to hire Fitzgerald.

Fitzgerald's income that year hit a low ebb—only $10,180. And that included the $2000 fee he received for an improbable fourth-rate love story titled "Trouble," which involved a nurse with that nickname, an alcoholic suitor, and a resident in orthopedics. It was the last story he sold to *The Saturday Evening Post,* which had been the mainstay of his career as a popular writer. His stories and articles were not selling well. One of them, in fact—originally titled "Thumbs Up"—was turned down by thirteen publications and re-vised over a three-year period before it was finally accepted by *Collier's.* The dismal statistics of Ober's difficulties in placing Fitzgerald's work is evidence of his doggedness on his client's behalf. Fitzgerald, staying at Oak Hall in Tryon, North Carolina, tried hard to convince his agent that he was hard at work; he referred to a pile of false starts on his desk and assured him that he had been off liquor for months. But he produced little that was notable during the early months of 1937.

It was not until June that he heard from Ober that negotiations with MGM had started up once more and that Knopf would be in New York for a personal interview. Fitzgerald was hesitant. He was looking forward to the trip to New York, he said, except for "meeting Mr. Knopf of the movies & being looked over." But evidently he had been convincing enough for Metro, at the end of the month, to make an offer of $1000 a week for six months for a position as screenwriter with an option for renewal at $1250. Fitzgerald wired his acceptance on July 2 and made plans for leaving. He also outlined a schedule of payments that Ober was to take out of his weekly checks in order to pay off his debts to the agency, as well as money borrowed from Perkins and Scribner's. Writing to Scottie after a hasty departure, he confessed: "I feel a certain excitement. The third Hollywood venture. Two failures behind me, though one no fault of mine." But he planned to profit from those earlier experiences, he told his daughter in a spate of professional talk. "I must be very tactful but keep my hand on the wheel from the start." The most important thing was to be in charge of the script himself, whatever the appearances might be. Given a break, he felt, he could make them double his contract in less than two years. He seemed to be having a revival of his old ebullience.

Fitzgerald took an apartment in one of the two-story bungalows in the Garden of Allah Hotel on Sunset Boulevard. It had once been the estate of the silent screen star Alla Nazimova, and was populated with friends and acquaintances from Fitzgerald's past. They were mainly the old crowd of Algonquin wits who had been transplanted bodily to the West Coast and settled beside the Baltic-shaped swimming pool among the tall, scrawny, and obscene-looking palm trees. Dottie Parker was living at the Garden of Allah with her husband, Alan Campbell; so were Marc Connelly and Robert Benchley. Benchley had been immensely touched when Fitzgerald sent him an inscribed copy of *Tender Is the Night*. "I would have given my two expensively-filled eye-teeth to have written just one page of the book," he said. Benchley's bungalow was the perennially convivial meeting place for the group, which also included Fitzgerald's old Minnesota protégé Donald Ogden Stewart, now a well-established screenwriter and an activist in Communist Party causes. Fitzgerald's opinion of him had softened not at all. Stewart, it appears, was claiming that he was a much better radical for having gone through the tempering fires of living at ease among the Whitneys and surviving the big money of Hollywood. After Stewart's "long pull at the mammalia of the Whitneys," Fitzgerald wrote a friend, "he ought to be able to swim under a long way." Dottie Parker, "the precious lazybones," seemed to complain a lot that she had never had to work so hard in her life. It was obviously difficult to continue with his own writing, but Fitzgerald said that he had contrived a "special stunt to beat the game"; he got up at six and worked until nine on his own writing before he reported to the studio.

When Fitzgerald arrived in Hollywood, Irving Thalberg was already a legend of the past. He had died of pneumonia in September 1936. The studio building in which Fitzgerald worked had been named after the wonder boy of the film industry, but Louis B. Mayer was now the mogul of the back lots and the fake streets. ("Isn't God good to me?" Mayer was supposed to have said, riding back from the funeral of his younger rival.) But though Fitzgerald stated that he admired Thalberg enormously, he came to the odd conclusion that Thalberg's death was the death of an enemy. Thalberg, he declared, had had "an idea that his wife and I were playing around, which was absolute nonsense." It is difficult to tell whether Fitzgerald's idea of Thalberg's jealousy had preceded or followed the writing of his story "Crazy Sunday." But what mostly had turned him against his former idol was his belief that it was Thalberg who had killed his hopes of selling *Tender Is the Night* to Metro. He was unwilling to acknowledge that his drunken phone call had not helped his prospects very much.

Things seem to have started well with the first script he was given, a rewrite of *A Yank at Oxford,* which was to star Robert Taylor and Maureen O'Sullivan. And he was, it seems, impressed when the actress invited him out to Malibu to discuss changes in those of her lines which she found unsatisfactory. A mint julep or two warmed Fitzgerald up. The actress remembered, "He strode about the room, with his arms waving in the air. It was a wonderful afternoon." But like many of Fitzgerald's Hollywood projects, the script went through endless revisions and conferences and only a few lines and a few scenes of his were left in the final version.

The glitter of Hollywood at first sifted down into his letters. He wrote to Anne Ober, Harold's wife, "I have seen Hollywood — talked with Taylor, dined with March, danced with Ginger Rogers (this will burn Scottie up but its true) been in Rosalind Russel's dressing room, wise-cracked with Montgomery, drunk (gingerale) with Zukor and Lasky, lunched alone with Maureen OSullivan. . . ." But Anita Loos, working in the Thalberg Building, had rather a different impression of Fitzgerald, who, it was clear, was making a conscientious effort to stay on the wagon. Loos wanted to avoid him, finding his sobriety rather more trying than his manic behavior when he was drunk. Scott had a habit of dropping by her office in apologetic fashion. "You don't really want to see me!" he would say. And after some brief chit-chat, he would leave, with the comment, "I know you want to get rid of me so I'll go now." Loos decided that "between being dangerous when drunk and eating humble pie when sober, I preferred Scott dangerous."

Shortly after his arrival, at a party at Robert Benchley's, Fitzgerald first saw Sheilah Graham, an up-and-coming young gossip columnist. The party was a double celebration, of Bastille Day and Graham's engagement to the Marquess of Donegall. Neither of them spoke to the other on that occasion, but Fitzgerald was studying her carefully from a corner of the room. He was smoking heavily but not drinking. He seemed to be struck by some fancied resemblance to Zelda. In fact, he would later romanticize that first meeting in his unfinished novel, The Last Tycoon, in the meeting of Monroe Stahr and Kathleen: "Smiling faintly at him from not four feet away was the face of his dead wife, identical even to the expression." But Fitzgerald left early. When Benchley told Graham who the man was, she was surprised. She had never read any of Fitzgerald's books, but when she found herself describing a woman no longer at her best, she thought she was talking about a Fitzgerald heroine.

Shortly after that, the two met at the Coconut Grove, at a dinner dance held by the Screen Writers Guild. Graham boldly suggested they dance. Unfortunately, Fitzgerald had promised the next one to Dorothy Parker, and it proved to be the last one before the speeches began. Then, on a Saturday night, Edwin Mayer, who had the other apartment in Fitzgerald's bungalow, asked Graham to dinner. Fitzgerald, he told her, was to be the other guest. The trio met for drinks at the Garden of Allah and then went on to a gambling place, the Clover Club, for dinner. Graham noticed that when Humphrey Bogart and his wife asked them to join them for a drink, Fitzgerald passed it up. She also noticed that people adopted a deferential tone when they spoke to the writer. When she danced with him, she was charmed by his conversation and his obvious and flattering attention.

Fitzgerald's first months at the studio were both busy and unsettling. In July, just before he met Sheilah Graham, Hemingway turned up in Hollywood for charity showings of *The Spanish Earth,* a film that he and Joris Ivens had shot in Spain for the benefit of the Loyalists in the Spanish Civil War. Fitzgerald had seen him only a month before, when Hemingway spoke at the Writers' Congress at Carnegie Hall in New York. The meeting had been seemingly cordial, in spite of their recent differences. "I wish we could meet more often," Fitzgerald wrote Hemingway afterward. "I don't feel I know you at all." But with Hemingway's arrival in Hollywood, Fitzgerald was overcome by a strange reluctance even to be in Hemingway's presence. There was a special showing of the film at the home of Frederic March and his wife, the actress Florence Eldridge, at which Hemingway, an effective fund-raiser, managed to raise several thousands of dollars for ambulances. Dorothy Parker invited a number of people, including Fitzgerald, to her apartment for a nightcap. Fitzgerald offered to bring Lillian Hellman, whom he had met earlier in Paris, though he seemed strangely vague about their meeting. When they drove off, she noticed how tentative he was, driving his secondhand car at a mere ten or twelve miles an hour down Sunset Boulevard. She also noticed that his hands were trembling, and she placed her own over his as a steadying gesture. At the Garden of Allah, Fitzgerald was very reluctant to go in; he said he was "riding low" in Hollywood. Hellman countered, "Not for writers." Fitzgerald, who was on the wagon, said, "I'm afraid of Ernest, I guess, scared of being sober when . . ." Hellman managed to get him inside, but at just that moment Hemingway, standing with his back to the doorway, threw a glass into the fireplace. That unsettled Fitzgerald even more. It was the last time the two men met, and it is uncertain whether they talked together. Hellman tried to get Dashiell Hammett to talk to Fitzgerald, but Hammett was drinking heavily himself and seemed to block out the whole conversation in order to continue discussing with someone a theory he had about Hemingway's inability to portray a woman in his books. When Hellman turned to look for Fitzgerald, he was gone. Fitzgerald later sent Hemingway an ambiguous telegram: THE PICTURE WAS BEYOND PRAISE AND SO WAS YOUR ATTITUDE. A letter that Fitzgerald sent to Max Perkins about their meeting does not suggest any hard feelings, only that awed attitude Fitzgerald had toward Hemingway. "Ernest came like a whirlwind. . . ." Fitzgerald wrote Perkins. "I felt he was in a state of nervous tensity, that there was something almost religious about it."

In August, Scottie came for an Alice-in-Wonderland visit to Hollywood, accompanied by Helen Hayes. She stayed with Hayes and her husband, Charles MacArthur, at the Beverly Hills Hotel, rather than with her father. There were dinners with the poet Stephen Vincent Benét and his wife and Zoë Akins, as well as Norma Shearer; Scottie thought them glamorous. Helen Hayes felt that Fitzgerald was distinctly uncomfortable with Norma Shearer, perhaps remembering his last, awkward party at her house. But Fitzgerald seemed in bright spirits about Scottie's visit. "All goes beautifully here so far," he told Perkins. "Scottie is having the time of her young life, dining with Crawford, Scheerer, ect, talking to Fred Astaire & her other heroes. I am very proud of her."

It was just after Scottie arrived that Fitzgerald and Sheilah Graham became sexually involved. He had called to break a date, and she suggested that he bring Scottie with him. Fitzgerald was reluctant, then agreed. Fitzgerald also brought along two young boy friends of Scottie's, and the company went to the Trocadero for the evening. Fitzgerald was nervous and fidgety all evening, correcting his daughter in front of the boys, telling her to sit straight, to finish her meat. Graham felt sorry for the girl as her father sat at the table, chain-smoking, drumming his fingers, and ruining his daughter's evening. That night, after she and Fitzgerald took the boys home and dropped Scottie off at the MacArthurs', Sheilah Graham had a rather different glimpse of the man who had been so charming on their earlier date. Now he was a graying father with thinning hair, and she was nonplussed. And then, unexpectedly, she asked him in.

She would write two lengthy accounts of her three-and-a-half-year affair with the writer — an affair that lasted to the end of his life. The first, *Beloved Infidel,* written in collaboration with Gerald

Frank, was published in 1958. And though it is revealing enough about their quarrels and reconciliations, about Fitzgerald's disastrous binges and equally disastrous behavior, it has some of the taint of the celebrity memoir. She later recalled that it was filmed through gauze, partly because of her memories about the many good times they had had together and partly because of her unwillingness to face up to the more destructive qualities of Fitzgerald's nature. The second, *The Real F. Scott Fitzgerald,* was published in 1976, thirty-six years after Fitzgerald's death, and takes into account the more difficult sides of Fitzgerald's personality, which she had come to know about through biographies that dealt with his life before he met her. *The Real F. Scott Fitzgerald,* a franker book than its predecessor, attempts to put to rest some of the gossip and rumors about Fitzgerald and about their affair. It also seems a more balanced account of Fitzgerald as a man and as a writer. Graham maintains that Fitzgerald was not a passionate lover, but a gentle and satisfactory one; she thus presumably counters the charges that Zelda made about her husband's sexual inadequacies and that Hemingway broadcast to inquiring biographers after Fitzgerald's death. There was one oddity about their intimate relationship that Graham also reveals. "In all our time together, I don't remember seeing him naked. But I was just as shy about my own body." Despite the modesty, she says, "We satisfied each other and could lie in each other's arms for a long time afterwards, delighting in our proximity."

They were talkers: "In those first weeks Scott and I talked incessantly." Fitzgerald called Graham every day, wanting to know what she was doing, what she was wearing. His insistence on finding out everything about her past life, her British background, may have been partly the inquisitiveness of a novelist interested in a new character — which she did become, in *The Last Tycoon.* But there were some details of her past life that she concealed at first. She was born Lily Shiel in an East End London slum. At an early age she was sent to an orphanage. There had been a secret marriage to an English major, John Gillam, from whom she was now divorced. She had been presented at Buckingham Palace. When still very young, she had determined to become famous, and she had taken the name Sheilah Graham when she became a member of Charles Cochran's Young Beauties — the English equivalent of the Ziegfeld Girls. She had had a remarkable success as a musical comedy star before she came to the United States. If Fitzgerald was struck by Sheilah Graham's resemblance to Zelda, there may have been another association in his mind, as well—with the little English actress and musical comedy star Rosalinde Fuller, whom he had known at the outset of his career and whom he had used in his earliest stories.

❧❧

After the disappointment of *A Yank at Oxford,* Fitzgerald was involved in his most successful screen venture, the only film for which he received a screen credit during his various assaults on Hollywood. For Fitzgerald, the condition of success was to be able to work without collaborators, and he was given the opportunity in this project, a screen treatment of Erich Maria Remarque's *Three Comrades,* an anti-Nazi drama set in Germany during the rise of Hitler. It was to be a starring vehicle for Robert Taylor, Franchot Tone, and Robert Young, the young comrades, and Margaret Sullavan, playing the tubercular heroine who dies in a hospital. He was under the supervision of Joseph Mankiewicz, who was both a producer and a writer and who had definite ideas about film scripts. Fitzgerald worked steadily on the project and seems to have been confident enough about the major part of the script that he turned in to Mankiewicz just before leaving in early September to bring Scottie back east and to visit Zelda in Asheville. But he was concerned that Mankiewicz might assign him a collaborator. On September 9, Mankiewicz wired him that he should stop reading "ALL THOSE NASTY STORIES ABOUT MOTION PICTURE PRODUCERS THEY'RE NOT TRUE." The rumor that he was assigning another writer was "BUSHWAH."

The trip home was not all that happy. He took Scottie and Zelda to Charleston, South Carolina, and to Myrtle Beach for a few days of swimming and sunning. Zelda was no better, Fitzgerald wrote Beatrice Dance: "She held up well enough but there is always a gradual slipping. I've become hard there and don't feel the grief I did once — except sometimes at night or when I catch myself in some spiritual betrayal of the past." She was restless and wanted to be allowed to pay a visit to Montgomery on her own, but Fitzgerald felt she wasn't ready for it. Writing to Zelda's psychiatrists, he said that she didn't have judgment enough, that a few drinks of sherry or a few highballs would set her off into "completely irresponsible channels," and there wasn't anyone strong enough in Montgomery to handle her. It was a worry he referred to often; at times, it seems to have been a projection of his worries about his own sobriety. But the content of his letters to Dr. Carroll and Dr. R. Burke Suitt was that he was clearly weaning himself from the hurt of the relationship. Distance seemed to be making it possible.

When Fitzgerald got back to Hollywood, he learned that Mankiewicz, in spite of the reassuring words, had assigned Ted Paramore as Fitzgerald's collaborator. Paramore, Edmund Wilson's high-flying, heavy-drinking friend of the twenties, was now a practiced screenwriter. Zelda, learning of the new collaboration, recalled Paramore's visits to the honeymoon cottage in Westport, and she wrote to Fitzgerald: "Give Paramour my regards and affectionate remembrances — Tell him how good looking he is — We used to have a lot of fun." But Fitzgerald, during the time they worked together, considered him a weak sister and a hack. Occasionally, it seems, the two hurled charges of pedantry and prudery at each other. Paramore was too ready to consult with Mankiewicz, and Fitzgerald clearly wanted to make decisions himself.

Perhaps because of disappointment and frustration, or as a result of his visit east, Fitzgerald slipped off the wagon. The excuse that he gave was that Sheilah Graham had been out on a date with another man. Fitzgerald, who knew of the date, had called her home several times. Graham had gotten home a few minutes later than expected, and when Fitzgerald finally reached her, he told her he had started drinking and she was the cause of it. He seemed to be punishing her. But Graham noted afterward that Fitzgerald had had more than one excuse for what turned out to be a week-long binge. Ginevra King, recently divorced and visiting in Santa Barbara, invited Fitzgerald to come see her. His hesitation is evident in a letter he sent Scottie:

> She was the first girl I ever loved and I have faithfully avoided seeing her up to this moment to keep that illusion perfect, because she ended up by throwing me over with the most supreme boredom and indifference. I don't know whether I should go or not. It would be very, very strange. These great beauties are often something else at thirty-eight, but Ginevra had a great deal besides beauty.

Ginevra decided to meet him in Hollywood. They had lunch, and Fitzgerald, nervous, began drinking. It upset her, because she knew he had been on the wagon. Then for several days after the lunch, still on the bender he blamed on Sheilah Graham, Fitzgerald gave up the pursuit of old illusions. "She is still a charming woman," Fitzgerald wrote Scottie, "and I'm sorry I didn't see more of her."

Sheilah Graham was unaware that Fitzgerald had been on a binge until he turned up at the airport to accompany her on a trip to Chicago. She had been having problems with the sponsors of her radio broadcast, who objected to her nervous delivery and more so to her pronounced British accent. They thought that it might be better for her to give her five-minute talk from Chicago, without the interference of relays to Hollywood. At the airport lounge Fitzgerald ordered a double gin, then another and another — gulping them down. During the flight, he became boisterous, telling the other passengers what "a great lay" Sheilah was, announcing that he was F. Scott Fitzgerald, the author of *The Great Gatsby*. At Albuquerque, she told him to get off and go back to Hollywood: he was of no help and would only make her more nervous. Fitzgerald left, only to return with another bottle of gin, the purchase of which was the real purpose for his getting off the plane.

It got worse; at the Drake Hotel in Chicago, Fitzgerald chased a busboy around the room when he brought another bottle of gin and stood waiting for a tip. Then he threatened Graham's sponsor when he called at the hotel and would not give a definite commitment that Sheilah's broadcast would be aired. He finally punched the man in the mouth. Graham went into hysterics, lying on the floor, kicking her feet, and screaming, "You have ruined me! I hate you, I never want to see you again!" Fitzgerald left, but he turned up at the rehearsal hall, trying to direct her performance. He had to be escorted out by stagehands. Somewhere in the midst of his mindless behavior during the trip he also managed to call her a "cunt" in front of the film critic for the *Chicago Daily News*. But the most gruesome vignette (it is included in her earlier memoir) was the sight of Fitzgerald in his hotel room, being fed by Arnold Gingrich, the editor of *Esquire,* whom Fitzgerald had called. Scott, wearing a napkin tucked under his chin like a bib, tried to bite Gingrich's hand as he shoveled forkfuls of steak into his mouth. Fitzgerald was not allowed aboard the midnight flight to Hollywood; Graham had to ride him around in a taxi until the next flight, which was five hours later. When they did manage to get back to Los Angeles, Fitzgerald was unable to work; he called the studio to say he was sick, with the expectable result that rumors about his drinking began to circulate again. As he had done in the past—in Baltimore—Fitzgerald, after a long bout of drinking, would hire a trained nurse and go through the process of drying out. It became standard practice for him not to see Graham during these periods. He would call her when he was all right.

Fitzgerald and Paramore had only the poorest of working relationships, which worsened after Fitzgerald's drinking became noticeable. "We got off to a bad start," Fitzgerald wrote to his collaborator late in October, "and I think you are under certain misapprehensions founded more on my state of mind and body last Friday than upon the real situation. My script is in a general way approved of. There was not any question of taking it out of my hands." The studio renewed his option for another year—at $1250 a week—but his drinking and behavior did not help with the scriptwriting of *Three Comrades*. Fitzgerald and Paramore turned in the final version in February 1938, but Mankiewicz was dissatisfied and began rewriting it himself. When Margaret Sullavan complained about the original dialogue, Mankiewicz improvised new material on the set. Fitzgerald wrote angry and snide letters to Mankiewicz and the studio executives, but Sheilah Graham apparently managed to persuade him not to send them. His letter to the executives had pointed out that he was a highly successful author, capable of producing what the audience wanted. It contained pompous statements about his "writing over a hundred and fifty stories for George Lorimer, the great editor of *The Saturday Evening Post*." In the letter to Mankiewicz, he wrote:

> To say I'm disillusioned is putting it mildly. For nineteen years, with two years out for sickness, I've written best-selling entertainment, and my dialogue is supposedly right up at the top. But I learn from the script that you've suddenly decided that it isn't good dialogue and you can take a few hours off and do much better. I think you now have a flop on your hands—as thoroughly naive as *The Bride Wore Red* but utterly inexcusable because this time you *had* something and you have arbitrarily and carelessly torn it to pieces.

Aside from disgruntled writers, Mankiewicz had other troubles over the screening of *Three Comrades*. The German consul in Los Angeles had been given a private viewing of some of the scenes and had objected to the anti-Nazi ideology of the film. When Joseph Breen, the industry censor, suggested that the problem might be solved by turning the Nazis into communists, Mankiewicz threatened to resign from MGM. According to one story, when Fitzgerald learned of this act of courage, he stopped Mankiewicz in the studio commissary, threw his arms around him, and kissed him. But it must have been only a passing truce, and he did not seem to believe in the studio's resolve. Writing to Harold Ober, he complained, "The truth of the matter is that the heart is out of the script and it will not be a great picture, unless I am very much mistaken." Somewhat caustically, he added, "I have been watching the taking of the mob scenes which ought to be excellent if they were about anything, now that the German Consul has had its say."

It was part of the marvelous magic of Hollywood in the mid-thirties that inconvenient political realities could be altered, that a few retakes could change Nazis into communists. Despite the fact that Fitzgerald railed against left-leaning friends like Donald Ogden Stewart and Dorothy Parker, who were active in the Screen Writers Guild, he still professed to be a liberal, if not a fellow traveler. (He had an odd disdain for Marxist-oriented writers. "They try to be Jesus . . . while I only attempt to be God, which is easier," he wrote in his notebooks.) But his views often seemed to be a matter of expediency rather than conviction or commitment. Concerned as he was about his daughter's education, he wanted to instill in Scottie a sense of the political probabilities at the outset of her freshman year at Vassar.

> You will notice that there is a strongly organized left-wing movement there [he wrote her]. I do not particularly want you to think about politics, but I do *not* want you to set yourself against this movement. I am known as a left-wing sympathizer and would be proud if you were. In any case, I should feel outraged if you identified yourself with Nazism or Red-baiting in any form. Some of those radical girls may not look like much now but in your lifetime they are liable to be high in the councils of the nations.

But if Fitzgerald had developed a leftist reputation in Hollywood, it was of little use to him. Ring Lardner, Jr., a young screenwriter at the time, active in the Screen Writers Guild, recalled: "Scott thought of himself as quite a communist at this time, but the CP wouldn't have permitted him to join even if he'd wanted to since he was considered too unreliable because of his drinking. But he did speak in 'progressive terms.' "

Joseph Mankiewicz maintained that he had never received Fitzgerald's letter. He said that Fitzgerald's problem in Hollywood was that he was too literary as a screenwriter, that he wrote "very bad spoken dialogue." The published script of the Fitzgerald screenplay for *Three Comrades* suggests that Mankiewicz was not altogether wrong. The dialogue is indeed pedestrian, but the greater problem seems to have been that Fitzgerald wrote down to his audience in a vein of maudlin sentimentality and heavy-handed cleverness. At times, he was positively mawkish. In one incredible scene, his hero, Bobby, puts through a telephone call to the heroine, Pat. It goes through a switchboard operated by a white-winged angel:

> *Angel* (sweetly)
> One moment, please — I'll connect you with heaven.
> CUT TO:
> > THE PEARLY GATES
> > St. Peter, the caretaker, sitting beside
> > another switchboard.
> *St. Peter* (cackling)
> I think she's in.

When Fitzgerald wrote what he considered his trashy commercial stories, the sheer literary style, the command of atmosphere, the perfected insights — the elements that could not be conveyed by camera — managed to redeem the contrived plots, the sometimes corny dialogue. Screenwriting mercilessly exposed his weaknesses.

Even so, Fitzgerald clung to his Hollywood ambitions, however cynically. To Anne Ober, he wrote, "The point is once you've got it — Screen Credit first, a Hit second, and the Academy Award third — you can count on it forever — like Laurence Stallings. . . . But till we get those three accolades we Hollywood boys keep trying." The remainder of Fitzgerald's career at MGM, however, was a case of piecemeal efforts, shunting from one job to another, putting in time on screenplays that were not used or not produced. Fitzgerald worked on *Infidelity,* a script based on a short story by Ursula Parrott, a screenwriter herself, intended for Joan Crawford under the direction of Hunt Stromberg. That film, too, ran into problems with the industry censors, who objected to the title. At MGM, one of the more ingenious solutions considered was simply to change the title to *Fidelity*. But Fitzgerald's script was not used. The most significant achievement of that episode in his film-writing career was Fitzgerald's vivid description of Joan Crawford's acting talents. "You can never give her such a stage direction as 'telling a lie' because if you did, she would practically give a representation of Benedict Arnold selling West Point to the British," Fitzgerald wrote Gerald Murphy. The remainder of his career at MGM was not much more productive; he put in time on *Marie Antoinette, The Women,* and *Madame Curie* — but in Hollywood fashion, after revisions and conferences, his work was not used.

He did, however, earn his screen credit for *Three Comrades,* the first of the rungs up the ladder to Hollywood success. The movie, with Mankiewicz's revisions, was a critical success when it was released in the summer of 1938. Margaret Sullavan's performance was nominated for an Academy Award. Zelda, when she saw the film, wired her congratulations: MISTERS FITZGERALD AND PARA-MORE HAVE ADAPTED THE BOOK FAITHFULLY AND DISCRIMI-NATELY RETAINING ITS LIGHTER PASSAGES WITHOUT SAC-RIFICING ITS HEAVIER ONES. . . . But Fitzgerald was under no illusions. He wrote Beatrice Dance: "I am now considered a success in Hollywood because something which I did not write is going on under my name, and something which I did write has been quietly buried without any fuss or row — not even a squeak from me. The change from regarding this as a potential art to looking at it as a cynical business has begun." If she should see the film, Fitzgerald told her, "only credit me with the parts you like."

He must have had a sense of being a man who had lost touch with his own identity, lost faith in his own talents. The evidence for this is a comic postcard that he wrote to himself during his stay at the bungalow-hotel on Sunset Boulevard. It read: "Dear Scott — How are you? Have been meaning to come in and see you. I have [been] living at the Garden of Allah. Yours, Scott Fitzgerald."

III

Early in 1938, Sheilah Graham began to dread the trips Fitzgerald took east to visit Zelda. He had weathered the first one in a relatively stable mood, but another one, early in the year, had been a different story. Fitzgerald had taken Zelda to Miami and Palm Beach. He reported to Scottie that Zelda was better than expected and that the trip would have been more fun if he hadn't been so tired. But something apparently had set him off, because on his return, he called Sheilah from the airport to say that he was getting divorced. When he arrived at her apartment, he was visibly drunk and made trips to his car, where he had stashed a bottle.

Writing to Dr. Carroll, Fitzgerald said that his slip off the wagon had lasted only three days; he had taken precautions that it would not occur again. He presented himself as a man with no more illusions about his future relationship with Zelda: "Certainly the outworn pretense that we can ever come together again is better for being shed. There is simply too much of the past between us. When that mist falls — at a dinner table, or between two pillows — no knight errant can traverse its immense distance. The mainsprings are gone." The letter was self-consciously literary, a muddle of metaphors. Fitzgerald could not be satisfied with presenting himself to Zelda's psychiatrist as a man and a husband confronting the inevitable; he wanted to be seen as a "literary" man. One of the more genuine portions of his letter is his admission that he could not quite let go of all that they had meant to each other: "So long as she is helpless, I'd never leave her or ever let her have a sense that she was deserted."

He was being harried by Zelda's family to let Zelda go home for extended periods of time. But Fitzgerald insisted that Mrs. Sayre was an "entirely irrational and conscienceless woman with the best intentions in the world." If it ever came to the point of a divorce, he would rather have Zelda continue under Dr. Carroll's care than her family's. But in an odd admission, Fitzgerald acknowledged that when he was with Zelda, sometimes "in order to turn her gratitude toward me" he gave her a few cigarettes and a few glasses of sherry, "in the spirit of a wickedly indulgent grandfather." In his letters to Dr. Carroll, there was usually a plea for sympathy for himself, as well. He worked hard, he said, and took care of himself. "I had a scare a few months ago when, for a long stretch, tuberculosis showed signs of coming back — just portents — weakness, loss of appetite, sweating. I took an X-Ray, lay very low for a few weeks, and the feeling passed."

In the spring Fitzgerald make a disastrous trip to Virginia Beach with Zelda and Scottie for what was supposed to be a family reunion. Fitzgerald got drunk, and Zelda went through the hotel corridors, telling everyone that her husband was dangerous and ought to be confined. Fitzgerald explained to the doctors that there were exonerating circumstances. Zelda had violently ambivalent reactions to Scottie, and they took the form of her coming to Fitzgerald, red-faced, and talking about the girl as if she were a criminal. They could stand being together for only a few hours at a time. His excuses for his own behavior took the usual medical form: "I had been physically run down and under a doctor's supervision for two months, working with help of injections of calsium, sodium, iron and liver, living on too much caffeine by day and sleeping on cloral at night and *touching no liquor*."

When he was in Hollywood, Zelda continued, through letters, to harass him. She alternated between pleading that she be allowed to leave the sanitarium to live with her mother, thus saving money, and being angry and abusive about his niggardliness in paying for extras for her. She asked for special gifts — clothes, belts, perfumes, slippers — and could be comical in her harping when they weren't received. "Did Mr. Goldwyn eat my slippers?" she asked in one of her letters. At other times, she was adamant. "I am a very extravagant woman; I am a Jezebel — However that may be the money is gone," she wrote him during one of her visits to Montgomery. In a hodgepodge inventory and in an angry scrawl, she carefully listed every recent expense — hats, dresses, onions, strawberries, loaves of bread, two cakes, laundry, Kotex, and hair tonic. "It seems a lot: it is a lot, but its all indispensible and as you know I cant shop in Asheville due to restriction."

But there were, too, the tender, grateful letters, thanking him for money, vacations, gifts:

> Dearest, I am always grateful for all the loyalties you gave me and I am always loyal to the concepts that held us together so long; the belief that life is tragic, that a mans spiritual reward is the keeping of his faith; that we shouldn't hurt each other. And I love always your fine writing talent, your tolerance and gener-

osity; and all your happy endowments. Nothing could have survived our life.

In a long and considered letter to Dr. Carroll, written in the spring of 1938, Fitzgerald tried to make plans about his financial arrangements for Zelda and her future treatment and to summarize the prospects for their lives. He wrote a first draft, but after many careful deletions he sent the doctor the second. He had been slowly and patiently paying off his old debts on the installment plan. (During the eighteen months he worked for Metro he earned about $85,000, but much of this had been used up in repayments of loans.) Zelda's hospitalization was costing $500 a month, and he had fallen into arrears. He was also planning to send his daughter abroad that summer with a friend, and he was arranging for her enrollment at Vassar in September. He was being forced to economize. (Sheilah Graham soon found him a house at Malibu Beach at half the rental he was paying at the Garden of Allah.) For economic reasons, therefore, he was trying to arrive at an arrangement for continuing Zelda's treatment.

Dr. Carroll's program, Fitzgerald felt, didn't offer enough hope to Zelda that she would be free from the hospital regimen for reasonably long periods. The psychiatrist wanted to keep her hospitalized more rather than less. In poetic fashion, Fitzgerald explained:

> Hope meant a lot in the best part of our lives, the first eight years we lived together, as it does in the lives of most young couples — but I think in our case it was even exaggerated, because as a restless and ambitious man, I was never disposed to accept the present but always striving to change it, better it, or even sometimes destroy it. There were always far horizons that were more golden, bluer skies somewhere.

He believed that if Zelda thought her stay in the hospital was forever, the effect might be very dangerous.

Nor, Fitzgerald claimed, did Dr. Carroll's plan leave any hope that Zelda might some time in the future look forward to a physical, a sexual relationship. In the deleted portions of his letter, Fitzgerald maintained that he could no longer sleep with Zelda; it was like "sleeping with a ghost." Nonetheless, she was, at thirty-seven, still an attractive woman and, when she was not too outrageously dressed, an extremely personable one. He had even contemplated the possibility that in time she might meet someone else and marry. But during his recent visits, he confessed, he seemed to be the worst person for her rather than the best. In another deleted section, he admitted that some part of him hated her for all the trouble and suffering that her illness had cost him. But part of him, he said in his letter, "will always pity her with a sort of deep ache that is never absent from my mind for more than a few hours; an ache for the beautiful child I loved."

And there was also the inevitable lie. When he was advocating the importance of sex in life, the hope of intimate relations, he gave himself as an example: "Judging by myself and the anchorite life that I perforce led during the years when I had T.B. and the broken bones, I know what a difference all that can make in morale." The anchorite years, of course, had included his mad summer in Asheville.

IV

The blows began to rain down on Fitzgerald at the end of 1938. At Christmas, he learned that Metro-Goldwyn-Mayer did not intend to renew his contract, which expired in January. He was working on *Madame Curie* (a production that was temporarily dropped) and was somewhat mystified as to why he was being let go. But during the year and a half he had worked at the studio, he was paid a high salary and received only one screen credit. Fitzgerald pretended that he was pleased that Metro had let him go, though he was plainly miffed. "I've hated the place ever since Monkeybitch rewrote 3 comrades!" he told Harold Ober. Over the next two years he grew increasingly sour on the subject: "Isn't Hollywood a dump—in the human sense of the word?" he wrote a friend. "A hideous town, pointed up by the insulting gardens of its rich, full of the human spirit at a new low of debasement." And there were other evidences of failure. He learned that *This Side of Paradise* was out of print, and it moved him to write to Max Perkins: "Isn't my reputation being allowed to slip away? I mean what's left of it. I am still a figure to many people and the number of times I still see my name in *Time* and *New Yorker* ect. make me wonder if it should be allowed to casually disappear—when there are memorial double-deckers to such fellows as Farrell and Steinbeck."

For a while, he considered going back to work on his medieval stories about Philippe, but fortunately gave them up for a novel about Hollywood. But when Charles Scribner asked about the Hollywood book, Fitzgerald wrote Perkins promptly: "I am in terror that this mis-information may have been disseminated to the literary columns. If I ever gave any such impression it is entirely false: I said that the novel was about some things that had happened to me in the last two years. It is distinctly *not* about Hollywood (and if it were it is the last impression that I would want to get about.)"

It was not only with Perkins that Fitzgerald was being mysteriously furtive about the book and its subject. It was during this period that Fitzgerald discussed "Crazy Sunday," the story that prefigures *The Last Tycoon,* with Sheilah Graham. He tried to convince her that Miles Calman was not based on Thalberg, but on the director King Vidor. He may have had an ulterior motive for saying that, since he had learned that Sheilah had had an affair with Vidor and had considered marrying him before she met Fitzgerald. Vidor had even asked her to approve the drawings for the new house he was planning to build high above Beverly Hills. In his proxy fashion, Fitzgerald used that bit of real life — as he used his own relationship with Sheilah — in *The Last Tycoon.* It is in Stahr's unfinished house at Malibu Beach that Stahr and Kathleen have sex for the first time, in what Fitzgerald, with near-accuracy, described as "an immediate, dynamic, unusual, physical love affair."

Fitzgerald continued to work as a free lance on film assignments for various producers and studios. On loan from MGM, he did a three-week stint on *Gone With the Wind,* polishing dialogue. Often the assignments were minor, lasting a day or a week or more, and the pictures, like *Air Raid* and *Open That Door,* were never produced. With others — *Raffles, Life Begins at Eight-Thirty* — it was only a matter of a week's work, or his screenplay was not used. He tried to promote screen versions of his own work — a musical version of his Basil stories, intended for Mickey Rooney and Judy Garland, who were then on the rise — but without success. He took up his commercial stories once again, mostly for *Esquire,* which paid little. He wrote a series for the magazine on a rundown screenwriter named Pat Hobby, even though he had hesitated to write about Hollywood society.

Whether the loss of his contract with MGM triggered the reaction is not clear, but at the outset of 1939, Fitzgerald seemed to be a man in a state of panic, bent on destroying the present. His Hollywood film agent, H. N. Swanson, managed to get him an assignment on the Walter Wanger film *Winter Carnival,* which was being shot at Dartmouth College during its annual Winter Carnival. Fitzgerald and a young, aspiring novelist and screenwriter, Budd Schulberg, the son of the producer B. N. Schulberg, had been assigned the script. The younger Schulberg had graduated from Dartmouth three years earlier. Wanger asked the two men to fly to New York, early in February, and take the train to New Hampshire to work while the production was going on; he hoped in this way to bring some fresh ideas to the script. Sheilah Graham, who was on the flight to New York, was plainly anxious about Scott, because he was running a temperature. But she went to her night berth, unaware that Schulberg's father had presented his son with two bottles of champagne. Fitzgerald and Schulberg spent the night reminiscing about college days and drinking. It was the beginning of a long binge, during which Fitzgerald, boisterous and insulting, disgraced himself at Dartmouth, argued with the producer, and was ordered off the campus. When he returned to New York with Schulberg, Fitzgerald was in terrible shape. Sheilah managed to locate a sympathetic psychiatrist, who gave him some momentarily helpful support. He was taken to Doctors Hospital, where he remained for a few days of medical and psychiatric treatment. After a week in a hotel, he returned to Hollywood. He had little place to go but down. Being rehired by Wanger was out of the question.

Over the next several months he had a series of vicious quarrels with Sheilah Graham. She had found him another house, this one at Encino, on the estate of the actor Edward Everett Horton. After the Dartmouth episode, Fitzgerald went through phases of depression, insomnia, and heavy drinking. He was taking Nembutal at night and pep pills in the morning. Again, he hired a nurse to see him through periods of drying out. One morning he woke in a drugged state, so wrapped up in the bedclothes that he could not move his arm. He shouted for the nurse, who decided to give him a scare, and convinced him that he had a temporary spell of paralysis owing to his drinking. The doctor, who was called, played along with the deception and corroborated the nurse's diagnosis. Fitzgerald, convinced, later played up the episode in a letter to Scottie. Since his movie work had ended, he told his daughter, "I have been through not only a T.B. flare-up but also a nervous breakdown of such severity that for a time it threatened to paralyze both arms — or to quote the doctor: 'The good Lord tapped you on the shoulder.' "

There were other episodes that were not so harmless. Very early one morning, he called Sheilah Graham to say that he was trying to sober up and had called the nurse, but he wanted her to come and stay with him until the nurse arrived. But once Sheilah was there, rather unaccountably Fitzgerald told her she should leave. As she started to go, she caught sight of his revolver in a partly opened drawer and grabbed for it. A struggle followed, and feeling that Fitzgerald was getting the gun from her, she slapped him hard. (There is the possibility that the strategically timed phone call and the strategically placed revolver had been arranged for melodramatic effect.) She managed to wrestle the gun from him and throw it at the wall. By this time, she was hysterical. "Shoot yourself, you son of a bitch! . . ." she screamed. "I didn't pull myself out of the gutter to waste my life on a drunk like you!" When she called the next day, she learned that Fitzgerald had flown east.

It was the beginning of a nightmare. Fitzgerald had gone to Asheville, taken Zelda out of the hospital, and then gone with her to Cuba. At the hotel in Havana, Zelda had one of her religious episodes; she shut herself up in her room, praying and reading her Bible. Fitzgerald, drunk, wandered the streets and was badly beaten when he tried to stop a cockfight. Zelda somehow managed to get him back to New York, where they registered at the Algonquin. Fitzgerald continued on a prolonged bender. Taking a cab out to Harold Ober's house in Scarsdale, he got into another terrible fight, this time with the cab driver, and was beaten again; his eye was badly hurt. Back at the Algonquin, he threatened to throw a waiter down an elevator shaft. It took Frank Case, the owner of the hotel, and John Palmer, husband of Zelda's sister Clothilde, to get him to a hospital for treatment.

Zelda remained in New York for a few days, staying at the Hotel Irving, to make sure that he was all right. She was afraid that she had created the problem by having antagonized him in some way. She wrote to him in the hospital: his eye, she said, looked terrible, but she was sure he was getting the necessary treatment. "Please take care of yourself," she said, and then added in a peculiarly stilted way, "There is a possibility of so much happiness if you will be of a more conservative intent." Like a small girl on a holiday, she had made use of the adversity, seeing an exhibition of American Scene painters at the Metropolitan Museum, taking in a newsreel, paying a visit to Harold Ober. But when it was time to go back to

Asheville, she became concerned that their stories might not jibe. She wrote Fitzgerald what her version would be: that it had been an enviable trip and everything had gone according to the rules, particularly concerning wine and cigarettes, which she was not supposed to have. She would tell her doctors that Fitzgerald's lungs were bad and he had needed medical treatment. Therefore, she had returned to the hospital on her own.

After his release from the hospital, still recuperating in Encino, Fitzgerald wrote her a reassuring letter:

> You were a peach throughout the whole trip and there isn't a minute of it when I don't think of you with all the old tenderness and with a consideration that I never understood that you had before. . . . You are the finest, loveliest, tenderest, most beautiful person I have ever known, but even that is an understatement because the length that you went to there at the end would have tried anybody beyond endurance.

One of the most damaging blows to his ego and his eroding confidence came in midsummer. Although he had largely cleared up his outstanding debts, he was now back to his old financial problems and began wiring Ober for advances once more. Fitzgerald seems to have completely ignored the warning signs in Ober's earlier letters, that he was feeling the financial pinch like many others. In January, having learned that Fitzgerald's contract would not be renewed, he sent the author memos about savings banks and advised him to put aside whatever he could from his free-lance assignments: "I would like to see you cut down expenses just as much as you can . . ." Ober wrote. "This doesn't mean that I think you have been living extravagantly but there is always a period of readjustment after working in Hollywood and I would like to have you leave there with excessive security."

In June, when Fitzgerald wrote for an advance of $500, Ober decided to give Fitzgerald a well-meaning lecture. In a long letter, he explained that he was short of funds himself and cautioned Fitzgerald against returning to old habits. "It would be a great mistake for us to get back into the position we were in," he said. "I think it is bad for you and difficult for me." He hoped they could keep things on a pay-as-you-go basis. Instead of sending the letter, however, he sent the money Fitzgerald had requested. If Ober had sent his letter, it might have served as a warning of the blow that followed. Early in July, Fitzgerald wrote for another advance, and Ober turned him down. Fitzgerald hastily wired Perkins, his message carrying the usual references to ailing health and dire circumstances that were probably a mixture of truth and high drama:

> HAVE BEEN WRITING IN BED WITH TUBERCULOSIS UNDER
> DOCTORS NURSES CARE . . . OBER HAS DECIDED NOT TO
> BACK ME THOUGH I PAID BACK EVERY PENNY AND EIGHT
> THOUSAND COMMISSION AM GOING TO WORK THURSDAY
> IN STUDIO AT FIFTEEN HUNDRED CAN YOU LEND ME SIX
> HUNDRED FOR ONE WEEK BY WIRE TO BANK AMERICA
> CULVER CITY SCOTTIE HOSPITAL WITH APPENDIX AND AM
> ABSOLUTELY WITHOUT FUNDS PLEASE DO NOT ASK OBERS
> COOPERATION.

On July 13 he wired Ober, saying he was still flabbergasted by his abrupt change of policy after twenty years, especially when Ober had another story in his hands. His commercial value couldn't have sunk from $60,000 to nothing "BECAUSE OF A SLOW HEAL-ING LUNG CAVITY." He pleaded for an advance of a few hundred "SO I CAN EAT TODAY AND TOMORROW." Ober's answering telegram read, SORRY COLLECTIONS SLOW AND IMPOSSIBLE MAKE ADVANCE NOW SUGGEST ASKING SWANSON GET AD-VANCE ON JOB. It was a cold reply and Fitzgerald was obviously hurt and probably furious. He scribbled, "The insult to my intelligence in the phrase 'collections slow' makes me laugh." Then he initialed the telegram and returned it to Ober. His problems were complicated even further, because Scottie generally stayed with the Obers during her vacations from Vassar; she had become almost a member of the family. But what was equally wounding was his sense that Ober had lost confidence in him, and he cast about for reasons. "I think something to do with it," Fitzgerald wrote Perkins, "is the fact that almost every time I have come to New York lately I have just taken Zelda somewhere and have gone on more or less of a binge, and he has formed the idea that I am back in the mess of three years ago." In mid-July he sent Ober a letter with an opening statement that showed he was still bleeding from the wound: "This is not a request for any more backing — there will be no more requests." He acknowledged how much he had relied on Ober in the past — and mentioned that he had largely paid back his indebt-edness. What shocked him, he said, was not Ober's refusal to lend a specific amount, but the manner in which Ober had abruptly changed his policy. "I turned down several picture offers under the conviction that you could tide me over until I got through to a magazine (and this a few months after telling me there was no hurry about paying back that money and just after a year and a half during which I paid your firm over ten thousand dollars in commissions and you personally thirteen thousand dollars in advances.)" Fitzgerald mentioned, as he had to Perkins, that every time he had come east he had gone on a binge, "most often after a time with Zelda, and the last time I brought a good deal of inconvenience into your settled life," but in his rhetorical devices Fitzgerald seemed to wander off the point, not making that the reason for Ober's sudden withdrawal. He ended his letter, "Nothing would ever make me forget your many kindnesses and the good times and laughs we have had together."

He was edging close to a break; had even forewarned Scottie: "I am pretty definitely breaking with Ober but he doesn't know it yet." But that may have been a self-serving pose. He broached the possibility with Perkins and asked for the names of other literary agents in New York. Perkins did his best to discourage Fitzgerald from making a change: "But Scott, I think that Harold Ober is one of the very best and most loyal friends you have in the world. I hope to God you will stand by him." Fitzgerald wrote Ober once more, going over the same grounds again, in a letter written on August 2. He ended it by saying, "If it is of any interest to you I haven't had a drink in two months but if I was full of champagne I couldn't be more confused about you than I am now." It was perhaps the nearest he would come to admitting the probable cause of their break. But he had thoroughly understood the consequences. "When Harold withdrew from the questionable honor of being my banker," he wrote Perkins, "I felt completely numb financially and I suddenly wondered what money was and where it came from."

He had begun to wonder, too, about the loss of friends: Ernest with his "crack" in "The Snows of Kilimanjaro," and Ober's "sudden desertion at the wrong time." Only recently he had come across John Bishop's essay about him, "The Missing All," in the winter 1937 issue of *The Virginia Quarterly Review,* and was deeply offended by it. Among other things, Bishop had intimated that Fitzgerald had flunked out of Princeton. "A nice return for ten years of trying to set him up in a literary way," he wrote Perkins. They were all — Hemingway, Ober, Bishop — "something less than friends" now.

"Once I believed in friendship," he told Perkins, "believed I *could*
(if I didn't always) make people happy and it was more fun than
anything. Now even that seems like a vaudevillian's cheap dream of
heaven."

Bishop's report troubled him for months. Writing to Bunny
Wilson, he complained about the unfairness of it: "He reproached
me with being a suck around the rich. I've had this before but
nobody seems able to name these rich. I always thought my progress
was in the other direction—Tommy Hitchcock and the two Murphys are not a long list of rich friends." He especially resented its
coming from John Bishop: "It can't be jealousy for there isn't much
to be jealous of any more. Maybe it's conscience—nobody ever sold
himself for as little gold as he did."

Wilson was still a friend. Fitzgerald had last seen him during
one of his sober periods in the fall of 1938, when he and Sheilah
Graham had made a trip east. The pair had traveled up to Stamford,
Connecticut, where Wilson was living with his new wife, Mary
McCarthy. Wilson, more than any other of his friends, seemed to
have a cordial appreciation of the women in Fitzgerald's life—Zelda,
Rosalinde Fuller, for instance. He was especially impressed with
Sheilah Graham, who had brought a new sobriety to Fitzgerald's
life. He wrote Christian Gauss about the Fitzgerald visit with some
enthusiasm: "I have never seen so great and sudden a change in
anybody I knew. He doesn't drink, works hard in Hollywood, and
has a new girl, who, though less interesting, tends to keep him in
better order than Zelda (who seems to be fading out in the sanatorium)." He added, "It is melancholy to think of him in Hollywood,
which has such a stultifying and oppressive effect on everybody who
has anything to do with it. But I imagine he'll emerge from it
eventually. He may work through to something new in the literary
way. It's really a proof of his strength of character and physique that
he's been able to survive at all."

Fitzgerald had been particularly appreciative of the visit. "Believe me, Bunny," he wrote later, "it meant more to me than it
could possibly have meant to you to see you that evening. It seemed
to renew old times. . . ."

⊠━━⊠

Fitzgerald's efforts to break through to some new literary ground
did not go very easily. Acting as his own agent, in September 1939

he sent a synopsis of his novel to Kenneth Littauer of *Collier's*, hoping the magazine would make a substantial advance on the serial rights. He was counting on his reputation. But Littauer wrote him that the synopsis was too inconclusive; he would need something more substantial before making a decision. Fitzgerald was discouraged. He worked hard to send the editor the first chapter, some six thousand words, and was turned down again when Littauer wired that the sample was "PRETTY CRYPTIC THEREFORE DISAPPOINTING"; he preferred to wait until the story was more developed. Fitzgerald wired him that he had no hard feelings, but there hadn't been an editor with pants on since George Horace Lorimer. It was inevitable that there would be a breakdown in his self-confidence.

To make matters worse, he was being besieged with letters from Zelda and from Zelda's family, asking that she be released permanently from the hospital and be allowed to return home to stay with her mother. It was a move Fitzgerald was not ready to accept. In a bitter mood he wrote Zelda a letter that he did not send. In it, in a rather self-consciously literary style, he told her that she was not capable of organizing her life in any serious way. He asserted his own rights to life in a self-pitying fashion: "*We*—we consumptives, mistaken people, workers, die-ers, we must live—not at your expence, God knows, but in spite of you. We have our tombstones to chisel—and can't blunt our tools stabbing you back, you ghosts, who can't either clearly remember or cleanly forget."

In his relationship with Sheilah Graham, he became threatening and abusive. Once, when he was drunk, he began toying with his revolver at the kitchen table. "They don't want anything by F. Scott Fitzgerald," he said. "I'm not in fashion any more." A few nights later, she found him entertaining two bums he had picked up in his wanderings. He had given them his wardrobe—the pink shirts, the ties and handkerchiefs, his Brooks Brothers suits. His life seemed to have become a travesty of his fiction, the reverse of Gatsby's proud display of his haberdashery. Fitzgerald was sitting in his bathrobe, unshaven and drunk. Sheilah threatened to call the police if the guests didn't go, leaving the clothes behind. Fitzgerald went on a rampage, throwing bowls of soup against the wall. Then he began slapping Sheilah hard. When the nurse ran in to help, Fitzgerald started a manic dance around the room, exclaiming, "She's a fake! She's right out of the slums of London," and chanting, "Lily Sheil, Lily Sheil," over and over again. He kicked the nurse in the shins

and sent her scurrying; searching wildly for his revolver, he threatened to kill Sheilah. She had had presence of mind enough to call
the police and managed to leave, unharmed. For the rest of the night
she was besieged by his phone calls. Then Fitzgerald began sending
threatening special delivery letters: "Get out of town, Lily Sheil, or
you will be dead in 24 hours." Then, in his vindictiveness, he sent
a telegram to her sponsor, saying that she had been banned by every
Hollywood studio, suggesting that she be sent back to England
where she belonged, and informing him of her real name.

He sent her an apologetic letter, honest to some degree but
also full of self-pity and calculated appeals. "I'm glad you no longer
can think of me with either respect or affection," he wrote. "People
are either good for each other or not." Then he poured on the pathos:

> I want to die, Sheilah, and in my own way. I used to have my
> daughter and my poor lost Zelda. Now for over two years your
> image is everywhere. Let me remember you up to the end which is
> very close. You are the finest. You are something all by yourself.
> You are too much something for a tubercular neurotic who can only
> be jealous and mean and perverse. I will have my last time with
> you, though you won't be here.

It was either during this quarrel or one of the earlier ones that
Fitzgerald took the photograph of Sheilah Graham which she had
given him and scrawled on the back of it "Portrait of a Prostitute"
and replaced it in its frame. Possibly, he had been so drunk at the
time that he had forgotten what he had done. Or it may have been
part of the perverse streak in his nature that he had never bothered
to change it after their later reconciliation. Sheilah Graham did not
discover it until after Fitzgerald's death. Then it seemed like an
accusation from the grave, unanswerable, cruelly undermining the
happier moments of their relationship that she had tried to keep in
mind.

V

Then, in 1940, like the eye of the storm, there came a period of
calm. Fitzgerald and Sheilah were reconciled. He gave up drinking
and started to work seriously on his novel. His course of instructions,
the "College of One," that he had begun with Sheilah, was resumed.
They had quiet times reading together; they visited friends, attended

concerts. Fitzgerald became enthusiastic about writing a screen treatment of "Babylon Revisited" for the producer Lester Cowan. But though he was paid for the work he did, the project was among his more ill-conceived ones. He had real hopes that Shirley Temple would play the role of Honoria, named Victoria in the film version, but it was never produced. Perhaps it was just as well, because in his eagerness to succeed, he messed up what was a fine and sensitive story with Hollywood gimmickry, including the same kind of murder plot between business associates that he was contemplating for *The Last Tycoon,* but that had nothing to do with his original story.

Fitzgerald still felt a lingering resentment about his situation in Hollywood. He became suspicious that his failure to get screenwriting assignments was because he had been blacklisted, because some "sinister finger" had been pointed at him. Budd Schulberg assured him that, although the studio executives denied there was such a thing, an informal blacklist existed among the producers. He asked Leland Hayward, who was acting as his Hollywood agent at the time, to see what he could find out. He had the feeling "that there is some unfavorable word going around about me," and he found it demoralizing. "And I know," he said, "when that ball starts rolling badly, as it did in the case of Ted Paramore and a few other pinks, it can roll for a long time." But it was hardly likely that Fitzgerald's politics was the problem; it was more likely his drinking and the legend of his unreliability.

He did not find Hollywood society any more agreeable. People came to Hollywood for negative reasons — even the stage-struck girls. "All gold rushes are essentially negative," he wrote Gerald Murphy. The heroes of the moment were "the great corruptionists or the supremely indifferent — by whom I mean the spoiled writers, Hecht, Nunnally Johnson, Dotty, Dash Hammet ect." He was suspicious, it appears, of Dorothy Parker's conversion to communism, no matter how faithfully she read her office every day. He suspected it did not "affect her indifference."

And he was equally discouraged by the slippage of his own literary reputation. In the late spring of 1940, he wrote Max Perkins in one of his unhappier moments: "But to die, so completely and unjustly after having given so much. Even now there is little published in American fiction that doesn't slightly bear my stamp — in a *small* way I was an original." What irritated him was that the proletarian writers, the "psychological Robespierres," were parading through American letters. "The boys read Steinbeck like they once read Mencken!" he complained. Professionally, he knew that the next move would have to come from him. "I have not lost faith," he assured Perkins. "People will *buy* my new book and I hope I shan't again make the many mistakes of *Tender*."

In a matter of months, soon after he had moved to a new apartment, on North Laurel Avenue in Hollywood, he took up his novel again with a renewed seriousness. It was to be a planned and constructed novel, as *Gatsby* had been, and Fitzgerald plotted and designed it, making charts and outlines of the episodes and the character development. It would have poetic passages, but only when they fitted the dramatic action; it would avoid the ruminations and side shows of *Tender Is the Night*. He discussed his work with Sheilah, as he had done with Zelda in the early days. It was, he admitted, to be a story patterned after the career of Irving Thalberg. He had admitted as much earlier, when he sent his synopsis to *Collier's*. "This is my great secret," he had written Kenneth Littauer. "Thalberg has always fascinated me. His peculiar charm, his extraordinary good looks, his bountiful success, the tragic end of his great adventure." But the character was also drawn from other sources, as he indicated in a draft of a letter he had optimistically planned to send to Norma Shearer when his novel was finished. He meant to preserve some part of the dazzling impression Thalberg had made on him, "though I have put in somethings drawn from . . . other men and, inevitably, much of myself." But Fitzgerald, or aspects of Fitzgerald, crop up throughout the book. He is the troublesome drunk who turns up at the airport in the opening sequence and is not allowed to board the plane. He figures, as well, as the smart, cynical, hard-drinking screenwriter Wylie White, who becomes a symbol of a flawed profession. In the novel, the young narrator, Cecilia Brady, sums up what is obviously Fitzgerald's view. "Writers aren't people exactly," she observes about Wylie and his breed. "Or, if they're any good, they're a whole *lot* of people trying so hard to be one person." It is an eloquent statement of Fitzgerald's long struggle to achieve some sense of his own personal identity out of the welter of his hard and happy experiences, the propensity to hero-worship, the inveterate role-playing that made him the writer he was.

Even in its incomplete state, with its fragmentary notes and scattered drafts, *The Last Tycoon* strikes one as reaching out for a larger purchase on life than the more narrowly focused personal dramas of Fitzgerald's earlier novels. Hollywood is still the subject of his jibes — "a mining town in lotus land," Wylie White calls it. But it seems clear that he had intended the Hollywood studio to be a symbol of the twenty-four-hour purgatory of life, a world of illusions and harsh realities. In an evocative passage, Fitzgerald describes it:

> There is never a time when a studio is absolutely quiet. There is always a night shift of technicians in the laboratories and dubbing rooms and people on the maintenance staff dropping in at the commissary. But the sounds are all different — the padded hush of tires, the quiet tick of a motor running idle, the naked cry of a soprano singing into a nightbound microphone.

Fitzgerald had meant to produce a confrontation between the Hollywood merchants and the Russian idealists; between the unions, with their criminal connections, and the communist organizers. Stahr would act as the flawed hero in a corrupting society. It is one of the virtues of the novel that Stahr is depicted more like Thalberg, a capitalist manqué, than like Fitzgerald, an ambivalent liberal. But Stahr, like Fitzgerald, has a passionate loyalty to the status quo, all the same. Fitzgerald is both comic and condescending about Stahr's grasp of Marxist politics; the producer once had the studio script department get up a two-page "treatment" of *The Communist Manifesto*. When his negotiations with the Screen Writers Guild break down, he arranges a meeting with a Communist Party organizer named Brimmer. In advance of the meeting, he bones up — as Fitzgerald often did — but by running through the Russian films in his library and one or two Dada epics, like Salvador Dali's *Le Chien Andalou*, "suspecting that they had a bearing on the matter." The comedy, however, may have involved a bit of self-scrutiny on Fitzgerald's part. He wrote of Stahr's attitude:

> But his mind was closed on the subject. He was a rationalist who did his own reasoning without benefit of books — and he had just managed to climb out of a thousand years of Jewry into the late eighteenth century. He could not bear to see it melt away — he cherished the parvenu's passionate loyalty to an imaginary past.

Except for the ancestry, it suggests Fitzgerald's passionate attachment to the old order. In the confrontation scene itself, Fitzgerald does not divide the field into villain and hero. He gives an even-handed portrait of both men. But Stahr half-baits and nearly truckles to Brimmer — in much the same way that Fitzgerald acted with Hemingway — getting drunker and more abusive until he is knocked down in a humiliating fight that he himself has provoked.

There is, in *The Last Tycoon,* a new maturity even in Fitzgerald's treatment of the love affair, the one between Stahr and Kathleen. Knowing that Kathleen is about to be married to another man, Stahr hesitates and loses her. He learns the news on a Saturday morning in his studio office, by the usual means that crucial news was conveyed in Fitzgerald's life — a telegram. Kathleen's telegram reads, I WAS MARRIED AT NOON TODAY GOODBYE.

But Fitzgerald sees Stahr's bad news as only one item in a broader context of bad news. He had been following the war news and had gloomy presentiments about the war's outcome. Much to Sheilah Graham's dismay, he predicted that England would fall to the Nazis. And early in June 1940 he wrote to Max Perkins, "The Allies are thoroughly licked, that much is certain, and I am sorry for a lot of people. As I wrote Scottie, many of her friends will probably die in the swamps of Bolivia." That sense of the larger scene, of something more urgent than a love affair, crept into *The Last Tycoon.* There are other items of news among Monroe Stahr's stack of telegrams: "a company ship was lost in the Arctic; a star was in disgrace; a writer was suing for one million dollars. Jews were dead miserably beyond the sea." Stahr, too, is death-bound; he has a bad heart and has received a "grave sentence" from the doctor. In his plans for the book, Fitzgerald projected an important scene for the moment when Stahr learns he must quit work:

> The idea fills Stahr with a horror that I must write a big scene to bring off. Such a scene as has never been written. . . . He has survived the talkies, the depression, carried his company over terrific obstacles and done it all with a growing sense of kingliness — of some essential difference which he could not help feeling between himself and the ordinary run of man and now from the mere accident of one organ of his body refusing to pull its weight, he is incapacitated from continuing. Let him go through every stage of revolt.

As in "Babylon Revisited," written after Zelda's breakdown, the protagonist's wife is dead. Monroe Stahr's dead wife, Minna, haunts the novel: Fitzgerald describes Stahr as "in love with Minna and death together." The opening chapter of *The Last Tycoon,* in which the plane is headed toward the promised land of California, was to be balanced at the end with Stahr's fatal plane crash. The irony is that where it was the rival suitor who was killed off in this fashion in Fitzgerald's earliest stories, it was the hero himself who plunges from the skies in Fitzgerald's last novel.

Fitzgerald's disastrous trip to Cuba was his last meeting with Zelda. He was feeling pressured by her family and by Zelda herself, who wanted to be released from the hospital. Her letters were often pleas that made him feel guilty. "*Wont* you let me go home?" she wrote him. "Whats the use of wasting what short space of life remains in a routine so outworn that it no longer contribute[s] a sense of the possibility of progress? Or anything else save a living death." Then, abruptly, in the spring, Dr. Carroll wrote Fitzgerald that Zelda could be released in her mother's care. Fitzgerald was at first enthusiastic, then had some second thoughts; he insisted that the doctor write a formal letter, presumably to absolve him and the Sayre family from legal responsibility if anything should go wrong. "They have no recourses or mental preparation for dealing with any sudden homicidal or suicidal tendency," he warned. He also wanted to be assured that Zelda could return to the hospital if necessary. In mid-April, Zelda was released from Highland after four years of treatment. Somewhat apprehensively, she settled into the routine life in Montgomery in her mother's little bungalow on Sayre Street, in a neighborhood that was slowly slipping downhill. She wrote Fitzgerald weekly to thank him for the allowance he sent and for the small gifts — flowers, a watch, perfume. She never saw him again.

When they were young, they had clung to each other for dear life; now, despite the distance, they seemed to cling to each other till death. Their letters were often affectionate, frequently nostalgic. Fitzgerald had been following the war and its developments. He had spent a Sunday in bed, reading Churchill's *Life of Marlborough.* "Funny that he should be Prime Minister at last," he wrote her. "Do you remember the luncheon at his mother's house in 1920 and Jack Churchill who was so hard to talk to at first and turned out to be so pleasant?" He had written some "really brilliant continuity" for the script of *Babylon Revisited,* he told her. "It had better be for it seems to be a last life line that Hollywood has thrown me."

Zelda had been reading Gertrude Stein's *Paris France* just after the French surrender. "The Gertrude Stein book both Mamma and

I find extremely amusing and heartbreakingly reminiscent, for me
— Isn't it devastating thinking that there isn't any France any more?"
He kept her informed about the progress of his novel, how he had
covered his room with charts telling the movements of the characters,
as he had done with *Tender Is the Night*, and how he was living in
the book, and how it made him happy.

Fitzgerald's letters to Scottie had mellowed, too. "What little
I've accomplished has been by the most laborious and uphill work,
and I wish now I'd *never* relaxed or looked back — but said at the
end of *The Great Gatsby:* 'I've found my line — from now on this
comes first. This is my immediate duty — without this I am nothing.' "

One afternoon in November, in Schwab's drugstore, where he had
gone for a package of cigarettes, Fitzgerald felt a stab of pain and
was dizzy. When he went to the doctor on the following day, he
was told he had had a cardiac spasm. He lied to Sheilah Graham,
assuring her that it wasn't a heart attack. But he told her he would
have to take it easy, that he couldn't go up and down stairs. He
moved into her ground-floor apartment on North Hayworth. He
still hoped to keep the seriousness of his problem from her; he would
not allow her to talk to the doctor alone. He did, however, mention
it in passing in one of his regular letters to Zelda, saying that it
wasn't a major attack and that the cardiogram had shown it up in
time. He was only "a little angry" that the illness had slowed up
the progress of his novel.

On December 20, he had a similar attack when he was leaving
the Pantages Theatre, where he and Sheilah had attended the première of *This Thing Called Love*. He didn't want her to call the doctor,
who was scheduled to look in on him the next day.

Saturday, the twenty-first, was a bright, sunny day. Fitzgerald
and Sheilah had a late lunch. Somewhat restless, Fitzgerald was
reading the *Princeton Alumni Weekly* in the green armchair by the
fireplace when, suddenly, he started up, clutched at the mantelpiece,
and fell to the floor. His eyes were closed and he was breathing very
heavily. In a panic, Sheilah called the police, the fire department.
She ran for the apartment manager. But when the police and the
firemen with the pulmotor arrived, it was too late. Fitzgerald was
already dead.

That evening, from the apartment of friends, she called Harold Ober, and Ober gave the news to Scottie, who was staying with the family over the Christmas holidays. Sheilah told the agent that since Fitzgerald had hated Hollywood, she assumed he would have wanted to be buried back east, probably where his father was buried. With bizarre appropriateness, Fitzgerald's body was placed on view in the Wordsworth Room of a Los Angeles mortuary, for the benefit of his West Coast friends. Then it was shipped to Maryland.

Zelda, fortunately, was with her mother in Montgomery when she learned the news. She did not feel capable of attending the funeral, though she was consulted about the arrangements. For reasons of discretion, Sheilah Graham did not attend, either. The two women who had meant most to Fitzgerald stayed away. Despite the pleading of John Biggs and Fitzgerald's friends, the Catholic authorities in Maryland would not allow a Catholic funeral service from St. Mary's Church or burial in the cemetery where Edward and Mollie Fitzgerald were buried. Fitzgerald had not been a practicing Catholic and had not received extreme unction or a conditional absolution immediately after his death. Sheilah Graham had been too distraught to arrange for it at the time. Moreover, she said, Fitzgerald had "abandoned the Catholic religion years ago and was definitely against all that sort of thing." An Episcopal service was held in the Pumphrey Funeral Home in Bethesda. According to one account, it was a glum affair, the suave funeral director ushering the mourners to the open casket, where the corpse, more florid than the Fitzgerald legend, looked smooth and pretty and overly rouged, in clothes that suggested a shop window—a mannequin rather than the man. The minister droned the burial service in the airless room among the spindly poinsettias.

Aside from nineteen-year-old Scottie, the family mourners were Fitzgerald's cousin Ceci Taylor, her daughter, and Rosalind and Newman Smith. The friends who were gathered in the small room, sitting on stiff-backed chairs, included Max Perkins and Harold Ober and their wives, the Biggses and Turnbulls, Ludlow Fowler, and Gerald and Sara Murphy. Dick Knight, Fitzgerald's old rival for Zelda's affection, was also among the mourners—a figure of some concern in the writer's days, perhaps, an irritant like life itself, but of only minor importance to the writer's fame. Old friends had come to bury old quarrels, old follies, old memories.

❧❧ 12 ❧❧

Epilogue

ONLY MONTHS before he died, Fitzgerald wondered about the decline of his reputation as one of the top-flight fiction writers of his generation. He suspected it had something to do with Zelda, with their life together. "It's odd that my old talent for the short story vanished," he wrote her from Hollywood. "It was partly that times changed, editors changed, but part of it was tied up somehow with you and me — the happy ending . . . I must have had a powerful imagination to project it so far and so often into the past."

Now that he was dead, Zelda preferred to recall the better times when she wrote to friends. "In retrospect," she told Harold Ober, "it seems as if he was always planning happinesses for Scottie, and for me. Books to read — places to go. Life seemed so promisory always when he was around: and I always believed that he could take care of anything."

But John Biggs, Fitzgerald's executor, said, "He left the estate of a pauper and the will of a millionaire." Fitzgerald had always thought big. Once, in the flush of his first success in 1919, so Fitzgerald had remembered, he paid off his "terrible small debts" and bought a new suit. Now, after his death, his larger debts to Highland Hospital, to Scribner's and Max Perkins, were paid out of the estate. The remaining inheritance, something less than $35,000, provided for Scottie and Zelda over the next seven years. Zelda had an annuity that gave her about $50 a month and her pension as the widow of a veteran.

The newspaper obituaries and articles spoke of Fitzgerald as the symbol of the Jazz Age. The *New York Herald Tribune* mentioned the gaudy world he had pictured—"the penthouses, the long weekend drunks, the young people who were always on the brink of madness, the vacuous conversation, the lush intoxication of easy money"—a world that had been largely swept away in the Depression. *The New York Times* said that Fitzgerald was "better than he knew," acknowledged that he had "invented a 'generation' and did as much as any writer to form as well as record its habits." Edmund Wilson arranged an obituary tribute in both the February 17 and March 3, 1941, issues of *The New Republic,* which included commemorative essays by Dos Passos and Glenway Wescott and a poem by John Peale Bishop that recalled Fitzgerald's literary talent, his personal life, and its defeats. Bishop, in "The Hours," remembered the dissipations but also the startling image of the man.

> None had such promise then, and none
> Your scapegrace wit or your disarming grace. . . .

His friends kept his reputation alive during the years of limbo into which, following death, even the most famous writers and artists are apt to fall. And Fitzgerald's gaudy world was especially vulnerable, since it did not serve the politics of a time of economic depression and war. Edmund Wilson edited *The Last Tycoon* for publication in October 1941, convinced that "even in its imperfect state" it was perhaps Fitzgerald's "most mature piece of work." He also edited a collection of Fitzgerald's essays and selections from his notebooks and letters for the book he titled *The Crack-Up,* published in 1945.

Zelda continued to live at home with Mrs. Sayre, returning to Highland Hospital from time to time when she felt she could not cope with the world. Her life was rather like the marquee on a theater that has closed down; the main attraction, still announced in jumbled letters, a thing of the past. She worked on her chaotic novel, *Caesar's Things,* but the cleverness had gone awry and the mind wandered. She kept up her painting, and occasionally exhibits of her work were held at the Montgomery Museum of Fine Arts and the Women's Club. Sometimes the curious, or an interested biographer, called, but she was increasingly timid with people. She had become something of a local legend, a strange, once-pretty figure, wearing long dresses, clutching a Bible. When Scottie married Ensign Samuel Jackson Lanahan in February 1943, at the Church of St. Ignatius Loyola in New York, Zelda did not attend. Harold Ober gave the bride away.

In her last years, Zelda became fervidly religious and sent former friends of hers and Scott's apocalyptic letters. John Biggs received one in 1947, in which Zelda warned him that she had had a special revelation that he would die within a year and that he should conduct himself accordingly. She had a kinder vision for Max Perkins: "I brood about my friends; about their Christian virtues and their aspirational purposes and want them to find salvation. You have done so much for people and so endeared yourself and care so much about many things that, of course, the Lord takes care of you."

Her messages to Carl Van Vechten, the friend of better days and ribald remarks, were more ominous: "There is much need of faith and charity in this aching world where there is so much spiritual destitution," she wrote. "To be rejected of God is to be prey of the Devil." Later, she wrote, "The world angered God with vanities and its indulgencies. . . . Though the late sun bled with tragedy and roads were drenched with heartbreak and worlds were lost in the dust of story, God sent the Spirit of Truth. . . ."

But in her less apocalyptic moods, she remembered the legendary times. With pardonable exaggeration, she wrote to Scottie: "You are sweet to hold in such high regard our artistic endowments. Daddy had an inexorable interest in the human aspects of life; an infallible memory and a great appreciation of dramatic context. . . . I always feel that Daddy was the key-note and prophet of his generation and deserves remembrance as such. . . . Daddy loved glamour & so I also had a great respect for popular acclame." She wished, she said, that she had "been able to do better one thing" and had not been so given to running into a cul-de-sac, attempting to do so many.

In the fall of 1947, feeling apprehensive about her condition, Zelda returned to Highland Hospital for a stay of several months. Early in March 1948, she wrote her mother about the promising spring weather. The jasmine was in full flower and the lawns were dotted with crocuses. "Time," she said, "seems of less relevance every day." It was her last letter to Mamma.

Just past midnight, on Thursday, March 11, the blazing Spirit of Truth descended on the central building of Highland Hospital in which Zelda was staying. A fire, starting in the kitchen, swept through the structure. It took the lives of nine women before it was brought under control. Zelda's was one of the unrecognizable bodies among the women who had been trapped on the top floor.

ACKNOWLEDGMENTS

NOTES

BIBLIOGRAPHY

INDEX

ᵉ═ᵉ ACKNOWLEDGMENTS ᵉ═ᵉ

EVERY MAJOR WRITER has as many lives as he has biographers. My own interpretation of the lives of the Fitzgeralds, of course, owes a good deal to their previous biographers. But I am especially indebted to Professor Matthew J. Bruccoli, not only for his scrupulously thorough biography of F. Scott Fitzgerald, *Some Sort of Epic Grandeur*, but because he has been, for many years, the moving force behind the restoration of Fitzgerald's writing to print. (His entries in the bibliography will attest to that.) I am also greatly indebted to Nancy Milford, whose highly detailed life study, *Zelda*, turned the legend into a recognizable human being. I want to point out, however, that although I have resorted to both the Milford and Bruccoli biographies in attempting to puzzle out some of the hazier episodes in the Fitzgerald chronology, any errors of speculation or misplaced guesses are strictly my own. I also want to point out that, though I have several times gone through Zelda Fitzgerald's correspondence at the Princeton University Library, I have cited both *Zelda* and Bruccoli's edition of Fitzgerald's *Correspondence* as the most accessible published sources for extended quotations from Zelda's letters and from the clinical literature relating to her illness.

The advance notices for Scott Donaldson's *Fool for Love*, published late last year, indicated that its theme would be Fitzgerald's various love affairs and the relation of the women involved to his writing. Though my biography had a broader scope, it seemed likely that we would be covering much of the same territory. I purposely decided not to read his book until I had finished mine. Having spent three or more years attempting to interpret Fitzgerald's attitudes toward women, both in life and in the work, I did not want it to seem — to readers or to critics — that I had been handed the subject, ready to serve, on someone else's platter.

Every major writer is subjected to as many critical interpretations as he has critics. In dealing with a writer's novels or stories, I prefer to work from the life rather than to lean on the critical literature. Generally I chose to read few rather than many critical studies. But no writer on writers can live in a plastic bubble, safeguarded against infectious critical opinions. From all of the substantial critical literature that has grown up around Fitzgerald, the critical studies that I have read or browsed through or glanced at are listed in the bibliography. I would like to acknowledge, however, that of those that I have read, Robert Sklar's *F. Scott Fitzgerald: The Last Laocoön* seemed particularly useful and provocative.

During the course of researching and writing this book, I have acquired debts that I want to acknowledge: to Peter Shepherd of Harold Ober Associates, for securing permission to read restricted materials relating to the Fitzgeralds at the Princeton University Library and for his great patience in dealing with the tangled details of copyright permissions; to Mrs. C. Grove Smith (Scottie Fitzgerald), for permission to quote from previously unpublished letters and manuscripts as well as from published sources; to Charles Scribner, Jr., for permission to quote from the Fitzgerald and Hemingway works published by Charles Scribner's Sons.

I want to thank Jean F. Preston, Curator of Manuscripts at the Princeton University Library, and her always obliging staff for help and assistance throughout that period. I especially want to thank Ann Van Arsdale for her never-failing good will during highly concentrated spells of research, and Antoinette Branham, who proved to be very resourceful in finding illustrative materials. At the Beinecke Library at Yale, I am indebted to David Schoonover, the Curator of the Yale Collection of American Literature, for his assistance and offered help, and to Donald Gallup, the former Curator. On the thorny issue of whether, in biographies, it is advisable to emend misspelled and badly punctuated letters or to leave them as is, I thank Gary Jensen and Paul Smith at the Library of Congress for their advice and research into the matter. I want to thank the librarians of Clinton, Madison, and Guilford, Connecticut, for their patience on the matter of long-overdue books, and Mrs. Caroline Kirmss of the Henry Carter Hull Library for tracking down out-of-print volumes. Two neighbors have proved helpful: Miss Mary Buell, who shared her recollections of working at *The New Republic* when Edmund Wilson was a member of the staff, and Maggie Held, wife of the noted illustrator and artist John Held, Jr., who recalled her husband's life and career for me.

For their generosity in supplying information and documentary material on the life and extraordinary career of the actress Rosalinde Fuller, I am very deeply grateful to Rosalinde Fuller's sister, Mrs. Cynthia Dehn, and her niece, Carol Odell, who sent me needed chapters from Fuller's unpublished autobiography. I am also very grateful to Robert Penn Warren and Henry Strater for sharing their experiences with the Fitzgeralds. I also want to thank Robert Taft for information concerning the later life of his uncle, Alexander McKaig.

For their responses to random queries or for supplying useful hints and suggestions, I wish to thank: Harold Acton, Ellis Amburn, Matthew J. Bruccoli, Jennifer Dunning, Peter Galassi, Paul D. Gray, George C. Griffin, Technical Sergeant Martin E. James, Liza Kirwin, Hilton Kramer, Eva Le Gallienne, R. W. B. Lewis, Sue Davidson Lowe, Alma McArdle, Nancy McCall, Barbara S. Meloni, Nancy Milford, Vincent P. Murone, John Palmer, Vivian Perlis, Patricia Bodak Stark, and Judy Throm.

For help in securing photographs, I thank Kathryn Abbe, Margaret Lynne Ausfeld, Robert Gottlieb, Alfred A. Knopf, Joan Washburn, and Lee Witkin. It came as a marvelous surprise to me, at the end of tracking down Rosalinde Fuller, to discover that Lee Witkin had known her all along and had been in London when she died, at the age of ninety, in 1982.

At Houghton Mifflin, my editor, Nan Talese, deserves special gratitude for having patiently read through my usual three drafts and for having offered very constructive advice at each stage. I also want to thank Jonathan Galassi, my former editor, for his initial support for this project. Helena Bentz, once more, deserves a special commendation for the laborious task of getting another long book through production — this one with a good many more typographical oddities than either of us had anticipated. And I thank Frances Apt, for a rigorous manuscript-editing that — once again — proved to be an education in grammar, syntax, proper style. I owe a special debt of thanks to Gail Ross and Signe Warner, for their enthusiasm for this project and their unfailing good humor in handling the never-ending details of copyright permissions and the important matter of securing the illustrations for *Invented Lives*.

June Mellow, a pioneer in on-the-ward treatment of mental patients in state mental institutions, has given me useful advice on the history, treatment, and nature of schizophrenia.

Last, I thank Augie Capaccio; this time not for companionship on the road, but for his very capable research assistance during several raids on the Princeton University Library.

ᴨ☰⸗ NOTES ⸗☰ᴨ

Abbreviations

Preface

PAGE

vi   "Five years have rolled away from me": FSF to MP [ca. May 14, 1932]; *Letters,* 229.

The Past Is Forever

PAGE

5   "barbarian princess": Mizener, *The Far Side of Paradise,* 127.

6   "WE WILL BE AWFULLY NERVOUS": FSF to ZSF, March 20, 1920; Bruccoli, et al., *The Romantic Egoists,* 64.

     "Last year as a Catholic": *Ledger,* 172.

7   "because she says": ZSF to FSF [February 1920]; *Correspondence,* 52.

     "You be a good Episcopalian": Mizener, *The Far Side of Paradise,* 119.

     "I never make late dates": Mayfield, *Exiles,* 2.

8   "Remember there were 3 pines": ZSF to FSF, n.d. [1935?]; PUL.

9   "There seemed to be some heavenly support": *Save Me the Waltz,* 35.

     "He smelled like new goods": Ibid., 37.

     "overwhelmingly aware of the youth": *The Great Gatsby,* 150.

     "great animal magnetism": *Notebooks,* no. 1378.

     Lincoln Weaver: The clipping is reproduced in Bruccoli, et al., *The Romantic Egoists,* 47. Weaver's name also appears in Fitzgerald's *Ledger* under July 1918. In one of Zelda's scrapbooks, there is a telegram, dated July 8, 1918, that more or less orders her to have lunch with him at noon, Wednesday. I have checked Weaver's army pay vouchers; they indicate that he received his final pay in January 1919 and his bonus in March 1920, which tends to suggest that his accident was not fatal. I have been unable to locate any military records of the accident or of Weaver's hospitalization.

10   "Anyway, if she's good-looking": ZSF to FSF, n.d.; Milford, *Zelda,* 70.

"One man tried to elope to N.Y. with me": ZSF to FSF, n.d.; PUL.

"I know you've worried": ZSF to FSF, n.d.; Milford, *Zelda,* 73.

11   "After yielding, she holds Philippe at bay like Zelda & me in summer 1917": Bruccoli, *Some Sort of Epic Grandeur,* 93. Fitzgerald wrote four stories for this improbable sequence for a historical novel. Three of them were published in *Redbook* magazine. The fourth, "Gods of Darkness," was not published until after his death, in November 1941. Fitzgerald's daughter has discouraged republication of the stories, thinking them too inferior. "In the Darkest Hour," however, was reprinted in *The Price Was High.*

It is one of the oddities: Aside from the letters and telegrams that Zelda pasted into a scrapbook, Fitzgerald's early letters and telegrams have not survived. Her letters to him, on restriction in the Princeton University Library, are usually undated and have to be assigned dates by way of internal evidence and sequence. Fitzgerald's ledger entries, made in a ledger book bought from a St. Paul stationer, were begun some time between 1919 and the early 1920s. Whenever it was that he began keeping the ledger account, he recapped the dates up to his age at the time, with all the possibilities of errors from faulty memory. Nor did he keep the record on a day-to-day basis after that point.

"Sweetheart, I love you": ZSF to FSF [spring 1919]; *Correspondence,* 44.

"Darling heart, I wish and wish": ZSF to FSF, n.d. [summer 1919?]; PUL.

12   "He said his first word": *Ledger,* July 1897.

"I could now be sympathetic": *Ledger,* September 1916.

"I leave the house": Turnbull, *Scott Fitzgerald,* 199.

13   "straight 1850 potato-famine Irish": Bruccoli and Bryer, *In His Own Time,* 276.

"depresses me inordinately": FSF to EW, June 25, 1922; *Letters,* 337.

"dressed like the devil": Piper, *A Critical Portrait,* 8.

14   "The color of the water": Turnbull, *Scott Fitzgerald,* 6–7.

"just missed being beautiful": Mizener, *The Far Side of Paradise,* 2.

15   "I don't know how it worked": *Afternoon,* 184.

"He fell under the spell": *Ledger,* 158.

"freudian shame": See *Ledger* entries for August 1901 and July 1903.

16   "He took off John Wylie's shoes": *Ledger,* 158.

"and ran home in consequence": Ibid., September 1904.

"hit John Wylie with a stick": Ibid.

"son of an Army officer": Ibid., January 1903.

"fell madly into admiration": Ibid., January 1907.

"Perfection — black hair, olive skin": Ibid., March 1915.

"scared silly": Ibid., December 1907.

17   "I dont remember who was first": *Thoughtbook,* IX – X.

Fourth of July spanking: See *Ledger,* July 1903.

"I spent the day with a friend": See "The Death of My Father," Bruccoli, *Composition,* 124 – 125.

18   "his handsome little boy": Ibid.

"Dear God . . . please": Bruccoli and Bryer, *In His Own Time,* 296.

"Scott, say something": Ibid.

19   "I think Taft will": Ibid., 297.

"the black Irish half": FSF to John O'Hara, July 18, 1933; *Letters,* 503.

"inveterate author": *Ledger,* January 1911.

20   "They're here! They're here!": *The Romantic Egotist,* MS., Chap. I, 21; PUL.

"The Great Event," "Enter Success!": Bruccoli, et al., *The Romantic Egoists*, 18, 19.

"to wit — Margaret Armstrong and Marie Hersey": *Thoughtbook*, XXIX.

"Violet got very mad": Ibid., XII, XVI.

21   "One day Marie Hersey": Ibid., XX.

"strong as an ox": Ibid., XXIII.

"wrote about it": Turnbull, *Scott Fitzgerald*, 20.

"that I was polite": *Thoughtbook*, XVI.

"Will someone poison Scotty": *Ledger*, January 1909.

"I didn't know till 15": FSF to Scottie [summer 1935]; *Letters*, 5.

"pulled forward by an irresistible urge": *Notebooks*, no. 978.

22   "a king who ruled the whole world": *Afternoon*, 185.

"I had lived so much": *The Romantic Egotist*, MS., Chap. I, 5–6; PUL.

"sprang from his Platonic conception of himself": *The Great Gatsby*, 99.

"My father is a moron": FSF to MP, February 20, 1926; *Dear Scott*, 134.

"Advantages of children whose mother is dead": *Notebooks*, no. 1336.

"If you want to be a top-notch writer": Laura Guthrie Hearne, "A Summer with F. Scott Fitzgerald," *Esquire* (December 1964), 260.

23   "Mother and I never had": FSF to Annabel Sprague [June 1936]; *Letters*, 535.

"Fiction is a trick of the mind": *Afternoon*, 184.

"When I like men I want to be": *Notebooks*, no. 938.

24   "Good, he's free": Bruccoli and Bryer, *In His Own Time*, 3.

"a back door way out of facing reality": *Afternoon*, 186.

"I marked myself handsome": *The Romantic Egotist*, MS., Chap. I, 33–34; PUL.

25   Martin Amorous: Amorous, a minor writer, would recall that Fitzgerald had "the most impenetrable egotism" he had ever encountered. Fitzgerald, years later, would list Amorous among his tally of homosexuals in his *Notebooks:* "A fag — his ups and downs like Amorous (Martin) and others — humility and fatalism." *Notebooks*, no. 1985.

"It seems to me": Chanler, *Autumn in the Valley*, 37.

"genial sinner": Allen, *Candles and Carnival Lights*, 37.

26   "rather like an exiled Stuart king": *This Side of Paradise*, 24.

"too gorgeous for words": Monsignor Fay to FSF, June 6, 1918; PUL.

27   "an enormous peony": Chanler, *Autumn in the Valley*, 84.

"He was intensely ritualistic": *This Side of Paradise*, 24.

"the few things I ever learned": Bruccoli, *Composition*, 124.

"a dazzling, golden thing": Bruccoli and Bryer, *In His Own Time*, 134.

28   "What a thing it is": Monsignor Fay to FSF [1918]; PUL.

"I always think it such a shame": Monsignor Fay to FSF, August 17, 1918; *Correspondence*, 29.

29   "He was resentful against all those": *This Side of Paradise*, 27.

He had taken his entrance exams: See *Ledger*, May 1913, for "Cribbing."

"a dozen times when a page of notes": *Afternoon*, 76.

30   "Only when you tried to tear part of your past": Ibid., 70–71.

"I don't know why": *This Side of Paradise*, 25.

"Suddenly all around you": *Afternoon*, 72.

31   "shy little scholar of Holder Court": *The Crack-Up*, 24.

"intellectual conscience": Ibid., 79.

"Queer bird," "awful highbrow": *The Romantic Egotist*, MS., Chap. V, 33; PUL.

32   "like a jonquil": Kazin, *F. Scott Fitzgerald*, 47. Bishop, whose article "The Missing All" appeared in the Winter 1937 issue of *The Virginia Quarterly Review*, remem-

bered that their conversation took place in the "September twilight." Fitzgerald's *Ledger*, however, places it in April 1914.

"those I had read, which were not many": Kazin, *F. Scott Fitzgerald*, 47. Oddly, Bishop's recollection, presumably written around 1937, was a neat paraphrase of what Fitzgerald had written about himself nearly twenty years earlier in the manuscript version of *The Romantic Egotist*, describing the conversation: "I discussed books voluminously — books I had read, books I had read about, and books I had never heard of." MS., Chap. V, 33, PUL.

"series of endless scraps": FSF to Scottie, August 3, 1940; *Letters*, 88.

"Sir, you can't flunk me.": Piper, *A Critical Portrait*, 22. See also Wilson, *A Prelude*, 93, for Fitzgerald's run-ins with Frank MacDonald.

"When I stayed in hotels": Wilson, *A Prelude*, 148.

"That's one thing that Fitzgerald's never done!": Ibid.

33 "with the brightest writers": Turnbull, *Scott Fitzgerald*, 54.

34 "Drunk," "Passed out at dinner": See *Ledger* entries for January, March, July 1915.

"Why, I can go up to New York": Wilson, *A Prelude*, 106.

"Despair": *Ledger*, September 1915.

"Everything bad in it was my own fault": Ibid., 170.

"withdraw from the University January 3, 1916.": Bruccoli, *Some Sort of Epic Grandeur*, 64.

"This is for your sensitive feelings": H. McClenahan to FSF, May 8, 1916; Bruccoli, et. al., *The Romantic Egoists*, 29.

"I had lost certain offices": *The Crack-Up*, 76.

35 "sat alone upon the darkened and deserted verandah": EW to FSF, October 7, 1917; Wilson, *Letters*, 30.

36 "made luminous the Ritz Roof": *The Crack-Up*, 24.

"Even now, you may be having": Turnbull, *Scott Fitzgerald*, 56.

"Boys like to talk about themselves": FSF to Annabel Fitzgerald [ca. 1915]; *Correspondence*, 15.

37 "Margaret Armstrongs slouch": Ibid., 16.

"A pathetic, appealing look": Ibid., 16–17.

"I am half feminine": Hearne, "A Summer with F. Scott Fitzgerald," 258.

38 "fair hair and green-gray eyes": *Apprentice*, 85.

39 "undercurrent of sadness": Bruccoli and Bryer, *In His Own Time*, 117.

40 "flickered out": FSF to John Grier Hibben [June 3, 1920]; *Letters*, 462.

"Oh, I'll be frank for once": *Apprentice*, 98.

41 "I'm sorry you think": Ginevra King to FSF, July 7, 1917; Mizener, *The Far Side of Paradise*, 61.

"the most complete case": Wilson, *The Twenties*, 19.

"the crisp tearing open": *The Crack-Up*, 25.

"Saw your friend Larry Noyes": FSF to EW [fall 1917]; *Letters*, 319.

42 "Slowly and inevitably": *This Side of Paradise*, 147.

"literary month": FSF to EW, September 26, 1917; *Letters*, 317.

"Fluff, have you ever had": Eble, *A Collection of Criticism*, 11.

"I'm afraid Scott just wasn't": Ibid.

"For Fluff Beckwith, the only begetter": Ibid., 13.

43 "conversion of Russia": Monsignor Fay to FSF, August 22, 1917; *Correspondence*, 20.

"jolly glad to get anything": Ibid.

"as we shall have to keep": Ibid.

"Now, in the eyes of the world": Ibid., 19

"As soon as you have read": Ibid., 21.

"Wetzel, military tailor": Monsignor Fay to FSF, August 29, 1917, and P.S. dated August 31; PUL.

44 "If your summer has had a feminine tinge": Ibid.

"Like all prejudices": Ibid.

"We can not go to Russia": Monsignor Fay to FSF, n.d.; PUL.

"Everything around us seemed": *Afternoon*, 78.

"Yes — Jack Newlin is dead": FSF to EW [fall 1917]; *Letters*, 320.

45 "How magnificent Strater is": Monsignor Fay to FSF, December 10, 1917; *Correspondence*, 23.

"We're extraordinary, we're clever": Ibid., 24.

"What is the use of telling me": Ibid.

"I am Second Lieutenant": FSF to Mrs. Edward Fitzgerald, November 14, 1917; *Letters*, 451.

"I have never been more cheerful": Ibid., 452.

"the worst lieutenant": Drawbell, *James Drawbell: An Autobiography*, 176.

46 "smeary pencil pages": *Afternoon*, 85.

"The Romance of an Egoist": Monsignor Fay to FSF, December 10, 1917; *Correspondence*, 23.

"the picaresque ramble": FSF to EW, January 10 [1918]; *The Crack-Up*, 252.

"a tremendously conceited affair": FSF to Shane Leslie, December 22, 1917; *Letters*, 371.

"Conceit is the soul or germ": Shane Leslie to FSF, January 1, 1918; PUL.

"If Scribners takes it": FSF to EW, January 10 [1918]; *Letters*, 323.

"I don't think you ever realized": Ibid., 324.

47 "We have a terrible honesty": Monsignor Fay to FSF, December 10, 1917; *Correspondence*, 24.

"Do you realize that Shaw is 61": FSF to EW [fall 1917]; *Letters*, 320.

"Did you ever notice": FSF to Shane Leslie [early February 1918]; Ibid., 373.

"another of the best novels of the century": EW to FSF, October 7, 1917; Wilson, *Letters*, 30.

"I was intensely critical about him": *The Romantic Egotist*, MS., Chap. I, 11 – 12; PUL.

48 "in character": E. E. Paramore to EW, August 12 [1920?]; Beinecke.

"I can't rewrite": *The Romantic Egotist*, MS., Chap. I, 18 – 19; PUL.

"Don't put in everything you remember": JPB to FSF [January 1918]; *Correspondence*, 28.

"Though Scott Fitzgerald is still alive": Shane Leslie to Charles Scribner, May 6, 1918; West, *The Making*, 15.

50 "when I consigned you there and beyond": S. J. Malone to FSF, October 2, 1936; PUL.

"if we were given an important task": Turnbull, *Scott Fitzgerald*, 88.

Never the Same Love Twice

52 "You know your letters worry me": Monsignor Fay to FSF, June 30, 1918; PUL.

"visiting bows": *Ledger*, July 1918.

"Fell in love on the 7th": Ibid., September 1918.

"A gay wedding reception": Bruccoli, et al., *The Romantic Egoists*, 27.

53 "THE END OF A ONCE POIGNANT STORY": Ibid.

"is as pronounced a blond": Ibid.

"Beautiful Billy Mitchell": *Ledger,* August 1916.

"in fact no ms. novel": Charles Scribner's Sons [probably Maxwell Perkins] to FSF, August 19, 1918; *Correspondence,* 31.

It was late in October: See Maxwell Perkins to FSF, October 25, 1918; Bruccoli, et al., *The Romantic Egoists,* 35.

54 "The end of a dream": Ibid., 35.

"The range," "The range again": *Ledger,* August and September 1918.

"swore and cursed the collars": *Save Me the Waltz,* 39.

"to send back the parts of your novel": Monsignor Fay to FSF, October 19, 1918; *Correspondence,* 33.

"Finding that I had dragged the hero": *Preface to This Side of Paradise,* 13.

55 "in those days all infantry officers": *Afternoon,* 84.

"Here is my heart": ZSF to FSF, February 13, 1940; *Correspondence,* 580.

"took Daisy one still October night": *The Great Gatsby,* 149.

"He didn't despise himself": Ibid.

56 "Clay was no saint": *Apprentice,* 151.

"God damn it to hell": Drawbell, *James Drawbell: An Autobiography,* 176.

57 "Gold Dust Twins": Mayfield, *Exiles,* 43

58 "My affair still drifts": FSF to Ruth Sturtevant [December 4, 1918]; *Letters,* 454.

"just 'had supper' ": ZSF to FSF [1936/1937]; *Correspondence,* 468.

"And you said you would come back": Ibid.

"Oh God! . . . Well, I can't help it.": *Save Me the Waltz,* 40.

59 "a back door way out of facing reality": *Afternoon,* 186.

60 "I'll think of the days": FSF to C. Edmund Delbos, January 13 [1919]; *Letters,* 454.

"Oh God! I can't write": FSF to Shane Leslie, January 19 [1919]; Ibid., 374.

"fear of that blending of the two worlds": Ibid.

"Your letter seemed to start a new flow": FSF to Shane Leslie [late January 1919]; Ibid., 375.

"This has made me nearly sure": Ibid.

61 "Have a date with you Saturday": P[ete] B[onner] to ZSF, n.d.; Bruccoli, et al., *The Romantic Egoists,* 48.

"but she's a perfect baby": FSF to Ruth Sturtevant, March 26, 1920; *Letters,* 459.

"YOU KNOW I DO NOT"; FSF to ZSF, February 21, 1919; Bruccoli, et al., *The Romantic Egoists,* 48.

"DARLING HEART"; FSF to ZSF [after February 22, 1919]; *Correspondence,* 38.

"seven city editors"; *Afternoon,* 85.

"We Keep You Clean in Muscatine"; Bruccoli and Bryer, *In His Own Time,* 298.

"I walked quickly from certain places": *The Crack-Up,* 85.

62 "launching decently into life": Ibid., 25.

"the four most impressionable months": Ibid.

"Isn't it strange": Stephan Parrott to FSF, June 11, 1919; PUL.

"Your conjecture in the letter": Stephan Parrott to FSF ("April whatnot 1919"); *Correspondence,* 41.

"because I would naturally do it in a hot tub"; Ibid.

63 "I am so glad that what I told you"; Ibid., 42.

"I felt exactly about Leslie as you do": Ibid.

"I'm glad 'Peevie' is back": ZSF to FSF [after March 22, 1919]; PUL.

"I wish I could meet a Zelda": Stephan Parrott to FSF ("April whatnot 1919"); *Correspondence,* 42.

64 "As you say, it is a very human document": Stephan Parrott to FSF, April 2?, 1919.

"Wild letters": *Ledger,* February 1919.
"Some actor with this week's Keiths": ZSF to FSF [April 1919]; *Correspondence,* 42.
"People seldom interest me": Ibid., 43.
He would recall being so much in love: See Turnbull, *Scott Fitzgerald,* 399, note 89.

65   "except for the sexual recklessness": *Notebooks,* no. 552.
"when I decided to marry your mother": FSF to Scottie, July 7, 1938; *Letters,* 32.
"Scott — there's nothing": ZSF to FSF, n.d. [1919]; Milford, *Zelda,* 62.
"young authors turned out": ZSF to FSF, n.d. [1919]; Ibid., 61.
"wild and heated correspondence": ZSF to FSF [spring 1919]; *Correspondence,* 44.
"My brain is stagnating": Ibid.

66   "It excited him, too": *The Great Gatsby,* 148.
"[He] was proud of the way": *Caesar's Things,* MS., Chap. IV, 30; PUL.
"He had planned his life for story anyway": Ibid.
"Proxy in passion": *Notebooks,* no. 466.
"Feeling of proxy in passion": Ibid., no. 765.
"Give me your hand": *Apprentice,* 139.
"The implication was that": *The Crack-Up,* 86.

67   "They're the most adorably moon-shiney": ZSF to FSF, n.d.; Bruccoli, *Some Sort of Epic Grandeur,* 96n.
"Those feathers — those wonderful, wonderful": ZSF to FSF, n.d.; PUL.
"I'm going to save it": ZSF to FSF n.d. [spring 1919]; Milford, *Zelda,* 71.
"Scott, Darling, It really is beautiful": ZSF to FSF [after March 24, 1919]; PUL.
"You can't imagine": ZSF to FSF [March/April 1919]; Milford, *Zelda,* 64.
"I have always been inclined toward masculinity": ZSF to FSF n.d. [spring 1919]; PUL.
"Scott, you've been so sweet": ZSF to FSF [April 1919]; *Correspondence,* 43.

68   "Scott, my darling lover": ZSF to FSF [spring 1919]; Ibid., 44.
"Why should graves make people feel": Ibid., 45.
"told us to be married": ZSF to FSF [summer 1919]; PUL.
"to try my hand in new fields": ZSF to FSF n.d. [spring 1919]; PUL.

69   "They always dance till breakfast": Ibid.
"Wild nights and headachy mornings": ZSF to FSF [summer 1919]; PUL.
"about Zelda and me. All true": FSF to MP [June 1, 1925]; *Dear Scott,* 113.

70   "He seized her in his arms": *All the Sad Young Men,* 227.
"ridiculous letters," "ridiculous telegrams"; *Apprentice,* 168.
"She made me want to do something": Ibid., 169.

71   "I wandered around that ballroom": Ibid., 170.
"I've done my best": FSF to Ruth Sturtevant, June 24 [1919]; *Letters,* 455.
"I think of you as being unhappy": Stephan Parrott to FSF, April 2?, 1919; PUL.
"I was a failure": *The Crack-Up,* 26.
"After that I dug in": Bruccoli and Bryer, *In His Own Time,* 251. The version that Fitzgerald told Tom Boyd here was that he had read Walpole on the train from New York to Washington. Another version was that he read Walpole's *Fortitude* on his train trip home to St. Paul in July 1919. See *Ledger,* July 1919.
"Scott showed me a shoe box": Mayfield, *Exiles,* 50.

72   "turned him out to grass": *Notebooks,* no. 966.
"This is [a] definate attempt": FSF to MP, July 26, 1919; *Dear Scott,* 17.
"You never got abroad": EW to FSF, August 9, 1919; Wilson, *Letters,* 44.
"Since I last saw you": FSF to EW, August 15 [1919]; *Letters,* 324–325.
"scarcely more than a memory": Ibid., 325.

"I'll tell you what the situation is": Wilson, *The Twenties*, 52.

"Well this side of Paradise": *This Side of Paradise*, title page.

73   "It abounds in energy and life": MP to FSF, September 16, 1919; *Dear Scott*, 21.

"Pretty swell? Eh!": FSF to Ludlow Fowler [October 1919]; *Correspondence*, 45.

"You'll call it sensational": FSF to EW [probably September 1919]; *Letters*, 325.

"You will do things": George Jean Nathan to FSF [before November 15, 1919]; *Correspondence*, 47.

"first wild wind of success": *The Crack-Up*, 86.

"That week the postman rang and rang": Ibid.

"I have so many things dependent": FSF to MP, September 18, 1919; *Dear Scott*, 21.

"an erratic mistress if not a steady wife": FSF to MP, July 26, 1919; Ibid., 17.

74   "new Rosalind is a different person": FSF to MP, September 4, 1919; Ibid., 20.

"Here is the mentioned chapter": FSF to ZSF [after July 1918]; *Correspondence*, 32.

"You'll recognize much of the dialogue": FSF to MP [ca. February 21, 1920]; *Dear Scott*, 29.

"the most important year of life": *Ledger*, 173.

"to take a room at the Commodore": *This Side of Paradise*, 203.

75   "an ineffectual, inarticulate man": Ibid., 3.

"Beatrice is a new character": FSF to MP, September 4, 1919; *Dear Scott*, 20.

"known by name as a fabulously wealthy American girl": *This Side of Paradise*, 3.

"My nerves are on edge — on edge": Ibid., 5.

"My nerves are bad to-night": Eliot, *Complete Poems*, 40.

"I know myself, but that is all": *This Side of Paradise*, 282.

"People dressed like him": Ibid., 77.

"curious sinking sensation": Ibid., 78.

76   "I've enjoyed imagining": Ibid., 158.

"the last time that evil crept close": Ibid., 222.

"the problem of evil had solidified": Ibid., 280.

"Then, suddenly, Amory perceived the feet": Ibid., 113.

"I had to stop reading": Stephan Parrott to FSF ("April whatnot 1919"); *Correspondence*, 41.

77   "Over by the window": *This Side of Paradise*, 247.

"A Romance and a Reading List": *Notebooks*, no. 1021.

"so unformed that *Youth's Encounter*": FSF to Frances Newman, February 26, 1921; *Letters*, 469.

"a book that three people sent me": *The Romantic Egotist*, MS., Chap. V, 34; PUL.

"I have five copies of *Youth's Encounter*"; FSF to Frances Newman, February 26, 1921; *Letters*, 469.

The suspicion is that Mackenzie's influence: If Fitzgerald's error was not merely a slip of the pen, then it suggests that the Donahoe chapters are from the earliest version of the novel and not from a later revision.

"If you thought you couldn't deal": EW to FSF, November 21, 1919; Wilson *Letters*, 45.

78   "Your hero as an intellectual": Ibid.

"Hope you've guarded well the great secret": FSF to Ludlow Fowler [October 1919]; *Correspondence*, 45.

"I'm mighty glad you're coming": ZSF to FSF, n.d.; Milford, *Zelda*, 78.

" 'S funny, Scott": Ibid., 79.

79   "there are all kinds of love": *All the Sad Young Men*, 238.

"Somehow 'When love has turned to kindliness' ": ZSF to FSF, n.d.; Milford, *Zelda*, 80.

"I am very proud of you": Ibid.

"I explained to you the reasons": FSF to MP, February 21, 1920; *Dear Scott,* 29.

81 "his first serious love affair": Rosalinde Fuller to EW, September 17, 1967; Beinecke. Fuller was quoting back the phrase that Wilson had written her in a prior letter: "I was interested to hear about Scott Fitzgerald's thinking that mine was his first serious love affair. It didn't begin in a taxi — but one of those old hansom cabs that stand or stood so patiently outside the Plaza Hotel."

"Rosalind": *Ledger,* November 1919.

"gay challenging face": Unpublished autobiography by Rosalinde Fuller, MS., Chap. 6, 80.

"I have, all my life": Rosalinde Fuller to EW, June 15, 1969; Beinecke.

82 "Scott roused the driver": Unpublished autobiography by Rosalinde Fuller, MS, Chap. 6, 80.

"no end to our delight and discovery": Ibid., 81.

"We never talked of other people": Rosalinde Fuller to Carol Odell, n.d.

"I think he had met her": Ibid.

83 "back down South to Zelda": Ibid.

"Sometimes he spoke of writing": Unpublished autobiography of Rosalinde Fuller, MS., Chap. 6, 81.

"but often in his stories": Ibid., 82.

"I came home in a thoroughly nervous": FSF to MP [ca. January 10, 1920]; *Dear Scott,* 24.

84 "Venus of the hansom cab": *Six Tales of the Jazz Age,* 120.

"I've got several damn strange adventures": FSF to Ludlow Fowler, January 1 [1920]; PUL.

"I wanted to, for your sake": ZSF to FSF [February 1920]; *Correspondence,* 50.

85 "O, Scott, its so be-au-ti-ful": ZSF to FSF [February 1920]; Ibid., 52.

"I thought maybe it might interest her to know": Ibid.

"But you may have to marry a corpse": Ibid.

"I LOVE YOU DEAREST GIRL": FSF to ZSF, February 24, 1920; Ibid., 51.

86 "Darling Heart, our fairy tale is almost ended": ZSF to FSF, [February 1920]; Ibid.

"Any girl who gets stewed in public": FSF to Isabelle Amorous, February 26, 1920; Ibid., 53.

"You're still a catholic": Ibid.

"The man with the jingle of money": *The Crack-Up,* 77.

"never been able to stop wondering": Ibid.

87 "As you know, Zelda has had": Minnie Sayre to FSF [1920]; Turnbull, *Scott Fitzgerald,* 104.

"You were to be the stuffed dummy": FSF to ZSF [fall 1939]; *Correspondence,* 559.

"The assumption is that you were a great prize package": Ibid.

The Metropolitan Spirit

91 He claimed that he had had his first glimpse of it: See *The Crack-Up,* 23. In the manuscript of *The Romantic Egotist* (Chap. II, 12; PUL), however, Fitzgerald describes the dramatic ferry ride as having occurred when he was 15, en route from Manhattan to boarding school.

"melancholy love": *The Crack-Up,* 23.

"that new thing — the Metropolitan spirit": Ibid., 24.
"flashing, dynamic good looks": Notebooks, no. 158.
"as tense as singing wires": Ibid., no. 163.
"darkly mysterious": Ibid., no. 181.
"an interested glance": Apprentice, 108.
"water jewels": Notebooks, no. 247.

92 "its birth, its planned gaieties": Ibid., no. 187.
"the style and glitter": The Crack-Up, 24.
"You've got to help me!": Mizener, The Far Side of Paradise, 118.
"We are glad — oh, so relieved": The Crack-Up, 60.

93 "the strangeness and excitement of New York": ZSF to FSF [late summer/early fall 1930]; Correspondence, 245.
"very pretty and languid": Wilson, The Twenties, 53.
"appropriate for a Southern belle": Ibid.
"wistful": The Crack-Up, 27.
"the skull and crossbones": Hayes and Dody, On Reflection, 95.

94 "You may be the world to Bill, dear": Wilson, The Twenties, 133.
"common, graceless and dull": Ibid.
"not one bit drunk or disorderly": ZSF to FSF [spring 1919]; PUL.

95 "Within a few months": The Crack-Up, 27.
"had no interest in politics at all": Ibid., 14.
"political conscience": Ibid., 79.
"fair claim to membership": Bruccoli and Bryer, In His Own Time, 305.
"glorious spirit of abounding youth": Ibid., 310.

96 "best American novel": Ibid., 311.
"He sees himself constantly": Bruccoli, et al., The Romantic Egoists, 59.
"notably poor company": The Crack-Up, 88.
"Change Mckenzie to Mackenzie": FSF to MP [before April 24, 1920?]. See West, The Making, 101 – 103.
"F.P.A. is at it again": FSF to MP, July 17, 1920; Ibid., 109.
"rather gay party": The Crack-Up, 88.
"We were there three days": FSF to Marie Hersey [May 1920]; Letters, 460.

97 "I think he will be fairly tame": EW to Christian Gauss, April 28, 1920; Wilson, Letters, 53.
"Isn't it wonderful!": EW to Arthur Mizener, January 27, 1950; Beinecke.
"looking like a tarnished Apollo": Wilson, The Twenties, 60.

98 "better than any place on earth": FSF to John Grier Hibben [June 30, 1920]; Letters, 462.
"taken away the honors": Ibid.
"cleaner, healthier, better looking": Ibid.
"On that day in 1920": The Crack-Up, 89.

99 "A New England conscience": Afternoon, 134.
"I soon got over my shyness": Wilson, The Twenties, 16.
"When it comes to lovin' ": Ibid., 263.
"You couldn't have him in the room": Ibid., 139.
"more inexperienced girlfriends": Ibid., 30.
"And yet there are people": E. E. Paramore to EW, September 28, 1922; Beinecke.

100 "Oh, Teddy": Wilson, The Twenties, 179.
"choir boys of Hell," "the Great Queen": Ibid., 65.
"This had, I believe": Ibid., 28.
"I wonder you can spare them": Ibid., 29.

101 "cold fishy side": Ibid., 425.

"connoisseur of kisses": *The Beautiful and Damned,* 74.
"Sudden revulsion seized Amory": *This Side of Paradise,* 14.
"I don't want to": Ibid.
"She kissed him several times": *Notebooks,* no. 570.
"Her face, flushed with cold": Ibid., no. 479.
"Her body was so assertively": Ibid., no. 482.

102   "Mae Purley, without the involuntary quiver": Ibid., no. 589.
"Mae's pale face and burning lips": Ibid., no. 516.
"Zelda used to say that hotel bedrooms": Wilson, *The Twenties,* 214.
"She loves shocking stories": *This Side of Paradise*, 171.
"Women she detested": Ibid. This is one of the points at which Fitzgerald adapted material from Zelda's letters. She wrote him her views on women: "If they'd just awake to the fact that their excuse and explanation is the necessity for a disturbing element among them—they'd be much happier, and the men much more miserable —which is exactly what they need for the improvement of things in general." ZSF to FSF [spring 1919]; PUL.
"John, I like you better": Wilson, *The Twenties,* 55.
"a long line of bachelors": Eble, *A Collection of Criticism,* 10.

103   "neurotically jealous": EW to Arthur Mizener, January 27, 1950; Beinecke.
"Oh, yes, they really have kisses": Wilson, *The Twenties,* 55.

104   "We did not like women": ZSF to FSF [late summer/early fall 1930]; *Correspondence,* 245.
"I never thought she was beautiful": Dorothy Parker to Nancy Milford, *Zelda,* 94.
"beglamoured": Wilson, *The Twenties,* 48.
"This looks like a road company": Ibid.

105   "Did you ever meet": Hellman, *An Unfinished Woman,* 187.
"No, but don't remind her": *Notebooks,* no. 314.
"Revelry and Marriage": *Ledger,* 174.
"the happiest year since I was 18": Ibid.
"I remember riding in a taxi": *The Crack-Up,* 28.

106   "complete literary radical": FSF to Robert Bridges, October 25 [1919]; *Letters,* 140. See also FSF to MP [ca. January 10, 1920]; Ibid., 142.

107   "That was the shock of our lives": FSF to Ruth Sturtevant [May 14, 1920]; Ibid., 461.
"forcibly": Ibid.
"quarreled over morals once": ZSF to FSF [late summer/early fall 1930]; *Correspondence,* 245.
"As soon as we get a servant": ZSF to Ludlow Fowler, May 19, 1920; PUL.

108   "Called on Scott Fitz and his bride": Turnbull, *Scott Fitzgerald,* 112. Extensive portions of McKaig's diary have been published in both Turnbull and in Milford's *Zelda.* Citations are from both these sources.
"Terrible party": Turnbull, *Scott Fitzgerald,* 112.
"Zelda had decided to change": Wilson, *The Twenties,* 59.
"reveling nude in the orgies of Westport": EW to HLM, May 12, 1922; Wilson, *Letters,* 82.

109   "because I drove it over a fire-plug": ZSF to Ludlow Fowler, May 19, 1920; PUL.
"cindery aroma": *The Crack-Up,* 41.
"Touring South. Shy of money": FSF to EW, n.d. [1920]; Beinecke.
"It's a pity that a nice girl": *The Cruise of the Rolling Junk;* a facsimile edition of articles published in *Motor* (February, March, April 1924).
"summer whine of phonographs": *The Crack-Up,* 42.
"There were so many smells": Ibid.

"Suddenly Zelda was crying": *The Cruise of the Rolling Junk.*

110   "What's happened to you?": Mayfield, *Exiles*, 61.

"The joys of motoring": ZSF to Ludlow Fowler, August 16, 1920; Milford, *Zelda*, 101.

"no power on earth": *Save Me the Waltz*, 42.

"she hadn't been absolutely sure": Ibid., 50.

"I can't tell you how glad": ZSF to Ludlow Fowler, August 16, 1920; Milford, *Zelda*, 101.

111   "Stephan Parrot [*sic*] from his brother": See *Correspondence*, 64.

"moderately spaced affairs": Stephan Parrott to FSF, August 9, 1921; PUL.

"As a matter of fact, Mr. Mencken": FSF to HLM, March 20, 1920; *Correspondence*, 55.

"an exquisite burlesque of Compton Mackenzie": Ibid.

112   "an exquisite burlesque": EW to FSF, November 21, 1919; Wilson, *Letters*, 45. On the very same date that he inscribed the copy to Mencken, Fitzgerald also inscribed one to Wilson. He wrote, "This 'Exquisite burlesque of Compton Mackenzie with a pastiche of Wells at the end' is presented as *toll* to Bunny Wilson." See Wilson, *Letters*, 47.

"I'm not so cocksure about things": FSF to MP, February 3 [1920]; *Dear Scott*, 28.

Fitzgerald had certainly read Frank Norris' *McTeague:* See Sklar, *The Last Laocoön*, 72: "There is no definite indication that Fitzgerald had read either Dreiser or Conrad by June 1920; rather he is quoting directly from Mencken's *Book of Prefaces.*"

"My view of life, President Hibben": FSF to John Grier Hibben [June 3, 1920]; *Letters*, 462.

"Conrad . . . is of the firm and resolute conviction": Cooke, *The Vintage Mencken*, 48.

113   "guano": Angoff, *The World of George Jean Nathan*, 7.

"handsome pomposity": Loos, *Cast of Thousands*, 41.

"Why didn't you call me up": George Jean Nathan to ZSF, n.d. [summer 1920?]; PUL.

"The beach, and dozens of men": [late summer/early fall 1930]; *Correspondence*, 245.

"the quintessence of [his] second-rate generation": Wilson, *The Twenties*, 49.

"horrified compunction": Ibid., 59.

114   "Sweet Souse": George Jean Nathan to ZSF, n.d.; PUL.

"At present, I'm hardly able": ZSF to Ludlow Fowler, August 16, 1920; Milford, *Zelda*, 101.

"gained a lot of inspiration from them": Nathan, "Memories of Fitzgerald, Lewis and Dreiser," *Esquire*, October 1958, 148–149.

"all in more or less exalted": Ibid.

"a personal affront": Manchester, *Disturber of the Peace*, 159.

115   "wined, victualed, etc.": EW to William Manchester, July 21, 1950; Beinecke.

"It may be that both [Nathan] and Mencken": Wilson's handwritten note in response to Manchester's letter of August 1, 1950.

"Mind absolutely undisciplined"; McKaig "Diary," September 11, 1920; Milford, *Zelda*, 103.

"Practically everyone of us": McKaig, Midnight [August 1920]; Ibid., 102.

"I certainly will be glad": McKaig, September 11, 1920; Ibid.

116   "sounds awful — no seriousness": McKaig, September 27, 1920; Ibid., 105.

"When I'm with John": Wilson, *The Twenties*, 53.

"Modern Sappho. Eighteen love affairs": McKaig "Diary," September 11, 1920; Milford, *Zelda,* 103.

"damn stupid": McKaig, September 20, 1920; Ibid., 105.

"Zelda came in & woke me": McKaig, September 16, 1920; Ibid.

117   "They threatened to put him off": McKaig, September 15, 1920; Ibid., 103.

"Fitz should let Zelda go": Ibid.

"Went to Fitzgeralds": McKaig, October 12, 1920; Ibid., 106–107.

"Fitz made another true remark": McKaig, October 13, 1920; Turnbull, *Scott Fitzgerald,* 113.

"Spent evening at Fitzgeralds": McKaig, October 16, 1920; Ibid., 114.

118   "Millay's response": McKaig, October 18, 1920; Milford, *Zelda,* 107.

"Fitz is hard up now": McKaig, October 20, 1920; Turnbull, *Scott Fitzgerald,* 114.

"Went up to Fitzgeralds to spend evening": McKaig, October 21, 1920; Ibid.

"Follies with Scott & Zelda": McKaig, October 25, 1920; Ibid.

119   "She passed very quickly": Campbell, "The Fitzgeralds Were My Friends," MS, PUL.

"romanticly attached": ZSF to FSF [late summer/early fall 1930]; *Correspondence,* 245.

120   "a casual one or two night affair": Hellman, *An Unfinished Woman,* 57.

"DEAR SCOTT THEY JUST FORWARDED": Dorothy Parker to FSF, July 6?; PUL.

"current idol": FSF to Mr. and Mrs. Philip McQuillan, December 28, 1920; *Letters,* 466.

"brilliant analysis": Bruccoli and Bryer, *In His Own Time,* 119.

"Why has no one mentioned": FSF to Burton Rascoe, November 17, 1920; *Correspondence,* 72.

121   "Mencken's code of honor": FSF to Burton Rascoe, December 7, 1920; Ibid.

"rule by the best minds": Rascoe, *We Were Interrupted,* 24.

"quite entheusiastic about Main Street": FSF to Burton Rascoe, November 17, 1920; *Correspondence,* 72.

"an incident in American life": Schorer, *Sinclair Lewis,* 268.

"Main Street is rotten": FSF to Burton Rascoe, December 7, 1920; *Correspondence,* 73.

"I'm all for *Salt, The Titan* and *Main Street*": FSF to James Branch Cabell, Christmas 1920; *Letters,* 465.

"I agree on Main Street": FSF to HLM, December 30, 1920; *Correspondence,* 75.

"I want to tell you that *Main Street*": FSF to Sinclair Lewis, January 26 [1921]; *Letters,* 467.

122   "pleasant sheep": FSF to Thomas Boyd, February 9 [1921]; *Correspondence,* 79.

"Even the stupidest people are reading *Main Street*": Ibid.

"Beginnings of coldness": *Ledger,* October 1920.

123   "living royally": FSF to Shane Leslie, August 6, 1920; *Letters,* 376.

"I am not averse": FSF to Mr. and Mrs. Philip McQuillan, December 28, 1920; Ibid., 466.

"so beautiful, so blond, so clean and clear": Mayfield, *Exiles,* 59.

"immediately contemptuous": FSF to HO, February 8, 1936; *Letters,* 403.

"[Dorothy Gish] is a colorless wench": FSF to Mr. and Mrs. Philip McQuillan, December 28, 1920; Ibid., 466.

"The world of the picture actors": *The Crack-Up,* 28.

124   "Spent evening at Fitzgeralds": McKaig, "Diary," November 13, 1920; Milford, *Zelda,* 108.

"Fitz making . . . speeches before select audiences": McKaig, November 27, 1920; Ibid.

"Suggested to Scott": McKaig, November 28, 1920; Ibid.

"Lunch at Gotham.": McKaig, December 4, 1920; Ibid.

125 "many adventures": Ibid., 109.

From that winter of dissipation: See ZSF to FSF [late summer/early fall 1930] *Correspondence*, 245.

"black eye": *Ledger*, January 1921.

"Evening at Fitz": McKaig, "Diary," December 11, 1920; Milford, *Zelda*, 109.

"all aimed to hand down": McKaig, December 18, 1920; Ibid.

"Finding no nucleus": *The Crack-Up*, 27.

126 "I remember a lonesome Christmas": Ibid.

Life, Liquor, and Literature

PAGE

127 "the sacredness of a family heirloom": *Afternoon*, 89.

"I have been pacing the floor": FSF to MP, December 31, 1920; *Dear Scott*, 34.

"I've made half a dozen starts": Ibid.

"My family seem[s] to need a fur coat ect": FSF to MP [ca. November 7, 1920]; *Dear Scott*, 32.

128 "If I could have $1000": FSF to MP [ca. December 8, 1920]; Ibid., 33.

"the life of one Anthony Patch": FSF to Charles Scribner II, August 12, 1920; *Letters*, 145.

129 "silk pajamas, brocaded dressing gowns": *The Beautiful and Damned*, 8.

"sufficient linen for three men": Ibid., 11.

"Anthony dressed there, arranged his immaculate hair": Ibid.

"a war of muddled optimism": Ibid., 40.

"Tell me": Ibid., 60.

130 "We're twins": Ibid., 131.

"Boston society contralto": Ibid., 5.

"wedded to a vague melancholy": Ibid., 6.

"for the first and last time": Ibid., 189.

"He saw himself in khaki": Ibid., 206.

131 "At the last they were too far away": Ibid., 309.

"Afterward she was glad": Ibid., 369.

"Oh, my pretty face!": Ibid., 404.

"Its too obvious to have him go crazy": FSF to MP, March 30, 1921; *Dear Scott*, 35.

132 "There on Sunday nights": *The Beautiful and Damned*, 69.

"He tried to imagine himself": Ibid., 56.

"My publishers, you know,": Ibid., 423.

"In Scott Fitzgerald we have an author": FSF to MP, July 30, 1921; *Dear Scott*, 40.

"the half truths and evasions": *Notebooks*, no. 486.

133 "Work!" she scoffed. "Oh, you sad bird!": *The Beautiful and Damned*, 211.

"Throughout the previous winter": Bruccoli, et al., *The Romantic Egoists*, 77.

"I am editing the MS": EW to Stanley Dell, February 19, 1921; Wilson, *Letters*, 56.

134 "Then, I guess she commits suicide": Angoff, *H. L. Mencken: A Portrait from Memory*, 98–99.

"I married her eventually": FSF to Phyllis Duganne Parker [fall 1920]; *Correspondence*, 71.

"This book which I feel sure": FSF to Mrs. Edward Fitzgerald, February 6, 1922; Ibid., 95.

"Gloria was a much more trivial": FSF to Scottie, June 14, 1940; Ibid., 600.

135   "I wish the Beautiful and Damned had been": FSF to ZSF [summer (?) 1930]; Ibid., 241.

"in the old days": Bruccoli, et al., *The Romantic Egoists*, 79.

"I'm not strong for the uplift stuff": Ibid.

"very boiled": FSF to Ralph Block, May 2, 1921; *Correspondence*, 82.

136   "The trouble is": Ibid., 83.

"seemed a little crestfallen": EW to FSF, June 22, 1921; Wilson, *Letters*, 63.

"Tullocks, Seywards, Engalitcheff": *Ledger*, May 1921.

"furtively and impressedly": Turnbull, *Scott Fitzgerald*, 124.

"a fine quiet reticent English gentleman": EW to Arthur Mizener, November 10, 1949; Beinecke.

"Mr. Galsworthy, you are one": Mizener, *The Far Side of Paradise*, 145.

137   "I don't think he liked it much": Ibid.

"a gross public compliment": EW to Arthur Mizener, November 10, 1949: Beinecke.

"I was rather disappointed": FSF to Shane Leslie, May 24, 1921; *Letters*, 379.

"a shade of blue": Wilson, *The Shores of Light*, 380.

"big as tomatoes": ZSF to FSF [late summer/early fall 1930]; *Correspondence*, 246.

"turned out to be so pleasant": FSF to ZSF, May 11, 1940; *Letters*, 116.

"I liked him mighty well": FSF to MP, May 26, 1921; *Dear Scott*, 38.

"the most beautiful spot in the world": Ibid., 37.

"Come on Over": ZSF and FSF to EW, May 23, 1921; Beinecke.

138   "France is a bore and a disappointment": FSF to Shane Leslie, May 24, 1921; *Letters*, 379.

"These Wops!": Bruccoli, et al., *The Romantic Egoists*, 85.

"God damn the continent of Europe": FSF to EW [misdated May 1921]; *Letters*, 326.

"drinking, drinking": ZSF to FSF [late summer/early fall 1930]; *Correspondence*, 246.

"Men from the British Embassy": *The Crack-Up*, 42.

"as the place where Zelda and I": FSF to J. F. Carter [spring 1922]; *Correspondence*, 99.

139   "Of 20 reviews about half": FSF to EW [misdated May 1921]; *Letters*, 326.

"France made me sick": Ibid.

"The truth is that you": EW to FSF, July 5, 1921; Wilson, *Letters*, 63.

140   "I would not love her again": EW to JPB, July 3, 1921; Ibid., 67.

"Goofo and Baby": JPB to EW, July 14, 1921; Beinecke.

"You may be right": FSF to EW, July 2, 1921; Beinecke.

"acidulous (and rather silly) explosion": FSF to MP [ca. December 1, 1921]; *Dear Scott*, 44.

"The Fitzgeralds, as you may have heard": JPB to EW, August 15, 1921; Beinecke.

141   "best combatant story": Bruccoli and Bryer, *In His Own Time*, 144.

142   "No one has a greater contempt": Ibid., 143.

"He hasn't a very original mind": FSF to MP [ca. June 20, 1922]; *Dear Scott*, 61.

"one God-damned line": Turnbull, *Scott Fitzgerald*, 128.

"charming egotist": FSF to James Branch Cabell, March 4, 1922; *Letters*, 472.

Ironically, two decades later: See McGuire, *Bollingen*, 207.

In an unkind moment: *Notebooks*, no. 1791.

143 "I'm having a hell of a time": FSF to MP, August 25, 1921; *Dear Scott*, 41.

"delirious summer": E. E. Paramore to EW, September 23 [1921]; Beinecke.

"Oh God, goofo I'm drunk": *Ledger*, October 1921.

"CONGRATULATIONS FEARED TWINS": Bruccoli, et al., *The Romantic Egoists*, 87.

"I'm glad the damn thing's over.": FSF to EW [November 25, 1921]; *Letters*, 327.

144 "SHE THINKS NEW ENDING": FSF to MP, December 23, 1921; *Correspondence*, 89.

"dead right": MP to FSF, December 27, 1921; *Dear Scott*, 50.

"The girl is excellent": FSF to MP [ca. January 31, 1922]; Ibid., 52–53.

"He looks like a sawed-off young tough": Ibid., 52.

"the latest spud": FSF to HLM, December 30, 1920; *Correspondence*, 75.

"brave attempts": Bruccoli and Bryer, *In His Own Time*, 125.

145 "a bum art form": EW to FSF, November 21, 1919; Wilson, *Letters*, 46.

"dumping all one's youthful impressions": Ibid., 46–47.

"a wretched thing without a hint": FSF to Burton Rascoe, November 17, 1920; *Correspondence*, 72.

"This writing of a young man's novel": FSF to Thomas Boyd, February 9 [1921]; *Correspondence*, 79.

"the depths of banality": Ibid.

"freely from James Joyce": FSF to HLM, December 30, 1920; Ibid., 75.

"I'm . . . sorry I said": FSF to HLM, January 5 [1921]; Ibid., 77.

"the most brilliantly successful": FSF to MP, July 30, 1921; *Letters*, 146 and footnote.

"not *one* newspaper ad": Ibid.

146 "She is *awfully* cute": ZSF to Ludlow Fowler, December 22, 1921; Milford, *Zelda*, 114.

"We are both simply mad": Ibid.

"I've had the pleasure": FSF to James Branch Cabell [February 1922]; *Letters*, 472.

"a raised check by an employee": FSF to HO [received March 13, 1922]; *As Ever*, 40.

"etched hotel, dainty and subdued": *The Crack-Up*, 42.

147 "particularly Zelda, who has become more matronly": EW to Stanley Dell, March 25, 1922; Wilson, *Letters*, 78.

"He looks like John Barrymore": Ibid., 78–79.

"Zelda and her abortionist": *Ledger*, March 1922.

"His son went down the toilet": *Notebooks*, no. 1564.

"pills and Dr. Lackin": ZSF to FSF [late summer/early fall 1930]; *Correspondence*, 246.

Her friend and sometime confidante: See Mayfield, *Exiles*, 80.

"That is, I'm neutral": *The Beautiful and Damned*, 204.

"Well, can't you — why can't you talk": MS., Book II, Chap. 2, 22; PUL.

148 "Afterward I might have wide hips": *The Beautiful and Damned*, 203.

"after an all-night party": EW to Stanley Dell, March 25, 1922; Wilson, *Letters*, 79.

"My original plan": FSF to EW [spring 1922]; *Letters*, 334.

"the meaninglessness of life": Wilson, *The Shores of Light*, 32.

149 "Not only is it ornamented": Ibid., 28–29.

"nearly mature": Ibid., 34.

"into something iridescent and surprising": Ibid., 31.

"uncanny fascination": FSF to EW [January 1922]; *Letters*, 330.

"It's no blurb": FSF to MP [ca. January 31, 1922]; *Dear Scott*, 53.

"romantic, but also cynical": Wilson, *The Shores of Light*, 31.

"this thing would hurt me more": FSF to EW [January 1922]; *Letters*, 330.

"that's where Francis Scott Key comes in": Ibid., 331.

"The most enormous influence": Ibid.

150 "concocted a wonderful idea": FSF to EW, July 13, 1922; Ibid., 337.

"the best American comedy ever written": EW to FSF, May 26, 1922; Wilson, *Letters*, 84.

151 "Nathan and me": FSF to EW, November 25, 1921; *Letters*, 328.

"The pictures prove to me": George Jean Nathan to ZSF, May 29, 1922; PUL.

"I can probably place it for you": George Jean Nathan to FSF, February 14, 1922; PUL.

"I feel that he will confect": Nathan, *The Theatre, The Drama, The Girls*, 16.

"A very substantial performance": Fitzgerald quoted Nathan's remarks in a letter to Max Perkins [ca. March 5, 1922]; *Letters*, 154.

"his usual self": FSF to James Branch Cabell, March 27, 1922; Ibid., 473.

"Fitzgerald blew into New York": HLM to James Branch Cabell, [March 1922]; Colum, *Between Friends*, 254.

"going to make me rich forever": FSF to MP [before December 27, 1921]; *Correspondence*, 90.

152 "very satisfactory but not inspiring": FSF to EW, June 25, 1922; *Letters*, 336.

"*Cytherea* is Hergesheimer's best": FSF to EW [January 24, 1922]; Ibid., 329.

"both in plan and execution": Bruccoli and Bryer, *In His Own Time*, 323.

"twilight nymphs": Ibid., 320.

"not because she is the more vivid": Ibid., 322.

"a marvelous book": JPB to EW [1921?]; Beinecke.

"the bitter cry": Bruccoli and Bryer, *In His Own Time*, 317.

"another picture of a society upset by modernism": Ibid., 319.

"veracious in its way": Ibid., 318.

153 "By now you've seen": FSF to MP [after March 4, 1922]; *Correspondence*, 97.

"It dwells, one imagines": Bruccoli and Bryer, *In His Own Time*, 337.

"To begin with, every one must buy this book": Ibid., 332.

"convey a profound air of erudition": Ibid., 333–334.

"In fact, Mr. Fitzgerald": Ibid., 333.

"A most attractive fellow": EW to Stanley Dell, March 25, 1922; Wilson, *Letters*, 79.

154 "I'm writing you": FSF to Burton Rascoe [ca. April 1922]; *Correspondence*, 100.

"There is something faintly repellent": FSF to EW, June 25, 1922; *Letters*, 336.

"Rascoe is getting worse": FSF to EW [August 5, 1922]; Ibid., 338.

"silly story": FSF to Burton Rascoe [after April 30, 1922]; *Correspondence*, 103 and note. See also FSF to Robert Bridges [before May 13, 1922]; *Letters*, 159–160.

"blubberingly sentimental": quoted in Sklar, *The Last Laocoön*, 126.

155 "You are all wrong": FSF to Burton Rascoe, May 5, 1922; *Correspondence*, 105.

"I won't say she was rude": Mrs. C. O. Kalman to Nancy Milford, September 1964; *Zelda*, 123.

"I want to show that it was published": FSF to MP [April 21, 1922]; *Correspondence*, 102.

"the whole gorgeous farce": Bruccoli and Bryer, *In His Own Time*, 122.

"he will hear the YMCA men": Ibid.

"I regard it as more or less": EW to FSF, May 26, 1922; Wilson, *Letters*, 85.

"I think her a prime dumbbell": Ibid.

"Having the money": FSF to EW [May 30, 1922]; Beinecke.

"the most amusing piece of buffoonery": EW to FSF, June 20, 1922; Wilson, *Letters,* 87.

"His mother and sister": Ibid.

157   "Your description of the wedding": FSF to EW, June 25, 1922; Beinecke.

"as if in portent": EW to FSF, July 31, 1922; Wilson, *Letters,* 88.

"It was all very affecting": Ibid.

"I miss him terribly": EW to Elinor Wylie, July 13, 1922; Ibid., 89.

Innocence Is No End in Itself

PAGE

161   "such a handsome head waiter": *The Crack-Up,* 42 – 43.

"The most extraordinary thing": EW to JPB, September 22, 1922; Wilson, *Letters,* 96.

162   *"Enfants Terribles"*: Bruccoli, et al., *The Romantic Egoists,* 98.

"Isn't it dweadful of me": Wilson, *The Twenties,* 205.

163   "stopped Cummings in his tracks": Ibid., 207.

"something about him that was soft": Ibid., 323.

"the million dollar look": Dos Passos, *The Best Times,* 127.

"gaudy Liberty silk necktie": Ibid., 128.

"Their gambit": Ibid.

164   "Scott had good bootleggers": Ibid.

"When he talked about writing": Ibid., 129.

"one to x weeks": ZSF to C. O. and X. Kalman, n.d. [October 1922]; PUL.

"common": Ibid.

165   "Zelda and I kept saying things": Dos Passos, *The Best Times,* 130.

"It wasn't that she wanted me": Ibid.

"The gulf that opened": Ibid.

166   "They were celebrities": Ibid.

"my 14 kt. couple": ZSF to C. O. and X. Kalman, n.d. [October 1922]; PUL.

"nifty little Babbit home": ZSF to C. O. and X. Kalman [October 13, 1922]; PUL.

"We have had the most terrible": Ibid.

167   "The Follies themselves were wonderful": EW to JPB, September 22, 1922; Wilson, *Letters,* 98.

"looks like nothing so much as Times Square": ZSF to C. O. and X. Kalman, n.d.; PUL.

168   "most amusing after the dull healthy": FSF to Mrs. Richard Taylor [after October 1922]; *Correspondence,* 117.

"Dog, dog — I like a good dog — ": Wilson, *The Twenties,* 222 – 223.

169   "And please don't tell anyone": FSF to MP [April 21, 1922]; *Correspondence,* 102.

"a good laugh": FSF to Thomas Boyd and Cornelius Van Ness [after December 10, 1922]; Ibid., 120.

"by *far* the worst movie": FSF to C. O. Kalman [after December 10, 1922]; Ibid., 119.

170   "a pleasant affiliation": FSF to Thomas Boyd [March 1923]; Ibid., 127.

One of his minor film projects: See Lewis, *Edith Wharton,* 444.

"By the way, Mrs. Wharton": EW to JPB, June 30, 1923; Wilson, *Letters,* 106.

"full of ozone": ZSF to C. O. and X. Kalman [January 1923]; PUL.

"They paid me fifteen thousand": FSF to Thomas Boyd [March 1923]; *Correspondence,* 126.

"So you see I'm now": Ibid.

171   "No figures in this letter": Ibid., 127.

"It was an age of miracles": *The Crack-Up,* 14.

"a collegiate literary world": ZSF to FSF [late summer/early fall 1930]; *Correspondence,* 245.

"undisguisably a babel of tongues": Wilson, *The Shores of Light,* 398.

"There *was* something going on": Ibid., 399.

"They all came from the suburbs": Wilson, *The Twenties,* 45.

172   "I found this rather tiresome": Ibid.

"Listen Mom, put on your glasses": Gaines, *Wit's End,* 31.

"enormous reverence": Wilson, *The Twenties,* 48–49.

173   "Because he is quite unaware": Amory and Bradlee, *Vanity Fair,* 80. See also, FSF to EW [before March 1923]; *Correspondence,* 125.

"This has made me suspicious": Wilson, *The Twenties,* 42.

"a long and uneventful one": Amory and Bradlee, *Vanity Fair,* 35.

174   "the glossiest bounder": Wilson, *The Twenties,* 34.

"incapable of saying": Ibid.

"It always seemed undignified": FSF to EW [February 1921]; *Correspondence,* 82.

175   "rivaled in their way": *The Crack-Up,* 30.

"whose articles in The New Democracy": *The Beautiful and Damned,* 285.

"It contains some of the most brilliant": EW to Stanley Dell, May 26, 1922; Wilson, *Letters,* 83.

"probably one of the most remarkable": Ibid.

"Am undecided about *Ulysses'* application": FSF to EW [August 5, 1922]; Ibid., 339.

176   "the only criticism yet": FSF to EW [July 13, 1922]; Ibid., 337.

"I agree with you about Bunny and Mencken": FSF to Thomas Boyd [May 1924]; *Correspondence,* 141.

"the great novel of the future": Quoted in Bruccoli, *Some Sort of Epic Grandeur,* 178 and note.

"It seems that Mencken has studied": EW to Stanley Dell, March 25, 1922; Wilson, *Letters,* 79.

"conspiracy against the government": Edmiston and Cirino, *Literary New York,* 57.

177   "drawings and writings": EW to FSF, November 6, 1922; Wilson, *Letters,* 98.

"The idea is to make": Ibid.

"the most elaborate": *Playboy,* undated; back cover copy.

"It looked like Flanders Field": Wilson, *The Twenties,* 138.

"I feel ready to say 'Blaa!' ": Ibid., 138.

178   "blew up as usual": Ibid.

"Successful scrapping not being": *The Crack-Up,* 28.

"Come and bring a lot of drunks": John Dos Passos to FSF [January 1923 (?)]; Dos Passos, *The Fourteenth Chronicle,* 353.

"Any contestant": Ibid., 353–354.

"I read this book of Cabell's": Wilson, *The Twenties,* 79–80.

"Oh, I am Edna St. Vincent Millay!": Ibid., 80.

179   "lots of talk": Kellner, *Carl Van Vechten,* 141.

"Rilda and David tortured each other": Van Vechten, *Parties,* 203.

"Scott slumbered in the living-room": Brooks, *Days of the Phoenix,* 109.

"embarrassing habit of using": Mizener, *The Far Side of Paradise*, 167.

180   "Suddenly, as though in a dream": Gilbert Seldes to Nancy Milford, *Zelda*, 127.
"a résumé of *The Education of Henry Adams*": Bruccoli and Bryer, *In His Own Time*, 330.
"because it presents a definite American": Ibid.
"I thought to myself": Gilbert Seldes to Nancy Milford, *Zelda*, 128.
"deathly pale": Drawbell, *James Drawbell: An Autobiography*, 171.
"Parties are a form of suicide": Ibid., 173.
"I was always trying to be": Ibid., 175.
"Oh, I've had all the fun": Ibid., 177.

181   "You ought to get the hell": Ibid.
Quite possibly the most notorious: The Dreiser party crops up in several memoirs. Burton Rascoe in *We Were Interrupted*, 299 – 302, reprints portions of Llewelyn Powys' account from *The Verdict of Bridlegoose*, with his own contradictory report on the event. Other accounts appear in Kellner, *Carl Van Vechten*, Anderson, *Memoirs*, and Boyd, *Portraits: Real and Imaginary*.
"an aging madonna lily": Rascoe, *We Were Interrupted*, 300.
"Mr. Dreiser, my name is Fitzgerald": Mayfield, *Constant Circle*, 43.

182   "Another lie! Fitz came in": Ibid.
"Even now I go into many flats": *The Crack-Up*, 28.
"We had run through a lot": Ibid., 29.
"I'm running wild in sackcloth and ashes": ZSF to Ludlow Fowler, November 22 [1922?]; PUL.

183   "Besides, I'm about the only one": Wilson, *The Shores of Light*, 142.
"Think of it!": Ibid.
"Maybe it would bore you to death": Ibid., 154.

184   "worshipped from afar": *The Crack-Up*, 29.
"My God, you beautiful egg!": Turnbull, *Scott Fitzgerald*, 136.
Even the dumb song title: See Wilson, *The Twenties*, 306, 307.
"Parties at Allan Dwan's": *Ledger*, July 1923.
"I'm too much of an egotist": FSF to JPB [April 1925]; Beinecke.

185   "pantheon of heroes": FSF to Scottie [winter 1939]; *Letters*, 49.
"an old friendship": *Notebooks*, no. 426.
"Rebecca West and a rather": FSF to Thomas Boyd [early 1924]; *Correspondence*, 138.

186   It is not clear whether this was: See Ray, *H. G. Wells & Rebecca West*, 156.
"craggy homeliness": Rebecca West to Nancy Milford, *Zelda*, 130.
"Fitz and Zelda have struck": EW to JPB, June 30, 1923; Wilson, *Letters*, 106.
"Visitors are requested": Mizener, *The Far Side of Paradise*, 165 – 166.
"merely put on disorderly drunken acts": Wilson, *The Twenties*, 95.

187   "Shall we have our coffee": Turnbull, *Scott Fitzgerald*, 138.
"I didn't notice he'd been drinking": Loos, *Kiss Hollywood Good-by*, 121.
"I'm eating dirt": Ibid., 122.
but the uncomfortable fact: Fitzgerald's *Ledger* entry for September 1928, for instance, reads, "Dirt eating at hotel."

188   "charming and brilliant young couple": Bruccoli, et al., *The Romantic Egoists*, 112 – 113.
"A large, brilliant, gathering": Ibid., 113.
"She is the most charming person": Ibid.
"Still drunk," "Tearing drunk": *Ledger* entries, February, April, July 1923.

"In Great Neck, there was always disorder": ZSF to FSF [late summer/early fall 1930]; *Correspondence*, 245.

189 "The repression breaks out": *Ledger*, 177.

"I think one of the things": Ring Lardner, Jr., *The Lardners*, 164.

190 Lardner was earning approximately $100,000 a year: See Yardley, *Ring*, 254.

"Ring and I got stewed": FSF to C. O. Kalman [after November 17, 1923]; *Correspondence*, 135.

"exactly like a merchant selling": Hart-Davis, *Hugh Walpole*, 203.

191 "She didn't pay as much attention": Ring Lardner, Jr., *The Lardners*, 161–162.

"My God, he hadn't even saved them!": *The Crack-Up*, 38.

"the worst editor of his own stuff": FSF to John Lardner, September 20, 1933; *Letters*, 506.

The story rippled out: See John Chapin Mosher, "That Sad Young Man" in Kazin, *F. Scott Fitzgerald*, 67–71.

192 "a disillusioning afternoon": MP to FSF, August 8, 1924; *Dear Scott*, 74.

"Scott was always lost in admiration": EW to "Dear Don," June 16, 1963; Beinecke.

193 "During those years": *The Crack-Up*, 36.

"2,500 words and I'm not getting": Ring Lardner, Jr., *The Lardners*, 162.

"Mr. Fitzgerald is a novelist": Lardner, *What of It?*, 18.

"Of all the girls for whom I care": Bruccoli, et al., *The Romantic Egoists*, 104.

"Ring is drinking himself": Yardley, *Ring*, 264.

"the after life": ZSF to X. Kalman [summer 1923]; PUL.

194 "not-forgotten summer night": FSF to Robert Kerr [April 1925]; *Correspondence*, 156.

"mysterious yachtsman whose mistress": FSF to Robert Kerr [June 1924]; Ibid., 143.

"THE BEAUTIFUL AND DAMNED": Bruccoli, et al., *The Romantic Egoists*, 103.

"Enroute from the coast": Max Gerlach to FSF [July 20, 1923]; *Correspondence*, 134.

195 "a catholic element": FSF to MP [ca. June 20, 1922]; *Dear Scott*, 61.

"Scott has started a new novel": ZSF to X. Kalman [summer 1923]; PUL.

"modus vivendi for preventing Zelda": EW to JPB, September 22, 1922; Wilson, *Letters*, 96.

"awe-inspiring half-lines": *Preface to This Side of Paradise*, 13.

"the dark celibacy of greatness": Ibid.

"Celibacy goes deeper than the flesh": *This Side of Paradise*, 158.

196 "The fear of God": Monsignor Fay to FSF, n.d. [1917]; PUL.

"Of course you shot a tremendous bolt": Monsignor Fay to FSF, June 6, 1918; PUL.

"He was perhaps created": FSF to John Jamieson, April 15, 1934; *Letters*, 504.

197 "the ebony mark of sexual offenses": *All the Sad Young Men*, 112.

"He could not tell Father Schwartz": Ibid., 115.

"Sometimes, near four o'clock": Ibid., 109.

"and he grew careful": Ibid.

"sensuously along roads": Ibid., 132.

198 "It's a thing like a fair": Ibid., 130.

"But don't get up close": Ibid.

"My play is the funniest": FSF to HO [December 27, 1921]; *As Ever*, 32–33.

"would flop on the boards": FSF to Mary Colum [ca. September 1923]; *Correspondence*, 134.

"I have been coming every day": FSF to MP [ca. November 5, 1923]; *Dear Scott*, 67.

199 "I'm at the end of my rope": Ibid.
"It was a colossal frost": *Afternoon*, 93 – 94.
"In brief, the show flopped": Bruccoli, *Some Sort of Epic Grandeur*, 187, 189.
"The whole thing has already cost me": FSF to HO [March 2, 1925]; *As Ever*, 75.

200 "I really worked hard as hell": FSF to EW [October 7, 1924]; *Letters*, 341.
"Scott's play went so badly": EW to JPB, January 15, 1924; Wilson, *Letters*, 118 – 119.
"I like Zelda better and better": Ibid., 119.

201 "Fitz said he was going abroad": Wilson, *The Twenties*, 185.
"conveyed his disgust": Ibid., 186.
"Deep blue patches appeared at the windows": Ibid.

A Consciously Artistic Achievement

PAGE

202 "against the mosquitoes": FSF to Thomas Boyd [May 1924]; *Correspondence*, 141.
"So dearie when your tender heart": Bruccoli, et al., *The Romantic Egoists*, 115.

203 "Yes, John seemed to us": FSF to EW [October 7, 1924]; Beinecke.
"like a bowl of Renoir flowers": MacLeish, *Riders on the Earth*, 79.
"Well-laundered": Donnelly and Billings, *Sara & Gerald*, 9.

204 "*un monsieur qui est par hasard*": MacLeish, *Riders on the Earth*, 124.
"Not that I care": FSF to Thomas Boyd [May 1924]; *Correspondence*, 141.
"a little tight": Ibid.

205 "forced atmosphere of picturesqueness": ZSF to MP [May 1924]; PUL.
"It rather spoiled the streets": FSF to Thomas Boyd, June 23, 1924; *Correspondence*, 142.
"clean, cool villa": *Afternoon*, 112.
"a summerhouse and a sandpile": Ibid., 112 – 113.
"Everything's idyllic": FSF to Thomas Boyd, June 23, 1924; *Correspondence*, 142.

206 "The Riviera is a seductive place": *Save Me the Waltz*, 90.
"Josanne and Silve": *Ledger*, June 1924.
"the artistic son": *Save Me the Waltz*, 84.
"René and Bobbie protruded insistently": Ibid.

207 "He was bronze and smelled of the sand": Ibid., 89.
"I don't know how far it really went": Gerald Murphy to Nancy Milford, *Zelda*, 142 – 143.
"The Big Crisis — 13th of July": *Ledger*, July 1924.

208 "A sad trip to Monte Carlo": Ibid.
"Zelda swimming every day. Getting brown": Ibid.
And only a few days after the Big Crisis: See FSF to HO, June 30, 1924; also ca. July 17, 1924 [received by Ober July 28th] and July 24, 1924. Several days later, Fitzgerald sent photographs to be used by the illustrator, with a plea "not to make my wife so utterly impossible looking." Ober received it on August 7. *As Ever*, 63 – 65.
"distinguished looking young man": *Afternoon*, 113.
"Both of them were burned": Ibid.

209 "Out of the casino": Ibid.
"Hasn't it been a good summer!": Ibid.
"It is twilight as I write this": Ibid., 116.

210 "Good work on novel": *Ledger*, August 1924.
Fitzgerald told a relative: See Milford, *Zelda*, 149. This was the version Zelda used

in her unfinished novel, *Caesar's Things*: "So she told her husband that she loved the French officer and her husband locked her up in the villa." See segment MS. titled "Jacob & Janno," Chap. 5; PUL.

211   "He told me he was so furious": Graham, *The Real F. Scott Fitzgerald*, 61.
"While he was telling me this": Ibid.
"This first version that he told me": Hemingway, *A Moveable Feast*, 170.
"It was one of their acts together": Hadley Hemingway to Nancy Milford, *Zelda*, 147–148.
"Then there was Josen": ZSF to FSF [late summer/early fall 1930]; *Correspondence*, 246.

212   "Whatever it was that she wanted": *Save Me the Waltz*, 98.
"Last sight of Josanne": *Ledger*, October 1924.
"romantic, decorous, and slightly comic": Mayfield, *Exiles*, 97.
"But they both had a need": Edouard Jozan to Nancy Milford, *Zelda*, 145.

213   "Sara . . . don't make me": Calvin Tomkins to Nancy Milford, *Zelda*, 144.
"Zelda drugged": *Ledger*, August 1925.
"Upon the theme of marital fidelity": Turnbull, *Scott Fitzgerald*, 146.
"strange mixed-up Irish catholic monogamy": EH to Arthur Mizener, May 12, 1950; Hemingway, *Selected Letters*, 694.

214   "That September 1924, I knew": *Notebooks*, no. 839.
"The going to the Riviera": Ibid., no. 765.
"Do you think he actually *is* a god?": *Save Me the Waltz*, 84.
"consciously artistic achievement": FSF to MP [ca. April 10, 1924]; *Dear Scott*, 70.

215   "If I'd spent this time reading": Ibid., 69.
"Trust me that at last": Ibid., 69–70.
"I feel I have an enormous power": Ibid., 70.
"We are idyllicly settled here & the novel": FSF to MP, June 18, 1924; Ibid., 72.
"I'm not going to mention my novel": FSF to MP [ca. July 10, 1924]; Ibid., 73.
"The novel will be done next week": FSF to MP [ca. August 25, 1924]; Ibid., 75.
"Its been a fair summer": Ibid., 76.
"I think my novel is about the best": Ibid.

216   "My book is wonderful": FSF to EW [October 7, 1924]; *Letters*, 341.
"mentioning prominent Biblical characters": Lardner, *What of It?*, 19.
"I think that at last": FSF to MP, October 27, 1924; *Dear Scott*, 80.
"I feel old too, this summer": FSF to Ludlow Fowler [August 1924]; *Correspondence*, 145.

217   "Whenever you feel like criticizing": *The Great Gatsby*, 1.
"If he'd of lived": Ibid., 169.
"once had a father stagger in": *Notebooks*, no. 989.
"out of a caterer's basket": *The Great Gatsby*, 43.

218   "a gorgeous, scarcely human orchid of a woman": Ibid., 106.
"They were still under the white-plum tree": Ibid., 108.
"vague personal capacity": Ibid., 101.
"that you never loved him": Ibid., 132.
"I can't help what's past": Ibid., 133.

219   "Clarence Endive was from East Egg": Ibid., 62.
"incurably dishonest": Ibid., 58.
"Jordan of course was a great idea": FSF to MP [ca. December 20, 1924]; *Dear Scott*, 90.

220   "In *Gatsby*, I selected the stuff": FSF to Corey Ford [early July 1937]; *Letters*, 551.
       "almost as valuable as positive originality": FSF to ZSF, July 6, 1940; *Letters*, 120.
       "by this man Goddard": *The Great Gatsby*, 13.

221   "northward to defile the Nordic race": FSF to EW [misdated May 1921]; *Letters*, 326.
       "the nature of Mr. Tostoff's composition": *The Great Gatsby*, 50.
       "But what struck me": Quoted in Le Vot, *F. Scott Fitzgerald*, 166.
       "Did you? Tell me your frank *reaction*": FSF to MP [ca. December 20, 1924]; *Dear Scott*, 90.
       "and see what I've left out": FSF to MP, September 10, 1924; *Correspondence*, 146.

222   "Gatsby is somewhat vague": MP to FSF, November 20, 1924; *Dear Scott*, 83.
       "I myself didn't know what Gatsby looked like": FSF to MP [ca. December 20, 1924]; Ibid., 89.
       "He's the best character I've ever done": Ibid., 90.

223   "Mr. Nobody from Nowhere": *The Great Gatsby*, 130.
       "like glass against Tom's hard malice": Ibid., 148.
       "ineffable gaudiness": Ibid., 99.
       "I suppose he'd had the name ready": Ibid.
       "gorgeous pink rag of a suit": Ibid., 154.
       "living too long with a single dream": Ibid., 162.
       "Can't repeat the past?": Ibid., 111.

224   "He had come a long way": Ibid., 182.
       "no good": FSF to HO, November 25, 1924; *As Ever*, 70.

225   "We make an agreement with children": *Six Tales of the Jazz Age*, 158.
       "I won't get a nights sleep": FSF to MP, October 27, 1924; *Dear Scott*, 81.
       "I think the novel is a wonder": MP to FSF, November 18, 1924; Ibid., 82.
       "It is an extraordinary book": MP to FSF, November 20, 1924; Ibid.

226   "Your wire & your letters": FSF to MP [ca. December 1, 1924]; Ibid., 85.
       "too ripe": See *As Ever*, 70 note.
       "a lowsy sheet": FSF to HO [January 26, 1925]; Ibid., 74.
       "It makes me weep": FSF to HO [February 18, 1925]; Ibid., 75.
       "cold": FSF to MP [ca. May 10, 1926]; *Dear Scott*, 142.
       "For Carmel Myers": Mizener, *The Far Side of Paradise*, 224.

227   "I could sleep with Zelda": Wilson, *The Twenties*, 298.
       "Zelda was not so loose": Ibid.
       "Plus vite, plus vite": Mayfield, *Exiles*, 111.
       "just about the rottenest thing": FSF to Howard Coxe, April 15, 1934; *Correspondence*, 349.

228   "There was a rushing, crashing noise": *The Price Was High*, 174.
       "I hate Italy and the Italians": FSF to HO [January 23, 1925]; *As Ever*, 73. Fitzgerald eventually wrote an article titled "The High Cost of Macaroni," which he admitted was "the lowsiest thing I'd ever written." (See *As Ever*, 81.) It was turned down by several magazines, and Fitzgerald eventually destroyed it, saving the better pieces of it for his notebooks. (See *As Ever*, 91.)
       "not a bit dirty": FSF to MP, January 24, 1925; *Dear Scott*, 93.
       "Rembrandt butcher shops": *The Crack-Up*, 45.
       "Zelda's been sick in bed": FSF to JPB [March 1925]; *Letters*, 355.
       "I think it's great": Ibid.
       "This place is full of fairies": FSF to MP, March 31, 1925; Ibid., 178.

229   "Dodo Benson is here": FSF to JPB [March 1925]; Beinecke.
       "I have just been reading": FSF to EW [October 7, 1924]; *Letters*, 341.

"Give one to some poor motherless Poilu fairy": FSF to EW, January 10 [1918]; *Letters*, 322.

"I sat up (tell Bunny)": FSF to JPB [April 1925]; Ibid., 356.

"I asked him why he had petered out": Wilson quoted Fitzgerald to Arthur Mizener, November 10, 1949; Wilson, *Letters*, 562–563.

230   "The cheerfullest things in my life": FSF to JPB [April 1925]; *Letters*, 327.

"I don't want any signed blurbs": FSF to MP, October 27, 1924; *Dear Scott*, 80.

"If my book is a big success": FSF to MP [ca. December 20, 1924]; Ibid., 91.

"Anyhow, I think": Ibid., 90.

"My guess is that it will sell": FSF to MP, January 24, 1925; Ibid., 93.

"stinko": FSF to MP [ca. December 20, 1924]; Ibid., 91.

"As the day approaches": FSF to MP [March 31, 1925]; Ibid., 98.

231   "The book comes out today": FSF to MP, April 10 [1925]; Ibid., 99.

Perkins cabled him: See note, *Dear Scott*, 101, for Perkins telegram.

"Your telegram depressed me": FSF to MP [ca. April 24, 1925]; Ibid., 101.

"that the way of writing": MP to FSF, April 20, 1925; Ibid., 100.

"over the heads": Ibid., 101.

"quite wild about it": Ibid.

232   "from May 12th to January 12th": FSF to MP, May 1 [1925]; Ibid., 104.

"chemical trace of magic": Bruccoli, et al., *The Romantic Egoists*, 125.

"F. SCOTT FITZGERALD'S LATEST A DUD": Bruccoli and Bryer, *In His Own Time*, 345.

"He gets the exact tone": Ibid., 347.

"It is undoubtedly in some ways": EW to FSF, April 11, 1925; Wilson, *Letters*, 121.

"I think it is incomparably the best": HLM to FSF, April 16 [1925]; *Correspondence*, 158.

"in form no more than a glorified anecdote": Bruccoli and Bryer, *In His Own Time*, 348.

"It's so good, Scott": Gilbert Seldes to FSF, May 26 [1925]; *Correspondence*, 164.

"has mastered his talents": Bruccoli and Bryer, *In His Own Time*, 360.

"On Page 82": Ring Lardner to FSF and ZSF, March 24 [1925]; *Correspondence*, 154.

233   "The plot held my interest": Ibid.

" 'The best since Paradise' ": FSF to MP, April 10 [1925]; *Dear Scott*, 99.

"tremendously moved": FSF to HLM, May 4, 1925; *Letters*, 480.

"not one had the slightest idea": FSF to EW [spring 1925]; *Letters*, 342.

"In all events I have a book": FSF to MP [ca. April 24, 1925]; *Dear Scott*, 102.

234   "I think all the reviews I've seen": FSF to MP [ca. May 22, 1925]; Ibid., 106.

Just a Real Place to Rough It

PAGE

236   "If you're going to ask me": Janet Flanner to James R. Mellow, October 1969.

"If the reader prefers": Hemingway, *A Moveable Feast*, Preface.

"This is to tell you": FSF to MP [ca. October 10, 1924]; *Dear Scott*, 78.

237   "I haven't it here now": Ibid.

"Hemminway is a fine, charming fellow": FSF to MP [ca. May 22, 1925]; Ibid., 106.

"completely worthless characters": Hemingway, *A Moveable Feast*, 147.

"Scott was a man then": Ibid.

238   "praise to the face": Ibid., 148.

"the extraordinarily nice, unworried": Ibid., 147.

239 "as soon as he could get his last": Ibid., 151–152.
"To hear him talk of it": Ibid., 152.
"He was cynical and funny": Ibid., 151.

240 "I was delighted that I had used up": Ibid., 155.
"It was as exciting to him": Ibid., 160.

241 "I was getting tired of the literary life": Ibid., 163.
Every detail of the account: That Hemingway did not invent the story out of the whole cloth is evident from a letter he wrote Fitzgerald in December 1925: "Know you will be glad to read in N.Y. Herald that 2 men died of cold in Chalons Sur Saone where you nearly did same." Hemingway, *Selected Letters*, 182.
"We had a great trip together": EH to MP, June 9, 1925; Hemingway, *Selected Letters*, 162–163.
"Hemingway and I went to Lyons": FSF to Gertrude Stein, June 1925; Gallup, *The Flowers of Friendship*, 174.
Where Mollie McQuillan Fitzgerald: Kenneth S. Lynn's "Hemingway's Private War," *Commentary*, July 1981, 24–33, gives a remarkably perceptive account of Hemingway's relationship with his parents, particularly his mother.

242 "bogus": Donnelly and Billings, *Sara & Gerald*, 21.
"phony as a rubber check": Mayfield, *Exiles*, 112.
"as male as all that": Donnelly and Billings, *Sara & Gerald*, 21.

243 "strong Cockney accent": Hemingway, *A Moveable Feast*, 178.
"Ernest, don't you think Al Jolson": Ibid., 184.
"Pain's such an awful thing": EH to FSF [ca. December 24, 1925]; Hemingway, *Selected Letters*, 182.
But the truth is that during those early years: See Hemingway, *Selected Letters*, 165, 177, 201.
"lovely, golden, wasted talent:" EH to Arthur Mizener, April 22, 1950; Ibid., 689.
"He was romantic, ambitious, and Christ, Jesus": Ibid., 690.

244 "Ernest would always give a helping hand": *Notebooks*, no. 1819.
"pretty much the old stuff": FSF to MP [ca. May 22, 1925]; *Dear Scott*, 106.
"It simply had not occurred to him": *The Crack-Up*, 325.
"a finished second-rater": Mayfield, *Exiles*, 108.
"He was a charming cheerful companion": EH to Arthur Mizener, April 22, 1950; Hemingway, *Selected Letters*, 690.
"He probably had others": Ibid.

245 "Let me tell you about the very rich": *All the Sad Young Men*, 1–2.
"It is in large measure": FSF to Ludlow Fowler [March 1925]; *Correspondence*, 152.

246 "I don't think he was ever happy": *All the Sad Young Men*, 56.
"Poor woman, she had to get": EH to EW, November 25, 1923; Hemingway, *Selected Letters*, 105.
"It seems Stallings is a great critic": EH to Archibald MacLeish, December 20, 1925; Ibid., 178. Here, Hemingway was agreeing with a remark made by John Dos Passos.
"could be roused to enthusiasm": Ibid.

247 "the first authentic book": Bruccoli, et al., *The Romantic Egoists*, 124.
"the only intelligent review so far": FSF to MP, May 1 [1925]; *Dear Scott*, 103.
"boys who find a new genius": FSF to MP [ca. December 27, 1925]; Ibid., 126.
"crazy about *Points of Honor*": FSF to Thomas Boyd [spring/summer 1925]; *Correspondence*, 166.
"I haven't an enormous faith": FSF to MP [June 1, 1925]; *Dear Scott*, 109.
"dressing up a few heart throbs": Ibid., 111.

"going to tell us mere superficial 'craftsmen' ": Ibid.

248 "Did you ever read": EH to FSF, December 15, 1925; Hemingway, *Selected Letters*, 176.

"getting stirred up over Main Street": Ibid.

"that shit": EH to Harold Loeb, January 5, 1925; Ibid., 143.

"One house would be fitted up": EH to FSF, July 1, 1925; Ibid., 165.

"a beautiful vacuum": Ibid.

"This city is full of Americans": FSF to EW [spring 1925]; *Letters*, 342.

249 "1000 parties and no work": *Ledger*, June 1925.

"Sap was great": FSF to Ludlow Fowler, November 6, 1925; *Correspondence*, 181.

"looking by no means distinguished": Ibid.

"has certainly the best chance": Piper, *Fitzgerald's The Great Gatsby*, 126.

"I believe I'd rather [have] your": FSF to Gilbert Seldes [June or July 1925]; *Letters*, 485. For his remark to Mencken, see *Invented Lives*, 233. He had written much the same thing to Max Perkins: "I'd rather have you & Bunny like it than anyone I know. And I'd rather have you like it than Bunny." FSF to MP [ca. December 1, 1924]; *Dear Scott*, 86.

"I may go to Hollywood": FSF to Gilbert Seldes [June or July 1925]; *Letters*, 485.

250 "that you have a background": Gertrude Stein to FSF, May 22, 1925; *The Crack-Up*, 308.

"You make a modern world": Ibid.

"My wife and I": FSF to Gertrude Stein, June 1925; Gallup, *The Flowers of Friendship*, 174.

"sententious gibberish": Mayfield, *Exiles*, 220.

251 "the most complete example of human symbiosis": EW to John Dos Passos, January 11, 1935; Wilson, *Letters*, 257.

"the only ones worth having": ZSF to FSF, n.d.; PUL.

"You see, I am content": FSF to Gertrude Stein, June 1925; Gallup, *The Flowers of Friendship*, 174.

"strange steerage clothes": Hemingway, *A Moveable Feast*, 16.

252 "I feel that to your generation": Edith Wharton to FSF, June 8, 1925; quoted in Lewis, *Edith Wharton*, 467.

"My present quarrel with you is": Ibid.

"she was damned if she would go": Mizener, *The Far Side of Paradise*, 202.

"But Mr. Fitzgerald, you haven't": Ibid., 203.

"They beat me!": Ibid.

253 "a couple of — er — ": Turnbull, *Scott Fitzgerald*, 154.

"There must be something peculiar": Ibid.

"On the way back to Paris": Bruccoli, *Some Sort of Epic Grandeur*, 231.

"go out and get drunk": ZSF to FSF, n.d.; PUL.

"That was better than going": Mayfield, *Exiles*, 114.

"To tea, Teddy Chanler and Scott Fitzgerald": Lewis, *Edith Wharton*, 468.

254 "about several things, one of which": FSF to MP, August 28 [1925]; *Dear Scott*, 120.

"There was no one at Antibes": FSF to JPB [probably September 1925]; *Letters*, 359.

"pretty young man with machine oil": Bruccoli and Bryer, *In His Own Time*, 122.

255 "liked Archie MacLeish": FSF to JPB [probably September 1925]; *Letters*, 358–359.

"Just a real place to rough it": Ibid., 359.

"There *really* was a great sound": Gerald Murphy to FSF, September 19, 1925; *Correspondence*, 178.

256   "No one ever makes things in America": FSF to Marya Mannes [October 1925]; *Letters*, 488.

"My new novel is marvelous": Ibid.

"I doubt you will be after five more years": Ibid.

"America's greatest promise": Ibid.

257   "almost glacial impersonality": *The Crack-Up*, 321.

"the field of his vision": Ibid., 318.

"the legend of a moon which never rose": Ibid., 322. Writing to Fitzgerald after the publication of *The Great Gatsby*, Rosenfeld acknowledged that if he had had a copy before writing his essay, it "would have given me a diving rock better than any I had." Paul Rosenfeld to FSF [spring/summer 1925]; *Correspondence*, 171.

"However, it is only fair to say": FSF to EH [postmarked November 30, 1925]; *Letters*, 295.

"was not suffering from lack of care": Ibid.

"Dr. Gros said there was no use": ZSF to FSF [late summer/early fall 1930]; *Correspondence*, 247.

258   "We went to London": *Bits of Paradise*, 6.

"was very nice — anything else": FSF to EH [postmarked November 30, 1925]; *Letters*, 295.

"For some reason I told you": Ibid.

"garbled version": Ibid.

259   "McAlmon is a son of a bitch": EH to FSF [ca. December 24, 1925]; Hemingway, *Selected Letters*, 181.

"Its good you didn't": FSF to MP [ca. December 27, 1925]; *Dear Scott*, 126.

"The Passing of a Great Race": Hemingway, *The Torrents of Spring*, Part 4.

"almost a vicious parody": FSF to MP [ca. December 30, 1925]; *Dear Scott*, 127.

260   "I agree with Ernest": Ibid.

"He and I are very thick": Ibid., 128.

"Frankly, I hope you won't like it": FSF to Horace Liveright and T. R. Smith [before December 30, 1925]; *Correspondence*, 183.

"To hear him talk": FSF to MP [ca. January 19, 1926]; *Dear Scott*, 131.

261   "We agree that Scotty": Ring Lardner to FSF [February 23, 1926]; *Correspondence*, 188.

"depth and diversity": MP to FSF, December 17, 1925; *Dear Scott*, 125.

"a terrible winter in a Paris flat": *Save Me the Waltz*, 99.

"a perfect breeding place for the germs": Ibid.

262   "I was sick again at Christmas": ZSF to FSF [late summer/early fall 1930]; *Correspondence*, 247.

"I write to you from the depths": FSF to MP [ca. December 27, 1925]; *Dear Scott*, 125 – 126.

"not entirely well yet": Ibid., 127.

"disease of that year": *The Crack-Up*, 46.

"out-of-the-way hole": FSF to Henry Albert Phillips [winter 1926]; *Letters*, 490.

"a little discouraged about everything": *The Crack-Up*, 46.

"We thought the show was great": Ring Lardner to FSF, February 23, 1926; *Correspondence*, 189.

"You need not feel ashamed": MP to FSF, January 28, 1926; *Dear Scott*, 131.

263 "Think of that horse's ass": FSF to MP [ca. February 25, 1926]; *Letters*, 200.

"We had a play on Broadway": *The Crack-Up*, 46.

"a family of hammer and tongs men": *Afternoon*, 119.

"Many of us who have grown weary": Ibid., 122.

264 "pretty darn close to the book": EH to Louis and Mary Bromfield [ca. March 8, 1926]; Hemingway, *Selected Letters*, 196.

"I'm glad you got Hemmingway": FSF to MP [ca. March 15, 1926]; *Dear Scott*, 137.

"unbelievable, wrenching, killing happiness": Baker, *Ernest Hemingway*, 165.

265 "grace under pressure": Donnelly and Billings, *Sara & Gerald*, 22.

"It makes no difference your telling": EH to FSF [ca. April 20, 1926]; Hemingway, *Selected Letters*, 200.

"last unalloyed good time": Dos Passos, *The Best Times*, 158.

"It's great, Ernest": Hemingway, *A Movable Feast*, 207.

"The pilot fish leaves of course": Ibid., 205.

266 "I'm happier than I've been": FSF to MP [ca. March 15, 1926]; *Dear Scott*, 137.

"It will be about 75,000 words": FSF to HO [ca. May 3, 1926]; *As Ever*, 89.

"My book is *wonderful*": FSF to MP [ca. May 8, 1926]; *Dear Scott*, 141.

"every prospect of a marvelous summer": FSF to MP [ca. May 10, 1926]; Ibid.

267 "This is confidential": FSF to MP [ca. July 1926]; *Dear Scott*, 144 [misdated in *Dear Scott* as ca. June 25, but it is clearly after Zelda's hospitalization there and Fitzgerald wrote Ober from Paris as late as July 1].

And he promptly told the same news: See Archibald MacLeish to EH [ca. June 1926]; MacLeish, *Letters*, 179.

"The hero, like Gatsby": EH to FSF [ca. April 20, 1926]; Hemingway, *Selected Letters*, 201.

"all takes place in Newport, R.I.": Ibid.

268 "He really had the most appalling": Tomkins, *Living Well*, 125.

"You can't expect anyone": Sara Murphy to FSF [June 1926]; *Correspondence*, 196.

"some theory you have": Ibid., 197.

269 "exhaustive in his way": MS., "Janno and Jacob" segment of *Caesar's Things*, Box 3, Folder 9; PUL.

"Dear Ernest: Nowadays": FSF to EH [June 1926]; *Correspondence*, 193.

270 "sneers, superiorities": Ibid.

"Quarter being a state of mind": Ibid., 194.

"I can't tell you the sense of disappointment": Ibid., 195.

Hemingway agreed with him: See Hemingway to Max Perkins, June 5, 1926; Hemingway, *Selected Letters*, 208: "He [Fitzgerald] suggested various things in it to cut out — in those first chapters — which I have never liked — but I think it is better to just lop that off and he agrees."

"God! the bottom of p. 77": FSF to EH [June 1926]; *Correspondence*, 195.

"But remember this is a new departure": Ibid., 194.

"The heart of my criticism": Ibid., 195.

"Why didn't you touch more" FSF to Van Wyck Brooks [postmarked June 13, 1925]; Ibid., 170.

271 "Novelists like he (him)": Ibid.

"This is wonderful": Turnbull, *Scott Fitzgerald*, 163.

272 "I wanted you to swim with me": ZSF to FSF [late summer/early fall 1930]; *Correspondence*, 247.

"You left me lots alone": Ibid.

"sense of carnival and impending disaster": ZSF to MP [ca. November 1926]; PUL.

"Think of Walker looking for a job": Wilson, *A Prelude,* 69.

"bullfighting, bullslinging": Mayfield, *Exiles,* 112.

273 "However, I love you both very much": Quoted in Donnelly and Billings, *Sara & Gerald,* 25.

"In the end, you will probably save us all": Ibid., 26.

274 "I couldn't wait for them to come to dinner": Barbara Garamekian, "In the Circle of a Charmed Life": *The New York Times,* February 6, 1983, p. 56.

275 "We were in a back-house": FSF to EH [fall 1926]; *Letters,* 296.

"At this point in my letter": Ibid.

"Your letter depressed and rather baffled me": Ibid., 297.

"That is we got stewed": Ibid.

"Scott is working and still brooding": ZSF to MP [November 1926]; PUL.

276 "almost died": ZSF to FSF [late summer/early fall 1930]; *Correspondence,* 247.

"I go back with my novel still unfinished": FSF to EH [postmarked December 23, 1926]; *Letters,* 298.

"Is there any man present": Turnbull, *Scott Fitzgerald,* 168.

"And we were back in America": ZSF to FSF [late summer/early fall 1930]; *Correspondence,* 247.

Weekends at Ellerslie

279 "the movie business": FSF to MP [ca. April 24, 1925]; *Dear Scott,* 102.

"FINE MODERN COLLEGE STORY": John W. Considine to FSF [ca. December 30, 1926]; Latham, *Crazy Sundays,* 49.

"GOING TO COAST FOR THREE WEEKS": FSF to MP. January 4, 1927; Ibid., 50.

280 "on probation": *Bits of Paradise,* 258.

"Daddy got so nervous": ZSF to Scottie, n.d. [1927]; PUL.

"just between the leading vamps": ZSF to Scottie, n.d. [1927]; PUL.

"ducky little girl": ZSF to Scottie, n.d. [1927]; PUL.

"incredible, fantastic, colossal": Kellner, *Carl Van Vechten,* 227.

"in a climate where": Ibid., 228.

"the average domicile": Ibid.

"weaving along under the vast sky": *Bits of Paradise,* 260.

281 "Hollywood is not gay": ZSF to Scottie, n.d. [1927]; PUL.

"It's ROTTEN and awful and terrible": ZSF to Scottie, n.d. [1927]; PUL.

"There's nothing on earth to do": ZSF to Scottie, n.d. [1927]; Milford, *Zelda,* 163.

"This is a tragic city": FSF to Mrs. Richard Taylor [winter 1927]; *Letters,* 415–416.

"one of America's foremost": Bruccoli, et al., *The Romantic Egoists,* 147.

"impudent, superbly assured": Ibid., 149.

"Constance Talmadge is the epitome": Ibid.

"She is the prettiest lady": ZSF to Scottie, n.d. [1927]; PUL.

"It's money, it's money": Latham, *Crazy Sundays,* 52.

283 "perform a quick operation": Ibid., 53.

"God! But you look old!": Ibid.

"These charming young people": Ibid.

"They were sitting close together": Tynan, *Show People,* 269.

"Even in Hollywood the Fitzgeralds were unique": Moore, *Silent Star,* 141.

"the aura of House-detective": ZSF to FSF [fall 1939]; *Correspondence*, 556.

"I am trying to make 'ole Massa' ": ZSF to Scottie, n.d. [1927]; Milford, *Zelda*, 162.

"there's enough mischief": Ibid., 163.

284   "Romain Rolland, F. Scott Fitzgerald": Bruccoli, et al., *The Romantic Egoists*, 150.

"backless evening clothes": Ibid.

"It was the face": *Bits of Paradise*, 159.

"Daddy was offered a job": ZSF to Scottie, n.d. [1927]; Milford, *Zelda*, 163.

"flagrantly sentimental relations": ZSF to FSF [late summer/early fall 1930]; *Correspondence*, 247.

285   "Everybody here is very clever": ZSF to Scottie, n.d. [1927]; Milford, *Zelda*, 164.

"School was over": Latham, *Crazy Sundays*, 59.

"confident to the point of conceit": FSF to Scottie [July 1937]; *Letters*, 16.

"I woke up in Hollywood": FSF to ZSF [summer? 1930]; *Correspondence*, 239–240.

286   "Scottie, supposing": Bruccoli, *The Last of the Novelists*, 16.

287   "BOOTLEGGERS GONE OUT OF BUSINESS": Lois Moran to FSF, March 14, 1927; Mizener, *The Far Side of Paradise*, 227.

"Darling Scott": Lois Moran to FSF [spring 1927]; *Correspondence*, 206.

"The first was so tragically real": Ibid.

288   "Thank God you have escaped alive!": HLM to FSF, March 15 [1927]; PUL.

"Once he had possessed a tenor voice": *Bits of Paradise*, 162.

"NEW YORK DESOLATE": Ibid., 171.

289   "At the first tea": Ibid., 173.

"The totality of the cocktails": Ibid., 174.

"Hesitating tentatively": Ibid., 167.

290   "that you never loved him": *The Great Gatsby*, 132.

"an image that would endure": *Bits of Paradise*, 177–178.

"the fast-throbbing darkness": Ibid., 186.

291   "Oh, we're such actors, George": *Stories*, 228.

"He rode away in a mood of exultation": *Bits of Paradise*, 167.

"one of those people": *Stories*, 226.

"Her story, to date, was short": *Bits of Paradise*, 253.

"the heir to fantastic millions": Ibid., 254.

292   "She learned to accentuate": Ibid., 259–260.

"She was royalty in exile": Ibid., 257.

"People knew her by name": Ibid., 259.

293   "She married him, of course": Ibid., 264–265.

"It is in the thirties": *Notebooks*, no. 1263.

294   "Deluxe service": FSF to EW, July 29, 1927; Beinecke.

"followed a person about like a mop": Milford, *Zelda*, 300.

"She is a great trial": ZSF to CVV, September 6, 1927; Beinecke.

295   "Anita, what a friend": Loos, *A Girl Like I*, 217.

"honestly delighted": FSF to Ernest Boyd, February 1, 1925; *Letters*, 478.

"She had no definite characteristics": Milford, *Zelda*, 300.

296   "From the depths of my polluted soul": ZSF to CVV, May 27, 1927; Beinecke.

"You were very sweet": ZSF to CVV, May 29, 1927; Beinecke.

"I love 'Squeeze Me' so much": ZSF to CVV, June 9, 1927; Beinecke.

"a shining sword which collapses": Ibid.

"pederast": *Notebooks*, no. 1118.

"Carl is a great fan": HLM to FSF, May 23, 1935; PUL.

"One of them is splotchy": ZSF to CVV, June 14, 1927; Beinecke.

297   "Carl is divine": Milford, *Zelda,* 300.
       "an instrument of our lost republic": Ibid.
       "Call yourself an actor?": Kobler, *Damned in Paradise,* 225.
298   "Dear Charlie, Its occurred to me": FSF to Charles Green Shaw, July 6, 1927;
       Buck Pennington, "The 'Floating World' in the Twenties: The Jazz Age and
       Charles Green Shaw," *Archives of American Art Journal,* vol. 20, no. 4, 1980:
       19–20.
       "a damn good piece of humorous writing": FSF to Charles Green Shaw, June 21,
       1927; Ibid., 19.
       "congenitally shy": Bruccoli and Bryer, *In His Own Time,* 282.
299   "His preference in women": Ibid., 283.
       "is an autocrat in theory": Ibid., 284.
       "When writing, he is usually": Ibid., 283.
       "He ordinarily rises": Ibid., 282.
300   "A BITTER AND SENSATIONAL ARRAINMENT": FSF to HO, July 14, 1927;
       As Ever, 98.
       "ROTTEN": FSF to HO, September 1, 1927; Ibid., 100.
       "WILL BE UP WITH STORY FRIDAY": FSF to HO, August 3, 1927; Ibid., 99.
       "JUST AN AWFUL MESS": FSF to HO, October 3, 1927; Ibid., 102.
301   "the indestructible Dancing Drinking": Amory and Bradlee, *Vanity Fair,* 127.
       "Zelda prays nightly": FSF to Cecilia Taylor [August 1927]; *Letters,* 491.
       "the most famous young man": *Bits of Paradise,* 237.
       "I don't blame either of you": FSF to Gilbert Seldes [probably fall 1927]; *Letters,*
       492.
       "on account of pursuing pursuits": ZSF to CVV, September 6, 1927; Beinecke.
302   "I am painting again": Ibid.
       "You did not like it": ZSF to FSF [late summer/early fall 1930]; *Correspondence,*
       248.
       "stood over me": FSF to Paul Reynolds, received April 7, 1927; *As Ever,* 94.
303   "The editors knew this": FSF to HO, received February 2, 1928; *As Ever,* 109.
       "The men who at twenty-one": Bruccoli, et al., *The Romantic Egoists,* 162.
       "lots of magazines": ZSF to Scottie, n.d. [1927]; PUL.
       "I am *crazy* to own a house": ZSF to Scottie, n.d. [1927]; Milford, *Zelda,* 165.
304   "The man was old enough": *Afternoon,* 140.
       "party of sorts": ZSF to CVV, September 6, 1927; Beinecke.
       "good simple people": Ibid.
       "a regular wake": Wilson, *Shores of Light,* 376.
       "dinner was never served": Milford, *Zelda,* 168.
305   "magnetic voice": Ibid., 300.
       "supernatural apparition": Wilson, *The Twenties,* 356.
       "oblivious with a kind of happy desperation": Milford, *Zelda,* 300.
       "thoroughly entangled sentimentally": ZSF to FSF [late summer/early fall 1930];
       Correspondence, 248.
306   "cocktails, made-up girls": Berg, *Max Perkins,* 148.
       "more quality of its own": Ibid., 149.
       "You talk to me": Ibid.
307   "I'm afraid I was the world's greatest bore": FSF to Thomas Lineaweaver [1927 or
       1928]; *Letters,* 492–493. The earlier date seems the more likely, since Fitzgerald
       at the time was considering an article on "the managing kind of American woman."
       "It seems that life went to pieces": ZSF to CVV, October 14, 1927; Beinecke.
       "I have been on the absolute wagon": FSF to MP [ca. January 1, 1928]; *Dear Scott,*
       149.

"Just think — it's like this": Turnbull, *Scott Fitzgerald*, 173.

308   "I have been an admirer": Thornton Wilder to FSF, January 12, 1928; *Correspondence*, 212.

"God, I'm a lousy speaker!": Turnbull, *Scott Fitzgerald*, 174.

"Don't brood about your speech": Thornton Wilder to FSF [February 1928]; *Correspondence*, 217.

"small revel Saturday night": FSF to Zoë Akins [February 1928]; *Letters*, 493.

"All is prepared": Wilson, *Shores of Light*, 373–374.

309   "magnificent setting": Ibid., 376.

"Don't you hear something strange?": Ibid., 377.

"her iridescent best": Ibid., 379.

"She had no readymade phrases": Ibid., 380.

310   "All that memorized Shakespeare!": Ibid.

Although Fitzgerald blanked out the whole episode: See Harrison, *The Enthusiast*, 110.

"Please go away": Wilson, *Shores of Light*, 380.

311   "Why, the little fellow said": Ibid., 382.

"could be nice to them": Ibid.

"The aftermath of a Fitzgerald evening": Ibid.

"intellectual arrogance": Ibid.

313   "It had a child's quality": *Basil and Josephine*, 19.

"account of how the boys and girls": MP to FSF, June 28, 1928; *Dear Scott*, 151.

"Please clip it": FSF to Norris D. Jackson [postmarked March 23, 1928]; *Correspondence*, 217.

314   "that terrible door": *Notebooks*, no. 976.

"too much good material": FSF to Betty Markell, September 16, 1929; *Letters*, 495.

"CAN YOU DEPOSIT THREE HUNDRED": FSF to HO, February 28, 1928; *As Ever*, 110.

"BRINGING MANUSCRIPT UP TODAY": FSF to HO, March 10, 1928; Ibid.

"SENDING STORY OFF THIS MORNING": FSF to HO, March 11, 1928; Ibid.

"DEAR HAROLD MY INCOME TAX": FSF to HO, March 18, 1928; Ibid.

315   "Ring looking bad": *Ledger*, March 1928.

"nervous attacks": MP to EH, April 10, 1928; PUL.

"Terrible incessant Stoppies begin": *Ledger*, August and September 1927.

"but after seeing him": MP to EH, April 10, 1928; PUL.

"to keep from having to": EH to MP, April 21, 1928; Hemingway, *Selected Letters*, 276.

"Black eyes in the Jungle": *Ledger*, March 1928.

316   The actual source of the episode: Lawton Campbell, "The Fitzgeralds Were My Friends," MS; PUL. Campbell notes that the Jungle Club incident and a subsequent meeting with Scott and Zelda in Paris had "followed some time after" Zelda's visit to Montgomery during her first months of pregnancy. Fitzgerald's *Ledger* entry tends to suggest that it had occurred just before their 1928 trip abroad.

"No so-and-so bouncer": Ibid.

"In those days of going to pieces": *Bits of Paradise*, 327.

"prolific as a Gueinea pig (mis-spelled)": EH to MP, April 21, 1928; Hemingway, *Selected Letters*, 276.

317   "on the absolute wagon": FSF to MP [ca. July 1, 1928]; *Letters*, 210.

"and he works 11 hours": FSF to MP [ca. July 21, 1928]; Ibid., 211.

"Festival of St. James": See *Correspondence*, 218.

With his usual dubious flattery: Herbert Gorman, however, gives a different version of the famous story. He says it took place at the Joyces' apartment at 2, Square Robiac, and that Fitzgerald threatened to throw himself out the sixth-floor window if Nora Joyce did not declare that she loved him. See Gorman, "Glimpses of F. Scott Fitzgerald," *Fitzgerald/Hemingway Annual 1973*, 116. Joyce's comment on Fitzgerald was "I think he must be mad."

"You were constantly drunk": ZSF to FSF [late summer/early fall 1930]; *Correspondence*, 248.

"first trip to jail": *Ledger*, July and August 1928.

"Drinking & general unpleasantness": Ibid.

318   "There *can't* be that many words": *Notebooks*, no. 1911.

"Its right up to Bierce & Stephen Crane": FSF to MP [ca. July 15, 1928]; *Dear Scott*, 151.

"Scott professes great enthusiasm": JPB to EW, September 20, 1928; Beinecke.

"Perkins, do you think": EW to Burton Rascoe, September 6, 1929; Wilson, *Letters*, 168.

"head over heels the best young man": FSF to MP [ca. July 21, 1928]; *Dear Scott*, 152.

319   "I am Voltaire!": Chamson, "Remarks," *Fitzgerald/Hemingway Annual 1973*, 74.

"feeling drunk and Christ-like": FSF to EH [postmarked December 28, 1928]; *Letters*, 303.

"in a time of discouragement": Bruccoli and Bryer, *In His Own Time*, 225.

320   "Somewhere in there": FSF to ZSF [summer? 1930]; *Correspondence*, 240.

"You made no advances toward me": ZSF to FSF [late summer/early fall 1930]; Ibid., 248.

"where I got back my self esteem": FSF to ZSF [summer? 1930]; Ibid., 240.

"Thirty-two years old": *Ledger*, 183.

"You know, I am thirty years old today": Toklas, *What Is Remembered*, 117.

321   "Ominous. No Real Progress": *Ledger*, 183.

"Anything to be liked": FSF to ZSF [summer? 1930]; *Correspondence*, 240.

"abnormal": ZSF to FSF [late summer/early fall 1930]; Ibid., 248.

"Dirt eating at hotel": *Ledger*, September 1928. Fitzgerald placed his return and the dirt-eating episode in the wrong month.

"Think he's the best kid": FSF to EH [ca. July 1928]; *Correspondence*, 220.

322   "a good deal of Joyce": Ibid., 221.

"Well Fitz you are certainly": EH to FSF [ca. October 9, 1928]; Hemingway, *Selected Letters*, 287.

"built like a brick shithouse": Ibid.

"Since the age of fourteen": Ibid., 288

"How's to get stewed": Ibid., 289.

323   "Almost every bloody fool thing": EH to MP, October 11, 1928; Ibid., 289–290.

"I wish to god": Ibid., 290.

"It seems fine to be sending": FSF to MP, November 1928; *Dear Scott*, 153.

"Remember novel is confidential": Ibid., 154.

"some of the best writing": MP to FSF, November 13, 1928; Ibid.

324   She also took on a new instructor: Gavrilov may have conducted classes at the Cortissoz Studios in Philadelphia as well. Zelda's address book, at Princeton, has a listing for him there.

"stupid and insubordinate": Milford, *Zelda*, 299.

"He left me alone so much": Ibid., 300–301.

325   "My dancing teacher was a protégé": Ibid., 301.
      "a lovely person": Robert Taylor, "A Strater Retrospective: No Faces of Fame,"
      the *Boston Globe* magazine, August 6, 1981, 22–24.
      In an unpublished section of *A Moveable Feast*: See Bruccoli, *Scott and Ernest*,
      68–69.
326   "To add to Zelda's troubles": Mayfield, *Exiles*, 133.
      "THE SUN ALSO RISES": EH to FSF [ca. November 24, 1926]; Hemingway,
      Selected Letters, 231.
      "This tough talk is not really": FSF to EH [December 1927]; *Letters*, 302–303.
      "We had a wonderful time": EH to FSF and ZSF [ca. November 18, 1928];
      Hemingway, *Selected Letters*, 290.
327   "Aren't you the best piece of tail": Hotchner, *Papa Hemingway*, 121.
      "Hemingwayed to death": Taylor, "A Strater Retrospective," 12.
      "Those two, they were really awful": Strater to James R. Mellow, interview, August
      16, 1981.
      "Dear Max, I am sneaking away": FSF to MP [ca. March 1, 1929]; *Dear Scott*,
      154.

A Country Where Many Things End

329   "On the boat coming over": ZSF to FSF [late summer/early fall 1930]; *Correspon-
      dence*, 248.
      "Another spring—I would see Ernest": FSF to ZSF [summer? 1930]; Ibid., 240.
330   "We drank apéritifs at a blue café": Milford, *Zelda*, 301.
331   "Zelda's Beau": *Ledger*, March 1929.
      "brittly cold": *The Crack-Up*, 49.
      "the best dinner procurable": FSF to HO [March/April 1929]; *As Ever*, 132.
      "Chambéry Fraise with the Seldes": Bruccoli and Bryer, *In His Own Time*, 224.
332   "The Prison at Nice": *Ledger*, March 1929.
      "I'm happy to be back here": FSF to HO [March/April 1929]; *As Ever*, 132.
      "John is like a man": Tate, *Memoirs and Opinions*, 72.
      "Cummings is here": JPB to EW, May 26, 1929; Beinecke.
      "Dozens of people": FSF to Sinclair Lewis [after March 1929]; *Correspondence*, 224.
333   "a pansy with hair on his chest": Mayfield, *Exiles*, 141.
      The last time Fitzgerald was in Paris: See EH to MP, April 3, 1929; PUL.
      "Certain coldness": *Ledger*, June 1929.
      "Ernest apartment": *Notebook*, no. 728.
      "Ernest taking me to that bum restaurant": Ibid., no. 1437.
334   "114–121 is slow": FSF to EH [June 1929]; *Correspondence*, 225.
      "talks too much physically": Ibid., 227.
      "Remember the brave": Ibid.
      "A beautiful book it is!": Ibid., 228.
      "Our poor old friendship": Ibid., 226.
      "Kiss my ass E.H.": Ibid., 228.
      "one of the worst damned documents": EH to Arthur Mizener, January 11, 1951;
      Hemingway, *Selected Letters*, 719.
335   "Ernest's last letter": FSF to MP [ca. June 1929]; *Letters*, 215.
      "The trouble is Max": EH to MP, June 7, 1929; Hemingway, *Selected Letters*, 297.
      "genuine thing": MP to FSF, January 24, 1928; *Dear Scott*, 150.
      "Your frank opinion": Morley Callaghan to FSF [June? 1929]; *Correspondence*, 229.

"too deliberate": Callaghan, *That Summer*, 152.

336   "pretty damned Biblical": Ibid.

"Oh, my God! I let the round go": Ibid., 214.

"My God, he thinks I did it": Ibid., 215.

"so interested to see if I": EH to MP, August 28, 1929; Hemingway, *Selected Letters*, 302.

"One knockdown to Ernest": Callaghan, *That Summer*, 216.

337   "have something for herself": Ibid., 163.

"living in a dream": Milford, *Zelda*, 301.

"impersonal escape": Ibid., 215.

338   "place" Egorova's son: *Ledger*, May 1929.

"egotist and a bore": FSF to Dr. Oscar Forel [summer? 1930]; *Correspondence*, 242.

339   "This is a poor substitute": FSF to HO [received March 2, 1929]; *As Ever*, 130.

"it seems to me Zelda's name": FSF to HO [received October 8, 1929]; *As Ever*, 147.

"pretty strong draughts": Ibid., 146.

340   "a great original in her way": FSF to Scottie, June 12, 1940; *Letters*, 78.

"She isn't a 'natural story-teller' ": FSF to Dr. Mildred Squires, March 8, 1932; Bruccoli, *Some Sort of Epic Grandeur*, 274.

"When I suggested": FSF to HO [ca. August 1929]; *As Ever*, 142.

341   "Is this Fitzgerald's roadhouse?": *Bits of Paradise*, 255.

"I like it a lot": HO to FSF, March 5, 1930; *As Ever*, 165.

"I really felt a little guilty": HO to FSF, April 8, 1930; Ibid., 166.

"a mighty good piece of work": Ibid.

"Zelda was delighted": FSF to HO [received May 13, 1930]; Ibid., 167.

342   "At this time she was making": *Bits of Paradise*, 214.

"beloved Riviera": FSF to MP [ca. March 15, 1926]; *Dear Scott*, 137.

"really inexpensive menage": FSF to HO [received June 26, 1929]; *As Ever*, 137.

"I am working night & day": FSF to MP [ca. June 1929]; *Dear Scott*, 156. Internal evidence indicates that date should be July 1929.

343   "I've been working like hell": FSF to EH, August 23, 1929; *Letters*, 304.

"Work on novel. Stenographers.": *Ledger*, September 1929.

"I cant tell you": EH to FSF, September 4, 1929; Hemingway, *Selected Letters*, 304 –305.

"It was a nightmare": Milford, *Zelda*, 302.

344   "It's been gay here": FSF to EH, August 23, 1929; *Letters*, 305.

"given their whole performance": FSF to EH, September 9, 1929; Ibid., 306.

"older, less gay, more social": FSF to EH, August 23, 1929; Ibid., 305.

"You disgraced yourself": ZSF to FSF [late summer/early fall 1930]; *Correspondence*, 248.

"Being drunk & snubbed," "Fairies Breakdown": *Ledger*, July 1929.

345   "You were simply one": FSF to ZSF [summer? 1930]; *Correspondence*, 241.

"Zelda dancing & sweating": *Ledger*, September 1929.

"I've paid for it": FSF to EH, September 9, 1929; *Letters*, 306.

"anyone in my state of mind": Ibid.

"Here's a last flicker": Ibid., 307.

346   "I've sworn not to come back": FSF to HO [received October 23, 1929]; *As Ever*, 153.

"For the first time since August": FSF to MP [ca. November 15, 1929]; *Letters*, 216.

"Not a beautiful woman": Tate, *Memoirs and Opinions,* 62.

"present day status of the Flapper": See note, HO to FSF, September 24, 1929; *As Ever,* 147.

347   "Met your friend Allen Tate": FSF to EW [U.S. postmark September 14, 1930]; Beinecke.

"I feel that the same ideas": See note, HO to FSF, November 12, 1929; *As Ever,* 156.

"You were going crazy": FSF to ZSF [summer? 1930]; *Correspondence,* 241.

348   "With Ernest I seem to have reached": FSF to EW [probably March 1933]; *Letters,* 345.

"Ruth Goldbeck Voallammbbrrossa": FSF to EH, August 23, 1929; Ibid., 305.

"But you seem to have damned well forgot": EH to FSF, September 4, 1929; Hemingway, *Selected Letters,* 304.

349   "Incidentally I thought you wanted": FSF to EH, September 9, 1929; *Letters,* 305–306.

"I think it was foolish": FSF to HO [received October 23, 1929]; *As Ever,* 153.

"*Please* don't in any correspondence": FSF to HO [received November 16, 1929]; Ibid., 158.

"You wouldn't do anything": EW to MP, October 18, 1938; Wilson, *Letters,* 312.

"Max Perkins couldn't spell": EW to Malcolm Cowley, 1951; Ibid., 254.

350   "to a really big sale": MP to FSF, October 30, 1929; *Dear Scott,* 157.

"Ernest has cabled me": MP to FSF, November 20, 1929; *Correspondence,* 233.

"Came home from Berlin": EH to MP, December 15, 1929; Hemingway, *Selected Letters,* 315.

351   "She claims you are the one of all us guys": EH to FSF [ca. October 22 or 29, 1929]; Hemingway, *Selected Letters,* 308–309. As indicated in the text, this letter and the one written the day after the Stein party are misdated. In a postscript to this letter, Hemingway asks, "What about yr. suit against McCalls?" Since Ober did not write Fitzgerald until November 12 that *McCall's* had turned down the article, the Stein party must have taken place on a Wednesday in late November. The fact that he had cabled Ober on November 20, then wrote a follow-up letter on the twenty-third, suggests that he had just received the news. The most probable date for the Stein party would then have been Wednesday, November 27, or Wednesday, December 4.

"Gertrude has taken me back": Tate, *Memoirs and Opinions,* 64.

"the entelechy towards which": Ibid., 65.

352   "giving Hem a little dig": Toklas, *What Is Remembered,* 116.

"And Hem said rather bashfully": Ibid., 116–117.

"I was not annoyed": EH to FSF [ca. October 24 or 31, 1929]; Hemingway, *Selected Letters,* 309. Misdated letter should be ca. November 28 or December 5, 1929.

"you're getting touchy": Ibid., 310.

353   "Turning to me he said": Robert Penn Warren to James R. Mellow, December 13, 1981.

"Am damned fond of Scott": EH to MP, December 15, 1929; Hemingway, *Selected Letters,* 315.

354   "This is absolutely": MP to FSF, October 30, 1929; *Dear Scott,* 158.

"McAlmon is a bitter rat": FSF to MP [ca. November 15, 1929]; Ibid., 158–159.

"Now tell that": Bruccoli, *Scott and Ernest,* 103.

355   "HAVE SEEN STORY": Callaghan, *That Summer,* 243.

"no publicity attached": EH to Morley Callaghan, January 4, 1930; Hemingway, *Selected Letters,* 319.

"I know you are the soul of honor": EH to FSF, December 12, 1929; Ibid., 312–313.

"I only wish to God": Ibid., 314.

356 "I really loved him": *Notebooks*, no. 62.

"Nature's attempt"; Ibid., no. 1320.

"Fairy who fell for wax dummy.": Ibid., no. 706.

507 "Apropos of Cocteau": Ibid., no. 1241.

"lifted himself by his own jockstrap": Ibid., no. 386.

"He had once been a pederast": Ibid., no. 905.

"The great homosexual theses": Ibid., no. 2054.

"I am opposed to him": FSF to MP, January 21, 1930; *Dear Scott,* 163.

"Curious and poor fellow": René Crevel to Gertrude Stein [October 1926]; Gallup, *Flowers of Friendship,* 198.

357 "yincing": *Notebooks*, no. 1394.

"My mind is the loose cunt": Ibid., no. 1390.

"It was like holding on to a cold fish": Callaghan, *That Summer,* 207.

"To Scott from his old bedfellow": Inscription on photograph [October 1931]; see *Correspondence,* 269.

358 "Zelda is crazy": Hemingway, *A Moveable Feast,* 189.

"I've seen that everytime": *Notebooks*, no. 1293.

359 "This spring she was making him jealous": Hemingway, *A Moveable Feast,* 179.

"Zelda & Dolly Wilde": *Ledger,* May 1929.

"In all that horror": ZSF to FSF, n.d. [1930?]; PUL.

"the Beauty of homosexuality": ZSF to FSF, n.d.; PUL.

360 "We came back to the Rue Palatine": ZSF to FSF [late summer/early fall 1930]; *Correspondence,* 241.

"The nearest I ever came": FSF to ZSF [summer? 1930]; Ibid., 241.

She went for days without eating. The whole of Zelda's "monologue" during the course of her first breakdown has been constructed entirely of paraphrases from both unpublished and published documentary source material. My only interpolations in the course of this lengthy passage (from pages 360 to 367 in *Invented Lives*) consist of connective words and phrases.

    The sources are principally the published and unpublished letters of Zelda Fitzgerald to Scott Fitzgerald and Edmund Wilson at the Princeton University and Beinecke libraries; clinical reports and clinical autobiographies written by Zelda while under treatment at Malmaison, Val-Mont, and the Phipps Psychiatric Clinic at Baltimore, previously published in Turnbull, *Scott Fitzgerald,* Milford, *Zelda,* and Bruccoli, *Some Sort of Epic Grandeur;* first-person accounts of friends given in Turnbull and Milford. Several purely descriptive accounts of places and events have been taken from the 1934 autobiographical essay, " 'Show Mr. and Mrs. F. to Number ——— , ' " published in *The Crack-Up.* Only one descriptive passage, that of the flowers Zelda bought for Mme. Egorova, has been drawn from a fictional source, Zelda's account of the episode in *Save Me the Waltz.*

368 "The photograph is all I have": FSF to ZSF [summer? 1930]; *Correspondence,* 244.

"Please don't write to me about blame": ZSF to FSF [after June 1930]; Ibid., 238.

"This is not a treatise": Milford, *Zelda,* 225.

369 "Your heart betraying me": FSF to ZSF [summer? 1930]; *Correspondence,* 239.

"For all your superior observation": Ibid., 241.

370 "I was in [torture] and my head": ZSF to FSF [late summer/early fall 1930]; Ibid., 249.

"What with his drinking": ZSF to Newman Smith, undated fragment; PUL.

"If you want to know": ZSF to FSF, n.d.; PUL.

"My work *is done on coffee*": FSF to Dr. Oscar Forel [summer? 1930]; *Correspondence*, 242.

"*white and trembling*": Ibid.

371   "*a large insurance policy*": Ibid.

"of all people": Ibid., 243.

"except dancers": Ibid., 242.

372   "Give up strong drink": Ibid., 243.

"not that drink in any way": FSF to MP [ca. September 1, 1930]; *Dear Scott*, 169.

"I must not drink anything": Ibid.

"which is to say": FSF to EW [U.S. postmark September 14, 1930]; *Letters*, 344.

"a fine man and a fine writer": Ibid.

373   "I've grown to loathe it": Ibid.

"always hiding in closets": *Notebooks*, no. 965.

"The matter is terrible enough": FSF to Rosalind Smith [after June 8, 1930]; *Correspondence*, 236.

"sort of American hunch": FSF to Judge and Mrs. A. D. Sayre, December 1, 1930; Ibid., 253.

"a great imbecile": Milford, *Zelda*, 220.

"*skideophranie*": FSF to Judge and Mrs. A. D. Sayre, December 1, 1930; *Correspondence*, 253.

374   "someone who is close to you": ZSF to FSF [January 1931]; Ibid., 258.

"By the time the failures": Ibid.

375   "All these dead": *The Price Was High*, 329.

"Goodbye then Father": Ibid.

"in the dark middle": FSF to MP [ca. July 8, 1930]; *Dear Scott*, 166.

"I think you'll see": Ibid., 166–167.

"In my opinion": Ibid., 167.

"astonishing power of expression": MP to FSF, August 5, 1930; Ibid., 168.

376   "who doesn't know from what depths": FSF to MP [ca. September 1, 1930]; Ibid., 168–169.

"now they wanted the taste and smell": *Afternoon*, 147.

"a country where very few things begin": Ibid., 161.

377   "They're us! They're us!": Ibid., 165.

"He would come back some day": *Babylon Revisited*, 230.

378   "some American stories": HO to FSF, May 19, 1931; *As Ever*, 176.

"I realize that you are having": Ibid., 177.

"I believe, and others who are": Ibid.

379   "The water was greener there": *The Crack-Up*, 52–53.

"We walked at night": Ibid., 53.

"It is as peaceful": ZSF to Judge A. D. Sayre [July? 1931]; Bruccoli, et al., *The Romantic Egoists*, 180.

"The young Germans stalking": *The Crack-Up*, 53.

380   "It was like the good gone times": Ibid.

"had gone over to Communism": Ibid., 33.

381   "Come back, come back": Ibid.

"I'm going to like it here": Bruccoli and Bryer, *In His Own Time*, 285.

"an earnest student of political science": Ibid.

"In ideals I am somewhat of a communist": Ibid.

382   "They went to sleep easily": *Notebooks*, no. 631.

The Invented Part

PAGE

385 "fall through the eternal trapdoor": FSF to MP [ca. May 1, 1930]; *Dear Scott*, 166.
"*in* the *Post*": FSF to HO [received May 13, 1930]; *As Ever*, 168.
"for a damn": FSF to HO [received October 29, 1931]; Ibid., 178.

386 "It's unbearable to think": ZSF to FSF, n.d. [November 1931]; PUL.
"a lot of minor characters": ZSF to FSF [November 11, 1931]; *Correspondence*, 270.
"You were younger than anybody": Ibid.
"Reading your stories": ZSF to FSF [before November 17, 1931]; Ibid., 272.
"writing for myself": ZSF to FSF [November 11, 1931]; Ibid., 270.
"I can't seem to get started writing": ZSF to FSF [November 1931]; Ibid., 271.

387 "That was an awful dream": Ibid.
"Great Little Master": Loos, *Kiss Hollywood Good-By*, 31.

388 "I'm sorry your work": ZSF to FSF [after November 18, 1931]; *Correspondence*, 274.
"The struggle is over": ZSF to FSF [November 18, 1931]; Ibid., 273.
"The Capitol flag is flying": ZSF to FSF, n.d. [November 1931]; PUL.
"It's just the little personal things": ZSF to FSF [after November 18, 1931]; *Correspondence*, 275.
"Our fathers died": *Notebooks*, no. 1107.

389 "In Spain, they have the donkey": Taylor, *Joy Ride*, 244.

390 Taylor felt a glum kind: Ibid., 245.
"Come on, Scott": Ibid., 246.
"I THOUGHT YOU WERE": Norma Shearer Thalberg to FSF [ca. December 1931]; *Correspondence*, 282.
"Not so good": Taylor, *Joy Ride*, 247.
"People seem to like it": ZSF to FSF, n.d. [1931]; PUL.
"I *wish* you could teach me": Ibid.
"'Am moanin' low over your story": ZSF to FSF, n.d. [November/December 1931]; PUL.

391 "There's no use asking": ZSF to FSF [November 1931]; *Correspondence*, 277.
"a candy-store": ZSF to FSF [after November 18, 1931]; Ibid., 273.
"Aw go to hell": ZSF to FSF, n.d. [November/December 1931]; PUL.
"all those placative phrases": ZSF to FSF [December 1931]; *Correspondence*, 280.
"erroneously warned": FSF to Scottie [July 1937]; *Letters*, 16.
"a bastard . . . since a suicide": Ibid.
"running out on them": Ibid., 17.

392 "Scott tried to turn the silly book": Loos, *Kiss Hollywood Good-By*, 34.
"At last for the first time": FSF to MP [ca. January 15, 1932]; *Letters*, 226.
"When you come back": Ibid.
"because I've got a fine story": FSF to HO [received December 28, 1931]; *As Ever*, 181.
"had never made a cheap picture": *Taps at Reveille*, 179.

393 "cultural limitations": Ibid., 176.
"the sad, lovely Siamese twins": Ibid., 178.
"feeling of proxy in passion": *Notebooks*, no. 765.

394 "Just as Jupiter is said": Taylor, *Joy Ride*, 250.
"on the ground that it": FSF to HLM [July 1932]; *Correspondence*, 295.

395 "It seemed very sad": ZSF to FSF [February 1932]; Ibid., 283.
"Now it's money": ZSF to FSF [after February 1932]; Ibid., 283–284.
"God! the point of view of sanity": ZSF to FSF [March 1932]; Ibid., 285.
"I am that little fish": Ibid., 284.

396 "I am proud of my novel": ZSF to FSF [March 1932]; Ibid., 286.
"à la Ernest": Ibid.
"It's an amusing book": ZSF to FSF [March 1932]; Ibid., 287.

397 "Do you think": FSF to Dr. Mildred Squires, March 16, 1932; quoted in Bruccoli, *Some Sort of Epic Grandeur*, 325.
"But this mixture": Ibid.
"That's why she sent the book": Ibid.
"the counter-implications": FSF to Dr. Harry M. Murdock, August 28, 1934; *Correspondence*, 381.
"knowing that you were working": ZSF to FSF [March 1932]; Ibid., 288.

398 "Scott, I love you more": Ibid., 289. Fitzgerald probably underlined the emphasized portions of this letter.
"that the other material": ZSF to FSF [April 1932]; Ibid., 291. Fitzgerald may have underlined this passage.
"CERTAIN SMALL BUT NONETHELESS": FSF to MP, March 25, 1932; Ibid., 290.

399 "Zelda's novel is now good": FSF to MP [ca. April 30, 1932]; *Dear Scott*, 173.
"I'm not certain enough": Ibid., 174.
"Spring came and shattered": *Save Me the Waltz*, 39.

400 "nasturtiums of leather": Ibid., 102.
"deep-red roses": Ibid., 138.
"They had evolved a tacit arrangement": Ibid., 104.
"There wasn't a way": Ibid., 98.
"You took what you wanted": Ibid.
"the story of myself versus myself": ZSF to FSF [April 1932]; *Correspondence*, 291.

401 "I have not been showing anything": MP to FSF, May 2, 1932; *Dear Scott*, 175.
"I was left alone": Quoted in Milford, *Zelda*, 255.
"That was swell praise": FSF to Richard Knight, September 29, 1932; *Letters*, 500.

402 "You annoyed me": Ibid.
"When you city fellows": Ibid., 501.
"the happiest of my life": FSF to Dr. Adolf Meyer, April 10, 1933; *Correspondence*, 308.

403 "a streak of vulgarity": FSF to Margaret Turnbull, September 21, 1932; *Letters*, 435.
"Of course, I don't believe": Ibid., 434.
"I simply meant": FSF to Margaret Turnbull [probably spring 1933]; Ibid., 436.
"It is a good novel now": FSF to MP [ca. May 14, 1932]; *Dear Scott*, 176.
"but there has always been": Ibid.
"just finishing a fine novel": FSF to HLM [April/May 1932]; *Correspondence*, 294.

404 "raked up a lot of the past": FSF to Dr. Oscar Forel, April 18, 1932; Ibid., 292.
"instead of feeding her egotism": *Bits of Paradise*, 358.
"He hated the conflict": Ibid.
"nice Mozartian hollow": ZSF to JPB [summer 1932]; Milford, *Zelda*, 310.
"I'll perforate you, Andrew!": Turnbull, *Scott Fitzgerald*, 214.

405 "a broken clock": Margaret Turnbull to Nancy Milford; *Zelda*, 311.
"Just too late": EH to Janet Flanner, April 8, 1933; Hemingway, *Selected Letters*, 388.
"now go back to Baltimore": Ibid.
"The Community Communist": ZSF to MP [ca. October 6, 1932]; PUL.
"I have taken": Ibid.
"The novel now plotted & planned": *Ledger*, August 1932.

406   "a communist-liberal-idealist": Bruccoli, *Composition,* 77.
"For his external qualities": Ibid., 78.
"the weakness such as the social-climbing": Ibid., 78–79.
"Portrait of Zelda": Ibid., 80.
"Show a man": Ibid., 76.
"last will and testament": Bruccoli, et al., *The Romantic Egoists,* 189.
"a curious muddle": Ibid., 190.
"ludicrous lushness": Ibid., 189.

407   "Many reviewers did object": MP to ZSF, December 23, 1932; PUL.
"We had a most unfortunate meeting": FSF to EW [probably March 1933]; *Letters,* 345.
"He [McKaig] told me to my amazement": Ibid.
"Please not a word": Ibid., 346.
"Don't tell Ernest": FSF to MP, January 19, 1933; *Dear Scott,* 177.

408   "A decision to adopt Communism": Ibid.
"balconies and bulges": Wilson, *The Thirties,* 322.
"A little treat, honey": Ibid., 323.
"It seems so puritanical": Ibid.
"a notorious Parisien homo-sexual": FSF to Dr. Adolf Meyer, April 10, 1933; *Correspondence,* 306.

409   "back to the agonizing cat and dog fight": Ibid., 308.
"under a greenhouse": Ibid., 309.
"to spend a week": Ibid., 307.
"I will probably be carried": Ibid., 306.
"During the last six days": FSF to Dr. Adolf Meyer [spring 1933]; Ibid., 310.
"could never seem to appreciate": FSF to Dr. Harry M. Murdock, August 28, 1934; Ibid., 381.
"never really *believed*": Ibid.

410   Their confrontation came to a head: This section is a paraphrase of a discussion between Zelda and Fitzgerald held at La Paix on May 28, 1933, under the supervision of Dr. Thomas Rennie. Extracts from the microfilm of the stenographer's notes are in Bruccoli, *Some Sort of Epic Grandeur,* and Milford, *Zelda.*

413   "A short story": FSF to MP, March 11, 1935; *Letters,* 259–260.
"It was terribly sad to see": *The Crack-Up,* 34.

414   "Whatever Ring's achievement was": Ibid., 36.
"private shame": FSF to EW [October 1933]; Beinecke.
"A great and good American is dead": *The Crack-Up,* 40.
"didn't seem to meet the case": EW to FSF, October 21, 1933; Wilson, *Letters,* 231.
"Besides, Lardner": EW to FSF, November 4, 1933; Ibid.
"Now is your time": Ibid., 232.

415   "I'm sorry about the other day": EW to FSF, December 4, 1933; Ibid., 233.
"I've gotten very fond": FSF to MP, January 13, 1934; *Dear Scott,* 189.
"JUST READ SECOND INSTALMENT": Louis Bromfield to FSF [January 1934]; see *Correspondence,* 326, note 1.
"There are certain pages": Louis Bromfield to FSF [April 1934]; Ibid., 341–342.
"Great God Scott": Archibald MacLeish to FSF, n.d.; Bruccoli, et al., *The Romantic Egoists,* 200.
"I thought you'd be interested": Thomas Wolfe to FSF [March 1934]; *Correspondence,* 332.

"The first installment of the novel": JPB to FSF [December 1933/January 1934]; Ibid., 321.

416   "If the characters got real enough": FSF to EW [postmarked March 12, 1934]; *Letters,* 346.

"Except for the movies": EW to Malcolm Cowley, 1951; Wilson, *Letters,* 254.

"I could wish that you": FSF to EW [postmarked March 12, 1934]; *Letters,* 346.

"It's so tightly knit": John Dos Passos to FSF [April 1934]; *Correspondence,* 358.

"The central figures change": Bruccoli and Bryer, *In His Own Time,* 371.

"second-rate English society novelist": Ibid., 372.

417   "most engaging qualities": Ibid., 379.

"Is it laziness": Ibid., 372.

"It would be picayune": Ibid., 378.

"We now know that the gossip": Ibid., 372.

"The story is the story of the Divers": Ibid., 374.

418   "expensive blondes and yachting parties": Ibid., 383.

"Dear Mr. Fitzgerald": Ibid., 384.

"Sometimes, I don't know": *The Stories,* xii.

419   "rather than pass it along": Malcolm Cowley to FSF, April 13, 1934; *Correspondence,* 350.

"Fitzgerald has always been the poet": Cowley, *Think Back on Us,* 227.

"There is a streak of vulgarity": Ibid.

"I hope he changes his mind": Ibid., 228.

"Malcolm Republic": FSF to EH, June 1, 1934; *Letters,* 310.

"Freedom has produced": FSF to MP [ca. March 5, 1922]; *Dear Scott,* 57.

"For two years I've gone half haywire": FSF to Mrs. Richard Taylor [postmarked August 17, 1934]; *Letters,* 417.

420   "the Opposition Communist": FSF to MP, November 26, 1934; Ibid., 256.

"The Crash! Zelda & America": Ledger, 184.

421   "Goodby, you unfortunates": *Notebooks,* no. 1496.

422   "being careful not to reveal": Bruccoli, *Composition,* 80.

"with a novelized Kraft-Ebing": Ibid., 81.

"Did you like the book?": FSF to EH, May 10, 1934; *Letters,* 307.

"Then you started fooling": EH to FSF, May 28, 1934; Hemingway, *Selected Letters,* 407.

"nearly ruined you": Ibid., 408.

423   "Forget your personal tragedy": Ibid.

"I'd like to see you": Ibid.

"damned fond": Ibid.

"This may irritate you": EH to FSF, December 16, 1935; Ibid., 425.

"a very stupid little boy feeling": EH to MP, March 25, 1939; Ibid., 483.

"If you had never met": FSF to EH, June 1, 1934; *Letters,* 308.

"To take a case specifically": Ibid., 309.

424   "or that I didn't like her": Ibid., 310.

"My temporary bitternesses": Ibid.

"I hated the book": Donnelly and Billings, *Sara & Gerald,* 38.

"consideration for other people's feelings": Sara Murphy to FSF [ca. 1934]; *Correspondence,* 398.

"never did really understand our life": Donnelly and Billings, *Sara & Gerald,* 43.

"I know now that what you said": Gerald Murphy to FSF, December 31, 1935; *Correspondence*, 425.

425 "We wait now": ZSF to MP [ca. October 6, 1932]; PUL.

"What made me mad": Milford, *Zelda*, 342.

"It's a swell book": ZSF to FSF [March 1934]; PUL.

"It seems very careless of the Murphys": Ibid.

"It makes me very sad": ZSF to FSF [April 1934]; *Correspondence*, 338.

"You seem afraid": ZSF to FSF, n.d. [1934]; PUL.

426 "and it haunts me": ZSF to FSF [after June 9, 1934]; *Correspondence*, 367.

"browning ourselves": Ibid.

"Please say what you want": ZSF to FSF [March 1934]; Ibid., 335.

"Dear: I am not trying": Ibid., 334.

"Carved forms like golden heads": PUL.

"Except for Picasso": Cary Ross to FSF, August 26, 1932; PUL.

427 *"Parfois la folie est la sagesse"*: Bruccoli, et al., *The Romantic Egoists*, 195.

"full of confused sentiment": *The Beautiful and Damned*, 360.

"akin to some martyred and transfigured Christ": Ibid., 361.

"I left my capacity": *Notebooks*, no. 1362.

428 "greasy kid stuff": John O'Hara to Gerald Murphy, July 30, 1962; O'Hara, *Selected Letters*, 402.

"his characters always came back": Ibid.

"My message to the world": John O'Hara to FSF [April 1934]; Ibid., 93.

"John O'Hara is in a perpetual state": *Notebooks*, no. 1901.

"like an idiot": Ibid.

"He's awful": John O'Hara to William Maxwell, May 16, 1963; O'Hara, *Selected Letters*, 429.

429 "I wanted to kill him.": John O'Hara to William Maxwell, June 7, 1963; Ibid., 432–433.

430 "Sister, where'd you get": "The Kingdom of the Dark," *Redbook* magazine, August 1935.

"let the Post feel": HO to FSF, August 30, 1933; *As Ever*, 198.

"I want to try to create": Ibid.

"As far as it concerns myself": HO to FSF, December 5, 1934; Ibid., 206.

"Sometimes I think it would be better": Ibid., 207.

431 "when you are not in your most rational state": Ibid.

"Nevertheless, the assumption": FSF to HO, December 8, 1934; Ibid., 209.

"in the black hole of Calcutta": Ibid.

"I liked a lot of Tender is the Night": Gertrude Stein to FSF [November 1934]; *Correspondence*, 393.

432 "If she has been as kind to you": Turnbull, *Scott Fitzgerald*, 253.

"it doesn't leak": Ibid., 254.

"somewhat stupid-got": FSF to Gertrude Stein, December 29, 1934; Gallup, *The Flowers of Friendship*, 294.

"handsome face and wise mind": Ibid.

435 "I held [Hop] with my eyes": Hearne, "A Summer with F. Scott Fitzgerald," 242.

436 "The utter synthesis": FSF to Beatrice Dance [early September 1935]; *Letters*, 529.

"just another victim of self-indulgence": Ibid., 529–530.

"sharp shock of a *fact*": Ibid., 530.

"on an impulse": FSF to HO [received July 2, 1935]; *As Ever*, 220.

"awful strangling heart-rending quality": Ibid.
"Dearest and always Dearest Scott": ZSF to FSF [June 1935]; *Correspondence*, 413–414.
437 "There are emotions": FSF to Beatrice Dance [early September 1935]; *Letters*, 530.
"no one near": Hearne, "A Summer with F. Scott Fitzgerald," p. 254.
"I was all keyed up for action": Buttita, *After the Good Gay Times*, 117.
438 "a stinking parlor pink": Ibid., 164.
"It's the thing they were yapping about": Ibid.
"He talked like a dyed-in-the-wool Southerner": Ibid., 171.
439 "a white boy wasn't a man": Ibid., 172.

Too Much Anger, Too Many Tears

PAGE
440 "Of course all life": *The Crack-Up*, 69.
Several months before: See *Notebooks*, no. 1598.
"What a typically modern joke": FSF to HO [received December 12, 1935]; *As Ever*, 233.
441 "the tin cup of self-pity": *The Crack-Up*, 74.
"Life was something you dominated": Ibid., 69.
"too much anger and too many tears": Ibid., 71.
"a grave sentence": Ibid.
"But the doctor was disgusted": Buttita, *After the Good Gay Times*, 20.
442 "I had been only a mediocre caretaker": *The Crack-Up*, 71.
"that every act of life": Ibid., 72.
"All in the same month": Ibid.
"Like most Middle Westerners": Ibid., 73.
"intellectual conscience": Ibid., 79.
"So there was not an 'I' any more": Ibid.
443 "into the dark maw of violence": Ibid., 20.
"He is hopelessly and completely insane": JPB to EW, January 7, 1936; Beinecke.
"the idea of the Big Out": *The Crack-Up*, 81.
444 "If the gossips insist": Loos, *Cast of Thousands*, 85.
"the best qualities of a hotel manager": *The Crack-Up*, 82.
445 "The natural state of the sentient adult": Ibid., 84.
"The sign *Cave Canem*": Ibid.
"Remember it was written": FSF to HO, January 21, 1936; *As Ever*, 244.
"in some deep way": Berg, *Max Perkins*, 355.
"The writing of the articles": FSF to Roger Garis, February 22, 1938; *Letters*, 569.
"Christ man how do you find time": John Dos Passos to FSF [September 1936]; Dos Passos, *The Fourteenth Chronicle*, 488.
446 "shamelessness of defeat": EH to MP, February 7, 1936; Hemingway, *Selected Letters*, 437–438.
"There was more truth and sincerity": EW to MP, February 16, 1941; Wilson, *Letters*, 337.
"*Do* you feel better?": Sara Murphy to FSF, April 3 [1936]; *Correspondence*, 429.
"I can't express to you": John V. A. Weaver to FSF, February 17, 1936; PUL.
447 "about as effectual": FSF to Sara Murphy [postmarked March 30, 1936]; *Letters*, 425.

"*Won't* you say your prayers?": ZSF to FSF, n.d.; PUL.

"In an odd way": FSF to Sara Murphy [postmarked March 30, 1936]; *Letters*, 425–426.

"The voices fainter and fainter": *Notebooks*, no. 462.

448 "poor Scott Fitzgerald": Hemingway, *The Short Stories*, 170.

"When he found they weren't": Ibid.

"If I choose to write *de profundis*": FSF to EH [August 1936]; *Letters*, 311.

"To have answered it": FSF to MP, September 19, 1936; Ibid., 267.

449 "a hell of a letter": FSF to Beatrice Dance, September 15, 1936; Ibid., 542.

"quite as nervously broken down": Ibid., 543.

"those awful things about himself": Baker, *Ernest Hemingway*, 290.

"you'd hesitate to use on a yellow dog": Gingrich, "Coming to Terms with Scott and Ernest," *Esquire*, June 1983, 55.

"I am getting to know the rich": Berg, *Max Perkins*, 385.

"As for what Ernest did": MP to FSF, September 23, 1936; *Dear Scott*, 232.

450 "halting old lady": *The Prince Was High*, 736.

"She had by no means": Ibid.

"It was sad taking her from the hotel": FSF to Mrs. Clifton Sprague [July 1936], *Letters*, 535.

451 "the luckiest event of some time": FSF to Beatrice Dance, September 15, 1936; Ibid., 541.

"There is no use reproaching me": FSF to Annabel Fitzgerald Sprague, September 10, 1936; *Correspondence*, 449.

452 "Just one ounce?": Bruccoli and Bryer, *In His Own Time*, 295.

"A writer like me": Ibid., 296.

"Much against your better judgment": Ibid., 297.

"My views?": Ibid., 299.

453 "The nurse came in": FSF to HO [received October 5, 1936]; *As Ever*, 282.

"IF YOU EVER WANTED": FSF to EH, September 28, 1936, draft on Western Union form; *Correspondence*, 454.

"WIRED UNDER IMPRESSION": Ibid., Note no. 1.

"to say goodbye": FSF to Beatrice Dance [early 1937]; Ibid., 470.

"If I had thought": FSF to Scottie, December 12, 1936; *Letters*, 13.

"Remember that I expect": Ibid., 14.

454 "scared or embarrassed": Turnbull, *Scott Fitzgerald*.

"I'm all right now": FSF to HO, January 2 [1937]; *As Ever*, 291.

"I think those confounded *Esquire* articles": HO to FSF, August 26, 1936; Ibid., 279–280.

455 "meeting Mr. Knopf of the movies": FSF to Anne Ober, n.d. [June 18, 1937]; Ibid., 322.

He also outlined a schedule of payments: The schedule that Fitzgerald proposed, and that he seems to have maintained rather faithfully, is given in his letter to Ober, received July 6, 1937 (*As Ever*, 325). Out of the weekly salary of $1000, $100 in commission and $150 against his debt to Ober were to be paid weekly. Fifty dollars was to be paid against his debts to Perkins and Scribner's. Two hundred dollars was to be banked against his taxes; $100 banked for "vacation money." The remaining $400 was to be put to his own expense account, out of which he would pay his life insurance.

"I feel a certain excitement": FSF to Scottie [July 1937]; *Letters*, 16.

"I must be very tactful": Ibid., 17.

"I would have given": Robert Benchley to FSF, April 29, 1934; *Correspondence*, 357.

456 "long pull at the mammalia": FSF to Corey Ford [early July 1937]; *Letters*, 551.
"the precious lazybones": Ibid.
"special stunt to beat the game": Ibid.
"Isn't God good to me?": Marx, *Mayer and Thalberg*, 252.
"an idea that his wife and I": FSF to C. O. Kalman, September 19, 1936; *Correspondence*, 451.
"He strode about the room": Latham, *Crazy Sundays*, 111.

457 "I have seen Hollywood": FSF to Anne Ober [dated July 26, 1937]; *As Ever*, 330.
"You don't really want to see me!": Loos, *Cast of Thousands*, 128–129.
"Smiling faintly at him": *The Last Tycoon*, 26.

458 "I wish we could meet more often": FSF to EH, June 5, 1937; *Letters*, 311.
"riding low": Hellman, *An Unfinished Woman*, 57.
"I'm afraid of Ernest": Ibid., 58.

459 "THE PICTURE WAS BEYOND PRAISE": FSF to EH, July 13, 1937; *Correspondence*, 475.
"Ernest came like a whirlwind": FSF to MP [ca. July 15, 1937]; *Dear Scott*, 238.
"All goes beautifully here": FSF to MP [ca. August 20, 1937]; Ibid.

460 "In all our time together": Graham, *The Real F. Scott Fitzgerald*, 30.
"In those first weeks": Graham, *Beloved Infidel*, 184.

461 "ALL THOSE NASTY STORIES": Latham, *Crazy Sundays*, 130.
"She held up well enough": FSF to Beatrice Dance [postmarked November 27, 1937]; *Correspondence*, 482.
"completely irresponsible channels": FSF to Dr. Robert S. Carroll and Dr. R. Burke Suitt, October 22, 1937; Ibid., 481.

462 "Give Paramour my regards": ZSF to FSF, n.d.; PUL.
"She was the first girl": FSF to Scottie, October 8, 1937; *Letters*, 19.

463 "She is still a charming woman": FSF to Scottie, November 4, 1937; Ibid., 21.
"a great lay": Graham, *The Real F. Scott Fitzgerald*, 103.
"You have ruined me!": Ibid., 104.

464 "We got off to a bad start": FSF to Ted Paramore, October 24, 1937; *Letters*, 558.
"writing over a hundred and fifty stories": FSF to Eddie Mannix and Sam Katz [winter 1938]; Ibid., 565.
"To say I'm disillusioned": FSF to Joseph Mankiewicz, January 20, 1938; Ibid., 563.

465 "The truth of the matter": FSF to HO, February 9, 1938; *As Ever*, 350.
"They try to be Jesus": *Notebooks*, no. 396.
"You will notice": FSF to Scottie, September 19, 1938; *Letters*, 37.
"Scott thought of himself": Schwartz, *The Hollywood Writers' Wars*, 146.

466 "very bad spoken dialogue": *Three Comrades*, 263.
"*Angel* (sweetly)": Ibid., 44.
"The point is once you've got it": FSF to Anne Ober [Christmas 1937]; *Letters*, 560–561.

467 "You can never give her": FSF to Gerald Murphy, March 11, 1938; Ibid., 427–428.
"MISTERS FITZGERALD AND PARAMORE": ZSF to FSF, June 3, 1938; *Correspondence*, 504.
"I am now considered a success": FSF to Beatrice Dance, March 4, 1938; Ibid., 489.
"Dear Scott—How are you?": FSF to FSF, n.d. [1937/1938]; Ibid., 477.

468 "Certainly the outworn pretense": FSF to Dr. Robert S. Carroll, March 4, 1938; Ibid., 487.

"So long as she is helpless": Ibid., 488.

"I had a scare a few months ago": Ibid.

469 "I had been physically run down": FSF to Dr. Robert S. Carroll and Dr. R. Burke Suitt, April 7, 1938; Ibid., 492.

"Did Mr. Goldwyn eat my slippers?": ZSF to FSF, n.d.; PUL.

"I am a very extravagant woman": ZSF to FSF, n.d.; PUL.

"Dearest, I am always grateful": Milford, *Zelda*, 397.

470 "Hope meant a lot": FSF to Dr. Robert S. Carroll, April 19, 1938; *Correspondence*, 494.

"sleeping with a ghost": Ibid. (deleted portion; PUL).

471 "will always pity her": Ibid., 495.

"Judging by myself": Ibid., 494.

"I've hated the place": FSF to HO [received December 29, 1938]; *As Ever*, 380.

"Isn't Hollywood a dump": FSF to Alice Richardson, July 29, 1940; *Letters*, 603.

"Isn't my reputation": FSF to MP, December 24, 1938; *Dear Scott*, 250.

472 "I am in terror": FSF to MP, May 22, 1939; Ibid., 256.

"an immediate, dynamic": Bruccoli, *"The Last of the Novelists,"* 28.

473 "I have been through not only": FSF to Scottie [July 1939]; *Letters*, 60.

474 "Shoot yourself, you son of a bitch!": Graham, *Beloved Infidel*, 281.

"Please take care of yourself": ZSF to FSF [April 1939]; *Correspondence*, 530.

475 "You were a peach": FSF to ZSF, May 6, 1939; *Letters*, 105.

"I would like to see you cut down": HO to FSF, February 1, 1939; *As Ever*, 382.

"It would be a great mistake": HO to FSF, June 21, 1939; Ibid., 394.

476 "HAVE BEEN WRITING IN BED": FSF to MP, July 3 [1939]; *Correspondence*, 534–535.

"BECAUSE OF A SLOW HEALING LUNG CAVITY": FSF to HO, July 13, 1939; *As Ever*, 400.

"SORRY COLLECTIONS SLOW": HO to FSF, July 14, 1939; Ibid.

"the insult to my intelligence": FSF to HO, n.d.; Ibid.

"I think something to do with it": FSF to MP, July 19, 1939; *Correspondence*, 536.

"This is not a request": FSF to HO, July 19, 1939; *As Ever*, 402.

477 "Nothing would ever make me forget": Ibid., 403.

"I am pretty definitely breaking": FSF to Scottie [July 1939]; *Letters*, 59.

"But Scott": MP to FSF, July 26, 1939; *Dear Scott*, 257.

"If it is of any interest": FSF to HO, August 2, 1939; *As Ever*, 408.

"When Harold withdrew": FSF to MP, December 19, 1939; *Dear Scott*, 260.

"sudden desertion at the wrong time": FSF to MP, May 20, 1940; Ibid.

"A nice return for ten years": Ibid.

478 "He reproached me with being a suck": FSF to EW, November 25, 1940; Beinecke.

"I have never seen so great": EW to Christian Gauss, October 27, 1938; Wilson, *Letters*, 313–314.

"Believe me, Bunny": FSF to EW, May 16, 1939; *Letters*, 348.

479 "PRETTY CRYPTIC": Kenneth Littauer to FSF, November 28, 1939; *Correspondence*, 561.

"*We*— we consumptives": FSF to ZSF [fall 1939]; Ibid., 558.

"They don't want anything by F. Scott Fitzgerald": Graham, *Beloved Infidel*, 294.

"She's a fake!": Ibid., 296.

480 "Get out of town, Lily Sheil": Ibid., 299.

"I'm glad you no longer": FSF to Sheilah Graham, December 2, 1939; *Correspondence*, 564.

"I want to die": Ibid.

"Portrait of a Prostitute": Graham, *The Real F. Scott Fitzgerald*, 18.

481 "that there is some unfavorable word": FSF to Leland Hayward, January 16, 1940; *Correspondence,* 578.
"All gold rushes": FSF to Gerald Murphy, September 14, 1940; PUL.
"But to die, so completely and unjustly": FSF to MP, May 20, 1940; *Dear Scott,* 261.
"psychological Robespierres": Ibid.

482 "*This is my great secret*": FSF to Kenneth Littauer, September 29, 1939; *Correspondence,* 546.
"though I have put in somethings": FSF to Norma Shearer Thalberg, n.d. [ca. 1940]; Ibid., 615.
"Writers aren't people exactly": *The Last Tycoon,* 12.

483 "a mining town in lotus land": Ibid., 11.
"There is never a time": Ibid., 21.
"suspecting that they had a bearing": Ibid., 118.
"But his mind was closed": Ibid.

484 "I WAS MARRIED AT NOON TODAY": Ibid., 116.
"The Allies are thoroughly licked": FSF to MP, June 6, 1940; *Dear Scott,* 264.
"a company ship was lost": *The Last Tycoon,* 116.
"The idea fills Stahr with a horror": Quoted in Bruccoli, *"The Last of the Novelists,"* 6–7.
"in love with Minna and death together": *The Last Tycoon,* 96.

485 "*Won't* you let me go home?": ZSF to FSF, n.d.; PUL.
"They have no recourses": FSF to Dr. Robert S. Carroll, March 26, 1940; *Correspondence,* 591.
"Funny that he should be": FSF to ZSF, May 11, 1940; *Letters,* 116.
"The Gertrude Stein book": ZSF to FSF, [postmarked August 14, 1940]; PUL.

486 "What little I've accomplished": FSF to Scottie, June 12, 1940; *Letters,* 79.

487 "abandoned the Catholic religion": Joan M. Allen, "The Myth of Fitzgerald's Proscription Disproved"; *Fitzgerald/Hemingway Annual 1973,* 176.
An Episcopal service: Details of the service are taken from Andrew Turnbull's account in *Scott Fitzgerald,* 321–322, from Allen's article, above, and from an unpublished letter from Scottie to Arthur Mizener in the Beinecke Library.

Epilogue

PAGE
488 "It's odd that my old talent": FSF to ZSF, October 23, 1940; *Letters,* 128.
"In retrospect it seems": ZSF to HO [December 24, 1940]; *As Ever,* 424.
"He left the estate of a pauper": Bruccoli, et al., *The Romantic Egoists,* v.
"terrible small debts": *The Crack-Up,* 86.

489 "the penthouses, the long week-end drunks": Bruccoli, et al., *The Romantic Egoists,* 230.
"better than he knew": Ibid.
"None had such promise then, and none": *The Crack-Up,* 345.
"even in its imperfect state": *The Last Tycoon,* x.

490 "I brood about my friends": ZSF to MP, n.d.; PUL.
"There is much need of faith": ZSF to CVV, November 13, 1944; Beinecke.
"The world angered God": ZSF to CVV, September 1, 1945; Beinecke.
"You are sweet to hold in such high regard": ZSF to Scottie, n.d.; PUL.
"Time seems of less relevance every day": Bruccoli, et al., *The Romantic Egoists,* 238.

◁▬◁ BIBLIOGRAPHY ◁▬◁

Aaron, Daniel. *Writers on the Left: Episodes in American Literary Communism*. New York: Harcourt, Brace & World, 1961.

Adams, Samuel Hopkins. *A. Woollcott: His Life and His World*. New York: Reynal & Hitchcock, 1945.

Allen, Joan M. *Candles and Carnival Lights: The Catholic Sensibility of F. Scott Fitzgerald*. New York: New York University Press, 1978.

Amory, Cleveland, and Frederic Bradlee, editors. *Vanity Fair: A Cavalcade of the 1920's and 1930's*. New York: Viking Press, 1960.

Anderson, Sherwood. *France and Sherwood Anderson: Paris Notebook, 1921*. Edited by Michael Fanning. Baton Rouge: Louisiana State University Press, 1976.

Angoff, Charles. *H. L. Mencken: A Portrait from Memory*. New York: Yoseloff, 1956.

Arieti, Silvano, M.D. *Interpretation of Schizophrenia*. New York: Basic Books, Inc., 1955 (second edition, 1974).

Arlen, Michael J. *Exiles*. New York: Farrar, Straus & Giroux, 1970.

Baker, Carlos. *Ernest Hemingway: A Life Story*. New York: Charles Scribner's Sons, 1969.

Baker, Carlos, editor. *Hemingway and His Critics*. New York: Hill & Wang, 1961.

Berg, A. Scott. *Max Perkins: Editor of Genius*. New York: Pocket Books, 1979.

Blum, Daniel. *A Pictorial History of the American Theater*. New York: Crown Publishers, 1969.

Bode, Carl. *Mencken*. Carbondale and Edwardsville: Southern Illinois University Press, 1969.

Boyd, Ernest. *Portraits: Real and Imaginary*. London: Jonathan Cape, 1924.

Boyd, Thomas. *Through the Wheat*. Carbondale and Edwardsville: Southern Illinois University Press, 1978.

Brooks, Louise. *Lulu in Hollywood*. New York: Alfred A. Knopf, 1982.

Brooks, Van Wyck. *Days of the Phoenix*. New York: E. P. Dutton, 1957.

Bruccoli, Matthew J. *Apparatus for F. Scott Fitzgerald's The Great Gatsby*. Columbia: University of South Carolina Press, 1974.

———. *The Composition of Tender Is the Night*. Pittsburgh: University of Pittsburgh Press, 1963.

———. *F. Scott Fitzgerald: A Descriptive Bibliography*. Pittsburgh: University of Pittsburgh Press, 1972.

———. *Supplement to F. Scott Fitzgerald: A Descriptive Bibliography*. Pittsburgh: University of Pittsburgh Press, 1980.

———. *"The Last of the Novelists": F. Scott Fitzgerald and The Last Tycoon*. Carbondale and Edwardsville: Southern Illinois University Press, 1977.

———. *The O'Hara Concern: A Biography of John O'Hara*. New York: Random House, 1975.

———. *Scott and Ernest*. Carbondale and Edwardsville: Southern Illinois University Press, 1978.

————. *Some Sort of Epic Grandeur: The Life of F. Scott Fitzgerald*. New York: Harcourt Brace Jovanovich, 1981.

Bruccoli, Matthew J., and Jackson R. Bryer, editors. *F. Scott Fitzgerald in His Own Time*. New York: Popular Library, 1971.

Bruccoli, Matthew J., and C. F. Frazer Clark, Jr., editors. *Fitzgerald/Hemingway Annual 1973*. Washington, D.C.: Microcard Editions Books, 1974.

Bruccoli, Matthew J., with Scottie Fitzgerald Smith and Joan P. Kerr. *The Romantic Egoists*. New York: Charles Scribner's Sons, 1974.

Buttita, Tony. *After the Good Gay Times*. New York: Viking Press, 1974.

Cabell, James Branch. *Between Friends: Letters of James Branch Cabell and Others*. Edited by Padraic Colum and Margaret Freeman Cabell. New York: Harcourt, Brace & World, 1962.

————. *The Letters of James Branch Cabell*. Edited by Edward Wagenknecht. Norman: University of Oklahoma Press, 1978.

Callaghan, Morley. *That Summer in Paris*. Harmondsworth: Penguin Books Ltd., 1979.

Chanler, Mrs. Winthrop. *Autumn in the Valley*. Boston: Little, Brown and Company, 1936.

Cowley, Malcolm. *And I Worked at the Writer's Trade*. New York: Viking Press, 1973.

————. *A Second Flowering*. New York: Viking Press, 1973.

————. *Exile's Return*. New York: Viking Press, 1969.

————. *Think Back on Us*. Carbondale and Edwardsville: Southern Illinois University Press, 1967.

Dardis, Tom. *Some Time in the Sun*. New York: Charles Scribner's Sons, 1976.

Donnelly, Honoria Murphy, with Richard N. Billings. *Sara & Gerald*. New York: Quadrangle/New York Times Book Co., Inc., 1982.

Dos Passos, John. *The Best Times*. New York: New American Library, 1966.

————. *The Fourteenth Chronicle: Letters and Diaries of John Dos Passos*. Edited by Townsend Ludington. Boston: Gambit, Inc., 1973.

Drawbell, James. *James Drawbell, An Autobiography*. New York: Pantheon Books, 1964.

Eastman, Max. *Enjoyment of Living*. New York: Harper & Brothers, 1948.

Eble, Kenneth E. *F. Scott Fitzgerald*. Indianapolis: Bobbs-Merrill Educational Publishing, 1977.

Eble, Kenneth E., editor. *F. Scott Fitzgerald: A Collection of Criticism*. New York: McGraw-Hill Book Company, 1973.

Edmiston, Susan, and Linda D. Cirino. *Literary New York*. Boston: Houghton Mifflin Company, 1976.

Elder, Donald. *Ring Lardner*. Garden City: Doubleday, 1956.

Ellmann, Richard. *James Joyce*. New York: Oxford University Press, 1982.

Enyeart, James. *Bruguière: His Photographs and His Life*. New York: Alfred A. Knopf, 1977.

Fenton, Charles A. *The Apprenticeship of Ernest Hemingway*. New York: Viking Press, 1958.

Ferber, Edna. *A Peculiar Treasure*. New York: Literary Guild of America, 1939.

Fitzgerald, F. Scott. *Afternoon of an Author*. New York: Charles Scribner's Sons, 1957.

————. *All the Sad Young Men*. New York: Charles Scribner's Sons, 1926.

————. *The Apprentice Fiction of F. Scott Fitzgerald*. Edited by John Kuehl. New Brunswick: Rutgers University Press, 1965.

————. *As Ever, Scott Fitz: Letters Between F. Scott Fitzgerald and His Literary Agent, Harold Ober*. Edited by Matthew J. Bruccoli. Philadelphia and New York: J. B. Lippincott Company, 1972.

————. *Babylon Revisited and Other Stories*. New York: Charles Scribner's Sons, 1971.

————. *The Basil and Josephine Stories*. New York: Charles Scribner's Sons, 1973.

————. *The Beautiful and Damned*. New York: Charles Scribner's Sons, 1950.

————. *Correspondence of F. Scott Fitzgerald*. Edited by Matthew J. Bruccoli and Margaret M. Duggan. New York: Random House, 1980.

————. *The Crack-Up*. Edited by Edmund Wilson. New York: New Directions, 1956.

————. *The Cruise of the Rolling Junk*. Bloomfield Hills, Michigan: Bruccoli Clark, 1976.

————. *Dear Scott/Dear Max: The Fitzgerald-Perkins Correspondence*. Edited by John Kuehl and Jackson R. Bryer. New York: Charles Scribner's Sons, 1971.

————. *F. Scott Fitzgerald's Ledger: A Facsimile*. Washington, D.C.: Microcard Editions, 1972.

————. *F. Scott Fitzgerald's Preface to This Side of Paradise*. Edited by John R. Hopkins. Iowa City: Windhover Press, 1975.

————. *F. Scott Fitzgerald's Screenplay for Three Comrades*. Edited by Matthew J. Bruccoli. Carbondale and Edwardsville: Southern Illinois University Press, 1978.

————. *Flappers and Philosophers*. New York: Charles Scribner's Sons, 1959.

————. *The Great Gatsby*. New York: Charles Scribner's Sons, 1969.

————. *The Last Tycoon*. New York: Charles Scribner's Sons, 1969.

————. *The Letters of F. Scott Fitzgerald*. Edited by Andrew Turnbull. New York: Charles Scribner's Sons, 1963.

————. *The Notebooks of F. Scott Fitzgerald*. Edited by Matthew J. Bruccoli. New York: Harcourt Brace Jovanovich, 1980.

————. *The Price Was High*. Edited by Matthew J. Bruccoli. New York: Harcourt Brace Jovanovich/Bruccoli Clark, 1979.

————. *Six Tales of the Jazz Age and Other Stories*. New York: Charles Scribner's Sons, 1960.

————. *The Stories of F. Scott Fitzgerald*. Selected and with an introduction by Malcolm Cowley. New York: Charles Scribner's Sons, 1953.

————. *Taps at Reveille*. New York: Charles Scribner's Sons, 1935.

————. *Tender Is the Night*. New York: Charles Scribner's Sons, 1962.

————. *This Side of Paradise*. New York: Charles Scribner's Sons, 1970.

————. *Thoughtbook of Francis Scott Key Fitzgerald*. Princeton: Princeton University Library, 1965.

————. *The Vegetable*. New York: Charles Scribner's Sons, 1976.

Fitzgerald, F. Scott, and Zelda Fitzgerald. *Bits of Paradise*. New York: Charles Scribner's Sons, 1973.

Fitzgerald, Zelda. *Save Me the Waltz*. Carbondale and Edwardsville: Southern Illinois University Press, 1967.

Flanner, Janet. *Paris Was Yesterday*. New York: Viking Press, 1972.

Ford, Hugh. *Published in Paris*. New York: Macmillan Publishing Co., 1975.

Fussell, Betty Harper. *Mabel*. New Haven: Ticknor & Fields, 1982.

Gaines, James R. *Wit's End*. New York: Harcourt Brace Jovanovich, 1977.

Gallup, Donald, editor. *The Flowers of Friendship: Letters Written to Gertrude Stein*. New York: Alfred A. Knopf, 1953.

Gelb, Barbara. *So Short a Time: A Biography of John Reed and Louise Bryant*. New York: W. W. Norton & Company, 1973.

Gish, Lillian. *The Movies, Mr. Griffith, and Me*. Englewood Cliffs, New Jersey: Prentice-Hall, 1969.

Graham, Sheilah. *College of One*. New York: Bantam Books, 1968.

————. *The Real F. Scott Fitzgerald*. New York: Grosset & Dunlap, 1976.

Graham, Sheilah, and Gerald Frank. *Beloved Infidel*. New York: Henry Holt & Company, 1958.

Halliburton, Richard. *The Royal Road to Romance*. Garden City: Garden City Publishing Company, 1925.

Haney, Lynn. *Naked at the Feast: A Biography of Josephine Baker*. New York: Dodd, Mead & Company, 1981.

Harrison, Gilbert A. *The Enthusiast: A Life of Thornton Wilder*. New Haven: Ticknor & Fields, 1983.

Hart-Davis, Rupert. *Hugh Walpole*. New York: Harcourt, Brace & World, 1952.

Hayes, Helen, with Sanford Dody. *On Reflection: An Autobiography*. New York: M. Evans and Company, 1968.

Hayes, Helen, with Lewis Funke. *A Gift of Joy*. New York: M. Evans and Company, 1965.

Hecht, Ben. *Charlie: The Improbable Life and Times of Charles MacArthur*. New York: Harper & Brothers, 1957.

Hellman, Lillian. *An Unfinished Woman*. New York: Bantam Books, 1980.

Hemingway, Ernest. *A Moveable Feast*. New York: Bantam Books, 1969.

———. *Ernest Hemingway: Selected Letters, 1917–1961*. Edited by Carlos Baker. New York: Charles Scribner's Sons, 1981.

———. *The Short Stories of Ernest Hemingway*. New York: Modern Library, Random House, 1938.

———. *The Sun Also Rises*. New York: Modern Library, Random House, 1930.

———. *The Torrents of Spring*. New York: Charles Scribner's Sons, 1972.

Hemingway, Mary Welsh. *How It Was*. New York: Alfred A. Knopf, 1976.

Hergesheimer, Joseph. *Cytherea*. New York: Alfred A. Knopf, 1922.

Hotchner, A. E. *Papa Hemingway*. New York: Random House, 1966.

Israel, Lee. *Miss Tallulah Bankhead*. New York: G. P. Putnam's Sons, 1972.

Kazin, Alfred, editor. *F. Scott Fitzgerald: The Man and His Work*. New York: Collier Books, 1974.

Keats, John. *You Might As Well Live: The Life and Times of Dorothy Parker*. New York: Simon & Schuster, 1970.

Kellner, Bruce. *Carl Van Vechten and the Irreverent Decades*. Norman: University of Oklahoma Press, 1968.

Kert, Bernice. *The Hemingway Women*. New York: W. W. Norton & Company, 1983.

Klehr, Harvey. *The Heyday of American Communism: The Depression Decade*. New York: Basic Books, Inc., 1984.

Klein, Carole. *Aline*. New York: Harper & Row, 1979.

Kobler, John. *Damned in Paradise: The Life of John Barrymore*. New York: Atheneum, 1977.

Kuehl, John, editor. *Write & Rewrite*. New York: Meredith Press, 1967.

Lardner, Ring. *Some Champions*. Edited by Matthew J. Bruccoli and Richard Layman. New York: Charles Scribner's Sons, 1976.

———. *"What of It?"* New York: Charles Scribner's Sons, 1925.

Lardner, Ring, Jr. *The Lardners: My Family Remembered*. New York: Harper Colophon Books, 1977.

Latham, Aaron. *Crazy Sundays: F. Scott Fitzgerald in Hollywood*. New York: Viking Press, 1971.

Le Vot, André. *F. Scott Fitzgerald: A Biography*. Translated from the French by William Byron. Garden City: Doubleday & Company, 1983.

Lewis, R. W. B. *Edith Wharton: A Biography*. New York: Harper & Row, 1975.

Loos, Anita. *A Girl Like I*. New York: Viking Press, 1966.

———. *Cast of Thousands*. New York: Grosset & Dunlap, 1977.

———. *Kiss Hollywood Good-By*. New York: Viking Press, 1974.

———. *The Talmadge Girls*. New York: Viking Press, 1978.

Lowe, Sue Davidson. *Stieglitz: A Memoir/Biography*. New York: Farrar, Straus & Giroux, 1983.

Ludington, Townsend. *John Dos Passos: A Twentieth Century Odyssey*. New York: E. P. Dutton, 1980.

MacLeish, Archibald. *Letters of Archibald MacLeish*. Edited by R. H. Winnick. Boston: Houghton Mifflin Company, 1983.

————. *Riders on the Earth*. Boston: Houghton Mifflin Company, 1978.

MacShane, Frank. *The Life of John O'Hara*. New York: E. P. Dutton, 1980.

McGuire, William. *Bollingen: An Adventure in Collecting the Past*. Princeton: Bollingen Series, Princeton University Press, 1982.

Manchester, William. *H. L. Mencken: Disturber of the Peace*. New York: Collier Books, 1967.

Marx, Samuel. *Mayer and Thalberg*. New York: Random House, 1975.

Mayfield, Sara. *The Constant Circle: H. L. Mencken and His Friends*. New York: Delacorte Press, 1968.

————. *Exiles from Paradise*. New York: Delacorte Press, 1971.

Mellow, James R. *Charmed Circle: Gertrude Stein & Company*. New York: Praeger Publishers, 1974.

Mellquist, Jerome, and Lucie Wiese, editors. *Paul Rosenfeld: Voyager in the Arts*. New York: Creative Age Press, 1948.

Mencken, H. L. *The New Mencken Letters*. Edited by Carl Bode. New York: Dial Press, 1977.

————. *The Vintage Mencken*. Gathered by Alistair Cooke. New York: Vintage Books, 1955.

Milford, Nancy. *Zelda*. New York: Avon Books, 1971.

Millay, Edna St. Vincent. *Letters of Edna S. Vincent Millay*. Edited by Allan Ross Macdougall. Camden, Maine: Down East Books, 1952.

Mizener, Arthur. *The Far Side of Paradise*. Boston: Houghton Mifflin Company, 1965.

————. *Scott Fitzgerald and His World*. New York: G. P. Putnam's Sons, 1972.

Mizener, Arthur, editor. *F. Scott Fitzgerald: A Collection of Critical Essays*. Englewood Cliffs, New Jersey: Prentice-Hall, Inc., 1963.

Moore, Colleen. *Silent Star*. Garden City: Doubleday & Company, 1968.

Morgan, Ted. *Maugham: A Biography*. New York: Simon & Schuster, 1980.

Nathan, George Jean. *The Popular Theater*. New York: Alfred A. Knopf, 1918.

————. *The Theater, The Drama, The Girls*. New York: Alfred A. Knopf, 1921.

————. *The World of George Jean Nathan*. Edited by Charles Angoff. New York: Alfred A. Knopf, 1952.

Nelson, Raymond. *Van Wyck Brooks: A Writer's Life*. New York: E. P. Dutton, 1981.

Nijinska, Bronislava. *Early Memoirs*. New York: Holt, Rinehart & Winston, 1981.

Nijinsky, Romola. *Nijinsky*. New York: Simon & Schuster, 1980.

Nowell, Elizabeth. *Thomas Wolfe*. Garden City: Doubleday & Company, 1960.

O'Hara, John. *Selected Letters of John O'Hara*. Edited by Matthew J. Bruccoli. New York: Random House, 1978.

Olson, Stanley. *Elinor Wylie: A Biography*. New York: Dial Press/James Wade, 1979.

O'Neill, William L. *The Last Romantic: A Life of Max Eastman*. New York: Oxford University Press, 1978.

Overton, Grant. *American Nights Entertainment*. New York: D. Appleton, 1923.

Perkins, Maxwell E. *Editor to Author: The Letters of Maxwell E. Perkins*. Edited by John Hall Wheelock. New York: Charles Scribner's Sons, 1979.

Perosa, Sergio. *The Art of F. Scott Fitzgerald*. Ann Arbor: University of Michigan Press, 1965.

Piper, Henry Dan. *F. Scott Fitzgerald: A Critical Portrait*. New York: Holt, Rinehart & Winston, 1965.

Piper, Henry Dan, editor. *Fitzgerald's The Great Gatsby: The Novel, The Critics, The Background*. New York: Charles Scribner's Sons, 1970.

Rascoe, Burton, *We Were Interrupted*. Garden City: Doubleday & Company, 1947.

Ray, Gordon N. *H. G. Wells & Rebecca West*. New Haven: Yale University Press, 1974.

Rosenfeld, Paul. *Port of New York*. Urbana: University of Illinois Press, 1966.

Rosenstone, Robert A. *Romantic Revolutionary: A Biography of John Reed.* New York: Alfred A. Knopf, 1975.

Rosmond, Babette. *Robert Benchley: His Life and Good Times.* Garden City: Doubleday & Company, 1970.

Schorer, Mark. *Sinclair Lewis: An American Life.* New York: McGraw-Hill Book Company, 1961.

Schulberg, Budd. *The Disenchanted.* New York: Random House, 1950.

———. *Moving Pictures.* New York: Stein & Day, 1981.

Schwartz, Nancy Lynn. *The Hollywood Writers' Wars.* New York: Alfred A. Knopf, 1982.

Seebohm, Caroline. *The Man Who Was Vogue: The Life and Times of Condé Nast.* New York: Viking Press, 1982.

Selznick, David O. *Memo from David O. Selznick.* Edited by Rudy Behlmer. New York: Viking Press, 1972.

Sklar, Robert. *F. Scott Fitzgerald: The Last Laocoön.* New York: Oxford University Press, 1967.

Stein, Gertrude. *Everybody's Autobiography.* New York: Random House, 1937.

———. *Selected Writings of Gertrude Stein.* Edited by Carl Van Vechten. New York: Random House, 1946.

Stenerson, Douglas C. *H. L. Mencken, Iconoclast from Baltimore.* Chicago: University of Chicago Press, 1971.

Stern, Milton R. *The Golden Moment: The Novels of F. Scott Fitzgerald.* Urbana: University of Illinois Press, 1970.

Swanson, Gloria. *Swanson on Swanson.* New York: Pocket Books, 1981.

Tate, Allen. *Memoirs and Opinions, 1926–1974.* Chicago: Swallow Press, 1975.

Taylor, Dwight. *Joy Ride.* New York: G. P. Putnam's Sons, 1959.

Teichmann, Howard. *Smart Aleck: The Wit, World and Life of Alexander Woollcott.* New York: William Morrow and Company, 1976.

Thomas, Bob. *Thalberg: Life and Legend.* Garden City: Doubleday & Company, 1969.

Toklas, Alice B. *Staying on Alone: Letters of Alice B. Toklas.* Edited by Edward Burns. New York: Liveright, 1973.

———. *What Is Remembered.* New York: Holt, Rinehart & Winston, 1963.

Tomkins, Calvin. *Living Well Is the Best Revenge.* New York: New American Library, 1972.

Turnbull, Andrew. *Scott Fitzgerald.* New York: Charles Scribner's Sons, 1962.

Tynan, Kenneth. *Show People.* New York: A Berkley Book, 1981.

Van Vechten, Carl. *Excavations.* New York: Alfred A. Knopf, 1926.

———. *Parties.* New York: Avon Books, 1977.

West, James L. W., III. *The Making of This Side of Paradise.* Philadelphia: University of Pennsylvania Press, 1983.

Williams, Martin. *Griffith: First Artist of the Movies.* New York: Oxford University Press, 1980.

Wilson, Edmund. *Letters on Literature and Politics, 1912–1972.* Edited by Elena Wilson. New York: Farrar, Straus & Giroux, 1977.

———. *A Prelude.* New York: Farrar, Straus & Giroux, 1967.

———. *The Shores of Light.* New York: Farrar, Straus & Young, 1952.

———. *The Twenties.* Edited by Leon Edel. New York: Farrar, Straus & Giroux, 1975.

———. *The Thirties.* Edited by Leon Edel. New York: Farrar, Straus & Giroux, 1980.

———. *The Forties.* Edited by Leon Edel. New York: Farrar, Straus & Giroux, 1983.

Wiser, William. *The Crazy Years: Paris in the Twenties.* New York: Atheneum, 1983.

Wolff, Geoffrey. *Black Sun: The Brief Transit and Violent Eclipse of Harry Crosby.* New York: Random House, 1976.

Woollcott, Alexander. *The Letters of Alexander Woollcott.* Edited by Beatrice Kaufman and Joseph Hennessey. New York: Viking Press, 1944.

Yardley, Jonathan. *Ring: A Biography of Ring Lardner.* New York: Random House, 1977.

◁▰◁ INDEX ◁▰◁

JAMES R. MELLOW is the author of
Charmed Circle: Gertrude Stein & Company
and *Nathaniel Hawthorne in His Times,*
which received the American Book
Award for biography in 1983.